Emerging Financial Markets

David O. Beim
Columbia University

Charles W. Calomiris
Columbia University

 **McGraw-Hill**
Irwin

Boston   Burr Ridge, IL   Dubuque, IA   Madison, WI   New York   San Francisco   St. Louis
Bangkok   Bogotá   Caracas   Kuala Lumpur   Lisbon   London   Madrid   Mexico City
Milan   Montreal   New Delhi   Santiago   Seoul   Singapore   Sydney   Taipei   Toronto

McGraw-Hill Higher Education

A Division of The McGraw-Hill Companies

EMERGING FINANCIAL MARKETS
International Edition 2001

Exclusive rights by McGraw-Hill Book Co – Singapore, for manufacture and export.
This book cannot be re-exported from the country to which it is sold by McGraw-Hill.
The International Edition is not available in North America.

10 09 08 07 06 05 04 03 02 01
20 09 08 07 06 05 04 03 02 01
UPE   ANL

Library of Congress Cataloging-in-Publication Data
Beim, David O.
    Emerging financial markets/David O. Beim, Charles Calomiris.
        p.   cm.
    Includes bibliographical references and index.
ISBN 0-07-242514-8
1.   Finance—Developing countries. 2. Financial institutions—Developing countries. I.
Calomiris, Charles W. II. Title. III. Series.
HG195.B44 2001
332'.09172'4—dc21   00-059454

www.mhhe.com

When ordering this title, use ISBN 0-07-118997-1

Printed in Singapore

Emerging Financial Markets

The McGraw-Hill/IRWIN Series in Finance, Insurance, and Real Estate

CONSULTING EDITOR
Stephen A. Ross, *Franco Modigliani Professor of Finance and Economics,*
Sloan School of Management, Massachusetts Institute of Technology

FINANCIAL MANAGEMENT

Benninga and Sarig
Corporate Finance: A Valuation Approach

Block and Hirt
Foundations of Financial Management
Ninth Edition

Brealey and Myers
Principles of Corporate Finance
Sixth Edition

Brealey, Myers, and Marcus
Fundamentals of Corporate Finance
Third Edition

Brooks
FinGame Online 3.0

Bruner
Case Studies in Finance: Managing for
Corporate Value Creation
Third Edition

Chew
The New Corporate Finance: Where Theory
Meets Practice
Third Edition

**Graduate Management Admissions
Council, Robert F. Bruner, Kenneth
Eades, and Robert Harris**
Essentials of Finance: With an Accounting
Review, Fully interactive CD-ROM derived
from Finance Interactive 1997 Pre-MBA
Edition, Finance Interactive: Pre-MBA
Series 2000
Second Edition

Grinblatt and Titman
Financial Markets and Corporate Strategy

Helfert
Techniques of Financial Analysis: A Guide
to Value Creation
Tenth Edition

Higgins
Analysis for Financial Management
Sixth Edition

Hite
A Programmed Learning Guide to Finance

Kester, Fruhan, Piper, and Ruback
Case Problems in Finance
Eleventh Edition

Nunnally and Plath
Cases in Finance
Second Edition

Ross, Westerfield, and Jaffe
Corporate Finance
Fifth Edition

Ross, Westerfield, and Jordan
Essentials of Corporate Finance
Third Edition

Ross, Westerfield, and Jordan
Fundamentals of Corporate Finance
Fifth Edition

Smith
The Modern Theory of Corporate Finance
Second Edition

White
Financial Analysis with an Electronic
Calculator
Fourth Edition

INVESTMENTS

Bodie, Kane, and Marcus
Essentials of Investments
Fourth Edition

Bodie, Kane, and Marcus
Investments
Fourth Edition

Cohen, Zinbarg, and Zeikel
Investment Analysis and Portfolio
Management
Fifth Edition

Corrado and Jordan
Fundamentals of Investments: Valuation and
Management

Farrell
Portfolio Management: Theory and
Applications
Second Edition

Hirt and Block
Fundamentals of Investment Management
Sixth Edition

Jarrow
Modelling Fixed Income Securities and
Interest Rate Options

Shimko
The Innovative Investor
Excel Version

FINANCIAL INSTITUTIONS AND MARKETS

Cornett and Saunders
Fundamentals of Financial Institutions

Management

Rose
Commercial Bank Management
Third Edition

Rose
Money and Capital Markets: Financial
Institutions and Instruments in a Global
Marketplace
Seventh Edition

Rose and Kolari
Financial Institutions: Understanding and
Managing Financial Services
Fifth Edition

Santomero and Babbel
Financial Markets, Instruments, and
Institutions
Second Edition

Saunders
Financial Institutions Management: A
Modern Perspective
Third Edition

INTERNATIONAL FINANCE

Eun and Resnick
International Financial Management
Second Edition

Kester and Luehrman
Case Problems in International Finance
Second Edition

Levi
International Finance
Third Edition

Levich
International Financial Markets: Prices and
Policies
Second Edition

REAL ESTATE

Brueggeman and Fisher
Real Estate Finance and Investments
Tenth Edition

Corgel, Smith, and Ling
Real Estate Perspectives: An Introduction to
Real Estate
Fourth Edition

Lusht
Real Estate Valuation: Principles and
Applications

FINANCIAL PLANNING AND INSURANCE

Allen, Melone, Rosenbloom and VanDerhei
Pension Planning: Pension, Profit-Sharing, and Other Deferred Compensation Plans
Eighth Edition

Crawford
Life and Health Insurance Law
Eighth Edition (LOMA)

Harrington and Niehaus
Risk Management and Insurance

Hirsch
Casualty Claim Practice
Sixth Edition

Kapoor, Dlabay, and Hughes
Personal Finance
Fifth Edition

Skipper
International Risk and Insurance: An Environmental-Managerial Approach

Williams, Smith, and Young
Risk Management and Insurance
Eighth Edition

To our wives,
Elizabeth Beim and Nancy Calomiris,
with gratitude for their love and support

About the Authors

David O. Beim, *Columbia University*

David O. Beim is a Professor of Professional Practice at the Columbia University Graduate School of Business. He joined the faculty in 1991 after a 25-year career on Wall Street. Since that time he has taught MBA and Executive MBA courses in international business, corporate finance, international banking, and emerging financial markets, and is a regular participant in Columbia's executive education programs. Professor Beim has published articles in *Foreign Affairs* and *The Public Interest.*

Professor Beim's career began at The First Boston Corporation in 1966, where he served for three years as a corporate finance generalist. He transferred to London in 1969 to help establish First Boston's presence in the nascent international bond market. Returning to New York in 1971, he founded and ran First Boston's project finance group.

In 1975 Professor Beim was appointed executive vice president of the Export-Import Bank of the United States, where he served until 1977. He then joined Bankers Trust Company with a mandate to start and run an investment banking business. He became an executive vice president and head of the newly formed corporate finance department, which grew substantially over the subsequent 10 years and included functions such as capital markets and derivatives, lease financing, private equity, and mergers and acquisitions. He also became a member of the bank's management committee. After leaving Bankers Trust in 1987, Professor Beim served for three years as a managing director of Dillon Read & Co.

Professor Beim received a BA from Stanford University in 1962 and a M Phil from Oxford University, where he was a Rhodes Scholar, in 1964.

Charles W. Calomiris, *Columbia University*

Charles W. Calomiris is the Paul M. Montrone Professor of Finance and Economics at the Columbia University Graduate School of Business and a professor in the Department of International and Public Affairs at Columbia University's School of International and Public Affairs, where he teaches students in the MBA, Executive MBA, PhD, and International Affairs programs. He has also taught courses for senior World Bank and IMF staff on bank regulation and exchange rate policy in developing economies. Professor Calomiris co-directs the Project on Financial Deregulation at the American Enterprise Institute, is a member of the Shadow Financial Regulatory Committee, is a senior fellow at the Council on Foreign Relations, and is a research associate of the National Bureau of Economic Research. He served on the International Financial Institution Advisory Commission, a congressional commission to advise the U.S. government on the reform of the IMF, the World Bank, the regional development banks, and the World Trade Organization. His research spans several areas, including banking, corporate finance, financial history, and monetary economics. Among his recent publications is *U.S. Bank Deregulation in Historical Perspective* (Cambridge University Press, 2000).

Professor Calomiris is the recipient of research grants or awards from the National Science Foundation, the World Bank, and the Japanese Government. In 1995 he was named a University Scholar at the University of Illinois, where he served as associate professor of Finance. He is a member of the editorial boards of several journals, and serves or has served as a consultant or visiting scholar for the Federal Reserve Banks of New York, Chicago, Cleveland, and St. Louis, the Federal Reserve Board, the World Bank, and the governments of Mexico, Argentina, Japan, China, and El Salvador.

Professor Calomiris received a BA in economics from Yale University in 1979 and a PhD in economics from Stanford University in 1985.

In 1997, **Professors Beim and Calomiris** designed a new course in emerging financial markets, which they have both subsequently taught and which provided the genesis for this book. This course won the 1997–1998 Chazen International Innovation Prize at Columbia Business School.

Preface

Purpose of This Book

We believe that this is the first textbook to be written on emerging financial markets (EFMs), a subject that is very new, yet one with roots reaching back into history. In a narrow sense, the book grew out of a grant given by Citibank to Columbia Business School in 1996 for the purpose of designing a new course in emerging financial markets for our MBA program. This funding was used primarily to create seven original cases. These cases, described in greater detail below, are a complement to this textbook and are specifically designed to illustrate its themes. We use the book and all seven cases in our course.

In a larger sense, however, this book is made possible by the outpouring of research in recent years that seeks to explain the startling financial crises in Latin America and Asia during 1995–1998 and related issues such as capital flows, currency regimes, legal and regulatory matters, corporate governance, and the functions and structure of financial systems. Just as the optimism of the first half of the 1990s stimulated a wave of investment activity on Wall Street, so the crises of the second half of the 1990s stimulated a wave of academic activity. The hundreds of creative and thoughtful papers written to explain aspects of EFMs provide the intellectual foundation for this book.

We try to represent all sides of the relevant debates, so that the text can be used with confidence regardless of any professor's personal position on the key issues. On the other hand, we show what we believe to be central to the subject by the very titles of our chapters. Simply put, this is a book about the institutional foundations of all financial markets. It emphasizes three fundamental elements that any financial market needs to function well: sound law and regulation, reliable systems of information and control, and thoughtful management of the national government's fiscal balance and the value of its currency.

Why Study Emerging Financial Markets?

We understand "emergence" to mean the separation of financial systems from state domination through a process of liberalization that we examine in detail. We believe that liberalization is highly beneficial to sustained economic growth, but that it can be fraught with danger. The EFMs can be thought of as some 50 experiments in privatizing economies and building financial systems, none perfect, with different emphases and different problems. If we can penetrate from the surface phenomena to the foundations, we can learn which foundations are important, and what goes wrong when some foundational element is missing or flawed. It does not require any great leap of faith to believe that if the foundations are weak, the structure can be knocked down by any number of passing storms. It is, we think, the differences in foundational institutions that make EFMs behave so differently from developed financial markets and from each other.

There are at least three good reasons to study emerging financial markets. The first is their role in global portfolio management. While investments in EFMs must be viewed as the high-risk component of a global investment portfolio, no money management firm can afford to ignore them. Every serious investor needs to understand the unique mix of rewards and risks that these markets offer.

Second, financial institutions are being built all over the developing world. Students from Africa, Latin America, Asia, and Central and Eastern Europe are flocking to the universities of the developed world to learn more about how modern market institutions work so they can apply that knowledge to the task of building their own countries' financial systems. These students need to gain a clear understanding of the problems in EFMs to better understand the specific gaps that need to be filled to build stronger institutions in their own countries.

But there is a third and deeper reason to study emerging financial markets. By looking carefully at the patterns of what works and does not work, all of us can gain a richer understanding of the foundations of all financial markets. In other words, this subject is much larger than it seems. The EFM perspective takes one back to basics, to the foundations on which all financial markets rest, and this perspective enriches our understanding of financial markets everywhere.

Intended Audience

Emerging Financial Markets is designed primarily for use in postgraduate study, particularly but not exclusively at business schools. It should be read by students whose careers will take them into direct contact with emerging financial markets, who will be living and working in one or more developing countries or working for a firm with important operations in developing countries. It is also intended to help those who plan careers in investment management. Also, because bank management figures prominently in the performance and risk of EFMs, the book will be of interest to students planning a career in international banking. We trust it will be of interest to public officials charged with the often frustrating task of developing and dealing with financial markets in an era of globalism and financial fragility. Finally, it should be read by all those who seek a richer understanding of what a financial market is, who want to see at a deeper level why some financial markets function so well and others so disappointingly.

This book and the related cases should provide a full set of materials with which a semester course in emerging financial markets can be taught. We have found at Columbia that the travails of the late 1990s by no means dampened interest in this subject. On the contrary, the need to penetrate the complexity of financial problems in developing markets has become increasingly clear and urgent, creating a fascinating curriculum of study. We offer this book in the hope of making such a curriculum more accessible. We also offer substantial data in the appendixes to the various chapters, in the hope that this will stimulate students and professional researchers as well to explore quantitatively the world of EFMs.

Outline of the Book

In the introductory chapter we survey the trends of finance in developing economies. We take a brief look at history, both the longer history of investment in developing countries and the more recent events, beginning with the great debt crisis of the 1980s, its reasons, and its aftermath. We then look at the capital flows into the emerging markets during the 1990s in more detail, examining them by region, by type of user, by type of capital inflow, and by type of investor. We note the connection between the development of external capital sources and the development of local financial institutions, and we pause to emphasize the importance of local institution building. We then take a more detailed look at the instruments and the performance. We examine the unique characteristics of risk and return patterns in EFMs, summarizing the aspects in which EFM portfolio risks differ from or mirror traditional risks borne in developed economies.

In Chapter 2 we begin the process of looking behind this financial performance to the underlying realities of developing countries' financial systems. Since many of these realities are political, we start with a description of the role of government generally and an account of the financial system's relationship to government. We describe a set of policies that have been called *financial repression*, which is a form of state domination of the financial process. We then characterize the functions of the financial system, emphasizing particularly its role in channeling capital to highest-return uses. We describe indicators of the extent of financial development (or its opposite, repression) and build a country-by-country index of financial repression and financial development. Finally, we connect this measure to the capital flows of Chapter 1 and to economic growth generally.

Chapter 3 is devoted to privatization, the key element in emergence and the most distinctive feature of EFMs in the 1990s. We develop a framework to explain why privatization has been such a powerful engine of economic growth, and why it is essential to the proper functioning of financial markets and intermediaries. After discussing the origins of state ownership, we focus particularly on the mass privatizations of Central and Eastern Europe, contrasting the approaches taken by different countries and asking which worked well and which worked badly. We then turn to financial liberalization. We define the phenomenon and consider pitfalls in the transition from financial repression to liberalization. We take a close look at two examples of financial liberalization: Chile in the 1970s and Korea in the 1980s. Lessons for successful liberalization are drawn from those and other recent experiences.

Chapter 4 is about the legal foundations of financial markets. We start with the rule of law itself: What does it mean and how can it be measured? We look particularly at the problem of corruption, which plagues all countries but which has particularly burdened many of the EFMs. We look at property rights and contracts, without which it is hard to imagine any financial market functioning well. We then turn to securities law and the prevention of securities fraud, which also plagues every financial market, but some disastrously. We examine the legal bases for shareholder and creditor rights, and consider in particular detail the need for good bankruptcy law and the various forms it can take.

Chapter 5 discusses information and control. We start with the academic under-standing of asymmetric information and its impact on financial markets. We then dis-cuss two types of information-related functions that effective financial systems provide: screening and monitoring. We explain adverse selection and the problems associated with risk monitoring, including principal–agent problems. We then consider the role of banks, institutions uniquely able to deal with screening and monitoring functions. This leads to a broader discussion of corporate governance, its goals, and various forms. We close the chapter with a discussion of the various institutions of information creation: accounting firms, credit rating agencies, security analysts, and the financial press, emphasizing the role that such institutions play in well-functioning capital markets.

Chapter 6 discusses the third foundational element of any financial market: cur-rency stability. We discuss the causes of inflation and its impact on both debt markets and foreign exchange markets. This discussion has a technical side, which places infla-tion in the broader context of government fiscal and monetary policy, and which exam-ines the desirability and risks of currency pegging and currency boards as devices to control inflation and stabilize currencies. We show that, in some cases, banks actually benefit from inflation, and examine what happens to banks in such instances when inflation subsides.

Because banks are the primary financial institutions in most EFMs, we devote Chapter 7 to a close look at the banking industry. The most obvious issue here is the stunning frequency and depth of banking crises that have erupted around the world during the past two decades. We examine the reasons for banking problems, including connected lending, moral hazard, and the decline of franchise value during liberaliza-tion. Finally, we turn to the resolution of bad loans and bankrupt banks—how best to resolve banking failures when they occur and what goes wrong when banks are bailed out inappropriately.

Chapter 8 describes the anatomy of a modern EFM crisis, a joint collapse of financial prices and financial institutions. We classify the explanations for these crises into three groups: those that focus on fixed exchange rates as the culprit, those that emphasize short-term debt and liquidity problems, and those that emphasize weak fun-damentals. We chronicle the "tequila" crisis of 1994–1995 and the Asian crisis of 1997–1998 in some detail, trying to find both common themes and special cases. We show the various linkages among the three explanations for these crises and consider lessons for government policy.

Finally, Chapter 9 is about building financial institutions. This provides a sum-mary of the learning in the entire book, with a particular emphasis on the micro or institutional perspective. We emphasize that a country will not have strong financial institutions unless the government sets out to support them, and offer examples of what good governments do when they are so motivated. We then consider the manage-rial problems of building a financial institution, emphasizing particularly the role of strategy, of a sustainable growth rate, of risk management, and of compensation con-tracts. As an antidote to the collapses studied in Chapters 7 and 8, we focus on some success stories and suggest reasons for optimism about the future.

At the back of the book is a glossary of technical terms and acronyms. When the text first mentions or first defines a term listed in the glossary, that term is often set in italics. We hope that the glossary will provide a useful way to refresh readers' under-standing of the numerous technical words and phrases.

Throughout, we hope to reflect the large amount of recent academic research, as well as practical experience in emerging financial markets. We often quantify character-istics of countries so that our comparisons and conclusions can be as well grounded as possible. We not only report some of the research results of recent academic studies, but also show some of the country-level data that underlie those studies. Thus, our chapters often have appendixes that list or quantify various attributes country by country.

It is not often that a fundamentally new subject comes along, but EFMs are in many ways a new and fascinating subject. Because the field is so new, our book certainly does not contain all the answers to the problems of successful investing or successful policy design. However, we trust that we will at least help our readers to formulate the right questions.

A Note on Cases

The seven original cases that have been written as complements to this book are summarized below. All of these cases have been refined based on our classroom experience with them, and comprehensive teaching notes are available for each. Next to each title is the chapter subject that the case is designed to illuminate:

Hungarian Telephone and Cable Corporation (Privatization)

A small American company has established a position in Hungary's telecommunications market during privatization. Having organized an advantageous dollar bond issue to finance its capital program, it shifts at the last minute to what seems to be a less attractive local loan from a weak Hungarian bank. Why?

Champacoal (Information and Control)

An American banker arrives in Hanoi to open an office for a large international bank in Vietnam. What clients should the banker pursue? The local state coal mining company looks potentially attractive as a business, and wants to borrow, but the only financial statements it can provide appear to be utter nonsense. Can this loan be made? How can one proceed?

Gazprom (Information and Control)

An international oil company is selected by Russia's largest enterprise to be its partner in field development, but the price is a large equity-linked investment. The stock has two prices, a local price and an external (ADR) price. The two prices appear wholly uncorrelated and of quite different magnitudes. Discounted cash flow analysis seems to produce a valuation lower than either stock price. Are the laws of finance suspended? What is the value of Gazprom?

Banco Itaú and the Real Plan (Inflation)

Banco Itaú has made a fortune on float during Brazil's period of hyperinflation. But that era may be coming to an end with the advent of Cardoso's *Real* Plan. How should the bank handle the "threat" of an end to inflation? What strategies are available? What speculative opportunities beckon? Should these speculations be tried?

Yuval Ran and Israel Credit Lines (Building Financial Institutions)

Yuval Ran dominates the "gray market" of high-rate, high-risk lending to individuals in Israel in the early 1990s. He is the kind of figure Michael Milken was in the United

States—charismatic, very successful, and living on the edge of legitimacy. His company, Israel Credit Lines, is rapidly expanding into corporate loans, challenging the entrenched banks. Is he a genius or a crook?

BancoSol (Building Financial Institutions)

A lending officer at a large international bank receives an unusual proposal to securitize a portfolio of very small loans from some of the poorest people in one of the poorest countries in the world. The underlying bank is Bolivia's BancoSol, originally founded by eleemosynary foundations but rapidly becoming one of the most profitable banks in South America. Does this marriage of village-level microfinance with modern securitization make sense? Is BancoSol as good as it appears?

Peregrine Investments (Financial Crises and Building Financial Institutions)

The hottest securities firm in East Asia crashes abruptly in 1997, despite the fact that its base of operations, Hong Kong, has escaped major damage in the Asian financial crisis. How could such a well-regarded firm fall so quickly? Were there underlying weaknesses that should have been visible prior to 1997? How could its mistakes have been avoided?

These cases are available through Primis Online, a large and growing McGraw-Hill/Irwin database that provides you the flexibility of choosing only the material that matches your course. In addition to obtaining cases, you can easily build a custom version of this text at <u>http://mhhe.com/primis/online</u>.

Acknowledgments

We gratefully acknowledge funding from Citibank in support of case writing. We are grateful to Professors Ray Horton, Ross Levine, Ronald McKinnon, Allan Meltzer, Anthony Saunders, and J. P. Mei, and to Dr. Gerard Caprio Jr. of the World Bank, for taking the time to review all or a portion of this volume. Their comments have helped to make it a better work. We owe special thanks to our students in the Emerging Financial Markets course at Columbia Business School, and to Becky Lane of the American Enterprise Institute, for numerous helpful comments on how to make the manuscript clearer. Becky Nordbrock, our project manager at McGraw Hill/Irwin, ably shepherded the manuscript through the production process. Remaining errors are, of course, our responsibility.

David O. Beim
Charles W. Calomiris

Brief Table of Contents

Contents

Emerging Financial Markets

The Emerging Markets Phenomenon

Questions:
What has been the history of developing countries' engagement with global financial markets?
What happened in the debt crisis of the 1980s?
Why did capital flows resume so quickly after the losses of the debt crisis?
What have been the investment characteristics and performance of EFM securities?
In what ways is the risk of investing in EFMs unique?

Introduction

Developing countries have existed for a long time, and for much of their history they have attempted two related tasks: to build their local financial institutions and markets, and to attract international investment. Some have succeeded quite admirably while others have a great deal of work left to do. As time has gone by, the words we use to describe these countries and their markets have undergone considerable change. In the 1950s and 1960s it was common to speak of an "underdeveloped country." This soon gave way to the more polite "less developed country" (LDC) that was prevalent in the 1970s and 1980s. Then the phrase "emerging financial market" (EFM) caught on in the 1990s, as a worldwide change of ideas away from state-sponsored development and toward the opening of free markets brought a burst of progress and performance.

The International Finance Corporation (IFC), the private sector arm of the World Bank Group, began using the phrase "emerging financial markets" to describe a set of countries for which they kept and published standardized stock indexes starting in 1981. Their original list contained only nine countries whose stock markets looked particularly promising. This list was later expanded to 25 countries, for which the informal criterion was 30 to 50 listed companies with a market capitalization of $1 billion or more and annual trading volume of $100 million or more. The phrase "emerging financial markets" is now widely used to describe all developing countries.

The year 1993 will be long remembered as the year of miracles in emerging financial markets. Portfolio investors from developed countries, who in 1992 had supplied $10 billion of new debt capital and $11 billion of new equity capital to EFMs, raised those amounts almost fourfold to $36 billion and $45 billion, respectively, in 1993. The IFC reported that stock price indexes, measured in U.S. dollars, rose dramatically in almost all developing countries, led by the Philippines (+133 percent), Turkey (+214 percent), and Poland (+718 percent). The total market capitalization of all EFMs nearly doubled from $884 billion to $1,591 billion.

It was a year of boundless optimism. The recession in the United States had come to an end and U.S. stock markets were rising. Communism had been swept almost totally from the world stage during 1989–1991. Democracy had spread so widely that for the first time every government in Latin America except Cuba's was democratically elected. Privatization was being aggressively pursued in every region of the world. The energy unleashed in world financial markets by these events caught the attention of portfolio managers everywhere. Academics began to publish studies of the astonishing behavior of EFMs.

This heady pace of financial expansion did not last. Important setbacks lay just a few years ahead for many countries in every major region. The Mexican currency and capital market collapsed abruptly at the end of 1994, sending the economy into a tailspin, with important spillover effects in Argentina and Brazil. This propelled average emerging market bond yields from a range of 400 to 800 basis points above U.S. Treasury bonds (from 1991 to mid-1994) to the range of 800 to 1,800 basis points (from mid-1994 through 1995). During 1996 and early 1997 yield spreads fell back to about 400 basis points, but then rose dramatically to 1995 levels again in the wake of the 1997–1998 East Asian crises, when Thailand, Malaysia, Indonesia, the Philippines, and Korea experienced collapses much like Mexico's.[1] The East Asian economies, celebrated as "miracles" in the early 1990s, saw large output losses during 1997 and 1998 in the aftermath of these events. The Russian default of August 1998 seemed to finish off any remaining investor enthusiasm for EFMs.

Many people assume that capital flows into EFMs dried up as a result of these crises, but the reality is somewhat more complex, as shown in Table 1.1. Foreign direct investment continued a path of almost uninterrupted growth during the 1990s, and accelerated rather than slowed down during the crisis years of 1995–1998. Portfolio investment has been more variable, but has been *net positive* in each year of the 1990s; that is, portfolio investors reduced their new commitments in the crisis years of 1995–1998 back to the level of 1991–1992 but continued to invest. It is the banks that have withdrawn capital as quickly and on as large a scale as they put it in. Furthermore, as we shall see in more detail in Chapter 2, the pace of privatization and financial liberalization did not slow but actually accelerated in 1998.

In the late 1980s and early 1990s, the financial world changed fundamentally in a way that is not likely to be reversed. For the first time, many countries in the developing world have adopted a strategy of international openness and private domestic ownership, a strategy embodied in newly liberalized trade relations and privatized corporations. International commodity and capital markets have demonstrated how quickly import demands and capital inflows from the developed nations could respond to new opportunities in developing countries, and have proved how quickly impressive economic results could be obtained for newly liberalizing economies. The financial crises of the late 1990s pose a new challenge to successful openness and liberalization—one that we will examine in detail in this book—but they have not undermined the core faith in these mechanisms as the necessary path to overcoming poverty.

A Brief Look at History

Cycles of Enthusiasm and Despair

The 1990s cycle of boundless enthusiasm followed by collapse and dismay in EFMs is, in many ways, not new. Because developing countries have attracted capital for a great many years, it is useful to look at the nature of capital flows and the experience of investors in the past. It is natural to assume that developing countries have long afforded interesting opportunities to obtain above-average returns although at the cost

---

[1]IMF (1998), p. 3.

TABLE 1.1   **Net Private Flows of Capital to Developing Countries (in billions of U.S. dollars)**

	1990	*1991*	*1992*	*1993*	*1994*	*1995*	*1996*	*1997*	*1998*
Foreign direct investment	18.4	31.3	35.5	56.8	82.6	96.7	115.0	140.0	131.0
Portfolio investment	17.4	36.9	51.1	113.6	105.6	41.2	80.8	66.8	36.7
Bank loans and other	11.9	55.6	32.7	11.5	−35.5	55.4	16.3	−57.6	−103.5
Total net private flows	47.7	123.8	119.3	181.9	152.8	193.3	212.1	149.2	64.3

Source: International Monetary Fund, 1999, Table 1.3.1.

of above-average risk. Certainly many private fortunes have been made in the developing world, though this has involved private equity or foreign direct investment (FDI) more often than investments in publicly held EFM stocks.

Equity markets in EFMs typically have a long history. For example, a stock market was organized in Turkey in 1866, in Brazil in 1877, and in Indonesia in 1912. Yet that history has been discontinuous; public securities markets frequently have not provided effective means for raising capital over long periods of time. The records of prices in these markets are often incomplete, and the markets themselves were often interrupted by war, revolution, or economic collapse.

A recent study pieced together a composite record of long-term stock market returns in many countries, which is summarized in Figure 1.1.[2] This figure shows real annual rates of return (nominal returns less actual inflation) in these stock markets against the number of years since 1921 the market has existed without interruption. Notice that in nearly half of the countries the returns were actually negative; that is, nominal returns did not keep up with inflation. The only countries that have sustained high real returns for many years are those considered as developed (see the upper right-hand corner). Figure 1.1 therefore offers a basic piece of wisdom about EFMs: They have often provided negative returns to arm's-length equity investors, frequently because of a major national or institutional collapse.

Debt investors have fared somewhat better, though they have suffered repeated periods of default and rescheduling. One study, for example, followed 10 developing countries from 1850 to 1970, comparing the returns promised and realized, expressed as a premium above the benchmark alternative of home-country government bonds.[3] The average promised return was 1.81 percent above the benchmark and the average realized return was 0.42 percent above the benchmark; that is, lenders not only did not lose their principal, but actually did better on average than they would have done on home-country bonds, though only by a small margin.

The Appendix to this chapter gives a listing of the many episodes of default and rescheduling of private loans to sovereign borrowers from 1800 to 1992. As can be seen, the list is very long and includes most countries of the world, some as many as six times. Interestingly, however, Asian countries, along with the independent Arab states, have rarely defaulted. The Appendix reminds us of another fundamental truth: that periodic default and rescheduling have been the norm of international lending in most regions since international lending began.

[2]Jorion and Goetzmann (1999).
[3]Lindert and Morton (1989).

FIGURE 1.1

Real returns on global stock markets sorted by years of existence

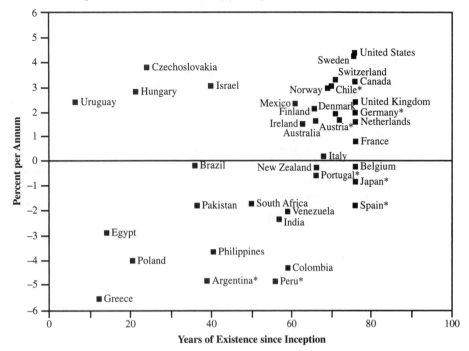

Note: An asterisk indicates that the market suffered a long-term break during its years of existence, the effect of which on returns cannot be measured but is almost surely negative.

Source: Jorion and Goetzmann (1999).

What explains these recurring cycles of high returns on equity and debt followed by stock market collapses and debt defaults? One point of view is that investors are only partially rational, and that they are prone to extremes of enthusiasm and despair. Some economic historians refer to historical cycles of "euphoria" and "revulsion" in international capital investment.[4] In this view of the world, people keep making the same mistakes because they have not learned from the past and let their temporary emotions shape their longer-term investment decisions.

Our view is rather different.[5] We believe that investors are rational for the most part, but that risks in emerging markets are inherently different. Investments in emerging markets are best viewed as complex institutional experiments with highly uncertain long-run outcomes. Unlike the returns histories of developed economies, which aggregate roughly into bell-shaped distributions of outcomes, emerging market countries tend to follow more discontinuous short-run paths and more "bimodal" long-run paths, oscillating between states with very high returns (when institutional experiments seem to be going well) and states with very low returns (when those experiments seem to be failing).

---

[4]Kindleberger (1989) is particularly associated with this view and expounds it with clarity and enthusiasm.

[5]For an introduction to the view of financial fragility that emphasizes the role of information problems and institutional constraints in capital markets rather than irrationality of investors see Hubbard (1990, 1991) and Calomiris (1995).

Adding to, and magnifying, the political uncertainties of EFM experiments in some countries are their undiversified export sectors. Particular commodities often dominate export earnings. Chile, for example, is heavily dependent on copper earnings, Brazil on coffee, and Mexico and Venezuela on oil. The lack of export diversity can produce extreme variations in the terms of trade for EFM countries (the prices of their exports relative to their imports) as international commodity prices fluctuate. Those fluctuations can undermine the more fragile EFM experiments and lead to collapses of equity and debt values. As shown in Figure 1.2, the terms of trade for countries with a lower gross domestic product (GDP) per capita tend to have substantially higher standard deviations than those of richer countries. As can be seen, oil producers have particularly volatile terms of trade.

Thus, EFMs pose new challenges for international investors. It will take time and experience for international investors, EFM governments, and EFM corporations to learn how to measure and manage the risks of economic liberalization. In particular, investors are learning about the importance of fundamental differences in legal and political institutions in determining long-run financial risk, and about how to measure the quality of those institutions. The measurement and management of risk are not static: countries evolve and investors learn. Market collapses are painful for all sides, and learning from them often guides important reforms in the next phase of capital market development.

The Longer-Term Picture

Figure 1.3 illustrates the longer-term history of capital flows to developing countries. This displays the annual real net investment by foreign creditors in the government debt of 10 countries during 1850–1982. The spike in 1894 is probably spurious, as it

FIGURE 1.2

Volatility of terms of trade

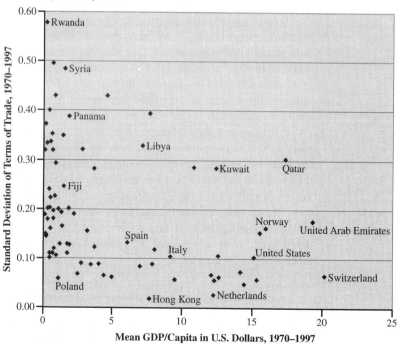

Source: International Financial Statistics (1999) and authors' calculations.

comes primarily from one large loan to the Russian government that was called external borrowing but that may well have come from internal sources. Note that the investment flows were relatively strong in the late 19th and early 20th centuries. This was a period of considerable stability and prosperity. It was the time of the gold standard, which effectively provided fixed exchange rates among currencies, and also a time of very free trade. Capital flows followed the trade flows, and Great Britain was the dominant country mediating both. In the decades prior to World War I, capital flows to developing economies were a larger fraction of world GDP than they are today, and the elasticity of those flows (the extent to which capital moved quickly in search of new opportunities) seems to have been greater as well.[6]

The era of enormous capital flows was brought to an end by World War I, but resumed in the 1920s as the United States became the world's principal source of international capital. The late 1920s witnessed a new period of euphoria, in which U.S. bond investors eagerly took up issues for Latin American and other sovereign governments in greater absolute value than any previous wave. Unfortunately, almost all of these bonds defaulted during the worldwide Great Depression of the 1930s. These defaults were not fully resolved until the 1950s or, in some cases, the 1960s. Although investors often eventually got their money back, even with a small positive return, the length of the workout period substantially interrupted the process of transferring capital to high-productivity uses in developing countries. Protracted default meant that developing economies could not sell bonds in the developed world again until the workout process was complete and international investors had regained confidence in the capacity and ability of developing economies to repay new debt.

FIGURE 1.3

Real net investment by foreign creditors in the government debt of 10 countries

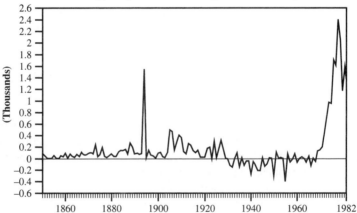

Notes: The vertical axis measures the real value of fresh lending to 10 governments—Argentina, Australia, Brazil, Canada, Chile, Egypt, Japan, Mexico, Russia, and Turkey—by foreign creditors, predominantly private, less retirements on the same external debt in the same year. The figures are in millions of dollars at 1913 prices, with flows in other currencies converted at the 1913 exchange rates. Payments of interest are not included, nor are changes in the real value of outstanding debt due to movements in the consumer-price deflator. The large "spike" of 1894 was a loan package of $1,489.5 million to the Russian government, much of which may have been purchased by Russian creditors. . . . The genuine rise after 1973 is slightly exaggerated in relative terms by a change in series. For developing countries the post-1970 data cover not only bonds but the other types of lending captured in the World Bank's loan disbursements data.

Source: Lindert and Morton (1989).

---

[6]Obstfeld and Taylor (1999).

Note in Figure 1.3 that net investment turns negative in the period 1930 to 1955. This reflects, of course, the devastation of the Great Depression and World War II. The gold standard had collapsed, foreign trade had contracted, and countries everywhere tried to protect their currencies with exchange controls and tariff walls. Bonds were in default and new investment was not replacing the workout payments on the defaulted bonds.

After World War II developing countries had few available sources of capital. Their first relief came from the World Bank, one of the multilateral "Bretton Woods" institutions set up to create a new international financial order after the war. The World Bank, whose official name is the International Bank for Reconstruction and Development, attended first to the need for the reconstruction of Europe and only later to the needs of developing nations. Toward the end of the 1950s, however, it began to make development a top priority. At the same time, the United States, and eventually other developed countries, began to experiment with foreign aid. But World Bank loans and foreign aid were strictly for governments.[7] Private companies in developing countries generally had to rely on local banks heavily controlled by local governments.

For most of modern history up to the 1960s, the large banks in developed countries were not important sources of capital for the developing world. The traditional view of bankers was that cross-border lending, particularly to developing areas, was simply too risky for the commitment of depositors' funds. But this began to change in the 1960s, primarily because the U.S. banking industry began to change.

During this period U.S. banks lost a major portion of their domestic corporate loan market to an efficient securities market alternative, namely commercial paper (i.e., short-term IOUs of corporations, sold either directly to investors or through the services of a securities firm).[8] It is invariably cheaper for a corporation with access to the commercial paper market to borrow short-term funds this way than through banks. The use of commercial paper by large U.S. firms with high credit quality exploded in the 1960s and deprived the banks of many of their best borrowers.

Furthermore, banks lost most of their low-cost sources of money (demand deposit accounts and low-interest savings accounts). They were able to raise large quantities of deposits in the international markets, but for this they had to pay the full market rate of interest. The London Interbank Offered Rate (LIBOR) is the benchmark short-term dollar interest rate announced daily by the British Bankers Association based on the offer side of the market for Eurodollar bank deposits with a 1 to 12 months' term, and is the international standard for bank loan pricing. What banks needed was a new category of borrower that could absorb large quantities of capital and pay LIBOR plus a reasonable *spread* (profit margin) for the banks. To meet this need, banks began to experiment with lending to developing countries.

In the 1970s another factor accelerated cross-border lending. The newly formed Organization of Petroleum Exporting Countries (OPEC) approximately tripled international oil prices in 1973 and again in 1979. The members of OPEC suddenly had billions of dollars in new cash. They deposited the bulk of those funds in the large banks

---

[7]Today the "World Bank Group" of institutions includes the International Finance Corporation (IFC), dedicated to financing the private sector in developing countries; the Multilateral Investment Guarantee Agency (MIGA), offering insurance to foreign direct investors against political risks; and the International Center for Settlement of Investment Disputes (ICSID) as well as the International Development Association (IDA), offering low-interest loans to governments of the poorest countries.

[8]See the discussion of loss of bank franchise value in Chapter 7. For a review of the growth of commercial paper, see Calomiris, Himmelberg, and Wachtel (1995).

of Europe and the United States. The banks in turn were then in a position to lend vast new amounts, but domestic markets for bank credit in industrial countries were insufficient to consume this new supply of funds.

Thus began the wave of syndicated loans to sovereign governments that dominated the international banking scene in the 1970s. Mexico and Brazil were the two largest borrowers, but many other governments joined the game. The early view was that banks were merely "recycling" oil money: Developing countries purchased oil from OPEC, OPEC redeposited the funds in banks, and banks re-lent the money to developing countries. That view, however, failed to note that the countries borrowing heavily had to repay the debt from their export earnings, and in most cases the increase in the relative price of oil had actually worsened their terms of trade. Furthermore, borrowing countries were borrowing far more than their oil import needs, and were using the new funds to promote large-scale, risky, government investments in transportation, power, and new import-competing industries.

Sovereign loans were syndicated to many small banks who had no knowledge whatsoever of the borrowing countries or the uses to which the funds were put. The period 1979–1982 became something of a feeding frenzy as banks lent and syndicated and countries borrowed ever-greater sums. In retrospect, LDC debt was growing much faster than LDC capacity to pay. This wave is represented by the large spike on the right-hand side of Figure 1.3. As can be seen, its volume was unprecedented, much larger than previous flows of capital to developing countries.

On the developing countries' side, foreign borrowing was fueled by the absence of domestic sources of funding. Banking systems were small and securities markets were virtually nonexistent in most developing economies.[9] The extremely low real rates of interest on offer from foreign banks during the 1970s were hard to resist. Most of the LDC lending was in U.S. dollars. A typical loan by banks to an LDC would be priced at LIBOR plus a spread of perhaps 0.5 percent to 3.0 percent.

LIBOR was unusually low in real terms (i.e., after adjusting for inflation) during the 1970s. Figure 1.4 shows a graph of three-month LIBOR and the inflation rate during the 1970s and 1980s. The LIBOR line was 2 to 3 percent above the inflation line in 1972 and 1973. But after 1973 real rates declined because dollar inflation was accelerating. Figure 1.4 shows a line for the typical interest rate at which an LDC might borrow (LIBOR + 1 percent) minus the actual realized rate of inflation. As can be seen, the realized real rate was close to zero. It is no wonder that borrowers were enthusiastic.

Because LDC borrowing cost was indexed to LIBOR, the low real rates of interest of the 1970s were not guaranteed to persist. LIBOR maintained a very different relation to inflation in the 1980s. Paul Volcker became chairman of the Federal Reserve Board in the autumn of 1979 with a mandate to squeeze inflation out of the dollar. Thus began the most massive monetary squeeze in modern times. Interest rates on the dollar, including LIBOR, were propelled into the mid-teens and stayed there even as inflation declined. The result was that real interest rates rose substantially. As can be seen in Figure 1.4, the real rate paid by a typical LDC went from near zero to approximately 10 percent by 1982.

Furthermore, the monetary squeeze induced a major recession in the United States, and by extension in other countries, during 1980–1984. This meant that the United States and other developed countries wanted fewer of the items that LDCs

---

[9]For an excellent review of emerging capital markets circa 1970, see Wai and Patrick (1973).

FIGURE 1.4

Real borrowing rates (%)

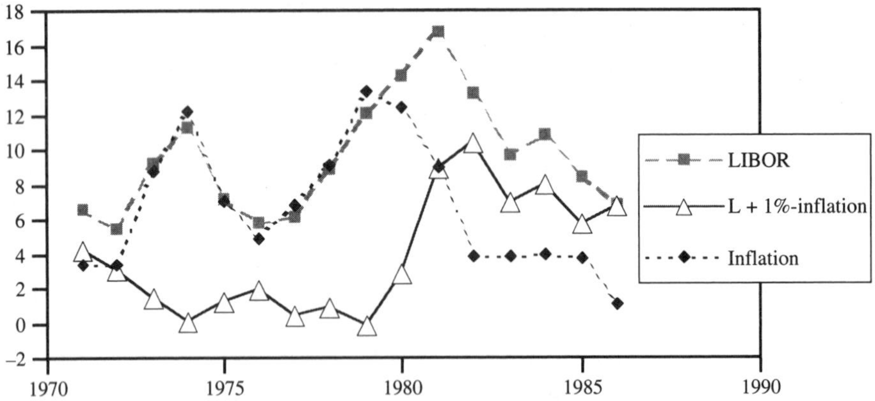

Note: The line designated "L + 1%-inflation" represents the *ex post* real borrowing rate for a typical country that borrows at LIBOR + 1% and experiences actual inflation.

Source: Citibase and authors' calculations.

exported. Lower exports combined with very high real interest rates to make LDC debt unmanageable. In August 1982 Mexico announced that it was unable to maintain interest payments on its foreign debt. This was followed in rapid succession by default announcements of governments throughout Latin America. Numerous other LDCs joined the wave of defaults, including the Philippines, Yugoslavia, and Nigeria. The great global debt crisis of the 1980s had begun.

The Debt Crisis of the 1980s and Its Aftermath

It is difficult to appreciate the magnitude of this crisis. Figure 1.3 suggested how very large the capital flows of the 1970s had been in comparison with earlier periods. Figure 1.5 gives a closer look at the debt and Figure 1.6 the debt service requirements of all LDCs. Official debt—that is, loans from governments and quasi-governmental entities such as the World Bank—rose by a factor of four, but private (i.e., bank) debt rose by a factor of 10 from 1972 to 1982. By the end of 1982, when the crisis began, total private debt stood at $255 billion.

At first the banks denied that the loan defaults implied losses. It was argued that LDCs had a temporary liquidity problem, not a fundamental problem of insolvency. It was widely believed that economic conditions were highly unusual and bound to improve soon. And there were some reasons to believe this: The world economy was deep in recession, interest rates were at all-time highs, and commodity prices (on which LDC export earnings often depended) were very low in comparison to the 1970s. An economic turnaround might restore the LDCs to health and allow them to service their debts.

In 1982 Walter Wriston, the chairman of Citibank, famously remarked that "a country does not go bankrupt." The remark was not as fatuous as it sounds in retrospect. Wriston was expressing confidence in the power of taxation. Government debt is supposed to be safer than corporate debt because governments, unlike corporations,

FIGURE 1.5

Long-term debt of all LDCs (in billions of $ U.S.)

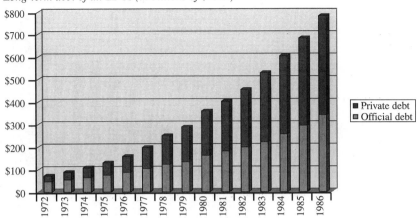

Source: World Bank, *World Debt Tables.*

can set their own revenues through taxation. As we shall see later in this book, that power is freely and ingeniously used to avoid default in EFMs on domestic debt. Local taxation does not, however, produce the foreign exchange needed to repay dollar-denominated international debt; for that, dollars must be earned through exports, and dollar debt must be written down if exports are insufficient to carry the debt.

Banks at first negotiated with the defaulting countries year after year, with the encouragement and support of the IMF, to lend new amounts that could pay the interest on the old amounts. This capitalization of interest would have been a sensible approach if the problem were indeed a temporary one. But insofar as the problem was fundamental and permanent, rolling up interest into more principal only made the debt overhang worse and the probability of full repayment lower.

That is why, despite the defaults in 1982, the total volume of debt kept growing without interruption through 1986, as is clear from Figure 1.5. The annual debt service requirements had actually grown faster than the debt principal during 1972–1982 because of rising interest rates. The rescheduling starting in 1983 slowed the growth of debt service only briefly; by 1986 it too had climbed to new heights, as can be seen in Figure 1.6.

Unfortunately, the LDCs did not recover their equilibrium as the banks had hoped they would. Table 1.2 tells the story clearly. The per capita growth in real GDP dropped from 3.6 percent into negative territory, and negative growth (i.e., a contraction of living standards) persisted for four years. Even after that time, per capita GDP remained essentially stagnant. Inflation, which had averaged less than 30 percent before the crisis, grew persistently into triple digits. Gross capital formation (i.e., new physical investment in capital goods) dropped from 25 percent to as low as 16 percent of GDP. And the ratio of debt to exports seemed to climb inexorably as each year's interest was capitalized. The overhang of excessive debt seemed to suppress the ability of developing countries to join the economic recovery taking place in the developed world by 1985.

By 1986 the LDC debt to private banks had grown to $437 billion, and still no major international bank had taken significant reserves against the likely losses.

FIGURE 1.6

LDC annual debt service requirements (in billions of $ U.S.)

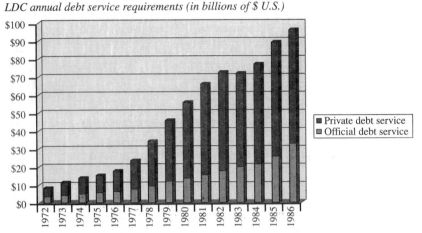

Source: World Bank, *World Debt Tables.*

Traders had begun to trade the defaulted loans. The prices depended on the country but in early 1986 ranged from about 5 percent of par for Bolivia to about 80 percent of par for Venezuela; of the biggest debtors Mexico was priced at 60 percent and Brazil at 75 percent.[10] By mid-1988, however, all such prices had fallen substantially (except for Bolivia, which rose from 5 percent to 11 percent because of a special buyback of half of its debt financed by donor nations). Mexico and Brazil were now both at 52 percent, and the highest value for any defaulted loan was Uruguay at 60 percent. It seemed that banks were facing losses of about 50 percent of the LDC loan exposure (i.e., at least $200 billion in the aggregate), which was especially painful for the U.S. banks that had led the lending binge. The situation seemed to get worse with each passing year.

This was quite different from earlier episodes in which countries defaulted on and rescheduled their bonds. First, the quantities were orders of magnitude larger: The lending and the defaults were of unprecedented size. Second, the lenders were banks rather than bondholders; banks are everywhere regulated by government and can be pressured by governments in a way that private bondholders cannot. Third, this time losses averaging about 50 percent began to appear inevitable. These losses greatly outweighed the interest spreads of 0.5 percent to 3 percent that banks had earned annually on these loans in the good years. Fourth, governments and the IMF encouraged banks and borrowers to postpone workouts by rescheduling debts. That policy error produced the ballooning debt problem—the size of debts grew while the capacity to pay debts shrank.[11] These four factors made the 1980s crisis unlike any the world had experienced before.

The crisis deeply depressed the stock prices of the banks with heavy LDC loan exposures. Indeed, the discounts implicit in the prices of LDC loans and the discounts implicit in the stock prices of heavily exposed banks moved together fairly closely throughout the period 1982–1987.[12] In mid-1987 the banks began to take loss provi-

---

[10]Huizinga (1989) lists prices for March 11, 1986, and June 9, 1988.

[11]For a review of the public policy debate surrounding the debt crisis, see Sachs (1989).

[12]Sachs and Huizinga (1987).

TABLE 1.2 The Economic Crisis in Heavily Indebted Countries

	Per Capita GDP (Annual Change)	Inflation (Annual Rate)	Gross Capital Formation/GDP	Debt/Export Ratio
Average 1969–1978	3.6%	28.5%	N/A	N/A
1979	3.6	40.8	24.9%	182.3%
1980	2.6	47.4	24.7	167.1
1981	−1.6	53.2	24.5	201.4
1982	−2.7	57.7	22.3	269.8
1983	−5.5	90.8	18.2	289.7
1984	−0.1	116.4	17.4	272.1
1985	0.9	126.9	16.5	284.2
1986	1.4	76.2	16.8	337.9

Source: International Monetary Fund, *World Economic Outlook*, April 1987.
Adapted from Lindert and Morton (1989).

sions (deductions from net income reflecting likely losses) of 20 to 25 percent of their LDC loans. By the end of 1987, developing country exposure as a percent of primary capital (equity plus reserves for losses) stood at 79 percent for Citibank, 80 percent for Bankers Trust, 97 percent for Chemical Bank, 112 percent for Chase Manhattan, 124 percent for Bank of America, and 145 percent for Manufacturers Hanover.[13] If half the exposures were lost, no bank would be wiped out but many would suffer severe reductions in their net worth.

Governments of developed countries had generally urged the banks to lend to the LDCs back in the mid-1970s, when the biggest problem the banks faced was how to "recycle" the incoming petrodollars. Furthermore, when the debt crisis first began, the same governments were very permissive in not forcing banks to take loss provisions against their LDC exposures, which would have severely depleted the book value of capital of many large banks. But that was then. Now (in the late 1980s) governments were alarmed at the deepening recession in the developing countries and began to fear political unrest and upheavals. So they began to pressure the banks to recognize their losses in order to bring the crisis to an end.

Numerous proposals were advanced to resolve the debt crisis. Many observers believed that the deeply discounted market prices of the loans held a key to resolution: By getting banks to accept these as losses already incurred, countries might be offered a reduction in the principal value of their debts. Several dozen proposals were advanced to establish a new international agency that would somehow buy up the discounted loans and exchange them for bonds or loans of lower principal amount but higher likelihood of payment.

No such proposals ever got close to realization, because each was fraught with incentive and resource problems. For example, what would prevent countries from acting uncooperatively with banks, breaking agreements and postponing reforms, to drive the price of their loans even lower and make resolution more favorable to themselves? Or what would prevent a bank from *free riding* on other creditors by refusing to make the exchange, knowing that if others made it, then the value of the bank's existing loans would surely rise toward face value? Furthermore, assuring the credit quality of any new instruments appeared to require commitment of government support in massive quantities, which was difficult to envisage politically. Alternatively, credit quality

---

[13]Huizinga (1989).

could be assured if all the old loans were subordinated to the new instruments, but then how much confidence could the agency holding the old loans have of ever being repaid?

Academics began to argue that voluntary debt reduction was in the banks' own interest, and some banks began experiments of swapping defaulted loans for new bonds, real assets, or corporate equity within the borrowing countries. Then in January 1989, Treasury Secretary Nicholas Brady called upon banks to negotiate voluntary debt reductions with the LDCs. His speech hinted that government resources could be marshaled to assist this process if the banks were willing to go along. Negotiations soon began with the government of Mexico to see if this formulation could work.

The promise of government support proved difficult to pin down and in the end scarcely materialized. Mexico offered to exchange new bonds for the defaulted Mexican loans held by the banks. The bonds, whose terms are summarized in Table 1.3, came to be known as *Brady bonds*. They had a 30-year term, with all principal repaid on the final day of the term.

The U.S. government did agree to sell to Mexico some 30-year zero-coupon bonds (ZCBs) at about 11 percent of face value. Since this was the fair market price for zero-coupon Treasuries, there was no government subsidy, just a market transaction. Mexico then pledged these bonds to a trustee to secure the principal payment of new 30-year bonds, whose annual interest would be paid by Mexico. Brady bonds were, in essence, a form of collateralized debt with the collateral held in escrow. This arrangement limited the potential magnitude of sovereign default in the future.

Brady bonds became the pivotal instrument for resolving the debt crisis and are still widely traded in the market. As shown in Table 1.3, there were two types of Mexican Brady bonds: one with a floating rate of interest and one with a low fixed rate. The combination of Mexican coupons and U.S. government-secured principal created an interesting valuation problem, and Table 1.3 shows the estimated values at the time the bonds were issued.

In the end, banks with loans to Mexico were offered three choices: (1) to swap their loans for 65 percent face value of Brady bonds with a floating interest rate; (2) to swap their loans for 100 percent face value of Brady bonds with a low fixed interest rate; or (3) to keep the loans and lend new money equal to 25 percent of their exposure. The fair market value of the first two options was 33 percent and 37 percent or par respectively—that is, somewhat less than the market price of Mexican loans, which by that time had fallen to about 40 percent. Banks would be taking an effective loss of nearly two-thirds of their loans whichever option they chose.

TABLE 1.3   The Mexican Brady Bonds

	Option (1)	*Option (2)*
Term	30 years	30 years
Principal paid	All at end of term	All at end of term
Security	U.S. 30-year ZCB	U.S. 30-year ZCB
Interest rate	LIBOR plus $\frac{13}{16}$ %	6.25% fixed
Market value of bond (M)	51% of face value	37% of face value
Face value of bond offered per dollar of defaulted loans (Q)	65% of loans	100% of loans
Value offered (MxQ)	33% of loans	37% of loans

Source: Authors' calculations.

Governments of all the major developed countries encouraged all banks with Mexican exposure in their jurisdiction to accept one of the three options, so as to minimize free riding. While banks could, in principle, have rejected the Brady approach, government encouragement was a powerful force for change. In the United States, government influence may have been enhanced by the increased dependence of weakened U.S. banks on the government safety net (the discount window and deposit insurance) and on continuing government tolerance of the high asset risk and low capital ratios of U.S. banks.

Mexico succeeded in reducing the economic worth of its bank debt by about two-thirds. This markdown was not necessarily reflected on the books of the banks, nor of Mexico, mainly because of the popularity of option (2) above. Under most bank regulatory and accounting regimes, provision for loss is taken if the principal value (not the economic value) is impaired. Because option (2) involved a low fixed interest rate but no reduction in principal value, and the full principal value was secured even though distant in time, the nominal amount of the banks' loans was not reduced by this choice. Nevertheless, it was an extraordinarily painful moment for the banks.

Seven more heavily indebted countries went through "Brady Plan" negotiations between 1990 and 1992: Argentina, Brazil, Costa Rica, Nigeria, Philippines (twice), Uruguay, and Venezuela. The menus of choices became somewhat longer and more refined, but all were variations on the pattern that Mexico had set. The value of the securities offered in exchange for the loans of these countries were closely calibrated to the trading price of the loans, and ranged from about 18 percent in Costa Rica to 52 percent in Uruguay.

By the end of 1992 the great debt crisis was over, having lasted an entire decade. Banks had taken an enormous loss. The developing countries had freed themselves from the largest of the debt overhangs that had dragged them down for a decade, but were not yet looking strong. The United States had again slipped into a recession in 1990, though it was not as severe as the recession of the early 1980s. It was a sober moment. But the seeds of a remarkable revitalization had been planted.

The Resumption of Capital Flows

Resurgence of the Private Sector

Even as the debt crisis was ending, private capital again began to flow into the developing countries. Figure 1.7 shows the aggregate net private capital flows by year and by region. East Asia, except for the Philippines, had not been part of the debt crisis, and that region benefited most from these new flows. The early 1990s were a high point of East Asian economic performance and prestige. The "Four Tigers" of Korea, Taiwan, Hong Kong, and Singapore had lifted themselves out of the developing category and were generally referred to as "newly industrialized nations." The "Tiger Cubs" of Southeast Asia were growing at a pace that was the envy of the world. And China had finally awoken from its long stagnation; although the government still called itself communist it seemed to be embracing private markets with exceptional enthusiasm. The growth rate of China's real GDP hit 14 percent in 1992 and continued in double digits through 1995. It is no wonder that East Asia attracted capital.

More remarkable, perhaps, was the resurgence of Latin America. The debt crisis, which had affected almost the entire region, might have left a stigma to frighten investors for some time. But the speed with which Latin America recovered was impressive, and a few countries (such as Chile and later Argentina) were setting

FIGURE 1.7

Net private capital flows to EFMs

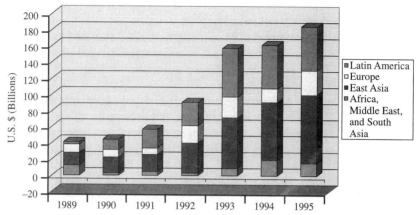

Source: World Bank, *World Debt Tables.*

standards of economic performance comparable to those of East Asia; Chile even harbored a frequently stated ambition to be "the Japan of South America."

As that phrase suggests, Asia imparted an important "demonstration effect" to many countries of Latin America. The export-led growth that had powered so many Asian economies led many Latin Americans to question their closed, inward-oriented systems. One result was a major round of trade liberalization, of which NAFTA (the North American Free Trade Agreement between Mexico, the United States, and Canada) is one expression. As we shall explore in more depth later in this book, several Latin American countries—including Brazil, Chile, Mexico, and Argentina—embarked on a remarkable series of innovations in exchange rate policies, pension reforms, financial market deregulation, and corporate privatization. For the first time, globalization and liberalization had reached Latin America, and with it came a new flow of capital.

The transition countries of Central and Eastern Europe and Central Asia were only modest beneficiaries of the capital boom. Having just shed communism, they had to make transformations of their economies and societies far more drastic than countries in other regions. The process of transformation to a market economy had serious ups and downs, periods of success and then periods of setback, as we will examine in detail in Chapter 3. Global investors were far more cautious about committing capital to this region than to Latin America and East Asia.

Finally, the group of other regions including Sub-Saharan Africa, North Africa and the Middle East, and South Asia attracted the least capital. Though there were individual success stories, these regions taken as a whole seemed to have much more difficulty in transforming themselves into vibrant economies. The process of political and social change seemed slower in these regions, and statism generally maintained a stronger grip here than anywhere else in the world.

Figure 1.8 divides these capital flows between public sector and private sector issuers. The most salient feature of this new rush of investment into emerging markets is how concentrated it was on the private sector. Financing of the public sector was small and static by comparison. Only in Central and Eastern Europe did the public sector rival the private sector in raising capital from private markets, primarily because

FIGURE 1.8

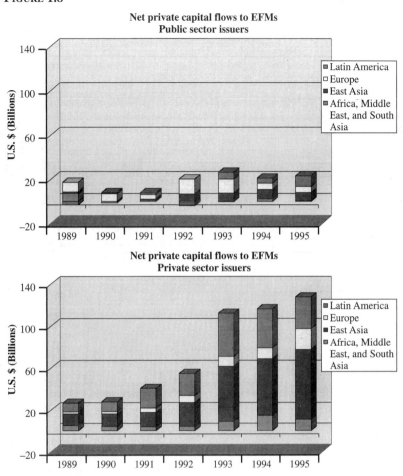

Source: World Bank, *World Debt Tables*.

the public sector was still very large and the private sector so new. Yet even in that region the public sector was declining and the private sector was growing by 1993 to 1995. This shift to the private sector is significant when contrasted with the public sector's previous dominance in raising capital.

Who Were the Investors?

When we break the flows down by type of investor, as in Figure 1.9, further interesting patterns emerge. First, it is obvious from this figure that banks were not important players in these markets through the first half of the 1990s. Having been badly burned by the debt crisis, they made only modest new commitments to the EFMs. They actually withdrew net capital from Latin America in 1989 and from Central and Eastern Europe in 1990 and 1991. The only region that drew significant commitments from banks was East Asia, and even here, despite the impressive economic performance, the banks were much more reticent than other investors. Finally, in 1994 and 1995 the banks began carefully to resume lending in Latin America.

FIGURE 1.9

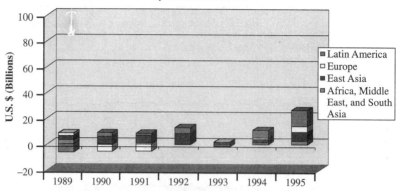

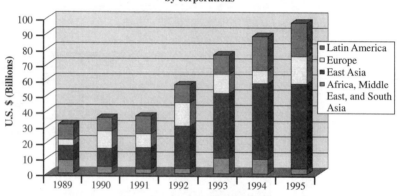

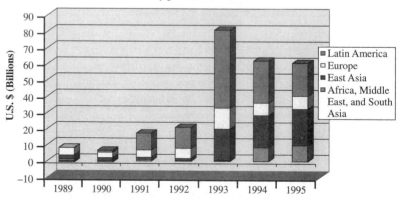

Source: World Bank, *World Debt Tables.*

Portfolio investors were similarly cautious during 1989 and 1990, but began buying Latin American bonds and stocks in serious quantities in 1991 and 1992. They got over any remaining inhibitions in 1993, with major plunges into Latin America and East Asia from 1993 to 1995. But why should bonds, which are debt instruments, have been so attractive so soon after the debt crisis of the 1980s? The answer may be that bonds did not default during the debt crisis. Very few Latin American bonds were outstanding in the 1980s, but those that existed paid off promptly even as banks were being forced into massive losses.

There was no legal or economic basis requiring debtors to pay on bonds but not loans; the sovereign countries simply chose to handle their debts that way. But the consequence was a marketplace impression that bonds were somehow safer than loans. This facilitated the use of Brady bonds in the debt crisis resolution, and it also facilitated the sale of new-money bonds in the 1990s. It also explains why Brady bonds, which were issued to and generally held by banks, required somewhat higher spreads (after adjusting for the presence of U.S. zero-coupon bonds) than new money bonds. Yields on Brady bond "strips" (the part of Brady bonds' future cash flows unrelated to U.S. zero-coupon bonds) have remained higher than yields on other bonds, suggesting that markets still treat Brady bonds differently than other bonds. Indeed, in August 1999, when Ecuador suffered a political and financial crisis, it defaulted selectively on its Brady bonds. This strongly reinforced the perception that Brady bonds are riskier than other bonds and further increased the market yield spreads between Brady strips and other bonds.[14]

It is interesting to note how often the relative preference for bank loans and bonds has been reversed. In the 1940s and 1950s, many foreign bonds were in default, while the small amount of bank credit that existed paid currently. In the 1980s many countries defaulted on bank loans but continued to pay the small amount of bonds outstanding. Then in the Mexican crisis of 1994–1995 and the Asian crisis of 1997–1998, bondholders suffered market losses (though few defaults) while both local and international banks were bailed out with public money. It must be remembered that debt is always at risk and that the relative safety of bonds compared to bank loans is a moving target.

The main message of Figure 1.9 is that corporations have been not only the largest but also the most consistent suppliers of capital to EFMs during 1989–1995. Portfolio investors rushed in during 1993 but then began to pull back, while corporations necessarily take a longer view because their investments are direct and illiquid rather than in the form of tradable securities. It is also clear from Figure 1.9 that the corporations heavily favored East Asia as the developing region of choice. While some commitments were made to Latin America and Central and Eastern Europe, the real growth in corporate commitments came from East Asia.

Some of the portfolio investment shown in Figure 1.9 may actually be disguised bank investment. The presence of banks in the market for EFM bonds may be inferred from the high percentage (35–50 percent) of such bonds with floating rates of interest. Floating rates appeal primarily to commercial banks because bank funding comes mainly from deposits whose cost varies from month to month. A bank protects itself from major interest rate fluctuations by letting the interest rate on its loans fluctuate with the interest rate on its deposits. Since its deposits are typically priced at or close to LIBOR, it prefers to earn LIBOR plus a spread on its assets. Therefore, when we see international bonds whose interest rate floats at LIBOR plus a spread, as we see

---

[14]There is a long history of government discrimination in the treatment of default on creditors. Governments may benefit from such discrimination, for a variety of reasons. For a discussion of these reasons, and the early U.S. experience with sovereign defaults and discrimination, see Calomiris (1991). For a discussion of the recent experience with Ecuadoran Bradys, see Vogel and Druckerman (1999) and *The Wall Street Journal* (1999).

for about half of the EFM bonds in the 1990s, we may reasonably infer that many of the buyers of these instruments are banks.

Furthermore, a bond-by-bond review of the issues in the World Bank's *World Debt Tables*[15] reveals that a disproportionate number of floating-rate issues come from a few major countries in East Asia: Indonesia, Thailand, and especially Korea. This may also explain the apparent bias of banks toward Latin America in Figure 1.9. In reality, banks were probably supplying more capital to East Asia than the figure suggests, through the mechanism of floating-rate bonds.

Debt versus Equity

The same data are cut between debt and equity in Figure 1.10. This shows another surprising pattern: Equity investments far outweighed debt investments. One might have imagined that debt, being generally safer than equity, would be favored in a risky region. On the contrary, investors seemed determined to participate in the much higher

FIGURE 1.10

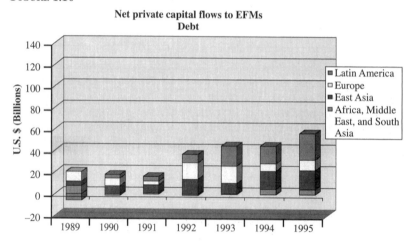

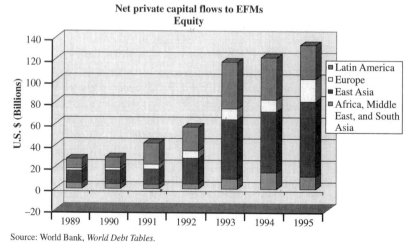

Source: World Bank, *World Debt Tables*.

---

[15]*World Debt Tables* changed its name to *Global Development Finance* in 1997, reflecting the new importance of equity flows.

returns of equity. This was again particularly true of Asia: Debt investments in Latin America actually exceeded those in East Asia in 1993 and 1995, while equity flowed more to East Asia than to Latin America throughout the 1990s.

We gain a somewhat different impression by looking just at portfolio debt (bonds) and portfolio equity (stocks) as in Figure 1.11. Here the division is more nearly equal, and the relative popularity of Latin America for equity investing is much higher. Thus, both the bias toward equity investment and the preference for East Asian equity came from the corporations; portfolio investors showed greater caution (greater relative preference for debt instruments). When they invested in East Asia, portfolio investors showed a slight preference for equity and in Central and Eastern Europe a distinct preference for debt. Indeed, very little equity from Central and Eastern Europe was sold to portfolio investors during this period.

These patterns are not difficult to understand. Since debt is safer than equity, those investors who are worried about the downside will prefer it. Portfolio investors make their capital commitments at arm's length, with much less information than corporations, who make direct investments in firms they are typically involved in managing. So it is natural that portfolio investors should tilt relatively more toward debt. This is doubly true in Central and Eastern Europe, where the problems of transition made

FIGURE 1.11

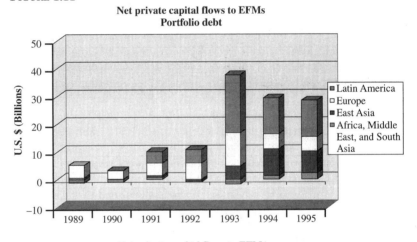

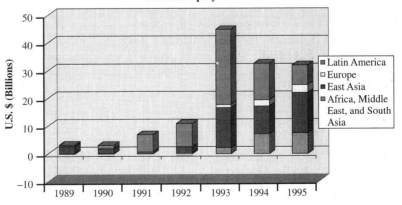

Source: World Bank, *World Debt Tables.*

portfolio investment particularly difficult. Only East Asia and Latin America were perceived as having the combination of opportunities and institutions to make the promised upside rewards of equity dominate the downside protection of debt for portfolio investors.

The net capital flows to EFMs that we have been examining need to be understood in a broader context. Not only was capital flowing to EFMs but across borders everywhere, particularly among the developed countries, and this was true for banks, corporations, and portfolio investors. Figure 1.12 shows in dramatic fashion how both banks and portfolio investors had increased their appetites for international investment over at least a decade before the EFM boom began.

Panel (a) shows how banks in member countries of the Organization for Economic Cooperation and Development (OECD), despite the debt crisis, had greatly expanded cross-border lending between 1980 and 1991. Since the OECD is essentially the set of developed countries, this shows the internationalization of bank lending among developed countries. Panel (b) shows the explosion of volume in international bonds again within the OECD, and panel (c) shows the astonishing increase in the appetite of portfolio investors in three developed countries for cross-border trades.

The forces underlying these changes included the expansion of international trade, which created a new demand for international finance; technological changes in communications, computing, and risk measurement, which facilitated the global reach of competing financial institutions and markets; and the deregulation of institutions and markets throughout the world, which was largely driven by the first two influences.

As in the 1970s, changes in interest rates also contributed to the attraction of global capital flows. The early 1990s saw nominal interest rates denominated in dollars drop to the 5–6 percent level. Debt investors in the developed world who had grown accustomed to higher returns first sought high-yield bonds, for which the market recovered fully by about 1993, and then increasingly debt from EFMs, which by the mid-1990s offered one of the few ways in which large amounts of capital could be lent at high spreads.

Thus, while the capital flows into EFMs in the 1990s reflected growing enthusiasm over the opportunities newly available in developing countries, it is also true that the attractive changes in the EFMs occurred at a very opportune time, when investors were ready to hear about international opportunities and equipped to take advantage of them.

FIGURE 1.12

Globalization of investors

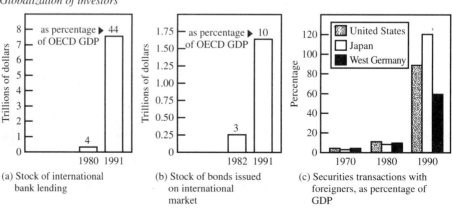

(a) Stock of international bank lending

(b) Stock of bonds issued on international market

(c) Securities transactions with foreigners, as percentage of GDP

Source: Bank for International Settlements; Crook (1992).

EFM Securities, Performance, and Risk

It is now time to take a closer look at the instruments behind these EFM capital flows and their risks.

International Bonds

Banks, of course, make loans with their own resources and corporations do much the same with their direct investment. But bonds come from a variety of markets. In a few cases, local bonds are available to foreign investors, but the majority of bonds sold by developing country issuers to portfolio investors are *international bonds*; that is, bonds designed for cross-border investors and not registered under the national rules of any country. These bonds are not denominated in local currency but in one of the developed country currencies such as U.S. dollars, Japanese yen, or German marks. Their interest is paid free of any withholding taxes.

International bonds were developed in the 1960s as a kind of freewheeling, unregulated securities market in which issuers from various countries could raise capital away from the internal markets of the developed countries. In the early days of the market, international bonds could only be sold if the issuer was of the highest credit with strong name recognition. Gradually, the international bond market has become more tolerant of lower credits and developing countries.

By 1994 the international bond market was offering a broad list of mainly private sector bonds from many countries and denominated in all major currencies. The largest issuers were from major countries such as Argentina, Brazil, Indonesia, Korea, Mexico, and Thailand, but a great many other countries also had access to this market, including in 1995 Estonia, Ghana, Jordan, Lebanon, Lithuania, Malta, Mauritius, Panama, Slovakia, and Sri Lanka.

International bond maturities in the mid-1990s were most often medium term (two to five years) for EFM issuers, but some bonds ranged out as far as 17 years. About half were at fixed rates of interest and about half at floating rates of interest tied, like a bank loan, to three-month or six-month LIBOR. The fixed interest rates can be best understood as a spread above U.S. Treasuries of comparable maturity. These spreads range from about 100 basis points (1 percent) to 500 basis points (5 percent). As can be seen in Figure 1.13, maturities and spreads are negatively correlated, with both dependent on the market's perception of the country's creditworthiness.

Creditworthiness is most commonly measured by bond ratings. Moody's Investor Services and Standard and Poor's Corporation (S&P), the two most widely followed rating agencies, were rating most EFM international bond issues by the mid-1990s. In 1995, for example, Korea was rated A1 by S&P and was upgraded from A+ to AA− by Moody's; Thailand was rated A2 by Moody's and A by S&P; the Czech Republic was rated Baa2 by Moody's and BBB+ by S&P. All of these were "investment grade" ratings; that is, they were not "junk bonds."

A study of bond ratings for sovereign risks[16] showed that a few factors affecting the capacity and willingness to repay debt (GDP per capita, growth of GDP, the historical record of default, inflation, and the amount of existing sovereign debt) explain more than 90 percent of the cross-country variation in bond ratings. Yet identifying the turning points in country risk assessment is notoriously difficult to do. Despite their high ratings in 1995, two years later Korea, Thailand, and the Czech Republic would

---

[16]Cantor and Packer (1997).

FIGURE 1.13

Terms of fixed-rate international bond issues, 1994–1995

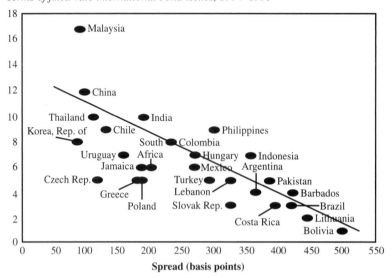

Note: Maturities and spreads are based on U.S. dollar–denominated fixed rate issues. Spreads are over the benchmark U.S. Treasury securities, except for Hungary, for which Deutschmark issues were used as a proxy.

Source: World Bank, *World Debt Tables* 1996.

all be on the brink of default. It is a sobering comment on EFM risk that the best financial professionals, including the bond rating agencies and the institutional investors pricing bonds in Figure 1.13, were unable to foresee (even months in advance) the kind of major setbacks that became realities in 1997. Despite an enormous amount of progress in quantifying risk throughout the world, EFM crises are very difficult to forecast.[17]

Equities

The riskiest of the EFM investments are publicly traded equities. The number and volume of traded EFM equities is far fewer than the number of traded bonds for three reasons. First, traded debt includes sovereign as well as private debt. Second, problems of information limit the number of firms that can qualify in equity markets since investors are relatively unprotected against downside losses on equity instruments. Third, a given company may have dozens of different bonds outstanding but it usually has only one stock, or at most two when voting rights are concentrated in a control stock kept in a few hands.

Most stocks, unlike bonds, are traded locally in stock exchanges. Thus, when international portfolio investors want to buy a local stock, it might seem natural for them to go directly to the local exchange. However, the complexities of multiple currencies, languages, taxes, and laws related to equity investments make it desirable to "translate" local stocks into a global format. Thus, for many years stocks with an international following have been offered as American Depository Receipts (ADRs) or Global Depository Receipts (GDRs). In this structure, a trustee holds a block of an EFM stock and issues "receipts" to investors for as many shares as it holds. The

---

[17]For a survey of approaches to forecasting crises, see Hunter et al. (1999).

receipts transmit the benefits of ownership to their holders, but they pay in a global currency and meet standards for listing on developed country exchanges. This arrangement avoids many problems that might arise if investors attempted to own EFM stocks directly, and the listing on developed country exchanges adds greatly to the investment's liquidity.

The need to diversify the risk of EFM stocks has led to the creation of hundreds of mutual funds, both redeemable (open-end) and nonredeemable (closed-end) that invest in the stocks of a particular country or region or EFM stocks generally. *Diversification* is one of the great lessons of modern finance theory: By investing in diversified portfolios, investors smooth out the idiosyncratic ups and downs of particular companies or countries. This reduces the overall risk of the investment without reducing the expected return, and should therefore be sought by all rational investors. Funds are the institutional expression of the need for diversification, and also allow investors to subcontract the job of particular stock selection to a professional engaged full-time in this difficult task. From the end of 1992 to the end of 1994, the total assets of EFM equity funds rose about tenfold from $2 billion to $23 billion.

The Unique Risk of EFMs

The rush of interest in EFM stock investments caused a number of academic researchers to take a longer look at performance in these markets compared with the risk, and the initial impression was quite favorable. Table 1.4 shows the average one-year returns on IFC global stock indexes for 20 EFMs from 1976 until 1992 (unless the market in question did not "emerge" until after 1976), omitting the extraordinary performance of 1993, and compares it with the performance of the Morgan Stanley Capital International (MSCI) index, a broadly based index of international equity investment.

As can be seen, the EFMs show a significantly higher mean return over this 16-year period; indeed, a mean 20 percent annual return over a long term is about as good as equity investments get even for the most aggressive investments, such as venture capital. Of course, the standard deviations are very high, and one cannot reject the possibility that the high mean return was merely random. Assuming, however, that the results are meaningful, it is important to compare them to risk. The sample standard deviation of returns is higher for EFMs than for the MSCI, but the standard deviation is a misleading measure of risk.

According to standard finance theory (the *Capital Asset Pricing Model*, or CAPM), if investors can diversify the idiosyncratic risks of particular countries by buying broadly based stock funds that invest worldwide, what should matter most for measuring and pricing risk is the correlation of EFMs with a broader portfolio index

TABLE 1.4 Average One-Year Returns from 1976 through 1992

	20 EFMs (%)	MSCI (%)
Mean return	20.4	13.9
Standard deviation	24.9	14.4
Correlation with MSCI	0.16	1.00
Auto-correlation	0.15	0.01

MSCI = Morgan Stanley Capital International index (value-weighted)
Source: Harvey (1995).

such as MSCI. From that point of view, EFM investments appear almost too good to be true, for they combine very high mean returns with very low correlation. This suggests that all rational investors should add large amounts of EFM stocks to their portfolios, and that doing so would raise the expected portfolio return while actually lowering portfolio risk.

Furthermore, the autocorrelation of EFM returns suggests elements of predictability: One good (or bad) year is more likely than not to be followed by another, which is also of considerable interest to investors. Although such patterns may be explicable by autocorrelation in risk, high autocorrelation of returns is sometimes viewed as an investing opportunity—a way for savvy investors to take advantage of stock market "momentum" by buying shares when returns rise and selling them when returns fall. The autocorrelation of EFM stocks may indicate special momentum opportunities in these shares.

When something appears too good to be true, it usually is. On closer examination of these results some problems emerge, and alternative interpretations of the data seem more reasonable. One problem with using the data in Table 1.4 to forecast future returns and risk is *survival bias*. This refers to the distortion of analysis that happens when we look back in time at a sample that disproportionately represents investments that have survived over time, and filters out many that have disappeared from the market. The easiest way to understand survival bias is to think about mutual fund performance, since poorly performing mutual funds are frequently shut down or merged out of existence. When we look at the historical average of the returns for funds that exist today, we form an overly optimistic view of expected future returns because the backward-looking data do not include the funds that have failed and disappeared.

An ingenious academic study[18] applied this concept to EFM stocks. It created a computer-based simulation in which a number of synthetic markets with the statistical characteristics of EFMs start their lives at a point in time and then evolve, subject to "submerging" whenever their level falls below a certain boundary. The study showed that the simple omission of "submerged" markets (i.e., those which had collapsed or which were not yet fully visible) could produce a pattern remarkably like that of Table 1.4—abnormally high returns right after "emergence," low correlation with world risk factors and autocorrelation—even if the actual expected returns of EFMs were no higher than those of the U.S. equity market.

But aside from survival bias there is a deeper problem with the logic that would use the data in Table 1.4 to suggest the availability of high risk-adjusted profits from EFM equity investments: Equity risk in EFMs is fundamentally different from that of equity markets in developed countries. In particular, a low country *beta* (the CAPM risk measure) provides a false signal of low risk in EFM equities.

Why are low country betas not indicative of low risk in EFM stocks? There are two reasons: First, the assumption that there are enough EFM countries in the world to diversify away idiosyncratic risk is highly questionable. Only a handful of countries in Latin America and Asia produce enough shares to offer international investors the chance to diversify their portfolios. Furthermore, EFM countries have interdependent risks in some states of the world, particularly during bad times. When one EFM country suffers an adverse shock (e.g., Russia in 1998), losses to international investors may lead them to shed other risky EFM assets, leading to a transmission of loss from one EFM equity market to another. Data on EFM equity returns show substantially

---

[18]Goetzmann and Jorion (1997).

larger correlation of returns across countries during the Mexican, Asian, and Russian financial crises.[19]

Second, the value of EFM stocks is highly dependent on the success of their countries' liberalization experimehts. Thus their long-run returns—during the early phases of economic development—have a certain *bimodal* (win or lose) character. In other words, investors in EFM stocks are learning over time and updating the probability of a successful economywide experiment in institution building. These experiments typically involve interrelated and risky changes in fiscal policy, bank regulation, foreign exchange and central bank policies, pension restructuring, and electoral reform. Economies that successfully graduate from this stage will enjoy highly positive long-run stock returns; those that do not will see their stock markets collapse alongside their exchange rates, banking systems, and, often, their governments. The opportunities available in Russian equities in mid-1999 discussed in the box below give an example of how potential stock returns are often perceived to be dramatically bimodal.

Russia's Shaky Options

The Russian stock market has become flavour of the year with emerging market investors once more in spite of the country's shattering financial crash, which occurred a year ago tomorrow, and continuing political turmoil. Since the start of 1999, the Russian stock market has surged more than 100 percent in local currency terms on the back of higher oil prices and a stronger than anticipated industrial recovery, making it one of the best performing markets in the world.

But the scarcely apprehended truth about Russia is that it still does not have a stock market. Rather, it boasts a highly volatile options market. Buying a Russian equity does not give investors enforceable ownership rights over a company's assets nor guarantee a slice of future cash flows. A Russian share is perhaps more accurately viewed as an exotic type of option, which may be converted into real equity one bright, shining morning in the future, when the country has built the infrastructure of an effective market economy and an independent judicial regime.

As Bill Browder, director of Hermitage Capital Management, says: "The Russian market is not really valuing anything on a fundamental economic basis. The market is more a perception of whether Russia will become a proper member of democratic, capitalist society. If Russia breeds an environment where equities really are equities, then everything is ridiculously undervalued. If they do not, then all of this speculation up and down is essentially a worthless exercise."

Of course, much the same could have been said of many other emerging markets at different points in the past. Brazil, for example, remained in the investment doldrums for decades as the country battled to get public sector deficits and inflation under control. But when Brazil introduced sounder monetary policies and more responsible government, the value of its corporate assets soared. The hope is that Russia's Gazprom—which trades at about a 95 percent discount to Exxon of the U.S.—could one day be revalued in a similarly striking way to Telebras in Brazil.

Reprinted from the *Financial Times*, August 16, 1999.

---

[19]Also, if there is a stable linear relationship between returns in one market and returns in another, reflecting economic interdependence, then the correlation of returns in the two markets will automatically increase when volatility of returns increases. See Forbes and Rigobon (1999).

The bimodal character of long-run outcomes for EFM stocks violates a basic assumption of the CAPM, on which the usefulness of beta as a risk measure depends: namely the normality of long-run stock returns. The violations of normality are also visible in short-run returns. It has been shown that short-run EFM returns are not normally distributed; instead the EFM return-generating process contains jumps or discontinuities (and these discontinuities are often correlated across countries, as during financial crises).[20]

The effects of these two problems—small numbers of significant stock issuing EFMs and nonnormal returns distributions—on risk are also interrelated. Bimodal long-run returns and discontinuities in short-run returns worsen the problem of diversification because the more extreme any one country's outcomes, the harder it is to diversify idiosyncratic risk by pooling stocks from different countries.

The autocorrelation of returns for EFMs is also explicable as a consequence of long-run bimodal outcomes of EFM experiments. Serial correlation could reflect the fact that, as the results of the EFM experiments unfold over time, investors update their beliefs about the relative probabilities of long-run success or failure—probabilities that evolve slowly over time, generating a degree of autocorrelation in returns.

Financial economists have sometimes considered the possible effect on asset prices of drastic events, which have low probability but large potential impact. This implies a major departure from normally distributed returns and is called, appropriately, the *peso problem*. It has been invoked to explain what seem to be unreasonably large forward discounts in inflationary currencies,[21] unreasonably large risk premiums in equity returns,[22] and apparent distortions in the term structure of interest rates.[23] Peso problems have not yet found their way into the mainstream theories that explain asset pricing, yet we need to keep them at the front of our minds as we consider market risk in countries where the peso lives.

A unique feature of EFM securities is the apparent pattern of *contagion*. On a day-to-day basis EFM stocks are not highly correlated across countries; but when a financial crisis (collapse of both stock and currency values) develops in one country, it sometimes seems to leap from that country to others like a contagious disease so that cross-country correlation is suddenly high. There are at least four reasons for this pattern, two related to trade and two to capital markets.

First, if the currency of country B collapses, its imports from country A may become prohibitively expensive, damaging A's real economy. For example, Argentina sells a substantial portion of its exports to Brazil; when the Brazilian *real* collapsed in early 1999, Argentina's exports contracted. Second, if the currency of country B collapses, it may become a far more attractive export competitor to country A. The collapse of the Thai baht, for example, which fell by about 25 percent in July 1997, put competitive pressure on Indonesia, Malaysia, and the Philippines, triggering collapses of their currencies. Then when the Indonesian rupiah lost 80 percent of its value during 1997–1998, it gained a competitive advantage over Thailand and the Philippines, complicating their recoveries.

Third, investors are often poorly informed and may imagine the worst. When one country suffers a financial collapse, it is natural to worry about which other countries might have a similar problem, without understanding the precise details. This may cause other countries' securities to be sold although if later information proves no real effects, they should soon recover. For example, Taiwan's currency and security values

---

[20]Harvey (1995).

[21]Krasker (1980).

[22]Rietz (1988)

[23]Lewis (1991).

fell during the early days of the Asia crisis in 1997, but soon recovered. Fourth, certain investors in EFM securities are leveraged (i.e., hedge funds and banks). When such investors suffer a serious loss in one part of their portfolio, they may need to protect the quality of their own debt issues by selling other risky assets to pay down debt. Thus, the losses created in Russia's 1998 collapse caused declines in other EFM securities.

In summary, the capital asset pricing model and its risk measure beta, while standard (if controversial) tools of analysis in developed markets, seem to be particularly ill suited to measuring EFM equity risk. CAPM is based on an assumption that pooling of idiosyncratic risks is feasible, that asset prices evolve continuously over time, and that the distribution of returns is stable and normally distributed.[24] The evolution of stock prices in EFMs is different, so the meaning of risk is also somewhat different, and the CAPM is not a sufficient tool for coming to grips with that risk.[25] In EFMs, the dominant concern is not the beta of a firm, an industry, or even a country, but the probability of failure of the liberalization experiment in which the country is engaged or the probability of a disruption to global capital markets coming from a similar failure in another EFM.

Consistent with that view, sovereign debt ratings are the most successful predictor of the cross-section of expected returns for different countries' EFM stock market indexes. Sovereign ratings themselves are largely governed by the risk of the institutional experiments in economic liberalization.[26]

Variation in the risk premium of EFM stocks and debts is often guided by sudden changes in perceptions about the long-term viability of the core institutions within EFM countries, since capital market risk is closely related to the health of the financial system and the government's fiscal balance. For example, as described in the nearby box, the Persian Gulf crisis had significant and sudden effects on various EFM securities through its effects on international trade and financial flows. Thus, one cannot fully understand EFM risk by extrapolating from day-to-day fluctuations of stock returns and their covariances under the standard assumptions used for developed markets. A standard analysis of those covariances would lead one to commit large amounts of resources to EFM stocks. Yet anyone who did so in 1993 based on these measures suffered a severe setback as the result of the discontinuities and correlations among EFM returns during the various crises of 1994–1998.

Perhaps when all countries are further up the financial learning curve, when EFM legal foundations are strengthened, information flows institutionalized and currencies stabilized, when banks and other financial intermediaries have learned what can go wrong and how to manage risk, when investors have learned better how to understand market anomalies and arbitrage them away, then perhaps large shocks will be fewer and securities returns may become more normally distributed.

EFM liberalization experiments are complex and multidimensional, involving at once financing market opening (discussed in Chapters 2 and 3), the privatization of state-owned enterprises (the subject of Chapter 3), legal system reforms (analyzed in Chapter 4), the development of new information, accounting, and corporate governance systems (the subject of Chapter 5), the restructuring of government finances and exchange rate policy (reviewed in Chapter 6), and the prudential regulation of the

---

[24]Alternatively, CAPM can be based on an assumption that investors have quadratic utility functions, which seems even less realistic.

[25]Interestingly, despite differences in the time series properties of returns for EFMs and developed equity markets, the factors that explain the cross-section of equity returns for individual firms within EFMs seem to be quite similar to the factors that work well in developed markets, as discussed in Rouwenhorst (1999).

[26]Erb, Harvey, and Viskanta (1997).

Shifting Sands of Risk: The Persian Gulf War

The standard determinants of sovereign risk change slowly: Long-run growth prospects, the volume of outstanding sovereign debt, a country's fiscal balance, and its history of default or repayment may remain unchanged for years or decades. But sovereign risk sometimes can shift suddenly in the face of important changes in import or export prices, or political events that otherwise influence the trade balance or the fiscal balance. After all, anything that interrupts the expected future flow of exports (which generate hard currency earnings), the cost of imports, or the government's tax receipts (the means for the sovereign to capture its share of export earnings) can threaten the government's ability to repay.

A particularly telling example of a sudden change of fortunes—with consequences that differed markedly across EFMs—was the Persian Gulf crisis of 1990–1991. Using the standard finance tool of *event study analysis,* Suk Hum Lee, Hyun Mo Sung, and Jorge L. Urrutia (1996) studied the effects of the crisis on the returns to holders of EFM syndicated bank loans. They found that the value of these debt offerings from oil exporting countries rose in response to the crisis, while the value of oil importing countries' debts fell. The size of the effect on bank loan values depended on the extent of a country's indebtedness. The debts of highly indebted oil importers were severely affected, while oil importers with little debt saw no significant change in their debt values.

The Middle East was also a destination for many foreign workers who remitted their earnings to their home countries, which sometimes provided those home countries with a significant share of their foreign currency receipts. The interruption of these remittances also had an adverse effect on the values of debt offerings by the remittance-dependent countries.

The consequences of the Persian Gulf War for the syndicated bank loans of EFM countries illustrate three points. First, sudden changes in the values of exports, import costs, and flows of remittances can have important effects on the sovereign risks of EFMs. Second, changes in sovereign risk are reflected in private debt claims as well as public debt claims; when an EFM's sovereign rating deteriorates, its private debt and equity issuers also suffer higher costs of funding. Third, the same event can have dramatically different consequences for EFMs depending on their risk exposures.

banking system (the subject of Chapter 7). The shape of EFM liberalization along each of these dimensions affects the risk of the securities issued by EFM governments and corporations. For example, one study found that successful privatizations of state-owned enterprises contribute to the reduction in "political risk" (the risk of a collapse of market-friendly government policies), and that this risk reduction is reflected in substantial reductions in EFM equity risk premiums.[27] That finding illustrates how market participants in emerging markets must be able to judge whether the sudden, dramatic, multifaceted changes accompanying liberalization are likely to succeed or fail, and price EFM securities accordingly. To make those judgments they must understand the determinants of success and failure along each of the crucial dimensions of reform, and how best to manage the risks of "experiment failure" to protect themselves from the costs of failure.

The issues of jump risk, financial crisis, and stock market survival make it clear that EFM securities not only involve more risk than those of developed countries, but

---

[27]Perotti (2000).

they involve a different kind of risk. On the surface, EFM stocks and bonds appear similar to the stocks and bonds of developed markets. But we need to understand what is happening beneath the surface. We will never understand EFM securities based on statistical behavior alone and developed-market models such as the CAPM. At a deeper level, the markets are based on quite different legal foundations, information flows, and currency considerations, and these factors in turn are connected with deep differences in culture, politics, and financial institutions. Penetrating to these levels is the primary task of this book.

APPENDIX

PRIVATE LENDING TO SOVEREIGNS: DEFAULTS AND RESCHEDULINGS, 1800–1992[a]

Country	Beginning of Period	End of Period	Form[b]	Notes
Albania	1990	1992	L	Soviet collapse
Angola	1988	1992	S, L	Civil unrest
Argentina	1890	1893	B	Refinancing problem (Baring crisis)
	1956	1965	S	Post-Peron budget crisis, beet export drops
	1982	1992	L	Oil and interest rate shocks, budget crisis
Austria	1802	1816	B	Napoleonic wars
	1868	1870	B	Coupon tax after Hapsburg dual monarchy
	1914	1915	B	World War I
	1932	1952	B	Depression, German occupation, and World War II
Bolivia	1875	1879	B	
	1931	1957	B	Depression
	1980	1992	L	Oil and interest rate shocks
Brazil	1826	1829	B	War with Portugal and United Provinces
	1898	1910	B	Coffee prices collapse
	1914	1919	B	End of rubber boom and coffee price drop
	1931	1943	B	Depression
	1961	1964	S	Budget crisis
	1983	1992	L	Oil and interest rate shocks and budget crisis
Bulgaria	1915	1920	B	World War I and civil unrest
	1932	1992	B	Depression, World War II, and Communist takeover
	1990	1992	L	Soviet collapse
Cameroon	1989	1992	L	
Chile	1826	1842	B	Independence war and civil unrest
	1880	1883	B	War of the Pacific
	1931	1948	B	Nitrate market collapse and Depression
	1965		S	Copper price drop
	1972	1975	S	Budget crisis and coup
	1983	1990	L	Oil and interest rate shocks
China	1921	1949	B	Civil war, World War II, and Communist repudiation
Colombia	1826	1861	B	Independence war and civil unrest
	1873		B	
	1880	1904	B	Trade depression, then civil war
	1932	1944	B	Depression
Congo	1986	1992	L	Oil and interest rate shocks
Costa Rica	1828	1840	B	Independence war and split from Central American Federation
	1874	1885	B	Central American chaos
	1895	1911	B	
	1932	1953	B	Depression
	1981	1990	L	Oil and interest rate shocks
Côte d'Ivoire	1984	1992	L	Oil and interest rate shocks
Cuba	1933	1934	B	Depression
	1960	1963	B	Communist revolution and repudiation
	1982	1992	L	Oil and interest rate shocks; Soviet collapse
Czechoslovakia	1938	1946	B	Nazi occupation, World War II
	1952	1959	B	Communist takeover and repudiation
Dominican Republic	1872	1907	B	Civil unrest and war, repudiations
	1931	1934	B	Hurricane and Depression
	1982	1992	L	Oil and interest rate shocks

Country	*Beginning of Period*	*End of Period*	*Form*[b]	*Notes*
Ecuador	1832	1855	B	Independence war and split from Colombia
	1868	1898	B	
	1906	1955	B	Civil unrest, then Depression
	1982	1992	L	Oil and interest rate shocks
Egypt	1816	1880	B	Budget crisis; British and French intervention
	1984	1992	L	Oil and interest rate shocks
El Salvador	1828	1860	B	Independence war and split from Central American Federation
	1921	1922	B	
	1932	1946	B	Depression
Germany	1932	1953	B	Nazi policy and World War II
	1949	1992	B	Communist takeover (East Germany only)
Gabon	1978		S	Interest rate shocks
	1986	1992	L	Oil price swings
Gambia	1986	1988	L	
Ghana	1969	1974	S	
Greece	1826	1878	B	Independence war and turmoil
	1894	1897	B	Budget crisis and political instability
	1932	1964	B	Depression and World War II
Guatemala	1828	1856	B	Independence war and split from Central American Federation
	1876	1888	B	Central American chaos
	1894	1917	B	
	1933	1936	B	Depression
Guinea	1985	1992	S, L	Oil and interest rate shocks
Guyana	1982	1992	L	Oil and interest rate shocks
Honduras	1828	1867	B	Independence war and split from Central American Federation
	1873	1925	B	Central American chaos
	1981	1992	L	Oil and interest rate shocks
Hungary	1932	1967	B	Depression, World War II, and Communist takeover
Iran	1992		L	
Iraq	1990	1992	L	Gulf War
Italy	1940	1946	B	World War II
Jamaica	1978	1990	L	Oil and interest rate shocks, budget crisis
Japan	1942	1952	B	World War II
Jordan	1989	1992	L	
Liberia	1875	1898	B	
	1912	1923	B	Budget crisis
	1932	1935	B	Depression
	1980	1992	S, L	Oil and interest rate shocks, civil unrest
Madagascar	1981	1992	S, L	Oil and interest rate shocks
Malawi	1982	1988	L	Oil and interest rate shocks
Mexico	1828	1850	B	Post-independence chaos and war with United States
	1859	1885	B	Civil war, French intervention, then repudiation
	1914	1922	B	Revolutionary period and partial repudiation
	1928	1942	B	
	1982	1990	L	Interest rate shocks
Morocco	1903	1904	B	
	1983	1990	L	Oil and interest rate shocks
Mozambique	1984	1992	L	Oil and interest rate shocks
Netherlands	1802	1814	B	Napoleonic wars
Nicaragua	1828	1874	B	Independence war and split from Central American Federation

Country	Beginning of Period	End of Period	Form[b]	Notes
	1894	1895	B	
	1911	1917	B	
	1932	1937	B	Depression
	1980	1992	L	Oil and interest rate shocks
Niger	1983	1991	L	Oil and interest rate shocks
Nigeria	1983	1991	L	Interest rate shocks and civil unrest
Panama	1932	1946	B	Depression
	1983	1992	L	Oil and interest rate shocks
Paraguay	1874	1885	B	Following war with Argentina, Brazil, and Uruguay
	1892	1895	B	
	1920	1924	B	
	1932	1944	B	Depression and war with Bolivia
	1986	1992	L	Oil and interest rate shocks
Peru	1826	1848	B	Independence war and civil unrest
	1876	1889	B	Guano price collapse and War of the Pacific
	1931	1951	B	Civil unrest, conflict with Chile, and Depression
	1968	1969	S, L	Fishmeal price drop and budget crisis
	1978	1992	S, L	Sharp exports contraction, oil and interest rate shocks
Philippines	1983	1992	L	Oil and interest rate shocks, natural disasters
Poland	1936	1952	B	Depression and World War II
	1981	1992	L	Soviet collapse, oil and interest rate shocks
Portugal	1834	1841	B	Repudiation of usurper's loan
	1850	1856	B	
	1892	1901	B	Budget crisis
Romania	1933	1958	B	Depression and World War II
	1982	1987	L	Soviet collapse, oil and interest rate shocks
Russia	1839		B	
	1885		B	Small coupon tax
	1917	1918	B	Revolution and repudiation
	1991	1992	L	Soviet collapse
Senegal	1981	1992	S, L	Oil and interest rate shocks
Sierra Leone	1977	1992	S, L	Oil and interest rate shocks
South Africa	1985	1992	L	Sanctions-induced capital outflows
Spain	1820		B	Troops mutiny against king
	1831	1834	B	Carlist wars
	1851		B	Civil unrest
	1867	1872	B	Civil unrest prior to Liberal uprising
	1882		B	
Sudan	1979	1992	S, L	Drop in cotton exports, interest rate shocks
Tanzania	1984	1992	S, L	Oil and interest rate shocks
Togo	1979	1992	S, L	Oil and interest rate shocks
Trinidad and Tobago	1989	1989	L	
Tunisia	1867	1870	B	
Turkey	1876	1881	B	Russo-Turkish War, budget crisis
	1915	1932	B	World War I, European occupation, Depression
	1940	1943	B	World War II
	1959		L	
	1965		L	
	1978	1982	S, L	Oil and interest rate shocks
Uganda	1981	1992	S	Oil and interest rate shocks
Uruguay	1876	1878	B	
	1891		B	
	1915	1921	B	
	1933	1938	B	Depression
	1983	1991	L	Oil and interest rate shocks
Venezuela	1832	1840	B	Independence war and split with Colombia

Country	Beginning of Period	End of Period	Form[b]	Notes
	1848	1881	B	Revolutions and civil unrest
	1892		B	Civil unrest
	1898	1905	B	Revolutions and European blockades
	1982	1990	L	Interest rate shocks and budget crisis
Vietnam	1985	1992	L	Oil and interest rate shocks
Yugoslavia	1895		B	Serbian default
	1933	1960	B	Depression and World War II
	1983	1992	L	Oil and interest rate shocks and civil war
Zaire	1961		B	Default following independence
	1976	1992	S, L	Budget crisis, and copper, oil, and interest rate shocks
Zambia	1983	1992	L	Oil and interest rate shocks
Zimbabwe	1965	1980	B	Repudiation following independence

[a]See below for methodology and sources.
[b]B = bonds, S = suppliers' credits, L = bank loans.
Source: This entire table and its accompanying notes are taken from Purcell and Kaufman (1993).

Methodology and Sources

This Appendix lists all the major periods of sovereign debt servicing incapacity from 1800 through 1992. There are, however, several important issues involved in compiling such a list:

Lender   Only private lending through bonds, suppliers' credits, or bank loans is considered. Intergovernmental loans, such as World War I debts, are excluded because of the heavily political nature of such lending, and because private sector investors are not directly affected.

Borrower   Only lending to sovereign nations is included. The volume of loans to states, provinces, cities, and private corporations generally has been much smaller than that to sovereign governments. Furthermore, data and commentary on subsovereign and corporate defaults are scarce.

Extent of Default or Rescheduling   Not every instance of technical default on bond or loan covenants is listed; to list them all would be virtually impossible. Instead, we identified extended periods (six months or more) where all or part of interest and/or principal payments due were reduced or rescheduled. Some of the defaults and reschedulings involved outright repudiation (a legislative or executive act of government denying liability), while others were minor and announced ahead of time in a conciliatory fashion by debtor nations. The end of each period of default or rescheduling was recorded when full payments resumed or a restructuring was agreed upon. Periods of default or rescheduling within five years of each other were combined. Where a formal repudiation was identified, its date served as the end of the period of default and the repudiation is noted in the notes (e.g., Cuba in 1963); where no clear repudiation was announced, the default was listed as persisting through 1992 (Bulgaria). Voluntary refinancings (Colombia in 1985 and Algeria in 1992) were not included.

Period Covered   The beginning of the 19th century was chosen as a starting point because of two important developments. First, the proliferation of constitutional forms of government led to more stable nation-states that recognized their continuing liability to lenders (in earlier periods, most loans were made to individual rulers). Second, financial relations were becoming more institutionalized as witnessed by the growth of incorporated banks and stock exchanges.

Unit of Analysis   National names and borders change. Where a national name is changed but the borders and population stay roughly the same, then defaults are listed under the nation's most recent name: New Granada is subsumed under Colombia, Santo Domingo under the Dominican Republic, and Rhodesia under Zimbabwe. Where a sovereign nation split into more than one country, defaults prior to the separation are listed only for the apparent successor country (e.g.,

Colombia, after Ecuador and Venezuela became independent; Turkey, when Bulgaria, Romania, and Montenegro left the Ottoman Empire; Russia, after the Soviet disintegration; and Austria, after the collapse of the Austro-Hungarian Empire). Defaults are not listed for six countries that no longer exist (Prussia, Westphalia, Hesse, Schleswig-Holstein, the Transvaal, and the Orange Free State). The East German default is listed under Germany. For an overview of the subject of state succession and public indebtedness, see Hoeflict (1982).

Sources   The primary sources were the annual reports of the Corporation of Foreign Bondholders and the Foreign Bondholders Protective Council, Borchard (1951), Hardy (1982), International Monetary Fund (1992), Suter (1992), Winkler (1933) and data provided by the Institute of International Finance. . . . When the sources differed as to the date or duration of a default or rescheduling (as they often did), we determined a consensus. Our list may not include small loans to minor debtors that were not publicly disclosed.

References

Borchard, Edwin. 1951. *State Insolvency and Foreign Bondholders: General Principles*. Vol. 1. New Haven: Yale University Press.

Calomiris, Charles W. 1991. The motives of U.S. debt-management policy, 1790–1880: Efficient discrimination and time consistency. *Research in Economic History* 13: 67–105.

———. 1995. Financial fragility: Issues and policy implications. *Journal of Financial Services Research* 9: 241–57.

Calomiris, Charles W., Charles P. Himmelberg, and Paul Wachtel. 1995. Commercial paper, corporate finance, and the business cycle: A microeconomic Perspective. *Carnegie-Rochester Conference Series on Public Policy* 42: 203–50.

Cantor, Richard, and Frank Packer. 1997. Determinants and impact of sovereign credit ratings. *Quarterly Review*, Federal Reserve Bank of New York 2, no. 2. pp. 37–53.

Corporation of Foreign Bondholders. Various years. *Annual Report of the Council of the Corporation of Foreign Bondholders*. London: Corporation of Foreign Bondholders.

Crook, Clive. 1992. Fear of finance. *The Economist,* September 19, 1992: 5–18.

Eichengreen, Barry, and Peter H. Lindert, eds. 1989. *The International Debt Crisis in Historical Perspective*. Cambridge: MIT Press.

Erb, Claude B., Campbell R. Harvey, and Tadas E. Viskanta. 1997. Country risk in global financial management. CIBER Working Paper 97–001, Fuqua School of Business, Duke University.

Forbes, Kristin, and Roberto Rigobon. 1999. No contagion, only interdependence; measuring stock market co-movements. Working Paper no. 7267, National Bureau of Economic Research.

Foreign Bondholders Protective Council. Various years. *Annual Report*. New York: Foreign Bondholders Protective Council.

Goetzmann, William N., and Philippe Jorion. 1997. Re-emerging markets. Working Paper no. 5906, National Bureau of Economic Research.

Hardy, Chandra S. 1982. *Rescheduling Developing Country Debts, 1956–1981: Lessons and Recommendations*. Washington, DC: Overseas Development Council.

Harvey, Campbell R. 1995. Predictable risk and returns in emerging markets. *Journal of Financial Studies* 8, no. 3: 773–816.

Hoeflict, M. E. 1982. Through a glass darkly: Reflections upon the history of the international law of public debt in connection with state succession. *University of Illinois Law Review* 1982, no. 1: 39–70.

Hubbard, R. Glenn, ed. 1990. *Asymmetric Information, Corporate Finance, and Investment.* Chicago: University of Chicago Press.

———. 1991. *Financial Markets and Financial Crises.* Chicago: University of Chicago Press.

Huizinga, Harry. 1989. The commercial bank claims on developing countries: How have banks been affected? In *Dealing with the Debt Crisis*. Washington, DC: World Bank.

Hunter, William C., George G. Kaufman, and Thomas H. Krueger, eds. 1999. *The Asian Financial Crisis: Origins, Implications, and Solutions*. Boston: Kluwer Academic Publishers.

International Monetary Fund. 1992. *Private Market Financing for Developing Countries.* Washington, DC: IMF.

———. 1998. *World Economic Outlook and International Capital Markets: Interim Assessment.* Washington, DC: IMF.

———. 1999. *International Capital Markets.* Washington, DC: IMF.

Jorion, Philippe, and William N. Goetzmann. 1999. Global stock markets in the twentieth century. *Journal of Finance* 54: 953–80.

Kindleberger, Charles P. 1989. *Manias, Panics and Crashes.* New York: Wiley Investment Classics.

King, Robert G., and Ross Levine. 1993a. Financial intermediation and economic development. In *Financial Intermediation in the Construction of Europe.* Ed. by Colin Mayer and Xavier Vives. London: Centre for Economic Policy Research: 156–89.

———. 1993b. Finance and growth: Schumpeter might be right. *Quarterly Journal of Economics* 108: 717–38.

———. 1993c. Finance, entrepreneurship and growth: Theory and evidence. *Journal of Monetary Economics* 32: 512–42.

Krasker, William S. 1980. The "peso problem" in testing the efficiency of forward exchange markets. *Journal of Monetary Economics* 6: 269–76.

Lee, Suk Hun, Hyun Mo Sung, and Jorge L. Urrutia. 1996. The impact of the Persian Gulf crisis on the prices of LDCs' loans. *Journal of Financial Services Research* 10: 143–62.

Levine, Ross. 1997. Financial development and economic growth: Views and agenda. *Journal of Economic Literature* 35, no. 2: 688–726.

Levine, Ross, and Sara Zervos. 1995. Stock markets, banks and economic growth. Working paper, World Bank.

Lewis, Karen K. 1991. Was there a "peso problem" in the U.S. term structure of interest rates: 1979–1982? *International Economic Review* 32: 159–73.

Lindert, Peter, and Peter Morton. 1989. How sovereign debt has worked. In *The International Financial System,* 1: *Developing Country Debt and Economic Performance.* Ed. by Jeffrey Sachs. Chicago: University of Chicago Press.

Obstfeld, Maurice, and Alan Taylor. 1999. *Global Capital Markets: Integration, Crisis, and Growth.* Cambridge: Cambridge University Press.

Perotti, Enrico. 2000. Privatization, political risk and stock market development in emerging markets. Working paper, University of Amsterdam.

Purcell, John F. H., and Jeffrey A. Kaufman. 1993. *The Risks of Sovereign Lending: Lessons from History.* New York: Salomon Brothers.

Rich, Jennifer L. 1999. The incredible shrinking markets. *Latin Finance* 109 (August): 17–24.

Rietz, Thomas A. 1988. The equity risk premium: a solution, *Journal of Monetary Economics* 22: 117–31.

Romer, Paul. 1998. Idea gaps and object gaps in economic development. *Journal of Monetary Economics* 32, no. 3: 543–74.

Rouwenhorst, K. Geert. 1999 Local return factors and turnover in emerging stock markets. *Journal of Finance* 54: 1439–64.

Sachs, Jeffrey D., ed. 1989. *Developing Country Debt and the World Economy.* Chicago: University of Chicago Press.

Sachs, Jeffrey D., and Harry Huizinga. 1987. U.S. commercial banks and the developing-country debt crisis. *Brookings Papers on Economic Activity* no. 2: 555–601.

Suter, Christian. 1992. *Debt Cycles in the World-Economy: Foreign Loans, Financial Crises, and Debt Settlements, 1820–1990.* Boulder, CO: Westview Press.

Vogel, Thomas T., Jr., and Pamela Druckerman. 1999. Ecuador buys time, but task remains tough. *The Wall Street Journal,* August 26, p. A13.

Wai, U Tun, and Hugh T. Patrick. 1973. Stock and bond issues and capital markets in less developed economies. *IMF Staff Papers,* July: 253–317.

The Wall Street Journal. 1999. Ecuador's bond deadline stirs wider tremors, August 23.

Winkler, Max. 1933. *Foreign Bonds, an Autopsy: A Study of Defaults and Repudiations of Government Obligations.* Philadelphia: Roland Swain.

Financial Repression and Financial Development

Questions:
From what do emerging financial markets emerge?
What goes wrong when business and government are too tightly linked?
What key roles does a private financial system play?
Why do many governments dominate and suppress their own financial systems?
What is "financial repression," what policies cause it, and how is it measured?
Does financial repression affect economic growth?

Introduction

"Emerging" is a curious word. It suggests that until recently developing countries were somehow in the shadows, or underwater, or otherwise hidden from view. Yet most developing countries have existed for a long time. What then is the implication of this word? The most likely answer is that it connotes movement away from statism and toward private markets, a trend of the entire world economy in the 1990s. In particular, financial markets almost everywhere have needed to be freed from government domination.

Most people do not realize that many developing country governments actively suppress their own financial systems. They may be even more surprised to learn that many economists once argued either that this does no harm or that it is actually helpful to development. In this chapter we will explore the various roles that a financial system can play and how those roles interact with the evolving role of government.

We need to understand the condition of finance prior to the changes of recent years in order to see the nature, magnitude, and meaning of the financial development that has occurred. But because the story involves the relationship between governments and markets, and between governments and their economies generally, we will be venturing into the arena of political economy. While this is not fundamentally a book about politics, we cannot understand EFMs without a clear grasp of the political setting.

If emergence is a movement away from government-dominated financial systems, then it is best understood as part of a broad historical movement away from authoritarian politics generally. Three hundred years ago, government was authoritarian almost everywhere: Monarchs governed with a firm and often arbitrary hand. Today, however, democracy is the norm. Even though elective democracy is not yet universal, the trend toward it is powerful and unmistakable. Even governments that are still purely authoritarian (e.g., North Korea) use phrases like "democratic republic" to describe themselves. While the North Korean government has no interest in real democracy, its attempt to cloak itself in the word amounts to a concession that "democracy," somehow defined, really is the standard to which nations aspire.

The trend toward political democracy is closely connected with the idea of free, private markets because both involve trusting ordinary citizens to make decisions that will affect the well being of all. It is certainly possible to liberalize the economy without first creating a political democracy—indeed this was the pattern in Korea and Taiwan, both highly successful cases of economic development—but in time the economic growth brought pressure to liberalize politically, and both countries are now full democracies. So political democracy and market economy are separable, but they tend to converge over the long term. Liberalizing an economy requires the government to take a new view of its role, and authoritarian governments do not find that easy to do. Thus, the two concepts are closely linked, and we need to explore the broader idea of political liberalization before returning to the discussion of markets.

Throughout, we must keep in mind that democratization and financial liberalization are long processes, not one-time changes. Those vested with political and economic power do not yield their privileges easily. Despite the enthusiasm for emerging markets in the early 1990s, a great deal of reform remains to be accomplished. The industrial countries took several hundred years to liberalize, and we should not be surprised if developing countries also take time to make reforms, with frequent setbacks and frustrations along the way. Nevertheless, financial repression as a concept has passed its crest and financial development is now recognized as a goal almost everywhere.

The Role and Fundamental Problem of Government

To start at the most basic level, the minimum function of government is control over the use of force. If we had no government at all, we would be subject to violence everywhere, including criminal attack, uprisings by organized groups, and invasions by other nations. The English philosopher Thomas Hobbes (1588–1679) wrote the classic description of this intolerable "state of nature," in which the life of man is "nasty, brutish and short."[1] He argued that rational human beings must agree to the existence of a state with absolute authority to monopolize the use of force. There are modern examples of areas in which state-of-nature anarchy prevails (e.g., Somalia in the 1990s) and they make it clear that a proper government providing public security needs to be established before an economy can function at much above subsistence level.

But once a government has arisen that monopolizes the use of force, it has the populace at its mercy. In general, people can do little to protect themselves against abuses by their own governments. And because governments consist of human beings with their own private interests, those who have gained a monopoly in the use of force quickly see that this position of power can be turned to substantial private benefit. Throughout history, rulers have tended to live with a great many more amenities than the rest of their societies. They do this by using force or the threat of force to extract part of the society's wealth.

This extraction of wealth takes two general forms: *taxes* and *rents*. Taxes are explicit wealth transfers and not very difficult to understand, though as we shall see, some may be cleverly disguised. Rents refer to payments for government-controlled goods or services that are higher than they would be in a free, competitive market; they may result from a pricing system distorted by monopoly or protectionism, or from outright corruption.

---

[1]Hobbes (1651).

Modern democratic states were founded on the basic principle espoused by another English philosopher, John Locke (1632–1704) that government should establish laws that reflect and serve the interests of individual citizens in their pursuit of happiness. According to that vision of government, laws are judged legitimate on the basis of how and why they empower and constrain free citizens, and we distinguish carefully between legitimate and illegitimate transfers of wealth to the government. That distinction requires a practical concept of *legitimacy*. A legitimate government adheres to principles that limit and specify its own proper behavior. A government with a clear basis of legitimacy must pursue bona fide public objectives using agreed procedures. A government without a clear basis of legitimacy either ignores its responsibilities to its citizens or confuses social objectives with the private well-being of the rulers.

This is why the *rule of law* is a central feature of legitimate modern states with vigorous private sector economies, and a focal point of this book. We shall explore the rule of law more fully in Chapter 4, but it certainly means more than the presence of laws—all governments have a large number of laws, but not all have the rule of law. The fundamental idea is that law should be based on a moral consensus regarding what is fair and just, and that laws should be reliably and uniformly enforced.

Above all, rule of law means that the rich and powerful cannot exempt themselves from the working of law and, in that sense, the rule of law is connected with the notion of limited government. Much of modern political thought is an effort to define the legitimate basis of government and to understand how the benefits of government can be obtained without the arbitrary intrusions and abuses of privilege. Modern elective democracy can be seen as the most durable institutionalization of limited government.

It is extraordinarily difficult to establish a rule of law that limits the behavior of government where that has not been the norm in the past. People who enjoy the privileges of unrestrained power rarely give them up without a fight or the threat of a fight. The past two centuries have seen numerous revolutions and upheavals as people have tried to limit the power of their governments. In these fights, privilege and taxation were often the central issue. The American Revolution against British rule was set off by disagreements over the granting of special privileges on an unequal basis among citizens (notably, the granting of special new privileges to the British East India Company at the expense of New England merchants) and over taxation—not so much over how much taxation but over the principle of whether the parties being taxed should be able to limit the authority of those imposing and collecting taxes.[2] Shortly thereafter, the French revolution was set off most fundamentally by popular disgust at the privileges and abuses of the aristocracy.

The transition to democracy is a gradual process, and rarely happens at a single stroke. France, for example, suffered several reversions to authoritarianism and several further upheavals before finally establishing a modern democracy. Many developing countries are in the midst of this transition, neither fully authoritarian nor yet fully democratic. In this transitional state, it is not surprising that the subjects of taxation and corruption should be both important and in a state of flux.

The flourishing of private business is closely connected to this deeper political evolution. An emerging middle class is almost synonymous with a growing private economy. Such a middle class can be a powerful agent of political change as well as the creator of economic growth. Since it is the primary target of taxation, the middle class takes the strongest interest in pressing for legitimacy, pushing the government to limit its taxes and be responsible for the use of tax proceeds, and often initiating serious revolts against authoritarianism.

---

[2]For an excellent review of that history, see the introduction to Freeman and Leonard (1915).

The Ming Legacy: Europe, China, and Democracy

The coevolution of democracy and markets is aptly illustrated by Europe's experience from the beginning of the second millennium until 1800, and the contrast between Europe and Asia during that period. Europe's political system began the second millennium as a feudal system characterized by a politically decentralized network of powerful local lords with legal rights over the labor of their serfs. Feudal lords, however, saw opportunities in the growing markets of Europe—opportunities to increase agricultural productivity with new methods of cultivation, and opportunities to build trade centers (Europe's merchant cities). Forward-thinking entrepreneurial lords saw that the best way to take advantage of those opportunities was to release serfs from bondage and create new incentives for them to act as free laborers, to build and populate cities, and to implement new agricultural technologies. Political and economic competition among lords was an essential ingredient spurring new markets, new cities, and new individual freedoms in the late medieval and early modern era.[3]

Markets thrived in Europe during this period. By the 16th century technological improvements in navigation and gunpowder changed the political shape of Europe, making it possible for powerful monarchs to establish nation states that reined in the power of local lords, allowing those new monarchs to transform their nation states into global empires of exploration, trade, and conquest. Those "mercantilist empires" defined a new set of rules for a partnership of interests between sovereigns and merchants. Sovereigns provided military protection, and often financing, while explorers, merchants, and settlers provided the entrepreneurial energy necessary to conquer lands and establish trade routes. Kings shared the fruits of exploration and conquest by conferring mineral, land, and trade rights on explorers and settlers.

The driving force of this expansion was royal greed and sometimes royal self-preservation in a world of intense international competition among monarchs. Certainly, not everyone gained from imperial expansion; notable exceptions were native Americans and African slaves. And yet monarchs could not afford to be entirely selfish. They were forced by necessity to establish incentives that rewarded others, and that necessity brought into being a new propertied class of merchants and (particularly in North America) landowners within their empires. The crown needed both to tolerate and to tax this new wealth. Struggles over taxation became generalized as struggles over economic and political rights, which culminated in successful armed revolt in both England (1640s) and America (1770s). The political revolution establishing American democracy was also an economic revolution in which the rules of mercantilism—special rules set by the crown governing who could produce and trade what and where—were displaced by a new free-market system based on Lockean principles of individual freedom. In that new system the

continued

Democracy typically evolves because even authoritarian governments need to negotiate with the holders of society's wealth. This can only be avoided if the economy does not grow or if the government preempts all of society's wealth and attempts to manage it centrally. This experiment (communism) was tried in a number of countries during the 20th century. For reasons that are discussed more fully in Chapter 3, it ultimately failed to produce economic growth and foundered on its own inefficiency and corruption.

---

[3]For reviews of economic history that underlie our account, see Duby (1979), Mokyr (1990), Jones (1988a, 1988b), North (1990), and MacFarlane (1978), and the references therein.

concluded

economic rights of individuals were expanded, and government influence over economic decisions was reduced.[4]

Interestingly, that history of simultaneous growth in political enfranchisement, average individual wealth, and international markets was a uniquely European phenomenon—what Eric Jones calls the "European miracle."[5] What were the barriers that prevented other parts of the world from following the European path to riches? Technical know-how was, in and of itself, not the decisive factor. Indeed, China had developed many of the most important technological advances that would fuel European expansion and industrialization centuries before Europe. Francis Bacon argued that three innovations—paper and printing, gunpowder, and the magnetic compass—had transformed the modern European world. All were Chinese inventions, as were a host of other essential ingredients of early capitalism, including such key contributors to Europe's Industrial Revolution as iron production and water-powered spinning. And yet, despite its advanced technological capabilities, China fell behind Europe during the miraculous era of European ascendancy from 1400 to 1800.[6]

Jones argues that Europe leapfrogged China because of shortcomings in the set of rules and institutions governing participation in the Chinese economy, and because of the political structure of China, which prevented an adaptation toward a more efficient set of rules. The central distinguishing features of Europe were the legal rights of individuals within countries that fostered entrepreneurial incentives, and the way intense competition among European nation states (military, as well as economic) spurred monarchs to encourage entrepreneurship both through the establishment of individual rights and the economic partnerships between monarchs and merchants, which were based on mutual advantage, not dictatorial fiat.

Ironically, the Chinese empire's political stability may have contributed to its relatively retarded economic growth. "Individual merchants might bribe their way to influence, but emperors never needed to rely on them as impecunious European kings did, and they did not gain influence as a class."[7] Emperors faced little external threat. Indeed, they perceived the main threat to their power as coming from within. A growing merchant class, which might increase its wealth and power if permitted to do so via free trade and expanded property rights, was perceived as the main threat.

The Ming emperors (1368–1644), in particular, felt threatened by the expansion of markets and went out of their way to put an end to industrialization, international trade, and foreign exploration. These emperors favored a shift back to agriculture, demolished the Chinese astronomical clock constructed in 1090, allowed their navy to decay from disuse, and banned foreign trade. By the mid-16th century the Chinese art of shipbuilding was forgotten.

The point of these sharply contrasting histories of Europe and China is that institutions (property rights, constitutional systems, the rules governing commerce) matter, and that the right kinds of institutions and business–government relations cannot be taken for granted. That history is quite relevant for understanding development and underdevelopment in today's world. The individual political rights and free-market property rights that Europeans and Americans may take for granted, and on which their economic progress depends, were an *exceptional* development in the history of mankind. At the dawn of the 21st century there remain many countries in which governments, or a small cadre of government-supported monopolists, own the bulk of their society's wealth and are bent on protecting that wealth through a variety of means that retard economic growth. The Ming legacy lives on.

---

[4]Government still maintained an important role in shaping the legal system, chartering corporations, and regulating competition. See Hughes (1991).

[5]Jones (1988a).

[6]Mokyr (1990).

[7]Jones (1988a).

Business/Government Overlaps and Separation

There is no doubt that some level of government intervention in business and finance is in the collective interest. For example, laws against monopolies are most important to ensure the competitive vitality of the economy. And government must set strong, well-conceived legal foundations for financial markets to function. These are both interventions for the purpose of maximizing economic performance. Other desirable government controls or interventions in the economy may diminish economic performance, but do so for a purpose that the society has determined is legitimate, such as environmental protection.

But many interventions are not so benign. Government efforts to maximize employment, for example, can create so much contractual rigidity in labor markets that they result in reduced employment, as the countries of Western Europe have found in recent years. Government efforts to direct the flow of capital to favored industries, firms, or individuals frequently steer it away from a value-maximizing use toward a lower-value or a "value-destroying" use (a concept described in detail in Chapter 3). What these interventions have in common is that government is attempting to perform direct economic functions that competitive markets can perform better.

The attitude of business toward government is somewhat ambiguous. On the one hand, business wants to minimize taxation and regulation, and in this sense tries to limit the role of government. On the other hand, business aggressively seeks any special privilege the government is empowered to hand out. A private firm will not be averse to a government intervention in capital markets to allocate a flow of capital to itself. Firms frequently lobby for and obtain protection from imports through tariffs, quotas, or other devices. They also want any subsidies the government may be willing to hand out. And finally, if government will grant any firm a monopoly or semimonopoly status through legislation or restrictive licensing, the firm will dramatically gain value. All of these special privileges constitute rents to the owners of the businesses. In some political systems, these rents are the price of the business community's support for the government. Too often, they become the basis for corrupt partnerships between government and favored recipients.[8]

In the prototypical early-stage developing country, business and government are too tightly linked and are controlled by the same privileged group of people. For this purpose it does not much matter whether the central government owns the business system (communism) or the business system owns the government (monopoly capitalism). These two apparent opposites have more than a little in common, as Russia's uneasy transition to capitalism illustrates.[9] What matters more is whether the same small group of people can make or powerfully influence decisions in both the economic and political domains. When economic and political power converge too closely and are concentrated in too few hands, both governmental and business decisions are likely to be made badly.

A government official with a business interest or a corrupt payment from a business firm is severely tempted to make decisions for private gain, not for the benefit of society. The resulting decisions are almost by definition different from those that would have been reached in the unbiased interest of society as a whole. Protectionism, monopolies, subsidies, and restrictive licensing tend to lower economic growth. However, such policies benefit particular firms or particular government officials.

---

[8]On the problem of rent seeking, see Krueger (1974), Bhagwati (1996), and the discussion of state-owned enterprises in Chapter 3.

[9]The Russian case is treated in detail in Chapter 3.

Conversely, a politician is often tempted to impose a political goal on business decisions. At their best, business decisions are made strictly to maximize firm value, which in most cases contributes to economic growth. But politicians often favor certain regions, industries, or firms for any number of possible reasons, and may try to direct business and employment accordingly. Private decisions are quickly rewarded or penalized by the market; governments can perpetuate their mistakes with further subsidies, which frequently reduces economic growth.

That is why successful modern democracies try to separate business from government. Each has a different logic, a different set of goals, and is best served when not overly influenced by the other. The payoff for this separation is both a stronger economy and a limitation on the power of government.

This digression into political economy and economic history is useful because it helps us to characterize and place in perspective the parallel processes of political and economic change that occur in developing countries. In Chapter 3 we will return to similar themes in our discussion of the creation of state-owned enterprises in the post–World War II era and their privatization in the 1980s and 1990s. In the remainder of this chapter we consider the particular problems of the financial system and its relationship to the state.

Financial Intermediation

Functions of the Financial System

The most primitive function of a financial system is to issue and safeguard money. The next function to evolve is a payments mechanism, typically a check-clearance system, which enables parties to transfer money among each other without taking the risk of delivering it in coin or currency. These basic functions are the domain of banks, which are invariably the first financial institutions to evolve in a developing country.

In a fully developed, competitive economy the financial system includes not only banks but also securities firms, specialized intermediaries such as finance companies and mortgage brokers, as well as institutional investors such as insurance companies, pension funds, and mutual funds. Such a financial system plays a large and sophisticated role: It encourages and mobilizes private saving and investment, and channels the capital so created into its most productive uses. It creates a diverse menu of saving and investment options for individuals—some at higher risk, some at lower risk, some for the long term, and some for a shorter term.

When *financial intermediation* is performed effectively, firms compete for savings by offering financial returns in various forms. The competition not only benefits savers but also causes capital to flow toward those uses that promise the greatest creation of value. The result is that society's savings are being put to the best possible uses, while savers are offered the most desirable feasible combinations of high expected return, low risk, and high liquidity.

One way to connect savings and investment is through *securities market intermediation.* Here corporations compete for capital by offering stocks, bonds, and other securities directly to individuals and institutional investors. Another way to connect savings and investment is through *bank intermediation.* Here individuals and institutions deposit their savings in banks, and the banks offer loans to the corporations. Securities market intermediation at its best is more efficient since there is no permanent middleman, but bank intermediation dominates EFMs for reasons we will explore throughout this book.

Banks and securities markets cannot function properly unless their institutional foundations are strong. Governments can play a critical role in creating or strengthening those foundations. But governments often neglect core institution building or, even worse, in pursuit of different objectives, purposefully weaken the core legal and economic institutions on which financial intermediation depends.

Government and the Foundations of the Financial System

Government and the institutions it creates or influences are central to the foundations of any financial system. The most basic foundational element is law (the subject of Chapter 4). Financial intermediation, whether through banks or securities markets, creates contractual claims between companies and individuals. In a securities market those claims are traded among strangers, making investors particularly vulnerable. Intermediation can only work well when investors have confidence that the claims will be honored. This requires laws, fairly and uniformly enforced, that protect the rights and interests of investors in those claims. Securities markets, in particular, offer massive opportunities to defraud investors. Strong laws, fairly enforced, are the only effective way to control market manipulation, insider trading, and outright fraud. All of this requires a government determined to create a strong financial system.

Banks also depend on laws and courts to clearly define and protect their rights as creditors. Banks rely on the law to enforce loan covenants (which restrict the behavior of their borrowers and the uses made of bank credit), to provide adequate procedures for registering and enforcing collateral interests in land, structures, equipment, and working capital (which facilitates lending by making it less risky), and to establish bankruptcy codes that help resolve problems of financial distress expeditiously and predictably (thereby reducing lenders' risks and avoiding wasteful delays in investment and production by illiquid firms).

In addition to the legal base, a second foundational element is information (the subject of Chapter 5). Through intensive investments in information collection, banks may be able to obtain some private information from their clients, which they can then use to enforce their contractual rights and to limit the risk of default on their loans. This is one reason why banks can be effective intermediaries when information is difficult to obtain. But for securities markets to function well, public disclosure of information is essential, so that all material facts about companies are passed along to investors as soon as they are generated. Some economists argue that the government has no justifiable role in mandating disclosure requirements since private firms can gain the trust of investors by establishing credible means of revealing information to the market (by hiring accountants, rating agencies, or underwriters to act as information intermediaries), and without that trust they would not be able to finance themselves in securities markets. Thus, the argument goes, private firms face strong incentives from the market to establish credible disclosure policies, and gain little from government intervention.

But the primary motivation for government disclosure rules—which also can justify regulatory limitations on sales practices in securities markets—is to protect unsophisticated investors. Disclosure rules force firms to meet minimal government standards for the quality and breadth of information they provide, and thus make it harder for firms to trick unsophisticated investors into buying their securities at inflated prices. Second, the government may be in a unique position to help standardize disclosure practices, which can facilitate comparisons by investors of different securities offerings, thus making markets work better.

The third foundational element is a sound currency. In Chapter 6 we explain how that too requires a supportive government that controls its own spending and raises sufficient taxes such that it does not need to print money to finance government expenditures. If the government is driven to print money, either continuous currency depreciation or periodic collapses of exchange value must ensue. Periodic collapses are especially disruptive to international trade and to capital markets, and have become a frequent phenomenon in recent years (the subject of Chapter 8). But we will show in this chapter that even continuous, predictable depreciation of the currency can be inimical to the savings and investment process, because it magnifies the taxation of the financial sector.

Finally, limiting government regulations that tax banks and establishing effective prudential regulation and supervision of banks are of central importance to financial health and economic growth. The role government plays in regulating banks can make the difference between a healthy financial system that promotes growth and one that stands in the way of growth. The taxation policies of governments toward banks and their effects on the economy are the subject of the remainder of this chapter, while prudential regulation and supervision of banks is treated in Chapter 7.

Why do some governments fail to provide these basic institutional foundations? Sometimes governments lack the ability to establish proper institutional foundations quickly, perhaps because they are constrained by inefficient preexisting legal traditions (e.g., the Napoleonic approach to developing commercial law).[10] In other cases, government officials may lack the power necessary to reduce taxation of the financial sector because doing so requires politically difficult tax increases elsewhere or expenditure cuts.

But in many cases institutional failure reflects the goals of rulers and the interests they represent, rather than the constraints under which they operate (a reprise of the Ming dynasty example). Governments that serve the interests of a small private elite at the expense of the public at large have little interest in promoting efficient, arm's-length transactions in the financial system. Indeed, doing so can reduce their ability to extract and distribute rents. For example, the absence of effective commercial laws, collateral registration procedures, and efficient bankruptcy laws favors inside dealings within bank-centered conglomerates and makes competitive entry into either industrial activities or financial intermediation more difficult. The absence of these core institutions, therefore, serves the interest of the existing elite.

Thus, it is not surprising that the governments likely to provide proper institutional foundations for the financial system are those most constrained to act in the public interest, and that usually means a government under a significant degree of democratic control. If this minimum condition is not met, authoritarian government will often purposely eschew efficient institutional reform.

Even worse, those same authoritarian governments will not only undermine the institutional foundations of the financial system, but also will often seize control of the financial system and use it to further their interests. Corrupt political systems prefer a financial system in which they can allocate capital directly to politically favored industries, as well as allocating some into the pockets of the rulers themselves.

---

[10]See LaPorta et al. (1997), Levine (1998, 1999), and Chapter 4.

Financial Repression

Prior to the 20th century, the widespread adherence to an international metallic money standard and the general openness of capital movements limited a sovereign's power to exploit savers and other holders of money through inflation. For example, if a sovereign committed to a hard-money standard wanted funds to wage a war, he would have to raise them by taxes or find a willing lender, who in turn would be looking to taxes for repayment. But taxes usually brought a parliament into the picture, even when democracy was otherwise quite rudimentary.

In the 20th century, however, the rise of fiat money as a unit of account and medium of exchange has greatly increased governments' ability to finance pet projects by printing money and exploiting savers, away from the budgetary process, thereby avoiding both taxes and parliaments. This actually undermines the development of democracy. Russia and the Ukraine were extreme examples of this in the 1990s.

Researchers have identified six ways in which governments often repress their financial system:

1. By imposing ceilings on interest rates paid by banks for deposits.
2. By imposing high reserve requirements on banks.
3. By lending to industry and/or directing bank credit.
4. By owning and/or micromanaging banks, leaving them little autonomy.
5. By restricting entry into the financial industry, especially by foreigners.
6. By restricting international capital inflows and outflows.

Note that most of these actions concern the relationship between government and banks. All of them are to the disadvantage of savers and/or efficient allocation of capital, but to the advantage of government. Many such advantages and disadvantages are magnified by inflation. We will examine each of these behaviors in detail.

1. Interest Rate Ceilings on Bank Deposits

It is very common for governments to impose a ceiling on the interest rate that banks pay to depositors. The rationale for this restriction is to prevent "excessive competition" for deposits, increasing the profitability and thereby presumably the safety and soundness of banks. Even the United States had interest rate controls (Regulation Q) from the 1930s until the 1970s. What finally forced their repeal in the United States was competition from money market funds—an efficient securities market offering better values than banks in a period of rising rates. Any government that is determined to maintain interest rate controls needs to suppress such efficient market alternatives to make the system work. It must also suppress the flow of capital abroad in search of better rates.

Controls on deposit rates do increase the franchise value of banks, providing them with *rents*—that is, sources of income that would not be available in a fully competitive market. Those rents are paid for by savers and by *private* borrowers (or would-be borrowers) not favored by the government. In Figure 2.1 we show these effects using a simple supply and demand graph for real loans as a function of real interest rates.

Figure 2.1 shows a demand curve for real loans $(L/P)^{\text{Demand}}$, representing the amount of loans L, adjusted for changes in the price level P, which creditworthy

FIGURE 2.1

Bank spreads and deposit interest rate limits

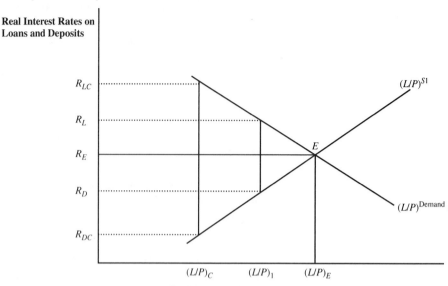

L = Loans
P = Price level

$(L/P)^{\text{Demand}}$ = Private borrowers' demand for real loans, as a function of real interest rates
$(L/P)^{S1}$ = Lenders' supply of real loans, as a function of real interest rates

E = Initial equilibrium of supply and demand
$(L/P)_E$ = Quantity of real loans in initial equilibrium
R_E = Real interest rate on loans in initial equilibrium

$(L/P)_1$ = Quantity of real loans when banks charge a spread between their deposit rate R_D
and their lending rate R_L

$(L/P)_C$ = Quantity of real loans when government imposes a ceiling R_{DC} on deposit rates
and hence forces private lending rates to R_{LC}

borrowers want as a decreasing function of the real (inflation-adjusted) interest rate on loans, R_L. The supply curve $(L/P)^{S1}$ shows the quantity of real loans that savers are willing to provide as in increasing function of the real interest rate on deposits R_D. Figure 2.1 shows the equilibrium point E at which the market would clear, where the loan rate equals the deposit rate and where the volume of real loans is $(L/P)_E$.

In reality, bank lending will not be able to reach point E. The operating costs of banks must also be factored into the determination of interest rates on loans and deposits: Banks must earn a spread between deposit and loan rates to recoup the costs of running their institutions (labor costs, the opportunity cost of maintaining zero-interest cash reserves on hand to cover withdrawals, and so forth). The vertical line represents the amount of that requisite spread ($R_L - R_D$). The need to channel some of bank earnings on loans into payments for overhead thus reduces the return depositors can receive, and shrinks the volume of real loans from $(L/P)_E$ to $(L/P)_1$.

The imposition of a deposit interest rate ceiling at R_{DC} reduces the available supply of deposits by constraining the ability of banks to attract depositors. To equate the new (lower) amount supplied with the amount demanded by borrowers, the size of the spread between deposit and loan rates must rise, which implies an enlargement of the vertical line separating the two rates. Thus, an interest rate ceiling not only lowers the real return R_{DC} paid to savers, but also reduces the volume of loans outstanding and thereby enables higher rates to be charged to private borrowers.

The difference in length between the two vertical lines measures the bank's rents per dollar of loans. Banks become more profitable, but at the expense of both savers and borrowers, and the volume of private loans available is less than it would be in the case without the controls.[11] How does the government benefit? Primarily, it benefits by not allowing the banks to keep most of their rents, but requiring them to offer subsidized loans to government-favored borrowers.

Interest rate ceilings, particularly in inflationary economies, especially victimize savers. As we shall examine in more detail in Chapter 6, when nominal bank deposit rates are lower than the level of inflation, savers receive negative real rates of return (i.e., they get back money with less purchasing power than the money they deposited). Because this happens in many repressed financial systems, the level of real bank deposit rates will be one of the measures we use to quantify how serious financial repression may be. It is not surprising that captive savers earning negative real returns are often very enthused to be offered a chance for positive market returns (see box).

2. High Bank Reserve Requirements

Banks in almost all countries are required to redeposit (usually without interest) a certain fraction of their own deposits as *reserves* at the central bank. This practice, when pursued within limits, can benefit banks and the public. Central banks can be a reliable repository for reserves and can use those reserve balances to facilitate clearing among banks. Banks need accessible reserve balances, both to handle the normal flow of deposit transfers among banks and as a precaution against financial crises when withdrawal demands can be heavy.

The practice of not paying interest on reserves, however, has no justification from the standpoint of promoting efficient banking. Its only advantage is the revenue it generates for the government: Reserve requirements provide revenue to the government by forcing banks to deposit funds in the central bank without earning any interest on those deposits. That reduces the amount of interest-bearing debt the government must issue, and therefore reduces government debt service costs. Zero-interest reserve requirements thus constitute an implicit tax on banking. In most cases, the high required ratio of reserves and the low interest rates banks earn on those reserves reflect governments' desire to maintain a tax device capable of generating substantial implicit revenue. That tax device has the political advantage that many depositors (who ultimately are the ones paying the tax) are unaware of it. When this tax becomes large, it has a serious negative effect on the financial system.

---

[11]Banks will have an incentive to offer nonpecuniary payments to depositors to attract them away from competitors. If they are permitted to do so, that would increase the supply of deposits to a level somewhere between the quantities in the constrained and unconstrained cases shown in Figure 2.1.

China's Stockmarkets: Open Outcry

WHEN Deng Xiaoping began whipping up pro-reform sentiment in China earlier this year, he is reported to have said that "a little chaos" could be expected as the economy was opened up. Even Mr Deng might hesitate to describe the stock-market riots that began on August 8th in the southern town of Shenzhen as only "a little" chaotic.

As many as 1m people from all over China had poured into Shenzhen (usual population 2m) to queue for share applications. In the ensuing barney [loud argument], which lasted on and off for three days, would-be shareholders smashed windows and cars and attacked each other and the police, who swung wooden clubs and fired shots. Many people were injured, and some reports (denied by the authorities) say one or two were killed. On August 11th the Shenzhen stockmarket was closed for the afternoon, and China's cabinet met in Beijing to talk about what should be done.

The main comfort for the leadership was that China's worst televised disturbances since the Tiananmen Square demonstrations in 1989 had nothing to do with politics. The motive was money. Shenzhen, which borders Hong Kong, was one of China's first "special economic zones" and, with industrial growth of 40 percent or so a year, remains the most spectacularly successful of them. It boasts the bigger and zippier of China's two authorised stockmarkets (the other being Shanghai's).

These markets have proven extremely popular—both with Chinese investors, who are allowed to buy and sell what are called A shares, and with foreigners, who can trade only in B shares. With 1 trillion yuan ($183 billion) of savings stashed away in bank accounts alone, and possessed of the touching belief that share prices only go up, ordinary Chinese have been eager to get their hands on A shares.

The question that has plagued both the Shanghai and Shenzhen authorities is how to distribute share offerings when demand so vastly outstrips supply. Perhaps taking too much to heart this newspaper's argument last week that "stockmarkets are lotteries, thank goodness for that," Shenzhen's officials set up a real lottery to allocate the 500m yuan-worth of new A share issues they expect to allow this financial year.

The city printed 5m application forms, for sale at 100 yuan apiece (proceeds to "welfare spending" in Shenzhen). Up to ten forms were available per customer, first-come first-served, to whomever queued up for them in Shenzhen on the weekend of August 8th. Later in the year one-tenth of the forms will be picked by lot. The lucky winners will be entitled to buy up to 1,000 shares per form in the 14 companies being floated on the exchange this year.

It seemed to faze nobody that the unlucky 90 percent would get nothing back from the 100 yuan they had paid for each form; nor that the identities, let alone the balance sheets and prospects, of the 14 companies to be listed have yet to be disclosed. The weekend fiasco did nothing to blunt the appetites of would-be investors. To atone a bit for its initial blundering, Shenzhen's government on August 11th put on sale 500,000 "exchange tickets" at 1,000 yuan apiece, each entitling the holder to ten application forms. If, as seems likely, these forms are added to the same lottery as the original 5m, the number of winning forms will drop to a mere 5 percent of the total. Never mind. The tickets, too, sold out, and were traded promptly (and illegally) on the street at twice their original price.

China's government can flatter itself that much of the trouble is encouraging. Like the B share market, where an estimated $1 billion in overseas "China Funds" is chasing no more than $50m worth of actively traded shares, the Shenzhen affair showed how strong the demand is for a piece of the Chinese action—at least until it soaks in that, even in China, markets fall as well as rise.

The dark side of the incident, from the leadership's point of view, is the cause of the would-be investors' anger. The Shenzhen police say they were weeding out trouble-

continued

The effect of the reserve tax on the loan market is diagrammed in Figure 2.2, which is an extension of Figure 2.1. A reserve tax means that banks must charge higher interest rates on private loans and/or pay lower interest rates to savers in order to pay the cost of holding low-interest or zero-interest reserves at the central bank; that is, the vertical gap between the supply and demand schedules must widen as the reserve tax increases. In Figure 2.2 the spread becomes $(R_{L2} - R_{D2}) = q R_{L2}$, where q is the percentage reserve requirement; that is, assuming for simplicity no overhead costs other than zero-interest reserves, if a bank has real deposits D/P on which it pays a real interest rate R_{D2}, and has to redeposit qD at the central bank at no interest, the real direct cost of the reserve requirement is $q(D/P)R_{L2}$; banks must adjust their spreads upward to accommodate that cost, reducing the supply of loans to $(L/P)_2$.

The above example implicitly assumed that the inflation rate is zero. The reserve tax on banks is aggravated by inflation, which further raises the real cost of holding reserves, since the *real* opportunity cost to holding zero-interest cash is the *nominal* interest rate on loans. As we shall see in more detail in Chapter 6, inflation functions like a kind of tax on all parties who hold currency and low-interest or zero-interest monetary assets. Since reserve requirements oblige banks to hold such assets, banks pay a significant part of the inflation tax. Inflation, therefore, further shifts the supply curve of loanable funds upward and to the left, further lowering the quantity of available loans from $(L/P)_2$ to $(L/P)_3$. The vertical distance between the real rates of interest on loans and deposits grows as a proportion of the rate of inflation (π). The real interest rate gap between loans and deposits will now be: $(R_{L3} - R_{D3}) = q(\pi + R_{L3})$. The higher spread reflects the fact that the market must compensate banks for a real opportunity cost that is higher. Forgone earnings on lending are now higher in real terms because the interest differential has increased between earnings on loans, which are indexed for inflation, and earnings on cash, which are zero regardless of the rate of inflation.

In summary, the banking system is often an important source of government revenue, which ultimately reflects the government's monopoly over the power to print money (which allows it to set the rate of inflation), and its regulatory power over banks (which allows it to enforce zero-interest reserve requirements). Banks provide governments with a relatively docile and unprotected part of the economy to tax. Since borrowers tend to be knowledgeable and are often favored by government, savers are in most cases the primary victims of these hidden financial taxes. Savers pay these taxes through reduced real rates of interest on their savings. Deposit rate ceilings reduce them explicitly; inflation reduces them by taking away part of the nominal rate of interest. And reserve requirements oblige the banks to lower the real returns paid to savers.

FIGURE 2.2

Effects of reserve requirements, inflation, and directed credit

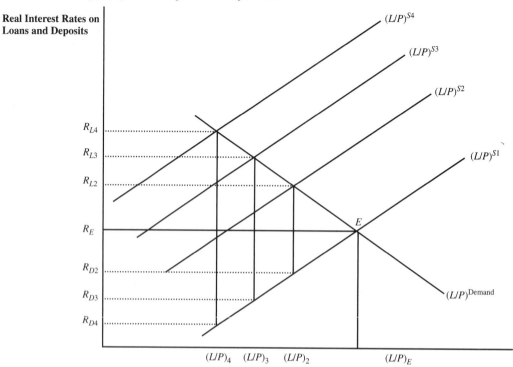

$(L/P)^{S2}$ = Lenders' supply of real loans when government taxes banks with reserve requirements

$(L/P)^{S3}$ = Lenders' supply of real loans when inflation imposes a further tax on banks

$(L/P)^{S4}$ = Lenders' supply of real loans to nonfavored borrowers when government additionally forces banks to lend to favored borrowers at low rates

R_{D2-4} = Real deposit rate in each of the above cases

R_{L2-4} = Real lending rate in each of the above cases

3. Government Credit and Government Direction of Bank Credit

When the banking system is obliged to redeposit a significant portion of its deposits in the central bank, the central bank then has resources that it can lend directly to industry. Most politicians find it highly desirable to have such funds at their disposal. A more straightforward way to accomplish the same goal is to nationalize some or all of the banks. In extreme cases, such as Mexico in the 1980s, the government nationalized all the banks and simply preempted the public savings to finance its own deficits and projects.

As noted above, few government officials really want to leave decisions about the allocation of funds either to disinterested banks or to an efficient securities market. Government control of credit flows can be a powerful vehicle for realizing policy objectives. Furthermore, control over credit flows enhances the personal power of government officials and can increase their wealth when the firms receiving subsidized credit are owned by, or are otherwise related to, those officials.

Even democratic or partially democratic governments find it hard to leave the business of capital allocation entirely to the marketplace. Politicians quite committed to acting in the public interest often believe that they can see more clearly and act more wisely than those unruly people who populate the capital market. Investors are often accused of making decisions for short-term benefit only. Politicians often maintain that the guiding hand of government, or government-controlled banks, is necessary to make the optimal capital allocation decisions for the long run.

Governments that are otherwise quite enlightened often find it very hard to let go of this control. In Japan, for example, the Ministry of Finance (MOF) maximized the role of banks in funding industry and (to a decreasing extent over time) gave detailed guidance to the banks on which industries, firms, and projects to support. Reportedly, the government also went beyond guiding loans into certain favored industries and in some cases encouraged banks to hire certain senior persons, either as a reward to such persons for good service elsewhere or to help ensure that the banks remained compliant with future suggestions from MOF. MOF actually prevented the formation of a corporate bond market or a commercial paper market until the mid-1980s, and it yielded then only because the large Japanese firms had gained full access to international capital sources so that MOF's traditionally firm grip on capital flows could not be sustained.

When banks are forced to channel some of their funds to government-owned firms or to government-favored borrowers at subsidized interest rates, the government is absorbing some of the supply of credit available for private (nondirected) uses. Figure 2.2 shows the effect of this further contraction in the supply of nondirected credit available to bank borrowers: The supply of private credit shifts again to the left and the spread between R_L and R_D widens—which is shown in Figure 2.2 as the movement from $(L/P)_3$ to $(L/P)_4$.

4. Government Ownership and Micromanagement of Banks

The simplest way for the government to repress the financial system is to own all the banks or at least some or all of the largest banks; this has been commonplace in developing countries from the 1960s through the 1980s. Ownership of banks gives government the unequivocal right to direct credit wherever it sees fit, with no pretense of a market system. Alternatively, even though the ownership of banks is left in private hands, the government may give strong "guidance" not just in lending decisions but also in hiring, funding, and all other aspects of bank management.

In addition to Japanese government guidance of private bank lending, Japan also has been one of the prime examples of direct state control of banking. The Japanese Postal Savings System has long been one of the largest financial institutions in the world, and it has been a protected source of low-cost funds used by the Japanese government to finance its directed credit programs to favored borrowers through the Japan Development Bank and other government lenders.[12] By limiting competition for retail customers from private banks (until very recently), the government was able to fund its directed credit policies at very low cost.

---

[12]For a detailed review of that experience, see World Bank (1994).

Not all government ownership of banks is the result of a conscious government effort to control banks. Sometimes government ownership occurs in the wake of a banking collapse and bailout, events that have become astonishingly commonplace throughout the world, when some of the insolvent banks (typically those which surviving banks have little interest in purchasing) become wards of the state. We will study bank crises in detail in Chapter 7, and also examine there the alternatives faced by the government in bailouts. To anticipate the outcome of that discussion, we will argue that the optimal bailout policy is one that wipes out the previous equity and dismisses the management that caused the problem. The bank can then be liquidated or recapitalized. Often, however, the government finds it politically difficult to wipe out one private group and immediately transfer the bank to another private group. In such cases, the most expedient solution may be for government to own the bank directly, with the intention of selling it in the future. An early case of bank nationalization following a banking crisis was that of Chile. Chile had a banking collapse in 1982 after a failed experiment in free banking, a story that we shall recount in detail in Chapter 3. Even though the government was strongly committed to the market economy, it ended up taking over about two-thirds of the banking system. Similarly, Mexico nationalized its entire banking system in 1982 as its sovereign default triggered the global debt crisis.

While the extent of government ownership of banks can easily be measured, it can be far more difficult to measure the effective control of bank lending decisions by government through the regulatory process. Government intrusion into bank management is not readily quantifiable. It can be hard to distinguish appropriate bank prudential regulation (which may include government restrictions of some bank lending practices) from hidden government lending mandates enforced under the threat of regulatory retaliation.

Do state-controlled systems perform well? At several points in the 20th century, state-dominated economic systems, whose financial flows were managed by state-controlled banks, appeared to produce economic and technical results superior to those of market economies. In the 1950s, for example, the Soviet Union grew rapidly, both in volume of production and in some elements of technical leadership. When that country launched the first space satellite ("sputnik") in 1957, many in the United States and Europe became alarmed that the market economies were falling behind. In retrospect, those fears now seem excessive. What the Soviet Union had done was to mobilize massive quantities of previously underutilized resources, particularly labor, and to focus disproportionate attention on military and military-related goods. It turned out that its formula was not a long-term means for generating productive use of resources, but rather an unsustainable way of producing impressive short-term growth.

Similarly in the 1970s and 1980s, East Asia produced substantial economic growth using a model of partial democracy, private enterprise, export orientation, and state-dominated finance. Japan had pioneered this model in the 1950s, 1960s, and 1970s, and by the 1980s had reached world dominance in several industries including automobiles and computer memory chips. Many observers attributed that success to the wise hand of government in partnership with organized private enterprise. Five-year plans, constructed in consultations between government and the private sector, guided capital into the long-term projects of specific industries. Corporate managers were beholden to government planners and to the so-called main banks that helped to shape government five-year plans and to orchestrate flows of funds within the industrial conglomerates they controlled. Government agencies and conglomerates (*keiretsu*) were perceived as having better information and more long-term goals, in contrast to U.S. firms that were guided by the short-term whims of investors.

Much of East Asia had followed the Japanese path, and its collective success shook the confidence of many Western observers in the Western approach to finance, where government has little say in the allocation of funds, and competition rather than coordination is deemed the desirable organizing principle for the private sector. Japanese management and manufacturing techniques were widely admired and imitated in the West, and unquestionably served to improve much Western management and production. But the Asian economic model of government control over credit allocation and a close partnership between government planners and bank-centered private conglomerates proved hard to sustain for the long run. By the 1990s Japan had entered a protracted recession, and by 1997–1998 much of East Asia suffered an economic collapse. Beginning in the late 1990s, Japan began gradually to reform its systems of finance and corporate governance.

In 1994, prior to the Asian crisis, the international economist Paul Krugman published an influential article that shocked many readers.[13] Though he did not predict an imminent collapse, he did argue that Asia's economic miracle was a myth and that its growth would soon slow. He showed that much of Asia's growth resulted not from efficiency in the use of resources but in massive new infusions of labor, machinery, infrastructure, and education that would not be sustainable. He called Singapore's growth a virtual economic twin of Stalin's Soviet Union, and argued that sustained growth would require efficiency gains, that is, higher-return use of resources. A related article in 1999 by Michael Porter and Hirotaka Takeuchi, which examined Japan's performance sector by sector, attributed many more failures than successes to Japan's governmental interventions.[14]

We will study the Asian crisis of 1997–1998 in considerable detail in Chapter 8. It is relevant to our discussion of financial repression because it was a *financial* collapse, a failure of a particular version of financial intermediation and capital allocation. Various countries had differing problems, but a common theme was that financial institutions were close to failure because poor capital allocation decisions had been made. East Asia had been doing a great many things right, but bad loans, failed banks, and low-return capital projects brought their progress to a halt. Ironically, the guiding hand of government and bank-centered company governance—extolled by admirers for its farsightedness—had become an obstacle to sustained long-term growth.

That lesson puts new emphasis on the importance of private control of financial intermediation and institutions. There is no doubt that in the short run economic growth can be rapid even where government-controlled or subsidized financial intermediation is inefficient. But in the long run, finance matters. Capital allocation is one of the key categories of economic decision making in any economy, and for long-run success capital must flow to the projects offering the highest returns.

5. Restrictions on Foreign Bank and Domestic Nonbank Entry

Countries that repress their domestic banking systems also typically restrict access to the financial system by would-be substitutes for domestic banks. There are two forms

---

[13] Krugman (1994). See also Young (1995).

[14] Porter and Takeuchi (1999). For a review of current reforms, see Hoshi and Patrick (2000).

of this restriction: one that makes it difficult for local entrepreneurs to enter the financial business, and the other that restricts foreign firms from opening local branches or buying local financial institutions. Such restrictions are widespread and represent a kind of protectionism for local financial institutions, including banks and securities firms. They are closely connected with protectionism in general.

In addition to outright prohibition of entry, there are other more subtle protective barriers. Just as virtually all governments have found it important to regulate the capital and behavior of financial institutions, so virtually all governments have some standards that must be met by those who want to build financial institutions. Some barriers to entry are appropriate. As in regulatory restrictions on bank credit, however, there is a fine line between appropriate regulatory standards for entry and the kind of abuse of regulatory authority associated with implicit protectionism or corruption.

It is not surprising that many countries feel uneasy about admitting foreign companies into their financial systems. After all, finance is one of the key industries in any modern economy, and its policies affect the well-being of most other industries. Defensive nationalists may fear that larger neighbors will take over their financial system and thereby develop power over the whole economy. Although regulation has the power to curb most abuses, people may doubt whether the foreign financial institutions have any interest in the longer-term well-being of the country.

On the other hand, those who encourage liberalization of EFMs, including notably the IMF, often put special emphasis on admitting foreign financial institutions in the hope that this kind of competition will bring improvements in bank performance. Not only does free entry into banking by foreigners provide an important source of capital, but it also helps to diversify both the ownership base and the loan portfolio of lenders in developing countries (since global banks naturally hold more diverse portfolios), which makes banks more resilient in the face of adverse domestic shocks. Finally, foreign banks provide important competitive pressure that improves the quality of domestic bank management.[15] The financial industry is rapidly changing, with risk management systems and communications technology evolving with each passing year. There is no faster way to introduce such new ideas into the local industry than to welcome foreign institutions as full players.

To be sure, foreign-owned financial institutions (which can choose among countries when deciding to expand abroad) will be less willing to comply with informal guidance from governments concerning "strategic industries" and so on. That may be the primary concern of those who want to restrict foreign entry. Because such guidance is itself a form of financial repression, another benefit to permitting foreign entry is the consequent weakening of the power of the government to control financial flows. Some of the most determined liberalizers, including Argentina and New Zealand, appear to have benefited in this way from permitting a large majority of their financial institutions to be foreign owned.

It is difficult to obtain accurate measures of the state's share of bank assets, and in any case this does not incorporate the intensity with which the state may micromanage banks they do not own. Nevertheless, Table 2.1 shows a compilation of state-owned banks' share of total bank assets for selected developing countries. Note that this

---

[15]See Demirgüç-Kunt and Levine (1998) and Kane (1998).

TABLE 2.1   **State-Owned Banks' Share of Total Assets (%)**

Country or Economy	One Year Prior To Reform	Most Recent Year
East Asia		
Hong Kong	N/A	0
Indonesia	76	40
Korea	81	32
Malaysia	N/A	8
Philippines	28	22
Singapore	N/A	16
Taiwan	78	58
Thailand	N/A	19
Latin America		
Argentina	52	39
Brazil	50	48
Chile	100	14
Colombia	N/A	23
Mexico	100	18
Venezuela	N/A	30
Middle East and Africa		
Egypt	50+	50+
Israel	90	N/A
South Africa	0	0
Turkey	50	48
South Asia		
Bangladesh	74	68
India	90	87
Nepal	85	64
Pakistan	89	63
Sri Lanka	82	70

Source: Williamson and Mahar (1999), Table 2.3.

measure still indicates that, as of the mid-1990s, a great deal of liberalizing remained to be done.

Governments may also deliberately restrict the development of securities markets. In Japan, for example, domestic corporate bonds and commercial paper were effectively forbidden until the mid-1980s. Clearly, such alternatives to bank lending can undermine the government's desire to control capital flows. But this only works if the companies themselves are contained within the national borders. It was access to global securities markets by large Japanese firms that finally undermined Japanese government control over capital allocation in the 1980s.[16]

Natural obstacles to securities market finance can be as formidable as government barriers to entry. To function effectively, securities market dealers and brokers themselves

---

[16]For a review of the progress of bond issues in Japan and the competition between bond and bank finance, see Hoshi, Kashyap, and Scharfstein (1990) and Campbell and Hamao (1994).

need access to bank credit.[17] Thus, in a repressed financial system the absence of bank credit can make it hard for domestic securities markets to function.

Another natural barrier to the reach of securities markets pertains to the information and transaction costs that limit the use of securities market finance. Securities offerings are generally reserved for "seasoned" credit risks—firms that already have a track record as clients of banks or venture capitalists. For a firm to appeal to the public as an issuer of stock, its accounts must be credible and its management and governance structure must be perceived as sound. Among U.S. manufacturing firms in the early 1990s, only roughly 3,000 had publicly traded equity. The public bond market is even more selective. Of the 3,326 publicly traded manufacturing firms in the Compustat database from 1985 to 1991, 2,684 had no public bond rating.[18] Thus, even if foreign and domestic securities markets can finance the largest, most mature firms, they will have a harder time funding the needs of smaller, younger firms, which are often the engine of growth in developing economies. Thus, the burden of financial repression falls particularly hard on what is often the most dynamic sector of the economy.[19]

6. Restrictions on Capital Flows

Emerging market countries are, almost by definition, locations of high investment opportunity. Access to global financial markets reduces financing costs and enables firms in EFMs to take advantage of opportunities. A firm's funding cost can be decomposed into two parts: the baseline (riskless) interest rate in the economy, and the risk premium it pays over and above that rate, which reflects the market's charge for bearing the risks created by the firm. Foreign inflows reduce both components of firms' financing costs. First, capital market integration leads to a convergence among the interest rates on riskless assets, as savings flow to markets where opportunities are high relative to domestic savings. Second, capital market integration permits greater diversification by investors, which reduces the risk premium component of the cost of funds. EFM firms that used to rely on domestic investors with relatively undiversified portfolio opportunities are able to raise funds from diversified foreign investors who demand a lower risk premium to finance EFM firms' risks. Studies of the impact of liberalization on the financing costs of EFM firms tend to find significant effects from both sources.[20]

Governments can limit entry into capital markets by placing any of a number of explicit or implicit taxes on capital inflows. Economists and government officials sometimes defend such taxes on capital inflows as a means of supporting a country's exchange rate policy. For example, many fear that excessive capital inflows can promote unsustainable booms that ultimately result in economic contractions and exchange rate collapses when foreign capital retreats.[21] The massive capital flows of the 1990s, which rushed into and then out of the EFMs, left many officials and economists skeptical about the merits of free trade in capital.

---

[17]Interbank deposits placed in New York City banks in the 19th century (owing to New York's position as a commercial center) allowed New York to overtake Boston as the locus of America's capital markets.

[18]Calomiris, Himmelberg, and Wachtel (1995).

[19]For evidence see Schiantarelli et al. (1994) and Rajan and Zingales (1996).

[20]Henry (2000) and Bekaert and Harvey (2000).

[21] McKinnon (1993) and McKinnon and Pill (1996).

Others argue that capital inflows can provide a boost to growth and increase the incentives for rapid reforms (to gain access to capital). Furthermore, those who favor open capital markets argue that taxes on short-term flows are unnecessary in the presence of market discipline—that is, so long as borrowers are not immune to the costs created by the risks they undertake, borrowers and lenders will not pursue unsustainable capital flows. From the perspective of that view, government subsidies that insulate domestic borrowers from defaulting on their foreign debt are the prime culprit for excessive foreign borrowing. Finally, critics of capital controls argue that capital controls are not easily enforceable in today's world, and are therefore no longer a real policy option.[22]

Capital controls were widespread in all countries during the Bretton Woods period of fixed exchange rates (1948–1973). Most of these controls in industrialized countries were lifted after 1973, when foreign exchange rates began to float freely. They remained in place, however, in the 1970s in many developing countries, especially in those that attempted to maintain fixed or semifixed exchange rates. Most such controls were substantially eased or eliminated in the period of liberalization that began in the late 1980s.

It is noteworthy, however, that despite the upheavals of emerging capital markets in the 1990s, few countries actually implemented new capital controls. The most prominent exception was Chile, which from 1992 to 1998 required that 30 percent of bank and portfolio inflows be deposited without interest for one year at the central bank. In 1998, however, Chile reduced this reserve requirement to zero on the grounds that more foreign capital was needed.

Similarly, Malaysia imposed some severe restrictions on capital outflows in 1998, but repealed or reduced the majority of them less than a year later. The fact is that developing countries need capital, and restricting the flow of capital can seem a cure (for instability) worse than the disease. In August 1999, Brazil followed suit and eliminated its taxation of short-term capital inflows in the hopes of accessing more foreign capital.

Nevertheless, capital controls remain a feature of the lower-income developing countries, and a form of repression of financial markets that still tends to dominate the countries of Africa, the Middle East, and South Asia. Capital controls can take many different forms and are inherently difficult to measure quantitatively. We will revisit them in Chapter 8.

Measuring Financial Repression

We now turn to the question of measuring the extent of financial repression or development. Some elements are easier to quantify than others. Effective reserve ratios are among the easiest measures to construct; we have only to divide reserves on bank deposits by bank deposits. Figure 2.3 shows this measure averaged over major regions from 1970 to 1998. The trend everywhere is clearly toward lower reserve ratios. Note that the transition countries start from a base of financial repression far deeper than any other group of countries, though their reserve ratios had come down to the level of most other regions by the mid-1980s. Latin America, which had

---

[22]Edwards (1999).

FIGURE 2.3

Bank reserves / bank deposits by region

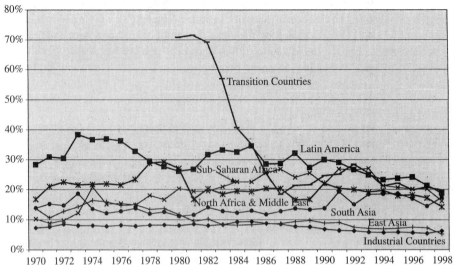

dropped from nearly 40 percent to about 20 percent by 1998, was the most highly reserved region of the world other than the transition countries during most of the period from 1970 to 1998.

During 1970–1980 East Asian reserve ratios dropped from the group of developing countries toward that of the industrial countries. The industrial countries on average dropped their own reserve ratios from about 10 percent to about 5 percent over 1984–1994, with East Asia following a similar path. Appendix Table 2.A1 shows country-by-country measures of reserve ratios in 1998.

While restrictions on deposit interest rates are hard to quantify, we can observe the effect of such restrictions by examining *real interest rates;* that is, the amount by which savers gained or lost the ability to buy real goods and services as a result of saving.[23] Ideally, we would adjust nominal deposit rates, which look forward in time, for *expected* inflation over the same forward time period. But since expectations cannot be observed or even estimated without extensive survey data, we use instead actual *realized* inflation in our measures of real interest rates. The fact that realized inflation can be significantly different from expected inflation creates quite a lot of noise in this measure. A further source of anomalies in these data, particularly in hyperinflationary economies, is a likely mismatch in timing of deposit interest rate measures and inflation measures, which sometimes lead to unbelievably large real interest rates.

We try to mitigate the noise problem by using a three-year moving average of real interest rates for each country in the IFS database.[24] Figure 2.4 shows the average of

---

[23]For a detailed explanation of real interest rates, please see "The Impact of Inflation on Debt Markets" in Chapter 6.

[24]The formula is real rate = (1 + deposit rate) / (1 + inflation rate) −1, averaged over the three years up to and including the year to which the measure is attached.

FIGURE 2.4

Real interest rates by region

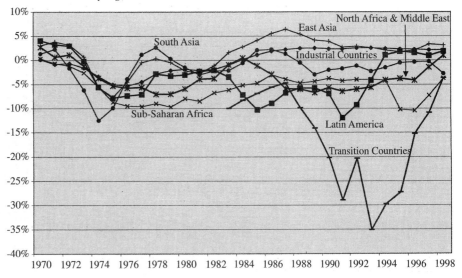

this measure by geographic region during 1970–1998. Notice how many regions spend many years below the zero line; that is, how prevalent and persistent are negative real rates. The depth of financial repression in the transition countries until the last years of the century is again an outlier, though on this measure the repression is worst during the transition out of communism, 1989–1996. Sub-Saharan Africa stayed consistently in the range of −10 percent to 0 percent real rates throughout the three decades. By 1998 only the transition countries, Sub-Saharan Africa, and South Asia remained in negative territory.

Latin America and North Africa and the Middle East had real rates ranging from −10 percent to 0 percent until the burst of financial liberalization in the 1990s, which brought both regions up to the levels of the industrial countries and East Asia, which have offered consistently positive real rates since the late 1970s, when realized inflation was racing ahead of expected inflation, pulling the measure down for all countries. The country-by-country three-year moving average measure of real interest rates up to 1998 is shown in Appendix Table 2.A1.

The only defense that private savers have against taxation of the banking system through deposit interest ceilings and reserve requirements is to hold as little of their wealth in bank deposits as possible. Thus, a consequence of taxing banks is that the supply of credit and the use of money (bank deposits and currency) are minimized. To capture that effect, we show a measure of relative money holdings among countries, namely the ratio of liquid liabilities (M3) to GDP.[25] This liquidity measure should be associated with greater economic and financial development.

Figure 2.5 shows the distribution of the liquidity measure by region from 1970 to 1998. During the 1970s, most developing areas were much like each other, with liquidity at 20 percent to 40 percent of GDP, while the industrial countries showed almost

---

[25]Following King and Levine (1993b), if M3 is unavailable, then M2 is used instead.

FIGURE 2.5

Liquidity (M3/GDP) by region

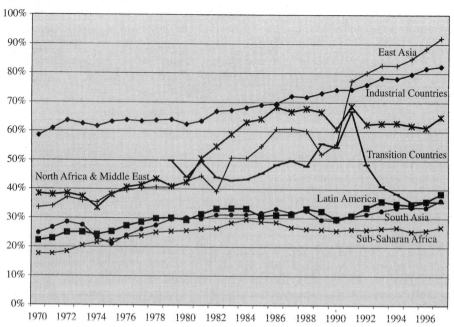

twice as high a level of liquid assets. During the 1980s and 1990s, however, East Asia and North Africa and the Middle East saw dramatic improvements in financial depth. East Asia, in particular, rose to surpass the liquidity of the industrial countries, reaching more than 90 percent of GDP by the end of the 1990s.

On this measure, Latin America is more of a laggard, staying quite consistently at the level of South Asia and only somewhat ahead of Sub-Saharan Africa. The transition countries again appear as fundamentally different from the other groups, rising in liquidity through 1993 and then collapsing to approximately the level of Latin America and South Asia. The Appendix shows country-by-country measures of liquidity in 1998.

It is somewhat more difficult to measure the intensity of government involvement in the lending process, particularly when the effect is through guidance and persuasion. We offer two measures, one related to borrowing and the other to lending. The borrowing measure gives the fraction of domestic credit that is granted to the private sector. The lending measure gives the ratio of commercial bank assets to the sum of commercial bank and central bank assets. This is designed to capture the importance of private lending compared with government lending.

The private sector share of borrowing during 1970–1998 is graphed by region in Figure 2.6. Throughout most of this period East Asia had the highest percentage of private sector borrowing of any region. At the same time, East Asia's ratios may overstate the extent of private control over capital, since government's guiding hand over private capital flows is not captured in this measure. The industrial countries also sustained a relatively high level of about 80 percent private borrowing. During the 1990s, Latin

FIGURE 2.6

Private sector share of borrowing by region

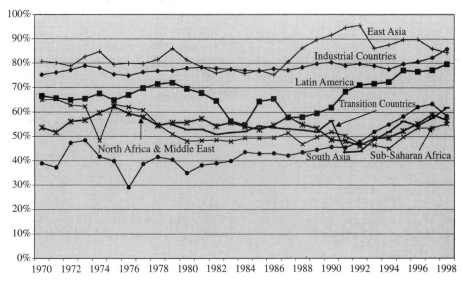

America climbed from the group of other developing regions to a level comparable with the industrial countries, a reflection of the intensity of privatization activity in Latin America during that decade. By the end of the 1990s, the private sector share of borrowing had settled into a common range of 55 percent to 60 percent in all the other regions, well below that of East Asia, the industrial countries, and Latin America.

Figure 2.7 shows the commercial bank share of combined commercial bank and central bank assets from 1970 to 1998. The industrial countries stand at the top of this measure, with commercial banks holding 94 percent of the combined assets, since central banks in industrial countries do little more than manage monetary policy. East Asia increased from about 70 percent to more than 80 percent as the central banks gradually reduced their role. North Africa and the Middle East also score highly on this measure, reflecting the importance of international banking to the region. Latin America and the transition countries showed a strong increase during the 1990s to the level of East Asia and North Africa and the Middle East, reflecting their moves away from government-directed credit. South Asia and Sub-Saharan Africa by this measure fell behind the liberalizing trend of most other regions during the 1990s. Both the borrowing and the lending measures are shown country-by-country for 1998 in Appendix Table 2.A1.

Our sixth measure of financial repression and development is the relative size of the stock market. Economists sometimes undervalue the importance of a functioning stock market, since public equities are a major source of investment capital in only a handful of developed countries, and banks dominate the financial systems of virtually all developing economies. Nevertheless, stock markets have an importance beyond their role in raising capital: The existence of public stock prices focuses the attention of managements and investors alike on value and value creation. The concept of *emerging* financial markets is closely connected with stock markets and interest in

FIGURE 2.7

Commercial bank (versus central bank) lending share by region

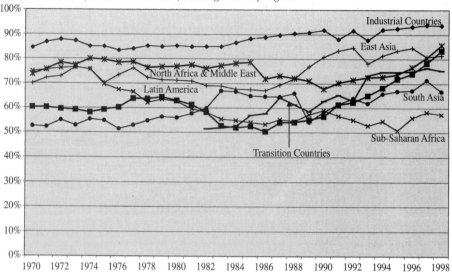

their values. Furthermore, research has shown that stock market valuation is closely correlated with economic growth.[26]

Aggregate stock market capitalization figures are not contained in IFS, which is the source of most of the measures used in this chapter. However, the IFC has been following emerging stock markets for several decades and publishes an annual fact-book with market capitalizations and much more.[27] We express *market value* as the ratio of this series on market capitalization relative to GDP. These ratios are graphed for major regions over the years 1980 to 1997 in Figure 2.8.

Figure 2.8 offers a new perspective on financial development by region. East Asia appears as the leading region on this measure throughout the 1990s. It peaked at more than 160 percent in 1993 and then slowly descended to the level of the industrial countries by the end of 1997. On the market value measure, East Asia as a region was essentially a peer of the industrial countries, even at the end of 1997 when the East Asian financial collapse had begun. Meanwhile, the industrial countries as a group grew steadily in this measure during the 1990s. North Africa and the Middle East are the most impressive of the emerging market regions measured by stock market capitalization at around 30 percent of GDP, while the other regions mostly converge in the 15 percent to 20 percent range.

The six measures of financial development are summarized in Table 2.2. Each of them, or a variant of them, has been found useful by a number of economists in studies of financial development and economic growth, and we shall summarize the results of their research in the next section. None of the measures is more than a

---

[26]Levine and Zervos (1998).
[27]International Finance Corp. (1999).

FIGURE 2.8

Stock market capitalization / GDP by region

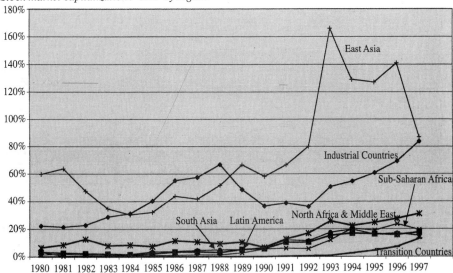

crude indicator of financial development, however, and each taken alone can easily give a false signal.

A combined measure of financial development is less susceptible to the errors that affect the individual measures. It is therefore useful to combine the six measures into a single numerical index that roughly summarizes where a country stands on the spectrum from full financial repression to full financial development. Armed with such an index, we can evaluate the progress of regions, examine the correlation between finance and economic growth, and quantify the extent to which financial development contributes to growth.

To combine the measures of Table 2.2, we map each of them onto a scale of 0 to 100 (taking account of whether the measures are positive or negative indicators of financial repression) in such a way that the average value among all countries over 1970–1998 is about 50 and the standard deviation is about 20, and where a larger number means more financial development and less repression. The six measures are then simply averaged to give an overall measure of financial repression and development. The method of doing these calculations, and the country-by-country results, are described in more detail in the Appendix to this chapter.

The index of financial repression or financial development by country is listed in the Appendix, Table 2.A2, for 1970, 1990, and 1997. These measures are summarized by region in Table 2.3 and are graphed in Figure 2.9. As of 1970 the industrial countries were far more financially liberal (averaging an index value of 60–70) than any other group of countries. In the developing world, most countries were mildly repressed (40–50), while South Asia (and no doubt the transition countries, if we had sufficient data) was severely repressed (30–40).

East Asia's climb into the liberalized mode of the industrial countries took place on a slow, steady curve. The curve began rising in the 1980s and then climbed

FIGURE 2.9

Index of financial repression and development

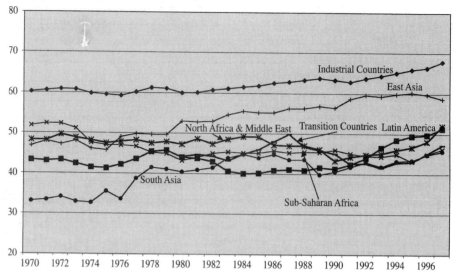

toward 60. South Asia similarly climbed, paused, and climbed again, but it started from such a deeply repressed point that by the mid-1990s it had only reached the level of Sub-Saharan Africa (40–45). The transition countries also progressed from a very low base, reaching about the same point. Latin America moved more deeply into financial repression during the great debt crisis of the 1980s, but then climbed very sharply in the 1990s, as did North Africa and the Middle East. Note particularly that the progress of most regions toward financial liberalization continued into 1997, despite the crises of that year and the immediately preceding ones.

The regions that attracted the most capital during the early 1990s were those that already were financially liberal (East Asia) or that were rapidly liberalizing (Latin America). It seems that external capital is most attracted to areas where financial liberalization is high and/or growing. Internal financial development—probably a consequence of a favorable institutional, political, and economic climate—is also associated with a greater ability to attract external funds.

TABLE 2.2   Six Measures of Financial Repression and Development

Reserve ratio	Bank reserves/Money plus quasi-money (*M2*) less currency held outside of banks
Real rates	Nominal annual interest on bank deposits (*i*) adjusted for realized annual inflation (π): $r = (1 + i)/(1 + \pi) - 1$
Liquidity	Short term liquid liabilities (*M3* if available, else *M2*) / GDP
Private borrowing	Claims on private sector/Total domestic credit
Bank lending	Deposit bank assets/Deposit bank assets plus central bank assets
Market value	Aggregate stock market capitalization/GDP

FIGURE 2.10

Finance and wealth

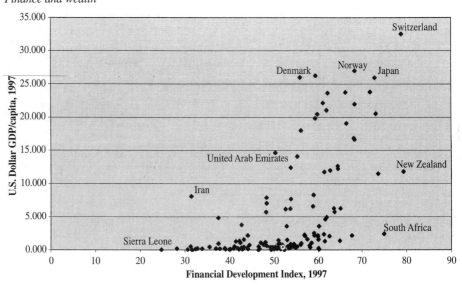

Financial Development and Economic Growth

There is an important connection between financial repression and the level of economic activity or wealth. Figure 2.10 is a graph of countries mapped by 1997 GDP per capita compared with the index of financial repression or development for 1997. The correlation of wealth with financial development is quite clear, if not uniform. As can be seen in Figure 2.10, only one severe financial repressor (index less than 45) had a GDP per capita greater than $5,000. Similarly, only three countries with high financial development (index greater than 70) had a GDP per capita less than $20,000. The graph seems to say that financial development is not a sufficient condition for high

TABLE 2.3   Index of Financial Repression and Development

	1970	1990	1997	27-Year Change
Industrial countries	60.3	63.3	67.8	7.6
East Asia	46.8	56.4	58.7	11.9
North Africa and Middle East	48.3	43.3	52.0	3.7
Latin America	43.3	41.3	51.3	8.0
Transition countries	N/A	45.0	47.2	N/A
Sub-Saharan Africa	51.8	46.0	46.2	−5.6
South Asia	33.1	40.6	45.7	12.7

Source: See Appendix.

FIGURE 2.11

Finance and growth

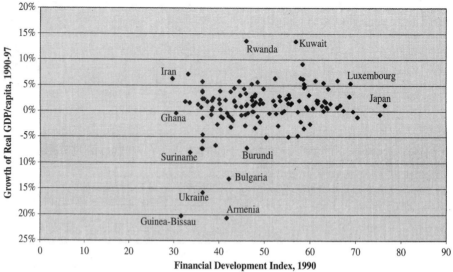

wealth (i.e., there are numerous countries with financial development and still low wealth), but that significant wealth is highly unlikely to materialize without a liberal financial system.

In more technical terms the correlation coefficient between the index and GDP per capita is 0.58. If we regress GDP per capita on the index of financial repression and development, the R^2 is 0.34 and the t-statistic on the index coefficient is 8.33, indicating a high degree of statistical significance. Of course, this analysis is incomplete because there are many other factors leading to wealth, and because the causality could easily be the reverse: One could argue that financial development reflects wealth rather than produces it. For that reason, a closer look at the causal role of finance is desirable.

The connection between financial development and economic development visible in Figure 2.10 is mirrored by a similar connection between financial development and growth (the process of attaining economic development) as shown in Figure 2.11. That figure shows a mapping of countries onto a grid relating their index of financial development in 1990 to their subsequent mean annual growth rate of real GDP per capita during the years 1990–1997. The growth rate is computed annually for each country as $(1 + g)/(1 + \pi) - 1$, where g is the annual growth of GDP measured in local currency and π is the rate of consumer price inflation in the local currency that year.

Perhaps the most striking feature of Figure 2.11 is the number of countries (52) whose average annual growth in real wealth was negative during 1990–1997. Much of Sub-Saharan Africa, for example, lost economic ground during the 1990s (though a few countries such as Rwanda and Gabon grew rapidly). Most of the transition countries of Central and Eastern Europe and Central Asia suffered major economic contraction as the first step toward a noncommunist system. Most of Central America and part of South America failed to take part in the emerging markets boom of the early 1990s. Some countries such as Mexico grew rapidly and then just as suddenly gave back the ground they had gained.

Figure 2.11 displays a general trend upward to the right, suggesting that on average higher financial development is associated with subsequent economic growth. However, a number of countries grew rapidly despite a financially repressed condition (e.g., Iran). This demonstrates that financial development is not a necessary condition for growth.

In statistical terms, the correlation between the index of financial repression and development and subsequent growth in real GDP per capita is 0.28. A regression of growth on the index shows an R^2 of 0.08 and a t-statistic on the growth coefficient of 3.50. Again, such a simple regression is merely suggestive because many other factors influence growth. The results of more comprehensive empirical studies are noted below.

In Theory, Should Financial Development Cause Economic Development?

Before turning to the empirical literature in economics that tries to disentangle the links between financial development and economic development, it is worth reviewing how controversial the causal role of finance in economic development has been until recently. Perhaps surprisingly, mainstream economic thinking until the mid-1970s held that financial development and financial institutions should not matter very much for economic growth. Indeed, the absence of any causal role for financial institutions in economic development was a rare point of agreement between Keynesian and classical economists.

In classical economic models, real activity is viewed as separable from monetary and financial matters, which overlay the real economy like a "veil." Financial transactions in that view are a sideshow. In these classical models, capital markets are perfectly efficient and all agents have full information, so there is no important function served by financial intermediaries. That sort of thinking, however, has trouble making sense of the fact that financial intermediaries themselves account for a large share of GDP in industrial countries.

Economic theory from the 1930s to the 1970s was dominated by the thinking of John Maynard Keynes, in whose theories money and interest rates mattered a great deal, but often in a negative sense. Furthermore, Keynes never attached much importance in his writings, to the productive role of financial institutions in the economy, except to remark on the disarray that a collapse of the banking system can cause.[28] Indeed, Keynes advocated suppressing interest rates to discourage the holding of money. In that sense, Keynes was a supporter of financial repression.

One must remember that Keynes's essential problem was to explain the depth and duration of the Great Depression of the 1930s. That indeed was a puzzle, since classical analysis held that recessions and depressions would be self-correcting as a new equilibrium evolved after some shock. Keynes observed that individuals and firms were holding large cash balances and were not willing to make the kind of investment

---

[28]Keynes (1931). See also Minsky (1975).

in productive assets that could rekindle the economy. He argued that people had an excessive preference for liquidity.

More precisely, Keynes postulated that money demand is sensitive to interest rates, and that interest rates can fall to some lower bound but not below. At this point (the "liquidity trap"), full-employment saving may exceed full-employment investment. If only interest rates could be forced lower, investment would be stimulated:

> The destruction of the inducement to invest by an excessive liquidity-preference was the outstanding evil, the prime impediment to growth of wealth, in the ancient and medieval worlds. And naturally so, since certain of the risks and hazards of economic life diminish the marginal efficiency of capital whilst others serve to increase the preference for liquidity. In a world, therefore, which no one reckoned to be safe, it was almost inevitable that the rate of interest, unless it was curbed by every instrument at the disposal of society, would rise too high to permit of an adequate inducement to invest.[29]

Presumably "every instrument at the disposal of society" would include interest rate ceilings imposed by the government.

Keynes's theory of the liquidity trap has been criticized as logically flawed and empirically irrelevant.[30] Nevertheless, in the postwar period Keynesian economists such as James Tobin created a new set of models, quite different from the liquidity trap framework, which echoed the theme that investment can be spurred by government policies that reduce the rates of return available to money holders. Whereas money was irrelevant in classical economics, it became the enemy in Keynesian economics.

The Keynesian view of money as deadweight baggage may have been true for gold coins but was not true for credit money in the form of bank deposits (i.e., money supplied by financial institutions as their way of raising loanable funds). When an individual deposits money in a bank, it does not disappear, but instead is often made available by the bank in the form of loans to companies and individuals. Far from preventing investment in productive projects, this kind of money makes possible such projects. In other words, banks are institutions designed precisely to reconcile the liquidity preference of individuals with the needs of entrepreneurs for long-term capital funding.

Many modern economists long puzzled over exactly what kind of market imperfections or information asymmetries could lead economies to expend the substantial resources we do spend (some 6 percent of U.S. GDP) on the activities of financial institutions. The economists who specialized in the areas of economic development and corporate finance first articulated the macroeconomic role of finance most explicitly and explained its importance for economic development.

For example, the great Austrian development economist Joseph Schumpeter, writing in the early years of the 20th century, emphasized the connection between entrepreneurship and credit. He saw that granting credit to an entrepreneur was an act of faith that the entrepreneur could use to create economic value. The banker, in this view, "is essentially a phenomenon of development, though only when no central authority directs the social process. He makes possible the carrying out of new combi-

---

[29]Keynes (1936), quoted in Fry (1995), p. 11.
[30]Brunner and Meltzer (1968), Meltzer (1999), and Hanes (1999).
[31]Schumpeter (1912), quoted in Fry (1995).

nations, authorizes people, in the name of society as it were, to form them."[31] But mainstream macroeconomists were reluctant to pick up this theme.

The notion that the financial system is actually necessary for growth was argued with new vigor in two important books by Ronald McKinnon (1973) and Edward Shaw (1973), both financial experts knowledgeable about developing economies. McKinnon and Shaw distinguished between inside money, meaning bank deposits supporting private sector loans, and outside money, meaning central bank liabilities such as bank reserves and cash. Economic growth is stimulated by encouraging people not to hold true deadweight assets such as gold, jewelry, and other physical objects often prized as inflation hedges, but to trust the banking system and create more inside money. Higher interest rates and lower reserve requirements would stimulate growth through this channel.

McKinnon and Shaw were followed by a school of economic thinkers who expanded on this theme and utilized econometric tests to demonstrate its validity. McKinnon and Shaw also generated some skepticism and rebuttal among numerous established economists, and those commentaries have served to refine and modify the claims that are made about the connection between finance and development.

One empirical qualification to the McKinnon-Shaw view has been a lack of evidence supporting the claim that allowing higher real rates of interest leads to substantially increased saving. Numerous econometric studies in developed countries suggested that saving has been driven by many factors, among which the level of real interest rates was relatively unimportant. Japan, for example, has had an extremely high savings rate despite a history of low interest rates. Only in cases of severely negative interest rates does it appear that savings is significantly responsive to interest rates.

The weak relationship between savings and real interest rates contradicts an element of the McKinnon-Shaw view, but does not overturn its fundamental insights. Even if the quantity of savings is relatively inelastic over most ranges of real interest rate variation, there *are* ranges in which it does respond strongly, and those tend to be in countries that have suffered disastrous economic performance. Furthermore, much of the McKinnon-Shaw view focuses on the *efficiency of the allocation of savings*, not just its quantity. Private intermediaries operating in a liberalized financial environment (as distinct from government planners) make better use of the funds at their disposal.

A second objection to McKinnon and Shaw is that some countries have grown rapidly without liberalizing their financial systems. The case of the Soviet Union has already been mentioned, and certain small countries such as Iceland and Cyprus are also sometimes mentioned as examples. What this shows is that financial development is not a *necessary* condition for economic growth, at least in the short to medium term.

With respect to the examples of growth experiences in which financial repression coincided with high growth, it is important to recognize that such counterexamples are allowed by the theory. Rajan and Zingales (1996) found that financial development operates largely through its effects in lowering the cost of external finance, which is more important for some industries and firms than for others. In economies where inside finance is available (through entrepreneurial wealth or abundant retained earnings), the contribution of financial intermediaries to growth may be relatively small. Iceland and Cyprus may be examples of this sort of coincidence of economic opportunities and financial resources in the same entrepreneurial hands.

Finally, critics of the McKinnon-Shaw school note that financial liberalization has sometimes seemed to cause more problems than it has solved, as suggested in the title of one well-known study, "Good-bye financial repression, hello financial crash,"[32] which tells the story of Chile's financial liberalization during 1976–1979 and subsequent collapse during 1980–1983. We will examine this story in Chapter 3, and the related stories of Mexico and East Asia in the 1990s in Chapter 8. At the very least, we have learned that sudden financial liberalization can create instabilities when the underlying institutional structure contains serious weaknesses.

Despite anxieties about instability, the mainstream of economic thought clearly has shifted toward recognizing an active, productive role for financial institutions in the economy, and the consequent advantages of allowing financial institutions to thrive. This view is grounded in market imperfections, such as transaction costs and asymmetric information among agents. Financial institutions arise, in this framework, to handle market imperfections; banks, for example, are now most often explained as collectors and users of information whose existence reflects the problems that would otherwise arise if savers tried to deal directly with users of capital. A large new microeconomic literature in corporate finance on the information-production of financial institutions (summarized in Chapter 5) has provided a wealth of empirical evidence in support of the McKinnon-Shaw macroeconomic paradigm of the role of banks in the economy.

Does Financial Development Cause Economic Development?

Financial economists have expended an increasing amount of effort over the past three decades to disentangle the linkages between economic and financial development and to resolve the question of whether the correlation between the two reflects a causal contribution of financial development to economic development.[33] Three different approaches to that problem have proved particularly informative, and all three have indicated strong causal effects of financial development for economic development.

The first approach, pioneered by Robert King, Ross Levine, and others, has been to use careful econometric analysis to separate the exogenous components of financial development (the extent to which financial development is predetermined with respect to economic development) from its endogenous components (the extent to which financial development simply reflects economic development). The first set of tests following this approach was published in 1993 in three related papers.[34] In this research, four different growth measures were regressed on a large number of control variables generally believed to have explanatory power for growth, plus various measures of financial repression or development, such as those shown in Table 2.1. This was done for contemporaneous growth and also for growth subsequent to the measurement point of the financial variables. In all cases the financial variables had coefficients that were sizable and highly statistically significant.

A set of follow-up papers constructed an additional set of tests using the econometric technique of "instrumental variables" to provide an alternative means for identifying the component of financial development that is truly exogenous to economic

---

[32]Díaz-Alejandro (1985).
[33]See Fry (1995) for a summary.
[34]King and Levine (1993a, 1993b, 1993c).

development. Measures of *predicted* financial development were constructed, using exogenous legal and institutional characteristics of countries as predictors. The variation across countries in that predictable component of financial development provided important explanatory power for economic development. In other words, aspects of financial development that are clearly traceable to the deep institutional history of a nation (and which therefore cannot be plausibly viewed as endogenous to the recent economic growth experience) go a long way to explaining the links between financial and economic development.[35]

A second approach to sorting out financial–real sector linkages is structural modeling. Structural modeling requires that one take a position on the specific channels through which financial development operates on economic development, and construct a model of the economy to estimate the effect of exogenous financial factors. Perhaps the most careful and convincing example of this line of research is the work of Alan Taylor.[36] Taylor approached the broader question of why Asian growth had outpaced that of Latin America in recent decades, and asked whether financial development promoted growth by lowering the cost of investment. He found a strong link between financial development and the cost of financing investment, and that these costs had large explanatory power for the growth difference between Asia and Latin America in the 1980s.

A third approach is to examine the economic performance effects of identifiable institutional changes associated with financial liberalization. A recent survey of research of this type concludes that "there is little evidence to support the claim, initially advanced in support of liberalization, that liberalization will increase saving . . . [but] there is much more support for two other claims, namely, that liberalization will lead to financial deepening and that it will foster a more efficient allocation of investment."[37] Another study found that reductions in government ownership of banks are associated with higher subsequent growth of per capita income and higher productivity growth.[38]

Together these three lines of research offer robust and convincing evidence that financial development contributes importantly to economic development. But as we shall discuss further in the following chapter, the way financial liberalization occurs also matters, particularly for ensuring that financial development rests on sound institutional footings.

Winners and Losers

If financial repression is so debilitating to economic growth and efficient capital market allocation, then why have governments been so willing to repress their economies? The answer is that not everyone loses from financial repression. Financial repression is a device for taxing savers (whose wealth suffers as a result) and nonfavored firms (for whom financing remains very expensive or unavailable) to transfer those resources

---

[35]See Levine (1997, 1998, 1999) and Levine and Zervos (1998).

[36]Taylor (1997).

[37] Williamson and Mahar (1998). For further evidence that financial deepening improves the quality of capital allocation, see Wurgler (1999), summarized in Chapter 4.

[38]LaPorta, Lopez-de-Silanes, and Shleifer (2000).

either to government itself or to borrowing firms that are part of the government's ruling coalition.

Each of the six tools of repression can be understood as a tax-and-transfer scheme. Ceilings on deposit interest rates deprive savers of the competitive market return they otherwise might have earned. This transfers wealth to the banks, and the government often mandates the pass-through of those transfers to favored borrowers. High reserve requirements transfer wealth from savers and nonfavored borrowers to government since reserves provide interest-free credit to the government. Directed credit policies, like state ownership and micromanagement of banks, give government control over the distribution of bank resources, which becomes an implicit government expenditure. Restricting competition, either by means of domestic bank entry limits or restrictions on foreign capital inflows and outflows, preserves the rents the government can extract from the protected and controlled financial sector.

Just as the Ming emperors chose to limit openness and growth in the interest of maintaining the emperor's control over resources, modern governments often choose financial repression as a means to laying claim to a bigger piece of a smaller economic pie.

APPENDIX

This Appendix consists of two tables:

Table 2.A1   Measures of Financial Repression and Development
Table 2.A2   Summary Index of Financial Repression and Development

The ratios are those defined in Table 2.2 of the text. Data are from IFS and IMC.

TABLE 2.A1   Measures of Financial Repression and Development, 1997

Country	Real Rates (%)	Reserve Ratio (%)	Liquidity (%)	Private Borrowing (%)	Bank Lending (%)	Market Capitalization (%)
Albania	7.0	18.4	N/A	7.2	57.3	N/A
Algeria	−70.8	2.8	N/A	9.3	71.9	N/A
Angola	0.1	28.6	73.5	51.6	41.7	N/A
Antigua and Barbuda	N/A	9.7	N/A	84.5	97.8	N/A
Argentina	7.3	4.2	54.9	71.9	89.6	4.2
Armenia	−37.2	42.3	8.9	73.7	74.9	1.0
Aruba	1.1	9.5	69.2	102.1	89.5	52.2
Australia	3.9	2.6	86.6	92.1	96.1	158.3
Austria	0.0	3.7	91.2	78.2	97.5	17.9
Azerbaijan	5.9	31.0	N/A	18.9	62.7	N/A
Bahamas	3.5	6.2	N/A	82.5	95.3	N/A
Bahrain	4.1	8.5	N/A	N/A	35.2	N/A
Bangladesh	−1.4	10.6	N/A	73.0	86.8	N/A
Barbados	1.0	6.7	69.5	77.0	97.6	N/A
Belarus	−41.8	26.4	16.2	48.8	63.7	N/A
Belgium	1.5	3.2	88.2	52.6	98.2	58.3
Belize	5.6	10.0	N/A	86.7	86.6	N/A
Benin	9.2	15.4	16.9	76.8	65.1	19.3
Bhutan	−9.6	61.3	18.9	75.9	97.3	18.3
Bolivia	7.8	21.2	30.1	98.3	76.5	N/A
Botswana	N/A	7.2	21.9	−13.1	0.0	N/A
Brazil	5.7	18.3	45.2	65.4	77.6	98.0
Bulgaria	−29.4	18.5	33.6	41.9	75.3	0.0
Burkina Faso	1.7	9.0	86.3	N/A	66.7	124.6
Burund	−1.1	7.3	N/A	58.8	66.9	N/A
Cambodia	4.0	476.3	N/A	91.4	74.7	N/A
Cameroon	−2.5	14.0	N/A	43.2	62.5	N/A
Canada	3.2	0.9	77.5	87.0	95.6	93.6
Cape Verde	−2.0	22.4	9.9	52.3	75.7	N/A
Central African Republic	−3.3	10.2	28.2	40.7	51.3	10.4
Chad	−3.7	38.7	19.7	31.8	42.2	N/A
Chile	5.4	4.3	N/A	94.8	78.5	N/A
China	−11.1	64.8	120.8	96.9	81.2	22.5
Hong Kong	−3.1	0.6	49.6	104.5	98.4	19.0
Colombia	7.7	15.4	N/A	80.6	94.9	8.8
Comoros	−77.2	32.7	24.1	80.8	70.1	N/A
Congo, Democratic Republic	N/A	N/A	27.4	N/A	N/A	N/A
Congo, Republic of	N/A	14.5	N/A	47.0	56.1	N/A
Costa Rica	0.1	30.3	31.4	48.9	59.8	0.9
Côte d'Ivoire	N/A	4.4	N/A	67.5	73.4	N/A
Croatia	−23.6	11.1	N/A	81.8	99.9	N/A
Cyprus	2.9	10.5	22.8	78.6	89.9	13.0
Czech Republic	−0.8	20.4	71.2	84.6	93.5	26.8

Country	Real Rates (%)	Reserve Ratio (%)	Liquidity (%)	Private Borrowing (%)	Bank Lending (%)	Market Capitalization (%)
Denmark	0.9	11.3	59.1	57.4	89.6	57.0
Djibouti	−6.2	1.9	15.7	81.6	4.4	N/A
Dominica	2.2	10.5	83.9	86.3	97.4	N/A
Dominican Republic	4.9	25.5	36.1	85.9	89.9	11.9
Ecuador	9.5	10.1	46.0	101.3	97.0	4.5
Egypt	N/A	17.8	44.2	50.8	77.1	N/A
El Salvador	4.9	29.4	21.5	83.8	80.6	0.8
Equatorial Guinea	0.6	38.2	36.7	45.0	47.7	43.7
Estonia	−1.9	26.1	41.7	86.5	99.5	33.7
Ethiopia	8.6	16.3	67.9	52.3	58.2	0.0
Fiji	3.0	10.3	43.8	85.4	100.0	4.6
Finland	1.6	7.1	51.7	96.5	98.2	63.9
France	2.2	0.9	71.5	81.1	97.7	49.7
Gabon	−6.6	12.8	106.2	54.0	83.7	24.4
Gambia	−15.0	15.7	42.0	107.9	76.9	9.5
Germany	1.4	3.8	71.8	80.5	95.4	40.6
Ghana	N/A	13.4	86.4	30.0	49.1	47.1
Greece	5.2	38.4	47.7	44.0	79.5	29.5
Grenada	2.5	11.1	75.0	88.1	97.4	N/A
Guatemala	−2.2	33.0	34.1	103.2	98.9	N/A
Guinea	3.4	21.6	82.7	64.3	29.6	8.6
Guinea-Bissau	8.3	N/A	102.2	N/A	N/A	77.2
Guyana	2.9	23.3	52.8	40.6	44.1	N/A
Haiti	−8.1	23.9	41.7	60.2	51.4	0.0
Honduras	−6.1	28.0	30.9	112.9	90.5	39.7
Hungary	3.7	N/A	N/A	N/A	N/A	N/A
Iceland	1.4	7.3	38.0	94.0	94.0	0.0
India	9.2	10.3	27.1	51.7	78.4	N/A
Indonesia	4.2	5.4	N/A	105.2	85.0	N/A
Iran	−23.6	35.2	20.7	45.5	43.9	N/A
Ireland	−1.5	4.4	84.4	93.9	99.7	35.0
Israel	3.4	18.1	13.8	91.5	95.9	N/A
Italy	2.1	9.9	54.7	62.0	88.1	31.1
Jamaica	1.9	30.4	N/A	76.4	68.2	N/A
Japan	−0.1	1.8	210.0	85.6	93.3	56.8
Jordan	4.3	52.7	N/A	84.5	78.9	N/A
Kazakhstan	−8.4	27.9	N/A	79.5	56.4	N/A
Kenya	N/A	17.0	32.8	64.0	81.6	44.0
Korea	−1.0	3.6	20.4	98.2	81.0	N/A
Kuwait	3.8	1.1	N/A	50.8	99.5	N/A
Kyrgyzstan	−1.0	24.8	13.8	19.3	23.1	N/A
Laos	3.0	22.0	14.2	78.8	68.5	N/A
Latvia	1.0	19.0	27.9	70.8	85.9	6.2
Lebanon	N/A	18.7	N/A	56.8	96.5	N/A
Lesotho	−3.9	18.0	N/A	−66.0	97.7	N/A
Liberia	−10.8	69.7	49.8	N/A	100.0	40.6
Libya	N/A	45.1	N/A	N/A	45.7	N/A
Lithuania	7.0	15.8	19.0	82.3	98.8	17.7
Luxembourg	2.4	0.6	N/A	110.5	98.9	N/A
Macedonia	0.0	12.1	N/A	92.5	81.0	N/A
Madagascar	N/A	27.2	N/A	72.5	59.2	N/A
Malawi	4.0	39.8	82.2	46.9	75.1	27.5
Malaysia	0.5	19.5	24.1	81.1	88.7	N/A
Maldives	3.0	69.3	N/A	56.5	54.4	N/A
Mali	N/A	14.9	39.8	111.7	68.5	N/A
Malta	1.3	7.5	160.5	79.6	96.2	8.6
Mauritania	N/A	14.9	N/A	294.8	66.4	N/A

Country	Real Rates (%)	Reserve Ratio (%)	Liquidity (%)	Private Borrowing (%)	Bank Lending (%)	Market Capitalization (%)
Mauritius	N/A	5.9	N/A	70.0	96.7	N/A
Mexico	−3.3	6.5	60.2	62.5	92.3	N/A
Moldova	−1.5	5.5	22.2	26.8	69.2	N/A
Mongolia	0.9	11.2	23.1	69.5	76.4	6.0
Morocco	−15.9	6.6	67.3	56.0	84.2	37.0
Mozambique	0.9	21.0	49.3	462.7	84.6	12.7
Myanmar	3.7	19.5	N/A	21.7	23.3	N/A
Namibia	N/A	4.5	38.9	96.2	100.0	4.5
Nepal	−1.1	12.2	79.0	70.4	72.9	42.5
Netherlands	1.6	0.6	86.4	84.6	98.3	134.4
Netherlands Antilles	0.5	0.3	N/A	91.0	96.7	N/A
New Zealand	5.5	1.9	50.2	102.2	96.0	189.9
Nicaragua	0.4	22.5	73.3	22.4	21.7	25.0
Niger	3.3	15.0	38.2	32.3	42.5	5.0
Nigeria	9.7	22.7	40.5	80.5	42.0	N/A
Norway	2.1	3.3	52.3	114.0	97.9	44.8
Oman	N/A	6.5	N/A	107.2	98.6	N/A
Pakistan	2.1	11.3	N/A	52.5	71.5	N/A
Panama	5.9	22.5	32.9	113.0	77.5	4.6
Papua New Guinea	−68.1	2.8	N/A	64.0	74.9	N/A
Paraguay	6.4	29.8	25.8	90.7	65.0	27.6
Peru	4.4	32.4	43.0	127.0	98.5	1.1
Philippines	1.7	9.2	10.7	72.4	87.1	N/A
Poland	0.0	10.3	39.7	48.9	85.9	9.6
Portugal	3.2	9.9	97.0	89.0	98.1	39.9
Qatar	5.7	4.6	15.1	57.0	97.7	N/A
Romania	0.0	15.6	24.9	44.6	87.6	2.0
Russia	3.1	22.7	17.8	35.9	67.4	29.8
Rwanda	−9.0	23.9	N/A	64.9	53.8	N/A
Samoa	−39.3	34.0	N/A	251.4	100.0	N/A
Saõ Tomé and Príncipe	2.9	46.2	32.4	−456.9	27.8	14.4
Saudi Arabia	3.4	11.1	N/A	N/A	99.7	N/A
Senegal	−0.9	7.5	18.4	73.9	62.3	N/A
Seychelles	−36.3	40.7	46.9	17.3	62.5	32.3
Sierra Leone	−5.4	42.2	N/A	5.4	7.0	N/A
Singapore	4.8	7.5	N/A	138.9	38.1	N/A
Slovak Republic	−7.8	12.6	68.2	61.6	91.6	9.7
Slovenia	0.0	5.5	42.5	79.9	97.3	9.5
Solomon Islands	2.5	6.2	N/A	38.1	79.1	N/A
South Africa	6.0	3.9	24.1	95.5	94.7	18.3
Spain	2.4	6.3	74.0	76.5	94.3	56.6
Sri Lanka	−1.5	15.1	26.8	74.9	86.5	12.7
St. Kitts and Nevis	2.8	12.6	65.9	97.8	99.6	N/A
St. Lucia	4.2	11.1	N/A	107.5	99.0	N/A
St. Vincent and the Grenadines	2.7	13.3	N/A	110.5	98.4	N/A
Sudan	N/A	29.1	48.7	33.6	31.3	20.1
Suriname	−22.6	19.0	56.1	85.1	78.2	53.5
Swaziland	2.3	12.8	169.7	N/A	96.4	238.2
Sweden	2.5	1.9	46.4	56.0	92.7	123.5
Switzerland	0.2	2.0	144.6	91.7	98.8	226.0
Syria	1.3	N/A	23.4	N/A	100.0	N/A
Tanzania	N/A	9.3	55.6	28.5	61.1	21.6
Thailand	N/A	5.1	N/A	91.8	87.9	N/A
Togo	0.7	13.2	48.3	77.5	71.0	16.9
Tonga	5.3	49.5	N/A	89.5	93.7	N/A
Trinidad and Tobago	3.2	17.0	N/A	75.1	89.7	N/A

Country	Real Rates (%)	Reserve Ratio (%)	Liquidity (%)	Private Borrowing (%)	Bank Lending (%)	Market Capitalization (%)
Tunisia	−3.7	9.6	126.8	94.0	99.5	132.3
Turkey	−3.2	25.3	67.2	75.2	86.6	201.6
Uganda	0.3	19.2	61.5	72.3	28.3	51.7
Ukraine	−5.2	14.6	13.6	14.4	51.6	7.5
United Arab Emirates	−13.3	14.8	N/A	99.3	100.0	N/A
United Kingdom	0.6	0.3	106.5	95.8	68.8	153.4
United States	0.0	0.0	0.6	0.8	0.9	1.4
Uruguay	−1.1	22.7	23.2	80.2	68.4	17.0
Vanuatu	−6.3	5.9	N/A	103.9	86.9	N/A
Venezuela	−27.2	25.7	69.1	74.3	78.6	N/A
Yemen	2.3	20.8	N/A	17.6	29.3	N/A
Zambia	−0.2	12.0	96.1	17.7	18.6	23.0
Zimbabwe	N/A	15.9	25.6	57.6	52.8	N/A

Source: IFS and IMC.

Table 2.A2 shows the summary index of financial repression and development for all countries in the IFS database in 1970, 1990, and 1997. For comparison, we also show average annual growth in real GDP per capita for 1970–1980 and 1990–1997, together with wealth (GDP per capita measured in U.S. dollars) in 1997.

The index of financial repression or development is constructed by averaging indexes for each of the six measures, or as many of them as are available in a given time frame. Each measure is mapped onto a 0 to 100 scale to produce an index that is approximately normally distributed, with a mean of 50 and a standard deviation of 20. Before constructing this mapping, each variable's empirical distribution is examined. Distributions that appear more lognormal than normal are first transformed by taking their natural logarithms (this applies to liquidity and market capitalization)

The following mapping translates each ratio or logarithm onto a 0 to 100 index:

Index = $\alpha + \beta x$,
  where
x = ratio or ln(ratio)
$\alpha = 50 - \beta$ mean(x)
$\beta = 20$/standard deviation(x)

When this formula produces an index less than 0 or greater than 100, the index is set at 0 or 100, respectively. As would be expected at 2.5 standard deviations in a normal distribution, such censoring is relatively infrequent.

The market value measure is derived from the IFC Emerging Markets Database, which contains information on 105 stock markets around the world. When a country is in the IFC database but a measure is not available, it is marked N/A. However, when a country is not in the IFC database it is assumed that the country does not have a significant stock market and the measure is set to 0. The 105 IFC countries are then mapped onto a 0 to 100 scale as described above.

TABLE 2.A2   Overall Index of Financial Repression and Development

Country	Index 1970	Growth 1970–1980 (%)	Index 1990	Growth 1990–1997 (%)	Index 1997	Wealth 1997 ($)
Albania	N/A	N/A	N/A	N/A	32.4	N/A
Algeria	44.8	9.6	52.2	2.1	46.9	753
Angola	N/A	N/A	56.3	N/A	45.2	N/A
Antigua and Barbuda	51.2	6.7	58.1	N/A	57.4	6,223
Argentina	54.5	3.5	42.6	−0.9	60.1	101
Armenia	N/A	5.2	N/A	−20.6	48.1	1,096
Aruba	N/A	N/A	56.3	N/A	58.4	N/A
Australia	55.7	1.7	62.6	0.6	71.6	16,645
Austria	62.3	2.6	62.0	1.7	63.5	20,478
Azerbaijan	N/A	N/A	N/A	N/A	23.2	N/A
Bahamas	70.1	0.6	61.1	−4.8	64.4	11,775
Bahrain	41.9	0.9	36.0	2.0	46.1	7,885
Bangladesh	29.3	4.4	46.8	3.3	45.2	161
Barbados	69.2	2.2	52.4	−0.3	61.8	6,591
Belarus	N/A	N/A	N/A	−7.3	46.3	N/A
Belgium	55.5	1.4	61.6	1.6	63.8	19,842
Belize	44.0	−14.8	63.3	0.9	62.7	2,018
Benin	58.0	N/A	45.8	1.4	53.4	401
Bhutan	25.9	4.3	35.7	2.3	48.5	112
Bolivia	37.1	2.3	37.9	1.5	52.2	527
Botswana	61.5	3.6	58.3	0.6	44.0	2,271
Brazil	43.6	−2.9	41.7	3.0	55.1	N/A
Bulgaria	N/A	N/A	36.8	−13.0	42.0	N/A
Burkina Faso	58.8	N/A	43.5	−1.3	53.5	346
Burundi	48.1	1.8	55.2	−7.1	51.7	177
Cambodia	0.0	N/A	40.7	N/A	41.4	N/A
Cameroon	57.4	4.4	58.4	−3.4	50.5	1,175
Canada	62.1	2.1	68.6	0.0	73.7	20,567
Cape Verde	65.9	N/A	46.5	N/A	53.6	N/A
Central African Republic	62.0	11.8	51.0	−2.1	48.9	511
Chad	59.8	N/A	51.2	−0.8	32.6	224
Chile	39.9	6.4	50.3	4.5	64.3	1,514
China	N/A	N/A	54.3	9.2	49.3	N/A
Hong Kong	N/A	N/A	62.8	2.1	74.3	11,832
Colombia	44.5	2.0	47.3	1.6	57.8	675
Comoros	N/A	N/A	40.7	N/A	38.0	N/A
Congo, Democratic Republic	22.3	7.3	29.5	−13.7	59.4	2
Congo, Republic of	55.3	8.4	54.3	−5.0	40.4	1,355
Costa Rica	50.0	3.4	36.3	2.1	43.3	1,077
Côte d'Ivoire	49.9	−0.2	50.5	−0.5	51.9	1,024
Croatia	N/A	N/A	N/A	N/A	62.7	N/A
Cyprus	44.2	4.8	48.7	2.3	57.4	7,670
Czech Republic	N/A	N/A	N/A	3.9	56.0	N/A
Denmark	57.2	0.8	64.4	2.0	57.2	25,995
Djibouti	43.9	N/A	60.7	N/A	40.9	N/A
Dominica	64.6	8.4	57.9	3.2	63.9	2,191
Dominican Republic	36.5	0.6	44.8	3.5	55.3	477
Ecuador	38.0	5.9	44.9	0.3	58.6	406
Egypt	27.5	5.5	35.6	1.4	41.1	448
El Salvador	45.2	−2.9	38.9	0.4	49.4	768

Country	Index 1970	Growth 1970–1980 (%)	Index 1990	Growth 1990–1997 (%)	Index 1997	Wealth 1997 ($)
Equatorial Guinea	56.3	N/A	49.8	5.3	38.1	450
Estonia	N/A	N/A	N/A	−0.7	56.3	N/A
Ethiopia	51.1	−6.5	42.4	2.6	54.0	162
Fiji	65.9	N/A	65.0	2.1	55.2	N/A
Finland	68.5	2.6	57.8	0.5	64.6	23,756
France	63.2	2.1	65.5	0.8	69.7	21,076
Gabon	64.1	18.5	56.9	4.6	49.6	5,704
Gambia	37.4	3.3	45.5	−2.1	45.3	246
Germany	65.5	1.6	61.7	0.1	64.1	23,661
Ghana	33.4	−8.5	37.0	−0.4	40.3	249
Greece	51.0	1.7	43.9	1.2	48.7	6,160
Grenada	60.8	0.1	58.9	2.7	64.2	2,367
Guatemala	50.0	1.4	46.0	1.8	48.0	525
Guinea	N/A	N/A	58.6	N/A	41.7	N/A
Guinea-Bissau	46.7	N/A	37.3	−20.2	53.5	954
Guyana	53.7	N/A	37.7	2.9	47.8	107
Haiti	21.3	−0.8	31.5	−3.5	39.3	207
Honduras	43.0	0.2	45.1	−0.1	46.8	387
Hungary	N/A	2.4	38.7	−2.6	66.7	2,191
Iceland	52.4	4.3	52.2	1.2	57.5	22,164
India	46.2	1.9	44.9	4.4	54.0	216
Indonesia	41.8	7.9	49.7	6.4	52.6	503
Iran	43.0	5.4	26.2	6.3	33.9	8,088
Ireland	47.3	2.0	57.1	5.3	65.6	12,671
Israel	46.4	2.5	48.7	2.2	53.7	8,283
Italy	58.3	3.9	53.6	1.6	56.1	17,997
Jamaica	65.5	−4.4	48.0	1.5	51.6	456
Japan	69.9	1.6	74.2	1.3	72.2	25,956
Jordan	53.1	6.4	38.2	−0.3	55.9	851
Kazakhstan	N/A	N/A	50.4	N/A	41.4	N/A
Kenya	61.5	−1.4	49.8	−5.1	57.4	246
Korea	50.1	9.5	57.3	6.3	55.7	4,619
Kuwait	70.2	5.3	33.6	13.5	61.3	12,257
Kyrgyzstan	N/A	N/A	N/A	3.7	23.6	N/A
Laos	45.0	N/A	43.3	2.5	50.3	149
Latvia	N/A	N/A	N/A	−4.5	50.1	N/A
Lebanon	53.0	N/A	50.9	N/A	50.9	N/A
Lesotho	35.0	1.6	44.6	3.8	52.3	288
Liberia	55.0	N/A	59.1	N/A	51.6	N/A
Libya	57.4	12.5	36.3	N/A	42.2	7,039
Lithuania	N/A	N/A	0.0	−5.8	51.8	N/A
Luxembourg	73.9	1.9	78.4	5.4	77.3	23,802
Macedonia	57.1	N/A	51.8	−1.3	58.0	N/A
Madagascar	64.5	−2.8	44.3	−1.4	47.7	179
Malawi	63.1	−2.7	34.0	1.9	41.7	197
Malaysia	61.6	5.8	64.9	6.0	62.6	2,168
Maldives	39.6	N/A	34.8	N/A	40.5	N/A
Mali	42.8	N/A	36.9	1.2	60.8	309
Malta	64.8	7.3	63.6	4.4	64.1	6,265
Mauritania	59.8	N/A	54.7	−0.6	45.8	537
Mauritius	47.8	5.2	50.7	2.9	53.8	2,205
Mexico	39.9	4.3	51.3	1.3	56.6	2,121
Moldova	N/A	N/A	N/A	7.2	44.2	202
Mongolia	N/A	N/A	46.0	−6.6	41.7	132
Morocco	45.2	2.1	48.2	−0.4	57.9	1,004
Mozambique	57.1	N/A	34.9	1.7	54.0	38
Myanmar	13.7	2.0	25.1	3.3	31.6	511

Country	Index 1970	Growth 1970–1980 (%)	Index 1990	Growth 1990–1997 (%)	Index 1997	Wealth 1997 ($)
Namibia	37.5	N/A	54.6	0.8	58.3	1,448
Nepal	48.9	−0.1	43.3	2.2	50.9	118
Netherlands	67.6	1.2	69.7	1.6	77.7	19,082
Netherlands Antilles	64.1	N/A	69.9	N/A	75.5	N/A
New Zealand	58.4	0.0	64.3	0.2	77.9	11,500
Nicaragua	51.2	2.3	35.0	1.6	35.2	0
Niger	57.5	0.6	47.2	−3.3	45.1	343
Nigeria	52.4	4.2	48.4	−3.1	55.1	244
Norway	59.1	4.5	68.4	2.9	67.9	27,007
Oman	N/A	N/A	54.8	N/A	56.1	4,942
Pakistan	42.5	2.7	45.6	1.0	42.3	286
Panama	54.7	2.0	34.7	4.4	59.9	2,080
Papua New Guinea	N/A	N/A	65.5	4.8	44.6	1,055
Paraguay	41.8	4.3	32.0	−0.3	53.7	816
Peru	41.9	2.8	42.2	−1.3	50.4	5
Philippines	44.0	1.6	52.7	0.1	58.1	578
Poland	N/A	0.9	35.1	−3.9	49.2	284
Portugal	64.2	0.9	54.5	3.2	64.8	6,277
Qatar	77.2	−2.7	52.5	−2.5	55.8	14,104
Romania	55.5	−1.3	62.7	−2.8	48.0	183
Russia	N/A	N/A	74.6	−7.3	48.1	N/A
Rwanda	30.1	−4.4	37.1	13.6	41.2	226
Samoa	109.5	0.9	35.7	N/A	56.1	881
São Tomé and Príncipe	63.8	N/A	66.3	N/A	33.4	N/A
Saudi Arabia	55.9	12.8	52.0	1.8	55.7	5,752
Senegal	66.8	−1.9	44.7	0.0	49.3	803
Seychelles	N/A	7.6	43.6	2.8	21.5	4,856
Sierra Leone	43.4	−1.4	21.2	−2.8	22.3	33
Singapore	32.3	5.7	49.8	5.7	52.9	12,422
Slovak Republic	N/A	N/A	N/A	5.8	54.4	N/A
Slovenia	N/A	N/A	N/A	5.8	58.4	N/A
Solomon Islands	47.3	N/A	54.5	N/A	52.8	266
South Africa	55.2	2.7	71.7	−1.1	75.8	2,421
Spain	58.7	1.1	58.3	2.1	63.5	12,010
Sri Lanka	39.6	7.3	45.4	3.1	52.6	351
St. Kitts and Nevis	N/A	2.9	60.4	6.4	65.0	3,579
St. Lucia	N/A	6.5	61.0	2.1	61.0	2,545
St. Vincent and the Grenadines	N/A	5.8	58.4	2.4	51.6	1,613
Sudan	44.9	−1.0	16.5	2.1	34.4	220
Suriname	63.7	1.0	38.1	−8.0	52.5	3,799
Swaziland	53.5	1.5	46.7	0.9	53.3	900
Sweden	61.4	1.7	58.6	−0.1	66.4	26,256
Switzerland	65.7	0.9	72.4	−0.6	84.2	32,540
Syria	34.6	5.5	36.5	2.5	73.6	1,588
Tanzania	41.9	−2.2	30.7	−1.1	43.9	109
Thailand	51.2	3.3	57.9	6.0	55.0	1,330
Togo	70.4	−1.8	36.5	−1.8	52.1	468
Tonga	N/A	N/A	32.7	2.1	33.4	N/A
Trinidad and Tobago	56.4	8.8	56.6	1.4	56.6	3,573
Tunisia	58.0	N/A	59.9	5.5	60.7	1,392
Turkey	43.7	N/A	38.7	1.9	54.7	790
Uganda	44.7	−6.2	53.5	4.0	39.2	80
Ukraine	N/A	N/A	45.0	−15.7	34.1	N/A
United Arab Emirates	46.2	N/A	49.6	N/A	50.0	14,660
United Kingdom	48.7	1.4	72.6	1.2	77.2	16,827
United States	59.7	0.0	65.5	0.8	70.7	21,989

Country	Index 1970	Growth 1970–1980 (%)	Index 1990	Growth 1990–1997 (%)	Index 1997	Wealth 1997 ($)
Uruguay	43.7	0.4	33.5	0.7	39.2	632
Vanuatu	N/A	3.0	66.2	1.1	41.5	1,587
Venezuela	46.2	2.7	48.1	−1.0	49.8	1,279
Yemen	26.7	N/A	23.5	−7.1	33.2	N/A
Zambia	48.2	N/A	27.2	−3.5	28.1	80
Zimbabwe	50.2	1.6	55.7	−2.8	51.4	376
Industrial countries	60.3	3.1	63.3	1.5	67.8	18,518
East Asia	46.8	6.3	56.4	4.7	58.7	4,779
Latin America	43.3	3.2	41.3	1.0	51.3	755
N. Africa and Middle East	48.3	9.0	43.3	2.1	52.0	5,736
South Asia	33.1	4.3	40.6	2.1	45.7	238
Sub-Saharan Africa	51.8	2.7	46.0	−0.9	46.2	775
Transition countries	N/A	N/A	45.0	−3.0	47.2	543

Source: IFS, IMC, and authors' calculations.

Note: "Growth" is the mean annual growth rate of real GDP. "Wealth" is the dollar value, at the year-end exchange rate recorded in IFS for 1997, of GDP per capita.

References

Bekaert, Geert, and Campbell R. Harvey. 2000. Foreign speculators and emerging equity markets. *Journal of Finance* 55: 565–613.

Bhagwati, Jagdish. 1996. *Political Economy and International Economics.* Cambridge, MA: MIT Press.

Brunner, Karl, and Allan H. Meltzer. 1968. Liquidity traps for money, bank credit and interest rates. *Journal of Political Economy* 76: 1–37.

Calomiris, Charles W., Charles P. Himmelberg, and Paul Wachtel. 1995. Commercial paper, corporate finance, and the business cycle: A microeconomic perspective. *Carnegie-Rochester Conference Series on Public Policy* 42: 203–50.

Campbell, John, and Yasushi Hamao. 1994. In *The Japanese Main Bank System: Its Relevance for Developing and Transforming Economies.* Ed. by Masahiko Aoki and Hugh Patrick. Oxford: Oxford University Press: 325–49.

Demirgüç-Kunt, Asli, and Ross Levine. 1998. Opening to foreign banks: Stability, efficiency, and growth. Working paper, World Bank.

Díaz-Alejandro, C. F. 1985. Goodbye financial repression, hello financial crash. *Journal of Development Economics* 19: 1–24.

Duby, Georges. 1979. *The Early Growth of the European Economy.* Ithaca: Cornell University Press.

Edwards, Sebastian. 1999. How effective are capital controls? *Journal of Economic Perspectives* 13: 65–84.

Freeman, Archibald, and Arthur W. Leonard, eds. 1915. *Conciliation with the Colonies: The Speech by Edmund Burke.* San Francisco: Houghton Mifflin.

Fry, Maxwell J. 1995. *Money, Interest and Banking in Economic Development.* Baltimore: Johns Hopkins University Press.

Hanes, Christopher. 1999. The liquidity trap, the supply of reserves and U.S. interest rates in the 1930s. Working paper, Federal Reserve Board.

Henry, Peter Blair. 2000. Stock market liberalization, economic reform and emerging market prices. *Journal of Finance* 55: 525–64.

Hobbes, Thomas. [1651] 1996. *Leviathan.* New York: Cambridge University Press.

Hoshi, Takeo, Anil Kashyap, and David Scharfstein. 1990. Bank monitoring and investment: Evidence from the changing structure of Japanese corporate banking relationships. In

Asymmetric Information, Corporate Finance, and Investment. Ed. by R. Glenn Hubbard. Chicago: University of Chicago Press: 105–26.

Hoshi, Takeo, and Hugh Patrick, eds. 2000. *Crisis and Change in the Japanese Financial System.* Amsterdam: Kluwer Academic Publishers.

Hughes, Jonathan R. T. 1991. *The Governmental Habit Redux: Economic Controls from Colonial Times to the Present.* Princeton, NJ: Princeton University Press.

International Finance Corp. 1999. *Emerging Stock Markets Factbook.* Washington, DC: World Bank.

Jones, Eric L. 1988a. *The European Miracle: Environments, Economies, and Geopolitics in the History of Europe and Asia.* Cambridge: Cambridge University Press.

———. 1988b. *Growth Recurring: Economic Change in World History.* Oxford: Oxford University Press.

Kane, Edward. 1998. Capital movements, asset values, and banking policy in globalized markets. Working Paper no. 6633, National Bureau of Economic Research.

Keynes, J. Maynard. [1931] 1968. The consequences to the banks of the collapse of money values. *Essays in Persuasion.* New York: W.W. Norton.

———. 1936. *The General Theory of Employment Interest and Money.* London: Macmillan.

King, Robert G., and Ross Levine. 1993a. Financial intermediation and economic development. In *Financial Intermediation in the Construction of Europe.* Ed. by Colin Mayer and Xavier Vives. London: Centre for Economic Policy Research: 156–89.

———. 1993b. Finance and growth: Schumpeter might be right. *Quarterly Journal of Economics* 108: 717–38.

———. 1993c. Finance, entrepreneurship and growth: Theory and evidence. *Journal of Monetary Economics* 32: 512–42.

Krueger, Anne. 1974. The political economy of the rent-seeking society. *American Economic Review* 64: 291–303.

Krugman, Paul. 1994. The myth of Asia's economic miracle. *Foreign Affairs* 73, no. 6: 62–78.

La Porta, Rafael, Florencia Lopez-de-Silanes, and Andrei Shleifer. 2000. Government ownership of banks. Working Paper no. 7620, National Bureau of Economic Research.

La Porta, Rafael, Florencia Lopez-de-Silanes, Andrei Shleifer, and Robert W. Vishny. 1997. Legal determinants of external finance. *Journal of Finance* 52: 1131–49.

Levine, Ross. 1997. Financial development and economic growth. *Journal of Economic Literature* 35: 688–726.

———. 1998. The legal environment, banks, and long-run economic growth. *Journal of Money, Credit and Banking* 30: 596–613.

———. 1999. Law, finance, and economic growth. *Journal of Financial Intermediation* 8: 8–35.

Levine, Ross, and Sara Zervos. 1998. Stock markets, banks, and economic growth. *American Economic Review* 88: 537–58.

McFarlane, Alan. 1978. *The Origins of English Individualism.* Cambridge: Cambridge University Press.

McKinnon, Ronald I. 1973. *Money and Capital in Economic Development.* Washington, DC: Brookings Institution.

———. 1993. *The Order of Economic Liberalization: Financial Control in the Transition to a Market Economy.* Baltimore: Johns Hopkins University Press.

McKinnon, Ronald I., and Huw Pill. 1996. Credible liberalizations and international capital flows: The "overborrowing syndrome." In *Financial Deregulation and Integration in East Asia.* Ed. by Takatoshi Ito and Anne O. Krueger. Chicago: University of Chicago Press: 7–50.

Meltzer, Allan H. 1999. Monetary policy at zero inflation. Working paper, Carnegie-Mellon University.

Minsky, Hyman P. 1975. *John Maynard Keynes.* New York: Columbia University Press.

Mokyr, Joel. 1990. *The Lever of Riches: Technological Creativity and Economic Progress.* Oxford: Oxford University Press.

North, Douglass C. 1990. *Institutions, Institutional Change, and Economic Performance.* Cambridge: Cambridge University Press.

Porter, Michael E., and Hirotaka Takeuchi. 1999. Fixing what really ails Japan. *Foreign Affairs,* May–June: 66–81.

Rajan, Raghuram, and Luigi Zingales. 1996. Financial dependence and growth. Working Paper no. 5758, National Bureau of Economic Research.

Schiantarelli, Fabio; Izak Atiyas; Gerard Caprio, Jr.; John Harris; and Andrew Weiss. 1994. Credit where it is due? A review of the macro and micro evidence on the real effects of financial reform. In *Financial Reform: Theory and Experience.* Ed. by Gerard Caprio, Jr., Izak Atiyas, and James A. Hanson. Cambridge: Cambridge University Press: 64–84.

Schumpeter, Joseph. 1912. *Theorie der wirtschaftlichen Entwicklung.* Leipzig: Dunker and Humbolt.

Shaw, Edward S. 1973. *Financial Deepening in Economic Development.* New York: Oxford University Press.

Taylor, Alan M. 1997. On the costs of inward-looking development: Price distortions, growth, and divergence in Latin America. *Journal of Economic History* 58: 1–28.

Williamson, John, and Molly Mahar. 1998. *A Survey of Financial Liberalization.* Princeton, NJ: Princeton University Press Essays in International Finance, No. 211, November.

World Bank (Japan Development Bank and Japan Economic Research Institute). 1994. Policy-based finance: The experience of postwar Japan. World Bank Discussion Paper 221.

Wurgler, Jeffrey. 1999. Financial markets and the allocation of capital. Working paper, Yale University School of Management.

Young, Alwyn. 1995. The tyranny of numbers: Confronting the statistical realities of the East Asian growth experience. *Quarterly Journal of Economics* 110: 641–80.

Privatization and Financial Liberalization

Introduction

In this chapter we discuss the major economic policy trend of the 1990s not only in EFMs but throughout the world, namely the trend toward privatization and financial liberalization. This virtually defines "emergence"—countries liberating the energy of their private sectors. The massive turn away from government ownership or government domination of productive assets is a trend of considerable breadth and power, affecting virtually all countries of the world. It brings closure to an earlier movement away from free enterprise that began in the 19th century and reached a crest during the half century from 1930 to 1980.

To understand the origins of the privatization movement, one must begin by understanding the origins of the state ownership wave of 1930–1980, and how the forces that favored state ownership were undermined in the 1980s and 1990s. Governments have always owned some property, and throughout history they have promoted and often owned major public works projects; the building of canals in America during 1815–1840, for example, was largely an activity of state governments. Furthermore, governments have sometimes seized control of the economy during wars by regulating wages and prices and industrial production. But 1930–1980 was an era of unprecedented, pervasive government ownership of enterprises; all over the world and in many different industries, government seized control of industry. In a similar vein, governments increased their authority in the regulatory process, moved toward increasing control of prices and wages, and further influenced the allocation of resources by providing large subsidies and credits for favored producers.

Three related trends in thinking about economic policy underlay the growth of government ownership: (1) socialism, the view that private ownership produces undesirable exploitation of workers and inequality of wealth; (2) the new economics of "market failures," which emphasized inefficiencies from private allocations of resources; and (3) the new critique of global openness, a protectionist doctrine rejecting the desirability of relying on free trade and unfettered private capital flows to promote economic growth. All three of these trends supported the movement to state ownership. Socialists argued that state ownership would create a more equal division of the gains from development. Advocates of "market failures" argued that government ownership could permit resource allocation to take into account the public gains of limiting some activities (e.g., pollution and overcrowding) and providing public goods that private markets would undersupply. Protectionism promoted public ownership by making local monopolies feasible, thereby weakening external competitive pressures that would have checked the growth of state-owned enterprises. Indeed, the inefficiencies of state-owned enterprises in many countries only became apparent after those enterprises were forced to compete in international markets, where the forces of global supply and demand dictated output prices.

These three trends in thinking were not simply exogenous to the economic process; each one reflected changes that were occurring in the economy. The privatization movement reflected a fundamental shift in thinking about the benefits of market allocation and global openness, given the economic collapse of the 1930s and the power of state action demonstrated during the war years:

> It is not difficult to understand—looking at the manifest failure of the American and British economies during the 1930s and their tremendous success in the Second World War, and looking at the success of the Latin American economies during the 1940s when they were cut off from international trade—why a rather *dirigiste* economic doctrine came to be established after the Second World War. And it is not hard to understand, looking at the experiences of the last 25 years, why the right doctrine for the time emphasizes markets, emphasizes openness, emphasizes the benefits of competition.[1]

The story of the rise of state ownership and subsequent (re)privatization has been a philosophical odyssey in which the ship of public policy has been pushed by the winds of economic experience.

Socialism

Socialism as a movement originated in the industrialized countries of Western Europe in the mid-19th century. Its strong appeal was its championing of the welfare of the poor, a reaction to the great inequality of wealth and class divisions within those societies. A hallmark of the Marxist socialist paradigm is the need to take the capital (what Marx called the means of production) away from the capitalists, and place it in the hands of workers (the proletariat). According to Marx, socialist government control of the means of production would result in a "dictatorship of the proletariat" and would prevent the exploitation of workers by preventing capitalists from gaining profits at workers' expense. During the first three decades of the 20th century, socialist parties gained power for at least some period of time in most of Western Europe. Yet their power was never so absolute that they could realize the dream of the "dictatorship of

---

[1]Summers (1999).

the proletariat" and there was little state ownership of enterprises outside the Soviet Union until after World War II.

From today's perspective, it is difficult to realize how unpopular private enterprise had become by the end of World War II. Concerns about inequality were especially pronounced in the wake of the Great Depression—a time during which enormous proportions of the working population had been unemployed, and poverty had spread widely even in the richest economies:

> At the end of the war, in Europe and throughout much of the world, capitalism was discredited in a way that is not easily imagined today. It seemed infirm, inept, and incapable. It could not be counted upon to deliver economic growth and a decent life . . . Capitalism was considered morally objectionable; it appealed to greed instead of idealism, it promoted inequality, it had failed the people, and—to many—it had been responsible for the war.
>
> One other factor was at work as well. The Soviet Union enjoyed an economic prestige and respect in the West that is hard to reconstruct today. Its five-year plans for industrial development, its "command-and-control" economy, its claims of full employment were all seen to constitute a great oasis and antidote to the unemployment and failures of capitalism in the 1930s.[2]

Market Failures

Not only did the Great Depression provide a boost to socialist ideals and challenges to the sanctity of private property, the Depression also helped to spur a new wave of thinking about the inefficiencies of the market economy. After all, vast unemployment is a form of resource waste. The new economics of market failure—emphasizing the need for government to manage the economy on *efficiency* grounds—was a by-product of that manifest inefficiency. Government ownership of corporations, along with government management of the investment process, was one approach to solving the inefficiency of underinvestment. Here is a typical view from 1980:

> Because of incomplete markets or imperfect information or other reasons, capitalist economies have frequently been characterized by underutilization of resources (of a kind that creates a strong presumption of inefficiency). Most dramatic of these failures of the market economy are the fluctuations that periodically lead to substantial unemployment. It is now accepted as a responsibility of the government to ensure a low level of unemployment. More generally, the fact that the market economy can lead to such massive underutilization of resources calls in question the appropriateness of the competitive equilibrium model. It is not obvious that—as some economists have suggested—once the problem of unemployment has been "solved," the classical model of the market economy, with its welfare implications, becomes applicable. It is more reasonable to suppose that the problem of unemployment is only the worst symptom of the failure of the market. There are indeed many other examples that suggest the limited applicability of the competitive equilibrium model: persistent shortage of particular skills, balance of payments disequilibria, regional problems, unanticipated inflation, etc. Even if the economy is well described by the competitive equilibrium model, the outcome may not be efficient because of externalities. There are innumerable examples where the actions of an individual or firm affect others directly (not through the price system). Because economic agents take into account only the direct effects upon themselves, not the effect on others, the decisions they make are likely not to be "efficient." . . .
>
> A particular category of commodities for which the market will not necessarily ensure the correct supply are public goods, of which defense and basic research are conventional

---

[2]Yergin and Stanislaw (1998), p. 22.

examples . . . Finally, there are . . . "merit wants." This is a category of goods where the state makes a judgment that certain goods are "good" or "bad," and attempts to encourage the former (e.g., education) and discourage the latter (e.g., alcohol). This is different from the arguments concerning externalities and public goods, in that with merit wants, the "public" judgment differs from the private evaluation, rejecting a purely individualistic view of society.[3]

These are not the pronouncements of a Kremlin leader, but the views of two of the most prominent Western economists of their generation, one of whom (Joseph Stiglitz) would later serve as the chairman of President Clinton's Counsel of Economic Advisors and as chief economist of the World Bank. As this account suggests, the mainstream view of the market economy had become decidedly jaundiced after World War II. The market was perceived as the source not only of inequality, monopoly, and abuse of power (the grand socialist themes of the past), but also of resource waste, of undesirable by-products (congestion and pollution); markets, it was argued, were incapable of identifying the "right" objectives and delivering the right outcomes given a set of objectives. Governments, many believed, could do much better by taking direct control of the economy.

Protectionism

The third philosophical ingredient in support of state ownership was protectionism. The weakness of international trade during 1930–1960 insulated government-owned enterprises from global competition, hence protecting them from the embarrassing market price signals that would have attached less value to their products in the competitive global marketplace than those products commanded in the protected domestic environment. Why did a world that had enjoyed relatively free trade for many decades before 1930 turn toward protectionism?

The backlash against free trade from 1930 to 1960 among developing countries was in part a reaction to the betrayal of free trade these countries had suffered at the hands of the developed world. Throughout the world, the late 19th century had seen the spread of free market thinking, especially as embodied in the core institutions and doctrines of global trade and finance: the removal of trade barriers, nearly universal adoption of the gold standard, the chartering of private banks, and the firm commitment to the repayment of sovereign debts. That new openness to globalism and the adoption of orthodox economic doctrines in trade and capital market policies fostered a boom in developing countries in the two decades prior to World War I. But that same openness placed emerging market countries in a very vulnerable position, as they were soon to discover.

Developing economies relied heavily on developed economies as markets for their exports, which were mainly primary commodities. The income and price collapse of the Great Depression (which resulted from the mismanagement of monetary policy in the United States and misalignments of exchange rates by the other developed economies under the restored international gold standard) had a devastating effect on developing economies. The reaction to the Depression in the developed world—increasing protectionism, followed by the destruction of World War II—seemed to put the lie to the earlier claims by the developed countries that free trade and financial openness were the road to prosperity. No wonder developing economies were fertile ground for neo-Marxist theories of "dependency" (which argued that free trade was a

---

[3]Atkinson and Stiglitz (1980), pp. 7–8.

means of international exploitation) and more mainstream arguments of the desirability of protecting "infant industries" from foreign competition.[4]

Finally, in addition to the events of the 1930s and 1940s, which buttressed the three ideological trends we have identified that supported state ownership, more distant history also played a role. The historical political links between the developed and underdeveloped worlds—which had their origins in European empire building—contributed to the ill repute of capitalist economics in developing countries. Africa and much of Asia were colonized and controlled by the European powers. Independence movements grew in all of these areas, and the concepts of "anti-imperialism" and "anti-capitalism" seemed almost interchangeable. The Soviet Union's support for such independence movements, and for the newly independent states, strengthened that perceived association between capitalism and imperialism (which was also an article of Leninist dogma). The new governments in India after 1948 and Africa in the early 1960s all adopted socialist policies. The long war in Indochina, fought first by France and then by the United States, appeared to many as a continuation of the same pattern, identifying nationalism with anti-capitalism.

State Ownership

Following World War II, the governments of Britain and France nationalized most heavy industries, including coal, iron and steel, railroads, telecommunications, and part of the petroleum industry that was not already state-owned; France nationalized the largest banks as well. Italy had two massive state enterprises, one industrial conglomerate (IRI) from Mussolini days and one state oil company (ENI) created after the war. The Soviet Union, which occupied Central and Eastern Europe at the end of World War II, saw to it that local communist regimes were installed throughout the region, each of which completely nationalized their economies. Mao Zedong's victory in China in 1948 added that country to the list of communist states. In the 1960s and 1970s, particularly, governments in most developing countries intervened directly in their economies, often forming *state-owned enterprises* (SOEs) in capital-intensive areas such as mining, petroleum, telecommunications, and heavy manufacturing.

The wave of state ownership and the rejection of global openness in developing economies was facilitated by the developed world's creation of a new financing organ for intergovernmental lending, the World Bank, which was then imitated on a smaller scale by the regional development banks (the Inter-American Development Bank, the African Development Bank, and the Asian Development Bank). A central problem poor, closed economies would have to face in the post–World War II environment was how to finance their development. They would not generate the export earnings to finance the purchase of capital goods from developed economies, so private sources of funding of those purchases would not be forthcoming. Private lenders in developed economies seemed to have little appetite for lending to governments of developing countries at this point in time.

The answer to that funding problem was the establishment of a new set of institutions that would manage intergovernmental transfers of funds from the developed economies to the developing world. The World Bank was conceived during World War II as a multilateral agency created by governments to provide governments with the capital

---

[4]For a review of the history of globalization, capital flows, and economic growth, see Eichengreen (1992, 1996), Obstfeld and Taylor (1999), Bordo and Eichengreen (1993), Bordo and Kydland (1995), Temin (1989), and the references therein. For a discussion and critique of many of the justifications for protectionist policies in developing economies, see Bhagwati (1988, 1996).

to finance postwar reconstruction and development programs. The World Bank was created at a time when private capital flows were virtually nonexistent and prospects for the speedy return of private capital to international finance seemed remote. These new World Bank lending programs not only built infrastructure such as roads, ports, and communications, but also pumped capital into heavy industry. According to a World Bank report:

> The public sector began to carry out a steadily increasing share of domestic capital formation, reaching on average over 45 percent in 1985 in the developing world . . . By the early 1980s, SOEs are estimated to have accounted for an average 17 percent of GDP in Sub-Saharan Africa and around 12 percent in Latin America. Asia, on the other hand, revealed a relatively modest share of only 3 percent (excluding China, India, and Myanmar). while Eastern Europe's SOEs were responsible for up to 90 percent of domestic production.[5]

It may seem surprising that Western governments were willing accomplices in financing, and thus promoting, the closed, state-controlled development strategies of the post–World War II era. But it should not be. After all, Western governments and their public policy experts increasingly shared many of those anti–free market views. Recall that President Richard Nixon (a Republican) instituted wage and price controls in the United States, and supported the expansion of welfare programs and other antidotes to the perceived shortcomings of the capitalist marketplace. For example, Brazil's grand plans for state construction of power plants and industrial mills, or its idea of relieving urban congestion by building a new capital city in the middle of the Amazon jungle, were perceived as bold and creative initiatives, not ill-advised, far-fetched schemes. The idea that government would operate wisely in the public interest was an article of faith that few questioned.

There were of course economists and political leaders in the 1950s, 1960s, and 1970s who decried the worldwide move toward statism and protectionism. Among political leaders, Barry Goldwater in the United States is perhaps the most notable example. Among economists, the most notable early critics of statism included Frank Knight, Friedrich von Hayek (author of the classic 1944 treatise, *The Road to Serfdom*), Milton Friedman, Mancur Olson, and George Stigler.[6]

During the 1960s and 1970s, the so-called "Chicago school" of economists emerged, a group of University of Chicago professors who were critics of the growth of government control over the economy. One of the key contributions of that school was to point out that the existence of inequality, externalities, and public goods did not necessarily imply a preference for government solutions over market solutions. These economists insisted that advocates of market failure identify the magnitude of the costs associated with the alleged failings of private markets, and compare that cost to the magnitude of social loss from government involvement. The Chicago school emphasized the flaws inherent in government as an institutional mechanism, rejecting the implicit assumption of interventionists that government involvement was costless, and that, therefore, control was desirable whenever a market failure of any magnitude could be identified. As George Stigler famously quipped, preferring the government on those grounds is reminiscent of the emperor who, when judging a contest between two musicians, gave the prize to the second musician after hearing only the first.[7]

---

[5]Sader (1993), p. 5.

[6]Hayek (1944) and Knight (1947) emphasized that the unheeded lesson of World War II's destructive dictatorships was that state control of the economy has a tendency to destroy personal freedom, with wide-ranging undesirable implications.

[7]The reference to Stigler's quip is from Atkinson and Stiglitz (1980), p. 10. For an introduction to the critique of government intervention, see Olson (1965) and Stigler (1988).

The costs of government policy referred to by these economists were not merely the physical transactions costs of implementing government programs, or the risks that come from honest errors of judgment (which now could take on a scale as grand as government's newfound ambitions), or the incompetence of powerful government officials. Rather, Olson, Stigler, and others argued that government policies also served vested interests; therefore, government usually acted intentionally in ways contrary to the interests of average citizens. The Chicago school identified key weaknesses in the political process that fueled government policy failures. Chief among these was influence peddling by self-interested politicians. Furthermore, government bureaucrats had a similar incentive to sell favors and little incentive to perform efficiently since their livelihoods did not depend on the efficiency of their performance.

That "political economy" critique of government intervention was applied skillfully to the developing world by Anne Krueger, Jagdish Bhagwati, and others who documented the litany of government abuses of power in the realm of economic policy. Krueger coined the phrase, "the rent seeking society," to capture the essence of the problem: a society where market opportunities are few, where government power is great, and where the most profitable occupation for citizens is seeking special favors and privileges (nonproductive "rents") through a corrupt process of bribery and extortion. By the end of the 1970s, Stigler's "second musician" was playing loud and clear.[8]

Those who have studied the actual performance of SOEs generally agree that the central problem is *inefficiency*. While a few SOEs have performed well, most combine overstaffing with poor service and little or no innovation. Public enterprises often lose money, absorb a disproportionate share of capital, and require substantial subsidies from taxpayers. Their loss-making performance is sometimes a primary reason behind the pervasive inability of developing country governments to control their fiscal deficits.

Even countries otherwise noted for their efficiency had inefficient public enterprises.[9] Japan, for example, whose private automobile and computer chip companies were setting new standards for world-class performance, suffered the hugely inefficient state-owned Japanese National Railway (JNR), whose annual losses exceeded $7 billion in the 1970s and $10 billion by the mid-1980s. Over this period the company received subsidies of more than $57 billion and ran its long-term debt up to $286 billion or 11 percent of the GDP. A government report issued in 1982 called for the breakup and sale of JNR, and by 1987 JNR was divided into six passenger lines and a freight line. From 1986 to 1990 passenger transport increased by 5 percent a year, service improved, operating cost per passenger fell by 11 percent, and aggregate annual losses of $4.3 billion turned into annual profits of $3.6 billion. At the same time, fares, which had been increasing almost annually since 1981, were not increased.[10]

The pattern seems nearly universal and therefore highly noteworthy. On average, public enterprises everywhere are less efficient than private enterprises. It is not that their people are inherently incompetent or untrained, but rather that their ownership and governance structures seem to undermine important incentives individuals face in

---

[8]The classic reference is Krueger (1974). In Chapter 4, we revisit the problem of corruption in detail.

[9]For more details on this problem as it pertains to Japan, and on the broader question of the role of the Japanese government in promoting inefficient, quasi-private firms through targeted government assistance, see Porter and Takeuchi (1999) and the references therein.

[10]Kikeri, Nellis, and Shirley (1992), p. 19.

the private sector to be creative and efficient. Repeated efforts to reform (rather than privatize) SOEs in Europe, Asia, and elsewhere seem to work only briefly before the old patterns reemerge. Anyone who has stood in a long line at a U.S. post office understands that there is something intrinsically different about public enterprise.

The Privatization Wave

In the 1980s a broad-based change of thinking about state-owned enterprises began to take hold. The trend started in the United Kingdom with the election of the Conservative government, led by Margaret Thatcher in 1979, and even there it started quite slowly:

> What has become commonplace in the late 1990s [privatization] was considered so radical prior to the 1979 election that even Thatcher's most committed supporters dared not raise the idea. The most that could be advocated for state-owned industries was the introduction of "inflexible" financial targets, the exclusion of ministerial meddling, the promotion of efficiency and ending of government subsidies . . . State-owned companies, some said, should be "commercialized" and made to operate more like private companies.[11]

But after her victory in the Falkland Islands in 1982, Thatcher began to sell SOEs in huge public offerings. In the subsequent 13 years the U.K. raised an estimated $65 billion through the sale of its stake in companies such as British Airways, British Petroleum, British Gas, British Telecom, and many more.[12] During that period Britain's economic performance went from mediocre to quite robust, and the privatized companies in most cases gained substantially in profitability and value. The clear success of this program forced the French and other Western European governments to rethink their public corporations, and soon they began privatizing as well.

But it was the fall of communism that signaled the beginning of a new era. Communism was, in the first instance, an economic theory, and throughout the modern era communist governments had advocated their system for developing countries as the key to successful economic development. What brought communism to an end was its economic failure, a failure so obvious and inescapable that no one could miss its importance. No visitor to Eastern Europe in the late 1980s could overlook the poverty, inefficiency, and immobility of these systems. Lenin had once predicted that capitalism would fall "like an overripe fruit from a tree." Ironically, that is what finally happened to communism.

The resolution of the global debt crisis in 1989–1991 coincided with the fall of communism and created an opportunity for developing countries to reorient their thinking and their actions altogether. Some, such as Chile, had a long head start; despite some serious setbacks described later in this chapter, Chile had been committed to privatization since the mid-1970s and by the late 1980s was finally reaping major rewards from its policies. Bolivia, Argentina, Peru, and eventually almost all of Latin America had joined the privatization surge by the early 1990s.

The reconstruction of Central and Eastern Europe in the 1990s was not only a massive exercise in privatization but also one that required far more: the building of

---

[11]Yergin and Stanislaw (1998), p. 114.
[12]See ibid. pp. 118–122, for a detailed account.

democratic political institutions, the construction of a modern legal system, the introduction of free prices for all goods, the opening of the economies to world trade, and the reconstruction of the human habits that make economies work—the work ethic (which depends on the confidence individuals must have that their efforts will be rewarded), and the courtesies and reciprocities of business relationships. In the successful cases, building institutions and establishing a work ethic were mutually reinforcing: Proper attitudes were bolstered by an increasingly orderly legal and institutional environment that encouraged long-run thinking as opposed to short-run opportunism, and by placing boundaries on government powers that made it clear that productive activity was more rewarding than nonproductive rent seeking. The unprecedented project of reconstruction went better in some countries than others, and some of the stories are told country by country later in this chapter. On average, the gains from privatization have been tangible and large.

East Asia had enjoyed a greater earlier commitment to private enterprise than other regions, and that lay behind much of its economic success in the 1970s and 1980s. The countries of East Asia (other than China and other still-communist countries) had fewer SOEs and therefore less to privatize. Nevertheless, they joined the global trend of selling off what SOEs they had.

China was a truly special case. While the government still called itself communist, China began to encourage private sector growth starting in the mid-1980s. This began as joint ventures between foreign enterprises and government entities at the local, provincial, or national level; it soon seemed that every government unit had its "subsidiaries"; many government officials were rapidly gaining wealth. By the mid-1990s purely private companies were tolerated as well. Offshore Chinese poured in capital, and the country experienced a remarkable ground swell of entrepreneurial activity and rapid persistent growth.[13]

Some privatization also occurred in Africa, the Middle East, and South Asia, though here the commitment was often more tentative. India, the bellwether economy of South Asia, committed itself to economic reform in the early 1990s and privatized a few SOEs, but encountered substantial political opposition to this course. India's long tradition of central bureaucracy, government licensing of every phase of economic activity, and the related phenomenon of corruption had become so embedded that the country had great difficulty in effecting change. By the turn of the century, however, a new Hindu nationalist government seemed to be injecting new life into economic reforms.

In a similar manner, the countries of Africa and the Middle East had some successes in privatization, particularly of small-scale enterprises, but in most cases lacked the political commitment to undertake wholesale economic reform. It is not hard to understand why. Africa, the Middle East, and South Asia are precisely the areas where colonialism had survived into the post–World War II era, where national independence was most recent and most fragile, and where the Soviet model and ideas of socialism had found their deepest resonance. It may require another generation before the global trend to private enterprise is fully and enthusiastically embraced in these regions.

The World Bank maintains a comprehensive database recording all EFM privatization transactions it can document since 1988. For the 10-year period 1988–1997 the

---

[13]China is counted as one of the transition countries rather than as part of East Asia in the statistics reported in this book.

database shows 6,169 transactions in 101 developing countries totaling $228 billion of value. These figures exclude activities in the industrialized countries. They also exclude the transactions of the *Treuhandanstalt* in East Germany and the mass voucher-based privatizations of Central and Eastern Europe (which are described later in this chapter), although they include transactions in formerly communist countries that involved outright sale. The data include partial privatizations in which a fraction of the equity in an SOE was sold to private or public investors. The database was first published, for 1988–1992, in Sader (1993) and has been updated periodically since.

These transactions are summarized annually by region in Table 3.1 and are graphed in Figure 3.1. As can be seen, the volume ran at $20 to $25 billion per year from 1991 through 1996, though the regional mix changed. In 1997, however, privatization surged throughout the world, but it was particularly noticeable in East Asia, Latin America (which began its surge a year earlier), and the transition countries. The financial crises in Mexico, Argentina, and Brazil in 1995, and in Asia in 1997, seem to have had far-ranging implications for privatization. In part, this reflects a continuation of the learning process about the inefficiency of state-owned enterprises that had been underway for decades. It may also reflect the fiscal pressure faced by many emerging market countries in the wake of shrinking exports and declining income growth. Fiscal deficits can be a powerful motivating force for accelerating the pace of privatization, particularly for an emerging market government hungry for foreign reserves.

Latin America has accounted for the largest volume; with almost $120 billion of total transaction value, the countries of Latin America represent more than half of the total. The transition countries of Central and Eastern Europe, after a slow start, undertook more outright sales as the 1990s progressed, and also joined the large increase in volume for 1997, yet they still have a good deal of privatizing left to do.

Figure 3.2 shows the proportion of transactions by region in various sectors. Manufacturing accounted for less of the volume than might have been expected, except in the Middle East and North Africa. Media, primarily the privatization of huge national telecom companies, was a large factor in every other region. The same is true for energy, representing the privatization of national oil and gas companies, which again

TABLE 3.1   Privatization Transactions by Region
   (in millions of U.S. dollars)

	Latin America	East Asia and Pacific	Transition Countries	Sub-Saharan Africa	Middle East and North Africa	South Asia	Total
1988	2,530	21		10	34		2,595
1989	1,436	196	469	1,298	230	3	3,632
1990	10,915	375	826	74	438	30	12,658
1991	17,101	832	2,339	1,121	229	998	22,620
1992	15,560	5,151	2,846	207	850	1,567	26,181
1993	10,487	7,137	3,505	640	900	992	23,661
1994	8,407	5,507	4,308	602	1,136	2,666	22,626
1995	4,627	5,442	9,169	472	1,318	921	21,949
1996	14,143	2,679	5,246	745	1,774	889	25,476
1997	33,897	10,385	16,072	2,348	2,078	1,794	66,573
Total	119,797	37,689	44,780	7,517	8,986	9,860	228,629

Source: World Bank, *Global Development Finance* (1999).

FIGURE 3.1

Privatization transactions by region

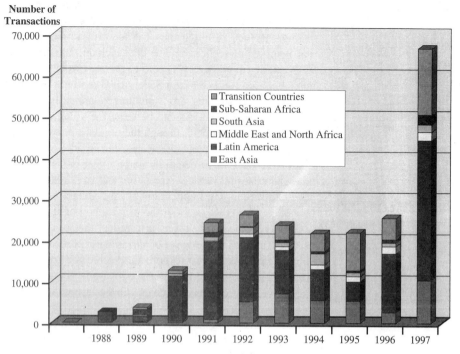

was a major feature of every region except the Middle East. The privatization transactions were closely associated with inflows of capital, not only in the sense that foreign companies bought some of the privatized firms, but also that the entire process of privatization attracted more investment than was needed just to buy the firms being sold.[14]

Table 3.A1 in the Appendix shows a country-by-country list of privatization transactions with information on whether the investors were local, foreign, or both. Some countries, such as Brazil and Malaysia, clearly favored local investors whereas others, such as Colombia and Mexico, tilted toward foreign investors. The totals show that joint ventures were the most frequently used form. Although joint ventures may not be stable for the long run, they are often the most acceptable compromise in the short run between a political desire to favor local investors and an economic desire to bring in foreign technology and management expertise.

Two Kinds of Growth

One goal of this chapter is to explore the underlying reasons why state-owned enterprises have underperformed relative to privately owned firms almost everywhere, contrary to the expectations and prescriptions of socialist politicians and many mainstream development economists throughout the 1960s and 1970s. To understand why privatization is so powerful and so important to economic success, one must reexam-

---

[14]See Sader (1995).

FIGURE 3.2

Proportion of privatizatons (1988–1997) by sector

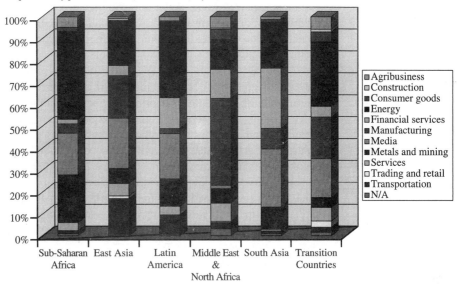

ine the concept of economic growth. In particular, when we apply the concepts of financial economics to the development problem, a new perspective emerges that illuminates the gains from privatization; financial economics provides a way of evaluating the *quality* of growth in national income, which is somewhat different from the macroeconomic perspective offered by national income accounting.

In the standard account of economic development, the goal is *growth per se,* defined as an increase in per capita GDP. To most people this seems obvious and axiomatic. Per capita GDP represents the total production of goods and services per person within the economy. If this number grows larger, it seems self-evident that people are on average better off, since on average each person has more goods and services available to him or her.

The socialist approach to growth was therefore to get larger as rapidly as possible: more production, more employment. The famous five-year plans of the Soviet Union set physical targets for output increases each year, and incentives were created for managers and workers to reach or exceed those physical goals. How could this be wrong?

A Digression into Corporate Finance

In corporate finance, *growth is not an unequivocal good.* Indeed, one of the first lessons taught in most introductory corporate finance courses at business schools is that growth is costly and often dangerous because growth requires the expenditure of resources—the cash needed to purchase productive equipment and to carry a growing quantity of inventories and accounts receivable. Companies that grow rapidly require ever-growing quantities of these inputs, and if the outputs are disappointing they can run out of funds, that is, fail financially.

The nexus of growth is *capital,* defined here in the financial sense of the total amount of funds available for investment in enterprises. In a well-functioning capital market, capital is available only at a substantial cost because capital is supplied by investors who require a certain minimal expected return on their investment in the firm. The future return supplied by the firm is of course uncertain, but it must have a sufficient expected value. Because investors are risk-averse, their expected return rises with the risk of their investment. Markets impose a distinct discipline. Firms that disappoint capital markets by earning less than the cost of capital must turn themselves around promptly or be cut off from the sources of funding.

A capital market has a rather cold-hearted way of feeding the strong and starving the weak: Capital will be showered on firms that can promise high expected rates of return while firms that are struggling may be left with no new sources of capital at all. Indeed, failing firms may be forced into bankruptcy and liquidation to repay their creditors, thereby also shedding their preexisting assets. The system transfers funds to industries and firms that can credibly be expected to earn returns above the cost of capital. In their personal affairs, ordinary human beings, including most corporate managers and government officials, rarely choose to act in such a heartless fashion when they have the freedom to do otherwise; they will typically want to tax the strong and support the weak. But the capital markets, if well informed and well structured, automatically do the reverse. They take away most of the freedom that corporate managers might use to act otherwise.

Corporate finance theory offers a clear but rigorous rule for corporate managers to follow when deciding whether to invest capital in some project—a rule that encapsulates the central criterion of market discipline. Managers should imagine that the prospective project is a freestanding company and decide what rate of return the capital markets would require to give it financing. They should then project the expected free cash flows (i.e., the amounts of cash that need to be put into their project or which can be taken out of it at various future dates) and discount those free cash flows at the estimated cost of capital. The result is the *net present value (NPV)* of the project. The *positive-NPV rule* says that managers should make the investment if the NPV is positive and reject it if the NPV is negative.

Since the value of the entire firm is the present worth of all its expected future cash flows, the market value of the firm (i.e., the sum of the market values of debt and equity claims upon it) will in principle rise to the extent that the NPV is positive and fall to the extent that the NPV is negative. That is, the NPV of a particular project is an estimate of the value that investment adds to or subtracts from the total value of the firm. The positive NPV investing rule thus implicitly says that a manager should invest in all projects that increase the firm's market value and reject all projects that diminish it. If that rule is followed (i.e., if managers prioritize investment opportunities according to their NPVs and reject all investments with negative NPV) then the firm's value will be maximized.

The pursuit of the NPV rule by managers is not just profitable for individual firms, but results in an efficient use of resources by the economy as a whole. Because firms compete for inputs, the market value of those inputs reflects the value those inputs create (in discounted cash flows) for the *marginal* purchaser of the inputs (the least profitable producer among those firms that purchase the inputs in pursuit of positive NPV projects). By following the positive NPV rule, managers ensure that productive resources are absorbed only by the firms that can make the most of them. In equilibrium, the price of the inputs is determined by (and equal to) their value to the marginal user.

The proof and measure of any firm's decision to invest should be a rising stock price in reaction to its decision, because the stock price is the yardstick by which the value of companies is judged in a capital market. A firm's stock price is a single, observable, unequivocal measure of corporate success or failure. That is why the positive-NPV rule is equivalent to the shareholder value–maximization rule. Thus, if firms serve their shareholders' interests, they must be following the positive-NPV rule. Why should firms maximize shareholder value? The shareholders own the company. They elect the board of directors and can in principle remove them. They invest in the stock solely to obtain greater value, and will judge the board and the management by how much their stock value rises. This is the fundamental link between private ownership and value-creating growth.

Corporate managers who are not shareholders, however, may undermine value maximization in a number of ways, including not working very hard, consuming corporate value through perquisites, and taking insufficient risk. That explains why such managers are commonly rewarded with stock options, so that their energy will be directed as far as possible toward maximization of corporate worth.

Note that following the positive-NPV rule is not the same thing as maximizing corporate growth. A manager who wants to maximize growth will accept *all* projects regardless of their NPV, and will prioritize projects on the basis of their size. But from the financial perspective, not all growth is good. Good growth consists of value-creating projects (i.e., projects expected to return more than the cost of capital). A manager who accepts all projects or targets projects with the highest sales (regardless of profit) is ignoring the cost of capital and very likely destroying value. This will usually lead to a static or falling stock price.

An example may help to clarify the paradox of growth without value. General Motors Corporation grew significantly in the 30-year period from 1965 to 1995. As shown in Table 3.2, investment in assets increased at a compound annual growth rate of 10.3 percent, sales increased at a rate of 7.2 percent, and net income at a rate of 4.0 percent. The number of common shares outstanding increased by 32 percent or on average 1 percent per year, but the price per common share did not rise at all. An investor could have bought a common share for $50 equivalent in 1965 and sold it for the same $50 in 1995.

Some people might look at this history and see nothing wrong with it. After all total production, and thus contribution to per capita GDP, was increasing steadily. Profit margins may have collapsed, but the company did not fail. If the shareholders did not make money for 30 years, that is their bad luck; after all, they may be just a bunch of speculators, so why should we feel bad about them?

TABLE 3.2 Growth without Value:
A Brief History of General Motors

	1965	*1995*	*Annual Growth Rate*
Assets ($ billions)	11.5	217.1	10.3%
Sales ($ billions)	20.7	168.8	7.2
Net income ($ billions)	2.1	6.9	4.0
Common shares (millions)*	571.2	753.0	0.9
Price range of common shares*	$45.63–$56.88	$37.25–$53.13	0.0

*Adjusted for 2-for-1 split in 1989.

Source: *Moody's Industrial Manual,* 1966 and 1996.

Those with a better knowledge of economics would note that asset efficiency was falling significantly: In 1965, $1.00 of assets could produce $1.80 of sales, while in 1995, $1.00 of assets produced only $0.78 of sales. Also, the decline in profit margins (net income/sales) from 10.0 percent to 0.4 percent means that many more operating costs are being incurred for each dollar of sales. Taken together, we see that while outputs were increasing, inputs were increasing even more rapidly, so that economic efficiency was being lost.

The aggregate market value of GM's common stock[15] rose from about $29 billion to $34 billion, but this increase was from new injection of capital (new shares) rather than value creation (increase in price per share). Financial analysis requires a rate of return to be assigned to the capital value tied up in any enterprise.

Since GM common stock did not grow in value, the investors' only return was dividends. Cash dividends were paid throughout the 30-year period, in amounts that fluctuated considerably from year to year. In addition, small dividends of Class E stock and Class H stock were paid to common shareholders in 1984 and 1985 respectively. Taking all of these into account and adjusting for the stock split in 1989, the 30-year average annual dividend was $2.09, representing a 4.2 percent yield on an assumed constant value of $50 per share.

We may compare this rate of return to the cost of equity capital—that is, the rate of return that investors expected or required during the period in order to hold the stock. Unfortunately, that number is quite difficult to estimate with precision. One benchmark is the average realized annual return over 1966–1995 for all large company stocks in the U.S. market, which is 11.9 percent.[16] The expected return on GM common stock might have been higher or lower than this during the period for a number of reasons, including the perception of its relative risk, but was surely higher than the average realized annual return for corporate bonds, which was 8.8 percent. Clearly, GM's performance of 4.2 percent was disappointing, and reflected the long-term inefficient use of resources by its management. Other firms in the U.S. economy operated far more efficiently during this period, and their shareholders enjoyed a boom in profits and stock price appreciation. Even those who have a hard time sympathizing with GM stockholders should have an easy time criticizing the abuse of resources by its management.

Michael Jensen estimated value creation and destruction by a number of large United States corporations during 1980–1990 by examining the efficiency of the management's spending on capital equipment and research and development.[17] According to his analysis, General Motors destroyed approximately $100 million of value during the 10-year period, the worst record of any firm he studied.

The reason that General Motors was able to continue destroying value for so long without failing or being forced to shrink is that it had very large internal sources of funding. It did not have to justify its projects to a bank or a capital market, but had merely to siphon off the considerable stream of internally generated cash coming from its established automotive business. In principle, if a firm is maximizing shareholder value, then when it does not have positive-NPV projects, it should distribute its free cash flow to its shareholders, either as dividends or as stock buybacks. That missing

---

[15]GM had several other classes of stock, which complicates the story but does not change the conclusion.
[16]Ibbotson Associates (1997).
[17]Jensen (1993).

cash was the value that GM shareholders failed to receive, which was instead pumped into rapidly growing but low-productivity assets.

Economists would say that GM was inefficient because it was not subject to a *hard budget constraint*—that is, it obtained cash too easily from its internal flows, with too little scrutiny of the returns on its investment projects. In this, GM is by no means alone. State-owned enterprises are the extreme case of firms that suffer from the lack of any hard budget constraint because their access to financing is generally unrelated to their profitability, but many conglomerate companies throughout the world also "soften" their budget constraints by relying on internally generated funds.

Soft budget constraints also go a long way toward explaining the poor performance of conglomerate companies, where managers can operate a politicized "internal capital market" and like government officials can direct capital into favored projects or bail out failing units. We will return to this phenomenon in detail in Chapter 5.

State-Owned Enterprises

Let us now translate this insight about growth back to the macroeconomic perspective. The Soviet Union grew in the 1950s and 1960s but its growth was not efficient. Like General Motors, it got substantially larger but that growth in measured output did not imply a commensurate growth in the wealth of its "stockholders" (citizens). First, real GDP was mismeasured because input and output prices did not reflect market values. But second, the true value of the capital stock created by investment was less than the value invested. The internal cash flow (government resources) that should have belonged to the citizens was instead plowed into inefficient investments that increased production while destroying value. The funds used by the state were not assigned a cost, did not have to earn a return, and did not earn a positive return.

Stated differently, the problem of state ownership is inefficiency: State-owned enterprises everywhere tend to consume more inputs, including capital inputs, than they produce in outputs. We translate this as value-destroying growth: SOEs grow but either lose money or fail to make enough money to compensate for the capital tied up. It took a long time and many deficits for governments to recognize that value destruction was a real cost paid by the suppliers of capital (i.e., the governments in question or their government-dominated banks) and indirectly by the taxpayers.

Why are state-owned enterprises inefficient? We can identify four significant factors:

1. Multiplicity of goals
2. Market structure (monopoly)
3. Weak incentives
4. Soft budget constraint

Let us look at these factors one at a time.

1. Multiplicity of Goals. This may be the most pervasive and important factor. The goal of a successful private company is simply and singly to maximize shareholder value, and we have seen how this is closely connected to the efficient use of resources. The goals of government are various, conflicting, and rarely related to efficient use of resources: maximize employment, promote regional development, ensure national security, reward loyalists, help junior's self esteem (as in the infamous case of the production of Indonesia's "Tommy car"), and many more. Multiple goals are inherently difficult to manage; trading off one goal against another is typically a political exercise reflecting the bargaining position of the players more than a rational reconciliation of priorities. In the course of the political bargaining, efficiency is an interest with no tangible constituency.

2. Market Structure.   Most SOEs are monopolies, and monopolies are rarely as efficient as enterprises obliged to compete. When SOEs compete in a genuinely private marketplace, like Air France or the Tennessee Valley Authority in the United States, they often perform much better than public or private monopolies. The advent of competitive pressure from private courier companies such as Federal Express and United Parcel Service has improved the performance of the U.S. Postal Service.

A competitive market structure affects results in two ways. First, it enables *prices* to be set through a normal market mechanism. Unless prices are correctly set, value cannot even be measured, so participants will never know whether they are adding value or not. Governments often cannot resist managing prices, but such efforts usually result in economic distortions. In monopolies, prices can be set quite arbitrarily, lowering efficiency by discouraging viable production of desirable goods and services.

The second reason why a competitive market structure leads to economic efficiency is its effect on human *effort*. Those who work in monopolies rarely feel the kind of pressure or intensity felt by those engaged in competitive enterprises. It is perhaps a sad comment on human nature, but we tend to do our best work when we look over our shoulders and see the competition gaining on us. For both of these reasons, competition matters. When monopolistic SOEs are privatized, they are typically broken into competing pieces (as the private monopoly AT&T was broken up in the United States) so that a competitive marketplace can form.

The reduction of trade barriers since 1960 has stimulated the wave of privatization by globalizing the prices of traded goods and thereby forcing state-owned monopolies to price goods correctly. Global competition forces domestic prices of SOEs' products to reflect global supply and demand, and allows new foreign entrants to take market share from low-quality, inefficient domestic producers. The shortcomings of SOEs are much more visible in this context, and this can spur managers to improve productivity.

3. Weak Incentives.   We noted above that managers of privately held firms are often given stock options as an incentive to maximize shareholder value. It is noteworthy that such incentives are necessary; we might like to imagine people perform well out of pride in their work or a sense of duty, but experience shows that most human beings need incentives as well. When an entrepreneur owns his or her own business, there is almost no limit to the effort that he or she will exert because every extra dollar of income is a dollar added to the owner's pocket. In contrast, most government employees usually exert less effort because they do not have ownership incentives.

Government employees have a different set of incentives. Because government is generally about the exercise of power, government employees often act in ways that enhance their personal power or that of their political master. Their payoff may be promotion within the government or popularity with various politically important constituencies. While managers of SOEs can be given contractual incentives based on the enterprise's performance, it is difficult to replicate the intensity of an entrepreneur who owns the business and captures all of its rewards.

4. Soft Budget Constraint.   A fundamental reason why SOEs are inefficient is their unconditional access to capital. As noted earlier, private capital markets require most enterprises to create value or be cut off. Governments, on the other hand, obtain capital primarily from taxation (including the printing of money) and generally do not assign the equivalent of a hard budget cost to that tax financing. They pass that funding on to enterprises through direct outlays or subsidies and cheap loans from the central bank or state-dominated banking system. Government enterprises are not put out of business if they fail to earn a return on those funds.

The standard of value-creating growth is a high standard, because it is not easy to create value. Positive-NPV projects are rare and valuable: You cannot return more than the cost of capital unless your strategy, technology, or franchise gives you opportunities of sufficiently high quality and you work very hard to realize those opportunities. Even companies that try hard to create value and think they are doing so often end up destroying it. SOEs most often destroy value because there is no equivalent of capital market pressure upon them to create it.

It is difficult to say which of these four factors is most important. A study based on a survey of more than 3,000 firms in 20 transition economies found that competition was the single unambiguous influence in promoting the efficiency of newly privatized firms, although it recognized the difficulty of measuring alternative influences.[18] Another study of manufacturing firms in Indonesia concluded that protectionism and soft budget constraint were the key issues, in that only SOEs that received loans from state banks or those shielded from import competition performed worse than private enterprises.[19] Of course, multiplicity of goals and weak incentives are inherently difficult to measure and incorporate in empirical studies.

As these issues have become better understood, many governments have tried to reform their SOEs to mimic some of the features of private firms. Merely introducing competition can improve performance. Managerial incentives for better bottom-line results can also help, provided that SOE managers are required to live with the consequences of their actions. So some countries try to improve SOE performance without privatizing.

France, for example, initiated "contract plans" with eight large public enterprises during the 1970s, and in 1983 extended the concept to 13 more.[20] The concept spread to a number of developing countries, many of them French-speaking. The basic idea was for government and SOE management to set out explicit goals, give management substantial autonomy to pursue those goals, and reward them to the extent the goals were reached. Such contract plans seemed to work well at first, but were not robust to shocks.

In particular, the oil price increase of 1973 made a mockery of all the carefully worked-out projections and plans that had been agreed upon before the oil price hike. The original contracts had been very detailed, and the participants realized that shorter and simpler contracts were better. Inevitably, those plans also were renegotiated, reflecting in part the shifting sands of multiple government objectives. Because the state is sovereign it cannot bind itself to any fixed agreement. Thus, the shorter, simpler plans became toothless guidelines for future negotiations, rather than vehicles for real management autonomy.

Governments can rarely keep their hands off the SOEs for long, and the full benefit of privatization can only be achieved if goals, prices, managerial incentives, and

---

[18]Carlin, Fries, Schaffer, and Seabright (2000).
[19]Bartel and Harrison (1999).
[20]Nellis (1989).

capital constraints are all reformed simultaneously.[21] That is why most efforts at reform of state-owned enterprises fall short or last only briefly. In the end, ownership itself is the simplest and best reform; private ownership of the means of production is the single credible reform for dramatically improving productive efficiency.

Detailed academic studies of various privatizations generally confirm that they lead to major improvements in performance. Table 3.3 shows the results of three such studies that used the same methodology, examining financial and operating performance before and after privatization in a variety of countries and industries. The first study noted in that table (MNR) covered 61 companies from 18 developed and developing countries and 32 industries divested during 1961–1989. The second (BC) analyzed 79 companies from 21 developing countries and 32 industries divested in 1980–1992. The third (DM) studied 85 share issue privatizations from 28 developed and developing countries during 1990–1996.

Taken together, the results are striking; all the improvements except those in employment are statistically significant at the 95 percent confidence level. We see

TABLE 3.3   Consequences of Privatization

Concept	Measure	Source	Median 3 Yrs. before Sale	Median 3 Yrs. after Sale
Profitability	Net income/sales	MNR	5.5%	8.0%
		BC	4.3%	11.0%
		DM	14%	17%
Efficiency	Sales/number of employees*	MNR	0.96*	1.06*
		BC	0.92*	1.17*
		DM	1.02*	1.23*
Investment	Capital expenditure/sales	MNR	12%	17%
		BC	11%	24%
		DM	18%	17%
Output	Sales adjusted by CPI	MNR	0.90*	1.14*
		BC	0.97*	1.22*
		DM	0.93*	2.70*
Employment	Number of employees	MNR	40,850	43,200
		BC	10,672	10,811
		DM	22,941	22,136
Leverage	Debt/assets	MNR	66%	64%
		BC	55%	50%
		DM	29%	23%
Dividends	Dividends/sales	MNR	1.3%	3.0%
		BC	2.8%	5.3%
		DM	1.5%	4.0%

*Ratio in year of sale set to 1.00 to avoid large differences among industries.
MNR: Megginson, Nash, and van Randenborgh (1994)
BC: Boubraki and Cosset (1998)
DM: D'Souza and Megginson (1999)
Source: D'Souza and Megginson (1999).

[21]See Kikeri, Nellis, and Shirley (1992), p. 17.

sharp increases in profitability, efficiency, investment, and aggregate output. Leverage was significantly lowered in all three studies and dividend payout increased very materially. The only ambiguous result was for aggregate employment, which rose slightly on average in MNR, stayed about flat in BC, and declined slightly in DM. Thus, there is no clear employment pattern, but in particular there is no evidence of massive layoffs and contraction that opponents of privatization so often fear. Rather, it seems that on average employees were kept on but obliged to work more productively.

The Mass Privatizations of Central and Eastern Europe

The collapse of communist regimes in Central and Eastern Europe over 1989–1991 was one of the defining events of modern times. No one who lived through those days will easily forget the images of the Solidarity movement in Poland, the "Velvet Revolution" in Prague, and the tearing down of the Berlin wall. No one had predicted these events, not the CIA, not the press, not the academic world, and not the wildest pundits who find a voice on television or in the newspapers. Each time a regime was overthrown in one country, it still seemed highly unlikely that the revolt could continue in others. The final, abrupt collapse of the Soviet Union after a failed coup in 1991 was as unexpected as all the other events of that dramatic period.

The cause of this collapse, in retrospect, was the economic failure of the state-owned enterprises that managed virtually the entire economies of the communist countries. To be sure, the regimes were unpopular because of their political repression. But when economic failure was added to the indignity of totalitarianism, popular support for communism vanished. Privatization of the SOEs became a high priority of reformers throughout the region.

But the job was much larger than simply selling off state enterprises. An entire culture and institutional framework had to be changed. Price liberalization was as important as privatization, for without market-determined prices Adam Smith's invisible hand cannot do its work. Competition was equally important because most of the SOEs operated as state monopolies. Legal frameworks for property ownership and contract rights had to be introduced. A work ethic had to be developed because incentives had been perverse and the workers at most SOEs had grown cynical and listless.

It is challenging to change everything simultaneously and suddenly, and so, despite the need for dramatic change along many dimensions, change inevitably must be phased in. If one begins with a totally state-owned system, as in Central and Eastern Europe in 1990, there seems to be a logical sequence of preconditions to privatization:

1. **Create legal structures for property rights, corporations, and contracts.** Unless there is a modern legal framework with enforceable contracts, no private sector can even be imagined. Law defines and protects the basic units of business; transformation has to begin with law.

2. **Restructure SOEs in corporate form.** Separate structure is a necessary first step to separating property rights of the enterprise from those of the state. Once corporate form is established, shares can be sold, assets can be leased to private managers, joint ventures can be formed, measurement of performance and incentives can be introduced, and monopoly firms can be broken up.

3. **Introduce competition.** Monopolies can be broken into competing pieces, as was done for AT&T in the United States and JNR in Japan. Also, government can permit

entry of new competitors into the industry and trade barriers can be removed to introduce the winds of global competition. Until competition is present, prices will be arbitrary and human effort will not be properly directed.

4. **Eliminate government price setting.** Value can only be created when it can be measured, and this requires fair market prices in alignment with world prices, where possible. Most governments try to control at least some prices in their economies. The more they can refrain from doing so, the more effective will be their privatizations.

5. **Introduce modern accounting and auditing.** The focus needs to change from the top line to the bottom line. The top line (sales) is easily observed, but the bottom line requires careful accounting. If managers are to respond to bottom-line incentives, the bottom line needs to be honestly computed. If shares in firms are to be sold, buyers need to understand the numbers and have confidence that they are not prone to manipulation at stockholders' expense.

Once these preconditions are met, the real work begins. Should firms be sold for cash or should they be given away? Should they be sold to foreigners or to locals? If sold to locals, should the buyers include the communist bureaucrats who have been running the enterprise or is this unjust?

From the perspective of value maximization, the most attractive buyers typically were foreign firms, which could also import modern management and technology as well as financial strength. But that option ran into a number of limitations in practice. First, it was not always clear that foreign firms wanted to buy very many formerly communist-run SOEs. Second, if too many of the best assets were sold to foreigners, a political backlash might have resulted over lost national independence.

If foreign firms were not buyers, then in most cases SOEs could not be sold for cash, since there was not enough real buying power in the entire savings pool of the domestic economies to purchase them. As noted in Chapter 2, even outside the formerly communist world financial repression had resulted in minimal saving and, therefore, minimal capital with which to buy SOEs. This led to a number of schemes for vouchers to effectively give away the SOEs to the people.

A complicating factor throughout the region was the *spontaneous privatization* that rapidly evolved during 1989–1991. In their last years, many communist regimes had sought to improve the performance of SOEs by giving them increased autonomy to make their own business decisions. As the central planning mechanism atrophied and then collapsed, SOE managers were left with no direction. Sensing their opportunities, many of them began to act as *de facto* owners of their enterprises.

Spontaneous privatization took a number of forms. In one variant, managers would form subsidiary companies to operate a segment of the business away from the general management of the SOE. In another, joint ventures would be formed in which the managers' contributions would be valued at a high price and the SOE contribution valued at a low price. In still another, SOE managers would sell or lease SOE assets under very favorable terms to new companies that they controlled.

From a purely economic point of view, these developments might well provide knowledgeable management with a suitable profit motive for efficiency. From a political point of view, however, spontaneous privatization looked a great deal like theft of public assets on the part of SOE managers, which produced outrage wherever it was publicized. Resentment against communist regimes was strong, and the thought of communist government bureaucrats stealing the entire economy was so outrageous that most governments moved promptly to bring order and fairness to the transformation process.

Each of the transition countries had a special set of circumstances that made its position and evolution somewhat different from the others. We now summarize the processes through which a number of the countries went.

East Germany

East Germany was unique because it was reunited with West Germany within a year of the collapse of the communist regime in 1989. West Germany had a powerful modern economy with ample capital to purchase the SOE assets for cash. West Germany had little reason to fear foreign investment, so state assets could be offered to non-Germans as well. And finally, West Germany offered generous welfare concessions, perhaps excessively generous (from the perspective of West German citizens), as the political price of reunification. All of these circumstances created a unique situation for East German privatization of state-owned enterprises.

Even prior to reunification a reformed East Germany created the *Treuhandanstalt* (trustee agency) to manage the privatization process. Its initial portfolio consisted of 8,500 enterprises with 44,000 plants and 4.1 million employees, about half the workforce of East Germany. Its mandate was to sell these enterprises as rapidly as possible. By June 30, 1993, nearly three years after reunification, 12,195 enterprises and parts of enterprises had been sold for a total of DM 32.0 billion, of which DM 4.8 billion, or 15 percent, came from purchasers outside Germany.[22]

In many ways, this is the best type of privatization: Knowledgeable buyers with technical and managerial skills became the new owners of the large enterprises and paid cash. As necessary, the *Treuhandanstalt* restructured large enterprises prior to sale. Smaller enterprises, those with less than 500 employees, were assigned to 12 regional subsidiaries of *Treuhandanstalt* with the freedom to sell in a variety of ways including sale to East German insiders (i.e., managers).

A disadvantage of the German approach was that East Germany deindustrialized very rapidly following privatization.[23] Indeed, because of the decisiveness of the privatization program, plant closings and job losses were greater in East Germany than anywhere else in the region. Total employment fell by about a third from 9 million to 6 million. The restructuring led to a doubling of productivity from the first quarter of 1991 to the last quarter of 1992, but at the same time wage levels rose to nearly West German standards, which was part of the political bargain of reunification. The result was unit labor costs in East Germany about twice the already high levels of West Germany. That high cost placed a drag on industrial growth in the former East Germany and fostered persistent unemployment.

Insider sales of small enterprises gained momentum because of concern over job losses. Regional offices of the *Treuhandanstalt* began to accept proposals from plant managers for management buyouts of the smaller enterprises. As of mid-1993 they had permitted about 2,400 management buyouts, accounting for about one-fifth of the total number of sales of enterprises or parts of enterprises.

---

[22]*Treuhandanstalt* (1993).
[23]Carlin (1994).

Czechoslovakia

Czechoslovakia had entered its communist phase as a sophisticated industrial country with the only prewar democracy in Central Europe. The distinguishing feature of Czechoslovakia's approach to privatization was the strong Czech sense of being part of the West, and a desire to privatize just as rapidly as East Germany, as expressed in the forceful leadership of the Czech premier, Vaclav Klaus, and the consensus for reform built by the reformist coalition known as the Civic Forum (also known as the "Velvet Glove" due to its success in spurring a "Velvet Revolution" of radical, but democratic and civil, change). Indeed, the determination of Klaus and his allies to rapidly transform the Czech lands caused a break with the more cautious and more Eastward-looking Slovaks, causing the country to split peacefully in two on January 1, 1993.

The Czech Republic became the first country in the region to implement a mass privatization by vouchers, particularly for large-scale enterprises. In 1991, about 10,000 small-scale enterprises, mostly retail stores, were rapidly sold for cash to local purchasers, including particularly local managers. But medium- and large-scale enterprises were obliged to come up with a plan for privatization. The rules were such that voucher plans got more rapid consideration than others, and so the roughly 3,000 medium- and large-scale enterprises were sold at auction through the voucher program in 1992 and 1993.

Czech citizens were able to buy a voucher book for 35 koruna, about one week's wages. Since the book value of all large-scale enterprises subject to voucher privatization was about 10 times that amount, the vouchers (which would be used exclusively to purchase the firms at auction) appeared to be an attractive investment. Why didn't the government simply give, rather than sell, vouchers to its citizens? It was argued that requiring citizens to pay something for their stake in privatized firms would encourage a view of privatized firms as bona fide investments rather than worthless gifts. Nevertheless, sales of voucher booklets began slowly.

What greatly accelerated voucher sales was the activity of various new mutual fund operators who encouraged citizens to purchase vouchers and resell them to the mutual funds. The most notable among these funds was Harvard Capital & Consulting, a company with no connection to Harvard University started by a brash young Czech who had attended Harvard, Viktor Kozeny. That company's funds offered to exchange their shares for voucher books, with a guarantee to repurchase the shares one year after operations began at 10 times the 35 koruna price. The funds had no resources with which to back up such a guarantee. They could point to the relationship between the relatively low price of vouchers compared to the book value of the SOEs to be privatized with them, but there was no clear relationship between market and book values.

Kozeny engaged about 25,000 agents to market the exchange offer and supported their efforts with U.S.-style television advertising unconstrained by U.S. legal restrictions on mutual fund sales (in particular, U.S. mutual funds are prohibited from offering guarantees to investors). His activity was imitated by other funds, some offering even more extravagant promises of redemption. Kozeny's companies obtained about 14 percent of all vouchers. Mutual funds as a whole, primarily sponsored by Czech banks, obtained 72 percent of all vouchers. The magnitude of the funds' activities and the dubiousness of their claims provoked much anxiety in Prague. The story is set forth in a published case.[24]

---

[24]Harvard Business School (1994).

Under many circumstances, mutual funds can be appropriate financial intermediaries since they offer effective means to concentrate corporate control and to diversify individuals' investments. Concentration of corporate control can focus attention and pressure on management to produce value, and low-cost diversification improves the risk-adjusted returns available to investors. However, in the absence of sufficient legal protection for fund shareholders, funds can also be exploitative. Kozeny ultimately used his position as fund manager to divert much of his funds' resources from the funds' shareholders.[25]

Despite this irregularity, the Czech program was deemed rather successful. In addition to the voucher sales, a few large enterprises were successfully sold to foreign firms. Volkswagen AG, for example, bought the Skoda automobile business. In the first wave of large-scale privatization, property worth over $23 billion was put up for sale, and $7 billion of this was purchased through vouchers. About 93 percent of the total shares offered were sold, and 99 percent of the vouchers were used up. Most of the shares ended up in the hands of active investors, although the dominance of banks in this group planted the seeds of later troubles in the banking sector.

An interesting feature of Czech privatization is that the demand for particular stocks was highest for stocks in which insiders held the largest blocks.[26] Although investors had good reason to mistrust such insiders, they also seemed to respect the capacity of insiders to manage assets that they understood better than outside investors could, and wished to associate themselves with the gains that the insiders might realize. In Chapter 5 we will return to the *principal–agent problem*, the complex relationship between inside managers and outside shareholders.

Hungary

Of all the Central European countries, Hungary had gone the furthest before the political changes of 1989–1991 in trying to reform its state-owned enterprises through partial measures that would provide them some if not all of the attributes of Western corporations. That history conditioned the approach to privatization that emerged during 1989–1991.

The year 1968 had seen reform movements take hold in several of the Central European countries. The movement in Czechoslovakia advanced so quickly that the Soviet Union saw fit to send in tanks to crush it and return that country to mainstream Stalinism. But the reforms in Hungary were subtler and lasted a good deal longer. Having already seen its share of Russian tanks in 1956, Hungary proceeded in 1968 in a cannier and less confrontational way than Czechoslovakia. Its New Economic Mechanism (NEM) was not a single blueprint so much as a license to try new approaches to revitalize SOEs. It incorporated four sets of ideas that were experimented with over the years. First came the separation of enterprises from direct state control by introducing intermediary structures such as holding companies, pension funds, and municipalities. This concept proved to have no practical effect, however, since the essential internal structures and incentives of the SOEs were unchanged and the government could easily reach through the new structures.

The second approach was to "corporatize" enterprises—that is, set them up as joint stock companies so that banks, pension funds, and other SOEs could hold stock

---

[25]Wallace (1996).
[26]Hingorani, Lehn, and Makhija (1997).

in them. Among other things, it was hoped that this would facilitate the division of SOEs into smaller, more coherent units, as well as provide a measure of independent governance. Furthermore, it might facilitate new capital accumulation through external sources of either debt or equity. While this approach gave rise to some experimentation, it also seems to have had little practical effect. Ultimately, the control that stockholders could exercise and the incentives managers faced to meet stockholders' expectations seem to have been too weak under the corporatized system.

The third idea was to permit individual entrepreneurship through the leasing of state assets to individuals or the creation of new enterprises with only a share of the ownership interest reserved for the state. This proved to be a useful initiative and was associated with significant changes in the economic structure. By 1988, for example, 11 percent of retail shops and 44 percent of catering enterprises were run by individual entrepreneurs. But this method was of limited use in restructuring large enterprises.

The fourth idea was to have the most lasting effect, particularly for medium- and large-scale firms. This proposed greater autonomy for SOE management and decentralization of decision making, with increasing control exercised at the local level through employee participation in ownership, workers councils, and similar devices. This approach was based on the Yugoslav model, which had generated significant interest in Central Europe in the 1970s and early 1980s. In 1984 Hungary passed a law enabling most SOEs to gain power over restructuring, mergers, and joint ventures. By 1987 many SOEs had formed one or more subsidiary companies that further insulated SOE management from state control. And in 1988 Hungary legitimized the corporate form generally and made possible the corporatization of whole SOEs within a structure of improved corporate governance and managerial incentives.

The popularity of this approach is very likely due to the preference by enterprise managers in virtually all settings for decentralized worker control to centralized state control. Managers can negotiate with local workers' councils for their mutual benefit, while state bureaucrats have little incentive to agree to efficiency-promoting improvements: Unlike local workers, bureaucrats do not share in the gains from such improvements and are averse to the risk of failure associated with any change. A major consequence of these reforms was that large SOEs, preferred by the government for control reasons, began to break into hundreds of smaller, more economically manageable units.

While this was in many ways a step in the right direction, local autonomy had a serious flaw; namely, that it gave freer rein to the self-interest of SOE managers, many of whom began appropriating subsets of SOE assets for themselves once the political changes of the late 1980s began to weaken the effective legal checks on managerial power. That spontaneous privatization took advantage of the ambiguity of ownership rights once central control started to dissipate, and was viewed as an outrage by most ordinary citizens. In 1990 the government established a State Property Fund to reestablish government ownership and control of SOE assets as a prelude to a more formal privatization.

What followed was a series of privatizations using various methods. The State Property Fund sold some assets and enterprises to foreign investors; indeed, the government's need for action on proper privatization created a strong connection between privatization and foreign direct investment, whose magnitude in Hungary during 1990–1994 was greater than that of all other countries in the region combined. Foreign investors' interest in Hungary reflected the right of foreign shareholders under Hungarian law to own controlling interests in Hungarian firms—a legal right the strength of which set Hungary apart from other transition countries.

In addition, the State Property Fund negotiated with Hungarian interests, including managements, to organize new firms. Inevitably, this had the effect of legitimizing much of the spontaneous privatization that had been taking place. A careful study of some of these cases[27] concluded that power and politics dominated the process and that the outcomes were far from economically rational in some instances. In Hungary, as elsewhere, privatization should be considered a somewhat messy and often unfair transitional process during which the old ways of doing business, and the special economic privileges of the preexisting ruling class, would dissipate only gradually.

Russia

Russia was of course the mother ship of communism. Russia had a long tradition of state ownership of enterprise dating back to Peter the Great. Its private sector in the late 19th and early 20th centuries had shallow domestic roots, and nearly half the industrial investment in this period was foreign-owned. Russia had been totally collectivized since the late 1920s and its privatization was bound to be more challenging than that of other countries whose experience with state ownership was more recent.

Furthermore, although the communists lost power they remained the largest political party in Russia, and the fear that they could easily regain control was foremost in the minds of reformers, many of whom sought to privatize Russia very rapidly so that reform would be as irreversible as possible. Russia under Boris Yeltsin engaged some high-profile Western consultants to assist in designing "shock therapy" based on a rapid decentralization of control.

The result was an economic collapse of enormous magnitude. The GDP in constant prices fell 13 percent in 1991, 19 percent in 1992, 12 percent in 1993, and 15 percent in 1994. Industrial output contracted by larger percentages and capital investment by yet larger ones.[28] Inflation ran at triple-digit levels and in 1992 exceeded 2000 percent.

Few of the preconditions listed above for privatization were in place. Legal foundations were totally inadequate since the rule of law itself was in doubt in Russia, a subject to which we shall return in Chapter 4. Spontaneous privatization was running rampant; state enterprise managers were rapidly transferring state assets to their personal firms. Government officials associated with the privatization, such as Prime Minister Viktor Chernomyrdin, were rumored to have assets valued at more than $1 billion. The great Russian hoard of state gold simply disappeared into private hands.

There was no time to prepare the state-owned enterprises by restructuring and introducing modern accounting, nor were monopoly SOEs broken up. The result was simply to transfer ownership of the great monopolies from the central government to private (or local government) hands with no true development of competitive markets.

The speed of the economic collapse, the need of the reformers to show positive results quickly, and the magnitude of the privatization challenge all created pressure for further rapid action. In June 1992 the government opted for a voucher-based scheme: Every adult citizen received a free 10,000 ruble (about $14) voucher enabling him or her to bid for enterprises.

The enterprises were obliged to change to corporate form. The employees then voted for one of three ownership formats, the most popular of which was (predictably)

---

[27]Antal-Mokos (1998).
[28]Blasi, Kroumova, and Kruse (1997), Table 3.2.

the one that gave employees 51 percent ownership. At least 29 percent of the shares were then sold through a voucher auction, in which the primary bidders were often the managers of the enterprise. Most individuals did not know what to do with their vouchers. Their market value fell to about 4,000 rubles and ambitious enterprise managers swept up most of them.

Russian law authorized investment funds, but many of those that formed turned out to be criminal enterprises that simply stole the assets they acquired. The more important financial intermediaries in the bidding process turned out to be newly formed banks. During 1992–1994 a large number of new banks were chartered, subject to very little regulation or control. These banks took some deposits but made rather few loans, making money instead on securities speculation. Many banks became the centers of industrial empires for new entrepreneurs; indeed, some of them began to look more like industrial holding companies than banks.

During 1995–1996, when the Russian government was running short of funds, banks were invited to bid to offer loans to the state, which would be collateralized by shares in remaining SOEs. Such loans were naturally not repaid, so the borrowing firms were liquidated and the banks assumed ownership of the enterprises in question. Furthermore, the banks did their best to suppress competition in these "loans for shares" swap arrangements by having the auctions of the firms' assets held in inaccessible locations. Banks thus obtained assets at prices far below what the state had hoped to realize.

Banks were not the only group that benefited from questionable privatization practices. Between December 1992 and June 1994 approximately 16,500 enterprises were auctioned. Insiders obtained on average 55 percent to 65 percent of the shares. Many critics protested that the process was too hasty and that the *nomenklatura* (former communist bureaucrats) ended up with more wealth and control than they deserved, but defenders of the process argued that speed was more important than exclusion of the previous masters. Spontaneous privatization was moving faster in Russia than in Central Europe, and through this device the *nomenklatura* were in any event rapidly gaining assets.

But the problem in Russia was far deeper than the unfair process of allocating SOE assets, which to a greater or lesser extent necessarily plagues all privatizations. An even greater problem in Russia was the failure to accomplish the true privatization of assets, which has undermined every aspect of economic performance. True privatization requires not only the nominal transfer of ownership, but also the transfer of the actual rights and privileges that the word "ownership" commonly implies.

A truly private firm not only has private stockholders, but can offer those stockholders and other claimants the assurance that the cash flows due to them will be calculated and delivered according to some set of well-defined rules. Those rules define the accounting practices and contractual and other legal obligations, rights, and means of redress that make the claims on firms' revenues meaningful. Without those rules, ownership rights can be worthless. Without credible *ex ante* rules, managers or local government bureaucrats, or anyone with the physical force to define the allocation of cash flows *ex post,* can lay claim to cash flows regardless of any legal ownership stake.

The failure to define and enforce such rules is the central failure of Russian privatization. The absence of the basic infrastructure of rules and property rights makes Russia's a "virtual" economy—one that appears to operate as a market system, but in fact does not.[29] The absence of enforceable rules undermines the incentives to invest and manage properly; it grants a sinecure to managers who are able to use their political power (and sometimes violence without fear of penalty) to maintain access to assets or government subsidies (e.g., by avoiding their legal obligations to pay private debts and taxes); and it undermines the tax resources on which the fiscal and monetary health of any state depend.

One commentator summarized the factors underlying Russia's failure, drawing especially the connection between the absence of well-defined claims on cash flows and its consequences: the fiscal weakness, monetary instability, capital flight, and low productivity that have plagued Russia:

> The first effort of reformers was . . . to limit inflation and liberalise prices. But this was only possible if they could impose hard budget constraints on enterprises. The more politically powerful the bosses were, the better they were able to resist the government, by accumulating arrears both to one another and to the state. As arrears grew and output collapsed, they demanded monetary expansion. Repetition of this cycle explains the damagingly slow achievement of monetary stability in countries such as Ukraine and Russia.
>
> Unfortunately, it was never politically possible to force enterprises to pay their taxes. So monetary stability could only be achieved if the government either refused to pay its contractual obligations, or borrowed. The Russian government did both. The first of these two options made it impossible to establish a culture of honest dealing: who would meet his contractual obligations if the government failed to do so? The second led to the default of last August.
>
> Meanwhile, the ruthless and amoral sought, successfully, to privatise as much of the wealth and income of the country as they could. Much blame is placed—rightly—on the privatisation of valuable assets at risibly low prices. One estimate is that in Russia assets worth between $50 billion and $60 billion were privatised for just $1.5 billion. But such privatisation was the icing on the cake. The exploitation of positions of influence to obtain valuable licenses, privileges or access to streams of income was pervasive. Privatisation often legitimised theft rather than caused it.
>
> The resulting symbiosis of property with illegal power has a host of malign consequences: it starves the state of resources for essential purposes; it allows inefficient enterprises to monopolise resources, at the expense of truly private business; it permits managers to steal property from companies they run; it allows established businesses to exclude competition; it encourages a culture of lawlessness; it undermines the legitimacy of private property; it encourages capital flight; and it discourages investment . . .
>
> More than 80 years ago [the Russian empire] suffered a ruthless revolution intended to create, by force, a selfless human being. Lenin's insane ambition has ended up in its opposite—in a capitalist economy more ruthless, more corrupt and more unequal than anything even he could have imagined.[30]

A contributor to Russia's failure to reform its institutions has been, ironically, its one strength: its military prowess and particularly its nuclear weaponry. Russia's military might has allowed its government to wrest enormous sums from other governments by accessing loans from the International Monetary Fund, to whom Russia owed some $18 billion by 1999 (making it the largest borrower from the Fund). Western governments feared the consequences of allowing a nuclear power to fall into complete chaos. The prospect of nuclear weapons being sold to belligerent powers, or of

---

[29]Gaddy and Ickes (1998).
[30]Wolf (1999a).

IMF Conditionality in Russia

In July 1999, Boris Fedorov, a former Russian Deputy Prime Minister and Minister of Finance, wrote an open letter to Michel Camdessus, Managing Director of the IMF, to encourage the IMF to adopt a less pliant position toward Russia, in the interest of the Russian people:

"I have observed with anxiety and frustration the way cooperation between Russia and IMF has developed over the last 7 years. It is usual for the IMF to be blamed for its toughness, but *in Russia it failed to adhere to its own Articles.* In fact, it blessed a lot of irresponsible actions not to speak of unsavory privatization deals, massive corruption and outright thievery.

"In August 1993 as deputy Prime Minister and Minister of Finance I wrote a letter to you refusing to take the second tranche of the STF [Systemic Transformation Facility] since Russia was not on track with reform. Still, IMF in 1994–1998 provided to Russia billions of dollars and this helped to stall and compromise reforms. *Not a single agreement with Russia was ever implemented.*

"In August 1998 as a deputy Prime Minister (appointed after the 17th of August) I wrote you another letter, the contents of which still stand true:

- Russian economy failed to pick up for a decade. Shadow economy is probably larger than the visible economy.
- Financial stabilization not achieved; inflation still a real threat.
- Tax reform not undertaken. Privatization corruption-ridden and did not improve efficiency. Enterprise reform and bankruptcy enforcement failed.
- Former state enterprises have immunity from paying taxes and Government failed to collect taxes; real tax intake is always dropping.
- Central Bank independence failed; it reverted to printing money and unsavory practices like FIMACO [the misuse of central bank reserves in speculative foreign investments abroad].

continued

those weapons falling into the wrong hands domestically, has led the Western governments that control the IMF to approach Russian assistance in a unique way. Many critics of IMF support to Russia have argued that the IMF has unwittingly aided the oligarchs and weakened pressures for deep reforms that might have come sooner if Russia had been forced to deal with its fiscal problem in the mid-1990s. (See box.)

What has emerged in Russia is not a free enterprise system and certainly not a healthy private financial system, but rather an oligarchic capitalism in which a powerful minority maintains excessive influence over the government and legal system, and uses that influence to extract value from firms in arbitrary ways. In particular, the plundering of Russia's oil companies (one of the few sources of real economic value in the country) by a handful of ruthless, criminal, and now very wealthy oligarchs has come into focus as perhaps Russia's central problem.[31]

Many enterprises still benefit from subsidies as if they were SOEs, and the arbitrary nature of tax collection constitutes hidden subsidies to some firms and destruc-

---

[31]Wolosky (2000).

concluded

- Not one budget adopted in a realistic form and implemented. Deficit financed with GKOs [government Treasury securities] at usury rates (crowding out private sector) or emission [bond issue].
- Artificial exchange rate regime leading to overvaluation of the ruble and then its collapse.
- Russia allows pervasive barter practices (i.e., corruption).
- Transfer pricing on major exports leads to losses of billions of dollars.
- Basic protection of shareholders' rights is extremely weak.
- Corruption at all levels of Government and not a single action to fight it.

"In view of the described facts one cannot help asking questions about the efficiency of Western financial assistance to Russia . . .

"I strongly believe that IMF money injections in 1994–1998 *were detrimental to the Russian economy* and interests of Russian people. Instead of speeding up reforms they slowed them. Conditionality was too weak, superficial and never really worked . . .

"Obviously, we cannot dictate to other countries how to spend your taxpayers' money but *it is we who will have to repay the loans which go down the drain. And this is unfair to Governments to come. Not to speak of ordinary people* . . .

"If only politics matter, it would be more honest to put a line in the U.S. budget with a title, 'Keeping Russia quiet.' 10–20 billion dollars per annum is nothing to the U.S.A., given their surpluses, but is enough to keep lifestyles of our elite. Then you will not have to send any missions to Moscow, to waste tons of paper on reports or to negotiate with people who do not care about economic reform or sound policies."

Source: Fedorov (1999). See also Wolf (1999b).

---

tive vengeance to others. Estimates of Russian GDP for 1999 place it (in dollar terms) at roughly half its preprivatization level. That is lower than that of Belgium and only 25 percent higher than that of Poland (a country whose GDP grew by 17 percent during the 1990s).

Russia is not a unique case of failure traceable to a lack of core capitalist institutions. Other countries of the former Soviet Union (outside of the Baltic countries) have faced legal and institutional problems similar to those of Russia and have seen similar declines in their national incomes alongside privatization. Georgia and Ukraine have lost roughly two-thirds of their preprivatization income.[32]

Poland

Unlike most other governments in Central and Eastern Europe, Poland had begun to permit an indigenous private sector to evolve in parallel with the state-owned enterprises starting as early as the 1970s. At the end of the 1970s the share of GDP produced by the local private sector began a steady increase. By 1989 it was producing 29 percent of GDP, which increased rapidly to 50 percent by 1990. Because of this history,

---

[32]Wolf (1999a).

privatization in Poland had more to do with new private businesses than with transformation of the SOEs, which proceeded more slowly in Poland than in East Germany or Czechoslovakia.[33] That "go-slow" approach to privatizing the SOEs was also favored because the reformist Solidarity government was essentially a labor union government, and unions tend to resist privatization.

From 1990 to 1993, Poland's privatization program consisted of two approaches: "commercialization" of potentially sound SOEs by putting them into corporate form, and liquidation of financially weak SOEs, whose assets were sold or leased primarily to their employees. The latter proved quite successful with small- and medium-sized firms; for example, between January 1990 and February 1991 most of the 100,000 enterprises owned by municipal governments had been privatized in this way. But large SOE commercialization proceeded much more slowly than anticipated. By 1993 sentiment had shifted in favor of mass privatization using vouchers, but the delay had given Poland the opportunity to witness the Czech and Russian experiments and to try to design a less chaotic process.

In April 1993 the Polish parliament passed the Mass Privatization Law, and implementation of the program finally began in March 1995. The key feature of this program was the explicit introduction of financial intermediaries. Fifteen National Investment Funds (NIFs) were created to own and restructure 512 medium- to large-scale SOEs. The Polish government, in consultation with the World Bank, hired consortiums of Western and Polish consultants, banks, and fund managers to run the NIFs. Each management consortium had its own makeup, strategy, and mix of advisors. The consortiums were hired on 10-year contracts and management was given an opportunity, through good performance, to earn up to 15 percent of the fund's shares.

Shares of the SOEs were then given the following initial distribution: 15 percent were given free to the employees, 60 percent were transferred to NIFs, and 25 percent were retained by the state treasury. Each fund became the "lead fund," with a controlling 33 percent stake, for approximately 30 companies and received a minority stake of about 2 percent in all the others. The controlling stakes were acquired by the funds in an orderly procedure in which the 15 funds successively picked one company at a time.

In November 1995 vouchers for purchase of *fund* shares were offered to the public at about $8 per voucher, and the exchange ratio for NIF shares was set so that all the NIF shares would be taken up through exercise of all of the vouchers. The vouchers themselves began to trade on the Warsaw stock exchange, which had been reconstituted, ironically, in the former headquarters of the Polish Communist Party. The price of vouchers rose to about $50 by mid-1997. By that time, 96 percent of all eligible citizens had purchased vouchers.

During 1997 the NIF shares began to trade separately on the Warsaw stock exchange, and gradually individual company stocks were listed as well. It is important to note that most of the underlying SOEs had not yet been restructured to the point that they could stand on their own as separate tradable stocks. Indeed, it was the explicit job of the lead fund to determine what level of restructuring was required and to pursue it—that is, not only to monitor but also to set policy for the SOEs for which they had primary responsibility.

Investors therefore selected not among companies but among NIFs based upon the reputations and strategies of their managers, long before the underlying SOEs they

---

[33]Gomulka and Jasinski (1994).

would control had been shaped to the point where public assessment of them would be feasible. By assigning a lead intermediary for each SOE, the government provided an institutional pathway for value-maximizing investors to guide and monitor the restructuring process.

As time has passed and the markets have evolved, weaknesses appeared at many of the NIFs. In one case, the Minister of Privatization dismissed most of the members of an NIF board that tried to prevent fund managers from aggressively pursuing restructuring. One fund dismissed all the foreigners on its board, one fund tried to do a hostile takeover of another, and one fund fired its management consortium and put itself in the hands of a Polish bank. By the turn of the century, only three of the funds had survived with significant ongoing support. While the transition was far from perfect, the emphasis on financial intermediaries made Poland's mass privatization the most successful of all the transition countries.

The Financial Sector and Mass Privatizations

The mass privatizations included few financial institutions. State banks tended to remain the property of the state, and financial repression continued to be official policy in many of the transforming countries. Among the transition countries, those with a strong orientation toward Western Europe tended to score highly by 1998 on the index of financial repression or liberalization described in Chapter 2. At the top of the list are Slovenia (66.8), Croatia (62.9), and the Czech Republic (58.1). The other, more eastward-oriented countries tended to score below average, with Russia (36.8), Ukraine (36.4), Azerbaijan (29.9), and Kyrgyzstan (27.7) at the bottom of the list.

There was some expansion of the private banking system throughout the region, which provided a measure of financial development. At an early stage Russia and the Czech Republic permitted relatively easy entry into the banking business, but the banking business was not yet a healthy industry and in both countries the number of troubled banks rapidly multiplied. Indeed, worries that a suddenly liberalized private banking system might spin out of control were widespread and justifiable.

Newly privatized firms were able to access funds through foreign direct investment (FDI) where that was encouraged. Hungary and East Germany in particular privatized by aggressively inviting foreign companies to bid on firms after the State Property Fund had established control over them, and by giving foreigners the right to maintain controlling interests in domestic enterprises. Hungary attracted about half of the region's total amount of FDI.

But there is a larger point to make. The urgent need everywhere was for effective monitoring and governance of corporations, and entities such as investment funds in Czechoslovakia and banks in Russia seemed to form spontaneously to perform that function. The privatizations highlight the need for such monitoring and the critical monitoring role that financial institutions play in a modern economy (a theme that we also emphasized in Chapter 2, and to which we will return again in Chapters 5 and 7).

In developed economies, the huge network of banks, mutual funds, pension funds, stock analysts, bond rating agencies, and financial press form a protective buffer between firms and ultimate holders of claims on those firms, scrutinizing the behavior and performance of businesses and reporting on current developments. Because of this watchful network and because of court systems that penalize wrongdoing with reasonable efficiency, cases of misbehavior by corporate managers are relatively rare.

It is natural that financial institutions are central figures in performing this monitoring function. Investors who entrust their savings to intermediaries such as banks and mutual funds expect them to protect those investments in an active way; individual investors have neither the time nor the training to do so for themselves, and if they did, the duplication of effort would be wasteful. Whoever makes choices for others about capital flows has a natural responsibility to be informed and to act carefully. Success as a financial intermediary depends on performing this function very well.

When there is no such network of monitors, management's temptations toward laziness, waste, fraud, and embezzlement are much greater. The spectacle of spontaneous privatization throughout Central and Eastern Europe shows how quickly managers will act in self-interest when the authorities requiring action in some other interest collapse. The fall of communism brought about a transitional situation in which the state's monitoring role collapsed and the financial system's monitoring role had not yet been constructed. It is a sobering reminder of the need for reliable monitoring.[34]

Imagine yourself as the holder of a voucher for privatization. What is the voucher worth? The great majority of people might find it nearly worthless. Unless you are prepared to inform yourself about the companies being auctioned, unless you can ally yourself with others interested in the same companies to control company decisions, and unless you can determine what the proper value of the companies might be, your voucher seems to do you little good.

Financial intermediaries offer the services of gathering information, amassing pools of capital, valuing investment opportunities, and limiting the abuse of shareholders or creditors by management. That is why the Czech privatization did not take off until funds began springing up to provide those services. The vouchers had inherent value in the sense that their cost was about one-tenth of the book value of the firms being sold. But until funds were formed, it was not easy for voucher holders to benefit from this value or even to ascertain it.

A frequently cited theoretical paper in financial economics[35] seeks to explain the existence of banks in terms of savers forming coalitions to gain cost efficiencies in monitoring the firms in which they want to invest. Like Hobbes's state of nature, "delegated monitoring" seems a curious abstraction until one observes some real-world situations that reflect its importance. Voucher privatization is the closest we may ever come to witnessing coalitions of agents forming financial institutions and delegating the monitoring of corporate behavior to them. The delegated monitors that actually were formed were more often funds than banks, but the idea is very much the same.

The need for such institutions in a liberalized environment had been understood for years even in the communist world. Intellectual and political debates in Hungary and Poland going back several decades considered the need for banks or funds to perform delegated monitoring if the SOEs were given greater autonomy. Without such monitors, giving greater autonomy to SOEs would simply be a license for misbehavior by SOE managers.

---

[34]For a review of the role of various intermediaries as monitors in the history of U.S. corporate finance, see Calomiris and Ramirez (1996).
[35]Diamond (1984).

But what makes banks or funds dependable? Who will monitor the monitors and reward or penalize them appropriately depending on their performance? One approach to answering that question focuses on the sources of market discipline that banks and funds face—the possibility that dissatisfied depositors or shareholders will withdraw their investments from incompetent or dishonest intermediaries.[36] Others argue that the government must play some role in ensuring that the monitors perform their duties faithfully—that the opportunities for misbehavior by financial intermediaries are greater than for industrial firms, and that market discipline of intermediaries may prove inadequate. That concern has sometimes delayed financial liberalization even as industrial privatization went forward.

Financial Liberalization

Just as we defined financial repression in Chapter 2 in terms of six constraints on the financial system, so financial liberalization can be defined as some combination of the following six kinds of constraint relaxation:

1. Elimination of interest rate controls.
2. Lowering of bank reserve requirements.
3. Reduction of government interference in banks' lending decisions.
4. Privatization of nationalized banks.
5. Introduction of foreign bank competition.
6. Facilitation and encouragement of capital inflows.

In general, financial liberalization proceeds more slowly than privatization. First, it is a more complex, multidimensional process. Second, control of the financial system is a more effective lever of power than ownership of SOEs, and politicians are therefore more reluctant to give it up. Third, two elements of financial repression (interest rate ceilings and bank reserve requirements) enhance the state budget while most SOEs drain the state budget. Fourth, there are authentic concerns that financial liberalization can be destabilizing.

Why would financial liberalization be destabilizing? There are a number of concerns, and they can be conveniently laid out against the above list of reforms:

1. Controls on deposit interest rates provide rents to banks. This makes the banks more profitable and arguably less vulnerable to failure.
2. Bank reserves provide the central bank not only with revenues but also with a large liquidity pool to help banks that get into trouble.
3. If the government does not monitor the lending decisions of banks, fraud and excessive risk taking could result.
4. If banks are privatized before SOEs, they may become centers of industrial empires as bank owners use their lending power to buy more companies for themselves.

[36]For empirical evidence in support of this argument, see Baer and Brewer (1986), Berger, Davies, and Flannery (1998), Calomiris and Mason (1997), Calomiris and Wilson (1998), and Flannery (1998).

5. Foreign banks may out-compete domestic banks and leave them seriously weakened.

6. Capital inflows, particularly short-term loans and portfolio flows, can easily go into reverse and create a major liquidity crisis.

These concerns can be answered, but they are not imaginary. Indeed, most of them will turn up later in our discussion of bank failure and financial crises (Chapters 7 and 8).

On the other hand, the benefits of financial liberalization are very substantial and there are risks in *not* liberalizing. Above all, financial liberalization imposes hard budget constraints on firms and pushes them toward value creation. There is, for example, evidence that privatization of state-owned enterprises is more successful when a financial system has been created to help impose hard budget constraints on firms, as in the case of Poland's NIFs.[37] We have already shown in Chapter 2 evidence that financial liberalization contributes materially to economic growth. We will find that the value destruction in cases where governments continue to dominate capital allocation can make financial crises far worse.

So financial liberalization is a kind of balancing act, with most governments attempting to get the benefits while avoiding the possible instabilities. This is most likely to succeed when strong foundations have been laid in law and regulation; indeed, a financial liberalization in the absence of appropriate law and regulation, as happened in Russia, gives rise to chaos. Most governments choose to go somewhat slowly.

Sequencing matters. Financial liberalization cannot occur in a vacuum. It works best when preceded by fiscal reform (i.e., the privatization of state enterprises), an end to state subsidies, and taxation reforms that allow the government to end its fiscal reliance on the taxation of the financial sector. If a government still has uncovered fiscal deficits that could lead to an inflationary explosion, it will have difficulty giving up capital controls, domestic interest rate restrictions, and high reserve requirements.

Furthermore, a sensible system of bank regulation should be in effect before banks are turned loose. Putting privatization of firms and bank regulation, along with insider lending limits, in place before financial liberalization would also prevent newly chartered, weakly regulated banks from using their deposits to build highly leveraged empires of weak industrial companies during the privatization process. The consequences of not following that sequence had dire consequences in Chile (1976–1982) and Russia (1993–1998), where alliances between self-aggrandizing conglomerates and newly liberalized banks ended in collapses of the banking system.

Appendix Table 3.A2 summarizes the changes in financial sector policy achieved in various countries between 1973 and 1996. This table is reproduced from Williamson and Mahar (1998), which is a comprehensive review of these changes and their effects. "The panel includes nearly all the economically significant countries; exceptions are some of the smaller industrial countries, the economies in transition (where the financial sector is merely a small subset of those undergoing liberalizations), and China (where data availability poses a particular problem)."[38]

The policy changes during this period are quite dramatic. As Table 3.A2 shows, the industrial countries were by no means fully liberalized themselves in 1973, and the great majority of the developing countries were quite severely repressed. Latin Amer-

---

[37]Demirgüç-Kunt and Levine (1994).

[38]Williamson and Mahar (1998), p. 4.

ica liberalized most rapidly in the 1990s after a late start, while East Asia built up financial reform more gradually over 25 years. This regional difference is reflected in Figure 2.9 in Chapter 2.

Figure 2.4 of Chapter 2 shows that negative real rates, having been the norm in developing countries (except in East Asia) prior to 1990, were a thing of the past in most regions by the late 1990s. Similarly, Figure 2.3 shows that reserve ratios in excess of 20 percent, which were common in the transition countries, Latin America, and Sub-Saharan Africa during the 1980s, were very nearly ended by the late 1990s.

Central bank lending to business was being substantially reduced or phased out everywhere except South Asia and Sub-Saharan Africa, as shown in Figure 2.7 of Chapter 2. By the late 1990s no country in East Asia maintained a directed credit program, nor did any in Latin America except for Brazil and Venezuela; Egypt, Israel, Morocco, South Africa, Turkey, and the South Asian countries had significantly scaled back directed credit.[39] Privatization of banks, however, was much slower to materialize. Indonesia reduced the state-owned banks' share of banking assets from 76 percent to 40 percent, Korea from 81 percent to 32 percent, and Mexico from 100 percent to 18 percent,[40] but few other countries showed such dramatic action in this area. Only three entries in Table 3.A2 get "perfect scores" for financial liberalization by 1996: the United Kingdom, New Zealand, and Hong Kong.

Yet even Great Britain, New Zealand, and Hong Kong have significant bank regulation. Would it be desirable to go further than these three, allowing what is sometimes termed "free banking" (i.e., permission to start banks with very few requirements and no government regulation)? Historical evidence suggests that relatively unregulated banking systems, which existed primarily before the 20th century, often performed quite well.[41] In the late 20th and early 21st centuries, however, when almost all governments have seen fit to guarantee the deposit liabilities of banks, free banking is no longer a viable option: If the government guarantees bank liabilities, it really must monitor their assets or it will likely suffer massive losses. Thus, all three of the fully liberalized countries above have both deposit protection and some form of bank regulation.

We will save the discussion of deposit insurance and appropriate bank regulation for Chapter 7. In this chapter, however, we want to look at Chile's experience with free banking in the late 1970s. That experience, which ended badly, is described in detail below. In the 1980s Chile tried a second approach to liberalization—one that was in some ways less free, but which had as its hallmark the need to enforce rigorous market discipline over banks to prevent the abuse of banks' political power.

A much milder approach to financial liberalization was followed in Korea during the 1980s, where government control of banks (and the conglomerates allied with those banks) remained extensive. That experience is generally admired because of Korea's strong performance throughout the 1980s. The financial crisis in Korea during the late 1990s will be discussed in Chapter 8 and has a complex connection with financial liberalization. Some commentators have attributed that event to excessive liberalization in the 1990s, meaning Korea's facilitation and encouragement of capital

---

[39]Ibid.

[40]Ibid.

[41]For several historical examples, see Rolnick and Weber (1983, 1984), White (1984), Gorton and Mullineaux (1987), Cowen and Kroszner (1989, 1994), Kroszner (1997), Gorton (1996), Calomiris and Kahn (1996), Calomiris and Mason (1997), and Calomiris and Wilson (1998).

inflows, while other commentators find the root of the problem in insufficient liberalization, notably a lagging of foreign bank competition and a continuation of government interference in bank lending decisions.

The contrasting stories of these two approaches to financial liberalization are worth examining in detail.

Chile in the 1970s

In the mid-1970s Chile, Argentina, and Uruguay all took major steps to liberalize their financial systems quickly. In all three cases the outcome was sobering. We will focus on the Chilean story because its motivation was particularly ideological and very explicit: to privatize the economy and to end financial repression in the shortest possible time.

Chile had suffered serious economic damage during the socialist regime of Salvador Allende, which ended in a military coup in 1973 after several years of hyperinflation and economic collapse. The revulsion against socialism caused a substantial consensus in favor of restoring free markets, including free financial markets. The new military government was authoritarian and in many ways repressive, but most unusual among military regimes in its ideological commitment to restoring private markets and giving them free rein to allocate capital resources.

Allende had nationalized the banking system in 1971, and followed a classic policy of state investment, low interest rates, and high reserve requirements, substantially impounding the national savings. The public sector received about half of all bank credit and paid 5 percent nominal interest, while inflation rose from 22 percent in 1971 to 163 percent in 1972 and 608 percent in 1973. As can be seen in Figure 3.3, the Chilean reserve ratio (Bank reserves/M1) rose from 36 percent in 1970 to 100 percent by the end of the Allende period and for several years thereafter, following which it was reduced to the 20 to 40 percent range. Real interest rates, as shown in Figure 3.4, became very high following Allende before settling into a normal range.

High inflation under Allende did not press money holdings to a low level as is the norm during financial repression; in 1973 the deposits in banks and savings associations reached 28 percent of GDP, slightly higher than in 1970. Chilean money holdings actually rose in the first few years of the 1970s, as shown in Figure 3.5, due to a significant amount of inflation indexing that had been permitted in various forms of deposits. Indeed, the major problem of SINAP, the central agency for savings associations, was what to do with the excess deposits, since government-tolerated attacks on land and home ownership had brought construction to a halt. This liquidity then contracted after Allende's fall, and only gradually rose thereafter as normal economic life resumed.

Allende was overthrown by violence in 1973 and the military dictatorship of General Augusto Pinochet followed. While this regime was highly repressive in the political arena, it was startlingly liberal in the financial arena, with a high commitment to free market economics. In March 1974 the government announced a classic plan of financial liberalization.

1. All interest rates with terms of more than one year would be decontrolled.

2. Credit controls and excessive reserve requirements would be ended.

3. All medium- and long-term debt could be indexed to inflation.

FIGURE 3.3

Chilean reserve ratio

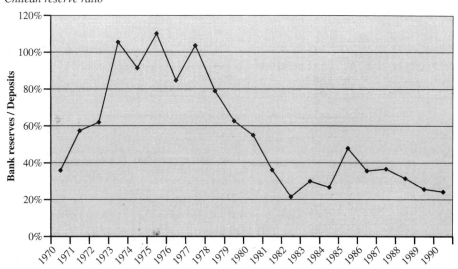

4. Inflation compensation would no longer be taxed as interest income.

5. Savings associations could lend long term for any purpose, not just for mortgages.

6. SINAP would be supported if rising interest rates brought it near insolvency.

7. Banks and savings associations would be free to extend consumer credit.

8. The government would no longer fix insurance premiums.

9. The state pension system would be privatized.

10. Healthy competition among financial institutions would be encouraged.

11. Securities laws would be reformed to increase disclosure requirements.

Implementation of this plan began with the first elements of (1) and (2) beginning in the autumn of 1974. Unfortunately, between then and January 1975 the price of copper, Chile's major export, fell by half on world markets. That greatly complicated the decontrol of credit, as the country went into recession and government revenues collapsed.

The complexities of changing interest rate and credit rules for existing institutions during an economic contraction were such that the government decided it would be preferable to authorize new intermediaries *(financieras)* free of all interest rate and credit controls, including the legalization of informal financial intermediaries, often run by wealthy individuals. The government explicitly disclaimed any guarantee of deposits in *financieras*. The freedom with which these new "banks" could be started and operated, in addition to a general lack of regulatory power by the Superintendency of Banks, led to *de facto* free banking in Chile.

Financial liberalization, in combination with the collapse of copper prices, caused the real rate of interest to rise dramatically. The damage to the government budget caused by the reduction of reserve requirements, the rise in borrowing costs, and the collapse of tax revenues caused some significant backpedaling. Reserve ratios were

Figure 3.4

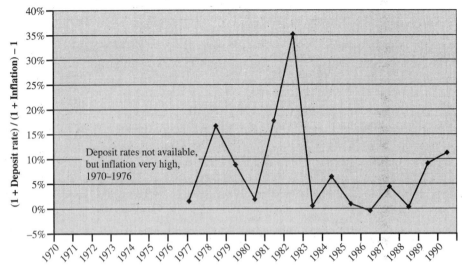

Chilean real rates of interest on deposits

periodically increased to levels as high as 100 percent throughout the mid-1970s, and the government began to "suggest" to banks that they lower their interest rates.

Consistent with its free market orientation, the government tried to disclaim any responsibility for bank deposits. Yet with rising real interest rates, the state-owned home mortgage bank SINAP began to lose money, much as savings banks did in the United States a few years later. Many depositors rushed to withdraw their accounts at the one point in the year when they had the right to do this, in January 1975. By March 1975 SINAP was near bankruptcy, and the government declared that its deposits enjoyed the guarantee of the state. Contrary to this declaration, some of the SINAP accounts were frozen and ultimately suffered losses of about 40 percent. The government's inconsistency on depositor protection seriously damaged its credibility.

In mid-1975 the government holding company (CORFO) sold its stock in 11 commercial banks, in 9 of which its position was the majority, offering generous credit terms to purchasers but obtaining exceptionally high prices. Following this, CORFO began to sell off its portfolio of industrial companies. This sequence of events enabled the purchasers of the banks to use the financing power of the banks to purchase the industrial companies. The result was a set of new, bank-centered conglomerate empires.

At the end of 1976, a number of *financieras* began to fail. These totally unregulated and unprotected financial institutions became serious centers of fraud. One informal *financiera* owner fled the country with his depositors' money. Another turned out to have only two lending clients, both companies controlled by the owner of the *financiera*. The private banks tried to form a pool to support one *financiera*, a move reminiscent of the early days of central banking. In January 1977 Banco Osorno y la Union failed, apparently pulled down by its close connection to a failed *financiera*. Several of its executives and major stockholders were arrested for irregularities, but

Figure 3.5

Chilean liquidity

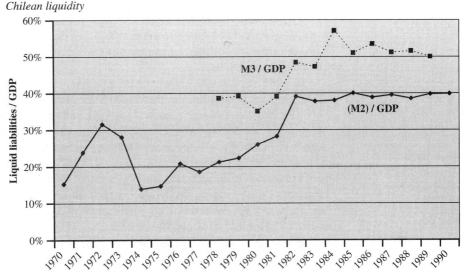

the bank was so large that the government felt compelled to announce complete protection of all deposits.

By the late 1970s it became clear that the newly privatized banks were heavily concentrated in loans to their industrial groups, and that *de facto* government protection would be provided to virtually all financial intermediaries of significant size. In essence, that combination of government protection of banks, and close links between banks and conglomerates, effectively nationalized prospective losses of banks and their closely affiliated industrial borrowers. What began as a financial liberalization had become transformed into a one-sided nationalization of the economy—one-sided because only losses of protected banks would be nationalized, while any future gains would accrue to private stockholders. That sort of protection can be extremely dangerous because it encourages banks and their affiliated firms that are insolvent, or nearly insolvent, to adopt risky "resurrection strategies" to undertake high risks (effectively at public expense) in the hope of restoring their solvency.

The government recognized the risks inherent in the close connections between banks and industrial firms. In 1981 the government passed a new banking law requiring banks to apply rules against concentration of risk to entire industrial groups, not just single companies. There followed a long struggle as the banks sought to evade the requirement to deconcentrate. This struggle was characterized by deceit, stock price manipulation, and other unsavory actions. The 1981 law also, for the first time, gave significant regulatory powers to the Superintendency of Banks.

The first sign of major trouble came with the default of CRAV, a Chilean sugar company, in June 1981. By November 1981 two Chilean banks and several *financieras* became insolvent and were taken over by the central bank, followed by more in early 1982. In the midst of the crisis, banks substantially expanded credit, presumably to stem the recessionary tide and to assist their affiliated firms: Between the end of December 1981 and the end of June 1982, domestic credit in Chilean pesos expanded by 41 percent.[42] This massive credit expansion, with its inflationary overtones, put the Chilean peso under further pressure. The peso, which had been pegged to the U.S. dollar since July 1979, lost more than half its value in foreign exchange markets when the peg broke in June 1982. That depreciation deepened the losses of Chilean banks and industrial firms because of their heavy dependence on borrowings denominated in dollars.

In 1982 the United States entered a serious recession that exacerbated Chile's problems. Real interest rates in the United States were exceptionally high, pulling capital back into the United States and out of developing economies, including Chile. Much of the developing world entered into a general financial crisis culminating in the default on sovereign debt by many countries in South America and elsewhere. Chile suffered in 1982 a 14 percent reduction in GDP and estimated nonperforming assets of banks rose dramatically. In January 1983 a large paper company failed, and eight more large banks were declared insolvent. The government closed three banks and recapitalized the other five. With this, the government had come full circle: It once again controlled 60 percent of bank deposits in Chile.

Having learned from its mistakes, however, Chile repeated the process of financial liberalization on a sounder footing in the 1980s. By the end of that decade, its stock market was soaring and its reprivatized banking system had gained considerable strength.

Korea in the 1980s

The Chilean experience is interesting because it was unusually rapid and extreme. Most attempts at financial liberalization proceed more cautiously, and typically err by making too little real reform. This more typical pattern is illustrated by Korea in the 1980s.

Korea had shifted in the early 1960s from a pattern of inward orientation and financial repression to the Japanese model of export-driven growth while still maintaining a firm government hand on capital allocation. That formula led to a decade of rapid economic growth. That growth slowed down substantially, however, with the oil price increases of 1973 and 1979.

Reserve ratios rose throughout the 1970s from less than 30 percent to more than 50 percent, as shown in Figure 3.6. Korean inflation during the 1970s was generally in the range of 10 to 25 percent, with the highest values in the two years following the oil price increases. The two bursts of oil-induced inflation were more responsible for negative real rates than any persistent effort to exploit savers, as illustrated in Figure 3.7. But inflation was not the essential problem in Korea, nor was liquidity abnormally low, as shown in Figure 3.8. The essential problem was continuing government allocation of capital.

By 1975, with inflation coming under control but growth still slow, the Korean government decided on a massive investment program in heavy industries: chemicals, petroleum and coal derivatives, metals, and machinery. Most of that investment was financed by foreign loans and central bank credit at very low rates to reluctant companies.

This turned out to be an excellent example of value-destroying growth; it was not driven by any assessment of demand, cash flows, or value added, but rather by a single-

---

[42]Díaz-Alejandro (1985). For additional accounts of the Chilean liberalization and crisis, see Edwards and Edwards (1991) and de la Cuadra and Valdés (1992).

FIGURE 3.6

Korean reserve ratio

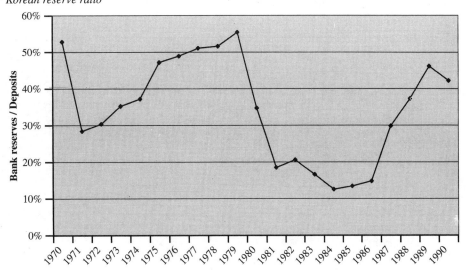

minded focus on top-line output. Production capacity expanded, but products were sold at a loss and much capacity soon lay idle. The firms that "benefited" from this government program were seriously weakened and exports failed to materialize. Elements of financial repression could be found in the reserve ratio, which rose to more than 50 percent by the late 1970s because of the budgetary pressures of the heavy and chemical industries investment program.

The second oil price increase of 1979 and the worldwide rise in real dollar interest rates seriously aggravated the situation. Debt service reached 18 percent of GDP in 1980, and the current account deficit rose to 8.7 percent of GDP by 1980. These troubles produced an important change in attitude. Government-dominated capital allocation had led to serious inefficiencies, and sound private projects had been crowded out. That experience set the stage for a period of moderate financial liberalization. The central features of this financial liberalization have been summarized as follows:[43]

1. Relaxing interest rate controls gradually.
2. Removing some barriers to entry into the financial industry.
3. Giving more autonomy to financial institutions.
4. Reducing specialization and moving toward universal banking.
5. Relaxing restrictions on exchange rates and foreign exchange transactions.
6. Freeing capital movements.

In 1980 the four leading banks in Korea were all owned by the government. The most important feature of the financial liberalization was a denationalization of banks and the opening of the industry to new competitors. This process was not perfect, as the large banks continued to take strong direction from the government after privatization,

---

[43]A detailed account of these events is found in Patrick and Park (1994).

FIGURE 3.7

Korean real interest rates on deposits

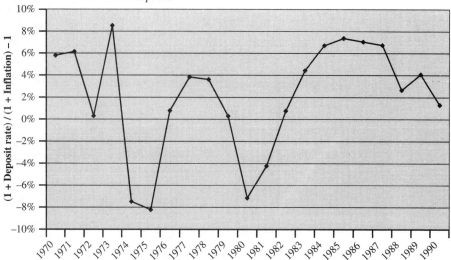

but it was a key first step in bringing private ownership, control, and incentives back into the financial sector.

Five new national banks and a large number of nonbank financial intermediaries were chartered, rather like the *financieras* in Chile. These organizations competed with, and in part formalized, what had up to then been a "gray market" or "curb market" of unofficial but substantial private lenders. Such informal intermediaries, including unregulated banks, moneylenders, merchants, pawnbrokers, loan brokers, and landlords, are a common feature of financially repressed economies.[44]

Like many developing countries, Korea also retained a set of state-owned specialized lenders for small enterprises, housing loans, fisheries, livestock, and so forth. With the reforms of the 1980s, these specialized institutions were gradually broadened in scope. Commercial banks were given powers to trade and underwrite securities. Foreign commercial banks were invited to establish and expand branches in Korea.

Bank-required reserve ratios were dramatically reduced after 1979, from over 50 percent of M1 to 13 percent by 1984, as indicated in Figure 3.6. Interest rates were gradually deregulated during the 1980s. The real rate of interest on bank deposits, which had been savaged by two rounds of inflation following the oil price increases of 1973 and 1979, rose steadily from −7 percent in 1980 to +7 percent by 1984, as shown in Figure 3.7. In January 1982 the government announced an end to direct control over bank lending.

However, as Figure 3.6 also shows, the reserve ratio was again raised from the mid-teens during 1983–1986 back to the mid-40s in 1988–1990. And the official privatization of banking overstates the real change that took place; the Korean banks continued to be subject to strong guidance from the Ministry of Finance, much as hap-

---

[44]See Adams and Fitchett (1992) for detailed descriptions.

FIGURE 3.8

Korean liquidity

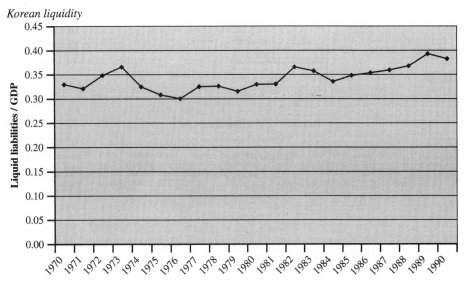

pened in Japan. In addition to *ex ante* guidance on credit allocation, the government also intervened to resolve corporate insolvencies of bank customers. Each major corporation had a designated "principal transactions bank" that served as its main bank intermediary and as the organizer and monitor of its financial links to other banks. When borrowing firms became financially distressed, taxpayers' funds would be made available through these principal transactions banks to bail out firms the government deemed worthy.

> During 1986–1988, for instance, as many as 78 corporations, largely selected by the Ministry of Finance, were involved in restructuring . . . The principal transactions banks selected candidate companies that might take over problem corporations and negotiated the terms with them. The terms of the financial support package were then examined and coordinated by the Office of Bank Supervision and Examination before they were confirmed by the Ministry of Finance through consultation with other involved ministries and agencies.[45]

Thus, not only were Korean banks subject to guidance, but their incentives for proper credit management were very weak in this insider-controlled, government-subsidized system. In that system, financial distress was less a problem for the lending bank and more a problem for the taxpayer. Distress also provided an excuse for further expansion in the size and scope of insider-run conglomerates with the authority of quasi-governmental bodies. Nam (1996) points out that in the Korean system, the business decisions of borrowers, business alliances, and the structure of conglomerates are often driven more by the need to maximize political influence and access to government-controlled credit and subsidies than by the criteria set by international competitiveness.

Although the reforms were imperfect, the financial markets deepened substantially. Private savings rose from 17.9 percent of GDP in 1980 to 27.3 percent in 1990.

---

[45]Park (1996), pp. 285–86.

Domestic credit (loans by banks and nonbank financial institutions) as a percentage of GDP rose steadily from 40.2 percent in 1980 to 56.9 percent in 1990.

The stock market rose by a factor of nine, from an index value of 106.9 in 1980 to a crest of 909.7 in 1989 before settling back to 696.1 in 1990, a level that was then maintained for several years. The market value of listed stocks as a percentage of GDP rose from 6.9 percent in 1980 to 46.1 percent in 1990. The value of stock traded rose from 3 percent of GDP in 1980 to 30 percent in 1990.

The degree of change was sufficiently impressive that the World Bank cited Korea as a leading example of the benevolent effects of financial liberalization in their 1989 *World Development Report,* which was devoted entirely to the subject of financial liberalization.[46] In this document, the World Bank went on record for the first time in support of the importance of financial liberalization to economic development. The World Bank went on to extol the "East Asian miracle" (of which Korea was a prime example) in its 1993 book on that subject.

> Financial sector policies . . . were designed to facilitate two crucial functions. First, they encouraged financial savings. Second, they channeled savings into activities with high social returns. There was great variety in the policies and institutions used to accomplish these ends, but several fundamental approaches were important in all eight economies. These included generally positive real interest rates on deposits and the creation of secure bank-based financial systems.[47]

The World Bank (1993), however, did not advocate full financial liberalization and, indeed, it praised Korea and other Asian economies for "fostering stable and secure banking systems through a combination of protection and regulation." The World Bank praised government policies that guided bank lending and pressured stronger banks to absorb weaker ones, as need be. The World Bank view was that unfettered competition of the Chilean kind was too dangerous, and that the Korean model struck the right balance between reform and government control.

Some economists disputed whether the general prosperity and the rise in Korean savings during the 1980s were really a consequence of financial liberalization (which itself was quite mild), arguing that increased saving was at least partly a simple consequence of the general prosperity. But few disagreed that the government was taking steps to let markets do more capital allocation than they had been permitted in the past, or that the liberalization created a climate of much greater confidence for investors.

The greater disagreement with the World Bank position and the Korean approach to financial liberalization was over two issues: (1) the desirability of retaining bank monopolies and the mutually protective "convoy system" of mutual support among banks and conglomerates that typified the Asian approach to financial liberalization, and (2) the linking of banks to closely affiliated conglomerates (the *chaebols* of Korea or the *keiretsu* of Japan). Critics argued that this system lacked sufficient competition, bred corruption, and failed to allocate capital to its best use; in short, it was not very different from a state-owned system.

There is no doubt that the financial system was both a tool for government control and a locus of corrupt practices. For example, Korea's liberalization did not end the practice of allowing individuals to own financial assets under assumed names. That

---

[46]World Bank (1989).
[47]World Bank (1993), pp. 349–50.

practice, with obvious overtones of criminality, was for decades an embarrassment to the Korean financial system. The government tried to ban it in 1972 and again in 1989, but ran into formidable political opposition, suggesting the complicity of powerful government figures in the criminality and corruption. It was not abolished until the election of President Kim Young Sam in 1993.

The Asian collapse of 1998–1999, in which Korea played a central role, revealed that capital allocation had still been quite flawed during the 1980s and 1990s: Too many investment projects of low productivity had gone forward with high leverage, often with debt denominated in dollars. The leveraged, low-productivity firms could not pay interest on their debts when the crisis struck.

Why did that happen, when Korea had been so widely admired? A sector-by-sector McKinsey study concluded that managerial practices were poor.

> In manufacturing, Korea has massively invested in the best available technology but because of protectionism and poor corporate governance in banks and companies, it was not forced to adopt best managerial practices. As a result, labor and capital productivity were found in most sectors to be less than half the U.S. levels.[48]

Additionally, the study found that the investments themselves were often flawed.

> The weakness of corporate governance in banks and industrial companies allowed for the continued injection of capital to industries/companies with capital returns below their cost of debt.[49]

In this view, government protection of powerful bank-centered conglomerates *(chaebols)* had changed their incentives and pushed them to keep building plants regardless of demand or profitability. Government protection against bad outcomes encouraged banks to lend where otherwise they would not, so capital allocation was flawed.

The central weaknesses of Korea's reforms of the 1980s were that they did too little to promote efficiency and too much to protect firms against the consequences of unwise investment decisions. Despite the fact that the liberalization was flawed, the changes of the 1980s undeniably pointed Korea in an important new direction. Just as Chile's policies during the mid-1980s indicate that it learned from its policy mistakes of the pre-1983 period, there are some indications that in the wake of the 1997–1998 crisis that Korea was coming to grips with the unfinished business of reform, particularly banking reform.[50]

Lessons for Financial Reform

In Chapter 2 we summarized the empirical literature linking measures of financial sector strength and depth with economic progress. That evidence points to the central importance of a liberalized financial sector as part of the development process. Certainly economic growth can occur, sometimes at impressive rates, in the absence of strong private financial institutions. It would seem, however, that such growth is often

---

[48]McKinsey Global Institute (1998), p. 1.

[49]Ibid., p. 3.

[50]For a discussion of the Chilean banking sector reforms of the 1980s, see Ramirez and Rosende (1992) and Calomiris (1997, pp. 30–34). For evidence that conglomerate reform may have begun in earnest, see Burton (1999a, 1999b) and Schuman and Lee (1999).

inefficient, and ends badly, as with the collapse of communism. At such moments the poor quality of many capital investment decisions is revealed.

Why is it so crucial that financial sector flows be placed in competitive, private hands? A successful financial system does much more than aggregate savings. It performs a selection role, sending funds to firms and projects that promise high levels of value added, and denying it to firms and projects that seem likely to destroy value. In doing so, it delivers better decisions than government-guided investment programs, which are typically affected by many goals other than value maximization.

Equally important is the monitoring function of private financial institutions. After an investment is made, the bank or fund that made it has responsibility to follow its progress, enforce creditors' or stockholders' rights, and bear the costs or benefits of the consequences of its initial investment decision. Incentives to select the best possible borrowers or stock issuers, to monitor their progress, and to enforce contracts properly all depend on the private banker who must bear the costs of failing to do so. If things start to go wrong with a loan, the financial institution is likely to suffer the loss and so shows substantial interest in taking corrective action, whether by pressuring management, by providing supplemental capital on stringent terms, or by forcing bankruptcy. And when loans go bad and losses are incurred, there is always something to learn from the result, and here too private banks have incentives to identify and internalize those lessons.

The mass privatizations of Central and Eastern Europe illustrate clearly the need for intermediary financial institutions, whether banks or funds. Such privatizations went best when, as in Poland, the government laid out the structure for such institutions and then let them be operated by the private sector. The most egregious problems of privatization occurred when, as in Czechoslovakia or Russia, the need for such intermediaries had not been thought through, and those that arose spontaneously were entirely unregulated and often criminal.

East Asia presents a special case. By our index of financial liberalization, the countries of East Asia did a great many things right. They relied on the competitive energy of their private sectors, they moved aggressively into world markets, and their governments provided strong and appropriate infrastructure support. Stock markets grew strong and banks were substantially freed from financial repression as measured by reserve requirements or interest rates. Korea looked quite good by these measures, yet its financial liberalization was imperfect.

A flaw in East Asia's growth, in Korea and elsewhere, was the continuing tendency of governments throughout the region to guide capital flows and to protect powerful conglomerates. Once seen as a strength, that tendency now appears to have been a major weakness so that the rapid growth of the region proved to be unsustainable. The Asian financial crisis of 1997–1998 has revealed the value destruction caused by many poor investment decisions. Such value destruction is not an abstraction, but accumulated as bad loans at the Asian banks. Sooner or later the bill for that value destruction had to be paid, and the paying of it brought Asia's growth to a halt. Japan's capital allocation proved to be one of the greatest value destroyers, with more than $500 billion of bad loans in its banks. Chinese bank losses are probably even larger, but they have not yet been accurately tabulated or acknowledged.

The experiences with privatization and financial liberalization during the 1980s and 1990s give us a new perspective on economic development. Sustainable growth is a financial concept. A firm grows at a sustainable rate when its return on equity, dividend payout, and growth rates of assets and liabilities are set at compatible levels, so that each year's retained earnings provide the basis for growth in balance sheet categories proportionate to sales growth. Translating that insight to development economics, a country grows at a sustainable rate when its capital investments earn returns in excess of the cost of capital, and when aggregate growth in profitability is high enough to sustain rising levels of debt. When that occurs, the financial institutions that fund investment can build their own capital base at a rate proportional to the growth of the economy. When that condition is not met, financial institutions fail alongside value-destroying borrowers, shutting off supplies of future credit.

Totally free banking, with no deposit insurance and no regulation, appears virtually impossible in a modern developing economy. The political economy of banking has changed since the 19th century.[51] In today's world, the near-universal government protection of deposits requires government to monitor and regulate banks in a variety of ways. Otherwise, well-intentioned liberalization will lead to excessive risks and the one-sided nationalization of banks (i.e., the nationalization of losses).

Countries also need regulation to protect consumers from fraud, particularly during the transitional phase when financial institutions and contracts are being established where they had not existed before. In that situation the inexperience of the public provides an undesirable opportunity for fraudulent practices. Minimal restrictions that protect consumers from fraud would have avoided the worst abuses of the Czech fund fiasco.

Perhaps most importantly, privatization and liberalization, to be successful, must be part of a broader and more fundamental set of reforms to the economic and legal environment.[52] The enforcement of contracts, the establishment of clear property rights and accounting practices, the creation of a private information network (to assist financial institutions in measuring and managing risk), and fiscal stability are all complementary reforms to privatization. Without clear property rights and enforcement of contracts, true privatization and liberalization are not possible because incentive structures of firms and financial institutions will be flawed. And without the development of standards for accounting and measuring risk (by private networks of accountants and risk analysts) it is much harder for private parties to measure and reward (or punish) performance. Legal foundations are the subject of Chapter 4.

Mechanisms for risk evaluation are critical in any market-based financial system. Published ratings by agencies such as bond rating agencies could play a role in assessing the risks of financial institutions. Normally, effective and sufficient disclosure is voluntary. Firms that wish to attract private funds have to find credible ways of revealing their condition to outsiders. But in some cases—particularly when firms are protected from market discipline by the government—those incentives cannot be relied upon. That is particularly true in protected banking systems where government deposit insurance permits banks to avoid the need to satisfy market concerns about concealed insider lending and undisclosed problem loans. To the extent that government protection

---

[51]For a discussion of the broad trends in political economy over the last century and the consequences for monetary and exchange rate policy (which parallel the changes in government protection of banks), see Eichengreen (1996).

[52]For additional evidence on the centrality of the broader legal environment, and prior fiscal reform, in determining the success of financial liberalization in many other countries, see Caprio, Atiyas, and Hanson (1994), Ito and Krueger (1996), Loriaux et al. (1997), and Faruqi (1993, 1994).

insulates banks or other firms from having to disclose information that the market would otherwise require, the coercive hand of government in regulating bank accounting standards is necessary to deal with these problems. Information and control are the subjects of Chapter 5.

In summary, a strong financial system based on the private incentives of financial institutions is needed to monitor the business system, and thoughtful government rules are needed to monitor the financial system. Experience suggests that no other way of organizing affairs can succeed for long.

This Appendix consists of two country-by-country tables. Table 3.A1, based on data from the World Bank's *Global Development Finance* (1999), shows the dollar value of privatization transactions during 1988–1997, divided between those involving control by a foreign investor and those involving control by domestic investors. These data exclude the voucher-based mass privatizations.

Table 3.A2 reproduces Table 3.5 from *A Survey of Financial Liberalization* by John Williamson and Molly Mahar (1998), describing the nature of financial liberalization achieved in each country between 1973 and 1996. The reader is referred to this publication for a more extensive discussion of these liberalizations and their effects.

TABLE 3.A1 **Dollar Value ($ millions) of Privatization Transactions, 1988–1997**
Divided between Foreign Investors and Local Investors

	Foreign Investors	Local Investors	Both	No Information	Total
Albania	$6	$22			$28
Algeria		9			9
Angola		4			4
Argentina	3,783	5,155	$18,836	$147	27,921
Armenia	150	32			182
Azerbaijan			2		3
Bahrain		10			10
Bangladesh		60			60
Barbados	51				51
Belarus		11			11
Belize	14	40			54
Benin	44	6		6	56
Bolivia	770	82	24	8	884
Brazil	6,269	12,877	13,668	1,747	34,559
Bulgaria	609	169	89	8	875
Burkina Faso	1			6	7
Burundi		2		3	5
Cameroon	41				41
Cape Verde					0
Chile	466	709	229	80	1,484
China	11,388	11	5,625	12	17,036
Colombia	3,346	1,063	1,029	247	5,685
Costa Rica		57			57
Côte d'Ivoire	221	127	128		476
Croatia	195	3	35	13	246
Cuba	706				706
Czech Republic*	2,043	163	60	103	2,369
Czechoslovakia*	1,862		47		1,909
Ecuador	94	35	40	1	169
Egypt	265	193	1,054	1,266	2,778
Estonia	36	313	53	65	467
Fiji			2		2
Gabon					0
Ghana	243	42	566	21	873
Grenada		6			6
Guatemala		43			43
Guinea	45				45
Guinea-Bissau		1			1
Guyana	44				44
Honduras	13	86			99
Hungary	7,138	196	2,078	3,374	12,785

continued

	Foreign Investors	Local Investors	Both	No Information	Total
India	$448	$757	$2,066	$3,802	$7,073
Indonesia	586	22	3,990	564	5,163
Iran		12	7		19
Jamaica	251	258		24	533
Jordan		15	33	11	59
Kazakhstan	5,347	25		426	5,798
Kenya	26	124	14	71	235
Kyrgyzstan				140	140
Laos	5	7	20		32
Latvia	223	145	58	5	431
Lithuania	16	99	1	784	900
Macedonia		608		3	611
Malawi	6	3	2		11
Malaysia	700	3,979	4,138	1,260	10,076
Mali				22	22
Mauritania		1			1
Mexico	4,423	16,940	11,842	148	33,353
Moldova		2			2
Montenegro	15				15
Morocco	636	591	587	32	1,847
Mozambique	19	31	38	22	111
Nepal	1	9	6		15
Nicaragua	5	121	4		130
Nigeria	500	262		1	763
Oman		55	5		60
Pakistan	258	585	1,085	23	1,951
Panama	724	30	70		824
Papua New Guinea			224		224
Paraguay			42		42
Peru	2,477	1,598	3,355	48	7,477
Philippines	942	986	755	1,127	3,810
Poland	2,359	1,173	1,882	431	5,846
Romania	411	348	8		767
Russia	1,227	5,079		374	6,681
Rwanda					0
São Tomé and Príncipe					0
Senegal	107		84		191
Serbia	907				907
Sierra Leone		2			2
Slovak Republic*	115	1,237	131	496	1,979
Slovenia	370			151	521
South Africa	1,261	2,483	1,269	1,052	6,065
Sri Lanka	317	198	188	24	726
Tanzania	121	16		4	141
Thailand	52	271	1,055		1,378
Togo	27		1	11	39
Trinidad and Tobago	413	6	30		448
Tunisia	27	88	34	22	171
Turkey	462	2,250	881	252	3,843
Uganda	72	36	31	13	152
Ukraine	32				32
United Arab Emirates				190	190

	Foreign Investors	Local Investors	Both	No Information	Total
Uruguay	$15		$2		$17
Uzbekistan	212				212
Venezuela	1,063	$265	4,522	$64	5,914
Vietnam		3			3
Yemen		1			1
Yugoslavia	360				360
Zambia	329	79		9	417
Zimbabwe	13		185		197
Total	$67,721	$62,274	$82,258	$18,712	$230,965

*Czechoslovakia split on January 1, 1993, into the Czech Republic and the Slovak Republic. The figures for Czechoslovakia in this table include both components for the period prior to the split.

TABLE 3.A2   Changes in Financial Sector Policy, 1973–1996

	Credit Controls	Interest Rates	Entry Barriers	Government Regulation of Operations	Privatization	International Capital Flows
Industrialized Countries						
United States	S&Ls deregulated in 1982.	Regulation Q suspended in 1982. S&Ls deregulated in 1982.	Foreign banks brought within federal regulatory framework in 1978. Interstate banking regulations eased in 1995, but restrictions remain.			Limited controls imposed in the 1960s, abolished in 1974.
Canada	Reserve requirements phased out in the early 1990s.		Foreign banks permitted within certain size regulations in 1980. "Four pillars" system largely eliminated in 1992.			
Japan	Window guidance discontinued in 1991. Special treatment for priority industries largely phased out by the 1990s.	Interest-rate deregulation began in 1979. Interest rates on most fixed-term deposits eliminated by 1993. Non-time-deposit rates freed in 1994. Lending rates market determined in the 1990s.	Bank specialization requirements significantly reduced by 1993. Foreign trust banks and securities companies allowed since the mid-1980s. Further liberalization to be implemented by 2001.	Dividend restrictions eased in 1980. Limits on advertising eliminated in 1993.	Government controls roughly 15% of financial assets through the postal savings system.	Controls on capital inflows eased after 1979. Controls on capital outflows eased in the mid-1980s. Foreign exchange restrictions eased in 1980. Remaining restrictions on cross-border transactions removed in 1995.

continued

	Credit Controls	Interest Rates	Entry Barriers	Government Regulation of Operations	Privatization	International Capital Flows
United Kingdom	Supplementary Special Deposits Scheme ("the corset") discontinued in 1980. Reserve-assets ratio abolished in 1981 and replaced by a universal 0.5% liquidity requirement.	Bank of England's minimum lending rate not published after 1981. Government withdrew guidance on mortgage lending in 1986.	Banks allowed to compete with building societies for housing finance after 1981. Building societies allowed to expand their lending business after 1986. All remaining controls on hire-purchase agreements eliminated in 1982. Fixed commissions on trading in government securities abolished in 1984. London stock exchange fully deregulated in 1986.			All remaining controls on foreign-exchange purchase eliminated in 1979.
France	Subsidized loans for exports, investments, housing, and to local authorities slowly phased out in the 1980s and 1990s but not eliminated.	Interest rates (except those on subsidized loans) freed in 1984. Subsidized loans, subject to a uniform interest ceiling, now available to all banks.	Financial institutions highly specialized until mid-1980s. Universal banks permitted after 1984. Unequal advantages still available to public sector banks.		Some banks nationalized since 1945. All larger banks national-ized in 1982. Several French banks privatized in 1987 and 1993, including Banque Nationale de Paris.	Capital flows in and out of the country largely liberalized over 1986–1988. Liberalization was completed in 1990.
Germany	In 1996, noninterest bearing minimum-reserve requirements stood at 12.1% for demand deposits and at less than 5% for time and savings deposits.	Interest rates freely market determined over entire period.	German banks allowed to enter directly or indirectly into all financial services over the entire period. Foreign banks permitted. New instruments slowly introduced since the 1980s. Stock market regulation eased in the 1980s. Money market funds permitted in 1994.			Most capital controls dismantled in 1973.
Italy	Credit ceilings eliminated in 1983 and reimposed temporarily between 1986 and 1987. Reserve requirements progressively lowered between 1989 and 1994.	Maximum rates on deposits and minimum rates on loans set by Italian Bankers' Association until 1974. Floor prices on government bonds eliminated in 1992.	CDs introduced in the early 1980s. Foreign banks permitted in 1993. Demarcation line between short-term and long-term lending banks abolished in 1993. Bank branching liberalized in 1990. Corporate bond and stock markets remain small compared to other G-7 countries.		Credito Italiano and some other public banks privatized in 1993–1994.	Foreign exchange and capital controls eliminated by May 1990.

	Credit Controls	Interest Rates	Entry Barriers	Government Regulation of Operations	Privatization	International Capital Flows
Australia	Quantitave bank-lending guidance eliminated in 1982. Reserve requirements on savings banks lowered in 1987. Statutory reserve deposit requirement was abolished and replaced by a new noncallable requirement of 1% of bank assets in 1988.	Deposit-rate controls lifted in 1980. Most loan-rate ceilings abolished in 1985. Deposit subsidy program for savings banks implemented in 1986 and removed in 1987.	Foreign banks permitted in 1985. Universal banking established for large domestic banks in 1980s. Nonbank financial institutions permitted to offer checklike intruments in 1986. Capital markets deregulated in mid-1980s.		Some state-owned banks privatized in the 1990s. Commonwealth Bank of Australia privatized in 1997.	Capital and exchange controls tightened in late 1970s after the move to indirect monetary policy increased capital inflows. Capital account liberalized in 1984.
New Zealand	Credit-allocation guidelines removed in 1984. Reserve requirements for trading banks removed in 1984. Requirement for financial institutions to purchase government securities removed in 1985.	Interest-rate ceilings removed in 1976 and reimposed in 1981. All interest-rate controls removed during summer 1984.	Unlimited entry of domestic and foreign banks meeting Reserve Bank criteria since 1985. Separate requirements for different types of financial institutions removed by 1987. Stock exchange liberalized in 1986.		Bank of New Zealand (one of the four largest banks) privatized in the early 1990s. Development Finance Corporation closed. Government sold all remaining shares in state-owned commercial banks by 1992.	All controls on inward and outward foreign exchange transactions removed in 1984. Controls on outward investment lifted in 1985. Restrictions on foreign-owned companies' access to domestic financial markets removed in late 1984. Controls on foreign direct and portfolio investment and repatriation of profits eased in 1985.

East Asia

	Credit Controls	Interest Rates	Entry Barriers	Government Regulation of Operations	Privatization	International Capital Flows
Hong Kong		Deposit-rate ceilings set by the Hong Kong Association of Banks. Since 1995, only interest rates on savings deposits controlled.	Moratorium on bank licensing lifted in 1978. Minimum capital requirement and licensing system remain. Some deposit-taking institutions subject to minimum-deposit restrictions.			
Indonesia	System of bank credit allocation phased out since 1983. Banks required to allocate 20% of loans to small business after 1990. Reserve requirements lowered to 2% of deposits in 1988. Banks must extend 80% of foreign currency lending to exporters.	Most deposit and loan rates freed in 1983. Some liquidity credit arrangements for priority sectors remained in place until 1988. Central bank guidance eliminated in 1991.	The monopoly of state-owned banks over the deposits of state-owned enterprises removed in 1988. Activities of financial institutions broadened in 1988. New foreign banks allowed to establish joint ventures in 1988.	State banks subject to political interference.	Stock exchange privatized in 1990.	Most transactions on the capital account liberalized in 1971. Some restrictions on inflows remain. The regulation requiring exporters to sell their foreign-exchange earnings to banks abolished in 1982. Foreign direct investment regula-tions eased further in 1992.

continued

	Credit Controls	Interest Rates	Entry Barriers	Government Regulation of Operations	Privatization	International Capital Flows
Korea	Targeted lending switched from heavy industries and chemical industries to small- and medium-size firms in 1980s. Most policy-based lending phased out by 1996. Bank of Korea's automatic rediscount facility replaced by an aggregate credit ceiling. Large banks still subject to moral suasion.	A series of decontrol measures adopted in the 1980s and later abandoned. All interest rates deregulated by 1995, except demand deposits and government-supported lending.	Branching of domestic financial institutions liberalized in 1986. Entry of NBFIs permitted in 1982. Limited foreign joint ventures permitted since 1983.	Government abolished or simplified directives regulating personnel, budgeting, and other operational matters in the 1980s.	Government divested its shares in commercial banks in the early 1980s. State-owned banks' share of total financial assets 13% in 1994.	Controls on foreign borrowing under US$200,000 with maturities of less than three years eased in 1979. Restriction on foreign borrowing under US$1 million eased in 1982. Controls on outward and inward foreign investment gradually eased since 1985. Significant restrictions on inward investment in place until 1998.
Malaysia	Fifty percent of net lending required to go to priority sectors in 1975. (Regulation quickly reduced to 20% and largely nonbinding.) Scope of priority lending reduced in the 1980s. Extension of bank credit below the cost of funds eliminated in the 1980s.	Initially liberalized in 1978. Controls reimposed in mid-1980s and completely eliminated in 1991.	No new license for foreign banks since 1973. Some foreign participation in joint ventures permitted recently. Local bank activities broadened in 1990s, but no new commercial banks allowed since the early 1980s. Foreign-currency accounts in selected local banks permitted in 1994.	Bank Negara Malaysia replaced managers of failed financial institutions during crisis (1985–1988).	Share of state-owned banks in total assets of the financial sector 8% in 1994 (BIS estimate). Government is the majority share-holder in the country's largest bank and wholly owns the second largest bank.	Capital account mostly liberalized in the 1970s. Inward foreign direct and portfolio investment deregulated further in the mid-1980s. Controls on short-term and portfolio inflows temporarily reimposed in 1994.
Philippines	Directed credit partly abolished in 1983. Remaining directed credit shifted to the relevant government agency and extended at market-oriented interest rates. Commercial banks still dependent on central bank rediscount window. Reserve requirements lowered in the early 1980s and again in 1993.	Interest controls mostly phased out over 1981–1985. (Some controls reintro-duced during the financial crisis of 1981–1987.) Cartel-like interest rate price fixing remains prevalent.	Offshore banking system introduced in 1975. Domestic financial institutions permitted to compete in various markets in 1983. Restrictions on foreign bank branching lifted in 1993.	Government continued to exert control over man-agement of Philippine National Bank and Development Bank of the Philippines throughout the 1980s.	Government took over some failed financial institutions during the early 1980s. Government's share of total bank assets was lowered to 22% by 1996. Govern-ment reduced stake in PNB to 47% in December 1995.	Foreign exchange and investment channeled through government in the 1970s. Interbank foreign exchange trading limited to 30 minutes per day after 1983. Off-floor trading introduced in 1992. Restrictions on all current and most capital transactions eliminated over 1992–1995.
Singapore			Only banks established prior to 1973 permitted to collect deposits in Singapore. Currently only offshore or foreign representative banking licenses available to nonresidents.			Government freed exchange and capital controls by 1978. (Exception: Offshore banks may not transact in Singapore dollars.)

	Credit Controls	Interest Rates	Entry Barriers	Government Regulation of Operations	Privatization	International Capital Flows
Taiwan	Priority lending to strategic, exporting, and small- and medium-size firms widespread since the 1960s. Budgets for subsidized credit continually modified in recent years.	Nominally liberalized in 1989. Remained uncompetitive until new banks were established in 1992.	Some liberalization of entry for foreign and domestic banks in 1989. New financial products introduced in 1989. 16 new banks established in 1992. New banks subject to NT$10 billion minimum capital requirement.	Government employee pool used to staff public and private financial institutions from the 1960s onward.	Privatization effort blocked by controlling interests in 1989.	Foreign-exchange controls removed in 1987. Inward and outward capital flows limited to US$5 million per person per year.
Thailand	Government gradually eliminated directed credit after 1980.	Interest rate ceilings on all types of deposits abolished in 1990. Ceiling on loan rates removed in 1992.	Foreign banks permitted with approval in 1990. Branching requirements for domestic banks loosened in 1986. Finance and securities companies permitted to set up banks outside Bangkok with approval in 1995. Scope of financial instruments for all financial institutions widened in 1992.		Share of state-owned banks in total assets 7% in 1994 (BIS estimate).	Restrictions on inward long-term investment eased in the mid-1980s. Controls on short-term flows and outward investment eased in the 1990s. The reserve requirement on short-term foreign borrowing is 7%. Currency controls introduced in May and June 1997 to deter currency speculators. Limits on foreign ownership of domestic financial institutions relaxed in October 1997.
Latin America						
Argentina	Credit controls initially removed in 1977 but reimposed in 1982. Controls reduced after 1992 to less than half the level before reforms. 100% reserve requirement freed in 1977. High reserve requirements reimposed in 1982. Reserve requirements on demand deposits lowered from 89.5% in 1987 to 15% by 1996.	Initial liberalization in 1977 reversed in 1982. Deposit rates freed again in 1987. Interest rates on some loans still regulated.	Approval requirements for new banks and bank branching eased in 1977. Free entry of domestic banks permitted since late 1980s. Foreign-owned banks also permitted.		Fifteen percent of the loan market privatized since 1992. Government still owns the largest commercial bank, Banco de la Nación Argentina.	Multiple exchange rate system unified between 1976 and 1978. Foreign loans at market exchange rates permitted in 1978. Controls on inward and outward capital flows loosened in 1977. Liberalization measures reversed in 1982. Capital and exchange controls eliminated in 1991.

continued

	Credit Controls	Interest Rates	Entry Barriers	Government Regulation of Operations	Privatization	International Capital Flows
Brazil	Directed credit partly reduced recently. Reserve requirements rationalized after 1988; requirements differ according to bank size. Reserve requirements remain over 80% on demand deposits.	Interest-rate ceilings removed in 1976 and reimposed in 1979. Deposit rates fully liberalized in 1989. Some loan rates liberalized in 1988. Priority sectors continue to borrow at subsidized rates.	Barriers reduced after 1991.			System of comprehensive foreign exchange controls abolished in 1984. Most capital outflows restricted in the 1980s. Controls on capital inflows strengthened and controls on outflows loosened in the 1990s.
Chile	Directed credit eliminated and reserve requirements reduced in the mid-1970s. Development assistance from multilateral agencies now auctioned off to eligible financial institutions.	Commercial bank interest rates liberalized in 1974. Some controls reimposed in 1982. Deposit rates fully market determined since 1985. Most loan rates market determined since 1984.	New NBFIs permitted in 1974. New foreign banks permitted after 1976. Currently, both domestic and foreign new financial institutions encouraged. "Traditional" and branch banking treated as separate.		Nineteen domestic commercial banks privatized in 1974. Banks nationalized during the 1982 crisis were reprivatized in the mid-1980s.	Capital controls gradually eased since 1979. Controls reimposed in 1982 and eased again in mid-1980s. Foreign direct and portfolio investment subject to a one-year minimum holding period. Foreign loans subject to a 30% reserve requirement.
Colombia	Directed lending to agricultural sector reduced to 6% of total loans for large- and medium-size farms (1% for small farms). Flexible interest rates implemented for these loans by 1994. Reserve requirements on time deposits drastically reduced in 1990s.	Most deposit rates at commercial banks market determined after 1980; all after 1990. Loan rates at commercial banks market determined since the mid-1970s. Remaining controls lifted by 1994 in all but a few sectors.	Competition and efficiency impeded by specialized banking regulations despite efforts to introduce domestic competition in the 1990s.		Two large banks and a large finance company nationalized in 1982. Government intervened in over 20 financial institutions between 1982 and 1986. 30% of loan market privatized by 1995.	Controls on capital inflows relaxed in 1991. Exchange controls also reduced. Large capital inflows in the early 1990s led to the reimposition of reserve requirements on foreign loans in 1993.
Mexico	Credit controls eliminated for commercial banks. Development assistance remains directed. Reserve requirements eliminated on local currency deposits.	Time deposit with flexible interest rates below a maximum rate permitted in 1977. Deposit rates liberalized in 1988–1989. Loan rates liberalized after 1988, except at development banks.	Legislation allowing the establishement of universal banks passed in 1974. Legal framework allowing development of NBFIs also passed in 1974. New entry of banks permitted in 1991. Foreign ownership restricted to 30%.		Authorities nationalized 18 commercial banks in 1982. Nationalized banks privatized in 1991.	Government given discretion over foreign direct investment in 1972. Ambiguous restrictions on foreign direct investment rationalized in 1989. Portfolio flows decontrolled further in 1989.

	Credit Controls	Interest Rates	Entry Barriers	Government Regulation of Operations	Privatization	International Capital Flows
Peru	Subsidized lending eliminated in 1992. Marginal targeted credit at market rates reimplemented in 1996. Reserve requirements on domestic deposits reduced to 9% in 1990.	Interest-rate controls abolished in 1991.			All five public development banks closed in early 1990s. All seven public commercial banks liquidated or divested over 1991–1995.	Capital controls removed in December 1990.
Venezuela	Targeted-credit programs reduced to about half the pre-reform level over 1991–1993. Reserve requirements reduced in early 1990s.	Interest rate ceilings removed in 1991, reimposed in 1994, and removed again in 1996.	Local barriers eliminated in principle. Barriers to foreign banks remain.		Four small public commercial banks liquidated or privatized in 1989. Public sector banks' share of total deposits 9% in 1993. Share increased to 29% after the national-ization of several banks during 1994–1996.	Foreign direct investment regime largely liberalized over 1989–1990. Exchange controls on all current and capital transactions imposed in 1994. System of comprehensive foreign exchange controls abandoned in April 1996.

Middle East and Africa

	Credit Controls	Interest Rates	Entry Barriers	Government Regulation of Operations	Privatization	International Capital Flows
Egypt	Ceiling on credit to private sector lifted in 1991.	Interest rates liberalized in 1991.	Foreign banks permitted to take majority stake in banks and to conduct business in foreign currency in 1990s.		Some privatization of smaller state banks. The four largest public banks not slated for privatization as of 1996.	Foreign exchange system decontrolled and unified in 1991. Some controls on inward portfolio and direct investment lifted in 1990s.
Israel	Directed-credit system abolished in 1990. Reserve requirements gradually lowered to international levels after 1987. Restrictions on investment instruments for institutional investors eased after 1987.	Subsidized rates on priority lending phased out by 1990.	Small number of large universal banks dominate banking sector. New licenses to expand small-bank operations issued after 1987.		Government nationalized leading banks in 1983. Union Bank (part of Bank Leumi) privatized in 1990s. 43% of Bank Hapoalim sold to Israeli-American consortium in 1997.	Capital controls eliminated in 1977 and reimposed in 1979. After 1987, restrictions on capital inflows gradually eliminated and restrictions on capital outflows gradually eased.

continued

	Credit Controls	Interest Rates	Entry Barriers	Government Regulation of Operations	Privatization	International Capital Flows
Morocco	Compulsory holdings of development bank bonds by commercial banks reduced from 15% to 2% of deposits after 1991. Incentives to provide credit to priority sectors virtually eliminated by 1996. Mandatory commercial bank holding of treasury paper reduced to 10% of short-term deposits over 1986–1996.	Interest rates gradually raised to positive real levels in the 1980s. Interest rate subsidies to priority sectors reduced in the 1980s. Lending rates liberalized in 1996. Deposit rates mostly free by 1996, but some controls and moral suasion remain.	Tangier offshore banking center now fully open to foreign banks. Foreign banks may own a majority share in domestic banks. Distinctions between commercial and specialized banks removed in the early 1990s.		The Casablanca stock market is state-owned. One state-owned bank was privatized in 1995.	Current account convertibility achieved in the 1990s. Surrender requirements or export revenue and outward investment restrictions relaxed in the early 1990s. Restrictions on inward foreign direct and portfolio investment and external borrowing by residents eased after 1993.
South Africa	Credit ceilings in effect from 1965 to 1972 and 1976 to 1980. Credit ceilings removed and reserve and liquidity requirements lowered in 1980.	Interest rate controls removed in 1980.	Register of Co-operation (which limited bank competition) eliminated in 1983. Some new banks permitted after 1983; 50 new banks since 1990. Capital and money markets (including derivative markets) exist but remain fairly thin.			Capital controls tightened in 1985. Exchange controls on nonresidents eliminated in 1995. Controls on residents relaxed in 1995.
Turkey	Reserve requirement reduced to 15% over 1986–1988 but raised to 25% in 1990. Directed credit phased out by 1989.	Interest rate ceilings on loans and deposits eliminated in 1980 and reimposed on deposits in 1983. Controls eliminated again in 1988.	Foreign banks permitted since 1980, with some restrictions. Scope of banking activities widened in 1980. Interbank money market established in 1987. Istanbul stock market operational again in 1986.		State-owned banks' share in total assets of the bank system remained constant over 1980–1990, at approximately 52%.	Capital flows liberalized in 1989.

South Asia

	Credit Controls	Interest Rates	Entry Barriers	Government Regulation of Operations	Privatization	International Capital Flows
Bangladesh	Directed and controlled credit largely phased out after 1989. Politically motivated lending remains prevalent. Cash reserve requirements lowered to 5% in the 1990s.	Interest rates raised to positive real levels in the early 1980s. After 1989, deposit rates on savings and time deposits subject to a floor. Floor abolished in 1996. Lending rates for loans freed, except for priority sectors. Priority sector interest rate bands fixed by central bank.	Private banks permitted, with approval, since early 1980s. In 1995, seven new banks established, including some foreign joint ventures. New banks largely occupy niche markets. Only public banks may lend to priority and public sectors. Capital and money markets remain weak or nonexistent.	Branching restrictions still in place for private banks.	Commercial banks nationalized in the 1970s. Two state-owned banks sold back to original owners in early 1980s. (These banks remain uncompetitive.)	Foreign exchange markets unified in 1991–1992. Restrictions on current transactions eliminated in 1994. Controls on capital inflows eased after 1991.

	Credit Controls	Interest Rates	Entry Barriers	Government Regulation of Operations	Privatization	International Capital Flows
India	Cash reserve requirement (CRR) raised rapidly after 1973. Statutory liquidity ratio (SLR) increased to 38.5% by 1991. The Reserve Bank extended discretionary credit to priority sectors and set credit ceilings for banks in the 1970s and 1980s. The CRR and SLR stood at 10.5% and 25%, respectively, in early 1998.	Complex system of regulated interest rates simplified in 1992. Interest rate controls on CDs and commercial paper eliminated in 1993. Minimum lending rate on credit over Rs 200,000 eliminated in late 1994. Interest rates on term deposits of over two years liberalized in 1995.	Entry restrictions eased in 1993. Ten new banks established in 1994–1995, including three foreign banks. Banks permitted to raise capital contribution from foreigners to 20% and from nonresident Indians to 40%. Money and securities markets fairly well developed.	Some branching and staffing regulations eased in the 1990s. Union work rules still represent a major restriction on branching and operations.	All large banks nationalized in 1969. Government divested part of its equity position in some public banks in the 1990s.	Regulations on portfolio and direct investment eased since 1991. The exchange rate was unified in 1993–1994. Current-account convertibility achieved in 1994.
Nepal	Statutory liquidity ratio of 27% from 1974 to 1989. Directed credit to "small" sector introduced in 1974 and substantially reduced since 1989.	Interest rate controls introduced in 1966; slowly phased out after 1986. Interest rates liberalized for almost all sectors by 1989, although marginal restrictions remain.	Foreign joint ventures permitted after 1983. The establishment of private sector banks made legal in 1983. Entry barriers further reduced in 1992.	Government influenced staffing, branching, and other bank managerial decisions. Nepal Bank Limited granted more autonomy through majority private ownership.	Two large public sector banks hold over half of total bank deposits. Goverment share of Nepal Bank Limited reduced to 41%.	Dual exchange rate system introduced in 1992. Current account became fully convertible in 1994. Some capital transactions liberalized in the 1990s, but restrictions remain.
Pakistan	Credit ceilings eliminated in 1995. Subsidized and targeted-credit programs scaled back in the 1990s.	Most lending rates freed in 1995. Interest on working capital and some deposits freed in the early 1980s.	Eleven new private banks, including three foreign, established since 1991. 19 branches of foreign banks established by 1997.	Comprehensive reforms in 1997 reduced government interference in public sector banks.	Muslim Commercial Bank privatized in 1991. Allied Bank privatized in stages between 1991 and 1993. First Women Bank privatized in 1997.	Rupee convertible for current transactions since July 1994. Capital controls eased in the 1990s.
Sri Lanka	Comprehensive Rural Credit Scheme terminated in the late 1970s. Reserve requirements of 14% in 1997. Directed credit programs still prevalent.	Deposit rates market determined since 1980. Lending rates for nonpriority lending freed in 1980. Subsidized rates for priority sector lending remained until the 1990s.	Foreign banks permitted since 1979. Restrictions on domestic banks and NBFIs eased after 1978. Private and public banks placed on equal footing in access to public enterprise deposits in 1990s. Development of stock, bond, and interbank markets increased in 1980s.	Government continues to influence portfolio management and staffing decisions in public banks.	Two development finance banks privatized in 1990s.	Exchange rate unified in 1978. Rupee made convertible for current transactions in 1994. Capital controls on inflows eased in 1978. Foreign portfolio investment restrictions eased further in 1991. Restrictions on capital outflows remain.

Note: NBFI: Nonbank financial institution; BIS: Bank for International Settlements.

References

Adams, Dale W., and Delbert A. Fitchett. 1992. *Informal Finance in Low-Income Countries.* Boulder, CO: Westview Press.

Antal-Mokos, Zoltan. 1998. *Privatisation, Politics and Economic Performance in Hungary.* Cambridge: Cambridge University Press.

Atkinson, Anthony B., and Joseph E. Stiglitz. 1980. *Lectures on Public Economics.* New York: McGraw-Hill.

Baer, Herbert L., Jr., and Elijah Brewer III. 1986. Uninsured deposits as a source of market discipline: Some new evidence. *Federal Reserve Bank of Chicago Economic Perspectives,* September–October: 23–31.

Bartel, Ann P., and Ann E. Harrison. 1999. Ownership versus environment: Disentangling the sources of public sector inefficiency. Working paper, Columbia University.

Berger, Allen N., Sally M. Davies, and Mark J. Flannery. 1998. Comparing market and regulatory assessments of bank performance: Who knows what when? Working paper, Federal Reserve Board.

Berger, Philip G., and Eli Ofek. 1996. Bustup takeovers of value-destroying firms. *Journal of Finance* 51: 1175–1200.

Bhagat, S., Andrei Shleifer, and Robert W. Vishny. 1990. Hostile takeovers in the 1980s: The return to corporate specialization. *Brookings Papers on Economic Activity* (Microeconomics): 1–72.

Bhagwati, Jagdish. 1988. *Protectionism.* Cambridge: Cambridge University Press.

———. 1996. *Political Economy and International Economics.* Cambridge: MIT Press.

Blasi, Joseph R., Maya Kroumova, and Douglas Kruse. 1997. *Kremlin Capitalism: Privatizing the Russian Economy.* Ithaca, NY: Cornell University Press.

Bordo, Michael D., and Barry Eichengreen, eds. 1993. *A Retrospective on the Bretton Woods System.* Chicago: University of Chicago Press.

Bordo, Michael D., and Finn E. Kydland. 1995. The gold standard as a rule: An essay in exploration. *Explorations in Economic History* 32: 423–65.

Burton, John. 1999a. Daewoo discovers it is not too big to be allowed to fail. *Financial Times,* August 17: 6.

———. 1999b. Creditors to dismantle Daewoo conglomerate. *Financial Times,* August 17: 1.

Butters, J. Keith, and John Lintner. 1945. *Effect of Federal Taxes on Growing Enterprises.* Boston: Harvard University Press.

Calomiris, Charles W. 1997. *The Postmodern Bank Safety Net.* Washington, DC: American Enterprise Institute.

Calomiris, Charles W., and R. Glenn Hubbard. 1995. Internal finance and investment: Evidence from the undistributed profits tax of 1936–1937. *Journal of Business* 68: 443–82.

Calomiris, Charles W., and Charles M. Kahn. 1996. The efficiency of self-regulated payments systems. *Journal of Money, Credit and Banking* 28 (November), Pt. 2: 766–97.

Calomiris, Charles W., and Joseph R. Mason. 1997. Contagion and bank failures during the Great Depression: The June 1932 Chicago banking panic. *American Economic Review* 87 (December): 863–83.

Calomiris, Charles W., and Carlos D. Ramirez. 1996. The role of financial relationships in the history of American corporate finance. *Journal of Applied Corporate Finance* 9 (Summer): 52–73.

Calomiris, Charles W., and Berry Wilson. 1998. Bank capital and portfolio management: The 1930s "capital crunch" and scramble to shed risk. Working Paper no. 6649, National Bureau of Economic Research.

Caprio, Gerard, Jr., Isaz Atiyas, and James A. Hanson, eds. 1994. *Financial Reform: Theory and Experience.* Cambridge: Cambridge University Press.

Carlin, Wendy. 1994. Privatization and de-industrialization in East Germany. In *Privatization in Central and Eastern Europe.* Ed. by Saul Estrin. London: Longman.

Carlin, Wendy, Steven Fries, Mark Schaffer, and Paul Seabright. 2000. Competition and enterprise performance in transition economies: Evidence from a cross-country survey. Working paper, University College London.

Cowen, Tyler, and Randall S. Kroszner. 1989. Scottish banking before 1845: A model for laissez-faire? *Journal of Money, Credit and Banking* 21 (May): 221–31.

———. 1994. *Explorations in the New Monetary Economics.* Cambridge: Cambridge University Press.

De la Cuadra, Sergio, and Salvador Valdés. 1992. Myths and facts about financial liberalization in Chile 1974–1983. In *If Texas were Chile.* Ed. by Philip L. Brock. San Francisco: Institute for Contemporary Studies: 11–101.

Demirgüç-Kunt, Asli, and Ross Levine. 1994. The financial system and public enterprise reform. Policy Research Working Paper #1319, World Bank.

Diamond, Douglas. 1984. Financial intermediation and delegated monitoring. *Review of Economic Studies* 51: 393–414.

Díaz-Alejandro, Carlos. 1985. Goodbye financial repression, hello financial crash. *Journal of Development Economics* 19: 3–24.

D'Souza, Juliet, and William L. Megginson. 1999. The financial and operating performance of privatized firms during the 1990s. *Journal of Finance* 54: 1397–1438.

Edwards, Sebastian, and Alejandra Cox Edwards. 1991. *Monetarism and Liberalization: The Chilean Experiment.* Chicago: University of Chicago Press.

Eichengreen, Barry. 1992. *Golden Fetters: The Gold Standard and the Great Depression 1919–1939.* New York: Oxford University Press.

———. 1996. *Globalizing Capital: A History of the International Monetary System.* Princeton, NJ: Princeton University Press.

Faruqi, Shakil, ed. 1993. *Financial Sector Reforms in Asian and Latin American Countries: Lessons of Comparative Experience.* Washington, DC: World Bank.

———. 1994. *Financial Sector Reforms, Economic Growth, and Stability: Experiences in Selected Asian and Latin American Countries.* Washington, DC: World Bank.

Fedorov, Boris. 1999. Open letter to Michel Camdessus, Managing Director of the International Monetary Fund, July 9.

Flannery, Mark. 1998. Using market information in prudential bank supervision. *Journal of Money, Credit and Banking* 30: 273–305.

Frydman, Roman, Cheryl W. Gray, Marek Hessel, and Andrzej Rapaczynski. Private ownership and corporate performance: Some lessons from transition economies. Policy Research Working Paper #1830, World Bank.

Gaddy, Clifford G., and Barry W. Ickes. 1998. Russia's virtual economy. *Foreign Affairs* 77 (September–October): 53–67.

Gillis, Malcolm, ed. 1989. *Tax Reform in Developing Countries.* Durham, NC: Duke University Press.

Gomulka, Stanislaw, and Piotr Jasinski. 1994. Privatization in Poland 1989–1993. In *Privatization in Central and Eastern Europe.* Ed. by Saul Estrin. London: Longman.

Gorton, Gary. 1996. Reputation formation in early bank note markets. *Journal of Political Economy* 104: 346–97.

Gorton, Gary, and Donald Mullineaux. 1987. The joint production of confidence: Endogenous regulation and nineteenth-century commercial-bank clearinghouses. *Journal of Money, Credit and Banking* 19 (November): 457–68.

Harvard Business School. 1994. Czechoslovakia's privatization: The fund phenomenon. Cambridge: Harvard Business School Publications, 9-292-124.

Hayek, Friederich A. von. 1944. *The Road to Serfdom.* Chicago: University of Chicago Press.

Hingorani, Archana, Kenneth Lehn, and Anil K. Makhija. 1997. Investor behavior in mass privatization: The case of the Czech voucher scheme. *Journal of Financial Economics* 44: 349–96.

Hubbard, R. Glenn, and Darius Palia. 1999. A reexamination of the conglomerate merger wave in the 1960s: An internal capital markets view. *Journal of Finance* 54: 1131–53.

Ibbotson Associates. 1997. *Stocks, Bonds, Bills and Inflation 1997 Yearbook.* Chicago: Ibbotson Associates.

Ito, Takatoshi, and Anne O. Krueger, eds. 1996. *Financial Deregulation and Integration in East Asia.* Chicago: University of Chicago Press.

Jarrell, Gregg A., James A. Brickley, and Jeffry M. Netter. 1988. The market for corporate control: The empirical evidence since 1980. *Journal of Economic Perspectives* 2: 49–68.

Jensen, Michael C. 1988. Takeovers: Their causes and consequences. *Journal of Economic Perspectives* 2: 21–48.

———. 1993. The modern industrial revolution, exit, and the failure of internal control systems. *Journal of Finance* 48, no. 3: 831–80.

Kaplan, Steven N., and Michael S. Weisbach. 1992. The success of acquisitions: Evidence from divestitures. *Journal of Finance* 47: 107–138.

Kikeri, Sunita, John Nellis, and Mary Shirley. 1992. *Privatization: The Lessons of Experience.* Washington, DC: World Bank.

Knight, Frank H. 1947. *Freedom and Reform: Essays in Economics and Social Philosophy.* Indianapolis, IN: Liberty Press.

Kroszner, Randall S. 1997. Free banking: The Scottish experience as a model for emerging economies. In *Reforming Financial Systems: Historical Implications for Policy.* Ed. by G. Caprio Jr. and D. Vittas. Cambridge: Cambridge University Press: 41–64.

Krueger, Anne. 1974. The political economy of the rent-seeking society. *American Economic Review* 64 :291-303.

Lang, L. H. P., and Rene E. Stulz. 1994. Tobin's q, corporate diversification and firm performance. *Journal of Political Economy* 102: 1248–80.

Lang, L. H. P., Rene E. Stulz, and R. A. Walking. 1989. Managerial performance, Tobin's q, and the gains from successful tender offers. *Journal of Financial Economics* 24: 137–54.

Loriaux, Michael, Meredith Woo-Cumings, Kent E. Calder, Sylvia Maxfield, and Sofia Perez. 1997. *Capital Ungoverned: Liberalizing Finance in Interventionist States.* Ithaca, NY: Cornell University Press.

McKinnon, Ronald I. 1993. *The Order of Economic Liberalization: Financial Control in the Transition to a Market Economy.* Baltimore: Johns Hopkins University Press.

McKinnon, Ronald I., and Huw Pill. 1996. Credible liberalizations and international capital flows: The "overborrowing syndrome." In *Financial Deregulation and Integration in East Asia.* Ed. by Takatoshi Ito and Anne O. Krueger. Chicago: University of Chicago Press: 7–50.

McKinsey Global Institute. 1998. *Productivity-Led Growth for Korea.* Washington, DC: McKinsey & Company.

Megginson, William L., Robert C. Nash, and Matthias van Randenborgh. 1994. The financial and operating performance of newly privatized firms: An international empirical analysis. *Journal of Finance* 49, no. 2: 403–52.

Mitchell, Mark, and Kenneth Lehn. 1990. Do bad bidders become good targets? *Journal of Political Economy* 98: 372–98.

Nam, Sang-Woo. 1996. The search for a new bank-business relationship in Korea. In *Financial Deregulation and Integration in East Asia.* Ed. by Takatoshi Ito and Anne O. Krueger. Chicago: University of Chicago Press: 277–306.

Nellis, John R. 1989. *Contract Plans and Public Enterprise Performance.* World Bank Discussion Paper no. 48. Washington, DC: World Bank.

Obstfeld, Maurice, and Alan M. Taylor. 1999. *Global Capital Markets: Integration, Crisis, and Growth.* Cambridge: Cambridge University Press.

Olson, Mancur. 1965. *The Logic of Collective Action.* Cambridge: Harvard University Press.

Park, Won-Am. 1996. Financial liberalization: The Korean experience. In *Financial Deregulation and Integration in East Asia.* Ed. by Takatoshi Ito and Anne O. Krueger. Chicago: University of Chicago Press: 247–73.

Patrick, Hugh, and Yung Chul Park. 1994. *The Financial Development of Japan, Korea and Taiwan.* New York: Oxford University Press.

Porter, Michael E., and Hirotaka Takeuchi. 1999. Fixing what really ails Japan. *Foreign Affairs,* May–June: 66–81.

Ramirez, Guillermo, and Francisco Rosende. 1992. Responding to collapse: Chilean banking legislation after 1983. In *If Texas Were Chile: A Primer on Banking Reform.* Ed. by Philip E. Brock. San Francisco: ICS Press: 193–216.

Rolnick, Arthur, and Warren Weber. 1983. New evidence on the free banking era. *American Economic Review* 73: 1080–91.

———. 1984. The causes of free bank failures. *Journal of Monetary Economics* 14: 267–91.

Sader, Frank. 1993. Privatization and foreign investment in the developing world, 1988–92. Washington, DC: Working Paper no. 1202, World Bank.

———. 1995. Privatizing public enterprises and foreign investment in developing countries, 1988–93. Washington, DC: Occasional Paper no. 5, World Bank Foreign Investment Advisory Services.

Schuman, Michael, and Jane L. Lee. 1999. Won world: Dismantling of Daewoo shows how radically Korea is changing. *The Wall Street Journal,* August 17: A1, A10.

Servaes, Henri. 1996. The value of diversification during the conglomerate merger wave. *Journal of Finance* 51: 1201–26.

Stigler, George J. 1988. *Chicago Studies in Political Economy.* Chicago: University of Chicago Press.

Summers, Lawrence. 1999. Summers questions development policy research. *World Bank Policy and Research Bulletin* 10 (April–June): 4.

Temin, Peter. 1989. *Lessons from the Great Depression.* Cambridge: MIT Press.

Treuhandanstalt. 1993. *Monatsinformationen der THA 06/93.* Berlin.

Valdes-Prieto, Salvador. 1994. Financial liberalization and the capital account: Chile 1974–1984. In *Financial Reform: Theory and Experience.* Cambridge: Cambridge University Press: 357–409.

Wallace, Charles P. 1996. The pirates of Prague. *Fortune,* December 23: 78–86.

White, Lawrence H. 1984. *Free Banking in Britain: Theory, Experience, and Debate, 1800–1845.* Cambridge: Cambridge University Press.

Williamson, John, and Molly Mahar. 1998. *A Survey of Financial Liberalization.* Princeton, NJ: Princeton University, International Finance Section, Essays in International Finance #211.

Wolf, Martin. 1999a. Caught in the transition trap. *Financial Times,* June 30.

———. 1999b. Price of forgiveness. *Financial Times,* August 11.

Wolosky, Lee. 2000. Putin's plutocrat problem. *Foreign Affairs,* March/April, :18–31.

World Bank. 1989. *World Development Report.* Washington, DC: World Bank.

———. 1993. *The East Asian Miracle: Economic Growth and Public Policy.* Washington, DC: Oxford University Press.

———. 1996. *World Development Report.* Washington, DC: World Bank.

———. 1999a. *Global Development Finance.* Washington, DC: World Bank.

———. 1999b. *World Development Report.* Washington, DC: World Bank.

Yergin, Daniel, and Joseph Stanislaw. 1998. *The Commanding Heights.* New York: Simon & Schuster.

Legal Foundations

Questions:
What does the "rule of law" actually mean?
Is corruption universal? Can countries make headway in battling it?
What does it mean for the law to protect property rights?
What sorts of legal protections and rights make equity holding attractive to outsiders?
What kinds of legal provisions do creditors rely upon?

Introduction

No set of institutions is of more fundamental importance to the effective operation of a financial system than the legal system that functions alongside it. Investors, whether private individuals, banks, or other institutions, normally have little direct control over the firms in which they invest. Those who invest through securities markets (i.e., public equity and bond investors) usually do not even have contact with the firms whose claims they purchase. Other stakeholders such as workers, suppliers, and customers have frequent direct contact with the firm; if they are not treated well, they can, unlike investors, withhold their cooperation until the treatment improves, even in the absence of legal remedies.

Investors place their funds at the disposal of firms and then hope for the best. Investors relinquish control of their funds to firms' managers, accepting in exchange pieces of paper that specify certain rights to the cash flows generated by the firms in which they have invested. Those rights are only meaningful and secure if the legal system clearly defines their meaning and ensures their enforcement. Thus, without an effective legal system, outside suppliers of funds will be unwilling to buy the debt and equity claims of firms, resulting in a shortage of funds to finance investment by firms, and slower economic growth.

Financial markets depend on the legal system in four general ways:

1. **Property rights.** The legal system defines property rights to assets, which entails not only establishing a system for registering interests in property and defining who can legally own property, but also clearly delineating the relative priority of

claims against firms' cash flows by workers, creditors, tax collectors, and shareholders. It is impossible to price a financial claim on a firm without a clear sense of how the holder of the claim stands to benefit from firm performance.

2. **Contracts.** The legal system specifies which kinds of contracts are permissible and the means for enforcing penalties for failure to comply with contractual promises.

3. **Companies.** The legal system establishes and enforces company law, specifying the range of rights and liabilities of corporations, their officers and directors, and how corporations can be governed.

4. **Finance.** Laws and regulations define and restrict specific aspects of the financial system itself: the legal means for purchasing and selling securities and for operating securities exchanges, the procedures required for chartering banks and the regulations to which banks are subject, the mechanisms for pledging collateral, and the process for resolving financial distress when firms become insolvent (i.e., bankruptcy law).

At a more fundamental level, all of these branches of the legal system presuppose an environment in which laws are adhered to and fairly enforced; that is, they presume a reliable legal structure where the *rule of law* is upheld. How could a financial market function if property rights associated with financial claims were not specified clearly in advance, and if agreements were not legally enforceable, at least to some degree? In such a world, raw power would prevail. Investors would need private enforcers and physical protection. The risk of investment would reflect not only the uncertain outcomes of the marketplace in which firms operate, but also the uncertain benefits and costs to using legal, or extralegal, means to lay claim to the revenues produced by firms. Some countries, such as Russia in the 1990s, show the consequence of such a pattern: weak and highly volatile public markets, built on the shaky foundation of an unreliable economic and legal system. In Russia, a powerful few control not only firms, but also the legal and political processes that govern transactions between firms and investors. Those oligarchs rely primarily on extralegal means (bribery, extortion, and physical force) to gain and maintain economic rights. *Ex ante* contracts and *ex post* outcomes often bear little or no relation to one another. Such countries lack a basic rule of law.

In many emerging financial markets, even where the rule of law prevails, important elements of law and regulation may be badly conceived, poorly enforced, or nonexistent. Indeed, emerging financial markets provide a kind of laboratory in which to examine the effects of different legal environments on the development of financial institutions. By studying EFMs we can better understand the legal foundations of financial markets in general.

Financial economists spend a lot of time puzzling over the shape of financial institutions and agreements. They ask why banks exist, why interest-bearing debt was invented, and why derivative contracts evolved. They also explore the legal factors that favor the development of deep and efficient financial markets and institutions, and that encourage the use of some forms of financial contracting over others. Numerous economists perceive connections between the legal framework and the structure and extent of the financial system. Pioneers of this area of research include Rafael La Porta, Florencia Lopez-de-Silanes, Andrei Shleifer, and Robert W. Vishny whose two related studies will be referred to repeatedly in this chapter. As these authors put it:

> Why do some countries have so much bigger capital markets than others? Why, for example, do the United States and the United Kingdom have enormous capital markets, while Germany and France have much smaller ones? Why do hundreds of companies go public in the United States every year, while only a few dozen went public in Italy over a

decade . . . ? Why do Germany and Japan have such extensive banking systems, even relative to other wealthy economies? If we look at a broader range of countries, why in fact do we see huge differences in the size, breadth and valuation of capital markets? Why, to take an extreme example, do Russian companies have virtually no access to external finance and sell at about one hundred times less than Western companies with comparable assets . . . ?[1]

These are the kinds of questions we shall consider in this chapter. We divide our discussion into two main parts: the general quality of the legal system and specific rules that govern financial claims and corporate control—that is, the laws most directly relevant to financial markets and institutions. Under the rubric of the general legal system, we discuss cross-country measures of the fair application of the rule of law, the efficiency of courts, and the extent of corruption (which undermines fair enforcement of laws and regulations). With respect to the laws governing finance and corporate control, we divide our discussion into laws that protect outside equity holders and those that protect creditors.

Figure 4.1 summarizes these various themes within a "legal pyramid." At the base of the pyramid are the fundamental requisites of an effective legal system: the fair enforcement of property rights and commercial contracts. Specific areas of law (shown above the base of the legal pyramid) can only be effective if the fundamental commercial rights and rule of law (the base of the pyramid) are enforced. The middle section of the pyramid refers to the rights all creditors and stockholders enjoy in their dealings with the firms whose claims they hold. The top section of the pyramid refers to the regulations that affect bundling of and trading in financial claims by intermediaries (banks, mutual funds, brokers, dealers, and securities exchanges). At the end of the chapter, we review the empirical literature that attempts to quantify the importance of these various legal underpinnings for financial development.

FIGURE 4.1

The financial system's legal pyramid

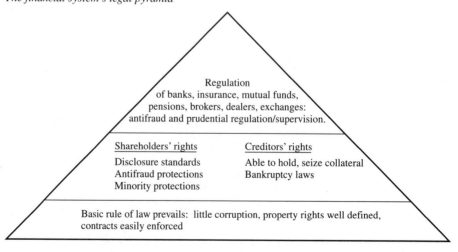

[1]La Porta, Lopez-de-Silanes, Shleifer, and Vishny (1997), p. 1131.

The Rule of Law

Where Does the Rule of Law Prevail?

We begin by asking to what extent the rule of law prevails in various countries. This requires us to specify more carefully what we mean by the *rule of law*. It surely means more than the presence of laws on the books. Every country has some kind of laws on the books, but not every country is said to live under the rule of law.

First of all, the rule of law means that all people are governed by the same rules, so that the rich and powerful may not exempt themselves from the rules that others are supposed to follow. The phrase is sometimes expressed as "the rule of law rather than the rule of men," meaning that powerful leaders cannot create special privileges for themselves. This is a function of enforcement, so that the judicial system is not afraid to punish people who break the rules based solely on their wealth and power. In particular, the rule of law means that government itself is constrained and cannot treat people arbitrarily.

This book has placed considerable weight on the general problem of restraining government. As emphasized in Chapter 2, that has been a central problem of political theory and practice in most countries of the world for the past several centuries. The institutions of representative democracy have proved to be the best institutional solution to this problem. They embody the rule of law as their most fundamental idea: They rely on a constitution, sometimes embodying basic human rights, which constrains even the sovereign government.

In the modern world, virtually every country has some sort of constitution. The communist countries all had constitutions, most of which purported to guarantee basic freedoms and human rights, even though the rulers had no intention of permitting such freedoms or rights in practice. The rule of law, then, requires more than a written document. The constitution needs to carry real authority, so that even rulers dare not flout its requirements. The constitution cannot be too detailed or it will require constant change; and a constitution should not be too easy to change lest it lose its authority. Rulers who find the constitution inconvenient should not be able to change it too easily or avoid its requirements.

Thus, part of the rule of law is about restraining the arbitrary exercise of power by government officials. But that is by no means the whole story. If government were reduced to zero, a state of anarchy would prevail, and that would be the opposite of the rule of law. Government needs to play a strong role in establishing and managing fair and uniform procedures for enforcing law and resolving disputes. For the rule of law to hold it must be feasible, and not too costly, for individuals to use the legal and political systems to define and protect a well-understood set of economic and political rights. That requires an effective legislative body and a complete judiciary system—courts, judges, public prosecutors, private lawyers, arbitrators, bailiffs, and so forth.

The United States may produce too many lawyers, but the great majority of developing countries produce too few. China, for example, had only 3,000 licensed lawyers during 1957–1980. This rose to more than 60,000 by 1995, and the government announced a target of 150,000 lawyers by 2000.[2] Furthermore, the lawyers need to be well trained and to share common legal theories and institutional traditions. There must be bar examinations and standards of professional conduct, with disciplinary

---

[2]World Bank (1995), p. 93.

procedures for violations. None of this is easy to produce on demand. It takes time and effort to reach consensus on basic legal and professional standards and to build the full range of public and private institutions needed to enforce them.

But the rewards for success are large. The payoff is increased confidence that the rules, contracts, and practices of business and personal life are fair and can be trusted. Strong legal institutions and traditions reduce arbitrariness and increase the confidence of people in the consistency and fairness of their system. The principle of fairness or justice states that like cases must be treated alike; or, to put it another way, people will only be treated differently insofar as differences among them are logically and appropriately connected to the differences in treatment. For example, if people are jailed, it must be for crimes that society believes deserve jail, and for which the guilty are predictably jailed.

Trust, a provocative book by Francis Fukuyama,[3] examined the importance of interpersonal trust in making societies and economies work. It distinguished between high-trust societies such as Germany and Japan, in which people have great confidence that known rules will be followed scrupulously, and low-trust societies such as Italy and China, where the extended family is the only social unit that inspires trust and any dealing beyond the family requires great care. In particular, low-trust societies are characterized by low confidence in government.

There seems to be a connection between rule of law, confidence in government, willingness to trust nonfamily, and economic well-being. Modern economies are so complex that they cannot function well without known, enforceable rules that encourage arm's-length dealings in the marketplace. In integrated market economies, dealing with strangers is inevitable, and that requires a commonly understood rule of law established by credible governments. Without that underpinning, individuals will eschew anonymous integrated markets in favor of narrow private associations based on extended families, which establish their own internal rules and means of enforcement.[4] Thus the gains from broad participation in financial markets depend on the establishment and enforcement of credible laws. The World Bank (1997) focused on government credibility as a factor that enables private parties to do business. Research showed that gross investment as a percentage of GDP, growth of per capita GDP, and the average profitability of projects financed by the World Bank all rose with government credibility measures.[5]

Various surveys have attempted to quantify the extent to which the rule of law prevails in various countries. One of these, the assessment (on average, for the years 1982–1995) of the law and order tradition in each country by International Country Risk, is reproduced in the Appendix to this chapter. Two related variables are survey-based indicators assessing the risk that the government will modify a commercial contract after it has been signed or that the government will expropriate a company or project. These measures are also displayed in the Appendix.

---

[3]Fukuyama (1995).

[4]Greif (1989) studied the development of international trade in the Mediterranean during the Middle Ages among the Maghribi, a sect of Jewish traders who lived throughout the region but retained close ties to each other and remained separate culturally from other groups. Greif showed that the Maghribi were able to form a private legal system of sorts, which set rules for international trade enforced by the threat of ostracism by other members of the group. This example shows that concern for reputation can substitute for formal legal penalties in enforcing contracts and resolving disputes in contracts, but only among members of a closed cultural group, and only if ejection from that group itself would be very costly to individual members. Thus, in general, the ability of private arrangements and reputational concerns to substitute for formal legal systems is quite limited.

[5]World Bank (1997), p. 37.

When one studies the details of the actual laws of various countries, it becomes clear that they fall into certain natural groups or families. LaPorta, et al. put it this way:

> Our starting point is the recognition that laws in different countries are typically not written from scratch, but rather transplanted—voluntarily or otherwise—from a few legal families or traditions (Watson 1974). In general, *commercial* laws come from two broad traditions: common law and civil law. Legal rules of civil law countries are derived from Roman Law and "are conceived as rules of conduct intimately linked to ideas of justice and morality" (David and Brierly 1985, p 22). These rules are usually developed by legal scholars, and incorporated into commercial codes. In contrast, common law is British in origin, and was "formed primarily by judges who tried to resolve specific disputes" (David and Brierly 1985, p 24). Furthermore, there are only three major civil law traditions or families that modern commercial laws originate from: French, German and Scandinavian. The French and German civil traditions, as well as the common law tradition, have spread around the world through a combination of conquest, imperialism, outright borrowing, and more subtle imitation.[6]

It turns out that these national origins have considerable explanatory power for the differences in laws governing finance and for the functioning of financial systems generally—a subject to which we will return at the end of this chapter. In the Appendix we reproduce a number of tables showing country-by-country measures, sorted by national origin, for a number of legal issues starting with the measures mentioned above for the rule of law itself. Note in Table 4.A1 that the countries with Scandinavian legal systems achieve perfect scores for rule of law, while those of German origin are next highest. The common law countries (English origin) come third and the French-based legal systems come last.

These average differences across countries according to legal origins, however, should not be viewed as definitive evidence of the inherent superiority or inferiority of any legal tradition. Before reaching any firm conclusions about the inherent qualities of different legal systems, one should control for other factors that might affect the quality of legal enforcement, including, for example, national wealth, education, the extent of political freedom, and political stability. Note, for example, that the sample of countries affiliated with the Scandinavian legal tradition is very limited—it includes only the four Scandinavian countries—and thus is very different in many ways from the sample of countries with British legal roots. Indeed, Table 4.A1 shows that most of the average difference between the English and Scandinavian groups is traceable to the low scores received by the poorest, most corrupt, or most politically troubled developing countries with English legal origins: Kenya, Pakistan, South Africa, Nigeria, Thailand, Zimbabwe, Sri Lanka, and India.

Incidence of Corruption

The rule of law is deeply undermined when judges, police, and government officials can be bribed to favor some person or company. Almost by definition, a bribed judge or policeman or other public official will do something unfair—that is, contrary to what an impartial agent would have done under whatever laws prevail. Corruption is about *illegitimate* payments and favors (i.e., payments and favors outside the rule of law). It is necessarily illegal and therefore is almost always concealed.

Corruption occurs to some extent in all countries and at all times. A pioneering study of the subject[7] traces corruption back to biblical times but predicts that it will someday be

---

[6]La Porta, Lopez-de-Silanes, Shleifer, and Vishny (1996), p. 4.
[7]Noonan (1984).

Trans-World Metals and the Rule of Law

Dear Vice President Gore and Prime Minister Chernomyrdin:

A situation is erupting in Russia that now directly threatens the principles and progress of the Gore-Chernomyrdin Commission in opening Russia to international trade and investment. The very existence of foreign investors who have helped turn around Russian industry and brought hundreds of thousands of jobs, benefits and profits to the people of Russia is at stake.

I should know. My name is David Reuben, I am an international businessman, and one of Russia's largest foreign investors and employers. My story should serve as a warning to foreigners who wish to invest in Russia and to leaders who believe Russia is committed to true open market partnerships.

My company, Trans-World Metals, was among the first to enter the Russian marketplace six years ago, when dozens of industries were being privatized. We went where no one else would go. We made long-term investments of hundreds of millions of dollars in plant, equipment, and operations to revitalize Russia's moribund aluminum and steel industries. Even though we accepted the huge investment risk, we did not seek out majority shareholder control, believing it to be more appropriately placed in the hands of Russian nationals.

The record will show that with our Russian national team, we turned these industries profitably around into well-run, productive enterprises. In the process, the market infrastructure was enormously strengthened; reliable, well-paying jobs with medical, housing, and day care benefits of tens of thousands of formerly unemployed Russian workers were created; and local community sponsorships in health care, education, culture, sports, and the arts were established. Every region we operated in has benefited. The free market system succeeded.

We took all the risks, encouraged by the Commission's effort, and have been fortunate enough to reap some of the rewards. Yet today we stand on the edge of seeing all our investments and achievements destroyed. Why is this happening today to Trans-World Metals and other major foreign investors in Russia?

The answer: a craven political power play, Russian-style. This power play is aimed at confiscating certain foreign investments and facilities *without* due process. The tools being used are a well-organized political effort and a media disinformation campaign at high levels. Led by officials within the Ministry of the Interior who want to "reprivatize" these companies and by renegade Russian banks who see an opportunity to profit without taking risk or making real investments, the attempt to steal our company places all private enterprise at risk.

Just last week, Mr. Kulikov, the Interior Minister, made a rare speech and demanded control of the aluminum industry for national security reasons, citing old and discredited allegations as his rationale. The Russian people are being told that curtailing foreign capitalists' independence and retaking control of the aluminum industry is essential for their survival. The reality is that if established foreign investors are forced out of the market, not only will the banks get a sizeable piece of the metals industry for free and the State will levy millions of new protectionist duties or taxes and impose nontariff barriers but the international market for investment in Russia will also totally dry up.

The takeover campaign is counterproductive to the long-term interests of the Russian people and completely foreign to the spirit of the Gore-Chernomyrdin Commission. If allowed to continue, this scheme will deliver a severe blow to U.S.-Russian trade relations and have immediate negative consequences on the world's second largest aluminum market and Trans-World's ability to stabilize it.

continued

concluded

If this Russian takeover agenda is allowed to succeed, it will close the book on what would have been substantial progress and a real East–West partnership envisioned during the past four years by the Gore-Chernomyrdin Commission.

How America and Russian officials respond to this strong-arm threat will have long-term consequences impacting both the political and economic stability of Russia, as well as that nation's economic relationship with capable long-term investors from around the world. The issue is now on the table; the choice is yours.

Source: Letter to the *New York Times*, March 2, 1997.

David Reuben was livid. Arriving at a shareholders' meeting of the Kazchrome metals company in Kazakhstan last October, the chairman of Britain's Trans-World Metals Ltd. was halted at the door by guards—even though Trans-World holds a 57 percent stake in Kazchrome. As Reuben stood fuming outside, other shareholders voted in a new management team hostile to Trans-World. That was only the start of Reuben's troubles. Within weeks, managers backed by the government had seized control of all of Trans-World's holdings in Kazakhstan.

Source: *Business Week*, International ed., February 16, 1998.

eliminated, just as slavery can be traced back to ancient times but is no longer a feature of modern life. Other observers are more pessimistic and believe that corruption is an inescapable fact of life that can never be eliminated and must simply be accepted.

Between these extreme positions lies a large middle ground. Countries vary considerably in the extent to which bribery is endemic. Some countries, such as Singapore and the Scandinavian countries, seem nearly free of corruption. Others, such as Zaire (now known as the Democratic Republic of the Congo) under its former president Mobutu Sese Seku, have been aptly described as *kleptocracy*, the rule of thieves, in which a significant portion of the GDP is siphoned off to the private accounts of a small oligarchic coterie of officials and their families. Countries can move back and forth on this spectrum. Hong Kong, for example, suffered significant corruption in the 1970s but made a determined and successful effort to control it in the 1980s.

Corruption can be viewed as a kind of tax collected by public officials and paid out to themselves. Most researchers agree that the cost of this tax is passed on to consumers through higher prices that are then distributed throughout the economy. Corruption is a kind of wasteful, inefficient spending, much like the excessive employment rolls at state-owned enterprises. However, the negative effects of corruption may be much more severe than those of ordinary state inefficiency.

Corruption is a predictable consequence of public–private interaction, and the more extensive that interaction, the greater the problem becomes.

> Corruption occurs at the interface of the public and private sectors. Whenever a public official has discretionary power over distribution to the private sector of a benefit or a cost, incentives for bribery are created. This corruption depends upon the magnitude of the benefits and costs under the control of public officials. Private individuals and firms are willing to pay to obtain these benefits and avoid the costs.[8]

---

[8]Rose-Ackerman (1997) in Elliott (1997), p. 31.

Bribery, Corruption Are Rampant in Eastern Europe, Survey Finds

A survey of more than 3,000 East European companies by the World Bank and European Bank for Reconstruction and Development paints a sobering picture of endemic corruption, favored lobbies and continuing state influence over business 10 years after the collapse of communism.

The survey, published as part of the EBRD's annual Transition Report, concludes bribery and corruption remain widespread due in part to the continued reliance of companies on direct ties to government officials. To assess the size of the so-called bribe tax, researchers from A.C. Nielsen polled entrepreneurs and businesspeople in 20 countries about their dealings with the state, and associated obstacles to doing business.

Among the findings: Companies in Eastern Europe pay bribes that amount from as little as 2 percent of annual revenue in Croatia to 8 percent in Georgia. "When added to what is already considered by firms to be an extremely high level of official taxation, the bribe tax imposes a severe burden on enterprises in the region," the survey said.

The average bribe tax in the former Soviet Union—5.7 percent of revenue—is almost twice the 3.3 percent of revenue in Central and Eastern Europe. Surprisingly, though, bribery remains widespread in countries considered transition success stories, the survey said. Companies saying firms in their country they bribe "frequently or more" totaled 31.3 percent in Hungary and 32.7 percent in Poland, compared with 29.2 percent in Russia. Private-sector companies pay a larger share of their revenue in bribes than do state companies.

Of concern to the EBRD is the impact on small companies, with about 40 percent of those surveyed saying they frequently pay bribes compared with 16 percent of large enterprises. EBRD President Horst Koehler said new firms are critical in driving economic growth in transition countries and must be protected and encouraged.

Source: *The Wall Street Journal*, November 9, 1999, p. A21.

The Cost of Doing Business under the Table

Country	Percent of Firms that Bribe Frequently	Average Bribe Tax as Percent of Annual Revenue	Country	Percent of Firms that Bribe Frequently	Average Bribe Tax as Percent of Annual Revenue
Azerbaijan	59.3%	6.6%	Russia	29.2%	4.1%
Romania	50.9	4.0	Kyrgyzstan	26.9	5.5
Uzbekistan	46.6	5.7	Czech Republic	26.3	4.5
Armenia	40.3	6.8	Bulgaria	23.9	3.5
Georgia	36.8	8.1	Kazakstan	23.7	4.7
Ukraine	35.3	6.5	Lithuania	23.2	4.2
Slovakia	34.6	3.7	Belarus	14.2	3.1
Moldova	33.3	6.1	Estonia	12.9	2.8
Poland	32.7	2.5	Slovenia	7.7	3.4
Hungary	31.3	3.5	Croatia	7.7	2.1

Source: Business Environment and Enterprise Performance Survey by the European Bank for Reconstruction and Development and the World Bank.

Consider India, for example, which during the period from independence through the 1980s created a massive "permit raj" in which every substantive element of economic activity had to be explicitly licensed by the government. If an Indian firm owned a fibers plant, for example, and wished to expand capacity by 20 percent, it would need a government license to do so. These licenses were not easy to obtain and were often denied. The opportunities for corruption created by this regime were overwhelming, and it should be no surprise that India developed one of the world's more serious corruption problems. It is said that Indian government jobs became so lucrative that a derivative market in government jobs developed in which individuals would pay large bribes to obtain a post.

Furthermore, once such a system is in place, many people come to possess vested interests in its perpetuation. Self-interested resistance to reform helps to explain why privatization has moved more slowly in India than in many other Asian countries. Privatization, and the related dismantling of the permit raj, was begun but not taken to completion by the Rao government in India during 1992–1994. Characteristically for India, Rao was brought down by accusations of corruption directed against him.

It is interesting to note that corruption is illegal and despised by a cynical population even in countries such as India where it is endemic. A similar case is Brazil, where Fernando Collor de Mello was elected president in December 1989 after a campaign promising to attack corruption that had reached epidemic proportions. Unfortunately, he enjoyed an excessively grand lifestyle and ultimately was perceived to be as corrupt as his predecessors. He was forced to resign in December 1992 under threat of imminent impeachment for corruption. He did not defend himself by arguing that bribery was just part of the Brazilian way of life; such a defense would have been ridiculous. Even where bribery is endemic, it is widely understood to be wrong.

Some businesspeople and academics from developed economies are tolerant of corruption in emerging market countries. That tolerance partly reflects the self-interested desire of business not to be placed at a competitive disadvantage. Some fear that strict rules against bribery, for example, when applied to international firms operating in developing economies, place them at a competitive disadvantage relative to domestic firms, for which bribery is often a profitable business investment. And others simply maintain that corruption is an unavoidable way of life in developing countries. The modern tendency to avoid criticism of other cultures also tends to discourage open criticism of other countries' political systems. But that attitude is patronizing in its own way. It implies that people in developing countries are inherently ("culturally") tolerant of theft in a way that citizens of developed economies would not be. The fact is that bribery is a form of theft and is both illegal and widely considered wrong in all countries.

We think that the more clear talk and action against corruption, the better. When government officials of any country engage in, or knowingly permit, behavior that is illegal and considered illegitimate, the government's credibility is damaged, the rule of law is undermined, and the mutual trust that makes economies function smoothly is reduced. Sooner or later, governments must clean up their acts if they want to promote sustainable economic growth.

For many decades economists have been interested in rent-seeking behavior, and have modeled and studied empirically the economic effects of bribery in various ways.[9] But the number of papers on the topic escalated significantly in the 1990s. In particular, the availability of survey-based indexes that estimate the degree of corruption in various countries has provided an important stimulus for empirical research.[10]

---

[9]Important contributions to this literature include Krueger (1974), Rose-Ackerman (1978), Klitgaard (1988), Shleifer and Vishny (1993), and Mauro (1995).

[10]Students interested in up-to-date studies of the issues and literature are referred to Elliott (1997).

Measures of corruption are based on surveys of businesspeople taken by a variety of organizations. Business International Corporation (BI), which was later purchased by the *Economist* Intelligence Unit, is one such source, though its results are generally made available only to subscribers. International Country Risk (ICR) publishes a monthly assessment of whether high government officials are likely to demand special payments and whether illegal payments are generally expected throughout lower levels of government. A publicly available source is Transparency International (TI), a German-based nonprofit organization loosely modeled on Amnesty International and dedicated to fighting corruption. TI's index is itself an average of a number of survey results conducted by various organizations at various points in time. The correlation of the BI and TI measures of corruption is 0.89,[11] which provides some confidence that a meaningful concept is being estimated. A country-by-country list of the average 1982–1995 ICR scores is given in Table 4.A1 in the Appendix, together with the TI scores for 1996 and 1997 in Table 4.A4. As with the rule of law scores, the Scandinavian systems score at the highest possible level, followed by the German-based systems, the English common law systems, and finally the French-based systems. Table 4.1 shows that the corruption scores are also highly correlated with the rule of law scores and similar measures.

Effects of Corruption

Recent research results show that corruption, as measured by indexes such as these, has a substantial impact on economic growth, and that the most important channel for this effect is through capital investment. One study implies that if a given country were to improve its corruption measure by two points on the scale of 0 to 10, then its investment/GDP ratio would rise by almost 4 percentage points and its annual per capita GDP growth would rise by almost half a percentage point.[12] Another study connects foreign direct investment (FDI) with the local rate of taxation and the local level of corruption. It shows that a worsening of a country's corruption index from that of Singapore to that of Mexico is equivalent to a 21 percentage point increase in the marginal tax rate. Furthermore, each 1 percent increase in the marginal tax rate (or corruption equivalent) reduces inward FDI by about 5 percent. These effects are statistically significant as well as large in absolute magnitude.[13]

The latter paper contains a number of other interesting insights. It tests the hypothesis that Asia is different—that is, that corruption is more accepted in Asia as a

TABLE 4.1   Correlations among Measures of Legal System Performance

	Judicial Efficiency	Rule of Law	Corruption	Risk of Expropriation	Risk of Repudiation
Judicial efficiency	1.00	0.65	0.80	0.66	0.64
Rule of law		1.00	0.85	0.91	0.88
Corruption			1.00	0.85	0.85
Risk of expropriation				1.00	0.96
Risk of repudiation					1.00

Source: Authors' calculations.

[11]Wei (1997), p. 9.
[12]Mauro (1995).
[13]Wei (1997), p. 11.

way of life and people there have found ways to avoid its harmful economic effects; no support for that theory is found. The author particularly examined China, since corruption is known to be a major problem there, yet China has benefited from a great deal of FDI. He found that China's FDI is more than fully explained by its GDP level, its wage rates, and other normal explanatory variables, and has actually been reduced from what it might otherwise have been by China's high level of corruption.[14]

Of particular interest in measuring the effects of corruption are two recent papers that employ microeconomic data at the firm level to see the effects of corruption on the financial valuation of firms and on firms' investment decisions. The first uses the methodology of *event study* to examine the responses of firms' stock prices on the Jakarta stock exchange to rumors about the health of President Suharto. Indonesia under Suharto was widely reputed to have suffered one of the most corrupt governments in the world. The study asks whether firms with close ties to Suharto (as measured by an index of political connectedness, which tracks the identities of major stockholders, firm managers, and board members, and their connections to Suharto) were valued higher than other firms, and whether those valuations changed at moments when Suharto's health was rumored to have declined.

The study finds that firms with close political ties to Suharto suffered large declines in their stock prices when his health was rumored to have deteriorated. Other firms without close connections to Suharto saw stock price appreciation on the same rumors. The study concludes that political connections accounted for roughly 16 percent of the market value of firms traded on the Jakarta stock exchange: "The large proportion of value that some firms derive from connections provides support for the perspective that political connections have distorted rates of return, and therefore the allocation of capital, in Indonesia."[15]

A second paper studies the effect of corruption on firm growth in Uganda.[16] It employs a unique data set based on surveys of individual Ugandan firms, which estimate the size of bribery payments those firms made in 1997. The study shows that the higher the bribery expenses, the lower the firm's sales growth. A one percentage point increase in the bribery rate (defined as bribe payments divided by sales) is associated with a reduction in firm growth of 3 percent. The size of that effect is much larger than the measured effect of increased taxation on firm growth—that is, bribery seems to be a uniquely damaging form of taxation.

To what extent can, and should, developed countries restrict bribery payments by multinational firms in emerging markets? In 1978 the United States, in the wake of the Watergate scandal and several revelations of bribery by major corporations, passed the Foreign Corrupt Practices Act (FCPA). While bribery of government officials is always illegal within the country of those officials, the FCPA made it a crime in the United States for a U.S. firm to bribe government officials in another country. This was initially ridiculed by other developed countries as another show of American puritanism and an example of the tendency by the United States to extend its laws to other jurisdictions. Many European countries at that time actually permitted tax deductions for foreign bribes.

By the 1990s, however, much had changed. A group of courageous magistrates in Milan successfully launched a broad attack on corruption, which ended with a significant part of Italy's political and business establishment humiliated and/or jailed. Two

---

[14]Ibid., pp. 18–24.
[15]Fisman (1999).
[16]Fisman and Svennson (1999).

former presidents of South Korea, Chun Doo Hwan and Roh Tae Woo, were led off to jail on corruption charges. Three Latin American presidents—Fernando Collor de Mello of Brazil, Carlos Andrés Pérez of Venezuela, and Abdalá Bucaram of Ecuador—were driven out of office for taking bribes, and a fourth, Ernesto Samper of Colombia, escaped impeachment but suffered a severe loss of political power. Important prime ministers such as Felipe González of Spain, Václav Klaus of the Czech Republic, P. V. Narasimha Rao of India, and Benazir Bhutto of Pakistan were defeated due to corruption allegations. And two of the most corrupt presidents in the world, Mobutu of Zaire and Suharto of Indonesia, both multibillionaires, were driven violently from office.

Institutional momentum against corruption has been building rapidly. Transparency International, organized in 1993, developed a network of over 60 national chapters by 1997. The Organization of American States approved a convention against corruption. The International Chamber of Commerce adopted strict anticorruption rules for member firms. The World Bank revised its guidelines and sharpened its rhetoric against corruption and the IMF began to do likewise. The United Nations approved an anticorruption declaration and the World Trade Organization initiated a study of the problem.[17]

But perhaps the most important such action was that of the Organization for Economic Cooperation and Development (OECD), whose members are the primary industrialized nations, and which in 1989 began an anticorruption initiative. By 1994 its members—the very developed countries that had been unimpressed with the FCPA—called on each other to take effective measures to deter, prevent, and combat the bribery of foreign government officials. In 1996 they recommended ending the tax deductibility of bribes wherever that embarrassment still persisted and in 1997 they recommended that all members adopt the approach of America's FCPA and make the paying of bribes to foreign officials illegal in their own countries. As of this writing, the tax deductibility of bribes has been ended in Denmark, Norway, Poland, and the Netherlands and appears near in France and Germany. National legislation implementing the OECD agreement on banning foreign bribes has yet to be implemented but is on the various legislative agendas with a seriousness it had not previously achieved.

It is no accident that this change of mood happened during and immediately after the great shift in global thinking away from state control of economies. Since, other things being equal, the amount of corruption is a function of the size of the public/private interface, major reductions of government economic control facilitated efforts to reduce corruption. The world's new suspicion of government economic activism translated into pressure for a more effective rule of law.

Nevertheless, despite the official rhetoric decrying corruption, governments of developed countries and multilateral institutions continue to reward corrupt governments in practice with high levels of economic aid. One recent study[18] asked four questions about the relationship between foreign aid and corruption: (1) Do corrupt governments receive more or less multilateral and bilateral aid, after controlling for other determinants of aid flows? (2) Do multilateral donors, such as international organizations, pay more attention to corruption than individual countries, and which countries are least willing to provide aid to corrupt governments? (3) Do private flows and official aid react differently to evidence of corruption? (4) Does foreign aid to corrupt governments increase or decrease corruption?

---

[17]Elliott (1997), p. 2.
[18]Alesina and Weder (1999).

The study found that greater corruption is rewarded by foreign aid—that is, the more corrupt the government, the more aid it is able to attract, after controlling for other influences. They found no statistically significant difference between bilateral and multilateral assistance to corrupt governments, although their regression estimates indicate that multilateral organizations are somewhat more likely to reward corruption. They further found that the United States, among individual donor countries, tends to reward corruption the most while the Scandinavian countries penalize corruption in their bilateral aid. They found that in contrast to foreign aid, private capital flows (depending on how they are measured) either punish corruption or do not react significantly to it. Finally, the authors found no evidence that foreign aid to corrupt governments reduces corruption; indeed, if anything their results support the opposite conclusion: Aid makes corrupt governments even more corrupt. These findings suggest a need to reform the facts of foreign aid to be more consistent with the rhetoric of donor countries, the World Bank, and others who, while formally opposing corruption, seem in practice to reward it.

More fundamentally, increased global competition is a force working against all forms of high domestic taxation—including income and sales taxes, and implicit taxes like excessive regulation and corruption. As countries vie for market share in the international arena, excessive taxation can hamper export growth. Once a country has chosen to open itself to international trade, the growing export sector becomes a powerful voice against taxes that limit its competitiveness, including corruption. One cause for optimism, then, is that as the export sectors of developing countries expand, the political constituency for fighting corruption also will continue to grow.

Shareholder Protection

We now turn to those specific elements of law that protect investors and thereby strengthen the capacity of financial markets to allocate capital to its highest uses. We begin with shareholder protection. Shareholders owning a majority of shares and their chosen managers ("insiders") generally have few problems of information and control. But those owning a minority of shares outside the controlling group ("outsiders") are highly vulnerable to expropriation of value by insiders. They need certain rights such as the right to information, the right to receive the same per share dividends as majority owners, the right to vote on important corporate matters including election of the board of directors, and the right to sue the company for damages.[19]

The word "tunneling" has been used to describe the transfer of resources out of a company and into the hands of its insiders to the detriment of its outsiders. This can include outright theft, which is everywhere illegal, but also many subtler forms such as selling or leasing corporate assets or services to insiders at bargain prices, preemption of corporate opportunities by insiders, excessive executive compensation, and making or guaranteeing loans to insiders. Many such practices can be attacked in common law jurisdictions as a violation of the insiders' fiduciary duty to minority shareholders, but there is no such concept in the civil law countries. Indeed, court decisions in continental European countries have typically refused to interfere in even blatant cases of tunneling.[20]

It is therefore important to examine in detail what legal protections outside shareholders need, and what recourse they have when their rights are violated.

---

[19]La Porta, Lopez-de-Silanes, Shleifer, and Vishny (2000).
[20]Johnson, Shleifer, and Lopez-de-Silanes (2000).

Wealth and Theft in Nigeria

Nigeria, Africa's most populous country, is rich. It has vast reserves of oil and minerals, fertile land, more than 30 universities and many talented, highly educated people. But after decades of gross mismanagement under military rulers, it is also marked by sweeping poverty and ethnic tensions . . .

"This is a land that lives in self-imposed poverty," said Samuel Aiyeyimi, 60, a former worker for the Lagos port authority. "If we had invested some of the billions of dollars from oil in agriculture, then we would have provided work and food for the millions of jobless. Instead, we import food and people are hungry."

Like many of Nigeria's problems, the failure to develop agriculture—which thrived until the 1960s and the move toward an oil-dominated economy—has an explanation that seems to reside in the pockets of the powerful.

Sugar cane, for example, would thrive here, but its cultivation would end the highly lucrative trade in smuggled sugar controlled by a coterie of powerful business people. Similarly, repair of the refineries would halt senior military officers' profits from transactions in imported fuel, and the refurbishing of petrochemical plants would shave the big profits on imported fertilizers.

Ismaila Gwarzo, security advisor to Gen. Sani Abacha, the dictator who died unexpectedly in June, was arrested recently in connection with the disappearance of $2.45 billion from the Nigerian central bank. The arrest appeared to indicate a determination to set new standards and recover some of the money stolen by the Abacha government.

With official theft on this scale it is little wonder that the state lacks the funds to fix the lights. Or to build schools. Or to pay a decent wage to customs officers, civil servants, police officers and young soldiers, who with monthly salaries in the $40 range have little incentive to work and overwhelming incentive to procure dash—the bribes that almost universally grease the wheels here.

The "What do you have for me today?" greeting at military roadblocks often comes close to armed robbery. At airports, the small baskets intended to ferry objects like keys or coins through the metal-detector machines are instead proffered by officials with a whispered "Dash me something!" In any event, the machines do not work.

By Western standards the sums involved are usually small, but by the same standards these practices are corrupt.

The system in Nigeria, from top to bottom, has become based on such behavior. Any right, even any notion, of redress or the rule of law has disappeared through years of dictatorship. In their place Nigeria has succumbed to an army-run system where any contract requires a payoff.

Source: *New York Times*, August 23, 1998, p. A1.

Accounting Standards and Disclosure

The first and most important legal protection for shareholders is to ensure their access to meaningful and accurate information. Anyone who is contemplating an equity investment, or who has made one and wants to decide whether to hold, sell, or initiate a shareholders' insurrection, needs quite a lot of detailed information. This includes reliable numbers. Shareholders own shares of a firm's profits, which are defined as the difference between revenues and costs. Costs include workers' wages, materials and depreciation, managers' salaries and bonuses, interest payments, and taxes. For outside shareholders to be treated fairly and to be able to measure and control the behavior of senior managers, they must be able to judge whether costs are real and warranted. Nothing matters more than knowing the facts.

Why is it that companies cannot be relied upon to disclose accurate information voluntarily, without any legal requirement? After all, companies that disclose useful information should attract more interest in their shares and obtain financing more easily. There are several answers. Very few people disclose negative information unless the law requires it. In many cases the long-run gains firms receive from being forthright about their distress are exceeded by the short-term costs of revealing weakness. Second, not all investors are sophisticated, and some legal protections (particularly against fraud) are necessary to protect unsophisticated investors. Third, the capital-raising advantage of unilateral disclosure may be more than offset by its competitive disadvantage. No company wants its competition to see the details of its business. Most firms face intense competition every day, while raising capital is an occasional event. So legal requirements can result in beneficial disclosure.

We reserve for the next chapter our detailed discussion of disclosure laws and related accounting rules.

Antifraud Protection

Closely related to information disclosure is the problem of outright fraud. This may take the form of nondisclosure of important information or the publication of information that is deliberately false or misleading. It can also take the form of people trading on their inside information about companies to the detriment of public stockholders. Finally, it can involve stock price manipulation of various sorts.

All of these actions are illegal in the United States and most are illegal in other industrialized countries. In EFMs, there may or may not be specific prohibitions of such behavior and written laws may or may not be effectively enforced. The definition of insider trading or stock price manipulation is not easy or obvious. Insider trading, in particular, has been the subject of controversy and close judicial judgment in developed countries. These nuances have not been addressed in most emerging markets. An Indian student cheerfully told us he had put himself through college on the profits from insider trading on the Bombay stock exchange.

The basic problem is simple and stark: Fraud and deception occur in all countries. Such behavior is not subtle and is illegal under general antifraud statutes almost everywhere. But the problem is not just to write laws prohibiting fraud; rather, it is to create a climate of strict enforcement in which such behavior is not tolerated. Nowhere is such enforcement more needed than in the transition countries of Central and Eastern Europe.[21]

During Russia's voucher privatization, a number of voucher funds arose, much as they had done elsewhere in the region, although as noted in Chapter 3 banks were the privatization intermediary of choice for aggressive entrepreneurs. The voucher funds caused no particular problems for the economy as a whole. Another class of new institutions, however, caused very serious problems. About 800 unlicensed investment

---

[21]The following accounts of the circumstances in Russia, Albania, and Romania are drawn from numerous newspaper sources. Some examples include Dascalu (1995), Bale (1996), Marsh (1996), and Popeski (1997).

companies began to take deposits from a gullible public, promising returns up to 3,000 percent a year.

The most notorious of these Russian companies was MMM, a creation of Sergei Mavrodi, who did not claim to have any business other than the taking of deposits. MMM was a classic "Ponzi" or *pyramid scheme*, paying high returns to early depositors out of the proceeds of later deposits. Pyramid schemes depend on rapid growth in deposits. Extraordinarily high returns received by initial depositors, paid out of new deposits, along with impossible-to-keep promises of high future returns, spur further deposit growth. Growth continues until the perpetrators decide to cash in on their scheme by halting payments and pocketing the firm's resources.

Mavrodi was a charismatic individual who like Viktor Kozeny in the Czech Republic (whose stock manipulations were discussed in Chapter 3) became by far the largest advertiser on local television. He set the price of his "shares" arbitrarily and paid out dividends arbitrarily. He claimed to have attracted more than 10 million shareholders when his scheme collapsed, as all pyramid schemes eventually must. His shareholders clearly wanted to believe that the astronomical returns he promised were feasible. Mavrodi was arrested in 1994 and spent time briefly in jail on charges of tax evasion. Some of his shareholders were so eager to believe in him that they went on a hunger strike to seek his release.

Mavrodi then discovered that he could obtain immunity from jail if he became a member of the Duma (parliament). He consequently campaigned for public office, promising to spend $10 million on his constituents, and won election without ever setting out a political program. Total losses by his shareholders are difficult to measure but are thought to be on the order of a billion dollars.

Although Mavrodi escaped justice, the Russian regulatory response was appropriate. A decree issued in November 1994 established a new regulatory agency to oversee the securities industry: the Federal Securities and Stock Market Commission, which consolidated and expanded the regulatory powers of several previous agencies. It initiated a licensing regime for securities professionals and prescribed universal registration rules for securities to be distributed, following basic practices in almost all developed countries.

The newly established commission estimated that over 2,000 Russian companies were engaging in illegal securities transactions with the sole purpose of defrauding the public, of which about 800 were unlicensed investment companies like MMM. In August 1995 the commission ordered all such investment companies to transform themselves into mutual funds or be shut down. Mutual funds were to comply with a presidential edict of July 1995 mandating a modern fund structure in which the fund, the management company, and the share depository all must be separate companies with defined responsibilities and reporting requirements. These requirements and others were codified in a major securities law passed by parliament and signed by President Yeltsin in April 1996.

Similar events happened in other postcommunist transitions. In Romania about 600 pyramid schemes have been counted, the largest of which was Caritas, founded by Ion Stoica, who was hailed as a god and a savior of poor Romanians until Caritas collapsed in early 1994. Caritas drew in about $1 billion of deposits from about 4 million Romanians, promising eightfold returns in three months. Even in a country where inflation crested at 300 percent a year in 1993, this was an unbelievable and unkeepable promise. Like Mavrodi, Stoica was politically astute and showered benevolence on his home city of Cluj. This did not save him, however, from going on trial and being convicted of fraud in 1995.

Even as the Stoica trial proceeded, however, another large pyramid scheme called Orion was being aggressively marketed in Romania. It escaped local securities fraud law by styling its certificates as "tickets." It was owned by three Russians, who disclaimed any connection with MMM despite the face of Sergei Mavrodi on their tickets. Authorities said they were powerless to stop Orion.

But the most outrageous pyramid scandal took place in Albania. Whereas MMM and Caritas burned out in 18 months, the Albanian pyramids remained in business for six years before collapsing in 1997. Economists estimated that $2 billion had been sunk into the schemes, representing a startling 80 percent of 1996 GDP.

Two of the funds, Xhaferri and Populli, were structured as charities and promised depositors that they could triple their money every three months over two years. Offices were set up all over Albania, and many farmers sold land and cattle in order to participate. The largest scheme was called Vefa Holdings, which used its deposits to purchase hotels, supermarkets, gas stations, and breweries. Vefa also promised heroic returns, but soon reduced its monthly interest payments to 3 percent. Meanwhile, it had become Albania's largest corporation by far.

The government did nothing to stop the spread of the pyramid schemes, and there seems little doubt that the largest ones contributed heavily to President Sali Berisha and other important politicians. In October 1996 the IMF urged the government to put an end to the fraud. It estimated that 7 Albanians out of 10 had put their savings into one or another of the schemes. When the collapse finally came, it was accompanied by bombings, riots, and the collapse of the Albanian government.

Although these stories from Eastern Europe are extreme and the victims unusually naive and vulnerable, fraud is a feature of securities markets in every country of the world. It would be nice to imagine that over time investors would learn to distinguish between the honest and the fraudulent, but experience suggests that even the most sophisticated markets contain millions of willing victims. It is simply too difficult for most untrained people to make the distinction, perhaps because we all want to believe in miracles of sudden wealth. A quick search of the Internet will reveal the continuing allure and professional presentation of obvious frauds. Antifraud enforcement against "bucket shops" (high-pressure marketers, usually by telephone, of dubious securities), get-rich-quick schemes, and Ponzi games requires a rigorous and constant enforcement effort in all countries. It is the minimum shareholder protection that good government should offer.

Antidirector Rights

Shareholders are the owners of the companies in which they invest; management, including the board of directors, is appointed by and should be responsible to the shareholders. Yet, when one views the reality of most firms in most countries, management and controlling shareholders (insiders) are vastly more powerful and in control than shareholders outside the controlling group (outsiders). This gives rise to a *principal–agent problem,* which we will discuss at length in Chapter 5.

The first need of shareholders is for accurate accounting and other information. But supposing that shareholders have at least some information and are unhappy with the direction their company is going, then they have two general paths of redress: *votes* and *takeovers*. Using votes means trying to elect a new board of directors to replace the offending one at an annual meeting. Using takeovers means selling shares to a new owner. Both require the protection of law to be effective. Following are the typical issues in the category of shareholder voting.

One-Share, One-Vote.   In a few countries (10 as listed in Table 4.A2 in the Appendix) the principle of one-share, one-vote is mandated by law. This ensures that economic value and voting power travel together. The great majority of countries, however, permit a variety of structures that separate voting power from economic interest. For example, there can be two classes of stock, identical economically but widely different in voting power. This will permit a family to go on controlling a company long after the majority of shares in economic interest have been sold to the public.

Defenders of flexible voting structures argue that each investor sees at the outset whether he or she has adequate voting rights; if not, the investor need not invest or may do so only at a significantly lower price. Indeed, the market value of the corporate vote can be measured by comparing the prices of such classes of stock where more than one exists.[22] It turns out that such price differences are small in Sweden and the United States, where other shareholder rights or incentives for good managerial behavior may make the voting right less valuable, but are large in Italy and Israel where other shareholder protections are less numerous.

Proxy and Other Voting Processes.   A basic question is whether shareholders must attend the meeting in person or may vote by proxy (i.e., by mail). If they must attend in person, the door is open to all sorts of obstacles, such as holding the meeting in remote locations or at inconvenient times. In Japan until recently, four out of five companies held their annual shareholder meetings in the same week and for many years mail proxies were not allowed, making it very difficult for shareholders to exercise voting control. Similarly, the law in many countries requires shareholders who wish to vote to deposit their shares physically several days before the meeting and leave them there until several days afterward, a cumbersome set of mechanics which clearly discourages shareholder voting.

If shareholder voting is to be meaningful, it must be possible for minority shareholders to put forward a competing slate of directors and solicit the support of other shareholders. Since management will naturally try to stifle any such initiative, legal protection for this exercise is important. In the United States, for example, a detailed set of proxy rules is mandated by the Securities and Exchange Commission (SEC), which not only require companies to allow voting by mailed proxies but also force companies to surrender the shareholder mailing list to dissidents. *Proxy contests*, as they are called, involve setting forth the positions of both sides in one or more proxy statements that are filed with the SEC and mailed to all shareholders. Actual proxy contests are relatively rare, but the threat of them can often force management to listen to dissident shareholders.

Cumulative Voting.   Since shareholders vote for an entire board and not just for one person, the question arises whether a shareholder can cast all of his or her votes for the same individual. If such cumulative voting is possible, then a relatively small coalition of shareholders can elect at least one representative to the board, an important element of shareholder control on management. The company law of some countries permits cumulative voting and in other countries does not.

Extraordinary Meetings.   Countries vary considerably in the percentage of equity interest needed to call an extraordinary meeting of shareholders, apart from the annual

---

[22]Zingales (1994 and 1995).

Poland versus the Czech Republic: An Experiment with Law and Regulation

In broad terms, Poland and Czechoslovakia share similar histories over the past 50 years. Both countries turned communist and became Soviet satellites shortly after World War II, and spent the next 40 years building socialism. In 1989 both countries spearheaded the anticommunist revolution. Both were fully industrialized, with an industrial structure largely shaped by decades of Soviet-style central planning. Both border on Western Europe and, in particular, Germany. By 1994, the two countries were virtually finished with basic reforms. The similarity between Poland and the Czech Republic should be contrasted with the difference between them and most other transition economies, particularly those in the former Soviet Union, which in the early 1990s were much further behind in their reform programs.

Despite the many crucial similarities, the two countries followed different approaches to reform in terms of the government's interest in regulatory intervention. This difference did not escape the early observers of the two countries, who viewed Polish economic policy as less laissez-faire than Czech economic policy. Václav Klaus, the Czech Finance Minister and later Prime Minister, was both tremendously articulate and unabashedly anti-government in his vision of reforms. Leszek Balcerowicz, the champion of Polish reforms, was a bit more cautious.

Poland's company law is somewhat more protective of minority shareholders than is the Czech law. The oppressed minority mechanisms have played some role in stopping investor expropriation in both countries, largely because a company cannot expand its capital while a complaint from minority shareholders is being litigated. The ability of a significant minority shareholder in Poland to elect a director has apparently also proved useful to some large domestic and foreign investors, who have put their candidates on the boards. At the same time, the exercise of some of these minority rights, such as the oppressed minority mechanism, relies on the judicial system, which is not particularly effective in either country. Although company laws have played some role in protecting minorities from expropriation, in Poland they have done so largely in conjunction with an elaborate system of securities regulation.

There are significant differences in the institutions of securities regulation in the two countries. In particular, similar to the U.S. model established in the 1930s, much of securities regulation in Poland takes place through tight administrative regulation of intermediaries operating in the securities markets. The Czech regulation of such intermediaries is less stringent. The Polish regulation of the issuers themselves is more extensive as well. In the area of securities regulation, the two countries appear to be very far apart.

Stable prices, rapid privatization, and openness to the West combined to generate extremely favorable initial assessments of the Czech economic reforms. By 1996, however, there was mounting evidence of systematic expropriation of minority shareholders by IPFs [investment funds] and company insiders colluding with them. In a typical scheme, the managers of an IPF holding a large stake in a privatized company would agree with the managers of this company to create a new (possibly offshore) entity, which they would jointly control. The IPF might then sell its shares in the company to this entity at below market price, thereby expropriating the shareholders of the IPF. The company could also sell some of its assets or its output to the new entity, again at below fair value, thereby expropriating its own minority shareholders. These arrangements between corporate managers and their large shareholders (i.e., IPFs) enriched them at the expense of minority investors in both the firms and the IPFs.

continued

continued

The laxity of the securities law accommodated tunneling. First, since transactions did not need to take place on an exchange, large blocks of shares could change hands off the exchange at less than the prevailing market price. Even on an exchange, there was no guarantee of price uniformity. Moreover, brokers and brokerage firms had no restrictions on facilitating such transactions, nor did the custodian banks have any regulatory duty to stop them. Second, since there was no requirement of ownership disclosure, the acquirers of large blocks could remain secret. Third, without a mandatory bid, these acquirers had no obligation to buy out the remaining minority shareholders. Fourth, the IPFs appear to have been under no restrictions in pursuing such transactions, since their management did not owe any clearly regulated duty to their investors let alone to the minority shareholders of the companies they tunneled. Fifth, there was no reason to disclose any financial transactions between the new owner of shares and the company, since such transactions were generally allowed and did not need to be disclosed except perhaps in the annual report several months later. Finally, the minority shareholders had virtually no legal recourse in stopping such expropriation except in a very few cases when the oppressed minority mechanism came into play, and even substantial minority shareholders could not elect their own directors to represent their interests.

During the mid-1990s, the heyday of tunneling in the Czech Republic, the regulators did very little to stop it. Part of the problem may have been a lack of interest. But equally important, most tunneling was probably legal under existing Czech law. In March 1996 the *Central European Economic Review*, a publication of *The Wall Street Journal*, surveyed assorted brokerages and fund managers on corporate governance in four transition economies. The survey asked respondents to comment on the disclosure of large shareholdings, transparency of markets, quality of reporting, protection of small shareholders, and insider trading. The Polish market came out as the best of the four, followed by the Hungarian market. The Czech market came third, ahead of the Russian market, which received the lowest score on every dimension. The Polish market outscored the Czech market on every dimension, with large spreads on the disclosure of ownership and transparency. Consistent with this general assessment, the International Federation of Stock Exchanges admitted the Warsaw Exchange as a full member as early as 1994 on the grounds that the regulation of securities markets met its standards. As of this writing, the Prague Stock Exchange still had not been admitted even as an associate member.

An examination of financial scandals in Poland suggests that they are typically less egregious than those in the Czech Republic, and often invite an aggressive regulatory response. Perhaps the best known Polish scandal involves a failure of a large conglomerate, Elektrim, to reveal in a prospectus an existing agreement to sell some shares in a valuable subsidiary to a third party at below market price (allegedly as a payment for services). When the existence of the agreement came to light, Elektrim's shareholders complained, and the Securities Commission quickly referred the case, which is still underway, to a public prosecutor. The top manager of Elektrim was forced to step down. The Elektrim case illustrates the crucial interaction between the corporate and securities law in the enforcement of investor rights. The failure by the company to disclose possibly material information in a prospectus was the source of the Commission's investigation under the securities law. This failed disclosure also brought about an effort by the outside shareholders to change the board of directors using the commercial code, which ultimately brought down the CEO. This pattern of interplay between securities law and company law appears in other countries as well: The securities law forces disclosure, which in turn invites shareholder activism using the provisions of company law.

The Polish regulator has also been aggressive in its administrative oversight of the intermediaries. In 1994, Bank Slaski, one of the largest Polish banks, which owned the largest broker at the time, was privatized. In response to the evidence that the brokerage

concluded

arm of the bank favored the insiders in allocating shares in privatization, the regulators took away its brokerage license. This was done even against opposition from the Ministry of Finance.

The available evidence shows that the Polish regulators relied on the actual legal rules to protect investors; it was not just their ideology that made a difference. They relied on specific rules to promote disclosure and investor rights that did not exist in the Czech law. A comparison with Russia may illustrate this issue as well. In the mid-1990s, Russia had a very aggressive securities regulator, who made daring efforts to protect minority shareholders. Yet the Russian regulator had few enforcement powers of his own, and the courts refused to back him up. As a consequence, investor protection in Russia was extremely weak—and the tunneling overwhelming—despite the best intentions of the regulator.

The vast majority of Czech companies barely trade, and most of the firms trading on the free market were delisted by the late 1990s. The number of firms on the main market, having risen to 62 in 1995, fell all the way down to 10 by 1998, with most of the firms being transferred to the less liquid secondary market. By 1998, most listed Czech firms emerging from privatization had been either delisted or transferred to an exchange with only limited liquidity. In contrast, despite a much lower initial level, the number of listed Polish firms has risen steadily over time, and hardly any firms have been transferred to the parallel market. If the number of actively traded securities is a measure of success, then the Polish market has significantly outperformed the Czech market over this period.

Between 1991 and 1998, no Czech company sold equity for cash as part of initial privatization, whereas 50 Polish companies did. No private Czech company has done an initial public offering (IPO) on the Prague exchange. By comparison, 136 nonprivatizing companies have gone public on the Warsaw exchange. No new or already listed Czech company has raised equity funds on the exchange through a public offering. In contrast, the Polish data show rapidly growing equity financing by both new and already listed firms. In 1998, over US$1 billion of new equity funds was raised on the Warsaw exchange.

By 1996 and especially 1997, the Czech stock market had become severely criticized by domestic and foreign investors, as well as the Czech legislature. The initial government response to this criticism was hostile, yet slowly the government introduced a number of measures protecting minority shareholders.

Source: Abridged from Johnson and Shleifer (1999). Ellipses are too numerous to be shown explicitly.

---

meeting. This percentage can be as low as 1 percent in certain states in the United States or as high as 33 percent in Mexico. The lower this percentage, the more likely it is that minority shareholders can force management to hear their point of view.

Redress of Grievances. Legal systems may give alternative forms of redress to minority shareholders who cannot otherwise make their viewpoints heard. In the United States the threat of a class action lawsuit, a special form of protected litigation in which a few shareholders can force the management to pay damages to all shareholders who have been somehow abused, is vivid and effective, and it goes a long way toward keeping managements responsive to shareholder interests. In other countries, shareholders who disagree with management decisions on certain fundamental issues such as mergers can force the company to buy back their stock.

These shareholder protections were tabulated country-by-country by LaPorta, Lopez-de-Silanes, Shleifer, and Vishny, whose data are reproduced in the Appendix together with a combined score for *antidirector rights.* Finally, the authors also tabulated another shareholder protection, the mandatory payout of a certain fraction of earnings as dividends. They pointed out that this device exists only in French-based jurisdictions, which offer the fewest protections of shareholder votes. It is negatively correlated with the others, and seems to serve as a "consolation prize" in these jurisdictions.

It is clear from Table 4.A2 in the Appendix to this chapter that the common law (generally the English-speaking) countries have the highest scores for shareholder protection. It is no accident that they also have some of the largest and most vigorous stock markets, as the empirical findings at the end of this chapter will attest. One recent study of equity markets in Brazil predicted that weak protection of minority shareholders' rights would cause the late 1990s slowdown in equity offerings to continue, and that the Brazilian equity market would remain primarily one for trading in utilities shares. Brazilian disclosure laws are weak, and if a controlling shareholder is able to amass only 17 percent of a firm's equity he is effectively insulated against the actions of dissident shareholders.[23]

Creditor Protection

The problem of creditor protection is quite different in flavor from that of shareholder protection because creditors have a firm contractual commitment to certain specific cash flows. The primary problem is to specify what happens when debts are not repaid or debt covenants are not kept. This can be looked at in two ways, one dealing with specific debts and the other with the failure of entire companies.

Property Rights and Collateral

Specific debts can be secured by specific *collateral*—that is, a company can pledge certain defined assets to secure specific loans. Such assets might be receivables, inventory, vehicles, machinery, or real estate. The implication is that if the debt is not promptly paid, the lender can step in and repossess the collateral, selling it to recover whatever value it brings in full or partial settlement of the debt. This does not necessarily cause the failure of the entire company.

Secured lending is very common. In most developed countries, well over half of all bank loans are collateralized; this is by number of loans, not dollar volume, as the larger loans tend to be made to large companies that do not need to use security to borrow. Collateral makes credit available to an entire class of companies that otherwise might not be able to borrow, especially where there is poor information about the firm's true credit risk. If one does not entirely trust the financial statements of the borrower and the total picture of the firm is cloudy, one can nevertheless lend if the collateral is good. When entire firms fail, secured lenders are entitled to and typically get a higher percentage recovery of their investment than unsecured lenders. The simplicity and clarity of collateral helps to solve problems of imperfect or nonexistent bankruptcy processes as well as problems of imperfect or nonexistent financial information.

In EFMs, secured lending is even more important. Not only does it protect lenders from the uncertainties of credit risk in an environment of poor information, but also it allows lenders to avoid the risks and costs otherwise associated with enforcing the repayment of debt. Collateral helps to avoid those costs by giving creditors a means to

---

[23]Rocca, de Carvalho, and da Silva (1998).

protect themselves without depending on court adjudication of debt repayment. That protection also strengthens the hands of banks in disputes with borrowers, helping to lower the probability of default. Indeed, bankers and bankruptcy lawyers in the United States often argue that the main benefit of secured debt is its strategic value to the lender, owing to its special claim on valuable firm assets and to the greater voting rights secured creditors enjoy in bankruptcy proceedings.[24]

However, secured lending cannot play these roles unless the legal framework supports it. This is more complex than it seems. To begin with, property rights in collateral must be clearly defined. One of the problems of state-owned enterprises is that no clear line of demarcation separates corporate property from state property, and in communist societies any private ownership of business property is typically limited to leaseholds.

Even when full private property is defined and protected by law, there may be many restrictions on its transfer. The concept of a lien or security interest may be ill defined or not defined. Even when liens are defined, there may be no simple way to determine whether prior liens exist; without this the same property might be pledged to many different lenders without their knowledge. Developed economies have public registries of security interests, but these are often missing in EFMs, and where they do exist, registries are sometimes not centralized to ensure that liens filed in all regions are easily observable.

A World Bank report on transition economies notes the following issues in particular countries:

> Bulgaria and Estonia forbid the pledging of goods not currently held by the borrower, making it difficult to finance crops and livestock. In Hungary and Poland only banks may formally lend for property that remains in the borrower's hands; this limits development of nonbank lending. Vietnam forbids the sale of pledge items, making it difficult to finance inventory . . . In Bulgaria the priority of a security interest is determined by the date it is agreed to; without a central registry, this can only be uncovered by searching through hundreds of scattered notarial records. The pledge registry in Poland is open only to banks. In China and Lithuania a security interest in movable property can only be registered if the underlying asset requires registration—fine for cars, trucks, ships and airplanes but useless for tractors, drill presses and grain silos.[25]

An article in *Latin Finance* attributes the severe scarcity of credit in Mexico to the legal obstacles creditors face in trying to obtain secured interests.

> In Mexico, the legal devices used in secured lending are the remains of Roman law mechanisms not well suited to modern-day financing. Consequently, creditors do not enjoy the essential confidence provided by a functioning secured finance system. This deficiency makes credit in Mexico both expensive and difficult to obtain . . .
>
> For instance, the current framework requires that enforcement follow legal procedures developed in the 19th century for the enforcement of real estate mortgages, a procedure that often takes between three and five years. This framework fails to consider the opposing nature of real and movable property. Unlike real property, movable property may be transferred from one location to another, depreciates rapidly, may be perishable, and, when consisting of instruments or documents, may have a set maturity date.[26]

The absence of strong institutions for arm's-length lending in Mexico and elsewhere may not be an accident. The high cost of arm's-length lending favors growth by insider-controlled bank-industry conglomerates, which wield considerable political

---

[24]See Rosenberg (1984).

[25]World Bank (1995), p 89.

[26]Wilson (1999).

power. But pressures for reform in Mexico in the late 1990s, reflecting the political unpopularity of the bailout of the Mexican banks in 1995, and the scarcity of credit that plagues the Mexican economy have begun to produce changes in the legal institutions that govern credit markets.

Mexican authorities now seem to be instituting reforms that may facilitate secured lending. Reforms include a new bankruptcy code and new legal mechanisms for gaining title to collateralized assets and a new registry to accommodate security filings.[27]

Even when the laws appear to be well written, there is always the question of enforcement in EFMs. A common problem is mechanical obstacles to enforcement and collection. After all, repossession of inventories is likely to disrupt production and sales, and notice of repossession of receivables must be made to the firm's customers to the substantial embarrassment of the firm, so systems biased toward debtors may create scores of obstacles to enforcement of collateral interests. In some countries, receivables can only be repossessed with the customers' consent. In many EFMs the registration of liens is so obscure and local that a bank requires a small army of collectors negotiating with local officials and courts, with all the attendant problems of corruption.

The enforcement problems of real estate security interests (mortgages) are more formidable than those surrounding personal property. The enforcement problems begin with the basic question of who owns the land. Throughout most of Latin America and in much of East Asia, land ownership is ambiguous at best. Earlier regimes of large plantations or estates have been broken up, often without consent or documentation, and new users have moved in. Such new users typically contribute vigorously to national output, but do so without having clear title to the land they are using. This is equally true in urban and rural settings.

One can fly over large areas of rural Latin America, for example, and see land broken into farms, with clear lines of demarcation between them. Everyone on the ground knows whose farm is whose, but in many cases none of the users has clean title and there may be no mechanism for users to obtain one. Without title, land is poor security for loans; without security, credit is often not available.

Furthermore, the repossession of real estate is a far more emotional issue than the repossession of personal property—and often requires more complex court procedures—because land is such a permanent asset, literally underpinning the society and defining personal and national identity. Few EFMs are willing to allow land to be freely transferred among financial institutions, particularly foreign ones, so that collecting on mortgages may become costly, time-consuming, or in the end impossible.

Despite these limits to mortgage lending and despite the much greater lack of liquidity in real estate compared with personal property, which makes it so much harder for lenders to repossess and sell, mortgage lending has been an important source of finance for consumers and businesses alike in some EFMs. The permanence of land and buildings, and their representation of more than half the national wealth in most EFMs, give them worldwide appeal as security for loans. And in some countries—notably Argentina in the 1990s—the relatively favorable set of legal institutions available for mortgage foreclosure have encouraged the development of mortgages as an important means of personal and corporate finance.

In Argentina, title to land is relatively reliable and mortgage collateral is viewed as desirable, compared to collateral interests in other assets. In large part, that reflects differences in the laws governing the enforcement of contracts in various

---

[27]For more detail on these reforms see the box in Chapter 9.

debt instruments. Those differences translate into long delays in the adjudication of nonmortgage debts, and interest rates that are sometimes 20 percent higher for working capital loans than for mortgages. Mortgage debt in Argentina increased from $5.2 billion in 1994 to $9.4 billion in 1998. On a per capita basis, mortgage debt grew over 90 percent, from $137 to $264. The popularity of mortgages in Argentina has also spurred the development of a new mortgage-backed securities market—a means for Argentina to access international capital markets at relatively low interest rates.[28]

Bankruptcy

The financial failure of individuals and entire firms is a political and social issue with considerable history. In earlier centuries debtors were often thrown into prison for nonpayment of debt. Limited liability companies were invented so that entrepreneurs could avoid this risk: Corporations are separate legal persons, and in general the shareholders of a corporation cannot be pursued for debts of the corporation itself. The success of this format, and the decline of debtors prisons, suggest that society has moved away from maximum harshness toward debtors and toward solutions that stimulate entrepreneurship by removing from it the draconian personal risks of unpayable debt.

In the modern world, debt defaults can have two possible outcomes: voluntary renegotiation or bankruptcy. Bankruptcy is a legal procedure for sorting out companies that cannot pay their debts or that cannot renegotiate their debts to mutual satisfaction. A good bankruptcy procedure leads to the *liquidation* of nonviable firms—that is, those whose continued operation would destroy economic value—but also to the *restructuring* of viable firms—those that can create value, but cannot pay the full magnitude of the financial claims upon them.

In a liquidation the firm's assets are sold, the liabilities discharged as far as possible, and the enterprise is terminated. In a restructuring (whether voluntary or court-imposed) the capital suppliers recognize losses and typically exchange their claims for new ones of a reduced amount. Liquidation is appropriate when the enterprise has negative cash flow at the operating level and is unlikely ever to be a successful business. Reorganization is appropriate when the company can generate substantial positive cash flow but not enough to satisfy all existing claims.

If the bankruptcy procedure tilts too far toward debtors, it will discourage lenders and lower economic efficiency by enabling the unscrupulous or incompetent to borrow other peoples' money, lose it, and escape serious consequences. This may also lead to higher interest rates. But if bankruptcy tilts too far toward creditors, it may lead to the inefficient liquidation of viable firms that could add to economic welfare by continuing to operate. So a balance needs to be struck between protecting creditors' rights and protecting viable companies.

Most legal systems provide for both liquidation and restructuring. In the United States, for example, Chapter 7 is the liquidation procedure and Chapter 11 the restructuring procedure. But countries vary considerably in the balance they strike between debtors and creditors. Many developing countries have no effective procedures for adjudicating bankruptcy, whatever the law says, which biases the system entirely toward debtors. In these cases creditors' rights are not protected and debtors can escape their contractual obligations.

---

[28]Swafford (1999), pp. 30–32.

United States.   The United States bankruptcy system is also biased quite strongly in favor of debtors, more so than that of any other industrialized country. Corporate managers in the United States can put their companies into Chapter 11 without the consent of the lenders. This stays all creditor claims and protects the company from further efforts by lenders to force repayment. Nevertheless, U.S. law does recognize the special rights of secured creditors. Holders of secured credits are often able to seize collateral during bankruptcy, or at least to ensure that the value of their collateral is not reduced during adjudication.

Managers of firms filing for Chapter 11 have a 120-day exclusivity period in which they, but no one else, may put forward a plan of reorganization. If they do so, no one may submit a competing plan during a 180-day period in which the managers solicit support for their plan. The bankruptcy court may extend both periods. The managers remain in complete control of the firm during the bankruptcy proceeding. All of this is weighted very heavily in favor of the managers.

While the U.S. system has a debtor bias, there is little evidence that it fails to shut down most value-destroying enterprises. One clinical study did document a 50 percent value loss in Eastern Airlines during its Chapter 11 procedure, attributed by the authors to "overly optimistic managers and misguided judges," but this appears to be an extreme case.[29] Still, since the urgent problem of developing countries is to cut off value destruction, a debtor-biased system like that of the United States is a poor role model.

Europe.   Some of the major European countries—especially Germany, Great Britain, and Sweden—offer better models for adoption by EFMs. These codes have in common a strong procreditor bias, particularly when the creditor is secured.[30] Adopting such codes could facilitate developing countries wanting to strengthen their financial institutions, although each of the European systems also has shortcomings. In particular, some observers argue that their renegotiation procedures are sometimes inadequate to save viable companies, but that conclusion is not universally endorsed. Recent research on the Swedish system, in which liquidation of assets through auction is frequent, suggests that viable bankrupt companies are often preserved even when firms are liquidated because efficient managers are able to obtain financial backing for purchasing those firms at auction.[31] In any case, the direction of change in Europe seems to be toward reducing the ease with which creditors can force premature liquidations.

France.   The French bankruptcy law is among the worst in Europe, and clearly not a model to be imitated by developing countries. The French law, which was amended in 1994, specifies that the objectives of the law, in order of priority, are to maintain firms in operation, preserve employment, and only third to enforce credit contracts. Thus, on its face, French law appears to tilt strongly toward debtors. Either debtors or creditors can initiate French bankruptcy. It provides two basic procedures: reorganization (*redressement*) and liquidation. Control is given to a judge from the Tribunal de Commerce for an observation period. The judge decides whether the firm should be liquidated or reorganized. In practice, however, about three-fourths of all filings are moved immediately to liquidation, while about half the balance are eventually moved to liquidation.

---

[29]Weiss and Wruck (1998), p. 55.
[30]See Kaiser (1996) and Franks, Nyborg, and Torous (1996).
[31]See Stromberg (1998).

If the firm is not moved to liquidation, the court appoints an administrator to supervise management. The court also appoints a court officer to represent and act on behalf of the creditors, after which the creditors lose the right to speak directly to the court. Before the end of the observation period (usually eight months) the court must either accept a reorganization plan proposed by the administrator or move the case to liquidation. The French system reflects a strong belief in the wisdom of the state as opposed to the U.S. faith in negotiated settlements: In France neither managers nor creditors have much voice in any reorganization plan.

A common outcome is not a true reorganization but a sale of the firm, subject to maintenance of all employment and all secured debt. But this, of course, prevents exactly the kind of downsizing and debt reduction that is the central feature of most successful reorganizations. As a result, French reorganizations often fail. One study of the 1986–1991 period found that about half of all reorganized firms soon returned to the court for a second reorganization, and that the great majority of these (88 percent) were then liquidated.[32]

In summary, the outcome of the French system, despite its explicit goal of preserving enterprise, is to liquidate far more companies than other systems, almost surely including some that could have been salvaged to the ultimate benefit of managers, employees, and capital suppliers. This paradoxical outcome results primarily from excessive reliance on centrally mandated solutions without sufficient input from the parties at interest.

Germany. The German system also features two separate court processes, reorganization (*Vergleichsordnung*) and liquidation (*Konkursordnung*). But a critical feature of the German system is that only unsecured creditors are parties to a reorganization. Secured creditors are completely outside the process, and may continue pressing their claims without interruption, making it extremely difficult for the firm to continue operating. Furthermore, a debtor that files for reorganization must submit a complete plan of reorganization at the time of filing. This requirement is almost impossible to fulfill in a situation of any real complexity. Because of these two problems, reorganizations are rarely completed in Germany and most distressed firms are liquidated.

Under liquidation, control of the firm is taken by a court-appointed administrator whose mandate is to sell the firm for cash, though the administrator has considerable freedom to do this slowly, subject to the predations of the secured creditors. This is much the most common procedure in Germany.

One benefit of the German system is exceptionally strong protection for secured creditors. It should come as no surprise that secured lending is the most important source of external capital in Germany's bank-centered system. Also, the unlikelihood of successful reorganization under court protection creates strong incentives for distressed companies to reach negotiated reorganizations with their creditors outside the court system. New legislation was passed in Germany in 1994 that took effect in 1999. It is designed to limit the powers of secured creditors to repossess assets and give other creditors more voice in the proceedings. Under the new law, secured creditors are stayed for three months and the powers of the administrator in liquidation are somewhat reduced.

United Kingdom. The system in the United Kingdom relies mainly on two creditor-initiated procedures: liquidation and receivership. Receivership is used when a creditor

---

[32]Germain and Frison Roche (1993).

has a particular claim known as a floating charge. The distinctive feature of these procedures is that management immediately loses control to the liquidator or receiver, who then has wide powers to sell or dismantle the firm to satisfy as quickly as possible the claims of the creditor who initiated the procedure. However, the liquidator or receiver has ro responsibility to maintain the value of the firm for the benefit of other claimants, including other lenders.

The alternative channel is debtor initiated and also involves two procedures, company voluntary arrangement and administration, designed to be used together. The central idea of these procedures is that a qualified insolvency practitioner is appointed by the court and takes control of the firm. There is no automatic stay of creditors' claims, so the administrator must act quickly. Within one month of being appointed, the administrator must assess the feasibility of restructuring and propose a plan to the creditors. Approval of the plan requires a 75 percent vote of each class of creditors and shareholders, which is difficult to achieve in practice.

Strong financial markets require ample legal protection for both shareholders and creditors. At a time of bankruptcy, however, these interests are in conflict. In general, the European systems lean toward the creditors and the U.S. system favors management and shareholders. This helps to explain the greater relative reliance on debt financing in Europe and on equity financing in the United States.

Each country must decide to what degree its bankruptcy procedures offer creditor protection. Given the frequency of banking crises in developing countries, it would seem that a strong dose of creditor bias would help resolve bad loans and build a stronger foundation for the future. Table 4.A3 in the Appendix lists various creditor rights in a number of countries.

How Much Does Legal Protection Matter?

The impact of legal variables on external finance has been studied in several recent papers, including LaPorta, Lopez-de-Silanes, Shleifer, and Vishny (1997). They regressed the ratio of externally held stock market capital to gross domestic product on the GDP growth rate, the logarithm of GDP (i.e., country size), and legal variables. As would be expected, they found that GDP growth has an important effect on attracting equity capital, but that country size does not matter. Controlling for these, raising the rule of law specification from the sample average of 6.85 to a perfect 10 increases outsider-held market capitalization by about 13 percent of GDP. Raising the antidirector rights of shareholders from its French-origin average of 1.76 to its common law average of 3.39 raises the market capitalization to GDP ratio by 19 percentage points. Countries with mandatory one-share, one-vote rules have a ratio 27 percentage points higher.

Similar results were obtained when the dependent variable was the number of listed domestic firms per million population. The world average for this ratio is 22. In this regression growth of GDP did not matter but country size did—bigger economies have fewer listed firms per million, other things being equal. Controlling for this, moving the rule of law score from the world mean of 6.85 to a perfect 10 is associated with 15 more listed firms per million. Moving the antidirector rights from the French-origin mean to the English-origin mean raises the ratio by 12. The one-share, one-vote measure, however, is not significant for the number of listed firms.

The authors' third regression concerns the number of initial public offerings (IPOs) between mid-1995 and mid-1996 per million of population. The world mean is 1.0. Here the growth rate is significant and country size is not. Controlling for these, moving the rule of law variable from the world mean to 10 raises the number of IPOs by 0.8 per million. Moving the antidirector rights from the French-origin mean to the English-origin mean raises the ratio by 0.8 as well. The one-share, one-vote measure is not significant for the number of IPOs.[33]

Complementing and extending this research, Ross Levine (1997) used the creditor rights and legal enforcement variables to explain banking development and the relationship between banking and long-run economic growth. Specifically, three creditor rights are singled out: (1) whether the country's laws protect managers by automatically staying creditor claims when a reorganization petition is filed, (2) whether the managers are protected by enabling them to keep running the firm during the reorganization procedure, and (3) whether secured creditors come first in line for asset distributions or other claimants such as employees and government can take some or all of the collateral away from the secured lender. These three are combined into one indicator of creditor rights. A measure for rule of law is combined with another that assesses the risk that the government can and will modify a commercial contract, once it has been signed, to produce a combined variable for legal enforcement.

The ratio of loans made by deposit-taking banks to the private sector divided by GDP is then regressed on creditor rights and legal enforcement. The results are both statistically significant and economically meaningful. A one standard deviation increase in creditor rights is associated with a 13 percent increase in banking depth. A one standard deviation increase in legal enforcement is associated with a 38 percent increase in lending. These results are not significantly changed when GDP per capita is included to control for the level of economic development. Furthermore, regressing the lending variable on legal origin shows that countries with a German legal origin have significantly better-developed banks.

A second part of this research revisits the question raised in Chapter 2, whether banking development causes economic growth. It is clear that countries with more economic growth have better developed banks, but many academics have questioned the direction of causality: Perhaps the growth caused the banking development rather than the other way around. Even the relationship between banking development at one point in time and subsequent economic growth has been challenged: Perhaps banking development merely predicts subsequent growth rather than causing it.[34]

Levine (1997) helped to resolve that question by using first creditor rights and enforcement quality, and then legal origin, as instrumental variables: quantities well correlated with banking development that are unlikely to have been caused by economic growth. The one-way quality of these instruments enables a modern econometric technique known as generalized method of moments to give strong evidence that differences in legal systems do indeed cause economic growth and furthermore do so through their impact on banking development.

Jeffrey Wurgler (1999) also showed that legal protections for shareholders and creditors matter for economic performance, and that they do so by improving the effectiveness of the financial system, not just its size. Wurgler's measure of economic performance is the efficiency of investment, not economic growth. For the 65 countries in his sample, he measured investment efficiency at the industry level as the elasticity of investment with respect to value-added (i.e., how much a relatively productive industry can attract capital quickly relative to less productive industries). Wurgler found that increases in financial development (stock market capitalization relative to GDP and

---

[33]LaPorta, Lopez-de-Silanes, Shleifer, and Vishny (1997).
[34]Rajan and Zingales (1997).

Bankruptcy in Indonesia

Here is an illuminating exercise, recommended for those who think the worst of the Asian financial crisis is past. Visit the Hong Kong headquarters of Peregrine, the investment bank that collapsed earlier this month, and observe the walls stripped of pictures and empty rooms so efficiently scoured by the liquidators. Then visit the Jakarta offices of Infiniti Wahana, the holding company for Steady Safe, an Indonesian taxicab firm whose stated inability to pay back a $350 million loan from Peregrine was the final nail in the bank's coffin. The wood gleams, the pictures shine, the office bustles: business as usual.

When a company in Europe or America cannot pay its debt, its creditors force it into bankruptcy, where a judge can fix a repayment plan or liquidate the firm and divide up the assets. But in Asia's most troubled economies, it is more likely to be the creditors who end up in trouble.

In Indonesia, as Western banks are discovering to their horror, it is almost impossible to force a debtor into bankruptcy. In South Korea, filing bankruptcy papers is easy—but months of inaction inevitably follow. In Thailand and the Philippines, the best a lender can expect is "sorry." As Asia begins to clean up from the financial meltdown of 1997, this lack of legal process is becoming a serious hindrance. So long as insolvent companies can keep operating with impunity, the restructuring of Asia's overindebted corporate sector will be indefinitely delayed.

Source: *The Economist*, January 24, 1998.

A new Indonesian court to deal only with bankruptcy cases will open in August. But while foreign bankers applauded the move, it's not certain that the court will give them what they want: an effective legal mechanism to declare debtors bankrupt and deal with selling their assets.

The degree to which changes in the legal system announced on Friday function smoothly, and are viewed favorably, may prove pivotal to Indonesia's restructuring of some $68 billion in private foreign debt and to getting capital flowing into the country again.

Indonesia's State Secretariat released 49 pages of amendments to the country's 1905 Dutch colonial-era bankruptcy law and 37 pages of explanations of the changes. The amendments had been promoted by the International Monetary Fund as part of Indonesia's economic-reform package.

While it's still not certain that the changes will give Indonesia an effective legal mechanism to declare debtors bankrupt and sell their assets, foreign bankers applaud the effort. Many worry that the old bankruptcy law, especially when administered by Indonesia's often-criticized court system, wouldn't prove to be an effective channel for creditors to seek redress . . .

A key objective of the amendments is to offer creditors a fair choice between liquidating a debtor's assets and opting for a reorganization and moratorium on repayments.

Doubts remain about how smoothly the new court will function when it opens August 22. The Indonesian court system is stigmatized by a widespread public perception that some judges accept bribes and that the courts should be avoided if possible . . .

Since the collapse of the country's currency, the rupiah, last July, hundreds of Indonesian companies have been unable, or in some cases unwilling, to repay their dollar-denominated loans. Formal talks between an Indonesia debt committee representing international lenders opened last week in New York, and will continue in Tokyo next month. Creditors say that reforming Indonesian bankruptcy law and procedures is critical to negotiations on restructuring the debt.

Source: *The Wall Street Journal*, April 27, 1998.

outstanding credit relative to GDP) raise the efficiency of investment, and that a reliance on state-owned enterprises reduces investment efficiency. He also found that legal determinants (which he captures in a summary measure that combines measures of the extent of rule of law with creditor and stockholder rights) have a direct effect on the efficiency of investment, even after controlling for the extent of financial development.

Taken together, this research provides compelling evidence that legal systems matter. Countries that want to have value-creating growth need strong financial systems to allocate capital. Strong financial systems in turn need strong legal foundations, which must be explicitly constructed with a view to protecting investors so that they will be encouraged to invest. Countries that emphasize shareholder protection, such as the United States, end up with strong stock markets and market-related controls on management misbehavior. Countries that emphasize creditor protection, such as Germany, end up with strong banking systems and bank-related controls on management misbehavior. Developing countries that do not adopt at least one of these approaches are likely to end up with management misbehavior, disappointed investors, and a severe misallocation of capital.

APPENDIX

The following tables are reproduced from Rafael La Porta, Florencia Lopez-de-Silanes, Andrei Shleifer, and Robert W. Vishny, "Law and Finance," Working Paper #5661, NBER, 1996, and represent the fruits of meticulous research into legal systems around the world. Primary sources are listed in the original article. Three tables are shown:

Table 4.A1   Rule of Law Variables
Table 4.A2   Shareholder Rights
Table 4.A3   Creditor Rights

Explanations for the variables in each table are given following the table.

In addition, the following table is reproduced from the website of Transparency International at the University of Göttingen (**www.gwdg.de/uwvw**):

Table 4.A4   Corruption Indexes

TABLE 4.A1 Rule of Law Variables

Country	Judicial Efficiency	Rule of Law	Corruption	Risk of Expropriation	Risk of Repudiation
English origin	**8.15**	**6.46**	**7.06**	**7.91**	**7.41**
Australia	10.00	10.00	8.52	9.27	8.71
Canada	9.25	10.00	10.00	9.67	8.96
Hong Kong	10.00	8.22	8.52	8.29	8.82
India	8.00	4.17	4.58	7.75	6.11
Ireland	8.75	7.80	8.52	9.67	8.96
Israel	10.00	4.82	8.33	8.25	7.54
Kenya	5.75	5.42	4.12	5.98	5.66
Malaysia	9.00	6.78	7.38	7.95	7.43
New Zealand	10.00	10.00	10.00	9.69	9.29
Nigeria	7.25	2.73	3.03	5.33	4.36
Pakistan	5.00	3.03	2.98	5.62	4.87
Singapore	10.00	8.57	8.22	9.30	8.86
South Africa	6.00	4.12	8.92	6.88	7.27
Sri Lanka	7.00	1.90	5.00	6.05	5.25
Thailand	3.25	6.25	5.18	7.42	7.57
United Kingdom	10.00	8.57	9.10	9.71	9.63
United States	10.00	10.00	8.63	9.98	9.00
Zimbabwe	7.50	3.68	5.42	5.61	5.04
French origin	**6.56**	**6.05**	**5.40**	**7.46**	**6.84**
Argentina	6.00	5.35	6.02	5.91	4.91
Belgium	9.50	10.00	8.82	9.63	9.48
Brazil	5.75	6.32	6.32	7.62	6.30
Chile	7.25	7.02	5.30	7.50	6.80
Colombia	7.25	2.08	5.00	6.95	7.02
Ecuador	6.25	6.67	5.18	6.57	5.18
Egypt	6.50	4.17	3.87	6.30	6.05
France	8.00	8.98	9.05	9.65	9.19
Greece	7.00	6.18	7.27	7.12	6.62
Indonesia	2.50	3.98	2.15	7.16	6.09
Italy	6.75	8.33	6.13	9.35	9.17
Jordan	8.66	4.35	5.48	6.07	4.86
Mexico	6.00	5.35	4.77	7.29	6.55
Netherlands	10.00	10.00	10.00	9.98	9.35
Peru	6.75	2.50	4.70	5.54	4.68
Philippines	4.75	2.73	2.92	5.22	4.80
Portugal	5.50	8.68	7.38	8.90	8.57
Spain	6.25	7.80	7.38	9.52	8.40
Turkey	4.00	5.18	5.18	7.00	5.95
Uruguay	6.50	5.00	5.00	6.58	7.29
Venezuela	6.50	6.37	4.70	6.89	6.30
German origin	**8.54**	**8.68**	**8.03**	**9.45**	**9.47**
Austria	9.50	10.00	8.57	9.69	9.60
Germany	9.00	9.23	8.93	9.90	9.77
Japan	10.00	8.98	8.52	9.67	9.69
South Korea	6.00	5.35	5.30	8.31	8.59
Switzerland	10.00	10.00	10.00	9.98	9.98
Taiwan	6.75	8.52	6.85	9.12	9.16

continued

Country	*Judicial Efficiency*	*Rule of Law*	*Corruption*	*Risk of Expropriation*	*Risk of Repudiation*
Scandinavian origin	**10.00**	**10.00**	**10.00**	**9.66**	**9.44**
Denmark	10.00	10.00	10.00	9.67	9.31
Finland	10.00	10.00	10.00	9.67	9.15
Norway	10.00	10.00	10.00	9.88	9.71
Sweden	10.00	10.00	10.00	9.40	9.58
Total average	**7.67**	**6.85**	**6.90**	**8.05**	**7.58**

Notes:

Efficiency of the Judicial System is an assessment of the "efficiency and integrity of the legal environment as it affects business, particularly foreign firms" produced by the country-risk rating agency Business International Corporation. It "may be taken to represent investors' assessments of conditions in the country in question." Average between 1980 and 1983. Scale from 0 to 10, with lower scores for lower efficiency levels.

Rule of Law is an assessment of the law and order tradition in the country produced by the country-risk rating agency International Country Risk (ICR). Average monthly index for April and October between 1982 and 1995. Scale from 0 to 10 with lower scores for less tradition of law and order (changed by the authors from its original range of 0 to 6).

Corruption is ICR's assessment of the corruption in government. Lower scores indicate "high government officials are likely to demand special payments" and "illegal payments are generally expected throughout lower levels of government" in the form of "bribes connected with import and export licenses, exchange controls, tax assessment, policy protection, or loans." Average is monthly index for April and October between 1982 and 1995. Scale from 0 to 10, with lower scores for higher levels of corruption (changed by the authors from its original range of 0 to 6).

Risk of Expropriation is ICR's assessment of the risk of "outright confiscation" or "forced nationalization." Average of the months of April and October between 1982 and 1995. Scale from 0 to 10, with lower scores for higher risk.

Risk of Repudiation is ICR's assessment of the "risk of a modification in a contract taking the form of a repudiation, postponement, or scaling down" due to "budget cutbacks, indigenization pressure, a change in government, or a change in government economic and social priorities." Average monthly index for April and October between 1982 and 1995. Scale from 0 to 10, with lower scores for higher risks.

TABLE 4.A2   Shareholder Rights

Country	*One Share, One Vote Required*	*Proxy Vote by Mail*	Antidirector Rights — *Shares Deposited to Vote*	*Cumulative Voting Permitted*	*Oppressed Minority Protection*	*Percent Shares Required to Call Meeting*	*Antidirector Rights*	*Mandatory Dividend*
English origin	**0.22**	**0.39**	**0.00**	**0.17**	**0.92**	**9%**	**3.39**	**0%**
Australia	0	1	0	0	1	5	4	0
Canada	0	1	0	0	1	10	4	0
Hong Kong	1	1	0	0	1	5	4	0
India	0	0	0	0	0	10	2	0
Ireland	0	0	0	0	1	10	3	0
Israel	0	0	0	0	1	10	3	0
Kenya	0	0	0	0	1	10	3	0
Malaysia	1	0	0	0	1	10	3	0
New Zealand	0	1	0	0	1	10	4	0
Nigeria	0	0	0	0	1	10	3	0
Pakistan	1	0	0	1	1	10	4	0

Country	One Share, One Vote Required	Proxy Vote by Mail	Shares Deposited to Vote	Antidirector Rights Cumulative Voting Permitted	Oppressed Minority Protection	Percent Shares Required to Call Meeting	Antidirector Rights	Mandatory Dividend
Singapore	1	0	0	0	1	10%	3	0%
South Africa	0	1	0	0	1	5	4	0
Sri Lanka	0	0	0	0	0	10	2	0
Thailand	0	0	0	1	1	20	3	0
United Kingdom	0	1	0	0	1	10	4	0
United States	0	1	0	1	1	1	5	0
Zimbabwe	0	0	0	0	1	10	3	0
French origin	**0.24**	**0.09**	**0.43**	**0.19**	**0.33**	**14**	**1.76**	**14**
Argentina	0	1	1	1	1	5	4	0
Belgium	0	0	1	0	0	20	0	0
Brazil	1	0	0	0	1	5	3	50
Chile	1	0	0	0	1	1	3	30
Colombia	0	0	0	0	0	25	1	0
Ecuador	0	0	0	0	1	25	2	50
Egypt	0	0	0	0	0	10	2	0
France	0	1	1	0	0	10	2	0
Greece	1	0	1	0	0	5	1	35
Indonesia	0	0	0	0	0	10	2	0
Italy	0	0	1	0	0	20	0	0
Jordan	0	0	0	0	0	15	1	0
Mexico	0	0	1	0	0	33	0	0
Netherlands	0	0	1	1	0	10	2	0
Peru	0	0	0	1	0	20	2	0
Philippines	0	0	0	1	1	10	4	50
Portugal	0	0	0	0	0	5	2	50
Spain	0	0	1	0	1	5	2	0
Turkey	0	0	0	0	0	10	2	0
Uruguay	1	0	1	0	1	20	1	20
Venezuela	0	0	0	0	0	20	1	0
German origin	**0.33**	**0.17**	**0.67**	**0.17**	**0.33**	**5**	**2.00**	**0**
Austria	0	1	1	0	0	5	2	0
Germany	0	0	1	0	0	5	1	0
Japan	1	0	0	0	1	3	3	0
South Korea	1	0	0	0	0	5	2	0
Switzerland	0	0	1	0	0	10	1	0
Taiwan	0	0	1	1	1	3	3	0
Scandinavian origin	**0.00**	**0.25**	**0.00**	**0.00**	**0.25**	**10**	**2.50**	**0**
Denmark	0	0	0	0	1	10	3	0
Finland	0	0	0	0	0	10	2	0
Norway	0	1	0	0	0	10	3	0
Sweden	0	0	0	0	0	10	2	0
Total Average	**0.22**	**0.22**	**0.27**	**0.16**	**0.53**	**11**	**2.44**	**6**

Notes:

One share, one vote required equals 1 if the company law or commercial code of the country requires that ordinary shares carry one vote per share, and 0 otherwise. Equivalently, this variable equals one when the law prohibits the existence of both multiple-voting and nonvoting ordinary shares and does not allow firms to set a maximum number of votes per shareholder irrespective of the number of shares the shareholder owns, and 0 otherwise.

Proxy vote by mail equals 1 if company law or commercial code allows shareholders to mail their proxy vote, and 0 otherwise.

Shares deposited to vote equals 1 if the company law or commercial code allows firms to require that shareholders deposit their shares prior to a general shareholders' meeting, and 0 otherwise.

Cumulative voting permitted equals 1 if company law or commercial code allows shareholders to cast all of their votes for one candidate standing for election to the board of directors, and 0 otherwise.

Oppressed minority protection equals 1 if company law or commercial code grants minority shareholders either a judicial venue to challenge management decisions or the right to step out of the company by requiring the company to purchase their shares when they object to certain fundamental changes, such as mergers, assets dispositions, and changes in the articles of incorporation. The variable equals 0 otherwise.

Percent shares required to call meeting is the minimum percentage of ownership of share capital that entitles a shareholder to call for an extraordinary shareholders' meeting. It ranges from 1 percent to 33 percent.

Antidirector rights is an index aggregating (1) proxy vote by mail, (2) shares deposited to vote, (3) cumulative voting permitted, (4) oppressed minorities protection, and (5) an index equal to 1 if percent shares to call meeting is less than or equal to its median value of 0.10. This aggregate ranges from 0 to 5.

Mandatory dividend equals the percentage of net income that the company law or commercial code requires firms to distribute as dividends among ordinary stockholders. It takes a value of 0 for countries without such restriction.

TABLE 4.A3   Creditor Rights

Country	Reorganization Restrictions	Automatic Stay on Assets	Secured Debt Paid First	Management Remains
English origin	**0.71**	**0.29**	**0.94**	**0.24**
Australia	0	1	1	1
Canada	0	1	1	1
Hong Kong	1	0	1	0
India	1	0	1	0
Ireland	0	1	1	1
Israel	1	0	1	0
Kenya	1	0	1	0
Malaysia	1	0	1	0
New Zealand	1	0	0	0
Nigeria	1	0	1	0
Pakistan	1	0	1	0
Singapore	1	0	1	0
South Africa	1	1	1	0
Sri Lanka	N/A	N/A	N/A	N/A
Thailand	0	0	1	0
United Kingdom	1	0	1	0
United States	0	1	1	1
Zimbabwe	1	0	1	0
French origin	**0.42**	**0.74**	**0.68**	**0.74**
Argentina	0	1	1	1
Belgium	0	0	1	1
Brazil	1	1	0	1
Chile	1	1	1	1
Colombia	0	1	0	1
Ecuador	1	0	1	0
Egypt	1	0	1	0
France	0	1	0	1
Greece	0	1	0	0
Indonesia	1	0	1	0
Italy	1	1	1	1
Jordan	N/A	N/A	N/A	N/A
Mexico	0	1	0	1
Netherlands	1	1	1	1

Country	Reorganization Restrictions	Automatic Stay on Assets	Secured Debt Paid First	Management Remains
Peru	0	1	0	1
Philippines	0	1	0	1
Portugal	0	1	1	1
Spain	0	0	1	1
Turkey	1	1	1	1
Uruguay	0	1	1	0
Venezuela	N/A	N/A	1	N/A
German origin	**0.33**	**0.33**	**1.00**	**0.67**
Austria	1	0	1	1
Germany	1	0	1	1
Japan	0	1	1	0
South Korea	0	0	1	0
Switzerland	0	1	1	1
Taiwan	0	0	1	1
Scandinavian origin	**0.75**	**0.75**	**1.00**	**1.00**
Denmark	1	0	1	1
Finland	0	1	1	1
Norway	1	1	1	1
Sweden	1	1	1	1
Total average	**0.54**	**0.52**	**0.85**	**0.57**

Notes:

Reorganization restrictions equals 1 if the bankruptcy and reorganization laws impose restrictions, such as creditors' consent, to file for reorganization. It equals 0 if there are no such restrictions.

Automatic stay on assets equals 1 if the bankruptcy or reorganization laws impose an automatic stay on the assets of the firm upon filing of the reorganization petition. This restriction prevents secured creditors from gaining immediate possession of their security. It equals 0 if such restriction does not exist in the law.

Secured debt paid first equals 1 if secured creditors are ranked first in the distribution of the proceeds that result from the disposition of the assets of a bankrupt firm. It equals 0 if nonsecured creditors, such as the government or workers, are given absolute priority.

Management remains equals 1 if the debtor keeps the administration of its property pending the resolution of the reorganization process and 0 otherwise. Equivalently, this variable equals 0 when an official appointed by the court or by the creditors is responsible for the operation of the business during reorganization.

TABLE 4.A4   Corruption Indexes from Transparency International

Country	1997			1996		
	Rating	Variance	Surveys	Rating	Variance	Surveys
Argentina	2.81	1.24	6	3.41	0.54	6
Australia	8.86	0.44	5	8.60	0.48	6
Austria	7.61	0.59	5	7.59	0.41	6
Bangladesh	N/A	N/A	N/A	2.29	1.57	4
Belgium	5.25	3.28	6	6.84	1.41	6
Bolivia	2.05	0.86	4	3.40	0.64	4
Brazil	3.56	0.49	6	2.96	1.07	7
Cameroon	N/A	N/A	N/A	2.46	2.98	4
Canada	9.10	0.27	5	8.96	0.15	6
Chile	6.05	0.51	6	6.80	2.53	7
China	2.88	0.82	6	2.43	0.52	9
Colombia	2.23	0.61	6	2.73	2.41	6

continued

| Country | 1997 | | | 1996 | | |
	Rating	Variance	Surveys	Rating	Variance	Surveys
Czech Republic	N/A	N/A	N/A	5.37	2.11	4
Denmark	9.94	0.54	6	9.33	0.44	6
Ecuador	N/A	N/A	N/A	3.19	0.42	4
Egypt	N/A	N/A	N/A	2.84	6.64	4
Finland	9.48	0.30	6	9.05	0.23	6
France	6.66	0.60	5	6.96	1.58	6
Germany	8.23	0.40	6	8.27	0.53	6
Greece	5.35	2.42	6	5.01	3.37	6
Hong Kong	7.28	2.63	7	7.01	1.79	9
Hungary	5.18	1.66	6	4.86	2.19	6
India	2.75	0.23	7	2.63	0.12	9
Indonesia	2.72	0.18	6	2.65	0.95	10
Ireland	8.28	1.53	6	8.45	0.44	6
Israel	7.97	0.12	5	7.71	1.41	5
Italy	5.03	2.07	6	3.42	4.78	6
Japan	6.57	1.09	7	7.05	2.61	9
Jordan	N/A	N/A	N/A	4.89	0.17	4
Kenya	N/A	N/A	N/A	2.21	3.69	4
Malaysia	5.01	0.50	6	5.32	0.13	9
Mexico	2.66	1.18	5	3.30	0.22	7
Netherlands	9.03	0.23	6	8.71	0.25	6
New Zealand	9.23	0.58	6	9.43	0.39	6
Nigeria	1.76	0.16	4	0.69	6.37	4
Norway	8.92	0.51	6	8.87	0.20	6
Pakistan	2.53	0.47	4	1.00	2.52	5
Philippines	3.05	0.51	6	2.69	0.49	8
Poland	5.08	2.13	5	5.57	3.63	4
Portugal	6.97	1.02	5	6.53	1.17	6
Russia	2.27	0.87	6	2.58	0.94	5
Singapore	8.66	2.32	6	8.80	2.36	10
South Africa	4.95	3.08	6	5.68	3.30	6
South Korea	4.29	2.76	7	5.02	2.30	9
Spain	5.90	1.82	6	4.31	2.48	6
Sweden	9.35	0.27	6	9.08	0.30	6
Switzerland	8.61	0.26	6	8.76	0.24	6
Taiwan	5.02	0.76	7	4.98	0.87	9
Thailand	3.06	0.14	6	3.33	1.24	10
Turkey	3.21	1.21	6	3.54	0.30	6
Uganda	N/A	N/A	N/A	2.71	8.72	4
United Kingdom	N/A	N/A	N/A	8.44	0.25	7
United States	7.61	1.15	5	7.66	0.19	7
Venezuela	2.77	0.51	5	2.50	0.40	7

Sources: The above indexes represent a combination of survey results from various sources compiled by Transparency International and the University of Göttingen, available on their website at **www.gwdg.de/uwvw** on a scale of 0 (totally corrupt) to 10 (totally clean). Countries are not shown unless at least four surveys are available. The variance among surveys is reported as well as the mean.

References

Alesina, Alberto, and Bea Weder. 1999. Do corrupt governments receive less foreign aid? Working paper, Harvard University.

Bale, Peter. 1996. Romanian investors picket suspended fund. *Reuters European Business Report,* May 14.

Dascalu, Roxana. 1995. Russia's MMM pyramid seen heading to Romania. *Reuters European Business Report,* June 15.

David, Rene, and John Brierley. 1985. *Major Legal Systems in the World Today.* London: Stevens and Sons.

Elliott, Kimberly Ann, ed. 1997. *Corruption and the Global Economy.* Washington, DC: Institute for International Economics.

Fisman, Raymond. 1999. Estimating the value of political connections. Working paper, Columbia University.

Fisman, Raymond, and Jakob Svensson. 1999. The effects of corruption and taxation on growth: Firm-level evidence. Working paper, Columbia University.

Franks, Julian R., Kjell G. Nyborg, and Walter N. Torous. 1996. A comparison of U.S., U.K. and German insolvency codes. *Financial Management* 25, no. 3: 86–101.

Fukuyama, Francis. 1995. *Trust: The Social Virtues and the Creation of Prosperity.* New York: Free Press.

Germain, M., and M. A. Frison Roche. 1993. Le sort des plans de redressement des entreprises en difficultés. Laboratoire de Sociologie Juridique, Université de Paris.

Greif, Avner. 1989. Reputation and coalitions in medieval trade: Maghribi traders. *Journal of Economic History* 49: 857–82.

Johnson, Simon, and Andrei Shleifer. 1999. Coase v. the Coasians. Working Paper no. 7447, National Bureau of Economic Research.

Johnson, Simon, Andrei Shleifer and Florencia Lopez-de-Silanes. 2000. Tunneling. Working Paper no. 7523, National Bureau of Economic Research.

Kaiser, Kevin M. J. 1996. European bankruptcy laws: Implications for corporations facing financial distress. *Financial Management* 25, no. 3: 67–85.

Klitgaard, Robert. 1988. *Controlling Corruption.* Berkeley: University of California Press.

Krueger, Anne. 1974. The political economy of the rent-seeking society. *American Economic Review* 64: 291–303.

La Porta, Rafael, Florencia Lopez-de-Silanes, Andrei Shleifer, and Robert W. Vishny. 1996. Law and finance. Working Paper no. 5661, National Bureau of Economic Research.

———. 1997. Legal determinants of external finance. *Journal of Finance* 52, no. 3: 1131–49.

Levine, Ross. 1997. Banks and economic development: The legal determinants of banking development and the impact of banks on long-run growth. Working paper, University of Virginia.

Marsh, Virginia. 1996. Broken promises prove an expensive commodity for Safi. *Financial Times,* May 4.

Mauro, Paolo. 1995. Corruption and growth. *Quarterly Journal of Economics* 110: 681–712.

Noonan, John T., Jr. 1984. *Bribes.* New York: Macmillan.

Pieth, Mark. 1997. International cooperation to combat corruption. In *Corruption and the Global Economy.* Ed. by Kimberly Ann Elliott. Washington, DC: Institute for International Economics.

Popeski, Ron. 1997. Ruined Albanians latest victims of pyramid schemes. *Reuters Financial Service,* February 11.

Rajan, Raghuram G., and Luigi Zingales. 1997. Financial dependence and growth. Working paper, University of Chicago.

Rocca, Carlos Antonio, Antonio Gledson de Carvalho, and Marcos Eugênio da Silva. 1998. Mercado de capitais e a retornada do crescimento econômico. Working paper, University of São Paulo.

Rose-Ackerman, Susan. 1978. *Corruption: A Study in Political Economy.* New York: Academic Press.

————. 1997. The political economy of corruption. In *Corruption and the Global Economy.* Ed. by Kimberly Ann Elliott. Washington, DC: Institute for International Economics, pp. 31–60.

Rosenberg, Richard M. 1984. An overview of workouts from the perspective of the institutional lender. *Loyola University Law Journal* 16: 1–41.

Shleifer, Andre, and Robert W. Vishny. 1993. Corruption. *Quarterly Journal of Economics* 108: 599–617.

Stromberg, Per. 1998. Conflicts of interest and market illiquidity in bankruptcy auctions: Theory and tests. Working paper, University of Chicago Graduate School of Business, February.

Swafford, David. 1999. Launching a new market. *Latin Finance* 109: 30–32.

Watson, Alan. 1974. *Legal Transplants.* Charlottesville: University of Virginia Press.

Wei, Shang-Jin. 1997. How taxing is corruption on international investors? Working Paper no. 6030, National Bureau of Economic Research.

Weiss, Lawrence A., and Karen H. Wruck. 1998. Information problems, conflicts of interest and asset stripping: Chapter 11's failure in the case of Eastern Airlines. *Journal of Financial Economics* 48, no. 1: 55–98.

Wilson, John. 1999. Solutions for a credit shortage: Mexico leads Latin America in the creation of a new secured credit market. *Latin Finance* 109: 10–14.

World Bank. 1995. *World Development Report.* Washington, DC: World Bank.

————. 1997. *World Development Report.* Washington, DC: World Bank.

Wurgler, Jeffrey. 1999. Financial markets and the allocation of capital. Working paper, Yale University School of Management, August.

Zingales, Luigi. 1994. The value of the voting right: A study of the Milan stock exchange experience. *Review of Financial Studies* 7: 125–48.

————. 1995. What determines the value of corporate votes? *Quarterly Journal of Economics* 110: 1075–1110.

Information and Control

Questions:
What is the meaning and importance of asymmetric information?
What effect does adverse selection have on emerging financial markets?
How can investors or financial intermediaries monitor their investments?
Why do conglomerate companies arise and what problems do they cause?
What is the "best" model of corporate governance?

Introduction

Frictions and the Behavior of Markets

Financial economics, like other disciplines, has passed through phases of development and changes in perspective. The 1960s were a high-water point for efficient-market theory: Many financial economists believed that financial markets were almost fully efficient in the sense that the prices of stocks and bonds impound all public and even most private information that might be relevant to them. If this were true, then neoclassical economic models show that financial markets would optimally allocate savings, and the only public policy prescription would be to prevent government from interfering with this allocation process.

The 1970s and 1980s, however, witnessed a major change in perspective. Empirical research turned up a remarkable number of anomalies in the patterns of stock market returns, such as short-term positive momentum effects and longer-term mean reversion, "January" effects, day-of-the-week effects, and other apparent departures from the predictions of rational behavior in a fully efficient market. Credit markets were found to display inefficient means of allocating loans; instead of allowing debtors to bid for funds without limit, lenders allocate funds according to a combination of limited available quantity and price. Such *credit rationing* would not be efficient in a frictionless neoclassical world.

Theorists seeking reasons for these phenomena found that economic theory had a hard time explaining even simple facts. Many theorists began to turn their attention to some basic neglected questions about the shape of financial markets and institutions.

For example, why did debt contracts arise? Why is collateral so important in real-world debt contracting? Why do banks exist? In a market with full informational efficiency, banks would scarcely be necessary: Savers and borrowers would find each other through the securities markets, without the need for a costly institution to take deposits and relend them.

The recent literature in banking and financial contracts has developed a new consensus that financial markets are by no means fully efficient even in the most industrialized countries. Allocative inefficiencies abound even in our highly communicative, computerized turn-of-the-century world. This is not to say that financial markets and institutions are performing their missions poorly. Recognizing the existence of market imperfections is a little like recognizing that real-world engineering (unlike abstract theoretical physics) must be performed in a world full of friction.

To understand where many market frictions come from, imagine that you have saved some of your income and are interested in investing it in a worthwhile firm. How would you find the right firm in which to invest? Surely not all firms claiming to have highly profitable, low-risk opportunities really are worth investing in. And even the managers of firms that have profitable opportunities may choose to use your savings, once they are placed at the managers' disposal, for a different purpose—one that feathers their nest at your expense.

This is an example of the *principal–agent problem*: the difficulty the principal faces getting an agent to act in the principal's interest. It is a problem of information and control. If all attributes and actions of the agent (manager) were observable, and if the costs of writing and enforcing contracts in the legal system were sufficiently low, then principals (investors) would always be able to choose the right firms in which to invest, and would prevent abuse of their funds simply by specifying in detail exactly what the agent must do and not do. Principals would then enforce those contracts to prevent any cheating by agents.

But this is not the world in which we live. Principals do not have all the information they would like to have about agents prior to placing funds at their disposal, and they cannot costlessly observe how agents make use of those resources, and whether agents fulfill all their promises. In the real world, it costs resources to collect information and to enforce contracts that bind agents.

By looking closely at information and control problems (the analogue of friction in the financial system), one can find explanations for many of the important theoretical questions and empirical anomalies referred to above. The existence of debt contracts and banks is typically traced to their role in economizing on the cost of gathering information about borrowers and controlling the behavior of firms and individuals who receive loans. Anomalies in equity markets, at least to some degree, seem to reflect problems that arise when individual investors lack information about the risk and return opportunities in securities markets. For example, when individuals delegate decisions to mutual fund or pension fund managers without being able to closely observe what, how, and why money managers invest on their behalf, money managers may have incentives to invest in suboptimal ways, which in turn may account for some market anomalies.[1] When investors are unable to observe the true capabilities of money managers, money managers may have an incentive to herd (to follow one another's investment strategies) as a means of avoiding punishment by investors, or

---

[1]See Lakonishok, Shleifer, and Vishny (1992) for an introduction to the issues surrounding the principal–agent problem in money management.

Mexico Isn't Free with Information

In Mexico, information is power. And just try to get your hands on any, be it mundane or profound. Everything from the number of billboards in Mexico City to the details of past presidential lives is closely guarded by government and business. The first line of defense of a Mexican secretary is the phrase: *"No sabría decirle,"*—"I wouldn't know what to tell you."

This frustrates everyone from bankers to travel agents. John Donnelly, head of Chase Manhattan Bank here, says the lack of credible credit information has stymied renewed lending growth since the 1994 peso collapse. Iris de Buendía, an agent at the Viajes Wilfer travel agency, says it is nearly impossible to get a straight answer from Mexican airlines on the timing of price promotions. "Everything is always top secret here," she says, sighing.

This vagueness has deep roots in Mexican history. The Aztecs, who commanded the central valleys of this land from the 12th century to the 15th, kept their vassals in awe with a changing cast of hard-to-understand and unpredictable, but powerful, deities. The Spanish who followed were big on bureaucratic minutiae but rarely shared the details with the people they ruled. For the past 70 years, the reigning Institutional Revolutionary Party, or PRI, has worked hard to make sure inconvenient information doesn't end up in the wrong hands.

"In Mexico, powerful people have traditionally kidnapped information," says historian and novelist Hector Aguilar Camin. "Part of the process of democratization is freeing it." But, he adds, "there is still a tendency to want to hold it hostage for some kind of benefit."

History, particularly when it damages the reputations of the living, is closely guarded. When researchers sought to confirm the details of a childhood shooting incident involving former president Carlos Salinas de Gortari, they found newspaper morgues purged of any reference to the event. Nor did they have better luck at the National Archives. The head of security there says a squad of government functionaries arrived to mop up Mr. Salinas's personal files when he took office in 1988.

The debate over access to information has become more explosive with the growth of a free press, the rise of opposition political parties and a big jump in the number of foreign investors doing business here who are demanding more transparency . . .

Lawmakers haven't had much better luck, so far, clarifying exactly what happened during the post-1994 bailout of the banking system orchestrated by President Ernesto Zedillo and his team. Finance Ministry officials say they are reluctant to give sensitive information to Congress, citing the country's bank-secrecy laws which, uniquely, protect not just data on deposits but also on loans. Lawmakers suspect the ministry is trying to protect hundreds of well-connected businessmen whose bum debts ended up being bought by Mexico's deposit insurance fund and which will, in the end, be borne by taxpayers.

Source: *The Wall Street Journal,* September 10, 1998.

may engage in trading strategies known as "window dressing" (changing balance sheet composition just prior to reporting dates), and these behaviors may contribute to momentum, mean reversion, and calendar effects in equity returns.

The increased focus on emerging financial markets in the 1990s has brought to the fore examples of apparent allocative failures much more serious than those found in the industrialized world, and has made it clear that information and control problems go a long way toward explaining the unique characteristics and uneven performance of EFMs. In particular, these frictions explain why EFMs with rich natural resources and obvious economic opportunities still find it hard to attract and mobilize funds to finance economic activity. A focus on information and control problems also explains the dominant role of banks in EFMs and can help us to understand why these banks are often troubled with losses. Since these losses have now become a global public policy problem of the first magnitude, it is important to study carefully their underlying causes, many of which are rooted in information and control problems.

Impact of Asymmetric Information on Financial Markets

The central information problem of financial markets is *asymmetric information*; that is, situations in which the user of capital knows far more about his prospects and problems than the supplier of capital. It is not hard to see that this will impede the confidence of capital suppliers. But the details of how information problems are treated in financial markets are less obvious and quite revealing about the nature of financial contracts and intermediaries. We have learned a good deal about what particular effects information problems have on the shape of financial markets and instruments.

Information is of little value without credible control mechanisms designed to make use of that information.[2] Such control mechanisms include appropriate contracts and courts to enforce them, corporate governance rules, and financial intermediaries willing to act as corporate monitors. Increased control may reduce the amount of information an investor or intermediary needs to collect or may reduce the cost of collecting it. For example, a debt contract well secured with collateral requires less information than a stock investment, and a demand deposit in a government-insured bank requires almost no information at all. Well-written corporate governance rules oblige managers to take fairly conducted shareholder votes on key issues, giving shareholders more control over managers. Mandatory disclosure laws make it far easier and cheaper to collect information about management decisions, increasing the likelihood that managers will choose to act in their shareholders' interest.

The new literature on information problems in financial markets emphasizes four related implications of asymmetric information for financial contracting that are especially relevant in EFMs:

1. Asymmetric information tilts the market toward *debt* and away from public equity. Indeed, debt contracts exist primarily to overcome information problems. Debt creates simple, fixed obligations whose promised cash flows are the same regardless of how well or badly the firm fares. The claims are in principle enforceable, although we have seen that this varies according to the legal structure of the country. But almost everywhere, debt holders are in a stronger position than holders of public equity to obtain their return in an environment of imperfect information. It is no accident that public equity issues as a source of new capital for firms are of greatest importance in the United States, where financial information is so abundant and well disseminated.

2. Asymmetric information tilts the debt markets toward *banks* and away from securities such as bonds, notes, and commercial paper. Buyers of debt securities need to feel that either they are well informed or that someone such as a rating agency has been able to inform itself and share its results with the investing public. Banks, in contrast, generate their own private information and are thus the dominant suppliers of debt finance when public information is inadequate. It is no accident that banks play a far larger role in EFMs than in more developed markets.

3. Asymmetric information tilts debt toward *short maturities* or toward contractual rights for creditors to accelerate payment if a contractual covenant is violated. The option

---

[2]For theoretical and empirical reviews of information and control problems, see Jensen and Meckling (1976), Myers (1977), Myers and Majluf (1984), Baskin (1988), Hubbard (1990), and Calomiris and Ramirez (1996).

not to roll over maturing debt, or to accelerate debt, gives creditors a powerful continuing voice in debtors' affairs after the debt contract has been signed, which can prevent debtors from behaving in ways that harm creditors' interests. Short-term debt is even more effective in this regard than long-term debt with the right of acceleration; acceleration requires judicial approval of the creditors' claim while the decision not to roll over debt does not.[3]

4. Asymmetric information tilts bank lending toward *secured loans* and away from unsecured loans. In many ways, collateral substitutes for sufficiently reliable information about the borrower, assuming of course that the legal structure is sufficiently supportive of collateralized lending. Even in the United States nearly 70 percent of all commercial and industrial bank loans are made on a secured basis.[4] In Europe the figure is even higher; we have seen that most European laws offer their greatest protections to secured lenders. In EFMs, making collateral legally feasible is one of the strongest steps a country can take toward strengthening its financial markets. Empirical evidence shows that collateral is strongly and unequivocally associated with weaker borrowers and weaker loans.[5] Collateral helps weak and little-known borrowers to obtain loans that would not be available to them without security. This makes collateralized debt particularly relevant to EFMs, where the proportion of weak borrowers and extent of information asymmetry is typically higher than in developed markets.

All of the above characterize emerging financial markets to a much greater extent than they characterize developed capital markets; that is, EFMs rely excessively on *debt* and typically have underdeveloped equity markets. With the debt arena, they are dominated by *banks* and typically have underdeveloped bond markets. EFM debt tends to be *short term* in nature, and uses *security* very freely. Our focus on information and control helps us to understand why EFMs are shaped in this way. This in turn helps us to understand why they are so often in crisis, since high reliance on debt can magnify the effects of economic shocks, particularly when that debt is short term.

Screening and Monitoring

It is useful to distinguish between two distinct kinds of information-related tasks: screening and monitoring.

Screening and Adverse Selection

Screening is necessary before an investment decision is made. It refers to the basis for making investment decisions when investment quality cannot easily be observed. If a user of capital knows more about his or her quality than the supplier of capital, how can the supplier make an appropriate choice? And having made a choice, how can a supplier of capital set an appropriate price? Screening and pricing are subject to the problem of *adverse selection.*

Adverse selection is a very general problem in economics. The classic case is the market for used cars, of which some are quite good and some are "lemons"; this is the example used by George Akerlof in a classic article about information asymmetries.[6]

---

[3]For a more detailed discussion of the incentive problems that can limit the attractiveness of long-term debt, see Jensen and Meckling (1976) and Myers (1977).

[4]Berger and Udell (1990).

[5]Ibid.

[6]Akerlof (1970); see also Myers and Majluf (1984).

Akerlof asked why a new car loses such a large amount of value simply by being driven out of the showroom. His answer was that car owners know more about their car than anyone, and that those who suspect their car is a "lemon" are the ones most likely to sell; so anyone buying a used car, even a very new used car, must significantly discount the price to take into account the increased probability of low quality from a seller more knowledgeable about his car than the buyer.

More generally, the problem of adverse selection has two effects: It tends to *lower the price* of used cars or any other commodity about which sellers know more than buyers, and in some cases it can *close the market* altogether. The adverse price effect comes directly from the need of buyers to protect themselves from more informed sellers. The market closing effect can be modeled by imagining that the quality of any set of commodities is related to the price: The more the price is lowered, the greater the likelihood of being offered a lemon, as sellers of good quality products are increasingly reluctant to sell as the price falls. Under these circumstances it is possible that no market-clearing price exists.

To illustrate adverse selection in credit markets, Akerlof used the example of India, an emerging financial market, where the village moneylender charges his clients the apparently extortionate rates of 15, 25, or even 50 percent while the largest banks in India's central cities might have prime rates of 6, 8, or 10 percent.[7] The reason for this large disparity is that the moneylender is the only potential lender who personally knows the quality of the village borrowers, and even he may be unable to distinguish between good and bad risks.

To the extent that moneylenders spend resources to identify low-risk borrowers, they must be compensated for those information investments through higher interest rates. High interest rates, therefore, are not necessarily an indication of monopoly profits. Uninformed outside lenders who tried to compete with informed lenders would end up with a disproportionate number of unreliable borrowers, and would have to charge an even higher interest rate to compensate for their much higher expected rate of loan losses.

The adverse-selection problem is also the most common explanation for credit rationing. Replace the falling price of used cars in the example above with the rising rate of interest paid by borrowers. High-risk borrowers will be more willing to pay higher interest rates than low-risk borrowers, just as sellers of "lemons" will be more willing to accept low prices than sellers of good cars. Thus, as the interest rate charged rises, the proportion of low-quality borrowers served rises as high-quality borrowers increasingly drop out of the market. Knowing this, the lender realizes that at some sufficiently high interest rate a further rise in the interest rate causes the lender's expected profit to fall (i.e., at that interest rate, the increase in defaults from raising rates more than offsets the increase in promised payments for those who do not default). Thus, lenders may choose to limit interest rates to a maximum level to ensure a high average quality in the borrower pool, even though at that maximum interest rate there is excess demand for loans by borrowers. In that case, lenders will choose to ration credit, limiting the amount that any borrower can borrow to cope with the excess demand. Asymmetric information means that sufficiently high risks may be avoided rather than priced. It also means that high-quality borrowers are paying a premium because of the presence of low-quality borrowers.[8]

So adverse selection has two negative effects on debt markets: It makes them more expensive, and it closes them off to borrowers above a certain level of risk. This

---

[7]Akerlof (1970), p. 498.
[8]Stiglitz and Weiss (1981).

corresponds to two well-known features of EFM debt markets: Their real interest rates often seem extremely high, and the markets periodically shut down, either to all borrowers or to all but the best-known.

High-quality borrowers often seek to avoid rationing and excess risk premiums by attempting to *signal* that their quality is higher than the average. This motivates voluntary disclosure of information to lenders. It also motivates offers of collateral: borrowers willing to pledge assets must be particularly confident of their ability to repay the debt. Collateral is widespread in EFMs in part because it is a very convincing signaling device. Indeed, requiring collateral can itself help to screen out high-risk borrowers who will be less willing to pledge collateral.

Equity investment is inherently more information intensive than debt investment. As noted above, debt was developed in large part to enable capital to be supplied to firms whose condition and prospects were not easily understood. Debt investors can look at a few financial ratios and require the pledging of physical collateral to protect themselves against default risk. Equity investors, in contrast, own the residual claim on the company and so must understand the full range of risks and opportunities facing the firm. This is a difficult task. Equity investors and underwriters perform a complex screening assignment for which offering firms must ultimately pay. For a firm to gain access to the equity market, it typically has to acquire significant support from knowledgeable institutions (underwriters and investors) that express confidence in its prospects.

Furthermore, a company's decision to sell stock to the public can be understood by the public as an unintended signal that the company is worried about its future. If a company with substantial debt anticipates a downturn in its business, the outcome might be bankruptcy unless the company increases its equity base. Knowing this, investors need to be skeptical of companies eager to sell stock, just as automobile buyers need to be skeptical of owners eager to sell their cars. That is why, more often than not, a stock's price falls when a new issue is announced, and why the effect is sometimes very large.[9]

It is a strange paradox. Groucho Marx once said that he would not want to join any club that would have him as a member. In a similar way, investors might be entitled to say that they would not want to buy a stock from any company that would want to sell it. The company knows more than the investor and a decision to sell stock may signal unrevealed problems. It is one of the financial world's clearest examples of asymmetric information inhibiting market development and performance. Much of the time and in many countries, it means that outside investors simply avoid stocks. Information problems also account for the suddenness with which foreign portfolio investors desert EFMs, the small number of EFM equity issuers, and the underdeveloped state of equity markets in most EFMs.

Private equity investors and foreign direct investors behave quite differently. They make longer-term commitments based upon a deeper understanding of local opportunities and risks. Their investments are illiquid and they cannot quickly reverse their decisions. But more than this, private equity investors and foreign direct investors tend to be informed, so they continue to invest even in the face of adversity, quite unlike the less well-informed arm's-length public investor. They are less erratic because they do their own screening before they invest and because they retain much greater direct control over their investments, which limits the extent to which firm managers can take advantage of them after they have purchased stock.

---

[9]Higgins (1998), pp. 205–209.

Investor Monitoring

Monitoring refers to the task of following the fortunes of an investment after it is made. This is not done just to satisfy curiosity. Investors need to be assured that the firm is not acting in ways that are detrimental to investor interests.

In industrial countries and particularly in the United States, where management is often separated from widely dispersed shareholders, the fundamental monitoring problem is how to ensure that managers act in the shareholders' interest. This version of the principal–agent problem has been widely studied and is best solved by a combination of disclosure laws (so that shareholders can learn what management is doing) and well-enforced shareholder rights (so that shareholders can dismiss managers who misbehave).

In most EFMs, however, wealthy individuals or families control the majority of corporations and quite often the CEO is part of the family. In this setting, the important control conflicts are not between management and shareholders but between (1) inside and outside shareholders and/or (2) equity holders and debt holders. Having considered protection for minority shareholders in the previous chapter, we turn here to the conflict between equity and debt. After all, debt is the dominant form of developing country finance. Assuming that shareholders control the management and management acts in the shareholders' interest, in what way do lenders (banks) need to monitor to protect themselves?

Banks need to beware, just as minority shareholders do, of "tunneling"—the expropriation of corporate assets by managers and/or controlling shareholders described in the previous chapter. As we saw in Russia, the Czech Republic, and a number of other countries in transition from communism, this is just what happened with spontaneous privatization. The risk is that banks will lend to finance assets that are then transferred out of the firm, leaving the debt to default.

The box describing Alphatec in Thailand gives a vivid example of what can go wrong. First, Alphatec's financial statements were fraudulent. Revenues were constructed in misleading and fictitious ways, and were overstated by a factor of between 6 and 10 times. Instead of $1.6 billion in profits over five years, the firm actually had losses of $700 million. This speaks to the need that banks (as well as any outside shareholders) have for accurate, properly audited financial information.

The article about Alphatec also shows the necessity of controlling the behavior of borrowers. From the lenders' perspective, the most damaging action was the transfer of large quantities of corporate assets from Alphatec to other companies controlled by Mr. Charn, including some engaged in land speculation. This classic example of tunneling was probably legal under Thai law, though it would be a clear case of fraud against capital suppliers in common law countries. It seems that bankers were represented on, and may even have dominated, the board of directors, yet they either were not paying sufficient attention or lacked the means to stop the tunneling.

Finally, the article says that Alphatec plunged ahead with one of the industry's most ambitious expansions just as its debts were ballooning out of control. The board chairman, Mrs. Waree, a former central banker, says she warned Mr. Charn about the risk of that expansion, yet the board did not stop it. Why?

Stockholders can benefit from risk taking at the expense of creditors because stockholders get to keep the upside of increased risk while creditors absorb the losses on the downside. This is particularly true in EFMs with poor bankruptcy laws, where in a bad outcome equity holders can often simply stall and negotiate endlessly while not paying. The temptation to increase risk at the expense of creditors is a form of

Creative Accounting and Corporate Governance in Thailand

Always another loan, always another deal. That was how Charn Uswachoke, better known in Thailand as "Mr. Chips," fended off jittery bankers in February, when a group of them asked why Alphatec Electronics PCL had just violated some terms of its international debt. All would be set right, promised the kingpin of Thai electronics. Lehman Brothers Inc., Mr. Charn told lenders, would soon be unveiling an initial public offering of shares in a newly restructured Alphatec on the New York Stock Exchange. To tide over the debt-strapped semiconductor-packaging company, Lehman was asking banks to raise as much as $1 billion of new loans for Mr. Charn's enterprises.

Yet even as the Lehman Brothers Holdings Inc. unit's plans moved forward, Alphatec was headed for more trouble. An independent audit by Price Waterhouse in July revealed that Alphatec, once a star on the Stock Exchange of Thailand, overstated profits by at least $164 million between 1994 and this April, a period when the report says the company should have been reporting "significant losses." Revenue was said to be 6 to 10 times as high as it actually was, say current and former employees familiar with Alphatec's true numbers. Price Waterhouse also found Alphatec had transferred at least $160 million of corporate funds to other Charn-controlled companies, without board approval . . . And Price Waterhouse discovered Alphatec maintained two sets of widely divergent accounting books.

How such questionable dealings have brought Thailand's preeminent high-tech company to its knees is a parable of the economic rot in Thailand today. The fact that many big U.S. companies fell victim to Alphatec's deceit—from Texas Instruments Inc. to Bankers Trust New York Corp. and Lehman—shows how alluring Thailand and Alphatec once were . . .

Once lionized as Thailand's best hope for leapfrogging into the upper ranks of the world's technology producers, Alphatec now stands as an object lesson in the dangers of doing business in a country where management accountability is spotty at best. The stark absence of corporate controls at Alphatec—the mingling of funds among listed and closely held companies run by the same family, the use of multiple sets of accounting books and misleading accounting methods, the highly paid, rubber-stamp board—mirrors the problems at other Thai companies that have brought this country's economy to the brink of collapse.

During Thailand's go-go decade after 1985 such deficiencies could be papered over with easy credit and soaring stock prices. But now the reckoning has begun. Paribas Asia Equity, a regional securities brokerage firm, has reconstructed income statements of 20 listed Thai companies using stricter accounting standards. The result: about $1.6 billion of reported profits from the past five years turned into cumulative losses of more than $700 million.

In Alphatec's case, the financial books were originally audited quarterly by KPMG Peat Marwick's Thai affiliate, KPMG Peat Marwick Suthee Ltd., which declines to comment. The Stock Exchange of Thailand is questioning the company's auditors about the discrepancies uncovered in the Price Waterhouse audit.

In May, Alphatec stopped making payments on its $450 million of debt. Yet until recently, creditors say, the company and its board stonewalled efforts to resolve the financial morass, commissioning the Price Waterhouse audit only after receiving an ultimatum from creditors. After Price Waterhouse's conclusions became known internally, seven bags of shredded documents were found at Alphatec's finance department, says Leslie Merszei, Mr. Charn's senior financial adviser at the time. Mr. Merszei resigned from Alphatec on Aug. 1 . . .

As Alphatec's debts ballooned out of control last winter, Mr. Charn pushed ahead with one of the most ambitious expansions in the global chip industry. Banking on the refinancing efforts launched by Lehman and others, he managed to keep construction going

continued

continued

on three plants, valued at $2.3 billion. In a first for Thailand, two of the plants, in partnership with Texas Instruments, were to perform some of the most advanced processes in microelectronics: the actual production of silicon wafers, the bailiwick of such high-tech heavyweights as Intel Corp., AMD and Micron Technologies Inc.

The expansion was key to Mr. Charn's goal of gaining a foothold on every rung of the lucrative chip-making ladder. Following common Thai business practice, he created several new companies to develop these ventures, independent of publicly listed Alphatec, and put family members in charge. The units were financed with loans from Thai and foreign banks, which Mr. Charn expected to repay from stock offerings on Thailand's booming stock exchange.

Then, about a year ago, Thai stock prices began their long, steep fall, making initial public offerings of stock all but impossible. Mr. Charn was stuck.

Yet the questionable financial practices continued. From January to April this year, more than $80 million of Alphatec funds were transferred, without board approval, to a Charn-controlled company that was building an industrial park for the new semiconductor plants, according to Mr. Merszei. Then, to hide continuing losses, Alphatec overstated first-quarter earnings by roughly $20 million, the Price Waterhouse report says.

There is no evidence suggesting any Alphatec board members, aside from Mr. Charn, knew about the company's accounting irregularities. But that fact, too, is revealing, Thai industry observers say. Led by Chairman Waree Havanonda, 69, a management teacher and former assistant governor of Thailand's central bank, the board is composed primarily of bankers, none of whom have any prior experience with advanced-electronics companies.

"I warned Mr. Charn many times not to expand rapidly," says Mrs. Waree who first met Mr. Charn when he was her student at business school. "He said, 'We have an opportunity; we must do it.' He wanted to be the king of electronics." Mrs. Waree denies Alphatec maintained two sets of accounting books, but acknowledged that "misstatements occurred" when production data were consolidated by Alphatec's finance department.

Even if some directors did know Alphatec was bankrolling other Charn-controlled ventures, it isn't clear they would have objected. One reason is that the key banks represented on Alphatec's board are backers of Mr. Charn's other companies; concerns about directors' conflicts of interest and fiduciary responsibilities hardly exist in Thailand, executives say. And the practice of using public-company money to launch private companies is ubiquitous in Southeast Asia, where family-run conglomerates mingle funds at will.

The accounting irregularities surfaced in May. After several fruitless months trying to restructure Alphatec for an initial public offering, Lehman Brothers shifted strategies and embarked on a $300 million high-yield-bond proposal instead. On May 11, a team of New York lawyers and investment bankers, led by Lehman technology chief Jack Skydel, visited Bangkok to run through the numbers with Alphatec's people.

Fifteen minutes before the meeting, Mr. Charn dropped a bombshell on Mr. Merszei: Alphatec's debt had expanded not by $35 million, as Mr. Charn had recently indicated, but by $100 million. Most of the increase had resulted from financial transfers to Mr. Charn's other companies, Mr. Merszei says Mr. Charn told him.

In another office, Mr. Merszei and a colleague, Robert Book, took Lehman's Mr. Skydel aside. "I said, 'This company is not a candidate in any debt or equity market in the world,'" Mr. Book, a long-time financial consultant to Mr. Charn, recalls. "'The financial practices here are not in keeping with the Western value system, or any value system. I'm sorry you came.'" The New Yorkers flew home that night.

Mr. Merszei called a moratorium on servicing Alphatec's debts, then nosed around some more. Though Alphatec's financial executives refused to open their books to him, with the help of other executives he pieced together an alarming picture. There was no

concluded

way Alphatec, with its factories running as they were, generated the $493 million of revenue it reported in 1996, or earned any profit at all, they concluded. They figured Alphatec must have had big losses, on less than $80 million of sales in 1996.

To validate the hugely inflated revenue claims to KPMG's auditors, Mr. Merszei and several Alphatec creditors say, the company's finance department booked as revenue the full market value of each chip it shipped for several of its customers rather than the small fraction of that value that Alphatec actually earned for packaging and testing semiconductors produced by other companies.

Later, during the course of its audit, Price Waterhouse turned up what appeared to be fake invoices that Alphatec used to tap trade credits at Bangkok banks. The ruse was sloppy: Two of the fake invoices, complete with company logos, were on the misspelled stationery of "Cypres Semiconductors Corp." and "Phiilip International Inc."

In mid-June, Mr. Merszei brought his findings to Alphatec's board, which confronted Mr. Charn about them. At first, he denied everything, accusing Mr. Merszei of conspiring with others to put Alphatec into default so they could buy it out cheaply. Mrs. Waree, Alphatec's chairman, says the board pressed Mr. Charn to explain what happened. "He admitted the money went to purchase land and promised to pay it back."

Source: *The Wall Street Journal,* September 8, 1997.

---

moral hazard (sometimes referred to as the *asset substitution problem*).[10] Thus, creditors need to monitor borrowers to ensure that excessive risks are not taken at their expense.

Moral hazard of this kind is present whenever firms borrow but becomes severe when the equity shrinks to little or nothing. It is entirely likely that Mr. Charn knew that Alphatec was about to collapse, but entered into a massive expansion as a desperate gamble, hoping that it would pay off and get the firm out of the hole it was in. When the equity is already gone, incentives become totally skewed. The downside of large risks is no longer a deterrent since losses will be entirely for the account of the creditors, whereas a sufficiently large upside could restore the firm's equity. Such "resurrection strategies" are common in banks, which are themselves highly leveraged and which can change their asset mix more quickly and freely than industrial companies.

Creditors can protect themselves against excessive risk to some degree by holding short-term debt. Holders of short-term debt are relatively protected from asset substitution because they will be able to demand their money back in the near future when the debt matures, or roll the debt over only at a higher interest rate. Of course, this requires that creditors be observant, monitor the firm's actions, and penalize higher risk when they observe it.

Restrictive covenants may also help creditors. These oblige management not to do certain things that would be grossly unfair to the lenders. For example, covenants may limit the amount that managers can pay out as dividends; this prevents equity holders from looting the company at the expense of the lenders. Similarly, if the debt is unsecured, managers must promise not to secure new debt with any assets (which would make the new debt effectively senior to the old) unless the unsecured lenders are brought in under the same collateral; this is called a *negative pledge clause.* Finally,

---

[10]See Chapter 7 for a full explanation of moral hazard, and the risks of asset substitution as bank capital falls or vanishes. We show that this can be a deadly source of risk not only for banks, but also for the economy as a whole.

covenants often prevent managers from letting debt expand above a certain fraction of assets or set minimal liquidity ratios for borrowing firms.

But covenants will not work unless they are monitored and enforced. The larger group of lenders must have some agent functioning who is given regular reports and who checks compliance with the covenants. Furthermore, the lenders must have legal recourse if covenants are not followed. In developed capital markets, failure to keep a covenant is an event of default that if not cured can precipitate acceleration of repayment, seizure of collateral, and bankruptcy. But in many EFM legal frameworks, the failure to keep covenants is not enforced as an event of default, leaving lenders little recourse even if they monitor.

If lenders are not able to monitor borrowers and enforce covenants, they will need to charge substantially higher interest rates to compensate for the likelihood that some borrowers, who are better informed about their businesses than lenders, will misbehave. That is why it is in the interest of borrowers to agree to some disclosure, some restrictive covenants, and some level of monitoring. In other words, reducing the information asymmetry is in everyone's interest. Also, the willingness of borrowers to disclose information, agree to covenants, and allow monitoring is a signal of their good intentions and confidence in their prospects.

The Role of Banks

Monitoring is often a prohibitively expensive process that is difficult for individuals to conduct on their own. It is therefore natural that financial institutions arise to perform this role on behalf of many suppliers of funds. A seminal paper in financial economics visualized a "state of nature" in which investors band together and form banks to be "delegated monitors" of their investments.[11]

Indeed, we have seen in the privatization of Central and Eastern Europe that financial institutions did arise spontaneously to perform this role, whether they were banks or, in some cases, mutual funds. However, we have also seen that such intermediaries can misbehave, whether they are banks (in Russia) or funds (in the Czech Republic). So financial institutions solve the monitoring problem at one level, but they also create a new problem: how to monitor the monitors.

Banks dominate emerging financial markets because, in situations of imperfect information, they are so well suited to performing both screening and monitoring functions. Banks perform screening by investing in information. Their staff of lending officers can call on a wide variety of firms, elicit private information about their businesses and prospects, and make decisions based upon the nature and quality of that private information. Borrowers in need of loans are generally willing to supply this private information in order to make a loan feasible.

When banks have accepted a borrower and made a loan, they establish an ongoing relationship characterized by regular gathering of information. Banks are then natural monitors of the firms in question, using the same lending officers, and can help the firm through any difficult periods it may encounter, though always standing ready to call their loans if they lose confidence in the ability or willingness of the firm to pay its obligations. Banks recover the costs of screening borrowers, and monitoring and enforcing contracts, by charging interest rates and fees that cover those costs, in addition to the interest cost the bank pays for its own funds and a risk premium to compensate the bank for the riskiness of the loan.

---

[11]Diamond (1984).

In recent years banks have emerged as private equity investors, both in developed markets and in EFMs. Because of the shortage of equity in EFMs, their role is especially important there. If fast-growing firms are forced to rely on debt entirely for their external financing needs, the only source of equity finance will be retained earnings. In that case, the firm's ability to attract outside funding will be constrained by a maximum feasible leverage ratio (debt capacity) and by its growth of retained earnings. The recent growth of private equity finance in EFMs indicates that—despite the formidable challenges that face outside equity investors in EFMs—there are substantial benefits from being able to attract private equity capital. In our discussion below of institutional investors, we consider factors that can favor the development of public and private equity markets.[12]

Banks serve an important role as specialists in information processing and contract enforcement, and that role is enhanced to the extent that they can reuse information efficiently, develop long-term relationships, and use a combination of debt and equity financing, as circumstances require.

This is now the standard framework for explaining why banks exist, how they structure their contracts with borrowers, and why limits exist on banks' abilities to resolve problems of asymmetric information in the loan market. Thus far, however, our summary of the role of banks has not considered the problem of information asymmetry on the other side of the market: How can savers have confidence depositing their funds in banks if the banks' portfolios are based on investments about which the bank has private information and, therefore, whose quality cannot easily be confirmed by depositors? How can they choose among banks, and what will prevent the banks from looting the deposits?

The question is not a trivial one. We have seen that in several EFMs liberalization has given rise to rogue banks or to banks whose portfolios consisted primarily of firms in which the banks' owners had interests, as opposed to the firms most likely to repay. Mechanisms need to be in place to protect depositors against misbehavior by better-informed banks.

When considering mechanisms that limit bankers' incentives to misbehave, it is important to distinguish market-based monitoring and control from regulatory monitoring and control. *Market-based discipline* relies on the suppliers of funds to banks, primarily depositors. Many depositors are, of course, individuals with little capacity to monitor the banks. But some depositors are large, institutional, and informed; typically some are other banks. Such large depositors should make it their business to understand what is happening in their economy and to influence events when possible. They are likely to be aware of problems emerging in banks.

A bank gets into trouble when a sufficient number of its borrowers are unable to service their loans. Often the bank can cover up problems by making fresh loans to troubled borrowers so that they avoid immediate default. But if the problems are more than temporary, sooner or later the bank has to worry about significant loan losses. If

---

[12]For a discussion of the Japanese banks' system of mixing equity and debt claims on firms—which is currently evolving in important respects—see Hoshi, Kashyap, and Scharfstein (1990), Aoki and Patrick (1994), and Hoshi and Patrick (2000). The German approach is somewhat different from a system of direct bank ownership of equity (as in Japan). Historically (prior to World War I), German banks underwrote vast quantities of equity for their client firms, which they placed with their trust customers. The banks retained control of those shares and voted on behalf of their trust customer stockholders. Thus, although banks were typically not large stockholders directly, they maintained a stake in the performance of the equity they underwrote through their role as trust account managers. That system of corporate governance was retained in the post–World War II period, although equity offerings have been far rarer than during the pre–World War I period (see Calomiris 1995).

the potential losses are large enough, they can wipe out the equity of the bank, leaving liability claims (mainly deposits) that exceed the true value of assets. This implies that depositors will not get all their money back. When rumors of this kind begin to spread, large and informed depositors quickly withdraw their deposits. Smaller depositors are usually just behind them, wanting their money too. Such a *bank run* can quickly exhaust a bank's liquid assets and lead to its closure. A bank run is a particularly strong demonstration of the financial market's ruthlessness in taking control over funds from any user that might be destroying value.

Fear of bank runs tends to keep banks from taking excessive risk, and this is the point of market-based discipline. In particular, the short-term nature of bank deposits makes runs an ever-present possibility. This strengthens the incentive for banks to behave cautiously, thereby partially overcoming depositors' anxiety about insufficient information.

Indeed, it is possible to argue that the liability structure of banks was designed in large part as a means of providing discipline on bankers, which benefited all bank depositors by constraining the actions of bankers. While it is undoubtedly true that there are other explanations for the liability structure of banks that revolve around needs for liquidity and the role of bank claims as a means of payment, it is important to note that other banklike intermediaries (e.g., finance companies, whose liabilities are not used as a medium of payment) also finance themselves largely from short-term liabilities, mainly commercial paper.[13]

A disadvantage of market-based discipline, however, is that innocent and uninformed depositors can lose money when banks fail. Prior to the creation of deposit insurance in the United States, stranded depositors suffered the risk of loss on their deposits and had to wait until the bank's assets were liquidated to be repaid in whole or part. But average losses were small compared to those of corporate debt holders historically or to losses seen in bank failures today. From the Civil War through the Great Depression, failure rates of banks and nonbank companies were similar, but losses on bank failures averaged about 10 percent while losses on nonbank company failures averaged about 90 percent.[14] Deposit withdrawals swiftly put a troubled bank out of business before losses could continue or resurrection strategies could be tried.

Because bank runs are a fearsome sight to both depositors and bankers, governments in industrial and developing countries alike have decided almost universally to insure some or all bank deposits in the present era. Perhaps even more important to the history of government safety net policy has been the pressure exerted by banks for government protection. Given the influential role of bankers, particularly in EFMs, allowing banks to fail can be politically difficult. As Chile discovered in 1982, even a government that does not offer explicit deposit coverage may be forced into it when the crisis is sufficiently great. Deposit insurance reduces the incentive depositors have to monitor and control the behavior of banks. This means that government must step in to perform that role.

Regulatory discipline means that the government itself screens and controls bank riskiness through licensing procedures, capital requirements, and a variety of prudential regulations, and it monitors banks through periodic examinations by government officials. Unfortunately, as we shall see in greater detail in Chapters 7 and 8, bank

---

[13]For theory, see Calomiris and Kahn (1991). For empirical evidence of market discipline historically, see Calomiris and Mason (1997) and Calomiris and Wilson (1998). For modern day evidence, see Berger, Davies, and Flannery (1998), Flannery (1998), Jagtiani, Kaufman, and Lemieux (1999), Morgan and Stiroh (1999), and Peria and Schmukler (1998).

[14]Kaufman (1994).

regulation is often a poor substitute for market discipline. Bank supervisors and regulators frequently lack both the ability and the incentive to respond to bank weakness with the reliability and swiftness of market participants. They are often excessively sympathetic to the bankers and try to avoid confrontation by temporizing. The result is no more bank runs, but the aggregate costs of bank failures are far higher than those seen in the past.

One recent approach to capital regulation of banks aims to address the shortcomings of capital regulation by incorporating an element of market discipline into the regulatory process. In essence, the idea is to create a class of institutional investors that monitor banks. Banks would be required to issue a certain amount of *subordinated debt* (a form of debt specifically earmarked to be junior to deposits and to receive no protection from the government) to institutional investors, possibly with a ceiling on its interest rate to ensure a sufficiently low risk for the bank. The institutional investors would then perform a monitoring role on behalf of the government regulator, for which they would be compensated through the interest rate.[15] Government regulators could thereby require that banks meet market standards for risk management, and use market signals of bank risk (observed yield spreads) as a regulatory tool to identify weak banks. Argentina adopted such a subordinated debt requirement, which became effective in 1998. Subordinated debt is properly understood not as a replacement for government regulation—indeed it depends on regulatory enforcement of the subordinated debt requirement to be effective—but rather as a source of additional monitoring and information.

Institutional Investors

As financial markets develop, banks tend to play a smaller role and securities markets become increasingly important. Securities market growth encourages the development of *institutional investors* to perform screening and monitoring functions on behalf of their less-informed individual clients. Such institutional investors include insurance companies, pension funds, mutual funds, and, increasingly in recent years, private equity funds. Although these institutions often invest in *private placements* (i.e., securities that are not publicly traded), even this activity depends on the presence of an active market for public securities to benchmark its prices and terms.

The role of financial institutions can be seen in both primary markets, where offerings are initially sold by underwriters, and secondary markets, where stocks are traded on a continuous basis. In secondary markets, active trading by large block holders has added greatly to market liquidity. In primary equity markets, institutional investors have been even more important in reducing the costs of marketing offerings:

> These institutions, which first sparked the cult of common stocks, later attracted public attention to "growth" stocks and created the fashion for instant performance. Innovative and inventive, institutional money managers have ventured into areas where older and more prudent investment men feared to tread, taking positions in the stocks of unseasoned companies, setting up hedge funds, devising new types of securities.[16]

The effects of institutional investors on the fees or spreads charged by investment bankers to firms offering equity—which provides a rough measure of the costs that

---

[15]Calomiris (1997).

[16]Friend, Blume, and Crockett (1970). For reviews of the codevelopment of the equity market and the new institutional investors in the 1960s, see Securities and Exchange Commission (1971), Friend, Longstreet, Mendelson, Miller, and Hess (1967), and Calomiris and Raff (1995).

firms must pay investment bankers to help overcome adverse selection problems when marketing shares to outsiders—can be roughly gauged by comparing the spreads paid before institutional investors were important players in equity markets (in 1950) with the underwriting spreads paid after these investors had become fully active in equity markets (by the end of the 1960s). One study found that, controlling for other characteristics that affect the costs of placing equity, underwriting costs for small, unseasoned firms had fallen from roughly 14 percent of the amount offered to 9 percent of the offering.[17]

That pattern of codevelopment between the rising share of institutional investors' financial assets and the falling cost of raising equity in public markets has continued in the last three decades, and has spread from the United States to other countries. Institutional investors, especially pension funds, have also become important in spurring the growth of private equity markets, as pension funds are typically among the biggest investors in these funds. In EFMs like Chile—which was the leader in privatizing its pension system in the 1980s and 1990s—the creation of a new class of large-scale institutional investors has opened up new opportunities for local firms to access public markets for debt and equity. We review the experiences of Chile and other EFMs with pension privatization, and its effects on securities markets, in Chapter 9.

There are three reasons that institutional investors have been so important in spurring private equity financing, reducing the costs of public equity offerings, and thus expanding access to these markets. First, because institutional investors buy in large quantity, they economize on the physical costs of selling. Before investment banks were able to sell in large blocks to institutions, they had to sell all their offerings in the retail market. This involved communicating with investors through vast, decentralized, multilayered networks of securities dealers and brokers. It is not hard to see why the physical costs of credibly transmitting information would be lower when a large fraction of issues are sold wholesale to large investors.

Second, institutional investors maintain contact with investment bankers over many successive issues. Thus, these institutions can work together on any one deal, knowing that the other side has a large stake in preserving its reputation for candor and honesty. Recent models of information transmittal in these markets have argued that it is best to see institutional investors and investment banks as working together, sharing information before issues are brought to market to improve the accuracy of pricing and lower the risk of being unable to sell offerings in the market.[18] There is also continuity in the involvement of institutional investors with a given firm. Pension fund investors can now invest in a firm from cradle to grave—owning an interest in the private equity fund that finances the firm and also purchasing shares of the firm's initial public offering (IPO) and its subsequent equity offerings.

Third, the large size of institutional investors' holdings has also permitted them to play a new role in corporate governance. Large pension funds (e.g., the California state employees' fund) sometimes take an active role in criticizing management and influencing the policies of the firms in which they invest. The ability to concentrate large chunks of a firm's equity in the hands of a few large institutional investors provides protection to buyers against *ex post* abuses of management, which also makes equity offerings more attractive.

---

[17]Calomiris and Raff (1995), p. 147.

[18]See, for example, Beatty and Ritter (1986) Benveniste and Spindt (1989), and Benveniste and Wilhelm (1990).

Corporate Governance

The need to monitor management raises the larger question of proper corporate governance: Who controls the behavior of firms, and to what end? The question is a deep and fundamental one in all countries, industrialized and developing alike. But it has a critical importance in EFMs because many observers find a connection between weak corporate governance and large bank loan losses. The Asian financial crisis of 1997–1998 in particular seemed to reveal poor corporate investment decisions (too much investment at too low a return), which in turn may have reflected weaknesses in corporate governance throughout East Asia.

Conglomerates and Business Groups

A central issue that cuts across all approaches to implementing governance is the appropriate span of control: Are firms best organized into families of companies under common control, usually through a holding company, or is it better that each distinct business be organized into a separate, independent firm? In developed and developing economies throughout the world, one sees many examples of conglomerate organization. What benefits might this confer? Here is a list of possibilities:

1. **Personal gratification.** Some human beings have large egos and find great satisfaction in building an empire. Examples of empire building by one strong personality abound in both the developed and developing worlds. To the extent that such individuals can command sufficient resources to support their grand plans, personal gratification can be an important force in building conglomerates.

2. **Political influence.** Wherever financial repression occurs, capital and political favors are allocated to some degree by governments. In such settings, the largest players may have the strongest claims, and combining companies into groups may maximize these claims by increasing political influence.[19]

3. **Obfuscation.** Conglomerate structures are usually very complex and difficult to understand. Intercorporate payments may be quite different from payments that would occur at arm's length. This may suit the desires of the owners, who perhaps wish to avoid disclosure of information, minimize taxes, and reduce external monitoring.

4. **Diversification.** Conglomerates are often justified as a form of diversification. The risk-reducing benefits of diversification are well known, although they are usually undertaken at the investor level rather than at the corporate level.

5. **Internal capital markets.** Related to diversification is the convenience of having some profitable internal companies whose free cash flow can provide capital to other businesses, hopefully promising ones. If related companies have better information about one another than outsiders do, then the creation of internal capital markets can be a means for overcoming some of the costs of external finance related to asymmetric information. On the other hand, internal capital markets may be used to fund inefficient pet projects of management that otherwise would have a hard time attracting funds. Below we consider both positive and negative aspects of internal capital markets.

In the United States and to a lesser degree in Europe, conglomerate companies enjoyed a vogue during the 1960s and fell into disrepute in the 1970s and 1980s. The

---

[19]See Fisman (1998) for evidence of the economic importance of such influence in Indonesia.

original vogue arose from a merger boom during the buoyant years of 1964–1969. In this period many holding companies made dozens (in some cases hundreds) of stock-for-stock acquisitions, claiming major "synergies" from this activity. The holding companies were primarily financial rather than operating control centers, holding each subsidiary responsible for delivering planned performance, and "managing by exception" when some fell short of their plans.

By the 1970s, however, it started to become clear that many such companies were underperforming: The average operating performance of firms inside conglomerate structures was lower than the performance of similar firms not in a conglomerate setting, and the value of the conglomerate stock was at a discount from the sum of the estimated values of the component companies taken separately. This became especially apparent as the process of takeover and divestiture caused the inefficient conglomerates to be dismantled in the 1980s.[20]

Academic research has suggested two reasons why conglomerates tend to be inefficient. First and most obvious is the problem of competence: It is hard for holding company management to be competent enough in dozens of business lines to direct the activities of the subsidiaries. Consequently, management may often behave only reactively, trying to control problems after they appear, rather than getting ahead of possible problems with thoughtful strategies. In short, the holding companies had difficulty adding value to the subsidiaries. It is now accepted management wisdom that firms should not try to excel in everything, but should identify and build upon only their "core competence."

The second reason, though less obvious, may be even more important because it reveals how holding company management can actually degrade the performance of subsidiaries. It is a specifically financial point: Conglomerate holding companies act like a kind of bank, taking excess cash from some subsidiaries and providing cash to others. As noted above, this reliance on internal capital markets is a convenience for holding company managers.

The nature of internal capital markets is usually to draw cash from the cash-producing companies and pass it to the subsidiaries in need of cash. This is sometimes justified as milking the "cash cows" in order to feed the future "stars" (an efficient use of internal capital markets to mitigate high external finance costs for the "stars"). But it cannot be taken for granted that internal capital markets are always used to promote efficient redistribution of cash. Financial value equals the discounted present worth of cash flows; thus, the so-called cows may be among the most valuable subsidiaries while some of the alleged stars may be value destroyers. Internal capital markets can easily lead to value destruction.

Indeed, critics of internal capital markets argue that conglomerate management typically makes capital allocation decisions that are more political than financial. That tendency, one might argue, is inherent in human nature. Almost all human beings have a natural tendency to help the struggling; to do otherwise would seem quite cruel. This is also apparent in the socialist objectives of governments, which tax the rich to feed the poor. But it is not the behavior of external capital markets, which tend to be heartless and Darwinian. Indeed, external capital markets typically deny cash to struggling companies and lavish it on those with the best prospects.

---

[20]Important contributions to the literature on conglomerate performance include Auerbach (1988), Lang, Stulz, and Walking (1989), Mitchell and Lehn (1990), Shleifer and Vishny (1990), Servaes (1991), Healy, Palepu, and Ruback (1992), Kaplan and Weisbach (1992), and Lang and Stulz (1994). For a dissenting view, see Maksimovic and Phillips (1999).

The heartlessness of capital markets is one reason they engender deep mistrust among many people, above all in EFMs. Yet this apparent heartlessness is the simple consequence of maximizing the value of enterprises. Critics of internal capital markets argue that if we support value maximization as the goal of enterprise, then we should let external capital markets do their work and not permit the political workings of internal capital markets to distort capital allocation.

To make this same point in different words, each separate enterprise creates value only to the extent that its internal rate of return exceeds its cost of capital, which in turn is a function of the enterprise's level of risk. Value creation is reasonably well assured by an external capital market, which provides funds to each separate company at a price reflecting that company's risk. But internal capital markets may subsidize riskier enterprises. It is the same mistake that governments typically make when they intervene to subsidize struggling industries. Such subsidies often lead to misallocation of capital, especially if continued over an extended period of time.

Of course, not all conglomerates abuse internal capital markets. Some firms make use of internal capital markets to reduce the financing costs of "stars" that otherwise would face high costs in external markets. One notable success story for internal markets is the General Electric Company (GE), which is not only one of the best-performing companies in the United States but also one of its few surviving conglomerates: It still has approximately 30 separate businesses, though this is dramatically less than the nearly 500 that existed in the early 1980s. GE's CEO Jack Welch at that time declared that he would only support subsidiaries that were number one or number two in their industries; all others would be sold or closed. Although this rule was simple and apparently crude, it acted to channel capital to likely value creators and to deny capital to likely value destroyers, leading to hundreds of divestitures. The result was impressive performance.

The conglomerate form of organization is very common in the developing world. There has been relatively little research on the relative performance of conglomerates in developing countries. One study has suggested that such conglomerates sometimes perform better than independent companies in the same countries, partly because of the inadequacies of the legal system, the inadequacies of external finance, and the inefficiencies of government-controlled services. Because capital market imperfections are often pronounced in EFMs, the role of internal capital markets in these countries may be helpful in reducing costs to profitable subsidiaries that would otherwise face high costs of external finance.

But the role of industrial groups in developing countries can go farther than creating beneficial internal capital markets. Industrial groups may form to permit firms to obtain reliable services from one another without having to depend on legal enforcement of contracts across businesses or on government provision of essential needs (like communication and transportation networks). From this perspective, the large scale and diversity of business groups reflects the desire to create sufficient scale and scope so that individual business components can avoid the worst features of the legal and economic institutional environments in which they operate by creating a mini-economy of their own. Sometimes groups locate in less-developed regions and build roads and other essential services in those regions, so that they actually maintain a physical separateness from the rest of the economy, enabling them to internalize the benefits of their infrastructure investments.[21]

---

[21]Fisman and Khanna (1999).

There are other reasons that conglomerates may function relatively well in developing countries. Developing countries enjoy an abundance of opportunities but suffer a shortage of management talent; thus, good entrepreneurs may need to spread themselves across a variety of firms that otherwise would suffer from a lack of management skill. Alternatively, conglomerates may perform better because they have political connections that benefit the companies in their group.

Despite these advantages, many large conglomerates in emerging markets display the same dysfunctions as large conglomerates in the developed markets. The Korean *chaebols,* the Mexican *grupos,* and conglomerates in Indonesia, for example, have been widely criticized recently for their underperformance and for the protection these inefficient firms receive from their governments. A common feature of privatization in Central and Eastern Europe has been the breaking up of huge, conglomerated state enterprises into smaller, more manageable units. On balance, we believe that governance considerations will cause developing countries to gradually move away from conglomerate forms, particularly as improvements in legal systems and capital markets, and new competition in the provision of transportation, communication, and other services, reduce the legitimate need to operate conglomerates.

Goals of Governance

In the following section we will consider the four primary models of corporate governance, but we first consider what criteria a proper governance system should satisfy. One must first decide what the overall *goal* of private enterprise is, and then choose the governance system best suited to achieving that goal. But what is the appropriate goal? In Chapter 3 we argued that the long-term economic well-being of countries depends not just on growth of GDP per capita, but also on efficient, or value-creating, growth. Growth based on increasing inputs alone is not sustainable. Sustainable economic growth comes from increasing productivity, that is, improving the efficiency with which inputs are used. This comes from allowing enterprises to maximize their bottom lines. The congruence between the social goal of sustainable growth and the private desire of entrepreneurs to maximize their personal wealth is the fundamental justification of capitalism.

In the United States there is widespread agreement that the goal of private enterprise is to maximize shareholder value. This is increasingly accepted in Europe as well, although an important segment of European thought would supplement it with a concern for the welfare of employees. Germany, for example, institutionalizes employee goals in corporate governance with its policy of *Mitbestimmung,* under which unions have a right to several seats on large corporate boards.

Let us pause at this point to reflect on the complexity and even confusion that this extra goal seems to introduce. Maximizing shareholder value is simple, clear, and unequivocal; shareholder value is measured by the stock price, which is maximized by generating as much profit as possible for shareholders. Maximizing employee welfare would seem to imply paying out all free cash flow to employees, to the obvious detriment of shareholders. Logically, one cannot maximize two conflicting objective functions; some trade-off between them must be specified for a definable goal even to exist.

If pressed on this point, defenders of *Mitbestimmung* would probably say that employee welfare need not be maximized, but does need to be taken into serious account. So the corporate goal might be: Maximize shareholder value subject to the constraint that workers and unions be treated generously. But then, how generously? How can we know if the corporate goal is reached? Can the unions change their view of what constitutes sufficiently generous treatment over the years? Isn't it likely that they will?

Furthermore, looking at Germany's economic performance in the late 20th century, one notes that German labor costs became the highest in the world and that German manufacturing companies seemed reluctant to invest capital in Germany throughout the 1980s and 1990s. Indeed, the United States was an important beneficiary of this dilemma, as large numbers of German companies built manufacturing plants in the nonunionized American South, especially North and South Carolina, even as the eastern regions of Germany suffered unemployment at rates of 20 to 30 percent. This behavior of German companies suggests that maximizing shareholder value really *is* their corporate goal, subject to the costly constraints that *Mitbestimmung* imposes on their operations inside Germany.

Corporate goals in developing countries also may be less ambiguous than they sometimes appear. Governments have played a dominating role in many developing economies, and governmental goals such as full employment, community and regional development, and taking care of politically favored persons have often found their way into some statements of the mission of the private sector. Spokesmen such as Prime Minister Mohamad Mahatir of Malaysia have tried to articulate an "Asian way" based on "Asian values" of communal sharing and cooperation.

Yet the great majority of businesses in Asia and throughout the developing world are family owned, and one must ask whether these families genuinely want to pursue broad communal goals with their own resources, or whether they want to maximize their own wealth, subject to the need to respond to a government that presses them in a policy-related direction. We think it is self-evident that a family-owned business normally would seek to maximize its own wealth as a primary goal. Naturally, it wants harmony with its employees, customers, and communities, but so do all established businesses. No business anywhere can maximize shareholder value over the long term without such harmony.

When considering nonfamily-owned businesses, it is hard to see why stockholders in public firms would, or should, be asked to bear some special burden to accomplish objectives other than value maximization. Indeed, if they were, that in itself would discourage the formation of publicly owned businesses, which would place undesirable constraints on the scale of firms, the ways firms could raise capital, and the opportunities for diversification in the economy.

Furthermore, as we have already argued, maximization of firm value is compatible with social goals. In the long term, single-minded competition to create profit leads to the highest level of sustainable, value-creating growth in the economy as a whole, without which most governmental goals are difficult to achieve.

Clarification of the corporate goal is critical to choosing an appropriate governance system. If value maximization is the goal, then a governance system should be chosen that makes value maximization most likely. People respond very powerfully to incentives, so the task of corporate governance then becomes the creation of incentives to maximize the value of the enterprise. The central constraint to an effective governance mechanism remains, however, problems of information and control— finding ways to align the incentives of management with the value-creation objective of stockholders in a world where it may be difficult to measure managerial accomplishment and to reward or penalizé managers in a way commensurate with their accomplishments.

Models of Governance

Let us now examine the four primary models of corporate governance found around the world:

1. State ownership and control.
2. Family ownership and control.
3. Bank-centered control systems.
4. Control by dispersed shareholders.

Each of these systems has its adherents, and each has at one time or another been promoted as the best system. In our view, some of these arrangements are, on average, better than others—for example, government control is generally not an effective method of governance—but it is important to recognize that each system has characteristic strengths and weaknesses that vary in magnitude with specific circumstances. There is no one-size-fits-all optimal method of governance.

Before looking at the four alternatives individually, it is useful to estimate how widespread each system is. A recent study examined in detail the control structures of the 10 largest firms in each of 27 countries, most of them industrial countries, but including Hong Kong, Singapore, Korea, Israel, Argentina, and Mexico.[22] Using ownership of 20 percent or more as a definition of control, the authors report that only 36 percent of these large firms around the world are controlled by dispersed shareholders, 30 percent are family controlled, 18 percent are state controlled, 5 percent are bank controlled, and the remaining 10 percent are in miscellaneous residual categories. Furthermore, in Argentina, Greece, Austria, Hong Kong, Portugal, Israel, and Belgium there are hardly any widely held firms in this sample by this definition. The percentage of family-controlled large firms in this sample is 50 percent in Israel, 65 percent in Argentina, 70 percent in Hong Kong, and 100 percent in Mexico.

The same study reported that dispersed shareholders are common only in the subset of countries with strong antidirector rights as discussed in Chapter 4; these tend to be the common law countries, and dispersed shareholders control 48 percent of their large firms. In the other subset, primarily civil law countries, dispersed shareholders control only 27 percent of the large firms, a statistically significant difference.

State Ownership. One surprising result of the above study is that state ownership is still widespread (18 percent), even after the wave of privatizations described in Chapter 3. Yet by the test of what governance system best advances the goal of maximizing firm value, state ownership can be virtually ruled out: State ownership creates incentives to pursue many goals other than value maximization. The managers who operate state-owned enterprises might seek power, influence, security, or other goals, but have little or no incentive to maximize the value of the enterprise. Even when governments consciously try to create such incentives in a context of state ownership, they usually cannot resist interfering in and influencing the behavior of the firm in pursuit of one or more political ends.

One can imagine extreme situations of war, depression, or crisis in which the government needs to take a very strong role, including the possibility of managing production, to resolve an emergency. Experience shows that in bona fide emergencies people are often very supportive of strong government action. But having resolved the emergency, the government must again separate itself from managing the production

---

[22]La Porta, Lopez-de-Silanes, and Shleifer (1999).

process, and allow value maximization and private enterprise to return to its central position in the economy.

That leaves three models: family ownership and control, bank-centered governance, and control by dispersed shareholders. Each has strengths and weaknesses.

Family Ownership and Control.   In many ways, family ownership and control represents capitalism at its best. The identity between family wealth and corporate value is nearly perfect, so incentives for value maximization are at their highest. There is no possibility for fundamental conflict between ownership and management, nor any problems of asymmetric information between owners and managers, because ownership and management are not separated. Family ownership is clearly the norm of corporate governance throughout the developing world, and is an important form in all countries.

The primary disadvantage of family ownership is that the extent of equity capital is constrained. This means that growth is financed by retained earnings and debt, typically with a high level of bank borrowing, so that financial risk compounds operating risk. Thus, family ownership can lead to high leverage (and consequently a high risk of financial distress) and an inadequate supply of capital for growth. Indeed, this is what sometimes forces a family to cede control, as capital needs grow far beyond the capacity of the family to invest more equity. This can be avoided by keeping the growth rate no higher than the rate of return on equity, so that equity grows naturally at a pace that keeps up with sales. But often in EFMs, growth opportunities are larger than that, so family-owned companies tend to adopt a risky high-leverage strategy. As bankruptcy procedures modernize throughout the developing world, many family-owned businesses that relied on excessive borrowing to support their growth will lose control through bankruptcy.

Furthermore, family control is inherently hard to sustain over the long run. By their nature, families change over time. The original entrepreneur dies or retires and children take over. They may or may not have the same talent for business and they may or may not get along with each other. As one generation rolls into another, problems can emerge because the logic of family relationships is different from the logic of business relationships. This often leads the family to consider selling the business to another company.

Bank-Centered Control.   An alternative governance mechanism with more permanence is bank-centered control. It is, however, much less common than widely assumed. Most people associate bank-centered governance with Japan and Germany, but the study cited above indicated that only 15 percent of large German firms are bank controlled (a percentage matched by Portugal and Sweden and exceeded by Belgium at 30 percent), but that *none* of the large Japanese firms in the sample could be so classified based upon their stock ownership. Of course, "main banks" influence Japanese companies in informal ways not captured by stock ownership, but such informal ties can change and may even vanish over time.

In modern times, bank-centered governance arises primarily in EFMs where a period of free banking (or at least very open banking) has preceded a wave of privatization, as in Chile during 1974–1979; Mexico, 1989–1994; and Russia, 1991–1995. These preconditions enable entrepreneurs to buy a bank, sometimes with money borrowed from the bank itself, and then to use further bank loans to buy other privatizing companies. The bank then becomes the central feature in the growing corporate empire. The consequence is a family of companies that behave a good deal like a conglomerate. The controlling bank moves cash among the various components. Companies may not be worried about borrowing very large amounts because they are confident that a bank that directly or indirectly owns part of their stock will never force them into liquidation.

In theory, as noted earlier in this chapter, banks provide a natural solution to problems of asymmetric information, including both screening and monitoring. But how well do they perform this role in practice in EFMs? With respect to screening, loans to insider-controlled firms may be determined more by influence than by profitability. With respect to monitoring and control, the massive wave of bank losses and bank failures around the world during the closing decades of the 20th century (examined in Chapters 7 and 8) suggest that many or indeed most EFM banks have significantly failed to detect problems and alter the behavior of firms.

Numerous studies in the transition countries indicate that banks do not have the skills or incentives to monitor companies effectively.[23] If the banks are the center of an industrial empire, they have little incentive to discipline other members of the group. Even if they are somewhat at arm's length, they may have difficulty gathering information and enforcing contracts if the legal system and the disclosure and accounting norms are inadequate.

Furthermore, the banking system in many EFMs still includes a significant fraction of government-owned banks. State-owned banks tend to monitor as poorly as state-appointed managers manage because of the ambiguity of goals and the lack of market penalties for underperformance. For example, a study of Indian corporate governance reported that

> a landmark committee set up to review the state of the financial sector, the Narasimhan Committee, admitted that loans had not been monitored for decades. The first reason for poor monitoring of Indian firms is that the dominant financial institutions (almost exclusively state-run banks) did not have monitoring as their primary objective. Indeed, until 1991, the objective of government policy was to maximize loans to the industrial sector in the belief that this would lead to industrial development.[24]

Defenders of bank-centered governance argue that banks with control over their borrowers take a long view, that they represent "patient capital" which will sustain a firm through difficult times. They will not require short-term earnings performance, but will be content to wait until a longer-term goal is reached. Their direct participation as a partial owner in the governance of the firm provides excellent monitoring and gives the bank maximum access to private information, including strategies for the long term.

But another interpretation of the patient capital argument is that managements are not under the kind of pressures created by capital markets to either increase shareholder value or be dismissed. The lack of pressure can in turn lead to rates of return that are not only low in the short term but also in the long term. Bank control prevents the firm from shopping for banking services and may lead to excessive interest rates.

Furthermore, companies dependent on banks may suffer when the banks themselves get into trouble.[25] This may help to explain Japan's decade-long recession in the 1990s in the presence of massive and unresolved bank loan losses. During the long stock market collapse in 1990–1993, the market values of bank-dependent firms in Japan declined materially more than firms that were not bank dependent.[26]

---

[23]See, for example, the five studies in Part II of Aoki and Kim (1995).

[24]Khanna and Palepu (1999).

[25]See Slovin, Suska, and Polonchek (1993) for a U.S. example.

[26]Kang and Stulz (1997).

More Insider Control: Opportunity or Ploy?

The giant Argentine conglomerate, Perez Companc, had a deal for its outside stockholders. The family that ran the firm, and held 29 percent of voting stock, wanted to exchange existing outsiders' shares in the company for new shares in a holding company. Outsiders would get diluted voting rights, and the family's voting control would increase to 67 percent of the new entity. Why would any outsider agree to such a deal?

The selling pitch for the deal ran as follows. The company saw growth opportunities requiring it to raise more equity capital, but it also feared hostile takeovers. If its voting control were raised to 67 percent and it had public shares with few voting rights, then it could sell new shares without fear of takeover, and so make the company grow faster.

But shareholders might be forgiven for wondering whether they would receive any benefits from such a program. Their voting power would be dramatically reduced, and it was not obvious whether their economic interest might also be diluted by unspecified expansions financed by equity. Nor was it obvious that reducing the probability of a takeover was in the outside shareholders' interest. A report from ABN AMRO opined that "the company has not yet provided a compelling plan or adequately explained the strategy behind the need for this cash infusion." From November 1999 to January 2000, in the wake of the management's announced proposal for restructuring, the share price of Perez Companc fell more than 20 percent relative to the Merval index of stocks.

In the event, some 98 percent of outside stockholders agreed to the exchange. That popularity partly reflected the concern that the old shares would be hard to trade once the new shares were issued. Whether the newly strengthened position of the Perez Companc family, and its ability to raise equity and stave off takeover threats, will be in the interest of outside shareholders remains to be seen.

Sources: *Financial Times,* January 24, 2000, and *Latin Finance,* March 2000.

Control by Dispersed Shareholders   This form of corporate governance is the distinctively modern, Anglo-Saxon model. It is fraught with information asymmetries, and so requires strong disclosure requirements and a great deal of available public information. Entry into public markets is typically a long and arduous process. Firms typically have to establish track records of accounts and borrowing histories from banks before they can gain admittance to public markets. Firms often pass first through a stage of private equity finance and "mezzanine" finance before they develop a sufficient track record of performance to qualify for public markets. Thus, problems of adverse selection severely limit which firms are eligible for public market finance, although—as noted above—institutions such as private equity funds, investment banks, pension funds, mutual funds, and hedge funds can help to mitigate those costs.

Even for relatively seasoned firms that are eligible for entry into public equity markets and that would stand to benefit from the greater access to capital offered by those markets, there are long-run governance costs associated with going public. Because the separation of management from shareholders is large, there is a much greater risk of management misbehavior that a dispersed body of individual shareholders has trouble monitoring.[27]

---

[27]See Shleifer and Vishny (1996) for an extensive survey of the problems arising when ownership is separated from management.

Even when capital markets are effective in uncovering problems and disciplining management, this is not a costless process. When shareholders as a group come to focus on a problem within their firm, they turn against managers who appear to be value destroyers. The willingness to take on management is necessary for value maximization, but doing so through disruptive techniques such as proxy contests and takeover battles has real costs. Furthermore, the rapid turns in stockholder opinions about management may not always be based on an accurate reading of the case, so market-driven governance sometimes appears capricious and short term. Unsurprisingly, this is a favorite argument of a besieged manager.

Capital market control produces managerial concern about stock market valuation of the firm, which is wholly appropriate from a long-run, value-maximization standpoint. But some critics see stock markets as fickle and thus worry about stock prices as a focus of management attention. According to that view, shareholders are neither patient nor equipped with inside information, so management ends up behaving suboptimally by paying too much attention to, and perhaps trying to manipulate, short-run perceptions that may influence stock prices. While there is an element of truth to this argument, the point should not be overstated; so long as stock prices are reasonably accurate measures of firm value (allowing even for a lag of a year or two in market recognition of the true condition of the firm), managers will face strong incentives to maximize long-run fundamental value.

Capital market control only works if it is well supported by legal and information structures. For that reason, this model remains hard to implement today in many EFMs. But the record of achievement, when it has been possible to move toward public ownership, indicates that there are big potential gains from making this form of organization feasible in EFMs.

Global experience with restructuring provides a good example of the gains from dispersed public ownership. For a number of reasons, including globalization and rapid developments in computing and communications, firms around the world needed to *restructure* during the 1980s and 1990s.[28] That is, they needed to refocus on core competencies, sell or close money-losing operations, reduce excessive layers of middle management, and in general slim down in order to be more competitive. This need was strong in all countries of the world, but was recognized first in the United States, where capital markets forced restructuring by takeovers of hundreds of important companies during the 1980s.[29] Only in the 1990s did most European companies acknowledge the need to restructure. Many of the much-admired Japanese companies, with their bank-centered control systems, seemed to be immobilized and unwilling to face up to this need. Consequently, they lost considerable competitiveness in the 1990s.

In summary, family ownership is probably the best model of governance so long as it lasts, but growth and the passage of time can erode its effectiveness. Bank-centered governance seems to work well in times of stability but may not be as adaptable to change. Market-based control by dispersed shareholders is the most flexible and responsive governance system and seems to produce the most sustainable success, despite its being disruptive and fraught with information and control problems, which make it highly dependent on both good law and good information.

---

[28]See Jensen (1993) for an exceptional review and interpretation of restructuring.

[29]See Auerbach (1988), Lang, Stulz, and Walking (1989), Mitchell and Lehn (1990), Shleifer and Vishny (1990), Servaes (1991), Healy, Palepu, and Ruback (1992), Kaplan and Weisbach (1992), and Lang and Stulz (1994). For a dissenting view, see Maksimovic and Phillips (1999).

An extensive and important survey of corporate governance concluded that it was difficult to say definitively whether family control, bank-centered control, or control by dispersed shareholders represented a better system overall, since each has advantages and disadvantages.[30] To the extent that public ownership is relied upon as a means of governance, what seems to be most important are (1) the presence of at least one large shareholder who will have enough at stake to pay attention and (2) the existence of legal protection for shareholders. Since these conditions prevail in most industrial countries, public governance in all such countries is reasonably good compared with governance in EFMs, where information and legal protection for outside shareholders are often very much lacking.

Institutions of Information

Securities markets cannot possibly work well unless public, arm's-length investors have access to substantial information about the issuers of securities. Without this basic foundation, investors will risk only a small portion of their savings, hoping to "win a lottery," or invest in situations where they have private knowledge of the parties involved, which gives them confidence to part with their capital. Furthermore, as noted above, one cannot rely on companies to share voluntarily information about their true condition; invariably they fear that competitors will take advantage of whatever they disclose. Therefore, a fundamental need of securities markets is for full and uniform disclosure, mandated by law.

Disclosure Laws

Disclosure rules are part of the fundamental legal foundation of financial markets. The purpose of a disclosure law is to make issuers of securities criminally liable for committing fraud by withholding facts that are material to the pricing of their securities. In the absence of credible penalties for failing to disclose material facts, investors will be wary of issuing firms and will, therefore, pay less for securities issues. This is an unnecessary component of the normal adverse-selection discount (or lemons discount) on securities issues discussed above. Pooling firms that are hiding material facts and firms that are not hiding material facts penalizes good firms by reducing the prices of their securities and rewards bad firms by allowing them to avoid being separated from the good firms in investors' eyes. Obviously, then, disclosure rules do not mainly benefit investors (who, on average, receive an expected return commensurate with risk, including the risk of fraud), but rather help good firms to credibly signal that they are good. When the law fails to provide penalties for fraudulent disclosure, it makes the costs of capital for good firms unnecessarily high.

In the United States, the Securities Act of 1933 mandated for the first time that any firm selling an issue of securities must first publish a prospectus giving full and fair disclosure of audited financial data and all material risks. The prospectus is registered with the Securities Exchange Commission (SEC), and the new issue may not be sold until the SEC approves the prospectus. Over time, this requirement for disclosure at the time of a new issue has changed into a requirement that all material information be disclosed promptly and continuously, regardless of whether a new issue is pending or not. Regular quarterly and annual filings of all public companies with the SEC are voluminous, informative, and readily available over the Internet.

---

[30]Shleifer and Vishny (1996).

Most European jurisdictions have somewhat similar laws, although those of the United Kingdom go further than others to ensure complete and timely disclosure. Few developing economies, however, have comparable laws and where they exist they are often not enforced. EFM governments tend to favor their productive companies; the voice of investors is scarcely heard and, in any event, this voice is often a foreign voice rather than a domestic one.

Regardless of disclosure laws, information production does not happen by accident, but is the product of deliberate effort. This effort is much larger than separate individuals can exert and therefore requires *institutions*. Wherever securities markets work well, an institutional setting supports them by generating critical information.

Independent Accounting

Accounting firms are perhaps the most fundamental and important institutions of information in financial markets. Unless financial results are fully disclosed according to a well-understood set of rules, and have been audited and certified by outside accountants, the numbers will be opaque and suspect, and the work of credit and stock analysts will become a frustration.

Audits require detailed standards. Most countries have some set of national laws that specify those standards or empower a qualified group to set them. Some of these standards are based on U.S. generally accepted accounting principles (GAAP) and others are based on the various statements of the International Accounting Standards Committee (IASC). In many cases, these basic standards are modified, sometimes to suit local conditions (e.g., inflation adjustments in Brazil). A detailed description of official accounting standards country-by-country can be found in the *Information Guides* published by PricewaterhouseCoopers.

While written standards are a necessary condition for a proper accounting system, by themselves they are insufficient. Much depends on the quality of the local accounting profession, which in turn is affected by the rigor with which the government enforces the rules. The accounting market tends to be dominated by the large, international accounting partnerships. Their aggressive globalism comes from the needs of their clients: To audit a significant number of large U.S. or European multinational clients requires a presence in virtually every country of the world, because the multinational clients themselves have operations all over the world. Most often, the large accounting firms form alliances with accounting partnerships within each country, and then draw those partnerships into the practices of the firm.

The writing of good accounting standards and even the presence of well-known accounting firms are not enough to overcome a culture in which truth in numbers is not deemed as important as secrecy. In Russia, for example, one study reported that "there are no regulations (including the Company Law) that specify disclosure requirements in detail. Out of 5,000 enterprises privatized, about 100 publish financial statements. Their balance sheets, however, consist of three lines on the assets and two lines on the liabilities, without footnotes, which is just nonsense."[31]

A 1998 study by the United Nations Conference on Trade and Development (UNCTAD) reviewed accounting practices in five East Asian countries after the Asian crises (Korea, Thailand, Indonesia, Malaysia, and the Philippines) and concluded that the failure to follow accounting standards contributed significantly to the magnitude of the crises and the way they unfolded. Specifically, because users of accounting

---

[31]Akamatsu (1995) in Aoki and Kim (1995), p. 142.

standards were misled about the true condition of companies in the period before the crises, investors were not able to pursue precautionary and disciplinary actions that would have prevented financial mismanagement by firms. The suddenness of the withdrawal of capital from these countries in 1997 partly reflected the drastic revision in beliefs about the performance and condition of Asian firms once it became clear that their accounts were unreliable indicators of their true condition.

The UNCTAD study found that the five East Asian countries did not comply with the standards of the IASC in the categories of related-party transactions, foreign currency debt, derivative financial instruments, and contingent liabilities. Only a third of the companies sampled disclosed information regarding related-party borrowing and lending. Only 19 percent disclosed foreign currency translation gains and losses in a manner consistent with IASC rules. More than 80 percent of the firms that used derivative instruments did not disclose the amount of interest and losses related to derivatives, or the terms, conditions, and policies regarding those instruments. Nearly half of the firms failed to report the amount of their contingent liabilities. Loan loss provisions and nonperforming loans were not accurately reflected in accounts of banks.[32]

The quality of accounting standards and disclosure is the only information category for which survey-based assessments are available on a country-by-country basis. These are reproduced in the Appendix, which reports results by country and for groups of countries according to the origins of the countries' legal traditions. Countries with an English or Scandinavian tradition scored highest on accounting performance, followed by countries with German legal origins, with the French-origin countries coming in last by a large margin. The studies of institutional determinants of equity markets (discussed at the end of Chapter 4) included this accounting quality measure in their list of institutional determinants and found that it had significant predictive power for the size of stock markets.

Credit Rating Agencies

Credit rating agencies are important in promoting the smooth working of commercial debt markets. There are in general two types: those that rate public securities and base their views on public information supplemented by meetings with companies, and those that rate private companies based on whatever private information they can accumulate, including primarily reports from trade creditors concerning the promptness of the firm's payments. These amount to a sharing of information among trade creditors, who are both the primary source of the data and the primary users of the reports. In the United States, Moody's Investor Services and Standard and Poor's Corporation are examples of the first type, and Dun and Bradstreet is an example of the second.

These large firms have also tried to become as global as possible, rating international bonds issued by a large number of EFM governments and private companies during the period of high capital flows in the early 1990s. Of course, this requires them to rate not only the prospects of the issuing company, but also the sovereign risk of the country itself; in general, a company cannot be rated more highly than its government. Furthermore, as successive crises and collapses have shown, the primary risk of EFM bonds is not the issuing company so much as the country involved; if it goes into financial crisis, few of its companies escape.

But what exactly does sovereign credit analysis entail? What is being measured? One study found that the best variables for explaining cross-country differences in sovereign ratings include the amount of debt outstanding, GDP per capita, GDP growth, infla-

---

[32]Vishwanath and Kaufmann (1999).

Argentina's State Credit Risk Agencies

In the 1990s Argentina's central bank (BCRA) tried to promote the development of greater transparency in its banking system by requiring that banks obtain private ratings, and by developing databases that track the basic financial information, and lending obligations, of all bank borrowers. The ratings requirement was the less successful of the two innovations, as it quickly led to the formation of many new rating agencies, including some who would give companies a high rating for a healthy fee and without too much scrutiny.

The new database on bank loan customers has been more successful, but it too raises a problem: How much information about bank borrowers should be shared? Clearly, there are gains to creating more information and disseminating it widely. More information facilitates the examination of banks by the authorities, and greater public transparency of risk should lower the costs of funds for high-quality banks by providing a credible way of separating troubled banks from good ones. The BCRA hopes that over time these agencies can give support to the growth of public bond offerings as well. But one must also be careful not to encourage free riding on banks' investments in private information. If all the information that banks collect about their customers were publicized, then competing banks would be able to cherry-pick each other's best customers without having to spend much effort screening customers themselves.

With this trade-off in mind, the BCRA created two parallel agencies, the *Central de Riesgo* and the *Central de Información Crediticia*, to collect and distribute information about virtually every individual or corporation borrowing from an Argentine bank. The former handles large corporate entities and the latter covers any firm or individual that borrows more than $50.

Prior to September 1997 the data consisted only of the name of the borrower, the amount of the loan from each bank, the internal rating by the bank (on a standard 1–5 scale) of the borrower's creditworthiness, and whether the loan was collateralized. Since September 1997, however, the database has been expanded to include detailed information from the firms' financial statements and personal data on the individual borrowers such as age, marital status, income, and wealth. New information from the federal tax authorities and provincial credit bureaus is being added as well. Firms that have poor credit ratings (3–5) remain in the database for 24 months, even if they have ceased being borrowers.

Full access to customer information stored in the databases is given only to Argentine banks, and only when they request information about a specific firm. By limiting the release of information about loan customers to small lists of customers specifically named by the requesting bank, the BCRA hopes to limit free riding on bank information costs, while still capturing the advantages of greater transparency, and also helping banks to control credit risk (information sharing can prevent the double pledging of collateral, for example).

Despite the limits placed on access to information, some concerns remain about whether the information sharing weakens the incentive for banks to form relationships. The answer turns partly on whether the banks' most important contribution to a credit relationship is screening based on accounting information. If that were so, then the free-riding objection would be valid. But insofar as other information about borrowers, and the monitoring and enforcement technology of the bank, are what create the bond between the bank and its borrower, there may be little cause for concern about free riding. Time will tell whether this experiment is successful or not. If so, it may be copied by other countries.

tion, and debt repayment history.[33] These variables all make sense—either as indicators of a country's ability or willingness to repay its international debt—but these measures either are not observable or do not vary sufficiently month to month to make them useful for predicting sudden changes in sovereign risk. Predicting sudden change is quite difficult, particularly when relevant information is withheld for long periods of time (as in the case of the East Asian countries, according to the UNCTAD study, or the case of Mexico's foreign reserve holdings, which were falsely reported by the government during its crisis). The ratings agencies did not foresee the East Asia collapse of 1997–1998, and a glance at Figure 1.13 in Chapter 1 will confirm that the rating agencies and bond markets alike had a very high opinion of countries such as Malaysia as late as 1996.

Within countries, the rating job may be somewhat simpler, that is, the categorization of local firms into the strongest credits, the next strongest, and so forth. International banks have adopted a number of credit scoring models to give statistically reliable answers to this question. Some of these are based on classic analysis of default or bankruptcy events, using either discriminant analysis (as in the "Zeta" model of Edward Altman) or logit or probit regressions as in more recent models. Whenever a reliable stock price is available, it turns out that the relationship between the firm's aggregate market value and the principal value of its debt has substantial predictive power for default or bankruptcy (as in the model offered by KMV Corporation of San Francisco). Of course, all such approaches depend on good accounting and stock market information, which often is not available in EFMs.

Stock Analysts

Wherever there is a stock market there are stockbrokers, and brokers typically hire stock analysts to supply them with ideas and recommendations for clients. It is well known, of course, that because of this connection, sell-side stock analysts are biased toward optimism. Somewhat more reliable are the buy-side analysts within mutual fund management companies and other institutional investors, but their recommendations are not usually available to the public.

Nevertheless, stock analysts play a significant role in a healthy stock market. They are tenacious in chasing management and ferreting out details of complex risks and opportunities in the firms they track. They study the financial statements at a level of detail not usually possible for private individuals without a great deal of training and experience. Their business is communication, and they are quick to make their recommendations known.

Financial Press

Finally, one must emphasize the role of the financial press. There is a large market for business and financial newspapers and online services. Those who invest significant amounts of money want daily updates on the earnings and prospects of hundreds of companies since timeliness of information is as important as accuracy of information. As a result, every important stock market has an active press surrounding it.

Furthermore, careers of reporters are often made by breaking stories that others have not found or noticed, so that the reporters have a particular zeal for finding the negative information that sell-side stock analysts may not be quite so eager to uncover. All financial markets have an ample supply of fraud and scandal, and the job of revealing these is a never-ending source of interest for writers and readers alike.

---

[33]Cantor and Packer (1996).

APPENDIX: QUALITY OF ACCOUNTING STANDARDS AND DISCLOSURE

The following table is reproduced from La Porta, Lopez-de-Silanes, Shleifer, and Vishny (1996) Table 7. This provides a rating of each country about the quality of accounting standards. According to the authors, this index was "created by examining and rating companies' 1990 annual reports on their inclusion or omission of 90 items. These items fall into seven categories (general information, income statements, balance sheet, funds flow statements, accounting standards, stock data and special items). At least three companies in each country were studied. The companies represent a cross-section of various industry groups where industrial companies numbered 70 percent while financial companies represented the remaining 30 percent."

Country	Rating on Accounting Standards
Average English origin	**69.62**
Australia	75
Canada	74
Hong Kong	69
India	57
Ireland	N/A
Israel	64
Kenya	N/A
Malaysia	76
New Zealand	70
Nigeria	59
Pakistan	N/A
Singapore	78
South Africa	70
Sri Lanka	N/A
Thailand	64
United Kingdom	78
United States	71
Zimbabwe	N/A
Average French origin	**51.17**
Argentina	45
Belgium	61
Brazil	54
Chile	52
Colombia	50
Ecuador	N/A
Egypt	24
France	69
Greece	55
Indonesia	N/A
Italy	62
Jordan	N/A
Mexico	60
Netherlands	64
Peru	38
Philippines	65
Portugal	36
Spain	64
Turkey	51
Uruguay	31
Venezuela	40

Country	Rating on Accounting Standards
Average German origin	**62.67**
Austria	54
Germany	62
Japan	65
South Korea	62
Switzerland	68
Taiwan	65
Average Scandinavian origin	**74.00**
Denmark	62
Finland	77
Norway	74
Sweden	83
Total average	**60.93**

References

Akamatso, Noritaka. 1995. Enterprise governance and investment funds in Russian privatization. In *Corporate Governance in Transition Economies: Insider Control and the Role of Banks*. Ed. by Masahiko Aoki: and Hyung-Ki Kim. Washington, DC: World Bank 121–83.

Akerlof, George A. 1970. The market for "lemons": Quality, uncertainty and the market mechanism. *Quarterly Journal of Economics* 84: 488–500.

Aoki, Masahiko, and Hyung-Ki Kim, eds. 1995. *Corporate Governance in Transition Economies: Insider Control and the Role of Banks*. Washington, DC: World Bank.

Aoki, Masahiko, and Hugh Patrick. 1994. *The Japanese Main Bank System: Its Relevance for Developing and Transforming Economies*. New York: Oxford University Press.

Auerbach, Alan. 1988. *Corporate Takeovers: Causes and Consequences*. Chicago: University of Chicago Press.

Baskin, J. 1988. The development of corporate financial markets in Britain and the United States, 1600–1914: Overcoming asymmetric information. *Business History Review* 62: 199–237.

Beatty, Randolph, and Jay Ritter. 1986. Investment banking, reputation, and the underpricing of initial public offerings. *Journal of Financial Economics* 15: 213–32.

Benveniste, Lawrence M., and Paul A. Spindt. 1989. How investment bankers determine the offer price and allocation of new issues. *Journal of Financial Economics* 24: 343–62.

Benveniste, Lawrence M., and W. J. Wilhelm. 1990. A comparative analysis of IPO proceeds under alternative regulatory environments. *Journal of Financial Economics* 28: 173–207.

Berger, Allen N., Sally M. Davies, and Mark J. Flannery. 1998. Comparing market and regulatory assessments of bank performance: Who knows what when? Working paper, Federal Reserve Board.

Berger, Allen N., and Gregory F. Udell. 1990. Collateral, loan quality and bank risk. *Journal of Monetary Economics* 25: 21–42.

Besanko, David, and Anjan V. Thakor. 1987. Collateral and rationing: Sorting equilibria in monopolistic and competitive credit markets. *International Economic Review* 28: 671–89.

Calomiris, Charles W. 1995. The costs of rejecting universal banking: American finance in the German mirror, 1870–1914. In *The Coordination of Activity Within and Between Firms*. Ed. by N. Lamoreaux and D. Raff. Chicago: University of Chicago Press: 257–321.

———. 1997. *The Postmodern Bank Safety Net: Lessons from Developed and Developing Economies*. Washington, DC: American Enterprise Institute.

Calomiris, Charles W., and Charles M. Kahn. 1991. The role of demandable debt in structuring optimal banking arrangements. *American Economic Review* 81: 497–513.

Calomiris, Charles W., and Joseph R. Mason. 1997. Contagion and bank failures during the Great Depression. *American Economic Review* 87: 863–83.

Calomiris, Charles W., and Daniel M. G. Raff. 1995. The evolution of market structure, information, and spreads in American investment banking. In *Anglo-American Finance: Financial Markets and Institutions in 20th-Century North America and the U.K.* Ed. by R. Sylla and M. Bordo. Burr Ridge, IL: Business One Irwin: 103–60.

Calomiris, Charles W., and Carlos D. Ramirez. 1996. The role of financial relationships in the history of American corporate finance. *Journal of Applied Corporate Finance* 9: 52–73.

Calomiris, Charles W., and Berry Wilson. 1998. Bank capital and portfolio management: The 1930s capital crunch and scramble to shed risk. Working Paper no. 6649, National Bureau of Economic Research.

Cantor, Richard, and Frank Packer. 1996. Determinants and impacts of sovereign credit ratings. Research Paper no. 9608, Federal Reserve Bank of New York.

Diamond, Douglas W. 1984. Financial intermediation and delegated monitoring. *Review of Economic Studies* 51: 393–414.

Fisman, Raymond. 1998. The incentives to rent-seeking: Estimating The value of political connections. Working paper, Columbia University.

Fisman, Raymond, and Tarun Khanna. 1999. Facilitating development: The role of business groups. Working paper, Columbia University.

Flannery, Mark. 1998. Using market information in prudential bank supervision: A review of the U.S. empirical evidence. *Journal of Money, Credit and Banking* 30: 273–305.

Friend, Irwin, Marshall Blume, and Jean Crockett. 1970. *Mutual Funds and Other Institutional Investors.* New York: McGraw-Hill.

Friend, Irwin, James R. Longstreet, Morris Mendelson, Ervin Miller, and Arleigh P. Hess, Jr. 1967. *Investment Banking and the New Issues Market.* New York: World.

Healy, P. M., K. G. Palepu, and R. S. Ruback. 1992. Does corporate performance improve after mergers? *Journal of Financial Economics* 31: 135–75.

Higgins, Robert C. 1998. *Analysis for Financial Management.* 5th ed. New York: Irwin/McGraw Hill.

Hoshi, Takeo, Anil Kashyap, and David Scharfstein. 1990. Bank monitoring and investment: Evidence from the changing structure of Japanese corporate banking relationships. In *Asymmetric Information, Corporate Finance, and Investment.* Ed. by R. G. Hubbard. Chicago: University of Chicago Press: 105–26.

Hoshi, Takeo, and Hugh Patrick. 2000. *Crisis and Change in the Japanese Financial System.* Norwell, MA: Kluwer Press.

Hubbard, R. Glenn, ed. 1990. *Asymmetric Information, Corporate Finance, and Investment.* Chicago: University of Chicago Press.

Jagtiani, Julapa, George G. Kaufman, and Catherine Lemieux. 1999. Do markets discipline banks and bank holding companies? Evidence from Debt Pricing. Working paper, Federal Reserve Bank of Chicago.

Jensen, Michael C. 1993. The modern industrial revolution, exit and the failure of internal control systems. *Journal of Finance* 48: 831–80.

Jensen, Michael C., and William H. Meckling. 1976. Theory of the firm: Managerial behavior, agency costs and ownership structure. *Journal of Financial Economics* 3: 305–60.

Kang, Jun-Koo, and René M. Stulz. 1997. Is bank centered corporate governance worth it? A cross-sectional analysis of the performance of Japanese firms during the asset price deflation. Working Paper no. 6238, National Bureau of Economic Research.

Kaplan, Steve N., and Michael S. Weisbach. 1992. The success of acquisitions: Evidence from divestitures. *Journal of Finance* 47: 107–38.

Kaufman, George G. 1994. Bank contagion: A review of the theory and evidence. *Journal of Financial Services Research* 8: 123–50.

Khanna, Tarun, and Krishna Palepu. 1999. Emerging market business groups, foreign investors and corporate governance. Working Paper no. 6955, National Bureau of Economic Research.

Lakonishok, Joseph, Andrei Shleifer, and Robert Vishny. 1992. The structure and performance of the money management industry. *Brookings Papers on Economic Activity: Microeconomics:* 339–91.

Lang, L., and R. Stulz. 1994. Tobin's q, corporate diversification, and firm performance. *Journal of Political Economy* 102: 1248–80.

Lang, L., R. Stulz, and R. A. Walking. 1989. Managerial performance, Tobin's q, and the gains from successful tender offers. *Journal of Financial Economics* 24: 137–54.

La Porta, Rafael, Florencia Lopez-de-Silanes, and Andrei Shleifer. 1999. Corporate ownership around the world. *Journal of Finance* 54: 471–517.

La Porta, Rafael, Florencia Lopez-de-Silanes, Andrei Shleifer, and Robert W. Vishny. 1996. Law and finance. Working Paper no. 5661, National Bureau of Economic Research.

Maksimovic, Vojislav, and Gordon Phillips. 1999. Do conglomerate firms allocate resources inefficiently? Working paper, University of Maryland.

Mitchell, M. L., and K. Lehn. 1990. Do bad bidders become good targets? *Journal of Political Economy* 98: 372–98.

Morgan, Donald P., and Kevin J. Stiroh. 1999. Can bond holders discipline banks? Working paper, Federal Reserve Bank of New York.

Myers, Stewart C. 1977. Determinants of corporate borrowing. *Journal of Financial Economics* 5: 147–75.

Myers, Stewart C., and Nicholas Majluf. 1984. Corporate financing and investment decisions when firms have information that investors do not have. *Journal of Financial Economics* 13: 187–221.

Peria, Maria S. M., and Sergio L. Schmukler. 1998. Do depositors punish banks for "bad" behavior? Working paper, World Bank.

Securities and Exchange Commission. 1971. *Institutional Investor Study Report.* Washington, DC: U.S. Government Printing Office. U.S. House of Representatives. Document No. 92–64, 92nd Cong. 1st sess.

Servaes, Henri. 1991. Tobin's q and the gains from takeover. *Journal of Finance* 46: 409–19.

Shleifer, Andrei, and Robert W. Vishny. 1990. The takeover wave of the 1980s. *Science* 249: 745–49.

———. 1996. A survey of corporate governance, Working Paper no. 5554, National Bureau of Economic Research.

Slovin, M. B., M. F. Sushka, and J. A. Polonchek. 1993. The value of bank durability: Borrowers and bank stakeholders. *Journal of Finance* 48: 247–66.

Stiglitz, Joseph E., and Andrew Weiss. 1981. Credit rationing in markets with imperfect information. *American Economic Review* 71: 393–410.

Vishwanath, Tara, and Daniel Kaufmann. 1999. Towards transparency in finance and governance. Working paper, World Bank.

Inflation and Currency Stability

Questions:

How serious is the inflation problem in emerging financial markets?

What is the relationship between fiscal deficits, money supply growth, and inflation?

In what sense is inflation a form of taxation?

Can inflation be controlled by pegging the currency value?

What effects does inflation have on debt markets?

What effects does inflation have on foreign exchange markets?

What effects does inflation have on banks?

Introduction

We have so far discussed two basic foundations of all financial markets: law and information. We have seen that financial markets cannot flourish and perform their critical capital allocation function without explicit legal protection of investors and effective institutions of information. We now come to the third foundation, currency stability.

Inflation and Devaluation

When people save and invest, they put aside a certain amount of money with the hope of earning a profit. Eventually they liquidate their investment and receive some amount of money back. Their *nominal* return can be measured by comparing what they received with what they invested, using units of the currency in question. But the currency itself may have lost value.

Loss of currency value has two meanings, one internal and one external. Internal deterioration of currency value, of interest to domestic investors, takes the form of *inflation*: Does the money investors receive have as much power to purchase domestic real goods and services as the money they invested? Inflation measures the extent to which prices have risen, and therefore the extent to which money buys fewer goods and services. External deterioration, of interest to foreign investors, means exchange rate *devaluation*: Does the money investors receive translate into as many dollars, euros, or other strong currency as the money they invested? The exchange rate is the price of local currency as measured in units of dollars, euros, or other strong currency, and devaluation means that this price has fallen.

In characterizing the currencies of industrialized countries as strong, we imply that they are not themselves subject to much deterioration. We must not overlook, however, the bouts of inflation and exchange rate devaluation that the dollar and many of the European currencies have suffered, notably during the 1970s. Since that time, the industrialized countries have adopted numerous agreements to avoid currency deterioration; indeed the launching of the euro in 1999 is the most important such agreement and would not have been possible unless all member countries of the European Union had faith in each other's long-term commitment to currency stability.[1]

Inflation and exchange rate devaluation, the two types of currency deterioration, are closely related. If the condition known as relative *purchasing power parity* (PPP) holds, then inflation and devaluation are highly correlated. This condition is described in the accompanying box, but essentially means that the pace of exchange rate devaluation on average matches the pace of relative inflation, so that the relative ability of a currency to purchase real goods and services at home or abroad is unchanged. Relative PPP typically does not hold in the short term, but it holds better over the longer term, so that the two types of currency deterioration tend to coincide over long horizons.

Inflation and exchange rate devaluation would be perfectly correlated if both were caused by the same single factor: growth of the country's money supply at a rate faster than growth of the real economy. The actual long-term correspondence between inflation and depreciation suggests that just such a common causal influence is at work. This is illustrated in Figure 6.1, which gives a 25-year look at average annual inflation relative to the U.S. dollar[2] and average annual currency devaluation against the dollar of countries for which a 25-year record is available in International Financial Statistics

FIGURE 6.1

Annual inflation versus devaluation of local currency in various countries, 1972–1996

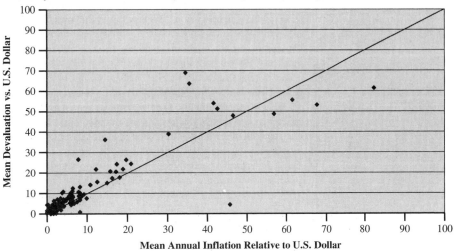

Mean Annual Inflation Relative to U.S. Dollar

---

[1]Some authors have argued that this faith is misplaced, that a lack of long-term credibility in fiscal policy will undermine the stable value of the euro. For discussions of this problem and potential remedies, see Calomiris (1999) and Casella (1999).

[2]Relative inflation is calculated as $(1 + \pi_i)/(1 + \pi_\$) - 1$, where π_i is the annual realized inflation of country i and $\pi_\$$ is the annual realized inflation of the dollar.

Purchasing Power Parity

Suppose that all tradable goods could be transported across countries with no costs, delays, or impediments. For example, if melons sold for $1 in New York and the equivalent of $5 in Tokyo, melon traders would buy them up in New York and send them instantly to Tokyo where they could be sold for a profit. In such a world the Law of One Price would prevail: Every traded good in the world would sell for the same currency-adjusted price. If prices deviated from this equality, goods *arbitrage* such as that described for melons would drive the prices together. In this perfect world, you could find the exchange rate between any two currencies by simply comparing the price of melons or any other tradable single good.

A related but different "law" is *absolute purchasing power parity (PPP)*. Suppose some typical basket of consumer goods costs P dollars in New York and P^* yen in Tokyo. Then absolute PPP says that the currency exchange rate will be $E = P^*/P$ yen per dollar. The idea is straightforward: Exchange rates are determined by the ratio of the average prices of a sufficiently broad set of goods. The basket of consumer goods is of course the concept on which consumer price indexes are based.

However, absolute PPP does not generally hold, for two reasons. First, consumers do not consume the same bundles of goods across countries or over time, so there is no "universal" basket of goods on which to base all price indexes. Second, any country's consumer price index contains nontraded goods such as housing, which can differ dramatically in cost across countries and whose prices are not driven together by goods arbitrage.

But even if absolute PPP does not hold, a weaker condition may prevail. Whatever the present exchange rate level, it may be that annual *changes* in exchange rates reflect primarily changes in the average price levels of the two countries. Suppose that E does not equal P^*/P but is related to it, and that we can approximate the relationship by $E = kP^*/P$, where k is a scalar that is slow to change and reflects differences such as the relative levels of industrialization or productivity. Then if inflation proceeds at an annual rate π in the first country and π^* in the second, the price levels after one year will be $P(1 + \pi)$ in the first country and $P^*(1 + \pi^*)$ in the second. We might reasonably expect that the exchange rate should move to $kP^*(1 + \pi^*)/P(1 + \pi)$, that is, last year's exchange rate times the relative inflation $(1 + \pi^*)/(1 + \pi)$.

The claim that the equilibrium exchange rate evolves according to relative inflation is known as *relative PPP*. Figure 6.1 can be interpreted as a simple examination of this claim. In that figure, the 25-year average annual relative inflation $(1 + \pi^*)/(1 + \pi) - 1$ is plotted against the 25-year average devaluation of the local currency against the dollar.

This long-term relationship is quite close on average. When mean annual devaluation is regressed on mean relative inflation for this set of countries, forcing the intercept to zero, the regression coefficient is 0.98 with a standard error of 0.04. Statistically, the average relationship is not distinguishable from a one-to-one equivalence. Furthermore, $R^2 = 0.76$, suggesting a high level of explanatory power for this relationship. The regression line is shown in Figure 6.1.

The number $k = EP/P^*$ used above has a name. It is called the *real exchange rate*; that is, the exchange rate adjusted by the ratio of the consumer price indexes in the two countries. PPP is equivalent to the claim that the real exchange rate is constant. When the real exchange rate is not constant, it implies that a country's exports are gaining or losing competitiveness. We will use this concept in Chapter 8 to examine the role of exchange rate competitiveness in financial crises.

(excluding a few outliers for which either mean was greater than 100 percent per annum). As can be seen, the relationship is strong, confirming that relative PPP tends to work reasonably well over long time horizons.

One reason why inflation and devaluation are not as well correlated in the short term is that the spot exchange rate, like all financial prices, reflects not only current and recent events but also expected future events. If investors believe that inflation is going to be much worse in the future than it has been recently, they will not wait for inflation to rise but will mark down the value of the currency immediately.

Thus, large currency moves sometimes occur in sudden jumps, when a new event or a new piece of information suddenly changes investors' opinions about future inflation. Like all financial markets, foreign exchange markets are subject to sudden changes of sentiment and unpredictable shifts in perceptions of the future. The abruptness of adjustment in foreign exchange markets compared with the more gradual realization of changes in inflation is a primary reason why inflation and devaluation do not match as closely in the short term.

Inflation Uncertainty

The most damaging effects of inflation come from its uncertainty. If it were known for certain that a particular currency would experience inflation at a rate exactly 10 percent higher than that of the dollar over the next 20 years, then the exchange rate might devalue quite smoothly at a rate of 10 percent a year against the dollar. All investors and other parties could plan on this and reflect it in their contracts. The interest rate on the local currency would be set at 10 percent above dollar interest rates so that both internal and external lenders would be exactly compensated for the currency value lost.

But life is not that simple. Investors must take a guess at future inflation and set today's interest rates and exchange rates accordingly. This is not too difficult if inflation is low, because low inflation tends to be stable and hence fairly predictable. But the higher the rate of inflation, the more variable it becomes.

Figure 6.2 shows the average annual inflation of many countries over 25 years, plotted against the standard deviation of annual inflation over the same period,

FIGURE 6.2

Mean versus standard deviation of annual inflation in various countries, 1972–1996

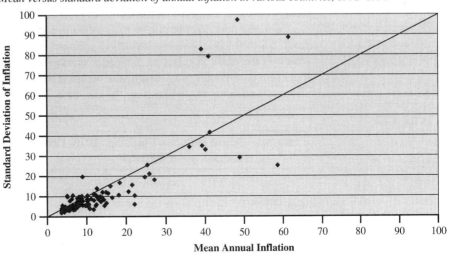

calculated for those countries for which a 25-year record is available in International Financial Statistics and excluding a few outliers for which either the mean or standard deviation exceeds 100 percent. The regression in this case shows a coefficient of 1.01 with a standard error of 0.05, so that again the relationship is not distinguishable from a one-to-one relationship in which the standard deviation simply equals the mean. The R^2 is 0.66. The regression line is shown in Figure 6.2. This illustrates quite clearly that high inflation tends to be variable inflation.

Extent of Inflation in Emerging Financial Markets

How serious is the inflation problem in EFMs generally? Are there patterns that we can study and learn from? It is useful to describe the overall magnitudes involved. The IFS database goes back to 1970, so that we can take a long view, but in many cases part of the data is missing, which complicates analysis. However, for 98 countries we have uninterrupted data from 1970 through 1995, and the comments in this section are based on these. The descriptive statistics for inflation in these 98 countries for 1970 to 1995 are summarized in Table 6.1 below.

A first observation from Table 6.1 is a further confirmation that the standard deviation of inflation (13.3 percent) is approximately equal to the mean level of inflation (14.7 percent). But it is also instructive to note that the median inflation over all countries (11.0 percent) is less than the mean (14.7 percent). This suggests that the inflation rate is not normally distributed among countries, but is skewed to the left, so that there are more low-inflation countries than high-inflation ones. This is confirmed by the positive skewness statistic in Table 6.1. Also, there is excess kurtosis, meaning that there are more extreme observations than a normal distribution would imply. This is caused by a number of unusually large observations, as is clear from the raw data.

Table 6.1 also shows descriptive statistics for the natural logarithm of 1 + inflation. For a small level of inflation, $\pi \approx \log(1 + \pi)$, so that the two numbers are close. But taking the logarithm moderates the swings out to large values. We see from the table that the median is somewhat closer to the mean in the logarithmic column, and that skewness and excess kurtosis are both reduced.

Table 6.2 shows the primary descriptive statistics for overlapping 10-year periods. We note that the means are surprisingly similar from one period to the next. Taken by itself, this would suggest that the distribution of inflation is quite stationary. However, we see in the next column that median inflation has been falling somewhat. This suggests that the median country is making progress in controlling inflation, but that this effect on the mean is offset by a smaller number of countries for which inflation is more of a problem recently than it was before. That interpretation is confirmed by the standard deviation, which rises slightly over time.

TABLE 6.1   Mean Inflation Statistics, 1970–1995
(Means of 98 Countries)

	Annual Inflation (%)	Log(1 + inflation)
Mean	14.7%	0.121
Median	11.0	0.100
Standard Deviation	13.3	0.091
Skewness	1.1	0.879
Excess Kurtosis	2.1	1.417

This review of the data confirms our intuition that inflation was particularly troublesome in the 1970s for the EFMs as it was for the industrialized world; that the 1980s continued to be inflationary for the developing world although inflation came more under control in industrialized countries; and that the 1990s have seen a reduction in inflation for most but not all EFMs, as many countries privatized and pursued fiscal reforms and thereby reduced their budget deficits and inflationary pressures.

The Appendix lists the country-by-country data that are summarized in the first column of Table 6.2 (i.e., the mean rate of inflation for each country in the four overlapping decades shown). This enables us to see which countries have become significantly more inflationary in recent years, contrary to the general trend. Such countries include Venezuela, Ecuador, Suriname, and Uruguay as well as Sudan, Sierra Leone, Turkey, and Lebanon. The table also shows some countries that have made particularly impressive progress in controlling inflation, including Saudi Arabia, Bahrain, Burkina Faso, Niger, Barbados, Dominica, and Korea.

Economists have studied at some length why inflation and inflation volatility should damage economic growth and capital allocation. While there is no unanimity in the profession, the following connections summarize the most widely held views. First, perhaps the most important connection is that uncertainty about the prices of goods and services makes it substantially more difficult for markets to do their job of optimally allocating resources. Uncertainty about price signals interferes with Adam Smith's invisible hand in the market for goods and services.

The same is true in the market for money and capital. If inflation is uncertain, real interest rates are uncertain and capital allocations are similarly suboptimal, but in the case of interest rates another factor is at work. Uncertainty about real interest rates will make investors nervous, which will be expressed as a risk premium in all rates of return, raising investors' required returns above where they would normally be. We will look at this phenomenon in more detail later in this chapter, but for now it should be clear that any such risk premium will make capital needlessly expensive and will depress and distort investment.

Second, inflation distorts capital gains taxation. If all prices trend upward, then the selling of a capital asset that had little or no real gain in value will nevertheless generate a taxable capital gain. This will make investors reluctant to sell capital assets at all, which impedes the work of capital markets.

Third, as discussed more fully in the following section, inflation imposes a tax on everyone who holds noninterest-bearing money, so people will wish to hold as little such money as possible. Too much cost and effort will be devoted to moving money rapidly before it loses further value.

To understand the magnitude of the above effects, empirical studies have tried to examine the effect of inflation and inflation volatility on economic growth. This is a

---

TABLE 6.2 **Mean Inflation Statistics in Overlapping 10-Year Periods**
(Means of 98 Countries)

	Mean of 10-Year Means	*Median of 10-Year Medians*	*Mean of 10-Year Standard Deviations*
1970–1979	13.3%	9.4%	9.4%
1976–1985	15.3	10.4	8.9
1980–1989	15.7	8.3	10.7
1986–1995	15.4	7.2	10.6

difficult job because economic growth is affected by many different variables. Furthermore, inflation and its volatility are highly correlated, as we have seen, so it is difficult to disentangle which has the actual impact on growth.

Despite these difficulties, many recent studies have found a significant negative correlation between inflation and growth.[3] Separating the effect of average inflation level from inflation volatility was accomplished in a further study, which used quarterly data.[4] This more frequent sampling shows volatility to be on average higher than the mean level of inflation and less highly correlated with it. This study found that both higher inflation and greater inflation volatility slow economic growth, though the impact of volatility was greater and the effect of the inflation level could only be detected if the level exceeded 10 percent.

The connection between high inflation and low output growth for EFMs is also apparent in simple comparisons of recent GDP growth rates across countries. *The Economist* reported in its August 21, 1999, issue that a sample of 25 EFMs posted an average GDP growth rate for the most recent year of 0.58 percent. Only three countries within this group (Russia, Turkey, and Venezuela) had CPI inflation rates in excess of 20 percent (the rates were 126.3 percent, 65.0 percent, and 23.0 percent, respectively), and these three countries all experienced substantially negative GDP growth rates (-3.9 percent, -8.5 percent, and -8.2 percent, respectively).

Thus, currency stability matters. Financial markets in high-inflation countries become restricted in ways that we will study later in this chapter, with serious consequences for capital allocation and economic growth. Investors value credible assurances that the currency in which they are repaid is not going to be worth a significant and indeterminate amount less than the value of the currency they invested.

Causes and Cures

What Causes Inflation?

If high and variable inflation is costly, why does it occur in the first place? The literature on the causes of inflation, like other literatures in economics, is populated by various schools of thought. Despite the many areas of disagreement within the inflation literature, there is substantial agreement on the narrowly focused question of what causes the high inflation that has plagued EFMs: excessive growth of the supply of money.

Milton Friedman famously remarked that inflation is "always and everywhere a monetary phenomenon." This statement can be viewed in two ways: as a definitional statement and as a causal theory. By definition, inflation (which measures the value of money) is a "monetary" phenomenon. But that does not necessarily mean that growth in the supply of money (controlled by the central bank) *causes* countries "always and everywhere" to experience inflation.

Many economists argue, for example, that real money demand (the ratio of desired money relative to the price level) relative to real income varies over time (the reciprocal of that ratio is defined as *velocity*). That variation implies that the money supply and the price level need not move together in lockstep. Other influences on the price level, therefore, can cause inflation to occur, even when money balances are not changing. For example, if fiscal policy causes output to expand, prices would tend to rise even if money balances are held constant. Or, if the world were physically to run

---

[3]For example see Fischer (1993), Motley (1994), and Barro (1995).
[4]Judson and Orphanides (1996).

short on basic inputs such as petroleum and minerals, the costs of those inputs would increase and this would be reflected in a rise of prices generally, alongside a decline in output because these inputs affect the great majority of physical goods produced. (This phenomenon, which gripped the world in the 1970s, became known as stagflation.) Similarly, if goods become more abundant and accessible because of a rise in productivity, then holding constant the level of money supplied in the economy, prices will tend to fall as output rises. So the connection between money supply changes and price changes is far from perfect.

These qualifications to Friedman's view of the causal role of money growth for inflation, however, are mainly relevant for explaining relatively small (single-digit) variations in inflation around its trend, associated with differences in money supply growth and inflation.[5] The significant differences in the *trends* of inflation across countries are "always and everywhere" traceable to different *growth rates* of the supplies of money. In particular, when one looks at the experiences of EFMs—where inflation rates can vary from zero percent per year to thousands of percent per year—there is a very clear and close connection between differences in money growth and differences in inflation.

It is important to recognize, however, that money growth itself has a deeper cause. High-inflation EFMs do not increase their money supplies unwittingly. They use high money growth as a fiscal device—a means of paying for expenditures when direct taxation is not sufficient. Thus, fiscal deficits are the ultimate driver of monetary expansion and hence inflation in EFMs. We note that at an early stage of his career Milton Friedman advocated a government debt rule as a means of controlling inflation, in recognition of the threat that rising government deficits pose to stable monetary policy.

Monetary Growth and Fiscal Deficits

In the modern world, as throughout much of history, money is a creation of government, so government is responsible for its quantity and quality. Governments do not usually set out to generate ballooning deficits, with their inflationary consequences, out of malice or stupidity; rather, deficits result from the political dilemma of managing government finances. Governments have legitimate goals that propel expenditures. They also face purely political constraints as constituents often demand pecuniary rewards for supporting a group of politicians. Most governments try to benefit as many groups, projects, and regions as possible so they can enjoy greater political support, while taxing as little as possible (since taxation is politically unpopular). This combination of large expenditures and small tax receipts produces deficits in the government budget. It is an ancient problem. The Roman Empire, as it tried to unify Europe during the first three centuries A.D., spent more than it could collect in taxes; it solved the shortfall by minting coins with less and less gold content. This degradation provides us with a physical record of currency devaluation during the period, which was mirrored over the long term by inflation of prices measured in such coins.[6]

Modern countries in Western Europe have had similar problems. They have a strong political commitment to state-sponsored social programs that have proven increasingly expensive. They have varied substantially in their willingness to raise taxes sufficiently to pay for such programs, and the resulting policy differences have

---

[5]The literature on the patterns and causes of cyclical variation in inflation around its trend is large. Important contributions include Phillips (1958), Phelps (1967), Friedman (1968), and Lucas (1972). The recent literature emphasizes that the cyclical pattern of inflation around its trend, particularly the correlation between inflation and economic activity over the cycle, and the extent to which money supply growth affects short-term inflation and output change are influenced by expectations of inflation.

[6]See DeCecco (1985).

led to differing rates of inflation that in turn caused their currencies' values to move away from each other during the 1970s and 1980s. Only in the 1990s have they sworn to stabilize their currencies by agreeing to common targets for inflation and budget deficits as part of their historic *Economic and Monetary Union* (EMU).

The United States experienced high inflation during the surge in spending on the Civil War; but this was followed by very low inflation, and sometimes even deflation, from the end of the Civil War (1865) until the beginning of World War I (1914). America experienced inflation in both world wars, but its worst bout of inflation in the 20th century came at the crest of enthusiasm for state intervention in the economy, during the 1960–1980 period. The cost of the war in Vietnam along with a domestic "Great Society" war on poverty in the 1960s caused serious budget deficits, and these spurred inflation through their direct effects on the demand for output and through the pressures they placed on the central bank to expand the money supply. But by the end of the 1990s, the United States had moved into a budget surplus and its rate of inflation had fallen to less than 2 percent per year. The long-term credibility of a low-inflation monetary policy stance on the part of the Federal Reserve has been buttressed by the government's strong fiscal position.

Developing countries, with less-developed tax bases but social problems and economic needs more urgent than those of the developed world, have particular difficulty in balancing their budgets. Furthermore, as noted in Chapter 3, developing countries became even more committed to statism than developed countries in the post–World War II era. Only by drastic privatization programs have some of them been able to bring their budget deficits under control. Thus, the problem of government budget deficits has been more intractable in EFMs than elsewhere.

In an open market economy a government facing a budget deficit has only three options: It can spend its international reserves, it can borrow, or it can *monetize* the deficit. Monetizing the deficit usually means that the government sells bonds to its own central bank. The central bank pays for the bonds by crediting the government's deposit account at the central bank. The government then writes checks against this account to pay for its purchases; the checks are deposited in commercial banks. The commercial banks redeposit a fraction of these as reserves at the central bank. The net effect is that the money supply is expanded, as both commercial banks and central bank expand their balance sheets. It is the modern equivalent of printing money to pay government expenses. Monetizing the deficit leads directly to inflation, as the larger money supply is spread over the same quantity of real goods.

Drawing down foreign exchange reserves or borrowing from bond investors other than the central bank to finance the deficit avoids the immediate inflationary impact of monetizing it, but neither action can be continued indefinitely. Reserves disappear when drawn down repeatedly. Borrowing abroad can only be done up to a certain limit, beyond which arm's-length lenders first raise the risk premium and finally refuse to lend more at any rate. Borrowing domestically has more scope, particularly when the government can sell its bonds to banks, but even this can be done only up to a certain limit. The real value of government debt outstanding cannot continue to increase unless the public expects future taxes to be levied to service that debt.

Therefore, drawing down reserves or borrowing can only be used as a temporary expedient unless the deficit is so small that sustainability ceases to be an issue. Sooner or later, a government with large deficits must turn to monetization, and the markets will see this coming. The currency value may fall when reserves fall even though inflation has not yet been realized. Most developing countries have already borrowed up to prudent limits (given their capacity to tax in the future to repay that debt) and do not have excess reserves, so monetization and consequent inflation are often the only option.

The relationship between deficits and monetary growth is much closer for EFMs than for developed economies. In developed economies, independent central banks typically maintain a low long-run target for the inflation rate and vary monetary policy over the business cycle in an effort to smooth economic fluctuations. The central bankers of developed countries can act independently of deficits because their governments' deficits are not a binding constraint on the long-run growth of the supply of money. In contrast, in many EFMs the need to spend without any politically viable prospect of paying for those expenditures with current or future taxes makes monetary policy subordinate to fiscal expediency. Many EFM central banks have little discretion over monetary policy, since there is a direct link between the amount the government spends and the amount of currency the central bank must print.

In What Sense Is Inflation a Tax?

Inflation takes value away from those who hold unprotected financial assets including money. For example, if you have a checking account containing 50,000 pesos and the peso loses 10 percent of its value while you hold the account, you have less ability to purchase real goods and services than you had at the beginning of the period. The value loss is 5,000 pesos. Where did this value go?

In the first instance, the bank in which you hold the account captures the value. This is why banks often prosper in times of high inflation, an idea to which we return in detail at the end of this chapter. On the other hand, the bank is required to redeposit a fraction of its deposits as noninterest-bearing reserves at the central bank. To the extent it holds such reserves, the central bank (government) collects the missing value. This makes inflation a kind of tax.

To be more precise, the quantity of money on which the government captures inflation tax is the sum of currency plus bank reserves deposited at the central bank—that is, all liabilities of the central bank that do not pay interest. This is known as the *monetary base* (M). Suppose the government decides to create some additional quantity of money (ΔM) to pay for its budget deficit. Then

$$\text{Deficit} = \Delta M = (\Delta M/M) \times M = \pi M$$

where we have associated the growth rate of the monetary base ($\Delta M/M$) with the rate of inflation (π). The monetary base M is the quantity being taxed and the inflation rate π is the tax rate. The inflation tax is precisely what pays for the deficit. We can also put the equation shown into *real* terms by dividing through by the price level P:

$$\text{Deficit}/P = \Delta M/P = (\Delta M/M) \times (M/P) = \pi(M/P)$$

Thus, inflation is not just the by-product of budget deficits; it is a solution to budget deficits. Inflation is a very expedient form of taxation: It is almost costless to collect and its effects are widely spread through the economy. It causes less political protest than the explicit effort to extract taxes from some target group. Indeed, it has such agreeable political qualities that governments can become quite addicted to financing their expenditures in this way. This is why inflation becomes endemic in most EFMs.

We have so far considered only noninterest-bearing claims because holders of interest-bearing claims can be compensated for inflation through the interest rate. As we shall examine later in this chapter, interest rates normally include both a real component and a component to compensate for expected inflation. For example, if the investor requires a real return of 4 percent and inflation is expected to equal 6 percent during the coming year, then one-year interest rates should be at least

10 percent. Provided actual inflation turns out to be 6 percent, such an investor is not taxed by inflation.[7]

But suppose there is a surprise burst of inflation. Perhaps actual inflation turns out to be 15 percent. Then the investor suffers a negative real return of 5 percent—a real value loss. If the government issued the debt instrument, then the government captures the missing value since it repays its obligations in a currency with much less real value than expected. Such a surprise burst of inflation could be described as a partial government default: Because of the surprise inflation, the government simply does not give back to the investor the full value that the investor had expected. Alternatively, we could call this the *unanticipated inflation tax,* whose base is M plus the total amount of interest-bearing government debt.

The real revenues that can be earned from the unanticipated inflation tax on domestic money and bonds can be large. For example, Robert Eisner argued that the inflationary burst in the United States in the 1960s and 1970s created one-time capital gains for the U.S. government that turned apparent deficits into surpluses, after properly accounting for the capital gains.[8] But large capital gains from surprise inflation are not a continuing source of revenue. Bondholders will raise yields in anticipation of higher inflation, and—following Abraham Lincoln's maxim about the difficulty of "fooling all of the people all of the time"—those yields will compensate bondholders for any inflation-induced capital losses on principal. And money holdings will decline in real terms from their pre-surprise levels, leaving the government with a smaller future steady stream of revenue from the anticipated inflation tax on money balances.

It is sometimes said that government debt is free of default risk because governments have unlimited power to tax and unlimited power to print money. But consider the sequence of sources to which a government may turn when it needs to make payments, particularly payments on its debt. The first recourse is taxation. But explicit taxation has a definite limit, beyond which political protest and noncompliance will frustrate even an authoritarian government. When this point is reached, the government can print money and collect the inflation tax.

However, the inflation tax cannot generate an infinite amount of real resources for the government. People will defend themselves against it by trying to reduce the amount of real currency and checking balances that they hold. The quantity M/P will shrink as they do this. At a sufficiently high rate of inflation, further increases in π may be more than offset by reductions in M/P. When the government cannot extract more real resources to cover its real deficit, what happens? At such a point the government is likely to save real resources by defaulting on its external debt. Thus, there is a subtle connection between inflation and default. Up to a point, inflation is a default substitute, but this cannot continue indefinitely.

Government debt denominated in local currency rarely suffers default because the government can always pay it by printing more local currency.[9] But foreign currency debt must be paid with real resources. Empirical studies of sovereign default risk on international debt find that domestic inflation is a powerful predictor of sovereign yield spreads: Countries that are fiscally weak display high rates of inflation.[10] A high-inflation country has likely come near the end of its fiscal rope; having exhausted its

---

[7]Except, of course, to the extent that the investor must pay income taxes on the entire 10 percent.

[8]Eisner (1986).

[9]In August 1998 the Russian government defaulted on its ruble-denominated treasury bills (GKOs) and then offered to settle them for a tiny fraction of face value.

[10]Cantor and Packer (1996).

capacity to tax directly or through inflation, any further fiscal deficit increase may have to be financed with outright default.

Coping with Inflation through Indexing

Some governments have attempted to deal with price instability by inflation *indexing*. That is, contracts of many kinds (including bank accounts and government debts) can come with built-in adjustment clauses keyed to the rate of inflation, so that wages, interest rates, and other cash payments rise to compensate for the currency's loss of purchasing power. Such indexing is always imperfect and generally favors the rich and sophisticated over the poor and uneducated. But even more important, it raises the government's cost of wages, interest, and the like, so that the nominal deficit in the next period is even greater and requires yet more printing of money. In these conditions inflation can soon escalate into hyperinflation.

The fundamental problem with indexing is that it attempts to protect people from the inflation tax while still collecting the tax. Viewed from this perspective, inflation must rise to ever-higher levels to succeed in solving the fiscal problem it is supposed to solve. The better people's protection against the tax, the more the inflation tax base will decline as inflation rises, and the higher the inflation tax rate must go to have the desired effect. That is why indexing often leads to acceleration of inflation.

Countries that suffer hyperinflation typically try to cure it with radical new plans. Such plans may include a variety of elements such as price freezes, business–union pacts, currency pegging, and extensive rhetoric. But the only countries that have succeeded in taming inflation have been those that committed themselves to the elimination of the fiscal deficits, primarily through privatization. This characterizes Bolivia (1985), Mexico (1989), and Argentina (1991). Brazil tried numerous stabilization plans in the 1970s and 1980s, but continued to suffer significant inflation primarily because it had not yet been sufficiently resolute about privatization and fiscal reform (including at the state level, since it has a federal political system); and Brazil continued to be addicted to inflation indexing.

Monetization of Brazilian deficits became so predictable during the 1970s that the exchange rate depreciated and the price level inflated in reaction to government debt growth even before it was monetized.[11] The extent of the inflation acceleration produced a substantial decline in the inflation tax base. Monetary velocity nearly doubled during the 1970s, as the real demand for currency and zero-interest reserves fell. Depositors with sufficient wealth were able to substitute away from zero-interest or low-interest cash and deposits, and into indexed bonds or bank repurchase agreements backed by treasury bills, which earned market returns that compensated for expected inflation. These opportunities, especially in the repurchase market, accounted for the remarkable increase in money velocity that occurred in the 1970s.

Even when indexing does not lead to hyperinflation, it can have the perverse effect of institutionalizing inflation, making it far more difficult to eradicate. Indexing creates a momentum effect whereby inflation can persist long after the underlying fiscal imbalances have been corrected.

An example may help to clarify this point. As illustrated in Figure 6.3, the Chilean government of Salvador Allende increased the fiscal deficit from 2.8 percent of GDP in 1970 to a peak of 12.8 percent of GDP in 1972. The inflationary impact followed

---

[11]Calomiris and Domowitz (1989)

FIGURE 6.3

Deficits and inflation in Chile

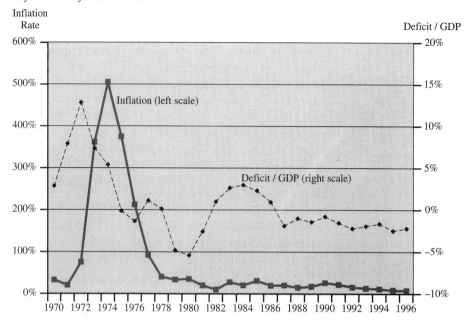

with a one- to two-year lag and was very largely due to indexing: Inflation rose from 20 percent in 1971 to 505 percent in 1974. The deficit fell to zero or even a slight surplus by 1975 and was in the 4 to 5 percent surplus range by 1979–1980. This should have brought inflation down more promptly, but indexing had created considerable momentum. Inflation fell steadily from 1974 to 1982, but did not fall to 10 percent until 1982. By that time the deficit was rising moderately but then subsided into balance by 1986 and was in surplus for every year thereafter through 1996. Inflation, however, remained stubbornly in double digits, although it finally reached single digits by 1995.

Having identified fiscal deficits as the ultimate cause of high, persisting inflation, we must add that the connection is often not immediate or direct, at least in the short term. Not only are there momentum effects, but in an open economy such as Chile's the time path of local inflation is affected by variables such as international oil prices, export prices, dollar inflation, and the currency exchange regime selected by the government.[12] Since the latter issue is particularly important to EFMs, we shall now examine it in some detail.

Currency Exchange Regimes

Fixed Exchange Rates as Inflation Control

We have seen that inflation and currency devaluation are intimately connected in the sense that expected future inflation will depress today's value of the currency. But it turns out that causality can work both ways. Not only can inflation cause devaluation,

---

[12]For a careful analysis of all such factors in the case of Chile, see Budnevich and Godoy (1995).

but devaluation can also cause inflation. A simple way to visualize this reverse connection is as follows: Imagine a small, open economy where *all* goods are traded on international markets. In such an economy, local prices would be set outside the country and simply reflect a translation of world prices into local currency. In this setting, any devaluation of the currency would immediately cause local prices to adjust upward. While this is an extreme example, it does show why devaluation causes inflation, especially in small, open economies.

Partly in recognition of this, many EFM governments seek to control inflation by anchoring the value of their currencies. The most radical and effective way to do this is simply to use another country's currency. Panama, for example, uses the U.S. dollar as its currency and hence follows roughly the U.S. level of inflation. With this type of currency regime, monetizing a fiscal deficit is not possible: There is no local currency to print. This means that any fiscal deficit must be paid out of foreign exchange reserves or borrowed in dollars. Panama was able to run budget deficits equal to 5 to 10 percent of GDP in the 1970s when banks were lending freely to developing countries; indeed the deficit reached 13.3 percent of GDP in 1979. But after the debt crisis of the 1980s such deficits could no longer be financed. Panama put its fiscal house in order because it had no choice—there was no way a deficit could be financed by printing money. Indeed, Panama was obliged to run a fiscal surplus in the first half of the 1990s, enabling some government debt to be repaid.

In countries suffering serious currency weakness, a strong currency such as the dollar may come into general use informally as a medium of exchange. In Russia, for example, dollars have circulated throughout the 1990s, particularly $100 bills, which became in many ways the safest way to store wealth—much safer than deposits in Russian banks, which collapsed in 1998. Similarly Argentina experienced significant "dollarization" during its hyperinflation of the late 1980s. The widespread acceptance of the dollar prepared the way for Argentina to adopt a currency board in the 1990s.

A *currency board* is a legal framework that enables local currency to be issued only under strictly limited circumstances. The goal is to ensure that local currency is at all times fully or almost fully backed by reserves of a strong currency such as the dollar, so that the two become nearly perfect substitutes. It involves a legislative commitment to exchange the two currencies at a fixed rate, usually one-for-one, combined with restrictions on the issuing authority (the currency board) such that new local currency is issued only in the presence of sufficient reserves of external currency, so that the exchange commitment is always credible.

Currency boards are sometimes adopted by small countries that want a local currency for reasons of symbolism and pride, but which in substance are willing to use the strong currency of another country. Thus, Bermuda, Brunei Darussalam, Cayman Islands, Djibouti, the Eastern Caribbean Central Bank, Estonia, the Falkland Islands, Gibraltar, Hong Kong, and Lithuania have adopted currency boards. The related external currencies have included the dollar, the German mark, and the pound sterling.[13]

These arrangements come closer in spirit to the classic gold standard than any others in the modern era. Like the gold standard under the classic "rules of the game" of the pre–World War I era, currency boards exert a harsh discipline by forestalling the option to monetize fiscal deficits. Deficits can only be paid for by borrowing or by drawing down the government's accumulated reserves. Insofar as government reserve holdings are drawn down to pay foreign debt (a form of capital outflow), domestic currency must be retired, so that the money supply actually shrinks.

---

[13]See Baliño and Enoch (1997) for a detailed analysis of currency boards.

The contractionary effect of this discipline means that countries that adopt this system (e.g., Argentina) must be prepared to suffer severe recession in times of stress, which tests the will of the government to maintain the currency board system. For this to work, there must be a strong anti-inflationary popular will. That was certainly present in Argentina in the 1990s given the suffering from inflation during the previous decades, but this will was severely tested by the speculative attack on the Argentine peso during the "tequila crisis" of 1995. By the end of the century, currency boards in Argentina, Estonia, Hong Kong, and Lithuania had all successfully withstood speculative attack, although Argentina remained in recession and continued to build its debt to cover deficits.

Since a currency board immediately translates deficits into debt or contraction of the money supply, it can hardly be recommended to a country whose fiscal deficits are quite large; this would quickly create unmanageable stresses. When President Suharto of Indonesia proposed to adopt a currency board arrangement after the collapse of the Indonesian currency and financial institutions in 1997, the IMF and most economists opposed this on the grounds that the country did not have sufficient reforms in place to create the stability that a currency board can reinforce but not single-handedly create.

While currency boards are still somewhat rare, a majority of EFM governments in the 1990s adopted some form of "peg" to the dollar or other strong currency that permitted some of the benefits of a currency board without the same rigidities. This usually amounted to little more than an announcement that the government would manage its foreign exchange market in such a way that currency would be bought or sold by the government in an effort to keep its price at or close to some stated value. The credibility of this promise is a function of the country's international reserves and its fiscal policies. Countries with large international reserves and good fundamentals that are determined to defend their currencies' values may be able to withstand major assaults on the pegged value, but no country has unlimited reserves nor unlimited will to spend reserves in this way.

When a country with a pegged currency spends reserves to defend the currency's value, this intervention is usually *sterilized.* This means that the central bank buys local currency bonds from local banks in quantities about equal to the foreign reserves it has drawn down, so that the overall monetary base (central bank liability structure) remains unchanged. Both foreign reserves and domestic bonds are assets of the central bank; sterilization is the replacement of a disappearing asset over which the central bank has little control (reserves) with an asset that the central bank can increase at will (government bonds purchased through open market operations). This action prevents conversions of domestic currency into foreign currency from having the contractionary effect on the money supply just described for a country with a currency board. But sterilization violates the classic gold standard "rules of the game," under which the deflationary action of reserve outflows is not offset. In other words, sterilization makes currency stabilization less painful, but it is very much akin to monetization of deficits. Sterilization can undermine the long-run credibility of the exchange peg by sending a bad signal about long-run monetary policy, and by increasing the ratio of domestic money to foreign reserves, which can encourage further reserve outflows. Sterilization cannot be pursued for very long without causing a collapse of the exchange rate peg.

If a country adopts another country's currency or establishes a currency board, it has literally surrendered the right to an independent monetary policy. Currency pegs other than currency boards formally permit the government to have a monetary policy separate from that of the external currency; that is, to print money through sterilization or otherwise to prevent an economic contraction. But unless the monetary policy adopted is very similar to that of the strong-currency country it will sooner or later become impossible to maintain the peg. The underlying idea is that differential inflation rates will sooner or later pull currencies apart (i.e., that relative PPP holds).

Crawling Pegs and Trading Bands

Crawling Pegs.   A variant on the currency peg that tries to accommodate differences in inflation is the *crawling peg*. This is an arrangement in which the pegged exchange rate is moved slowly but frequently in response to actual realized inflation, or to a longer-term inflation target, relative to inflation in the strong-currency country, following the relative PPP formula discussed earlier. The idea is to keep the peg at the relative PPP equilibrium point. This can work effectively if local inflation is not too severe and if the equilibrium real exchange rate remains relatively constant (i.e., if k— as defined on page 230—does not vary much over time). Otherwise, however, it will be hard to maintain and likely will be undone by uncertainty. High, uncertain, and variable inflation is likely eventually to overwhelm any peg system, even a crawling peg. If we cannot be sure where inflation is headed and what the real purchasing power of the currency should be in the future, then we cannot have confidence in the crawling peg.

The main argument in favor of a currency peg, fixed or crawling, is that it provides an anchor, enabling the local currency to capture at least some of the credibility of the stronger currency. Conceivably, this can control both actual inflation and inflationary expectations, which explains the great popularity of pegs. However, the arguments against pegging are also strong.[14] First, pegging severely limits the scope of monetary policy, as noted above. Second, it makes a country vulnerable to economic shocks taking place in the strong-currency country that need not otherwise have affected it. Third, and most importantly, it offers a tempting target for speculative attack: When a currency weakens against its peg, speculators pile on, selling the currency spot and forward with very little risk of its strengthening and with the possibility of huge gains if the peg breaks.

Indeed, the speculators involved in currency crises usually include and sometimes consist primarily of local individuals, companies, and banks, many of whom are intimately involved with the government. These insiders are often among the first to see a crisis coming because of a growing perception that the peg is holding the currency at too high a level, and they rush to sell their local currency and hedge their hard-currency borrowing before it is too late. This phenomenon, known as *capital flight,* is made possible by the obliging central bank, which continues to buy local currency at a price increasingly deemed too high by the market. This portrayal of capital flight by insiders explains why some observers described Indonesia's proposal to establish a currency board at the peak of the Asian crisis in 1997 as an "exit strategy for wealthy Indonesians."

Finally, when a currency peg does break, the consequences can be very severe. We will look at EFM financial crises in detail in Chapter 8, but there is no doubt that some of them were made much worse by first holding a peg in place and then releasing it. The resulting cascade can swamp even the best-run governments and result in extended periods of high interest rates and economic contraction much more severe than would have occurred if the currency had not been pegged in the first place.

In short, successful pegs are excellent and broken pegs can be catastrophic. The moral would seem to be that a country should not adopt a peg unless (1) its fundamentals

---

[14]See Mishkin (1998) for an excellent statement of the case against pegging.

are in very good shape, in particular with little or no fiscal deficit, and (2) the country is prepared to suffer periods of stress when the peg is attacked, including high interest rates and economic contraction. If these conditions are met, as they have been so far in Hong Kong and Argentina, then the country can and perhaps should adopt the strongest form of peg (currency board) to give it as much credibility as possible.

Trading Bands.   When these conditions are not met, countries sometimes opt for a soft form of pegging, a *trading band*. This means that the country declares a fundamental exchange rate that it believes to be sustainable and then promises to defend a band of, say, plus or munus 10 percent around it. If the currency falls to the bottom of the band, the government promises to intervene by buying currency; if it rises to the top, then the government will intervene by selling currency. The central rate and hence the entire band then may or may not crawl through frequent small adjustments in inflation according to relative PPP.

The best example of a noncrawling band is the experience of the European Community (EC) during 1975–1995, prior to the Maastricht Treaty, which committed the EC to EMU. For several decades, the countries of the EC tried to stabilize their currencies against each other through the *Exchange Rate Mechanism* (ERM), a system of pegging EC currencies to the dollar through a trading band. The results were less than satisfactory. The bands were frequently adjusted, generally to widen them and accommodate market movements. Finally, in 1992 the United Kingdom and Italy fell out of even the wide bands after fears about inflation (future more than present inflation) drove speculative attacks on their currencies.

Rather than abandon the goal of currency stability, the member countries of the EC resolved to coordinate their economic policies ever more closely together, and this led to the Maastricht Treaty and EMU. Since a common currency requires common policies, especially common monetary policies, policy conditions were agreed upon. The three key conditions were (1) a public sector deficit/GDP ratio less than 3 percent, (2) a national debt/GDP ratio less than 60 percent, and (3) inflation less than 3 percent. All of these were designed to keep inflation low enough in all member countries so that the various currencies could be combined. Despite widespread skepticism in other regions, the euro was launched on January 1, 1999. This nearly unprecedented event represented a significant surrender of monetary policy independence by sovereign countries, illustrating how far one must go to control inflation and make currency stability work.

Russia and Indonesia adopted crawling bands in 1996 and 1997, respectively, but quickly abandoned them in the collapse of 1998. Four other countries—Chile, Colombia, Ecuador, and Israel—were able to maintain their crawling bands. A commission in India recommended in 1997 an even weaker concept that it called a "monitoring band," which involves no commitment to intervene at the edges of a band, but reserves the right to do so when the currency is outside the band.[15] As bands become weaker and commitments to them less clear, the exchange regime becomes what has been termed a "dirty float," where intervention is decided upon on a case-by-case basis.

Finally, countries may simply let their currencies float freely. This is the default solution when no other system is in place, or a peg has been broken by an attack. Floating is simple and does not risk a sudden collapse. But its disadvantage is that volatility in the foreign exchange markets continues to be very high, so that not only a country's imports and exports, but also its own inflation rate, are likely to be blown around by erratic market events over which the government has no control.

---

[15]See Williamson (1998) for a defense of crawling and monitoring bands.

To summarize, there are two simple, polar choices of exchange rate regime: purely fixed and purely floating, with a variety of often unsuccessful efforts to construct alternative arrangements in between. Purely floating is low cost and easy to implement, but does not bring stability. Therefore, many EFM governments attempt to anchor their currency as firmly as possible to a strong external currency in the hope that this will help to control inflation. The system can work, but only under special conditions: Fiscal deficits must be small enough not to pose a threat to monetary discipline and the peg must be made as strong and credible as possible, backed by substantial international reserves that the government is prepared to pledge to support the currency. If these preconditions are not met, then currency pegs are most likely to lead to currency overvaluation, resulting capital flight, and eventual financial crisis. Following the Asian crisis, many countries shifted to floating exchange rates, though most were soon operating with trading bands, and one country (Malaysia) adopted a new peg to the dollar.

The Impact of Inflation on Debt Markets

Effect on Interest Rates

Inflation has a serious and negative effect on debt markets. Those who contemplate lending money must be concerned about the value of the money they later receive in repayment. In general, expected inflation raises interest rates, shortens the available lending maturities, and reduces the availability of loans.

The first-order effect on interest rates is to raise them by approximately the amount of the expected inflation. Consider inflation's effect on interest rates with a simple model in which a lender who will lend for a single period contracts to earn a nominal interest rate i. At the end of the period he or she finds that prices have risen by π percent, and thus real wealth has increased only by a smaller *real rate r*:

$$1 + r \equiv (1 + i) / (1 + \pi)$$

This is the definition of the *ex post* real rate r. We turn this relationship around and imagine that all lenders have in mind their target *ex ante* real rate r and combine it with their expected rate of future inflation π^e to produce a nominal interest rate i in the following way:

$$1 + i = (1 + r)(1 + \pi^e) \approx 1 + r + \pi^e$$

That is,

$$i \approx r + \pi^e.$$

This is, of course, quite an abstraction since neither the real rate r nor the expected inflation π^e can be observed directly in most cases.

Whenever interest rates are indexed to inflation, we have an opportunity to observe the real rate directly. For example, inflation-indexed Treasury bonds were introduced into the United States capital markets in January 1997 with a 10-year issue bearing a (real) rate of 3.375 percent plus an ongoing adjustment of principal to reflect changes in the consumer price index. One subsequent five-year issue was sold in 1997 with a 3.625 percent interest rate, and in 1998 10-year and 30-year issues were sold, both with coupons of 3.625 percent. By year-end 1998 all four issues were trading to yield between 3.8 percent and 4.0 percent, while the longer maturities among regular (nonindexed) Treasury bonds were trading to yield 5.2 percent to 5.4 percent. We may conclude that the market's expectation of inflation was about 1.4 percent, which seems consistent with 1998 inflation and with what most economists were saying about future inflation in the United States.

The above model must be considered only a first approximation, however, as it takes no account of inflation *risk*. Since future inflation is an unknown quantity, we must take into account the possibility that it will be higher than the value we reasonably expect; that is, our expectations may turn out to be wrong. Lenders at fixed interest rates are damaged by inflation, so unexpected inflation (i.e., the chance that inflation may be worse than its expected future value) must enter into their calculations. If lenders are risk averse, as they almost surely are, then they will require extra compensation for this risk: We can reasonably assume that lenders require some *inflation risk premium m*:

$$1 + i = (1 + r)(1 + \pi^e)(1 + m) \approx 1 + r + \pi^e + m$$

That is,

$$i \approx r + \pi^e + m.$$

The magnitude of the risk premium m depends on the variability of inflation, and we have seen that inflation variability is highly correlated with the level of inflation. In the case of the United States, m was essentially zero by the late 1990s because almost no one was seriously concerned about inflation risk. The greater the inflation risk, the higher the risk premium. A study of inflation-indexed and nonindexed bonds in the United Kingdom concluded that the risk premium in sterling was about 0.70 percent on average from October 1992 to July 1997, when the Bank of England adopted an inflation-targeting regime, and about 1.00 percent over a longer horizon reaching back to July 1982 when inflation risk was greater.[16]

When we look at EFMs, however, the inflation risk premiums become dramatically higher than in developed economies. Israel is another country with inflation-indexed bonds, which provide the basis for measuring real interest rates and hence inflation risk premiums. Furthermore, as is clear from the Appendix to this chapter, Israel is one of the most inflationary of all EFMs over a long period of time. Israel's rate of inflation averaged 3.179 percent per month or 45.6 percent a year during the period from September 1984 to March 1992. One study[17] estimated the inflation risk premium during this period to be 0.34 percent a month or 4.16 percent a year.[18] Furthermore, if one looks just at a period of runaway inflation from September 1984 to July 1985, prior to the adoption of a strict austerity program, average inflation was 15.2 percent a month or 443 percent a year, and the inflation risk premium rose to 2.36 percent a month or 32.3 percent on an annual basis! This level of risk premium, which appears to the borrower as additional real interest to be paid, makes borrowing prohibitively expensive.

The tendency for EFM currencies to command significantly higher interest rates than currencies of industrialized countries—because of expected and unexpected inflation—continues to be evident even in most cases where the EFM government has pegged its currency to an external anchor such as the dollar. If the peg were perfectly credible, external investors would have an easy, risk-free arbitrage opportunity: Borrow dollars, sell them for local currency, and lend the local currency at a much higher rate. Suppose, for example, that a bank pays 5 percent for dollar deposits and that local currency deposits pay 12 percent. The simple arbitrage described would yield 7 percent,

[16]Remolona, Wickens, and Gong (1998).
[17]Kandel, Ofer, and Sarig (1996).
[18]If r, π, and m are monthly, annual $1 + i = (1 + r)^{12}(1 + \pi)^{12}(1 + m)^{12}$. Then, $(1 + .0034)^{12} = 1.0416$.

an enormous spread. If this operation were conducted on $1 billion, for example, a perfectly feasible number given the size of international banks, it would pay $70 million a year provided the currency price did not change.

One of the most fundamental tenets of finance theory is that risk-free arbitrage opportunities cannot exist more than fleetingly, and that financial returns rise as risk increases. That makes it clear that the opportunity described, apparently so very profitable, is far from risk-free; its very magnitude suggests that the risk is also very high. The risk in question is that the peg will break and the EFM currency will devalue. The very existence of an interest rate differential indicates doubt that the currency peg is firm. Indeed, the magnitude of the interest rate differential is a reasonably good measure of the risk of the peg breaking.

A bank that acquired the asset-liability pair described would own an explosive package of risk and reward. The same package could be acquired off balance sheet through a forward purchase of local currency, if a forward market exists, since by interest parity (reviewed in the box in the next section) the asset–liability pair is exactly equivalent to a forward purchase. Similarly, many derivatives such as swaps, which amount to multiperiod forward purchases of currency, offer another off-balance-sheet method of taking the risk and attempting to earn the reward.

This is not just an abstraction; it is known throughout EFMs as the "short dollar position." Banks all over Asia were taking this bet prior to the Asia crisis, creating a kind of powder keg that would explode when the currencies collapsed. Mexican banks were not permitted to take such unmatched exchange risks in 1994 (except to the extent of 15 percent of their capital), but managed to do so anyway through derivatives, which greatly increased the damage from Mexico's currency collapse. We will look at these situations in detail in Chapter 8.

Lending Terms and Volumes

There is also a level of risk beyond which neither external nor internal investors will invest at all, and when this happens, markets simply shut down. For example, in the autumn of 1989 it became clear that the United States was entering a significant recession and that the future outlook was bleak and uncertain. This followed several years in which high-yield debt ("junk bonds") had been sold with interest coverage levels lower than at any other time in recent memory. When the change in circumstances happened, the market for these bonds temporarily dried up and the firm of Drexel Burnham Lambert, the most important underwriter and trader of junk bonds, failed.

Similarly, in 1998 currency instability that began in East Asia in 1997 spread to Latin America and Central and Eastern Europe. In late summer of that year, a currency collapse and debt default in Russia caused a major sell-off in stock markets around the world and virtually shut down the market for new issues of EFM stocks and bonds. Not since the great debt crisis of the 1980s had capital flows to EFMs come so close to a near standstill. Uncertainty and illiquidity had reached the point at which investors no longer tried to price risk but simply avoided some kinds of risks altogether.

This shutdown is not a discontinuity so much as the extreme end of a spectrum of risk. In almost all debt markets, strong borrowers can borrow more than weak ones. That is, the volume of new risky lending and the ability to sell risky assets at their previous peak prices will tend to diminish as investors' credit standings decline and/or the riskiness of investments increase. Firms that have experienced losses dump risky assets and try to lower their leverage to put themselves in a stronger position for the future. Those willing to lend become fewer in number as risk increases and liquidity declines, until a finite risk point is reached at which few will lend at any interest rate.

The phenomenon of market shutdown above a certain level of risk also explains why in every debt market there is a maximum term, the longest time period for which any investor will lend at a fixed rate of interest. This is a function of the level and volatility of inflation. When inflation becomes high, this maximum term may shrink to months or weeks. Indeed, during Brazil's hyperinflation of the late 1980s, the maximum term shrank to one or two days. In such an economy, there is no longer a yield curve but just a "yield point."

To summarize, inflation damages debt markets by increasing interest rates not only by the amount of expected inflation but also by a premium for unexpected inflation. In addition, inflation shortens the maximum term for which any investor will lend at a fixed rate of interest, sometimes quite dramatically, and reduces the volume of fixed-rate bonds that investors are willing to hold.

The Impact of Inflation on Foreign Exchange Markets

Volatility of Exchange Rates

The most important effect of inflation on exchange rates is to make them substantially more volatile. This happens because foreign exchange markets are dominated not by agents who trade goods, but by agents who invest and lend. Investors incorporate into foreign exchange rates their estimates of all future inflation, and opinions about the future can change suddenly and dramatically.

We have seen that much of the damage from inflation arises from its volatility, which increases with its level, and that foreign exchange rate determination has a great deal to do with expected inflation. The inescapable conclusion is that countries that tolerate even moderate levels of inflation are likely to suffer from periods in which their foreign exchange rates fluctuate in unexpected and sometimes extreme ways. As we have also seen, this cannot easily be fixed by just pegging the exchange rate.

In this section we will focus on a second impact of inflation on foreign exchange markets, namely its effect on the forward rate. This is a direct consequence of its impact on interest rates, as should be clear from the nearby box on *interest parity*.

Forward Exchange Rates

Covered interest parity makes it clear that forward exchange rates are not anyone's prediction of what later spot exchange rates will be; rather, they are a simple, mechanical consequence of interest rate differentials in the two countries. Nevertheless, we can gain some additional insight into forward rates by replacing the interest rates with their decomposition into required real rates, expected inflation, and risk premium. We will assume that the weaker currency ("pesos") has an inflation risk premium and that the dollar has none. Then:

$$F_{P/\$} = E_{P/\$}(1 + i_p)/(1 + i_\$) = E_{P/\$}(1 + r_p)(1 + \pi_p^e)(1 + m_p)/(1 + r_\$)(1 + \pi_\$^e)$$

Now we make a strong assumption: Suppose that the required real rate of interest (abstracting from inflation risk) is the same in both countries, so that $1 + r_p = 1 + r_\$$. This implies that capital earns the same real return in both countries, so that capital does not persistently flow from one to the other. The capital flows in the 1990s show how unrealistic this assumption is: Most of the time, capital is rapidly flowing either into or out of EFMs, reflecting changes in perceived real rates of return. But if we reached a state of equilibrium in which capital remained voluntar-

Covered Interest Parity

Covered interest parity is a relationship between the interest rates in two countries, the spot exchange rate of their currencies, and the forward exchange rate of their currencies. An easy way to understand it is with the diagram below. In this diagram, the top horizontal line represents dollars and the bottom horizontal line represents pesos. The left vertical line represents time today ($t = 0$) and the right vertical line represents a future point in time $t = T$.

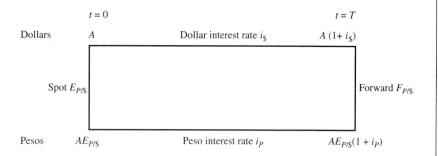

The upper left-hand corner therefore represents dollars today. The lower left-hand corner represents pesos today. The upper right-hand corner represents dollars at time T. The lower right-hand corner represents pesos at time T.

The upper edge of the box connects dollars today with dollars at time T and so is the dollar interest rate for term T. The lower edge of the box connects pesos today with pesos at time T and so is the peso interest rate for term T. The left-hand edge of the box connects dollars today with pesos today and so is the spot (current) exchange rate $E_{P/\$}$ expressed in pesos per dollar. The right-hand edge of the box represents the forward exchange rate $F_{P/\$}$ also expressed in pesos per dollar.

The point of covered interest parity is that these four quantities are not independent of each other: Given any three of them, one can compute what the fourth must be. In particular, if we know the spot exchange rate and the two interest rates, we already know what the forward exchange rate must be.

We reason as follows. Start with A dollars today in the upper left-hand corner. These dollars can be invested at the dollar interest rate and become $A(1 + i_\$)$ dollars by time T. Alternatively, the A dollars can be converted to pesos at the spot exchange rate, yielding $AE_{P/\$}$. This amount of pesos can then be invested at the peso interest rate and become $AE_{P/\$}(1 + i_p)$ by time T.

In all major currency markets and some smaller ones, traders are willing to trade forward exchange rates—that is, to agree today that come time T they will exchange dollars for pesos at a rate $F_{P/\$}$ that is agreed upon today. If there is a forward market for pesos, the peso investment in the lower right-hand corner can be today sold forward, guaranteeing that at time T we will have $AE_{P/\$}(1 + i_p)/F_{P/\$}$ dollars.

So we have two different ways to change our A dollars today into dollars at time T. One way is to go across the top of the box, investing them directly as dollars. The other way around the box is to convert them to pesos, earn the peso rate, and today sell the resulting pesos forward, guaranteeing our outcome. The financial principle of no risk-free

continued

concluded

arbitrage says that if two strategies are fully equivalent, they must have the same return; hence:

$$A(1 + i_\$) = AE_{P/\$}(1 + i_P)/F_{P/\$}$$

The A on each side cancels, since the amount for which we transact has no importance, and the result is the formula for the forward exchange rate:

$$F_{P/\$} = E_{P/\$}(1 + i_P)/(1 + i_\$)$$

This tells us that if the forward exchange rate is traded, its price is equal to the spot exchange rate times a fraction whose numerator is one plus the peso interest rate and whose denominator is one plus the dollar interest rate. This is called the *covered interest parity* relationship. The word "covered" means that the foreign exchange risk of moving into pesos has been hedged by also selling the pesos forward. The word "parity" means equality or equivalence. The formula tells us that it will do us no good to chase a high peso interest rate: If we hedge, the consequence is exactly the same as investing in dollars in the first place.

ily at rest, the real interest rates would cancel each other out in the above expression, leaving:

$$F_{P/\$} = E_{P/\$}(1 + \pi_P^e)(1 + m_P)/(1 + \pi_\$^e)$$

This is close to the statement of relative PPP, in which the future exchange rate will move to reflect the ratio of expected inflation. Indeed, it is exactly equivalent except for the presence of the risk premium term $1 + m_P$. What the risk premium does is to bias the forward rate away from the expected future exchange rate predicted by relative PPP. In particular, $F_{P/\$}$ will be higher, and hence $F_{\$/P}$ will be lower, than the expected future exchange rate predicted by relative PPP. The latter is the price of the peso measured in dollars, so we may say that the forward value of the peso will be depressed below its equilibrium level by the risk premium.

If there were no inflation risk premium in pesos (i.e., if $m_P = 0$), then the forward exchange rate $F_{\$/P}$ would be an unbiased estimate of the future value of the peso, according to relative PPP. When $m_P > 0$, though, $F_{\$/P}$ is biased low. This means that hedging peso holdings by selling pesos forward becomes very expensive. The inflation risk premium m_P discourages hedging currency risk, just as it discourages borrowing in pesos.

In summary, inflation distorts foreign exchange markets in two ways. The most important effect is that even moderate inflation will lead to significant exchange rate volatility, and that high inflation will lead to extreme exchange rate volatility. The only way to finally tame the volatility is to tame the fiscal deficits that are the ultimate drivers of high inflation risk. A secondary effect of inflation is to depress the forward foreign exchange rate below its equilibrium level because of the presence of inflation risk premiums in interest rates. This substantially raises the cost of hedging out of local currency.

Inflation and Banks

Banks and Float

While inflation has serious and negative effects on both debt markets and foreign exchange markets, raising risk premiums and creating troubling instabilities, the story is quite different when we come to banks.

EFM banks often benefit from inflation, primarily because inflation increases the velocity of money and the number of monetary transactions. When the currency is deteriorating by the day, no one wants to hold it any longer than necessary, and so it tends to be spent more quickly.[19] In periods of hyperinflation, people may run to stores rather than walk, to spend currency quickly on real goods before it loses more value.

Similarly, people will write checks rapidly, drawing down their checking balances to the lowest possible level. The money is not lost to the banking system as a whole, but merely passes from one account to another. What does grow is the *float,* the quantity of money in transition from one account to another. The float typically is "owned" by the banks for a day or two while it is in transit.

Banks do not pay interest on the float, so it becomes an interest-free source of funding. Furthermore, the balances in checking accounts pay little or no interest. The sum of checking account balances and checks in the process of collection represent a most attractive source of funding for the banks. A significant fraction of this free funding must be shared with the central bank (where banks hold zero-interest reserves), and to this extent the government also profits from inflation, but the rest greatly increases the profitability of the banks.

Thus, it often happens that the banking sector appears quite robust in inflationary economies. The fraction of the GDP represented by banking services can expand to as much as 15 percent of GDP (as in Brazil during the late 1980s and early 1990s) from the more normal level of 3 to 5 percent. Banks may be the most profitable of all business sectors in such economies.

One might imagine that prosperous banks would stimulate the entire business sector because a banking system flush with funds should want to lend those funds out to businesses. However, other factors intrude. First, inflation is often associated with reduced *real* money holdings (M/P) and hence a reduced supply of real loanable funds in the banking system. Second, the inflation risk premium appears to borrowers as a higher real rate, discouraging them from borrowing. Finally, banks do not need to take the default risks associated with lending in a highly inflationary environment; they can earn high returns on capital simply by putting most of their funds into government bonds.

Banks and Government Bonds

High deficits generate a growing supply of government bonds for the local market. The usual problem is to find sufficient local savings to support the purchase of these bonds. Banks that profit from float are natural purchasers of the liquid bonds. The liquidity of the bonds is attractive because in a rapidly changing market it is desirable to be able to change the composition of assets quickly. Volatility can be especially problematic when the source of financing bank assets is float.

In all countries, even the most developed, banks hold a certain fraction of their assets as government bonds. This has long been deemed essential for liquidity. But in inflationary economies, the proportion of bank assets held as government bonds is likely to be especially high. The government is issuing large quantities of bonds, and the banks need an asset liquid enough to be financed by float, so banks find it beneficial to hold large quantities of government bonds. Such holdings are typically quite profitable for the banks because the government bonds pay a high and often inflation-adjusted rate of interest.

---

[19]Widespread inflation indexing makes it unnecessary to quickly spend bank balances on which indexed interest is earned, but the above remarks hold for cash and checking deposits.

The consequence is that government funding often crowds out the private sector in inflationary economies. What the government is doing, first by its reserve requirements and second by its massive sale of bonds to the banks, is preempting the national savings for itself to pay for its deficits. Banks in inflationary economies can be "hollowed out" by their governments, so that skills in private sector lending actually decline and banking becomes a business of manipulating bonds, interest rate futures, inflation indexes, and other instruments unrelated to the private sector's need for loans. In an extreme case, such as Mexico in the 1980s, the government drops all pretense and simply nationalizes the banks, taking all the national savings for its own purposes.

In summary, inflation can make banks prosper, but beneath that prosperity often lies a deep distortion of capital allocation whose net result is to crowd out the private sector, preempt the national savings to pay for the government's deficits, and undermine the private intermediation function of banks.

APPENDIX: MEAN ANNUAL INFLATION, 1970–1995

The following table is based on the IMF's *International Financial Statistics* (1999).

Country	Mean 1970–1995	Means 1970–1979	1976–1985	1980–1989	1986–1995
Panama	3.78	6.01	5.08	3.15	0.80
Germany	3.78	4.89	3.97	2.90	2.46
Singapore	3.97	5.91	3.52	2.79	1.93
Switzerland	3.99	4.98	3.32	3.27	2.85
Malta	4.26	5.56	5.40	3.58	2.37
Netherlands	4.44	7.06	5.13	2.87	1.73
Malaysia	4.46	5.50	4.61	3.65	3.07
Austria	4.57	6.10	5.08	3.84	2.71
Japan	4.85	9.09	4.71	2.53	1.36
Luxembourg	4.99	6.50	6.63	4.72	2.27
Belgium	5.23	7.13	6.71	4.90	2.28
Saudi Arabia	5.33	12.47	4.64	0.04	1.06
United States	5.67	7.10	7.22	5.55	3.55
Netherlands Antilles	5.72	8.31	6.86	4.98	2.73
Cyprus	5.93	6.79	7.49	5.80	3.94
Canada	5.96	7.38	8.11	6.51	3.36
Bahrain	5.99	12.56	8.30	2.25	0.54
Bahamas	5.99	6.92	6.44	6.28	4.47
Burkina Faso	6.31	8.08	9.68	5.04	3.13
Thailand	6.47	8.00	7.42	5.82	4.35
Niger	6.60	10.35	11.40	3.57	1.82
Denmark	6.71	9.29	9.18	6.91	2.95
France	6.82	8.90	10.08	7.38	2.65
Norway	7.04	8.37	8.74	8.34	4.32
Morocco	7.34	7.79	9.80	7.58	5.40
Finland	7.47	10.41	9.67	7.32	3.57
Sweden	7.56	8.57	9.76	7.94	5.22
Togo	7.67	9.52	8.92	5.04	5.70
Australia	7.78	9.83	9.46	8.41	5.22
Senegal	7.88	9.79	9.39	6.91	3.87
Fiji	8.01	10.62	8.15	7.45	5.30
Jordan	8.30	10.81	8.53	7.02	6.97
St. Lucia	8.32	13.39	8.21	5.77	3.92
Gabon	8.50	11.06	11.44	6.49	4.87
Ethiopia	8.57	10.42	11.89	4.60	7.52
Barbados	8.69	13.87	8.92	6.89	3.42
United Kingdom	8.74	12.63	10.82	7.43	4.68
India	8.77	7.54	6.76	9.12	9.45
Côte d'Ivoire	8.93	11.71	11.20	6.75	7.23
Ireland	9.11	12.75	13.27	9.34	2.91
Congo, Rep.	9.12	8.15	10.34	7.60	9.20
Cameroon	9.26	10.28	11.37	9.10	6.79
Dominica	9.31	16.30	12.62	6.89	3.31
New Zealand	9.61	11.46	13.45	11.86	5.76
Nepal	9.65	7.81	7.85	10.84	11.20
Burundi	9.71	11.90	12.09	7.17	8.66
Pakistan	9.82	11.76	7.95	7.27	8.99
Italy	10.27	12.33	15.09	11.20	5.35
Honduras	10.32	6.63	8.40	7.40	14.92
Rwanda	10.33	12.45	8.98	4.70	10.42
Mauritius	10.39	10.97	13.27	11.15	7.30
Sri Lanka	10.39	6.89	11.25	12.83	11.42

continued

Country	*Mean* *1970–1995*	Means			
		1970–1979	*1976–1985*	*1980–1989*	*1986–1995*
Western Samoa	10.44	9.32	14.20	13.45	6.88
Korea	10.61	15.22	12.36	8.41	5.82
Spain	10.73	14.39	15.44	10.25	5.82
Trinidad and Tobago	10.77	11.66	12.70	11.72	8.38
Haiti	11.98	9.26	8.72	6.62	15.56
South Africa	12.07	9.67	12.95	14.61	13.31
Gambia	12.17	9.63	11.91	17.47	14.55
Indonesia	12.23	16.92	12.20	9.63	8.20
Swaziland	12.31	10.17	14.68	14.23	12.38
Guatemala	12.49	8.86	9.19	12.07	18.70
Algeria	12.64	8.23	10.56	9.03	19.10
Guyana	12.78	9.24	16.26	19.30	12.73
Bangladesh	12.98	19.60	9.98	11.26	6.89
Egypt	12.98	7.78	13.51	17.35	16.86
Zimbabwe	13.69	7.27	12.60	12.81	20.23
Myanmar (Burma)	13.94	10.86	4.44	10.09	23.03
Philippines	13.98	14.64	16.89	15.05	9.20
Kenya	14.12	10.92	13.20	11.74	17.71
El Salvador	14.15	9.39	13.78	18.52	18.29
Syria	15.17	9.25	11.74	22.61	21.74
Portugal	15.28	17.14	22.48	17.64	9.28
Madagascar	15.29	7.90	14.90	18.56	19.83
Greece	15.69	12.31	18.53	19.49	15.67
Dominican Republic	16.49	9.20	13.63	20.87	23.36
Paraguay	17.13	11.08	15.48	20.47	23.24
Iran	17.73	11.00	16.10	19.82	25.08
Costa Rica	18.65	9.79	22.78	27.09	18.21
Jamaica	21.39	17.27	19.66	15.60	27.17
Venezuela	21.59	6.61	11.14	23.02	41.88
Colombia	22.37	19.31	23.43	23.46	25.01
Tanzania	22.51	10.99	21.93	30.07	29.39
Nigeria	24.59	15.67	18.03	23.07	37.40
Ecuador	27.13	11.87	19.89	33.97	43.34
Iceland	27.72	29.55	45.84	39.16	11.97
Mexico	36.69	14.68	41.87	69.05	46.88
Sudan	39.25	15.34	25.49	37.96	80.52
Suriname	40.62	8.78	9.26	12.93	91.91
Ghana	40.79	38.84	66.18	48.27	31.05
Sierra Leone	41.90	10.83	33.25	62.95	70.62
Turkey	46.26	23.32	45.07	51.27	66.72
Lebanon	48.44	12.13	20.82	87.54	108.12
Uruguay	61.25	59.26	51.34	57.58	70.66
Israel	65.50	32.49	138.71	129.67	18.59
Chile	79.03	174.56	51.98	21.37	16.67

References

Baliño, Tomás J. T., and Charles Enoch. 1997. *Currency Board Arrangements: Issues and Experiences.* Washington, DC: International Monetary Fund.

Barro, Robert J. 1995. Inflation and economic growth. *Bank of England Quarterly Bulletin* 35: 166–76.

Budnevich, Carlos L., and Sergio Godoy. 1995. Un análisis empírico y de política económica de la inflación en Chile: 1984–1992. In *Análisis Empírico de la Inflación en Chile.* Ed. by Felipe Morande and Francisco Rosende. Santiago: Instituto de Economía, Pontificia Universidad Católica de Chile.

Calomiris, Charles W. 1999. The impending collapse of the European Monetary Union. *Cato Journal* 18: 445–52.

Calomiris, Charles W., and Ian Domowitz. 1989. Asset substitution, money demand, and the inflation process in Brazil. *Journal of Money Credit and Banking* 21: 78–89.

Cantor, Richard, and Frank Packer. 1996. Determinants and impacts of sovereign credit ratings. Research Paper no. 9608, Federal Reserve Bank of New York.

Casella, Alessandra. 1999. Tradable deficit permits: Efficient implementation of the stability pact in the European Monetary Union. Working Paper no. 7278, National Bureau of Economic Research.

DeCecco, Marcello. 1985. Monetary theory and Roman history. *Journal of Economic History* 45: 809–22.

Eichenbaum, Martin, and Charles Evans. 1993. Some empirical evidence on the effects of monetary policy shocks on exchange rates. Working Paper no. 4271, National Bureau of Economic Research.

Eisner, Robert. 1986. *How Real Is the Federal Deficit?* New York: Free Press.

Fischer, Stanley. 1993. The role of macroeconomic factors in growth. *Journal of Monetary Economics* 32: 485–512.

Friedman, Milton. 1968. Inflation: Causes and consequences. In *Dollars and Deficits.* Englewood Cliffs, NJ: Prentice Hall.

Judson, Ruth, and Athanasios Orphanides. 1996. Inflation, volatility and growth. Working paper, Board of Governors of the Federal Reserve System.

Kandel, Shmuel, Aharon R. Ofer, and Oded Sarig. 1996. Real interest rates and inflation: An ex-ante empirical analysis. *Journal of Finance* 51, no. 1: 205–25.

Lucas, Robert E., Jr. 1972. Expectations and the neutrality of money. *Journal of Economic Theory* 4: 103–24.

Marrinan, Jane. 1989. Exchange rate determination: Sorting out theory and evidence. Federal Reserve Bank of Boston, *New England Economic Review,* November–December: 38–51.

Mishkin, Frederic S. 1998. The dangers of exchange-rate pegging in emerging-market countries. *International Finance* 1: 81–101.

Motley, Brian. 1994. Growth and inflation: A cross-country study. Working Paper no. 94-08, Federal Reserve Bank of San Francisco.

Phelps, A. W. 1967. Phillips curve, expectations of inflation and optimal unemployment over time. *Economica* 34: 254–81.

Phillips, A. W. 1958. The relationship between unemployment and the rate of change of money wage rates in the United Kingdom, 1861–1959. *Economica* 25: 283–99.

Remolona, Eli M., Michael R. Wickens, and Frank F. Gong. 1998. What was the market's view of UK monetary policy? Estimating inflation risk and expected inflation with indexed bonds. Staff Report no. 57, Federal Reserve Bank of New York.

Williamson, John. 1998. Crawling bands or monitoring bands: How to manage exchange rates in a world of capital mobility. *International Finance* 1: 59–79.

The Trouble with Banks

Questions:

Why have banks failed in record numbers and at record cost in the 1980s and 1990s?

Is it all right for banks to lend to their owners, directors, and their companies?

Why do insolvent or nearly insolvent banks sometimes take extreme risks?

Why aren't failed banks liquidated like failed industrial firms?

What are the best approaches for government policy toward weak or failed banks?

Introduction

The Epidemic of Systemic Failures

Banks are the dominant financial institution in virtually all emerging financial markets. This is the direct consequence of legal frameworks and information institutions insufficient to support strong public capital markets. Banks, of course, benefit as well from a strong legal framework, but they are better able than public markets to survive in environments where legal foundations are insufficient. They are also very well adapted to private screening and monitoring in environments of imperfect information.

A central feature of banks is that they are relational: They invest in relationships with their customers and gain access to private information through these relationships. This investment is costly, but once made can give the bank that made it an informational advantage with the customer in question. Banks have more muscle than market investors in enforcing their rights when borrowers are recalcitrant. Banks can even profit from inflation and currency instability. Thus, it is no surprise that banks dominate EFMs.

Furthermore, EFM governments tend to favor banks in a number of ways. For example, if interest rates are regulated, government often lets banks collect a subsidy by limiting legally permissible interest payments from banks to savers. In some EFMs the banks are owned directly by the government, but even where this is not true, governments often lean on banks informally to direct and manage the flows of capital within their countries. Banks are the perfect instrument for this purpose. Whereas markets are diffuse and difficult to control, banks can be influenced quietly and privately to favor certain industries, firms, projects, or regions.

Nevertheless, during the 1980s and 1990s, banks in virtually all EFMs have been privatized and the links between them and their governments have weakened. Reserve requirements have been lowered and interest rate controls loosened or abandoned. Many banking markets have been opened to foreign competition. All of this gained general support by the early 1990s among economists and others concerned with the pace of economic development.

But something is going wrong. As countries develop and financial markets liberalize and grow increasingly intertwined, as banks are privatized, and as information technology expands, banks throughout the world are often in trouble in industrialized countries as well as developing ones. The United States experienced a collapse of its thrift institutions—savings banks and savings and loan associations—in the 1980s. Even before that was resolved, U.S. banks located in the southwestern states and in New England began to fail in large numbers; almost all banks and bank holding companies of significant size in Texas and Oklahoma failed between 1986 and 1990. The total number of U.S. (nonthrift) bank failures in this period exceeded 1,000.

During the same period, almost every large bank in Norway, Sweden, and Finland either failed or was bailed out by its government for fear of failure. The governments also intervened in several notable European banks such as Crédit Lyonnais in France and Banesto in Spain. Nonperforming loans in Japan's banks were rumored to be as much as $500 billion by 1990; though these estimates were initially denied by the government, it became apparent by 1997 that such estimates were actually low. In 1998 two Japanese banks, Long Term Credit Bank and Nippon Credit Bank, were taken over by the Japanese government. At this point the official estimate of total nonperforming loans rose to $400 billion; private estimates were as high as $1 trillion.[1] The Obuchi Plan of 1998 provided about $500 billion of public funds for resolution. That sum, however, will likely be insufficient to cover the large losses in banks, local cooperative banks, and credit unions.

In the developing world, it is difficult to identify a country that did *not* experience a banking crisis in the late 20th century. Celebrated cases include the "southern cone" collapse in Chile, Argentina, and Uruguay during the early 1980s, the Mexican collapse of 1994–1995, and the Asian financial crisis of 1997–1998. These three events had a particularly virulent quality because they affected countries that were highly admired and undergoing rapid liberalization. They involved the intersection of a banking crisis with the collapse of a pegged exchange rate regime and a rapid reversal of previous capital inflows. This now familiar and distinctively modern type of EFM crisis is studied in detail in Chapter 8.

It is important to see, however, that these well-known collapses are only a small subset of the much broader set of banking crises that seem to affect the great majority of the countries in both the industrialized and developing world. The immense global wave of bank failures has attracted a great deal of attention from the academic community, governments, and international organizations. An important starting point is simply to list all the banking crises that have happened and to agree on their magnitude. Gerald Caprio Jr. and Daniela Klingebiel, two World Bank researchers, have published the most comprehensive database of bank failures to date, and have analyzed it in detail.[2] The Appendix reproduces an updated summary of their database,

---

[1]*The Economist*, January 23, 1999.
[2]Caprio and Klingebiel (1996a and 1996b).

showing the countries, dates, and extent of each crisis during the period 1977–1979, and where possible an estimate of the cost of resolution.

This Appendix list is long and astonishing, and it warrants careful attention. Caprio and Klingebiel have divided bank crises into two categories: systemic and lesser cases. A *systemic* case is one in which *most or all bank capital is exhausted.* Note that the Appendix lists 112 systemic crises in the last 25 years of the 20th century, involving 94 countries! These are not minor events, but collapses of most or all banks within a country's banking system. Some countries suffered repeat systemic crises, and two countries (Kenya and Argentina) went through this experience three times in the 25-year time frame.

Many of these crises proved extremely expensive to resolve. Table 7.1 shows some of the higher resolution costs, those of 10 percent of GDP or more, as shown in the Appendix. Note that Caprio and Klingebiel were unable to estimate resolution costs in a substantial number of cases; had they been able to report resolution costs for all their cases, Table 7.1 might have been considerably longer.

Banking crises have occurred throughout history, as long as there have been banks, but the magnitude of losses recently has been a departure from the past. The United States suffered one of the most unstable banking systems of the 19th and early 20th centuries, and experienced 11 severe banking panics between 1800 and the beginning of World War I. In that era, when the losses of failed banks were borne by depositors rather than governments, the fraction of the banking system that failed during crises and the related losses were rather small. For example, the worst banking crisis of the so-called

TABLE 7.1   Resolution Cost of Selected Bank Crises

Country	Years	Cost as Percent of GDP
Argentina	1980–1982	55%
Benin	1988–1990	17
Bulgaria	1990s	13
Chile	1981–1983	41
China	1990s	47
Côte d'Ivoire	1988–1991	25
Czech Republic	1991–1994	12
Finland	1991–1994	11
Hungary	1991–1995	10
Indonesia	1997–1999	50
Israel	1977–1983	30
Japan	1990s	12
Korea	1997–1999	20
Macedonia	1993–1994	32
Malaysia	1997–1999	20
Mauritania	1984–1993	15
Mexico	1995	15
Philippines	1981–1987	19
Senegal	1988–1991	17
Spain	1977–1985	17
Taiwan	1997	11
Tanzania	1987	10
Thailand	1997–1999	42
Uruguay	1981–1984	24
Venezuela	1994–1995	18

Source: Appendix, page 279–87.

national banking era (1863–1913) occurred in 1893. The negative net worth of the banks that failed during that crisis was less than 0.10 percent of GDP.[3] The banking crises of the Great Depression of the 1930s reflected unprecedented strains on U.S. banks, resulting from deflationary monetary policy and the collapsing fortunes of bank borrowers. Yet during the Great Depression, when roughly a quarter of America's banks closed, the negative net worth of failed banks was only about 3 percent of GDP.[4]

Other countries historically had similar, or even better, records of infrequent banking system collapses and low banking system losses. Many emerging market countries of the pre–World War I era never experienced a banking crisis in which depositors or taxpayers suffered significant losses from failed banks. This was a period when most emerging market countries rigidly adhered to the gold standard, established competitive banking systems, and relied on large international flows of capital to finance their growth—capital flows that reached much higher levels relative to GDP than those of today. So in many respects the pre–World War I period was a precursor of the post-1980 period of EFM liberalization. Yet during that era, Canada, Germany, Japan, Mexico, Russia, and Sweden all avoided significant banking crises. Only Argentina (in 1890), Australia (in 1893), Brazil (in 1892 and 1901), Italy (in 1893), and Norway (in 1901) experienced banking crises in which the negative net worth of failed banks reached or exceeded 1 percent of GDP, and none of these six banking crises resulted in costs in excess of 10 percent of GDP.[5]

Why Are Losses So Large?

The magnitudes of banking crises in the 1980s and 1990s, in terms of number of countries, percentage of banks involved, and cost of resolution, were strikingly greater: The world had not seen anything like the epidemic of bank losses of the late 20th century. Furthermore, this was a period of substantial prosperity—nothing like the Great Depression of the 1930s was occurring, nor the economic volatility of the pre–World War I period, when shifts in the terms of trade often produced deep recessions in the real economy of many countries. What in the world was going on? Had there been a global outbreak of stupidity among bankers and bank regulators? How could it be stopped? This had become the most pressing question in the entire study of emerging financial markets by the turn of the century.

Economists have focused their attention primarily on the highly visible financial crises that are associated with massive external capital flows and collapses of currency value. The interaction of these elements is a particularly dangerous and complex phenomenon, associated with a general collapse of the real economy, and is studied in detail in Chapter 8. Such crises invite explanations in terms of international illiquidity and fixed, overvalued exchange rates, and we shall look at these interacting elements particularly in connection with the Mexican collapse of 1994–1995 and the East Asian crisis of 1997–1998.

For the moment, we simply note that banking crises before the 1980s have usually occurred independently of currency crises. Furthermore the pre–World War I period, as noted, was one in which exchange rates were fixed and in which very large capital flows took place into and out of developing countries; yet in that era we did not witness the powerful interaction of these elements with banking crises that we observe in the late 20th cen-

---

[3]Calomiris (2000).
[4]Calomiris (1998).
[5]Calomiris (2000).

tury. The magnitude and frequency of modern currency collapses is also impressive relative to past experience. Indeed, one study found that in recent years virtually no EFM fixed
exchange rate survives for more than a few years without collapsing.[6] Yet not all currency
collapses are associated with systemic banking failures and collapse of the real economy.

So we find it useful to study banking crises separately, and return to the interaction with currency collapse in the next chapter. How can it happen that in so many
countries the capital of entire banking systems has been wiped out? Where did the capital go? When banks repeatedly make loans that are not repaid, one must conclude that
their borrowers are destroying value. The existence of large bank loan losses, often
preceding a collapse of the banking system by months or years, is *prima facie* evidence that poor lending decisions were made. If the job of financial markets is to allocate funds to their most profitable uses, then EFM banks taken as a whole have failed
to perform acceptably. They have repeatedly directed resources to low-value uses that
have not even been able to pay interest, let alone repay principal.

Of course, this merely refocuses the question. Why have banks been such poor
fund allocators? Is it that they are unskilled and would do better with more training
and experience? Or are there structural problems in EFM banking that have led repeatedly to these outcomes? If something is deeply wrong, then the problems, costs, and
crises will continue until the underlying issues are addressed.

We suggest three factors that can explain bad banking decisions. Taken together
they may account for much of the unprecedented size and scope of losses that we now
observe in banks: connected lending, moral hazard, and overcapacity.

Connected Lending

Connected lending occurs when a bank directs loans to parties who are somehow connected with the bank: its owners, its board of directors, their families and friends, and
companies with which the bank has special ties, either because the bank owns equity
in them or because it maintains some important governance relationship with the
recipient. The opposite of connected lending is arm's-length lending.

At first glance, connected lending seems entirely normal, harmless, and inherent
to banking. After all, banking is supposed to be about relationships and private information. This seems to lead quite naturally to firms with which the owners and boards
of banks have personal connections.

But connected lending is a complex issue, which we might better understand
through an extreme example. Suppose a bank has assets of 1,000, deposit liabilities of
900, and equity of 100. The owner of the equity now takes out 600 of loans, steals the
proceeds, and flees to some tropical island. The bank fails, its equity is lost, and the
government closes it down. The owner nevertheless has a net gain of $600 - 100 =
500$, not a bad return on an investment of 100. In short, an unscrupulous bank owner
can profitably loot his or her own bank. This is by no means unrealistic. Willie Sutton
said he robbed banks because "that's where the money is," and there are modern
equivalents. If this sounds fanciful, consider the story of BCCI.

The Bank of Credit and Commerce International (BCCI) was formed in 1972 by
Agha Hasan Abedi, a Pakistani banker with a taste for rich and powerful friends. BCCI
expanded rapidly throughout the Muslim world, with deposits from rich and poor
alike. It practiced a special form of Islamic banking that in many cases replaced inter-

---

[6]Obstfeld and Rogoff (1995).

est income with lavish gifts and personal favors.[7] Loans were made to Abedi's friends without interest, without collateral, and in some cases without documentation. BCCI was closed in July 1991 after a meeting of regulators from several countries convened by the Bank of England. Its ultimate losses totaled between $12 and $14 billion, which were paid for primarily by depositors who did not benefit from deposit insurance, and who received 30 to 40 percent of their deposits in partial settlement.[8] This was a spectacular case of connected lending at a level that amounted to looting.

One recent study constructed a formal economic model of looting. Its key ingredient is a creditor that behaves inefficiently; that is, that supplies financing or guarantees it without monitoring adequately or protecting itself against self-dealing by the owners in the way that private lenders do through their contracts and their behavior. The creditor (or guarantor of the bank) is most often the government, but could also be a particularly naïve and uninformed set of depositors, like those of BCCI. When owners discover they can extract value through self-dealing, they sometimes do so to the maximum extent, driving the net worth deeply negative. The authors show how their theory might explain some cases during the thrift debacle in the United States and the Chilean collapse of 1982.[9]

Suppose bank owners use the bank's lending capacity almost exclusively to assist themselves and their associates to buy industrial companies. This would be particularly likely during a period of privatization in which financial liberalization preceded privatization of industrial enterprises. This is just what happened in Chile during 1977–1980 and in Russia during 1991–1994: In both cases depositors were trusting and no regulator existed to monitor bank behavior.

Banks that are used in this way become the centers of industrial empires. They enable entrepreneurs to leverage their own resources and acquire many more firms than they would otherwise be able to obtain. In some sense these are not true banks at all, for they do relatively little arm's-length lending. Furthermore, the criteria on which they lend are not likely to match the arm's-length criteria of profitability and economic value. In many developing economies plagued by connected lending, banks do not diversify their portfolios to reduce their risk-adjusted profits.[10] Instead of being purely for-profit enterprises, banks become instruments for channeling subsidized credit and control to favored entrepreneurs; their willingness to lend becomes a tool in the exercise of power.

Banks of this description usually fail, as happened in Chile in 1982 and in Russia in 1998. This fits the description of looting if the owners had no intention of continuing the banks in business, but were simply taking a short-term gain. Perhaps a less harsh description would say that the owners did not plan on failure, but neither would they be greatly harmed if failure occurred. Their goal was not the well-being of a bank but the aggrandizement of an industrial empire, which they acquired through the bank and would continue to own even if the bank failed.

A more respectable version of connected lending is found in Japan and Korea, where many of the largest enterprises are organized into large industrial groups, *keiretsu* in Japan and *chaebols* in Korea. The *keiretsu* have been studied extensively, and for a number of years were thought to represent an interesting model of governance

---

[7]Islamic law forbids charging interest, which is viewed as usury. Profit sharing is the typical form of compensation received for lending.

[8]Numerous books have been written about BCCI's failure. See, for example, Truell and Gurwin (1992).

[9]Akerlof and Romer (1993). See also Calomiris and Kahn (1991).

[10]Caprio and Wilson (1997) show that EFM banking systems often forgo important opportunities for diversification.

Banco Latino and the Venezuelan Banking Collapse

Venezuela's banking collapse of 1992–1994 gets less public attention than the events in Mexico and Argentina that soon followed. It had little to do with international capital flows or currency markets. But it did have a great deal to do with "crony capitalism." It resulted in estimated government losses of nearly $11 billion, approximately 13.5 percent of GDP. This figure is particularly striking in comparison with total Venezuelan bank deposits of $11.2 billion.

Venezuelan President Carlos Andrés Perez maintained an inner circle of the business elite widely referred to as the "twelve apostles," all of whom became very wealthy during his administration. Policies were enacted and enforced by the same few who stood to benefit most from them. These businessmen and their families controlled industrial empires with family-owned banks at their center.

The most influential of these banks was Banco Latino. In 1989 Perez appointed Banco Latino's president and major shareholder, Pedro Tinoco, as head of the bank regulatory commission under the central bank. Even while serving at the central bank, Tinoco remained very involved with Banco Latino. Four other "apostles" were represented on Banco Latino's board of directors, and Perez's brother was also a board member. At the same time FOGADE, the deposit insurance fund, decided to hold more than half of its assets on deposit at Banco Latino and a closely related bank, thereby putting the fund at the same risk as the deposits they were insuring.

Also in 1989, President Perez issued a presidential decree authorizing "debt reconversion." Designed to subsidize Venezuelan companies during a period of economic stringency, this decree enabled firms to buy Venezuelan public debt at low global prices and resell it to the government at full face value. Approximately half of all such transactions were passed through Banco Latino, and companies controlled by the "apostles" were the principal beneficiaries.

Banco Latino operated a "money desk" to lend money under favorable terms to companies controlled by the bank's directors and their friends. In some cases these companies were shells that simply siphoned cash to the personal offshore accounts of the directors. The bank also gave complimentary jet aircraft to many of the directors. These aircraft were either purchased by the bank or leased at inflated rates from companies controlled by directors. The bank also purchased real estate at up to three times market prices from companies controlled by its directors. By 1993, approximately 70 percent of Banco Latino's loans were to shareholders, directors, and other insiders. Nonperforming loans were officially stated at 7.2 percent.

Bank regulation was lax and ineffective. Neither the central bank nor the bank superintendency had any political autonomy or adequate regulatory staff. Yet the pattern of abuse was so obvious that the bank was forced to pay a premium in deposit markets. Toward the end of 1993 Banco Latino offered interest rates up to 105 percent, about twice the market rate, to keep depositors from withdrawing funds. A deposit insurance scheme was in effect, but in principle it covered only Bs 250,000 (about $1,000) per person. In the event, government insurance implicitly covered all bank liabilities, but the risk premium on bank debt reflected the fact that *ex ante* there was some risk that the government would be unwilling or unable to bail out *de jure* uninsured claimants.

Pedro Tinoco died in March 1993 and Perez was impeached on corruption charges in May. Rafael Caldera's election and inauguration as president in December provoked a run on the bank. The bank was closed in January 1994. Soon after, the government faced the additional bailout of nine of Banco Latino's affiliates. By the end of 1994 sixteen banks, representing nearly two-thirds of Venezuela's bank assets, had been taken over by the government.

Source: Numerous accounts from newspapers and magazines, including *The Wall Street Journal, The Washington Post, Financial Times, The Economist, Global Finance,* and *Euromoney.*

that appeared to have important advantages over the Western model of shareholder governance.

As the extent of bank losses in Japan have become known, however, fewer observers have been willing to defend this system as an attractive form of corporate control. While the Japanese banks have been reasonably professional and open to non-family business, they have also suffered from massive *nonperforming loans*, suggesting capital allocation decisions that were less than optimal. We may learn more in the future about why so many poor decisions were made, but some at least may be related to the political nature of the banks' role at the center of the *keiretsu*.

How can connected lending be controlled? It is difficult to think how a rule can be written to prevent the abuses of connected lending without somehow banning close banking relationships. Probably the best answer is disclosure and monitoring. Banks should be required to declare and list in detail all loans to parties connected with the bank. Government regulators should examine these declarations and review a selection of them to see if they conform to good lending practice. Finally, there needs to be a limit on the total percentage of assets that any bank can dedicate to each set of enterprises, to ensure diversification of risk.

Effective regulations limiting connected lending can be tricky to enforce. As part of the Mexican bank liberalization of the early 1990s, Mexican law forbade industrial firms from owning banks. But the concentration of wealth is so great in Mexico that a few families, who owned the large industrial conglomerates (*grupos*), were also able to acquire control of the banks and use them as tools for their own financing needs and as instruments of political patronage. The experience of Mexico, Chile, and Venezuela with connected lending led Argentina to develop strict rules in the mid-1990s to limit cross-holdings of ownership interests by individuals or firms in banks and their client firms. Enforcing these rules requires a detailed monitoring of the composition of stockholders of firms throughout the economy.

Moral Hazard

Definition of Moral Hazard

In a normal risk decision, the agent making the decision bears the full weight of its consequences: If the decision is a good one, the agent benefits proportionately, but if the decision is a bad one, the agent pays an equivalent price. Most bank lending decisions are normal in this sense: If the loan pays off, the bank's equity gains value and if it defaults the equity loses value. Similarly, the bank officer making the loan in a well-run bank will gain in reputation and compensation if his or her portfolio is sound, but will suffer personal penalties including dismissal if his or her portfolio is filled with losses. The owners' equity and the officer's personal risk aversion protect the bank from excessive risk taking.

Moral hazard is a problem of skewed incentives. It occurs when a risk decision is asymmetric: The agent making the decision stands to benefit if the decision is a good one, but for one reason or another does not pay a commensurate price if the decision is bad. It is a case of "heads I win, tails someone else loses." For example, when banks lack net worth, they have little to lose from bad outcomes (the bank is already insolvent) but much to gain from good outcomes (the possibility of financial resurrection). Agents faced with this kind of incentive structure will rationally want to massively increase the amount of risk taken. This can lead to exceptionally large losses. This simple concept can help to explain the magnitude of many banking losses observed around the world.

Moral hazard can also arise from conflicts of goals and incentives between bank stockholders and their employees as the result of faulty compensation systems. For this reason, traditionally, banks have not paid large cash bonuses to their loan officers. Bank managers have long understood that this could distort the loan officers' incentives and lead to large volumes of apparently profitable loans whose poor quality would only be clear after the passage of time. Among traders, however, the tradition of cash bonuses is strong, because the profitability of most trading positions is marked to market daily, and losing positions are quickly closed out. One need not wait several years to discover whether a trader made good decisions, so traders may be safely compensated in cash. However, traders understand how to game the system.[11] Moral hazard can pose a deadly risk for trading banks. (See the box on the fall of Barings.)

In a well-run bank in a healthy economy, moral hazard is not usually a problem. Bank owners and managers have a good deal to lose—their equity stake in the bank and their jobs, respectively—if the bank should fail, and so they will not want to take unreasonable risks. But the moral hazard problem becomes particularly pronounced when a bank's net worth is low or negative. Consider what happens when the bank's capital erodes and falls below regulatory benchmarks. If the regulators are alert, they should pressure the bank to increase its capital at once or shrink its assets. But regulators often do not perform this function appropriately.

For example, the entire thrift industry (savings banks and savings and loan associations) in the United States lived for many decades on taking short-term deposits and investing them in long-term, fixed-rate home mortgages. Because the value of fixed-rate mortgages declines when interest rates rise, the primary risk of this business was that some day interest rates would rise substantially; if that happened, the thrifts would face income losses if they carried the mortgages (because they would have to pay more interest on deposits than the mortgages earned) and record even larger capital losses if they tried to sell the mortgages at their reduced prices.

These events finally occurred in the period from 1979 to 1982, and the thrift industry suffered serious immediate losses. While some thrifts were in better shape than others, the losses were highly correlated across all thrifts—just the kind of event risk that could bankrupt the deposit insurance fund. The thrift regulators, with the aggressive encouragement of the U.S. Congress, pampered the industry rather than force it to deal with its weakened condition.

In 1982 Congress broadened the business definition of thrifts beyond home mortgages, so that they could move their business definition toward something more like a commercial bank. While in principle this was a good idea, most thrifts did not have the net worth, skills, and credit culture of a healthy bank, so that trouble might have been expected. The same law sanctioned "regulatory accounting," which created the illusion of capital when generally accepted accounting principles would have found little or none. When even this facade crumbled, the regulators engaged in "forbearance," meaning that they decided not to enforce their own rules.

The result was a disquieting number of what Edward Kane has termed "zombie thrifts"—the living dead—firms that had lost all their capital but still continued in business. In a normal industry, no one would fund such companies. But banks and thrifts are different because they benefit from deposit insurance. Some zombie thrifts began to grow at a phenomenal rate, taking a wild level of risk that led to some of

---

[11]For example, when trading in thin markets a trader can execute a small transaction, as a buyer, at an inflated price and thereby record a large capital gain on a preexisting position, entitling him to a large bonus.

Moral Hazard and the Fall of Barings

Barings PLC, one of the most venerable of British merchant banks with 233 years of history, failed on February 26, 1995. Its downfall was due to the activities of a single trader in its Singapore office, Nicholas Leeson. His portfolio of futures and options lost $1.3 billion, which exceeded the capital of the bank. The story is a lesson in moral hazard.[12]

Leeson's job was to trade futures on the Nikkei 225 index of Japanese stocks. He was in fact not a very good trader, but he had learned to conceal his losing trades in a secret "error account" and to show only the profitable ones, so that he enjoyed an undeservedly good reputation.

The Nikkei index had fallen from about 40,000 to 19,000 in the course of three years. But by 1994 the index seemed to have stabilized, and Leeson's bottom line in that year was less than he would have hoped. So he decided to sell options on the index. In particular, he sold 35,000 each of both puts and calls, a position known as a short straddle. This is essentially a bet against volatility; he showed immediate income because the options were sold for a significant premium, and he would only give that profit back if the index went quite far either above or below 19,000. Note how easy it is to show a short-term profit in a financial institution: You have only to take on risk.

All went well until the Kobe earthquake struck on January 17, 1995, when the Nikkei fell to below 18,000, then recovered to nearly 19,000 again, and then began a six-week slide down to about 17,000. At this level, Leeson's straddle would show a loss of about $150 million. A loss this large could not be concealed. Leeson knew he would lose his job and his reputation, the maximum sanction the bank had against him.

With his back to the wall and nothing left to lose personally, Leeson gambled on a comeback. He began to buy the Nikkei futures in unprecedented quantities, trying single-handedly to drive the price back up. He also sold futures on the Japanese government's 10-year bond, possibly in the mistaken belief that the government would have to borrow massively to repair the earthquake damage. He accumulated an astonishing total of $7 billion face amount of futures, and still was unable to get the index back up. He wrote fraudulent orders for customers to buy the futures as well.

What is interesting from a moral hazard point of view is that the total loss expanded to $1.3 billion. If only he had folded his position instead of defending it, his losses would have been less than $150 million. In other words, the losses expanded almost tenfold in a six-week period. But this additional loss was for Barings' account, not Leeson's. Had the strategy worked, his cash bonus might have been huge. The asymmetrical incentives created a situation in which risk massively expanded, turning a bad loss into a catastrophic loss and bankrupting the firm.

Sources: Fay (1997), Hunt and Heinrich (1996), and Jorion (1997).

the largest losses of the thrift crisis. It has been clearly documented that this risk taking occurred *after* the institutions had become insolvent.[13] The losses reached $180 billion by the time the government finally faced the consequences in 1989. This is far more than it would have cost the government to simply shut down the failed thrifts as they lost their capital. Moral hazard had turned a serious loss into a catastrophic one.

---

[12]Jorion (1997) provides a numerical analysis of Leeson's position.
[13]Barth and Batholomew (1992).

Government Safety Nets

An extreme kind of moral hazard can occur in a setting where the government not only guarantees bank deposits but also pampers the banks' owners and managers—and even the owners and managers of the firms unable to pay their debts to the banks. Such a regulator shows no sign of ever closing the banks in question.

The problem may begin with a government that wishes to promote certain favored industries and projects. It uses its persuasive powers to encourage banks to lend and companies to borrow in order to build these industries and projects. The result is an implied assurance that the government will take care of any problems. This is not a contract or a formal guarantee, but it affects bank and borrower behavior all the same.

Companies might not make such investments on their own because they appear too risky. But the government seems to say: Do this for us, and if the investment goes well we will all prosper; if it goes badly we will work with you to resolve any problems. Firms now face asymmetrical incentives—heads I win, tails the government loses—and so take greater risks than they otherwise would, including borrowing heavily to finance risky projects, thus compounding operating risk with increased financial risk.

The banks are in a similar position, since the government urges them to make loans to the companies with much the same kind of assurances. In the case of the banks, the assurances might imply that (1) the government will not close banks that get into trouble and/or (2) the government may simply provide cash infusions to banks that get into trouble. Indeed, one of the striking problems in Japan throughout the 1990s was the incapacity of the political system to resolve the increasingly obvious problems of banks with huge nonperforming loans. The dominant Liberal Democratic Party showed an astonishing preference for simply handing out cash to all banks, regardless of condition, rather than confronting those in the most serious trouble. Only in 1998, after the onset of the financial crisis throughout East Asia and increasing pressure from the opposition parties, did the government actually take over two important banks.

Some observers believe that this kind of diffuse, implicit, economywide moral hazard stimulated excessive risk taking throughout East Asia during the 1990s and lies at the root of Asia's financial collapse.[14] At the very least, say others, the message from the government was ambiguous and some agents might have felt they had protection against bad outcomes. If so, the result would be a general sense of overconfidence and overinvestment, both of which can be observed in Asia during this era.

Whether one accepts this interpretation of the Asian events or not, moral hazard clearly does encourage excessive risk taking by banks in cases where a bank is permitted to operate despite having exhausted or nearly exhausted its capital. The phenomenon is not a mere abstraction, but seems responsible for a significant part of the bank losses observed throughout the world.

Overcapacity, Franchise Value, and Liberalization

Securities Markets and Bank Disintermediation

There is another reason why banks so often find themselves in trouble in the modern era—namely, the evolution of all countries, over time, toward more efficient and

---

[14]See Corsetti, Pesenti, and Roubini (1998), Krugman (1998), and Pomerleano (1998).

competitive financial markets, and a related decline in the profitability of traditional bank lending. The consequence is typically overcapacity and loss of bank franchise value. In simplest terms, when banks' screening and monitoring services become less necessary, banks become less profitable, and we need fewer banks. The logical consequence should be the shrinkage, failure, or voluntary closure of at least some banks, yet governments and banks alike often resist this. From this point of view, the closure of many banks can be a natural process that governments should allow to proceed, rather than fight through repeated and increasingly expensive *bailouts*. But because banks are political as well as economic institutions—that is, institutions that broker political power as well as financial transactions—bankers and politicians will resist market solutions that eliminate the "intermediation" of political influence. We will start by describing the decline of traditional banking in developed countries and then return to the problem of banks in emerging financial markets.

As securities markets grow and communications technology improves, information about companies becomes widely available at low cost. Today, for example, anyone in the world can obtain detailed financial and other information about all public companies in the United States simply by downloading their required filings at the Securities and Exchange Commission from that agency's website. It takes no more than a minute and its marginal cost is zero.

When their financial information is widely disseminated, firms rely increasingly on securities markets to handle financial intermediation because these markets do not suffer the high operating costs of banks, and hence can deliver more attractive rates to savers and borrowers alike, so long as information production (i.e., screening and monitoring of borrowers by the lender) is not necessary. Consider, for example, the dilemma for banks shown in Figure 7.1.

The agents in this diagram are all institutions. The investors want short-term (one to six months) liquid investments of high quality. Such investors include money market mutual funds and corporate treasuries. They face a choice between two alternatives: They can deposit their money in a bank or they can buy *commercial paper*, which is a short-term promissory note of a borrowing corporation. From the investors' point of view, these are very similar. The commercial paper is a short-term I.O.U. of a company, and the deposit (e.g., a certificate of deposit, or CD) is a short-term I.O.U. of a bank. Provided the company and the bank are both strong credits, the investors are relatively indifferent between them. For this reason, the interest rates on bank CDs and commercial paper are very similar.

The bank now attempts to lend the money to a borrower. The interest rate it charges will equal its cost of funds (i.e., the deposit interest rate) plus a *spread*. For a high-quality borrower, the spread might be as low as 0.25 to 0.50 percent, but it cannot be zero because the bank needs to cover the cost of maintaining its staff, buildings, and

FIGURE 7.1

Disintermediation of banks

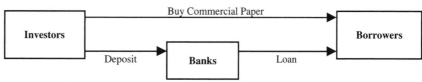

so forth. But now the borrower faces a choice: The commercial paper financing route will be cheaper if market purchasers of commercial paper have sufficient information about the borrower's high quality. In that case, by borrowing directly from the investors, the borrower saves on interest cost.

This phenomenon is called *disintermediation,* and it swept the U.S. financial system in the 1960s, 1970s, and 1980s.[15] During that period, banks lost a large portion of their highest-quality borrowers to less expensive securities markets. This included not only commercial paper, but also, in the 1980s, expanding bond markets for lower-quality credit. Banks are middlemen in the flow of funds, and as financial markets become ever more efficient, there is increasingly less room for middlemen to make money. If all investors and borrowers could find each other with little cost or effort, there would be little role for bank lending.

Of course, banks might be protected from this outcome if their cost of funds were lower than commercial paper rates. That is why some governments have continued controls on deposit interest rates, in an effort to provide a funding advantage to banks, even as markets liberalize. But in a sophisticated, modern financial system, depositors can avoid earning artificially low rates by putting their savings into a money market fund, which in turn buys commercial paper, an alternative form of disintermediation. This is precisely what happened in the United States from the late 1960s onward, forcing the United States government to abandon its own interest rate controls.

We have seen that a legitimate need for bank lending comes from information and control problems, which banks are well equipped to solve. But as financial information becomes more widely and easily available, banks tend to lose their informational monopolies. Alternatively, they can build informational monopolies only for small firms that are not publicly owned and widely followed.

This explains why, in developed economies, traditional deposit-and-loan business tends to shrink over time. In the United States, for example, banks provided 35 percent of funds to nonfinancial borrowers in 1974 and 22 percent in 1994; the banking industry's share of total financial intermediary assets fell from about 40 percent in the 1960–1980 period to less than 30 percent at the end of 1993.[16]

Strategic Response of Banks to Franchise Loss

What can a bank do in the face of declining value in its traditional business and franchise? One option is simply to shrink, though most institutions resist shrinking. Another option is to enter the securities business; if this form of financial intermediation is best for the clients, perhaps the banks can offer it as well, and build a new franchise in these services. Associated with securities is the derivatives business, which many large banks have entered in a major way.

But a third option is to replace the missing high-end business with larger quantities of low-end business—that is, the banks take more risk, pushing down into lower categories of creditworthiness where their predecessors would not have ventured in earlier times. Many U.S. banks that felt they had neither the resources nor the business culture to enter the securities and derivatives business chose this option during the 1970–1990 period.

In a purely market-driven system, banks that take more risk would face higher costs and declining availability of funds. But government protection of banks by

---

[15]Calomiris, Himmelberg, and Wachtel (1995).
[16]Edwards and Mishkin (1995).

means of deposit insurance and discount window lending (which lower banks' cost of funds) increases the banking system's ability to maintain market share and resist disintermediation. Government protection helps banks avoid the discipline of the marketplace that otherwise would have forced their shrinkage. But it does so at the cost of subsidizing increased risk taking as banks move into lower-quality credits without having to pay the penalty that this would normally entail.

That protection explains a large number of risk-seeking decisions by U.S. banks in the 1970–1990 period. For example, most banks did not lend across national borders until the late 1960s; for centuries, international lending typically was conducted by wealthy individuals or through bond markets, but was thought too risky a use for depositor funds. Then, in the late 1960s and 1970s, banks began a wave of lending to developing countries on an unprecedented scale, as shown in Chapter 1, Figure 1.3. Why? In large part, because they needed borrowers to replace those lost to disintermediation. Not wanting to shrink, banks pressed into higher-risk lending where most of them had little private information or insight. Not surprisingly, this ended in major losses during the 1980s. Such losses can properly be attributed to prior losses of franchise value in home markets.

Another example is real estate. Before the late 20th century, real estate lending was also thought a dubious activity for banks. The main exception was home mortgages, in which thrift institutions specialized. But from the 1960s onward, just as commercial paper usage was rapidly expanding, U.S. banks began to increase their commercial real estate lending. Real estate loans rose from 11 percent of total commercial bank assets in 1960 to 25 percent of assets in 1990.[17]

The first wave of this lending was through real estate investment trusts (REITs), a vehicle favored by U.S. tax law. But the bank-owned REITs collapsed in the 1970s, severely damaging a number of the largest banks. The second wave occurred in the 1980s, when commercial real estate lending by U.S. banks returned on such a scale that almost all U.S. cities were 20 to 30 percent overbuilt in commercial space by the end of the decade. This also ended in debacle during the late 1980s.

Increased risk taking might be a successful strategy if the risks are attractively priced. But U.S. banks do not seem to charge high spreads for these increasingly risky loans. Whether the borrower is a developing country, a real estate project, or a small company, U.S. banks in the 1980s and 1990s rarely charged a spread of more than 3 percent above their cost of funds.[18] These low spreads reflected overcapacity: Too many banks were competing for the risky loans. The failure of about 1,300 U.S. banks in the regional economic downturns of 1985–1989 and the general recession of 1989–1992 confirmed the high cost of the risks that banks had assumed so willingly. It was as if the market's "invisible hand" were trying to sweep away the excess capacity.[19]

The Japanese banking crisis also seems rooted to some degree in overcapacity and a decline in bank franchise value. Throughout the second half of the 20th century, Japan's Ministry of Finance (MOF) built and supported an exceptionally strong set of bank franchises. Banks were privileged, but the trade-off was strong direction from MOF on where capital should flow. Although the stock market flourished, no corporate bond market and no commercial paper market was permitted in Japan until the 1980s, and even then they were only allowed to grow slowly. By the end of the 1980s,

---

[17]Gorton and Rosen (1995), Figure 7.7.

[18]Loan Pricing Corporation database.

[19]Gorton and Rosen (1995) argued that the tolerance of low spreads and suboptimal profitability reflected managerial entrenchment, which was a consequence of regulatory limitations on bank acquisitions.

Japan's banks had become the largest in the world and provided more than 80 percent of all funding needs of Japanese firms.

But as the large Japanese firms grew more internationalized, they gained access to international capital markets. MOF's control was weakened because Japanese firms could not be restricted to Japan's borders. Over the long term, financial liberalization is hard to resist because firms will finally demand and get the efficiencies that modern financial markets can provide. As liberalization finally reached Japan, the country's oversized banking system began to develop problems.

Many of the banks' lending decisions turned out to be poorly conceived and/or poorly priced. As noted earlier, the nonperforming loans in Japanese banks reached more than $500 billion by the early 1990s, a level that threatened the survival of many large and small banks. The government did not force a cleanup, and the banks responded by taking new risks, notably in East Asia. It is an extreme example of banking overcapacity.

Effects of Financial Liberalization

In developing countries, the value of bank franchises can be adversely affected by financial liberalization. Governments control interest rates and limit entry into banking, particularly foreign entry. Rules of this sort substantially increase the profitability of banks, whether well or poorly managed. This creates franchise value, even though it is franchise based on government-protected rents rather than on the creation of economic value. When governments liberalize, they take away some of these privileges, which lowers the value of the bank franchise. This is an appropriate step, over time even a necessary step, that forces banks to create value in new ways. But during the transition period, liberalization can reduce the value of many bank franchises. When inefficient, protected banks lose franchise value, they are further tempted to take on lower value, riskier business. This adds to the systemic vulnerability of liberalizing banking systems.[20]

Furthermore, countries that liberalize rapidly without providing strong foundations for a private financial system can get into serious trouble. In Russia, for example, thousands of banks formed quickly in the early 1990s without the appropriate legal structure or control systems. In the infamous "loans-for-shares" program, the government financed its deficits by borrowing from these banks, offering shares of state-owned enterprises as security. When the loans defaulted, banks and their owners acquired empires at very low prices and became centers of connected lending. The entire system collapsed, leading to a sovereign Russian default in August 1998.

Two things seem quite clear. The first is that financial liberalization is important for the long-run health of the economy. We have seen its connection to economic growth in Chapters 2 and 3. The other is that *quasi*-liberalization—where banks' profits are privatized, but banks are protected from competition and subsidized by taxpayer bailouts of their losses—can be riskier than no liberalization. If privatization of banks creates a new set of banking institutions that act as the political and economic tools of oligarchs and their protected industrial firms, then those banks are liable to engage in excessive insider lending, take risky market positions, hold little capital, and undertake negative NPV investments. This is a recipe for disastrous banking collapses.

The task is to liberalize in a way that avoids the incentive distortions that produce banking collapses. Very few governments have gotten the pace and sequence of bank-

---

[20]Keeley (1990), and Hellman, Murdock, and Stiglitz (1998a, 1998b).

ing liberalization and regulation exactly right. And academics have devoted considerable effort to studying exactly what the optimal pace and sequence might be. This will depend in part on conditions unique to each country.[21] As bank competition increases and bank profitability declines, each bank must develop a plan for a new strategy in the changing environment. It should not be surprising that at least some banks cannot find a sensible way of doing business in the more demanding market environment and thus fail during the liberalization process.

The challenge for EFM governments is to manage the process of financial liberalization carefully and deliberately, allowing banks to come down from their protected positions and enter a more difficult but normal market world without collapsing. This typically requires some orderly bank capacity reductions, often through mergers, sometimes through failure of weaker banks. This does not happen easily, and getting it wrong undoubtedly accounts for some of the large banking losses seen at the end of the 20th century.

Government and Banks

Liquidity and Bank Runs

The three kinds of problems that plague banks around the world—connected lending, moral hazard, and excess capacity—are greatly magnified by the central problem of government protection of banks. Bank depositors and other debt holders historically were a powerful force for ensuring conservative behavior and value creation by banks. They limited insider lending, excessive risk taking, and wasteful lending of excess deposits by withdrawing their funds as soon as they sensed trouble.

Government protection insulates banks from such pressures. When the government guarantees deposits and other bank liabilities, bank depositors and other debt holders need not concern themselves with how well the bank is run. Instead, government agents must perform the monitoring. Banking risk becomes socialized and can grow very large because government discipline is much more permissive than market discipline.

Governments everywhere tend to embrace banks, protect them, regulate them, and use them as instruments of policy. Sometimes the government embrace smothers market efficiency. Part of successful financial liberalization involves changing the nature of this relationship from one in which governments treat banks as their instruments of policy to one in which governments accept banks as fully independent institutions but regulate them in ways that create appropriate incentives for good behavior.

To understand the complexity of the modern and evolving relationship between government and banks, it is useful to see why and how government involvement in banking evolved, and how that protection has become a political tool that is often abused.

The primary economic justification for government involvement in protecting banks is that banks are not only very important to the economy, but also they are uniquely vulnerable to economic disturbances because their most fundamental role is to provide *liquidity* to the real economy.[22] Firms are liquid when they have on hand or can readily obtain all the cash they need to meet their obligations and exploit their

---

[21]See McKinnon (1993) for a detailed discussion.
[22]Rajan (1996).

opportunities. Liquidity is the lubricant of business: When firms are liquid, bills are paid on time and investments move forward on schedule. When firms are illiquid, the economy slows down—firms feel short of cash, so they delay their projects, reduce credit extended to their customers, and minimize their obligations.

Firms are liquid when they have sufficient short-dated assets; that is, a net surplus of assets that will convert into cash within a short period of time. Assets that will convert into cash in less than one year are called current assets, and liabilities that must be settled in cash in less than one year are called current liabilities. An accounting measure of liquidity is working capital, the excess of current assets over current liabilities. Anyone attempting to set up a business needs ample working capital as well as fixed assets such as plant, property, and equipment. Firms can also enhance their liquidity by long-dated liabilities; that is, obligations that will not fall due in cash for many years. For liquidity reasons, most industrial firms borrow significant amounts of long-term debt.

So firms ensure sufficient liquidity by having substantial net quantities of short-dated assets and long-dated liabilities. Banks meet this need by putting themselves into the reverse position: They have long-dated assets and short-dated liabilities. A bank's long-dated assets are its loans of more than one year. Its short-dated liabilities are its deposits, almost all of which are repayable in less than one year and some of which are repayable at any time on demand. A bank's liquidity position is the mirror image of that of its customers. By accommodating its customers' needs for liquidity, a bank puts itself in constant risk of illiquidity.

In particular, a bank gets into trouble if too many customers want to withdraw their deposits at one time. This is particularly true since the bank's loan portfolio is inherently illiquid in the sense of being nonmarketable. In the prototypical case, the loans are based on private information about the borrowers, and thus cannot readily be sold to others who, because of asymmetric information, do not know the borrowers and would not trust a bank that wanted to sell loans about which it was better informed than any buyer could be.

Some depositors may learn that a particular bank has problems in its loan portfolio, or hear rumors to that effect, leading them to withdraw their deposits. Other, uninformed observers who notice this now begin to worry that the bank may not be able to meet all its obligations. So they decide to withdraw as well, and the result is a cascading demand for deposit withdrawal. This phenomenon is known as a *bank run*. Runs have occurred throughout banking history and have been extensively studied by theorists and empiricists. The ability of depositors to demand their money back is a form of monitoring system, encouraging banks to behave conservatively, thus counteracting the incentives banks might otherwise face to abscond with depositors' funds or to channel those funds into excessively risky ventures.[23]

Bank Failures in Earlier Eras

Bank runs can lead quickly to bank failures. The most frightening aspect of a bank run is the possibility that it would destroy healthy, solvent banks as well as those that, in retrospect, truly deserve to be shut down. To protect themselves against this risk, banks long ago learned to join together in associations for mutual support. A common institution was the *central bank,* which in some countries in earlier centuries was a private organization rather than a government agency. Commercial banks would leave a por-

---

[23]Calomiris and Kahn (1991).

tion of their deposits on reserve at the central bank, in a pool that could be drawn upon at a time of need. Countries without central banks formed similar pools (e.g., the New York Clearing House).[24]

A fundamental question is whether bank runs turn out to be well founded or flights of fancy—that is, were depositors aware of problems that in retrospect were real and serious threats to their bank's solvency, or did their actions arbitrarily destroy a sound and solvent bank based on whim, rumor, and emotion? One way to answer this is to see whether, once the crisis was resolved, many banks had actually failed, and if so why. In particular, how often did a solvent bank fail simply because it was subjected to a run?

Evidence from 19th-century U.S. history, when the United States was an emerging market, is particularly telling. From 1863 to 1913 (the national banking era) six major nationwide panics occurred. In all six cases, the panics were preceded by several months of unusually large declines in stock prices and unusual increases in business failures. Indeed, using dual threshold criteria—a minimum percentage decline in stock prices and a minimum percentage increase in business failures—one can predict the incidence of banking panics.[25] Table 7.2 reviews the history of national bank failures in each of these panics. It shows the number of bank failures that occurred during each crisis, and the reasons bank examiners gave for those failures.

It is clear from Table 7.2 that the number of failures was small, compared to the thousands of banks in the United States in the late 19th century, and the reasons for the failures apparently traceable to fundamentals. Another interesting fact about these panics was that they tended to occur either in the spring or the fall. The asset risk of banks increases with the loan-to-asset ratio, which tends to hit seasonal highs in the spring and autumn, and this may explain the seasonality in the pattern of banking panics. Similar studies of bank failures during the Great Depression have also traced the causes of failures to fundamental insolvency problems of banks. Market discipline over banks seems not to have been capricious.

Nevertheless, over time, the protection of banks and their insulation from market discipline became a governmental function in almost all countries. This did not eliminate banking panics, but it did change the way their costs were allocated. The total losses in historical banking panics were relatively small, rarely more than 1

TABLE 7.2   Causes of U.S. National Bank Failures during Panics

	Panic of:					
	1873	*1884*	*1890*	*1893*	*1896*	*1907*
Total number of failures	9	6	10	49	34	6
Attributed to asset depreciation alone	4	2	5	31	26	3
Attributed to fraud alone	0	2	0	7	3	2
Attributed to both asset depreciation and fraud	5	4	5	11	5	0
Asset depreciation attributed to monetary stringency	0	0	0	17	8	0
Asset depreciation only; attributed to real estate	0	1	2	0	4	0
Attributed to real estate depreciation and fraud	0	1	2	0	1	0
Attributed to run on bank	0	0	0	0	0	1

Source: Calomiris and Gorton (1991)

---

[24]Calomiris and Gorton (1991).
[25]Ibid.

percent of GDP. However, the losses fell primarily on individual depositors, which became a political problem, especially in more recent times, as the level of losses increased. Historically, bank borrowers also suffered during times of banking system stress. As banks scrambled to reassure depositors that bank loan losses would not result in losses to depositors, they cut back on lending and accumulated cash reserves (to reduce bank asset risk and enhance bank liquidity).[26] In those circumstances, borrowers found themselves in an illiquid position, facing higher interest costs.

Government Protection of Depositors

In the United States, small bankers and their depositors and dependent borrowers—all of whom were most vulnerable to banking crises and therefore stood to gain the most from government protection of banks—became vocal proponents of protection. That protection took the form of state-level bank insurance systems (some of which were founded as early as the 1820s), subsidized loans from the central bank (after the founding of the Federal Reserve System in 1914), and, later, federal deposit insurance and government injections of capital into banks in the 1930s.

The United States initiated the first national program of deposit insurance by government in 1933, primarily as an accommodation to small banks during the Great Depression. At first this was a modest program designed to protect only the smallest depositors; each depositor was insured only up to $5,000. Over time, however, the insured amount expanded in stages to $100,000, and in 1984 the United States extended *de facto* government protection to uninsured depositors, not by statute but by the actions of the Federal Deposit Insurance Corporation (FDIC) in bailing out the Continental Illinois National Bank.[27]

The same outcome has been reached along various paths in virtually all countries. Many countries had no formal depositor protection, but found themselves under political pressure to make depositors whole when crises erupted. As noted in Chapter 3, Chile tried to renounce depositor protection in the late 1970s, but was unable to resist the pressures created by multiple bank failures in 1982. Venezuela had a similar experience in the early 1990s, trying unsuccessfully to limit government losses to the low level of formal deposit insurance. Today many countries offer virtually complete governmental insurance to depositors, even if their laws do not explicitly say so.

This comprehensive *safety net* has indeed stopped bank runs from occurring, but it has done so at a significant price. Protected depositors have no incentive whatever to monitor the risk of their banks or to withdraw funds from banks that are clearly losing money. Indeed, the safety net enables banks that are certifiably insolvent to go on attracting deposits and making loans. This shifts the burden of monitoring and control from the bank debt market to the government regulatory agencies, which must act decisively to shut down insolvent banks or risk an explosion of bad loans caused by the moral hazard of low or negative capital.

---

[26]Calomiris and Wilson (1998).

[27]That bailout was justified by appeal to the "too-big-to-fail" doctrine—the view that the failure of a large bank would be too disruptive to the financial system. In response to growing criticism of that doctrine and concerns about its moral hazard consequences, the ability of the FDIC to bail out uninsured depositors was restricted in 1991.

This sea change alters the very nature of what constitutes a banking crisis. Bank runs are replaced by

> a more silent form of financial distress . . . when a significant portion of the system is insolvent but remains open, perhaps the most pernicious type of insolvency . . . Financial distress can persist for years, overlooked by weak supervisory and regulatory systems and obscured by bankers' ability to make bad loans look good by granting new loans.[28]

The critical variable at this point becomes the behavior of the bank regulators. Their optimal behavior is careful monitoring and decisive action to close insolvent banks. Such action is necessary for two reasons. First, insolvent banks have clearly destroyed value for the economy and are likely to go on destroying value unless they are stopped. Second, as we have seen, banks whose capital is zero or negative undergo a powerful change of incentives as equity and management are tempted to take massive new risks to resurrect their fortunes.

Bank Capital and Loan Losses

Standards for appropriate behavior by government regulators are widely recognized as crucial. In the 1980s an international agreement establishing minimal standards for the prudential regulation of international banks was adopted, and the Basel Committee (which set those guidelines) continues to offer its opinions on appropriate supervisory and regulatory standards.[29] One of its key tenets is that banking supervisors must set prudent and appropriate minimum capital adequacy requirements for all banks. Bank capital is the protective cushion, the "deductible" in deposit insurance. Any asset losses should first run down the capital and only second endanger the ability to repay deposits.

Optimal regulatory behavior also means that banks with low but still positive capital are not permitted to go on lending until their capital ratios are brought back to acceptable levels. If capital levels are kept sufficiently high, then deposit insurance alone may not cause major incentive problems. Managers and bank owners still have a good deal to lose and so are not subject to moral hazard. In this circumstance, the depositors are protected against all downside risk but the owners and managers are not, and it is owners and managers who make risk decisions.

Unfortunately, bank capital is a more elusive matter than it first appears. One would like to think of it as the bedrock on which the bank's balance sheet is built, but in reality it depends heavily on the policies of management and regulators toward nonperforming loans (i.e., loans on which scheduled payments of principal and interest are past due).

Under internationally accepted accounting standards, banks should take a *loss provision* for loans as soon as they suspect that a loan is in trouble, and certainly by the time it is nonperforming. Such a provision is deducted from income, and so reduces capital, but it is a noncash charge made wholly at the judgment of management. Such a loss can be avoided by extending a new loan to the troubled borrower so that the old loan will not default, or simply by ignoring the default and pretending it has no consequence.

The judgmental element in loss provisions means that actual bank behavior with respect to loan losses varies widely; some banks act conservatively by providing for losses and others cover up their problems. The conservative banks then show relatively less capital. A bank with massive loan losses may appear to have relatively more capital simply because it has not taken appropriate provisions for loss.

---

[28]Caprio and Klingebiel (1996b), p. 84.
[29]Basel Committee (1997).

For example, a bank may report capital equal to 8 percent of risk-weighted assets, the Basel Committee minimum standard. But if 16 percent of the loans are nonperforming and few provisions have been taken, the bank is likely to be insolvent because bank recoveries on nonperforming loans are substantially less than 50 percent in most EFMs. The bank should have taken a provision of at least 8 percent, wiping out capital. But this, of course, is tantamount to declaring bankruptcy, something few owners or managers will voluntarily do. If regulators are not sufficiently vigilant about the bank's practices and procedures for evaluating the quality of assets and taking provisions, they will not even know how much real capital the bank has. Regulators understand this arithmetic, but often they are very permissive with troubled banks. They may not press for larger loan provisions or they may indulge in "forbearance" of capital requirements—that is, not enforce the rules.

Resolving Insolvent Banks

The old-fashioned discipline of bank runs had the disadvantage of forcing individual depositors to bear the risk of loss, but like all market-based control systems, its action was swift and sure to stop value destruction. Unfortunately, few bank regulators act in this decisive way. One reason they do not is that most human beings find it hard to be as unfeeling as markets. But there are additional factors as well. Banks and their dependent borrowers are powerful political entities; government supervisors can find it politically difficult to discipline them. Furthermore, unlike private depositors, supervisors suffer little personal harm from turning a blind eye to bank weakness.

A key factor aggravating the political opposition to disciplining banks is that serious bank insolvency almost always occurs at a time of economic downturn. Closing a bank during an economic downturn or forcing it to reduce its lending so as to limit its risk, while essential to effective bank regulation, can be politically difficult when politicians look to banks to provide loans to stimulate a recovery. For this reason, bank regulators typically allow undercapitalized and even insolvent banks to continue in operation. Japan, for example, became mired in a recession during the 1990s that seemed never to end. The many weak banks were not purged by regulators for fear of aggravating the recession in the short term through the act of closure. Yet in the longer term, the most important step the government could have taken in Japan, and in many other cases, would have been to cleanse the banking system of bad loans at an early date, so that strengthened banks could begin lending on a sound basis once again.

Another factor is that closing insolvent banks requires substantial amounts of cash. Optimal economic behavior would be to close the bank, pay off all the deposits, take over the loan portfolio, and then realize the portfolio's value over time. But paying off the depositors in even a small bank requires billions of dollars of cash; in a very large bank it requires hundreds of billions. Governments have difficulty in mobilizing this amount of cash, and therefore often choose a nonoptimal course of resolution.

A favorite technique of embattled bank regulators is to promote a merger of the insolvent bank into a stronger bank. This avoids the need for cash and also avoids the possible criticism of closing a bank during a time of economic stress. It passes the entire resolution problem to a management that appears competent. The difficulty is that the strong bank is then saddled with all the problems of the failed bank, which may even drive the strong bank toward insolvency.

An even worse solution, though it was the one selected by the Japanese government in the mid-1990s and is often chosen by EFM regulators, is simply to give cash to the banks, either as a grant or as a purchase of a junior security such as preferred stock. This temporizes, providing an "instant recapitalization" of the weak banks. But its incentive effects are the worst possible: Nothing could be better designed to tell bank managements that taking excessive risk is an outstanding strategy, since the government will explicitly subsidize all the negative outcomes while the bank's owners and managements will benefit from all the positive outcomes. This is moral hazard at its most obvious and most destructive.

Finally, the strategy of simply doing nothing is also a terrible choice. Banks can go on functioning even if totally insolvent so long as the government is willing to guarantee all deposits. But, as noted before, the behavior of bank management changes when equity is low or negative. The pursuit of high-risk strategies by insolvent banks can be extremely dangerous, converting a modest bank crisis into a catastrophic loss.

In June 2000, the World Bank held a conference on the design and implementation of deposit insurance in developing countries, with a focus on the role of safety nets in promoting moral hazard in banking systems. This conference brought together some of the first careful academic studies that make use of new World Bank data sets that track the specific design features of deposit insurance systems and the extent to which governments go beyond deposit insurance with special bailouts of insolvent banks. The findings of these studies were remarkably consistent and uniform, despite the diversity of methodologies and backgrounds of the participants.[30]

One study by Edward Kane constructed measures of the quality of different countries' legal, informational, and regulatory environments and found that generous government protection of banks without effective regulation and supervision was highest in countries with weak "informational, ethical, and corporate-governance environment[s]." A second study, by Asli Demirgüç-Kunt of the World Bank and Enrica Detragiache of the IMF, found that the more extensive and credible the protection offered by government deposit insurance, the greater the likelihood of banking crises. A third paper, by Demirgüç-Kunt and Harry Huizinga, investigated the mechanism through which deposit insurance systems with relatively generous protection were able to create moral hazard. The authors found that generous protection made bank debt holders complacent and thus eroded market discipline, which freed banks to pursue excessive risk taking. The absence of market discipline is reflected in the absence of the risk pricing of bank debt (that is, interest rate charges that are relatively insensitive to the true risk of bank failure).

Three other papers, by Patrick Honohan and Daniela Klingebiel of the World Bank, by John Boyd and others, and by Robert Cull of the World Bank and others, examined the link between government bailout policies and the size of bailout costs (measured both in terms of the budgetary costs of paying insolvent banks' debts and the forgone GDP that results in the wake of bank credit collapses during and after banking crises). Honohan and Klingebiel found that "unlimited deposit guarantees, open-ended liquidity support [for banks], repeated recapitalizations [of banks], debtor bailouts and regulatory forbearance add significantly and sizably to [the fiscal] costs of resolving banking crises." Boyd et al. also found the size of post-crisis economic decline was larger when bailouts were more generous. Finally, the paper by Cull et al. found that relatively generous bank safety net policies tended to be associated with low long-run growth in output, and smaller and more volatile financial systems. Taken together, these six papers offer

---

[30]These papers include, among others, Boyd, Gomis, Kwak, and Smith (2000), Cull, Senbet, and Sorge (2000), Demirgüç-Kunt and Detragiache (2000), Demirgüç-Kunt and Huizinga (2000), Honohan and Klingebiel (2000), and Kane (2000). These and other papers presented at the conference are available at the World Bank's website, **www.worldbank.org/finance/html**.

strong and consistent evidence that government safety net policies have been a major contributor to banking crises and underdevelopment in emerging market countries.

The particular initiating causes for banking crises have not changed much through time: macroeconomic shocks, bank fraud and mismanagement, falling asset values. What has changed a great deal is the size of banking system losses and the allocation of responsibility for bearing losses and disciplining the banking system. Private markets used to assume both roles, but now government has assumed them. Government regulators in EFMs have in many cases only begun to realize what a difficult challenge this is. How can government regulators be smart enough, diligent enough, and imaginative enough to ferret out problems before they become crises? Once problems are uncovered, how can government be tough enough and fast enough to impose real costs on those bank owners and managements who destroy value? In particular, in settings where bank owners and managers have substantial political power, what will prevent the pernicious pattern of governments simply passing money to misbehaving bank owners and managers?

Within the framework of government protection of depositors, there may be room to restore at least some element of market discipline. For example, if governments require all banks to issue a layer of subordinated, uninsured debt to a class of arm's-length investors, then those investors may become effective monitors of the banks.[31] Argentina has implemented a version of this system and other countries are currently considering this approach. Time will tell its effectiveness.

In summary, the nature of government's relationship to banks may have more to do with bank losses than any other variable. If the government owns the banks and uses them as a conduit for capital flows to favored projects, as in China today, the result is almost sure to be large numbers of nonperforming loans. If the government quasi-liberalizes—privatizing profits within a protected, risk-subsidized banking system, without preparing a careful monitoring and control system—the result is likely to be even worse.

The only path to safety and lasting growth is a program of credible financial liberalization that is carefully designed and implemented to promote competition and discourage abuse of government protection. Government must subject the private banks to a well-crafted system of incentives, monitoring, and control. It must require a sufficient quantity of capital, honestly measured, to be maintained at all times. When banks develop problems, government must act decisively to bring the bank into compliance or close it. Finally, government must be prepared to act forcefully against owners and managers who destroy value, closing the banks where this occurs.

The world is still learning how to find the right relationship between banks and governments, and the job is not an easy one. Some EFMs have come a long way and seem closer to achieving the best practices than many industrialized countries. Argentina, Chile, and Singapore, for example, seem to be on a promising track. Argentina has allowed foreign banks to enter, buy local banks, and compete; foreign banks now control about half of bank assets. It also has one of the highest capital requirements in the world. Argentina's many banking reforms are described in detail in the box on page 339.

We are all learning. There is no single universal explanation for the cascade of bank loan losses, but there clearly are common themes, including those highlighted in this chapter. Countries that manage their banking systems inappropriately are now paying high prices for these mistakes. Still, there is room for optimism: No country can afford to do this for long.

---

[31]Calomiris (1997).

APPENDIX

The following appendix material is an updated summary of the data provided in Gerard Caprio and Daniela Klingebiel (1996a). We are grateful to the authors for supplying it to us. The data are divided into two sections: Systemic banking crises in which most or all of banking system capital is exhausted, and borderline or smaller cases. Each of these tables is grouped by region and shows the country, the origins and causes of each crisis, and its cost of resolution where possible.

TABLE 7.A1 Systemic Banking Crises:
Cases in which Most or All of Banking System Capital Is Eroded

Country	Scope of Crisis	Estimate of Total Costs
Africa		
Algeria		
1990–1992	Banking system nonperforming loan ratio (NPLs) reached 50%	
Benin		
1988–1990	All three commercial banks collapsed; 80% of banks' loan portfolio nonperforming	CFA95 billion, equivalent to 17% of GDP
Burkina Faso		
1988–1994	Banking system NPLs estimated at 34%	
Burundi		
1994–ongoing	Banking system NPLs estimated at 25% of total loans in 1995; one bank liquidated	
Cameroon		
1987–1993	In 1989, banking sector NPLs ratio reached 60–70%; five commercial banks closed, three banks restructured	
1995–1998	At year-end 1996, NPLs accounted for 30% of total loans; three banks restructured and two closed	
Cape Verde		
1993–ongoing	At year-end 1995, commercial banks' NPL ratio 30%	
Central African Republic		
1976–1992	Four banks liquidated	
1988–1999	Two largest banks, accounting for 90% of total assets, restructured; banking sector NPL ratio 40%	
Congo (Brazzaville)		
1992–ongoing	Two large banks placed in liquidation; the remaining three banks insolvent; situation aggravated by civil war	
Congo, Democratic Republic of (former Zaire)		
1980s		
1991–1992	Four state-owned banks insolvent; fifth bank to be recapitalized with private participation	
1994–ongoing	NPLs to the private sector 75%; two state-owned banks liquidated and two others privatized; in 1997, 12 banks in serious financial difficulties	
Chad		
1980s	Private sector NPL ratio 35%	
1992		
Côte d'Ivoire		
1988–1991	Four large banks affected, accounting for 90% of banking system loans; three definitely insolvent and one perhaps so; six government banks closed	Government costs estimated at CFA677 billion equivalent to 25% of GDP

Country	Scope of Crisis	Estimate of Total Costs
Djibouti 1991–1993	Two of six commercial banks ceased operations in 1991 and 1992; other banks experienced difficulties	
Equatorial Guinea 1983–1985	Two of country's largest banks liquidated	
Eritrea 1993	Most of banking system insolvent	
Ghana 1982–1989	Seven audited banks (of 11) insolvent; rural banking sector affected	Restructuring costs estimated at 6% of GNP
Guinea 1985	Six banks accounting for 99% of total system deposits deemed insolvent	Repayment of deposits amounted to 3% of 1986 GDP
1993–1994	Two banks insolvent accounting for 22.4% of financial system assets; one other bank in serious financial difficulties; these three banks accounted for 45% of the market	
Guinea–Bissau 1995–?	At year-end 1995, NPLs accounted for 45% of commercial banks' total loan portfolio	
Kenya 1985–1989	Four banks and 24 nonbank financial institutions faced liquidity and solvency problems; together accounted for 15% of total liabilities of financial system	
1992	Intervention in two local banks	
1993–1995	Serious systemic problems with banks accounting for more than 30% of assets of financial system facing solvency problems	
Liberia 1991-1995	Seven of 11 banks nonoperational; assets equivalent to 60% of total bank assets at mid-1995	
Madagascar 1988	25% of banking sector loans deemed irrecoverable	
Mali 1987–1989	NPLs of largest bank 75%	
Mauritania 1984–1993	In 1984, five major banks had nonperforming assets ranging from 45% to 70% of their portfolio	Cost of rehabilitation estimated at 15% of GDP in 1988
Mozambique 1987–1995?	BCM, main commercial bank, experienced solvency problems apparent after 1992	
Niger 1983–?	In the mid-1980s, banking system NPLs reached 50%; four banks liquidated and three restructured in the late 1980s	
Nigeria 1990s	1993: insolvent banks account for 20% of total assets and 22% of banking system deposits; 1995: almost half of banks reported in financial distress	
São Tomé and Príncipe 1980s, 1990s	At year-end 1992, 90% of Monobank's loans nonperforming; in 1993, commercial and development departments of former Monobank liquidated, as was the only financial institution; two new banks licensed, which took over many assets of their predecessors; credit operations of one newly created bank suspended since year-end 1994	
Senegal 1988–1991	In 1988, 50% of banking system loans nonperforming; six commercial banks and one development bank closed accounting for 20–30% of financial system assets	US$830 million, equivalent to 17% of GDP

Country	Scope of Crisis	Estimate of Total Costs
Sierra Leone 1990–ongoing	In 1995, 40–50% of banking system loans nonperforming; license of one bank suspended in 1994; recapitalization and restructuring of the banks ongoing	
Swaziland 1995	Central Bank also took over Meridien BIAO Swaziland and Swaziland Development and Savings Bank (SDSB), which faced severe portfolio problems	
Tanzania Late 1980s, 1990s	1987: main financial institutions had arrears amounting to half of their portfolio; 1995: National Bank of Commerce, accounting for 95% of banking system assets, insolvent since 1990–1992	1987: implied losses amount to nearly 10% of GNP
Togo 1993–1995		
Uganda 1994–ongoing	50% of banking system facing solvency problems	
Zambia 1995	Meridian Bank insolvent, accounting for 13% of commercial bank assets	Rough estimate of US$50 million (1.4% of GDP)
Zimbabwe 1995–ongoing	Two of five commercial banks recorded high NPL ratio	
<u>**Asia**</u>		
Bangladesh late 1980s–1996	In 1987, four banks accounting for 70% of total credit had estimated NPL ratio of 20%; since late 1980s, entire private/public banking system technically insolvent	
China 1990s	At year-end 1998, China's four large state-owned commercial banks, accounting for 68.3% of total banking system assets, deemed insolvent; total banking system NPLs estimated at 50%	Net losses estimated to reach US$427.6 billion, or 47.4% of GDP in 1999
Indonesia 1997–ongoing	By March 1999, Bank of Indonesia had closed down 61 banks and nationalized 54 banks, of a total of 240; NPL estimates for total banking system at 65–75% of total loans	Fiscal costs estimated at 50–55% of GDP
Malaysia 1997–ongoing	Finance company sector being restructured and number of finance companies to be reduced from 39 to 16 through mergers; two finance companies taken over by Central Bank, including MBF Finance, the largest independent finance company; two banks, deemed insolvent, accounting for 14.2% of financial system assets, to be merged with other banks; at year-end 1998, NPLs estimated at 25–35% of total banking system assets	Net loss estimated at US$14.9 billion, or 20.5% of GDP by 1999
Nepal 1988	In early 1988, reported arrears of three banks accounting for 95% of financial system, averaged 29% of all assets	
Philippines 1981–1987	Two public banks accounting for 50% of banking system assets, six private banks accounting for 12%, 32 thrifts accounting for 53.2% of thrift banking assets, and 128 rural banks	At its peak, central bank assistance to financial institutions amounted to 19.1 billion pesos (3% of GDP)
1998–ongoing	Since January 1998, one commercial bank, seven of 88 thrifts, and 40 of 750 rural banks placed under receivership; banking system NPLs reached 10.8% by August 1998 and 12.4% by November 1998; expected to reach 20% in 1999	Net loss estimated at US$4.0 billion, or 6.7% of GDP by 1999

Country	*Scope of Crisis*	*Estimate of Total Costs*
South Korea 1997–ongoing	By March 1999, 2 of 26 commercial banks accounting for 11.8% of total banking system assets nationalized; 5 banks, accounting for 7.8% of total banking system assets, closed; seven banks, accounting for 38% of banking system assets, placed under special supervision; overall, banking system NPLs expected to peak at 30–40%	Net losses estimated at US$68.3 billion, or 20.3% of GDP in 1999
Sri Lanka 1989–1993	State-owned banks, comprising 70% of banking system, estimated to have nonperforming loan ratio of about 35%	Restructuring cost amounted to 25 billion rupees (5% of GDP)
Taiwan 1997	Banking system NPLs estimated at 15%, at year-end 1998	In 1999 net losses estimated at US$26.7 billion, or 11.5% of GDP
Thailand 1983–1987	Authorities intervened in 50 finance and security firms and 5 commercial banks or about 25% of total financial system assets; 3 commercial banks judged insolvent (14.1% of commercial banking assets)	Government cost for 50 finance companies estimated at 0.5% of GNP; government cost for subsidized loans amounted to about 0.2% of GDP annually
1997–ongoing	To March 1999, Bank of Thailand intervened in 70 finance companies (of 91), which together accounted for 12.8% of financial system assets or 72% of finance company assets. Also intervened in six banks that together had a market share of 12.3%; at year-end 1998 banking system NPLs reached 46% of total loans	Net losses estimated at US$59.7 billion, or 42.3% of GDP in 1999
Vietnam 1997–ongoing	Two of four large state-owned commercial banks, accounting for 50.7% of banking system loans, deemed insolvent; other two experiencing significant solvency problems; several joint stocks banks in severe financial distress; total banking system NPLs reached 18.2% of total loans in late 1998	
Central America and the Caribbean		
Costa Rica Several instances	In 1987, public banks, accounting for 90% of total banking system loans, in financial distress; 32% of their loans considered uncollectible	Implied losses of at least twice the capital plus reserves
El Salvador 1989	Nine state-owned commercial banks recorded NPL ratios of 37% on average in 1989	
Jamaica 1994–ongoing	In 1994, a merchant banking group closed; in 1995, a medium-sized bank received financial support; in 1997, the Financial Credit Adjustment Company intervened in and effectively nationalized five of six commercial banks as a result of sharp deterioration of their asset quality and virtual erosion of their capital base	
Panama 1988–1989	In 1988, Panama's banking system underwent a nine-week banking holiday; financial position of most state-owned and private commercial banks weak; as a result, 15 banks ceased operations	
Mexico 1981–1982 1995–ongoing	Government took over troubled banking system Of 34 commercial banks in 1994, nine were intervened in and 11 more participated in the loan/purchase recapitalization program; these intervened banks accounted for 18.9% of total financial system assets and were deemed insolvent	Total estimated cost of bank rescue US$65 billion by February 1998, or nearly 15% of GDP
Nicaragua Late 1980s–1996	Banking system NPLs reached 50% in 1996	

Country	Scope of Crisis	Estimate of Total Costs
South America		
Argentina		
1980–1982	More than 70 institutions liquidated or subject to central bank intervention, accounting for 16% of assets of commercial banks and 35% of total assets of finance companies	55.3% of GDP
1989–1990	Nonperforming assets constituted 27% of the aggregate portfolio and 37% of the portfolios of state-owned banks; failed banks held 40% of financial system assets	
1995	Suspension of eight banks and collapse of three banks; overall through year-end 1997, 63 of 205 banking institutions either closed or merged	Direct and indirect cost to public estimated at 1.6% of GDP
Bolivia		
1986–1987	Five banks liquidated; total NPLs of banking system reached 29.8% in 1987; in mid-1988 reported arrears stood at 92% of commercial banks' net worth	
1994–ongoing	Two banks with 11% of banking system assets closed in November 1994; in 1995, 4 of 15 domestic banks, accounting for 30% of banking system assets, experienced liquidity problems and suffered from high levels of NPLs	
Brazil		
1990	Deposit to bond conversion	
1994–ongoing	By year-end 1997, Central Bank had intervened in or put under the Temporary Special Administration Regime (RAET) system, 43 financial institutions; nonperforming loans of entire banking system reached 15%	In 1996, negative net worth of selected state and federal banks estimated at 5–10% of GDP; costs of individual bank recapitalization, by year-end 1997: Banco Econômico, US$2.9 billion Bamerindus: US$3 billion Banco do Brasil, US$8 billion Unibanco, US$4.9 billion In 1998, cost of public support to private banking sector estimated at 1–2% of GDP
Chile		
1976	Entire mortgage system insolvent	
1981–1983	Authorities intervened in four banks and four nonbank financial institutions (with 33% of outstanding lbans) in 1981; in 1983, seven banks and one *financiera* accounted for 45% of total assets; by year-end 1983, 19% of loans were nonperforming	1982–1985: government spent 41.2% of GDP
Colombia		
1982–1987	Central Bank intervened in six banks accounting for 25% of banking system assets	Costs of restructuring estimated at 5% of GDP
Ecuador		
Early 1980s	Implementation of exchange program (domestic for foreign debt) to bail out banking system	
1996–ongoing	Authorities intervened in several smaller financial institutions in late 1995 to early 1996 and in the fifth largest commercial bank in 1996; seven financial institutions, accounting for 25–30% of commercial banking assets, closed in 1998–1999; in March 1999, authorities declared one-week bank holiday	
Paraguay		
1995–ongoing	Government Superintendency intervened in two interconnected commercial banks, two other banks, and six related finance houses, accounting for 10% of financial system deposits; by July 1998 government had intervened in six other financial institutions, including the country's largest public bank and the largest savings and loans; by year-end 1998 government intervened in most of remaining domestic private and public banks and a number of finance companies	By end of May 1998, government had spent US$500 million, equivalent to 5.1% of GDP

Country	*Scope of Crisis*	*Estimate of Total Costs*
Peru 1983–1990	Two large banks failed; rest of system suffered from high levels of nonperforming loans and financial disintermediation following the nationalization of the banking system in 1987	
Uruguay 1981–1984	Affected institutions accounted for 30% of financial system assets; insolvent banks accounted for 20% of financial system deposits	Costs of recapitalizing banks estimated at US$350 million (7% of GNP); Central Bank's quasi-fiscal losses associated with subsidized credit operations and purchase of loan portfolios amounted to 24.2% of GDP during 1982–1985
Venezuela 1994–ongoing	Insolvent banks accounted for 30% of financial system deposits; authorities intervened in 13 of 47 banks, which held 50% of deposits in 1994, and in five additional banks in 1995	Estimated losses at more than 18% of GDP
Middle East & North Africa		
Egypt Early 1980s	Several large investment companies closed	
Israel 1977–1983	Virtually entire banking sector affected, representing 60% of stock market capitalization; stock exchange closed for 18 days; bank share prices fell over 40%	About 30% of GDP in 1983
Kuwait 1980s	An estimated 40% of loans nonperforming by 1986	
Lebanon 1988–1990	Four banks insolvent; 11 banks resorted to Central Bank lending	
Morocco Early 1980s		
Turkey 1982–1985	Three banks merged with the state-owned Agriculture Bank and then liquidated; two large banks restructured	1982–1985: rescue cost equivalent to 2.5% of GNP
Yemen 1996–ongoing	Banks suffered from extensive nonperforming loans and heavy foreign currency exposure	
Transitional Socialist Economies		
Albania 1992–ongoing	31% of "new" (post-July 1992 cleanup) banking system loans nonperforming; some banks faced liquidity problems owing to logjam of interbank liabilities	
Armenia 1994–1996	Since August 1994, Central Bank closed half of active banks; large banks continued to suffer from high NPL ratios; savings bank financially weak	
Azerbaijan 1995–ongoing	12 private banks closed; 3 large state-owned banks deemed insolvent; 1 large state-owned bank faced serious liquidity problems	
Bosnia-Herzegovina 1992–present	Banking system suffers from high ratios of NPLs due to the breakup of former Yugoslavia and civil war	
Bulgaria 1990s	In 1995 an estimated 75% of all loans in banking system substandard; banking system experienced a run in early 1996; government then ceased carrying out bailouts, prompting the closure of 19 banks accounting for one-third of assets of the sector. Surviving banks recapitalized by 1997	By early 1996, the sector had a negative net worth estimated at 13% of GDP

Country	Scope of Crisis	Estimate of Total Costs
Croatia 1996	Five banks accounting for about 50% of banking system loans deemed insolvent and taken over by the Bank Rehabilitation Agency during 1996	
Czech Republic 1991–ongoing	Several banks closed since 1993; during 1994–1995, 38% of banking system loans were nonperforming	12% of GDP spent on bank support through 1994
Estonia 1992–1995	Insolvent banks accounted for 41% of financial system assets; licenses of five banks revoked; two major banks merged and nationalized; two large banks merged and converted to loan-recovery agency	Recapitalization outlays for new entity 300 million EEK (1.4% of 1993 GDP)
1994	Social Bank, which controlled 10% of financial system assets, failed	
Georgia 1991–?	Most large banks virtually insolvent; about one-third of total banking system loans nonperforming	
Hungary 1991–1995	Second half of 1993: eight banks, accounting for 25% of financial system assets, insolvent	Overall resolution cost estimated at 10% of GDP
Kyrgyzstan 1990s	80–90% of total banking system loans doubtful; four small commercial banks closed in 1995	
Latvia 1994–ongoing	Between 1994 and 1999, 35 banks either saw their license revoked, were closed, or ceased operations	In 1995, negative net worth of banking system estimated at US$320 million or 7% of 1995 GDP; aggregate loss of the Latvian banking system in 1998 expected to reach US$172 million, about 2.9% of GDP
Lithuania 1995–1996	In 1995, 12 small banks of 25 liquidated, 3 private banks accounting for 29% of banking system deposits failed, and three state-owned banks deemed insolvent	
Macedonia 1993–1994	70% of total banking system loans nonperforming; government took over banks' foreign debts and closed second largest bank	Costs of banking system rehabilitation, obligations from assumption of external debt, liabilities of frozen foreign exchange and contingent liabilities in banks estimated at 32% of GDP
Poland 1990s	Seven of nine treasury-owned banks with 90% share of total credit market, the Bank for Food Economy, and the cooperative banking sector experienced solvency problems in 1991	1993: recapitalization costs of US$750 million for seven commercial banks; recapitalization costs for Bank for Food Economy and cooperative banking sector amounted to US$900 million, together equivalent to 1.9% of GDP
Romania 1990–ongoing	In 1998, nonperforming loans estimated at 25–30% of the total loans of the six major state-owned banks	Agricultural Bank recapitalized on a flow basis; Central Bank injected $210 million into Bancorex, the largest state bank, about 0.6% of 1998 GDP; another $60 million to be injected in 1999

Country	Scope of Crisis	Estimate of Total Costs
Russia		
1995	On August 24, 1995, interbank loan market stopped working due to concern about connected lending in many new banks	
1998	Nearly 720 banks, one-half of all those operating, deemed insolvent; these banks account for 4% of the sector's assets and 32% of retail deposits; Central Bank of Russia estimates 18 banks, holding 40% of the sector's assets and 41% of household deposits, to be in serious difficulties, requiring rescue by the state	In 1999, cost of full bailout estimated at about US$15 billion, or 5–7% of GDP
Slovakia		
1991–ongoing	In 1997, total amount of unrecoverable loans was estimated at 101 billion crowns, equal to approximately 31.4% of total loans and 15.3% of GDP	
Slovenia		
1992–1994	Three banks, accounting for two-thirds of banking system assets, restructured	Recapitalization costs of US$1.3 billion
Ukraine		
1997	By 1997, 32 of 195 banks being liquidated; a further 25 undergoing financial rehabilitation; bad loans constitute 50 to 65% of assets of country's leading banks; in 1998, Ukraine banks further hit by government's decision to restructure government debt	
Industrialized Countries		
Finland		
1991–1994	Savings banking sector badly affected; government took control of three banks that together accounted for 31% of total system deposits	Recapitalization costs amounted to 11% of GDP
Japan		
1990s	Banks suffering from sharp decline in stock market and real estate prices; official estimate of NPLs: ¥40 trillion (US$469 billion) in 1995 (10% of GDP); unofficial estimates put NPLs at ¥1 trillion or 25% of GDP; banks have already made provisions for some bad loans. At year-end 1998, total banking system NPLs estimated at ¥87.5 trillion (US$725 billion), about 17.9% of GDP; in March 1999, Hokkaido Takushodu bank closed, Long Term Credit Bank nationalized, Yatsuda Trust merged with Fuji Bank, and Mitsui Trust merged with Chuo Trust	In 1996, rescue costs estimated at over US$100 billion In 1998, government announced Obuchi Plan, which provides ¥60 trillion (US$500 billion), about 12.3% of GDP, in public funds for loan losses, recapitalization of banks, and depositor protection
Norway		
1987–1993	Central Bank provided special loans to six banks, suffering from post-oil recession of 1985–1986 and from problem real estate loans; state took control of three largest banks (equivalent to 85% of banking system assets, whose loan losses had wiped out capital), partly through a Government Bank Investment Fund (Nkr 5 billion) and the state-backed Bank Insurance Fund had to increase capital to Nkr 11 billion.	Recapitalization costs amounted to 8% of GDP
Spain		
1977–1985	1978–1983: 24 institutions rescued; four liquidated, four merged, and 20 small/medium-sized banks (Rumasa Group) nationalized. In total, 52 of 110 banks experiencing solvency problems, representing 20% of total banking system deposits	Estimated losses of banks were equivalent to approximately 16.8% of GNP
Sweden		
1991	Nordbanken and Gota Bank insolvent, accounting for 21.6% of total banking system assets; Sparbanken Foresta intervened, accounting for 24% of total banking system assets; overall, five of six largest banks, accounting for over 70% of banking system assets, experienced difficulties	Cost of recapitalization amounted to 4% of GDP

TABLE 7.A2   Borderline or Smaller Banking Crises

Country	Scope of Crisis	Estimate of Total Costs
Africa		
Angola		
1991–ongoing	Two state-owned commercial banks experienced solvency problems	
Botswana		
1994–1995	One problem bank merged in 1994, a small bank liquidated in 1995, and state-owned National Development Bank recapitalized	Recapitalization cost of National Development Bank amounted to 0.6% of GDP
Ethiopia		
1994–1995	A government-owned bank was restructured and its nonperforming loans taken over by the government	
Gabon		
1995–ongoing	One bank temporarily closed in 1995	
Gambia		
1985–1992	In 1992, a government bank restructured and privatized	
Ghana		
1997–ongoing	NPL levels increased sharply during 1997 from 15.5% of loans outstanding to 26.5%; two state-owned commercial banks, accounting for 33.9% of market share, in bad shape; three banks, accounting for 3.6% of market share in terms of deposits, insolvent	
Kenya		
1996–ongoing	At end of 1996, NPLs reached 18.6% of total banking system loans	
Lesotho		
1988–ongoing	One small bank of four commercial banks suffered from large portfolio of nonperforming loans	
Mauritius		
1996	Central Bank closed 2 of 12 commercial banks for fraud and other irregularities	
Nigeria		
1997	Distressed banks accounted for 3.9% of banking system assets	
Rwanda		
1991–?	One bank, with well-established network, closed	
South Africa		
1977	Trust Bank	
1989–?		
Tunisia		
1991–1995	In 1991, most commercial banks undercapitalized	1991–1994, banking system raised equity equivalent to 1.5% of GDP and made provisions equivalent to another 1.5%; recapitalization through 1994 required at least 3% of GDP
Asia		
Brunei		
Darussalam		
Mid–1980s	Several financial firms failed in mid-1980s; second largest bank failed in 1986; in 1991, 9% of loans past due	
Hong Kong		
1982–1983	Nine deposit-taking companies failed	
1983–1986	Seven banks or deposit-taking institutions liquidated or taken over	
1998	One large investment bank fails	

Country	*Scope of Crisis*	*Estimate of Total Costs*
India 1993–ongoing	Nonperforming assets of the 27 public sector banks estimated at 19.5% of total loans and advances as of end of March 1995; nonperforming assets to total assets reached 10.8% in 1993–1994; at year end 1998, NPLs estimated at 16% of total loans	
Indonesia 1994	Classified assets equal to over 14% of banking system assets with over 70% in state banks	Recapitalization cost for five state banks expected to amount to 1.8% of GDP
Laos Early 1990s		Recapitalization of state-owned commercial banks amounted to 1.5% of GDP
Malaysia 1985–1988	Insolvent institutions account for 3.4% of financial system deposits; marginally capitalized and perhaps insolvent institutions account for another 4.4% of financial system deposits	Reported losses equivalent to 4.7% of GNP
Myanmar 1996–?	Largest state-owned commercial bank reported with large ratio of NPLs	
Papua New Guinea 1989–?	85% of savings and loan associations ceased operations	
Singapore 1982	Domestic commercial banks' nonperforming loans rose to about $200 million or 0.63% of GDP	
Taiwan 1983–1984	Four trust companies and 11 cooperatives failed	
1995	Failure of credit cooperative Changua Fourth in late July sparked runs on other credit unions in central and southern Taiwan	
Central America and the Caribbean		
Costa Rica 1994–ongoing	One large state-owned commercial bank closed in December 1994; ratio of overdue loans (net of provisions) to net worth in state commercial banks exceeded 100% in June 1995	
Guatemala 1990s	Two small state-owned banks had high nonperforming assets; these banks discontinued operations in early 1990s	
Trinidad and Tobago 1982–1993	In early 1980s, several financial institutions experienced solvency problems, resulting in merger of three government-owned banks in 1993	
South America		
Venezuela Late 1970s and 1980s	Notable bank failures: Banco Nacional de Descuento (1978); BANDAGRO (1981); Banco de los Trabajadores de Venezuela (1982); Banco de Comercio (1985); BHCU (1985); BHCO (1985); Banco Lara (1986)	
Transitional Socialist Economies		
Belarus 1995–ongoing	Many banks undercapitalized; forced mergers burdened some banks with poor loan portfolios	
Estonia 1998	Three banks failed in 1998: Maapank (Agricultural Bank), which accounted for 3% of banking system assets, and two smaller banks, EVEA and ERA	Maapank's total losses reached US$500 million
Tajikistan 1996–ongoing	One of largest banks insolvent; one small bank closed, and another (of 17) in process of liquidation	

Country	Scope of Crisis	Estimate of Total Costs

Middle East and North Africa

Egypt
1991–1995 — Four public sector banks given capital assistance

Jordan
1989–1990 — Third largest bank failed in August 1989 — Central bank provided overdrafts equivalent to 10% of GDP to meet a run on deposits and allowed banks to settle foreign obligations

Turkey
1994 — Three banks failed in April 1994 — Up to June 1994, authorities spent 1.1% of GDP

Industrialized Countries

Australia
1989–1992 — Two large banks received capital from government to cover losses; nonperforming loans rose to 6% of total assets in 1991–1992 — Rescue cost of state-owned banks estimated to be 1.9% of GDP

Canada
1983–1985 — 15 members of Canadian Deposit Insurance Corporation, including two banks, failed

Denmark
1987–1992 — Cumulative loan losses 1990–1992 were 9% of loans; 40 of 60 problem banks merged

France
1994–1995 — Crédit Lyonnais — Unofficial estimates put losses at US$10 billion, making it the largest single bank failure up to that time

Germany
Late 1970s — So-called Giroinstitutions faced problems

Great Britain
1974–1976 — "Secondary Banking Crisis"
1980s and 1990s — Notable bank failures: Johnson Matthey (1984), Bank of Credit and Commerce International (1991), Barings (1995)

Greece
1991–1995 — Localized problems required significant injections of public funds into specialized lending institutions

Iceland
1985–1986 — One of three state-owned banks became insolvent; eventually privatized in a merger with three private banks
1993 — Government forced to inject capital into one of the largest state-owned commercial banks after it suffered serious loan losses

Italy
1990–1995 — 58 banks, accounting for 11% of total lending, merged with other institutions

New Zealand
1987–1990 — One large state-owned bank, accounting for one-fourth of banking assets, experienced serious solvency problems due to high NPLs — Bank required a capital injection amounting to 1% of GDP

United States
1984–1991 — More than 1,400 savings & loans and 1,300 banks failed — Cost of savings & loan cleanup estimated at US$180 billion, equivalent to 3.2% of GDP

References

Akerlof, George A., and Paul Romer. 1993. Looting: The economic underworld of bankruptcy for profit. *Brookings Papers on Economic Activity* 2: 1–73.

Barth, James R., and Philip F. Batholomew. 1992. The thrift industry crisis: Revealed weaknesses in the Federal deposit insurance system. In *The Reform of Federal Deposit Insurance.* Ed. by James R. Barth and R. Dan Brumbaugh, Jr. New York: Harper Business.

Basel Committee on Banking Supervision. 1997. *Core Principles for Effective Banking Supervision.* Basel, Switzerland: Bank for International Settlements.

Boyd, John, Pedro Gomis, Sungkyu Kwak, and Bruce Smith. 2000. A user's guide to banking crises. Conference paper, World Bank.

Calomiris, Charles W. 1997. *The Postmodern Bank Safety Net: Lessons from Developed and Developing Economies.* Washington, DC: American Enterprise Institute.

———. 1998. The IMF's imprudent role as lender of last resort. *Cato Journal* 17: 275–94.

———. 2000. *Victorian Perspectives on the Banking Collapses of the 1980s and 1990s.* Manuscript.

Calomiris, Charles W., and Gary Gorton. 1991. The origin of banking panics: Models, facts and bank regulation. In *Financial Markets and Financial Crises.* Ed. by R. Glenn Hubbard. Chicago: University of Chicago Press.

Calomiris, Charles W., Charles Himmelberg, and Paul Wachtel. 1995. Commercial paper, corporate finance, and the business cycle: A microeconomic perspective. *Carnegie-Rochester Conference Series on Public Policy* 42: 203–50.

Calomiris, Charles W., and Charles M. Kahn. 1991. The role of demandable debt in structuring optimal banking arrangements. *American Economic Review* 81: 497–513.

Calomiris, Charles W., and Eugene N. White. 1994. The origins of federal deposit insurance. In *The Regulated Economy.* Ed. by Claudia Goldin and Gary Libecap. Chicago: University of Chicago Press.

Calomiris, Charles W., and Berry Wilson. 1998. Bank capital and portfolio management: The 1930s capital crunch and scramble to shed risk. Working Paper no. 6649, National Bureau of Economic Research.

Caprio, Gerard, and Daniela Klingebiel. 1996a. Bank insolvencies: Cross-country experience. Working Paper no. 1620, World Bank.

———. 1996b. Bank insolvency: Bad luck, bad policy or bad banking? In *Annual Bank Conference on Development Economics 1996.* Washington, DC: World Bank.

Caprio, Gerard, and Berry Wilson. 1997. On not putting all the eggs in one basket: The role of diversification in banking. Paper presented at the 1997 World Bank annual meeting, Hong Kong.

Cole, R., J. McKenzie, and L. White. 1995. Deregulation gone awry: Moral hazard in the savings and loan industry. In *The Causes and Consequences of Depository Institution Failures.* Ed. by A. Cottrell, M. Lawlor, and J. Wood. Boston: Kluwer Academic Publishers.

Corsetti, Giancarlo, Paolo Pesenti, and Nouriel Roubini. 1998. What caused the Asian currency and financial crisis? Part I: A macroeconomic overview. Working Paper no. 6833, National Bureau of Economic Research.

Cull, Robert, Lemma W. Senbet, and Marco Sorge. 2000. Deposit insurance and financial development, Conference paper, World Bank.

Demirgüç-Kunt, Asli, and Enrica Detragiache. 2000. Does deposit insurance increase banking system stability? Conference paper, World Bank.

Demirgüç-Kunt, Asli, and Harry Huizinga. Marker discipline and financial safety net design. Conference paper, World Bank.

Edwards, Franklin R., and Frederic S. Mishkin. 1995. The decline of traditional banking: Implications for financial stability and regulatory policy. Federal Reserve Bank of New York. *Economic Policy Review* 2: 27–45.

Fay, Stephen. 1997. *The Collapse of Barings.* New York: W.W. Norton.

Friedman, Milton, and Anna Schwartz. 1963. *A Monetary History of the United States, 1867–1960.* Princeton, NJ: Princeton University Press.

Gorton, Gary, and Rosen. 1995. Corporate control, portfolio choice, and the decline of banking. *Journal of Finance* 50: 1377–1420.

Hellman, Thomas, Kevin Murdock, and Joseph Stiglitz. 1998a. Liberalization, moral hazard in banking, and prudential regulation: Are capital requirements enough? Working paper, Stanford University.

———. 1998b. Financial restraint: Towards a new paradigm. Working paper, Stanford University.

Honohan, Patrick, and Daniela Klingebiel. 2000. Controlling fiscal costs of banking crises. Conference paper, World Bank.

Hunt, Luke, and Karen Heinrich. 1996. *Barings Lost*. Oxford: Butterworth-Heinemann.

Jorion, Philippe. 1997. *Value at Risk*. Burr Ridge, IL: Richard D. Irwin.

Kane, Edward. 2000. Designing financial safety nets to fit country circumstances. Conference paper, World Bank.

Keeley, Michael. 1990. Deposit insurance, risk and market power in banking. *American Economic Review* 80: 1183–1200.

Krugman, Paul. 1998. What caused Asia's crisis? Working paper, Massachusetts Institute of Technology.

McKinnon, Ronald I. 1993. *The Order of Economic Liberalization*. 2nd ed. Baltimore: Johns Hopkins University Press.

Obstfeld, Maurice, and Kenneth Rogoff. 1995. The mirage of fixed exchange rates. *Journal of Economic Perspectives* 9, no. 4: 73–96.

Pomerleano, Michael. 1998. The East Asia crisis and corporate finances: The untold micro story. Policy Research Working Paper no. 1990, World Bank.

Rajan, Raghuram. 1996. Why banks have a future: Toward a new theory of commercial banking. *Journal of Applied Corporate Finance* 9, no. 2: 114–28.

Truell, Peter, and Larry Gurwin. 1992. *False Profits: The Inside Story of BCCI, the World's Most Corrupt Financial Empire*. New York: Houghton Mifflin.

Financial Crises

Introduction

Banking crises, as detailed in Chapter 7, have occurred for as long as there have been banks. The great majority in earlier eras were modest in scope. A few banks would fail in a setting of economic downturn, but the outcome was not generally an economic catastrophe. Private associations of bankers experimented with various types of cooperation to control damage, and reserve-based central banks evolved as an additional form of mutual protection. Only in modern times have governments taken over central banking and assumed responsibility for preventing and resolving banking crises.

Currency crises have also occurred, though they are more modern in flavor. In previous centuries, international transactions were denominated in units of gold or silver, and the international means of payment took the form of gold and silver coins or currency that was usually credibly convertible into those coins, which were broadly acceptable around the world. Paper money was issued initially by banks, and only gradually did governments begin to manage their paper currencies through monetary policies. Currencies of various countries were sometimes linked together by fixed exchange rates—for example, during the pre–World War I era of the gold standard (1870–1914), the 1920s, the Bretton Woods era (1948–1973), and Europe's successive experiments with a European Monetary System and Economic and Monetary Union. In these settings, a currency collapse is defined as an abandonment of the commitment to a fixed exchange rate, usually by one or more weak currencies devaluing or falling out of the system altogether. But these events, which typically were not associated with a banking crisis, generally did not give rise to economic catastrophes.[1]

In the 20th century, however, and particularly since the liberalization of emerging financial markets and the growth of global financial integration, we have seen a new and frightening form of collapse: a combined currency and banking collapse, leading to high interest rates, capital flight, and a disastrous contraction of the real economy. The events in Chile, Argentina, and to a lesser degree Uruguay during 1982–1983 typified these "modern" financial crises, but the scenario was later replayed in Mexico, Thailand, Indonesia, Malaysia, Korea, Russia, and elsewhere. The intensity and damage done by these crises have attracted much attention from governmental, banking, and academic communities.

The common preconditions for this new type of "twin" crisis seem to be the following, all occurring jointly:

1. Financial liberalization in the years before the crisis.
2. A fixed or partially fixed exchange rate policy.
3. Large, optimistic capital inflows in the years before the crisis, some of which are withdrawn during the crisis.
4. Underlying weaknesses in domestic banks and firms that mount in the months immediately preceding the crisis.

An early sign of trouble is often the growth of nonperforming loans in the banking system; observers recognize (*ex post*) excessive leverage and poor investment decisions by both banks and firms, often following a period of rapid expansion but also reflecting structural weaknesses in areas such as corporate governance and bank supervision.

Figure 8.1 shows the anatomy of a prototypical modern financial crisis, portraying it as a kind of vicious circle. The crisis can begin at any point in the diagram. It might begin when some macroeconomic setback, microeconomic failure, or simply rumor and anxiety about future fundamentals (e.g., fiscal and monetary policy intentions of the government) cause both internal and external investors to lose confidence and begin withdrawing funds from the country. It could initially take the form of a capital outflow. It might start with an expansionary monetary policy undertaken for reasons of domestic macroeconomic stabilization that backfires by leading foreign investors to doubt the credibility of the fixed foreign exchange rate.

However it begins, the crisis builds because the four elements shown in Figure 8.1 intensify each other. As investors pull capital out of the country, the currency peg comes under pressure. Interest rates then rise substantially because investors now require a higher risk premium and the government might try to slow the capital outflows with a high-interest-rate monetary policy.

If banks and firms have borrowed extensively in foreign currency, as is often the case, a collapse of the currency value can imply that their debt obligations double or triple in terms of local currency, so that moderate or high leverage can become unmanageable leverage. Furthermore, the rapid rise in interest rates means that firms face rising interest costs on that debt. Few firms are so profitable that they can afford very high

---

[1]Indeed, the banking collapses of the Great Depression of 1929–1933, which were unusually severe, were associated with an unwillingness to devalue exchange rates. See Eichengreen and Sachs (1985), Temin (1989), Bernanke and James (1991), Eichengreen (1992), and Calomiris (1993).

FIGURE 8.1

Anatomy of a modern EFM financial crisis

real rates of interest. Thus, the collapse of the currency value may quickly lead to disaster if banks and firms have exposed themselves to extensive interest rate and foreign exchange risk through extensive borrowing at floating rates in dollars, yen, or euros.

The realization of this risk tends to further frighten investors, who now withdraw their capital in even greater quantity. The selling pressure on the currency is difficult and expensive for governments to resist, and in most cases leads to a collapse of the fixed exchange rate. Then the worst fears are realized, as real interest rates rise to unsustainable levels (20–50 percent) and overextended firms begin to default on their debts, further undermining the domestic banks that have foreign exchange and interest rate risks of their own.

The interest rate risk and foreign exchange risk inherent in the earlier borrowing pattern now explode, becoming credit risk and bringing the banking system to the edge of collapse. The potential claims on public funds to repair the banks aggravate fears of inflation and put further pressure on the currency value. They also aggravate capital outflows and the crisis gathers force. Like a hurricane, it generates its own circular energy as it accelerates.

Explanations of the Crises

As researchers have tried to understand these crises, a number of schools of thought have emerged, each differing in what it considers the essential source of the problem. It is somewhat like the ancient story of the blind men trying to describe an elephant, each holding on to a different part. All of these accounts have some merit. Indeed, what makes the modern crises unique is the conjunction of a number of troubling factors occurring at the same time and aggravating each other in a vicious cycle that makes a new equilibrium very difficult to establish.

The reason some studies emphasize a single central or fundamental cause is probably because such explanations lead to clearer policy prescriptions, and most of the participants in the debate wish to influence policy in a certain direction. With this in mind, and in search of a balanced perspective on these crises, let us review the various explanations.

Overvalued Currency

One school of thought emphasizes the role of fixed exchange rates and finds the heart of the problem in the tendency of pegged currencies to become overvalued because of continuing inflation. The gradual overvaluation acts like a kind of spring, storing up ever-larger amounts of energy against the day when it is finally released. Without this element, exchange rate adjustment might be gradual and manageable instead of abrupt and cataclysmic.

The situation is illustrated in Figure 8.2, which shows the actual evolution of Brazil's inflation and exchange rate relative to the U.S. dollar. In June 1994 Brazil instituted a new currency, the *real,* which was initially valued at 1.00 *real* to the U.S. dollar. The government attempted to keep the currency's value close to that of the dollar for a number of years, even though a weak fiscal policy kept inflation running at about 20 percent a year for several years. Indeed, by June 1997 the consumer price

FIGURE 8.2

Brazilian consumer price index and currency value

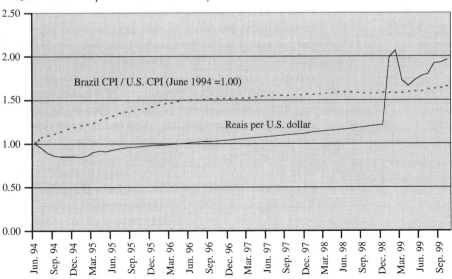

index was 66 percent above its value three years before and the ratio of Brazilian CPI to the U.S. CPI was up by 53 percent, while the currency had depreciated by only 8 percent. Inflation then slowed, but the currency was highly overvalued, which gave rise to continuing expectations of a crisis. When the peg finally broke in early 1999, the currency snapped abruptly to a level well beyond where it would have been if it had followed the evolution of inflation.

Overvaluation of currencies has occurred periodically in the industrialized world during the Bretton Woods period (1948–1973). During that time, all currencies were firmly pegged to the U.S. dollar and the dollar was pegged to gold. Problems arose when inflation in Italy, the United Kingdom, or elsewhere exceeded that of the other industrialized countries, causing the inflating currencies to become overvalued. The visible sign of overvaluation was deterioration in the current account. Under the Bretton Woods system, the current account deficit had to be financed by drawing down reserves or by borrowing dollars, so that another visible sign of crisis was a decline of reserves or a massive buildup of debt. Since reserves and borrowing capacity are finite, this could not be sustained indefinitely, and soon investors would sense trouble. Their flight from the weakening currency would put further pressure on reserves and borrowing capacity, in a cycle that often ended in devaluation.

The primary variables determining the short-run vulnerability of a country to such events were the magnitude of the reserves and the ultimate capacity of the country to borrow hard currency. External investors would not wait for reserves to be exhausted; as soon as the probability of exhaustion became significant, a phenomenon similar to a bank run would occur as all holders of the local currency sought to trade it for the government's reserves.[2] The most important variables for long-run vulnerability, however, were fiscal and monetary policy. A country bent on pursuing policies that require an aggressive expansion of its money supply will sooner or later lose the battle to preserve its fixed exchange rate (as discussed in Chapter 6), no matter what the level of its initial reserves and no matter how great its initial capacity to borrow.

This account describes reasonably well the currency crises in the industrialized world, and it can be extended to EFMs that attempt to fix the values of their currencies. Chile during 1979–1982 is a case in point. Chile had succeeded in most of its reform goals by 1979 but was still plagued with inflation, a policy problem that was aggravated, as noted in Chapter 6, by its policy of indexing. With inflation running initially at 30 percent a year, a policy decision was made in 1979 to fix the exchange rate at 39 pesos to the dollar. In the subsequent two years, inflation did decline dramatically to near zero, but the currency became significantly overvalued, as evidenced by a trade deficit of more than 10 percent of GDP. Yet economic growth was strong and capital inflows continued right up to the time that the peg broke in 1982.

To many observers, the collapse of the currency was inevitable because the real (inflation-adjusted) exchange rate had risen by 56 percent over the three-year period and reached an unsustainable level; that is, cumulative inflation relative to the dollar had run to about 56 percent since the currency was pegged. A currency level that seemed appropriate in 1979 looked very high by the end of 1981, and Chilean goods were less and less competitive on world markets. Reserves fell and debt increased. This did not by itself create a crisis, but it did create a vulnerability to shocks, which finally arrived in 1982. The Mexican crisis of 1994–1995, described in detail below, bears a considerable resemblance to the Chilean events.

---

[2]Krugman (1979).

An insidious feature of such scenarios is that the government's credibility is very much at stake. If the government's commitment to the peg seems unshakable, then speculators may stay away. But if the peg looks increasingly vulnerable because of deteriorating fundamentals—which could force the government to devalue—then speculators arrive in quantity, selling the currency spot and forward, and these actions precipitate a crisis. Anticipating that risk, the government feels it cannot show the slightest wavering or lack of confidence in its fundamentals. This may lead the government to make statements that sound increasingly unrealistic. Both the Chilean authorities in 1982 and the Mexican authorities in 1994 were adamant in denying any overvaluation of the currency, despite growing evidence to the contrary. The Brazilian authorities behaved similarly in 1998.

Some of the speculators against the currency, of course, may well be insiders in the country's business–government elite. There is ample evidence that the selling of the Mexican peso that began in late 1994 originated with Mexicans. Nevertheless, astute participants in financial markets all over the world will see a one-sided bet in such attacks on overvalued currencies. By selling the currency in spot markets and by selling it forward when forward markets exist, speculators stand to gain a great deal from a possible devaluation, but risk very little, since the chances of the currency increasing in value are almost nil. Few opportunities are more tempting than the chance to make a large profit with almost no risk of loss.

So pegged currencies often create a tension between governments determined to defend their credibility and speculators who have an appealing opportunity to challenge it. Small wonder that governments tend to demonize speculators and see them as the fundamental cause of their countries' problems. This has happened for decades. During the 1960s, for example, when the Bretton Woods agreement was starting to weaken, the Swiss banks ("the gnomes of Zurich") were portrayed as the greedy disrupters of tranquility for governments such as those of the United Kingdom and Italy.

In the modern era, it is George Soros and other hedge fund managers who are most frequently mentioned. Soros, whose Quantum Fund has made several billion dollars in currency speculation, including one highly successful attack on the pound sterling and the Italian lira just before these currencies dropped out of the EMS in 1992, has tried to reposition himself as advisor to governments, criticizing the instabilities of the global financial order, and showing developing countries how to defend themselves against people such as himself.[3]

The most vocal opponent of hedge funds and speculators in general is Dr. Mohamad Mahatir, prime minister of Malaysia. Because of the visibility of this criticism and the interesting questions it raises, researchers began investigating whether hedge funds in general or Quantum Fund in particular was in any way responsible for the collapse of the Malaysian ringgit in 1997. They found no such evidence. The estimated positions of the hedge funds in the ringgit were not unusual prior to the crisis, nor did they make unusual profits from the crisis. Quantum Fund was apparently long the ringgit. In the case of Korea in 1997, it is clear that domestic, not foreign, investors drove declines in securities prices during its stock market collapse.[4]

The unwillingness of governments to admit the slightest problem creates a certain blindness to emerging difficulties, a pressure to not even discuss a possible weakness. That is why reversals often have the appearance of sudden shocks.

---

[3]Soros (1998).

[4]Brown, Goetzmann, and Park (1998), and Choe, Kho, and Stulz (1998).

Policymakers are invariably surprised by how the market can suddenly turn on them, and by the extent to which they have underestimated their vulnerability. Markets, in turn, are surprised by how little liquidity there is when all the lenders scramble to get out at the same time. The combination makes for a chaotic collapse and the disruption of finance. Moreover, because the policy regime is typically sustained by strong appeal to credibility, any action that undermines this will profoundly disorient the lenders, thus aggravating the lack of credit.[5]

The policy advice that flows from the view that currency overvaluation is the essential cause of modern financial crisis is basically not to peg currencies; it is argued that floating exchange rates, though volatile, are preferable. Since currencies are generally pegged in an effort to control inflation, the related advice is not to worry so much about inflation—better a moderate level of inflation than a total financial collapse.[6]

Capital Flows, Overborrowing, and Illiquidity

Some analysts emphasize that a high level of foreign borrowing (a large capital inflow) seems always to precede a financial crisis, and that the crisis itself consists of a sudden reversal of this flow. They argue that the exchange rate alone is less important than the huge flow of capital transactions driving the exchange rate. They show how crises are much worse when the capital inflows are short-term debt, particularly debt denominated in dollars or other external currency. Their solutions are typically to regulate capital flows.

A common theme in this approach to understanding financial crises is the tendency for capital markets to overshoot—for lenders to be excessively optimistic and then suddenly to shift to excessive pessimism. That view connects the study of modern financial crises with the historical literature on crises, some of which sees investment booms and busts as the result of "euphoria" that turns suddenly to "revulsion."[7] On the borrowers' side, a similar perspective might explain why developing countries overborrow.

Related to overborrowing and overlending is the abruptness of reversal of capital flows. If the fundamentals are to blame in the case of East Asia, for example, why did investors lionize the region for so long and then change so suddenly and completely? In this view, "the collective result is disastrous and the panic is unnecessary, in the sense that the fundamentals could have supported a much more favorable outcome. In short, international financial markets are intrinsically highly unstable; or to put it another way, the East Asian crisis is as much a crisis of Western capitalism as of Asian capitalism."[8]

In the world of neoclassical economics, of course, markets do not, on average, overreact. While speculators will often be mistaken in their expectations (since no one has perfect foresight), they should learn from previous mistakes and thus not overshoot repeatedly. To explain why market participants fail to learn, one would need to specify some market failure or irrationality. One approach lies in the evolving willingness of financial economics to take into account decades of research in human psychology and admit that market participants might not be fully rational. This view, quite radical

---

[5]Dornbusch, Goldfajn, and Valdés (1995), pp. 245–46.
[6]Ibid.
[7]Kindleberger (1978) is the most prominent proponent of this interpretation of financial crises historically.
[8]Radelet and Sachs (1998), pp. 2–3.

among economists, began to be discussed publicly as a general issue in the early 1990s.[9] Financial economists opened the possibility that poorly informed "noise traders" would not necessarily be wiped out but might even come to dominate markets.[10] By the end of the 1990s, researchers were beginning to connect established anomalies in stock market behavior with established psychological results concerning overconfidence, a very widespread human phenomenon, and biased self-attribution (the tendency to hear news that confirms your beliefs and not to hear news that contradicts them).[11] Certainly these two traits can give rise to market overreaction.

However, most economists are reluctant to put much explanatory weight on psychological factors, preferring rational models when these are possible. Market collapses can be rationally explained by *multiple equilibrium* models; these assume rational behavior, but make expectations exogenous: If people for any reason expect a currency to rise in the future they will buy it today, causing its price to rise. Similarly, if they expect an exchange rate collapse, a collapse might well be precipitated. If we allow expectations to be formed arbitrarily, they can become self-fulfilling, and equilibrium will emerge where people expect it to emerge. This kind of framework can readily model market panics.[12]

Furthermore, the risk of such a collapse can be aggravated by problems of illiquidity. *Liquidity* means having access to sufficient cash whenever you need it. Firms or individuals that borrow substantial amounts gradually lower their liquidity by limiting their access to additional borrowing. The higher the debt level becomes, the greater is the vulnerability to shocks. A quantity of debt that looks manageable in good times may suddenly look unmanageable if negative news changes lenders' assessments of the borrowers' ability to service their debt. In such an event, liquidity can dry up and borrowers may be under pressure to repay debts falling due rather than being able to refinance them. In short, excessive borrowing creates the risk of a liquidity crisis.

At the national level, liquidity implies the existence of sufficient reserves of foreign exchange at the central bank and aggregate foreign exchange earnings relative to the foreign exchange payment requirements by agents in the country; that is, from both a stock and a flow perspective, the government wants to avoid any suggestion that the country as a whole cannot meet its foreign exchange payment obligations as they fall due. Low reserves and extensive foreign borrowing, especially at short term, seriously lower liquidity.

Governments with a large amount of short-term debt run the risk that a self-fulfilling bad equilibrium could develop where debt holders worry about *each other's* willingness to roll over maturing debt. Each debt holder worries that other debt holders may refuse to roll over their outstanding debts and thus force the borrower into default. As the risk of government illiquidity rises, debt holders become reluctant to roll over debt, which can itself precipitate a liquidity crisis.

Illiquidity is not to be confused with *insolvency,* which means a fundamental incapacity to ever repay all of one's debts. Insolvency occurs when the fundamentals of an economy turn out to be much weaker in a permanent way than had previously been realized. We will examine below the explanations of financial crisis in terms of weak fundamentals. The liquidity school argues that most financial crises are not caused by these deeper problems, but are simply the consequence of low reserves and high debt

---

[9]Thaler (1991).

[10]DeLong, Shleifer, Summers, and Waldmann (1991).

[11]Daniel, Hirschleifer, and Subramanyam (1998).

[12]Obstfeld (1986 and 1996), and Chang and Velasco (1998).

at excessively short term, which makes economies highly vulnerable to random fluctuations. This view considers crises to be unnecessary and avoidable, since they are not caused by any underlying insolvency.

When short-term debt is denominated in foreign currency, however, liquidity risk becomes compounded with foreign exchange risk, and this really can lead to insolvency. Capital outflows stemming from the failure to roll over short-term debt can produce reserve outflows from the central bank, which can precipitate a speculative attack and the collapse of the exchange rate. This in turn raises the domestic currency value of short-term debt, and possibly turns what began as an illiquidity problem into a massive insolvency problem for debtors.

When measuring liquidity risk, it is important to bear in mind that measures of the mismatch of the government's reserves and short-term international sovereign debt do not provide an adequate picture of liquidity risk. One must also consider the structure of private obligations and the possibility that sudden capital outflows could deplete reserves and create a sovereign liquidity crisis. Indeed, one must consider the short-term liabilities of a country's entire banking system. In a speculative attack, depositors will be among the first to try to convert their bank debt into hard currency and to exit before the crisis causes the hard currency value of their deposits to fall.

The notion that liquidity risk can create bad self-fulfilling equilibriums has its roots in the banking literature. Banks exist in part to provide liquidity transformation: Borrowers are more liquid if their liabilities are long term (so that they do not face refinancing), and savers with uncertain needs are more liquid if their assets are short term. Banks reconcile borrowers' need for long-term funding with savers' need for short-term investments, providing liquidity to both. But by offering this service, banks take the reverse position of long-term assets and short-term liabilities, making them inherently subject to liquidity risk. The consequence is the possibility of bank runs. The liquidity view of financial crises sees them as the international equivalent of a bank run.

This view can explain why financial crises erupt in some of the most promising countries, frequently following periods of privatization, deregulation, fiscal reform, and financial liberalization. It is precisely the beneficial qualities of these reforms that attract foreign capital, including abundant foreign loans, as if the government had given a signal that the future will be very good in contrast to a troubled past. Promising countries worry less about short-term, foreign currency debt than troubled countries, so they are more likely to tolerate an illiquid position.

If the essential problem is national illiquidity, then solutions that address capital flows may be desirable. In the short run, the IMF should be more generous in its lending so that liquidity is restored to the countries in question.[13] In the long run, countries should avoid getting into illiquid positions by not borrowing large amounts at short terms, which suggests possible advantages from controls on short-term capital inflows or outflows. The liquidity view, with its emphasis on market instability, sounds a retreat from the era of free capital movement. For the first time in decades, capital controls are being seriously advocated. In Malaysia, under the guidance of the profoundly antimarket Dr. Mahatir, comprehensive controls on capital outflows were instituted in 1998.

A basic question is whether, in the longer run, capital controls actually work. A study of that issue concluded that controls on capital outflows are largely ineffective: They not only change investment incentives, but are often circumvented and lead to

---

[13]Those who advocate this view suggest reforming IMF lending rules to increase liquidity assistance while discouraging abuse of IMF lending. See Calomiris (1998).

increased corruption as well as higher cost of capital.[14] Controls on capital inflows, some argue, seem more benign. The major EFM experiment of this kind was Chile's policy of *encaje* [reserve], in which 30 percent of all bank and portfolio inflows had to be put on reserve for one year at the central bank. The study concluded that this policy did increase the average maturity of Chile's debt but did not reduce the total volume of Chile's capital inflows. It had no significant effect on Chile's real exchange rate and only a very small effect on interest rates. It may have reduced stock market instability to some degree but did not isolate Chile from the East Asia crisis. It also significantly increased the cost of borrowing, particularly for smaller firms. Furthermore, derivative contracts could possibly enable borrowers and lenders to avoid the constraints of the *encaje*.

Troubled Banks and Moral Hazard

The third school of thought about financial crises blames them primarily on weak institutions, particularly on banks and firms that take too much risk and have too many losses. Such banks and firms are the main nexus of foreign exchange risk and illiquidity by borrowing short term in foreign currencies and so setting up the preconditions for crisis. They are also the main victims of a crisis when it hits. This view is not really at odds with the liquidity view, but it does focus on the parties making the decisions and asks why they would put themselves into this dangerous position.

Throughout this book we have emphasized the importance of strong institutions: strong banks, sound government and regulatory bodies, honest and efficient courts, appropriate institutions of information, and sound corporate governance. We have seen that weak fundamentals prevent the emergence of strong securities markets, so that banks dominate EFMs. But weak fundamentals can also lead quickly to weak banks. Excessive government domination of banks or, at the other extreme, insufficient government oversight of banks, can lead to connected lending and moral hazard that undermine the stability of the banking system.

In this view, modern EFM financial crises result from countries with weak institutions opening up to the global market economy before they have instituted appropriate reforms. Advocates of this viewpoint note that countries with strong banking sector fundamentals can withstand broken currency pegs and sudden liquidity needs with relatively little damage. For example, at the peak of the Asia crisis in late 1997, both Taiwan and Hong Kong suffered speculative attacks on their pegged currencies. Taiwan's peg broke and its currency depreciated 19 percent against the U.S. dollar between mid-October 1997 and mid-January 1998. Hong Kong's currency board withstood the attack and did not break. But neither Taiwan nor Hong Kong suffered a financial or macroeconomic collapse because both banking systems were strong.

Brazil's case was similar. As shown in Figure 8.2, the Brazilian foreign exchange regime collapsed and the *real* lost about 40 percent of its value in January 1999. This event had been widely anticipated based particularly on Brazil's weak fiscal policy and evident currency overvaluation. But despite these fears, there was no financial or macroeconomic collapse. The reason appears to be that Brazil's banks were not riddled with losses and had not exposed themselves to devaluation risk.[15] Indeed, a few may have profited from the devaluation. Thus, speculative attacks on pegged currencies

---

[14]Edwards (1999).

[15]Some observers have argued that Brazil's crisis was worsened by illiquidity resulting from the repatriation of retained earnings by foreign firms that had invested in Brazil. Repatriated earnings—which, like short-term debt, can exit quickly—reportedly placed significant pressure on Brazil's foreign exchange reserves.

do not seem to lead to economic collapse when the banks are strong and not severely exposed to devaluation.

Liquidity risk, too, does not seem to trouble economies whose banks are strong. Indeed, a problem with the liquidity view of crises is to explain why illiquidity by itself should ever be more than a temporary setback. It is an axiom of banking that borrowers with strong fundamentals (solvency) can refinance or restructure their liabilities, given sufficient time; this is the essential difference between illiquidity and insolvency. Restructuring may require a good deal of communication and negotiation, but banks in principle want to lend to solvent borrowers on terms they can live with. So without denying that overvalued currency and excessive short-term debt can cause problems, advocates of the banking viewpoint maintain that neither is likely to cause major damage unless financial sector fundamentals are not in order. It is fear of insolvency that causes capital to flee.

The "fundamentalists" note that, whatever the many differences among countries and regions, every country that has experienced a modern financial crisis has had weakness in its banking system prior to the crisis. Very few people or publications anticipated or predicted the Asian financial crisis that struck in the summer and autumn of 1997. But in April 1997 *The Economist* published a survey of banking in emerging markets in which it called attention to the weakness in Asia's banks and all but predicted the crisis that occurred several months later:

> *Spot the next crisis* . . . A surfeit of lending to overstretched property developers, state-owned smokestacks, politicians' cronies and other poor risks has left [Asian] banks' balance sheets riddled with holes. Excluding Japan and China, Asia's banks are burdened with something like $200 billion of nonperforming debt—equivalent to the GDP of Thailand . . . Banks in Thailand and Korea are lurching toward full-blown crisis. Unless regulators act quickly, one of these two might become the next Mexico or Japan.[16]

A work covering 76 balance of payment (BOP) crises and 26 banking crises in the 1970–1995 period examined the relationship between them and concluded the following:

> Most often, the *beginning* of banking sector problems predates the BOP crisis; indeed, knowing that a banking crisis was underway helps predict a future BOP crisis. However, the causal link is not unidirectional. Our results show that the collapse of the currency deepens the banking crisis, activating a vicious spiral. We find that the *peak* of the banking crisis most often comes after the currency crash, suggesting that existing problems were aggravated or new ones created by the high interest rates required to defend the exchange rate peg or the foreign exchange exposure of banks . . .
>
> While speculative attacks can and do occur as market sentiment shifts and possibly, herding behavior takes over (crises tend to be bunched together), the incidence of crises where the economic fundamentals are sound are [sic] rare.[17]

The mutually reinforcing effects that banking crises and currency crises have on one another warrant emphasis. Bank insolvency—when bank losses are borne by taxpayers—undermines fiscal credibility and can precipitate a currency run. Conversely, because bank debt is short term, a run on the domestic currency will produce a run on banks. Furthermore, if banks or their borrowers expose themselves to significant devaluation risk by borrowing in foreign currency–denominated instruments or speculating in currency and derivatives markets, devaluation can make banks insolvent.

---

[16]*The Economist,* April 12, 1997, p. 29.
[17]Kaminsky and Reinhart (1999), p. 474.

Why do banks in emerging financial markets generate so many nonperforming loans? The answers are different in different countries. In Thailand, banks had made many bets on the buoyant real estate market, and real estate values had started to fall in 1996, leading ING Barings to estimate that the sector's bad loans (again, prior to the crisis) exceeded 14 percent of outstanding credit.[18] In Korea the conglomerate *chaebols,* which formed the backbone of the economy, were showing surprisingly poor results: low returns and, increasingly, losses. In Indonesia, the business and banking systems were both thoroughly corrupted by the constant intrusions of President Suharto and his family. Similarly, prior to the Mexican crisis of 1994, Mexican banks were in poor shape. They had been privatized in 1990–1991, often sold at very high prices to wealthy industrialists, and then allowed to expand lending very quickly (often to insiders) despite the inexperience and lack of credit skills of the staffs.

In Asia, a common theme across crisis countries was overinvestment, which produced a low return on investment: too many projects purchased too carelessly at too high a price.[19] Some analysts blame corporate governance: Banks were not monitoring firms to ensure that the cash flows of projects would provide a rate of return sufficient to pay the cost of capital. The very impressive success of Asian economies created an ethic of growth for its own sake, often without sufficient attention to value creation. The magnitude of nonperforming loans in banks before the crisis broke is testimony to value destruction; that is, projects whose returns are below the cost of capital.

At a deeper level, however, economy-wide moral hazard may underlie the tolerance for poor governance. As noted in Chapter 7, EFM governments often give assurance to both banks and firms, implicitly or explicitly, that the government will stand by them in the event of trouble. This cuts off the lower tail of return distributions and lets both banks and firms focus solely on the good outcomes. The result is indistinguishable from extraordinary optimism and overconfidence; asset prices are driven up to what Paul Krugman termed "Pangloss values": values in the best of all possible worlds.[20]

This national-level moral hazard has an international parallel. If global lenders believe that the IMF will routinely bail out overextended countries, then debt flows into such countries will be greater than would otherwise occur, and the lenders and borrowers will both be less concerned about the foreign exchange risk and liquidity risk that such debt flows entail.[21] Efforts by government at the national or international level designed to reduce or eliminate risk in the financial system seem instead to increase risk. It is similar to the example of automobile safety, in which the presence of seat belts in cars often leads to more aggressive, overconfident driving and hence to more accidents.

If the essential problem is troubled banks, then the policy advice must be to repair the banks and the regulatory system. In particular, if the problem is massive bank loan losses and generalized moral hazard based on anticipations of bailout, the advice must be to close insolvent banks promptly and not bail out their shareholders or managements. If the loan losses have resulted from poor corporate governance, then governance should be reformed and corporations restructured. If the losses have resulted from lack of credit skills at the banks and poor bank supervision in the government, the prescription must be not only training but also mergers with foreign banks that have demonstrated such skills.

---

[18]Ibid, p. 32.

[19]Pomerleano (1998).

[20]After the incurably optimistic Doctor Pangloss in Voltaire's *Candide:* Krugman (1998), p. 5.

[21]See McKinnon and Pill (1996 and 1998), Calomiris (1998), and Calomiris and Meltzer (1999).

These are essentially the policy prescriptions of the World Bank and International Monetary Fund, which subscribe to the view that recent financial crises largely reflect weak fundamentals.[22] Unfortunately, they are the most painful of all the prescriptions because they cut the most deeply. It is understandable that the affected governments much prefer the liquidity view, under which they need more loans but not fundamental reforms. Furthermore, once a country finds itself in a financial crisis it is also suffering a deep recession, and politically it is extremely unpopular to restructure corporations by shutting down plants, selling assets, and closing failed banks. All such actions aggravate the immediate economic problem of falling production. The merits of fundamental reforms are found only in their longer-term effects, which political considerations encourage rulers to discount.

Reconciling the Explanations

It may not be possible to reconcile advocates of very different policy recommendations. But the purpose of this book is not to advocate policy but to increase understanding. As noted at the beginning of this chapter, financial crises happen when a number of circumstances occur jointly. From this perspective, the explanations are not alternatives so much as common elements that need to be reconciled.

For example, the emphasis on bank loan losses and moral hazard combines well with the view that crises are brought on by overborrowing. Indeed, moral hazard is precisely the explanation for overborrowing adopted by some researchers, and overborrowing is the consequence one would expect if government aggressively protects firms and banks against risk.[23] Even if moral hazard were not a factor, it would be hard to construct any model of overborrowing and overlending that did not result in serious bank loan losses. Therefore, the emphasis on weak banks and the concept of illiquidity as excessive debt are highly compatible.

Moral hazard and illiquidity also combine well in the following sense. Government safety nets are now almost universal, yet the sort of financial crisis described in this chapter seems to affect only a few countries that have exposed themselves to large-scale foreign exchange and liquidity risk. Yet when we dig deeper, asking which countries get into this position, we often find it is those such as Mexico, Thailand, Indonesia, and Korea that have the most troubled banks. We have seen that banks with high levels of nonperforming loans may be considered insolvent, and that insolvent banks are the most likely to take massive risks, gambling on resurrection. Moral hazard explains why countries whose banks have high levels of nonperforming loans are so frequently the countries that get into risky, illiquid positions.

Furthermore, the focus on weak banks can be directly connected with currency overvaluation where the exchange rate is pegged. In the early models of currency overvaluation, crises did not occur until actual inflation occurred and undermined the real exchange rate. Yet *anticipated* inflation can also trigger a speculative attack. Since bank deposits are now almost universally protected by governments, an observation of massive loan losses can be translated directly into a need for large-scale government expenditure, with all the inflationary consequences such expenditure would probably have.

If we therefore shift the emphasis from *current* deficits and inflation to *prospective* deficits and inflation, the fundamentalist and currency overvaluation views are easy to reconcile: Rational holders of the EFM currency will want to sell as soon as

---

[22]For the views of prominent economists at the World Bank and the IMF, see Caprio and Honohan (1999) and Fischer (1999).

[23]McKinnon and Pill (1996 and 1998).

they anticipate government action to bail out the banks.[24] This could explain why Asian currencies were attacked when their reserves were strong and their trade balances were either in surplus or moderate deficit, but their banks were weak. It explains why visibly weak banks often precede financial crises.

It is also undoubtedly true that a financial crisis makes the condition of banks and firms far worse than was true before the crisis. The vicious cycle of weakening banks, falling currency, and rising interest rates helps us to see the extreme nature of the events and to understand why equilibrium is not easily restored. If currency overvaluation were the only problem, devaluation might restore equilibrium, as happened in Taiwan and Brazil. If illiquidity were the only problem, a renegotiation of debt terms could restore equilibrium. It is the interaction of weak banks and overleveraged firms with currency collapse that leads EFM crises into a spiraling disequilibrium.

A central tenet of the liquidity view is that markets are erratic and possibly irrational, and that even if your fundamentals are strong and your currency is not overvalued you can be undone by speculative attack. The best defense against this is to build liquidity: to have plenty of reserves and unused loan commitments, and not to let the structure of debt become too heavily short term.[25] This is very sound advice and not at all incompatible with keeping fundamentals strong as well. A country that has both strong fundamentals and liquidity is well prepared for whatever markets may hold.

This integrated view of financial crises is supported by a study of 20 different countries during 1995, some of which experienced financial crisis and some did not. Through regression analysis, the researchers found three factors that taken together explain most of the 20 outcomes: high real exchange rate appreciation, low reserves (i.e., low liquidity), and a weak banking system. While contagion and self-fulfilling panic may well occur, it seems to strike selectively at countries where these three factors are simultaneously present.[26]

The Mexican Crisis of 1994–1995

Facts of the Crisis

Mexico was severely damaged during the debt crisis of the 1980s, but went through an impressive set of reforms in connection with its Brady Plan debt restructuring—opening to foreign competition, aggressive privatization, deregulation, and fiscal reform—all in the context of substantial political democratization as well. President Carlos Salinas of Mexico had acquired a strong international reputation, close to celebrity status, as a result of these accomplishments. The peso was attached to the dollar with a floating trading band as described more fully below. Inflation had declined substantially and Mexico had attracted substantial outside capital during the early 1990s. As a result, it had built up significant foreign exchange reserves. Table 8.1 summarizes a few macroeconomic indicators. In addition, Mexico benefited from a special relationship with the United States that was institutionalized in the North American Free Trade Agreement (NAFTA) in 1993. In short, everything seemed to be going exceptionally well as late as 1993.

The Mexican economy slipped into recession in late 1993 and capital inflows began to slow. Stock prices peaked in February 1994. A series of political setbacks in

---

[24]Burnside, Eichenbaum, and Rebelo (1999).
[25]Feldstein (1999).
[26]Sachs, Tornell, and Velasco (1996).

TABLE 8.1   **Mexican Macroeconomic Indicators**
(percentages)

	1990	1991	1992	1993	1994
Exports / GDP	15.8	13.8	12.6	12.4	13.1
Imports / GDP	16.9	17.0	18.1	16.7	18.9
Trade balance / GDP	−1.1	−3.2	−5.5	−4.3	−5.8
Private consumption / GDP	70.9	71.8	72.2	71.5	71.0
Private saving / GDP	12.5	10.3	9.5	8.9	10.7
Inflation of CPI	26.7	22.7	15.5	9.8	7.0
Exchange rate (pesos/$)	2.95	3.07	3.12	3.11	5.33

Source: Sachs, Tornell, and Velasco (1995) and IFS.

1994 began to shake confidence in Mexico's stability. In January a populist uprising began in the southern state of Chiapas. On March 23 the presidential candidate of the dominant Institutional Revolutionary Party (PRI), Luis Donaldo Colosio, was assassinated. He was replaced by the relatively unknown Ernesto Zedillo, who went on to win the presidential election in August. But in September the secretary general of the PRI, José Francisco Ruíz Massieu, was also assassinated. In November, Deputy Attorney General Mario Ruíz Massieu resigned, alleging a cover-up of the murder of his brother, which he suggested might involve drug traffickers in league with high-level politicians. And just before Zedillo took office in December, violence again erupted in Chiapas.

Capital inflows had reached a peak of $30 billion in 1993, primarily portfolio investments of both debt and equity. But in March 1994, following the Colosio assassination, there was a net outflow. To stem a possible flight of capital by both external and internal investors, the Mexican government shifted its financing strategy from peso-denominated notes (*cetes*), to notes payable in pesos but indexed to the peso–dollar exchange rate (*tesobonos*). From April to November the use of *tesobonos* was so predominant that it accounted for half of the value of all government debt outstanding at the end of November. Foreign exchange reserves crested at $29.0 billion in February 1994 but declined by $3.4 billion in March and by another $8.2 billion in April. After the shift to *tesobonos,* reserves stabilized until November.[27]

Mexico had instituted a fixed currency peg in 1988, but this was modified in 1989 to a crawling peg and then in late 1991 to a crawling trading band. There was a fixed limit on peso appreciation, but the range of peso depreciation widened gradually at a rate somewhat less than the rate of relative peso inflation. From late February to late April, the exchange rate drifted about 4 percent to the limit of its permitted depreciation. At that point interest rates on 91-day *cetes* rose from 10 percent in late March to 18 percent in late April, and stayed in the range of 16 to 18 percent through August, when they began to decline into the 13 to 15 percent range through mid-December. The exchange rate hovered near its intervention limit. Spreads on Brady bonds increased from 140 basis points (bp) in early 1994 to a peak of 528 bp on April 21 before settling into a range of 300 to 460 bp.

In November, however, selling of the peso and capital outflows resumed. Reserves dropped from $17.2 billion at the end of October, to $12.5 billion at the end of November, to $6.1 billion at the end of December; it was obvious that Mexico was on

---

[27]International Monetary Fund (1995).

an unsustainable path. On December 1, President Zedillo took office. International investors waited expectantly for an announced program to limit fiscal risk, reform the banking system, and raise interest rates in support of the currency peg. But no such announcement was made and markets quickly lost confidence in the new administration. On December 20 Mexico widened the intervention band for the peso, allowing a *de facto* devaluation of 15 percent. But the markets pushed rapidly through the new limit, and on December 22 the peso was allowed to float. The peso went into free fall, losing more than half of its value in the next few months.

The currency collapse was immediately followed by a collapse of the banking system and the real economy whose magnitude startled most observers. On January 2, 1995, an \$18 billion credit to Mexico from the governments of the United States and Canada, the Bank for International Settlements (BIS), and several U.S. commercial banks was announced, but it was quickly replaced with a \$50 billion package from the United States, the IMF, the World Bank, the Inter-American Development Bank, and the commercial banks. Peso interest rates rose to a high of 80 percent by March, and spreads on Brady bonds widened to more than 10 percent. Mexico's new economic plan, adopted in March 1995, featured bank bailout funds, increased taxes, cuts in spending, and curbs on wages.

Argentina and Brazil, in a bout of what appeared to be contagion, were hit by currency selling. By the end of March 1995, Argentina had lost one-third of its reserves. Its local interest rates rose from 9.5 percent on December 19 to 23.0 percent a week later. Its currency board system survived the attack but at a cost: The loss of reserves automatically contracted the money supply by a like amount, and the economy went into a severe recession. The combination of high interest rates and the collapsing real economy caused a number of bank failures and a need for bank restructuring.

Currency Overvaluation

What caused this financial crisis? Many economists pointed to currency overvaluation as the most obvious culprit, since some inflation had continued even as the currency was held relatively stable. Indeed, several economists had been expressing alarm since 1992 at the rising real exchange rate.[28] One must give considerable weight to any observers who correctly anticipate a financial crisis, because it suggests that these observers were looking at significant measures.

The real exchange rate can be computed against either consumer prices or wholesale prices. Table 8.2 traces nominal changes in the peso/dollar nominal rate (i.e., peso price of the dollar) and the real exchange rate index during 1991–1995. It can be seen by this measure that the peso appreciated (dollar depreciated) in real terms by about 20 percent between early 1990 and early 1994. Those who had sounded the alarm about this measure estimated that the peso was overvalued by approximately 20 to 25 percent.

Another way of understanding whether exchange rates are sustainable is to examine the trade balance, because if a currency is truly overvalued then its exports should come under competitive pressure while its imports would expand. As can be seen in Table 8.1, the trade balance deteriorated during 1990–1992. This seems to confirm that the currency was overvalued. Mexican officials, however, insisted that this interpretation was incorrect. They noted that Mexican exports are dominated by oil, whose world price fell steadily through the 1990s, lowering the exports of all petroleum

---

[28]Dornbusch (1993) and Edwards (1994).

TABLE 8.2   Mexican Inflation and Exchange Rates

Year	Quarter	Inflation (%)	Nominal Foreign Exchange Rate Change (%)	Real Foreign Exchange Rate Index (1980 = 100)
1991	I	7.32	0.67	127.09
	II	3.61	1.22	124.88
	III	2.74	1.30	124.08
	IV	4.60	0.90	120.61
1992	I	5.40	−0.03	115.15
	II	2.71	0.92	114.11
	III	2.00	0.10	112.82
	IV	2.52	0.73	111.68
1993	I	3.27	−0.42	108.58
	II	1.85	0.19	107.69
	III	1.62	0.10	106.46
	IV	1.66	0.30	105.80
1994	I	1.94	1.34	105.84
	II	1.54	5.51	110.66
	III	1.45	1.56	111.75
	IV	1.85	5.95	116.76
1995	I	8.00	58.09	172.41

Source: Sachs, Tornell, and Velasco (1995).

exporters. This can hardly be taken as evidence about the Mexican exchange rate, since oil is priced in dollars and the price decline was a world phenomenon. They pointed out that Mexican manufacturing exports were actually growing in the 1990s at about the pace of East Asian exports.[29]

Finally, it can be seen in Table 8.1 that private saving dropped materially in the 1990–1993 period. This has been interpreted as the result of a rise in imports and consumption financed by the capital flows, a distortion ultimately caused by an overvalued currency. While an overvalued currency could indeed stimulate excessive imports of consumer goods, Table 8.1 shows that imports and consumption were relatively stable over the 1990–1993 period.

Taking these observations as a whole, one can conclude that some currency overvaluation was doubtless present in Mexico during the early 1990s, but that its magnitude was not so large nor its effects so obvious that a crisis of this depth can be attributed solely to it. A consideration of other factors is warranted.

Illiquidity

Mexico began 1994 with very high reserves and by this measure appeared to have ample liquidity. However, a broader view of liquidity that takes into account the maturity structure of the government debt and the government-insured commercial bank debt reveals heavy reliance on short-term borrowing.

We have seen that in an inflationary economy such as Mexico's, local debt markets are distorted by high interest rates, including not only expected inflation but also an inflation premium, and by short maturities. Few investors were willing to hold long-term peso paper in 1994; the inflation risk was simply too great. Of necessity, the

[29]Gil-Díaz and Carstens (1997).

government financed itself at short term. To some extent the lack of liquidity was not a matter of choice.

The more interesting question about government funding is why it shifted from *cetes* to *tesobonos* in the spring of 1994, so that by the end of the year about half of the government's debt was linked to the dollar. The apparent answer is that the market required foreign exchange protection as well as short maturity to continue financing the government on the terms and in the quantities required. A consortium known as the Weston Forum approached the Mexican government soon after the March assassination and suggested issuing medium-term debt *tesobonos* to limit rollover risk. The government, however, maintained its short-term debt structure in order to economize on the cost of debt service.[30] By the end of 1994, however, as devaluation became more probable, even *tesobonos* could no longer be sold.

The Mexican case illustrates how fundamental problems that a government fails to address make that government increasingly vulnerable and erode its reserves. Whether one views the speculative attack on the peso as a rational response to fundamental weakness or as an irrational, self-fulfilling panic, in either case longer-term debt would have been helpful in mitigating the extent of the collapse. But it is not obvious what more the government could have done to enhance its liquidity position without simultaneously addressing the fundamental loss of confidence in its exchange rate policy.

Another influence favoring short-term dollar-denominated debt may have been the expectation by foreign investors that the IMF would most likely protect this kind of debt (partly because of the liquidity risk that failing to protect such debt entailed). In the event, the IMF/U.S. Treasury bridge loan to Mexico made it possible for short-term debt holders to exit whole.

At the end of 1993, Mexican external debt stood at $34.7 billion, most of which could have been immediately repaid from reserves. Yet these reserves were exhausted in a yearlong battle to defend the currency peg. Mexico's use of its foreign exchange reserves to purchase pesos during 1994 might have caused a major contraction in internal liquidity. Indeed, that is precisely what happened in Argentina, where the currency board system required such a contraction, much as the classic gold standard would have required a century earlier. But Mexico sterilized its reserve outflows; that is, it expanded domestic credit in amounts almost perfectly matched to its loss of reserves. The goal of sterilization is to avoid a domestic liquidity squeeze, which would have had (and did have in Argentina) a powerful contractionary effect. But this expands domestic credit, which implies future inflation and adds further to the risk of devaluation. In short, provision of internal liquidity can be at cross-purposes with the austerity required to maintain the credibility of a currency peg.

Troubled Banks

Mexico's bank problems are well known and date back to the nationalization of the banks in 1982, at the onset of the debt crisis. The government at that time preempted most of the national savings to finance its deficit, and the banks held few assets except government bonds. During this period, any skills in credit analysis and modern banking that Mexican banks might have had surely atrophied. Recognizing the need for much-improved banking, President Salinas decided to privatize the banks rapidly and liberalize the financial system relatively early on in his six-year term.

---

[30] *The Wall Street Journal*, June 14, 1994, p. A1.

By 1992 the program was substantially complete. The government sold banks at high prices, in some cases more than four times book value, generally to families that already controlled industrial groups and so had the financial resources to bid. Two Bank of Mexico officials who adamantly denied that the peso was overvalued in 1994 readily admitted the problems in the banking system. Following is their summary of the liberalization process:

- The financial sector was liberalized, lending and borrowing rates were freed, and directed credit was abolished.
- Bank reserve requirements were eliminated.
- To calculate nonperforming loans, banks applied "due payments" criteria: misleadingly, the amount of payments due past 90 days was recorded as delinquent loans instead of the value of the loans themselves.
- Banks were hastily privatized—in many instances with no due respect to "fit and proper" criteria in the selection of new shareholders or their top officers.
- Several banks were purchased without their new owners proceeding to their proper capitalization, since shareholders often leveraged their stock acquisitions, sometimes with loans provided by the very banks that had been bought out.
- Commercial banks had lost a substantial amount of human capital at the higher echelons while under public management. With these officials, institutional memory migrated as well.
- The problem of "moral hazard" (or perverse incentives) was enhanced by the full government backing of bank deposits. This backing did not distinguish between interbank borrowings, borrowings from abroad, or deposits by large treasuries. In addition, homogeneous premiums were applied to all banks, regardless of their creditworthiness.
- There were no capitalization rules based on portfolio market risk. This encouraged asset–liability mismatches that in turn led to a highly liquid liability structure—more than two-thirds overnight for the banks—with the potential to create huge strains on the lender-of-last-resort capabilities of the central bank.
- Banking supervision capacity was weak to begin with, and it became overwhelmed by the great increase in the portfolio of banks.
- Some commercial banks were able to have access in disproportionate amounts to money market funds because of their confidence that, on any particular day, they could rely on an unlimited supply of daylight overdraft facilities.
- Mexico did not have efficient credit bureaus.
- There was a phenomenal expansion of credit from the development banks.[31]

The financial liberalization resulted in greatly expanded credit from the banking system to the private sector. In 1988 commercial bank loans to the private sector equaled 10.6 percent of GDP. In just two years this had grown to 20.6 percent, and by 1993 it had reached 34.5 percent.[32] Loan growth as rapid as this often results in substantial credit losses, since rapid lending tends to be careless lending, and in the case of Mexico there were additional factors at work.

---

[31]Gil-Díaz and Carstens (1997), pp. 189–90.
[32]Rojas-Suárez and Weisbrod (1995), p. 31.

First, analytic skills were lost during the 1980s. Not only did the new bank owners have little or no experience in credit analysis, but they also inherited a staff that for a decade had done little more than fill the portfolio with government bonds. Second, the Banco de Mexico similarly lacked skills to monitor and examine the new banks, nor did it have clear prudential rules, as suggested by the above list.

Third, the new owners were almost by definition wealthy industrialists, because few others had the resources to bid. They had within their existing companies plenty of lending opportunities, so we would expect substantial connected lending. The above list tells us that in some cases the banks financed their own acquisition; this is a particularly dangerous form of connected lending, since it serves to reduce the bank's true capital without appearing to do so, greatly magnifying moral hazard. The list also tells us that some banks were significantly undercapitalized, which again leads us to expect serious moral hazard; the payoff-truncation problem underlying moral hazard worsens as capital declines, implying less downside loss from risk taking.

The industrialists who bought the banks were among the strongest supporters of President Salinas and some of the principal advocates of his liberalization program. Elections were scheduled for August 1994, and the PRI needed and obtained this group's support. In part, that support entailed a willingness to expand the amount of consumer lending prior to the election to mitigate the effects of economic deceleration on the PRI's popularity. There was a long and quite explicit tradition in Mexico of "compensating" such supporters for their support.[33] Although there is no public proof, we may plausibly surmise that bank owners could expect the PRI to support them in the event of trouble. Thus, all the ingredients for moral hazard were likely in place: little initial bank capital, insider lending, low-quality loans motivated by political considerations (which further erode bank capital), and the anticipation of a taxpayer-financed bailout of weak banks.

The official statistics for loan loss reserves of Mexican banks relative to average loans at year-end 1993 stood at 3.7 percent for large banks and 3.9 percent for small banks.[34] This represents the amount of loss that bank managers publicly declared that they anticipated. The reported level of nonperforming loans was 7.4 percent of total loans in 1994 but, as noted in the list above, this grossly understated the true amount of loan principal at risk since only the unpaid amounts are counted. Private sources estimated true levels of nonperforming loans at 2–3 times official estimates.

In short, there is every reason to believe that the Mexican banks were in trouble in 1994, with high levels of nonperforming loans and reasons to believe the government would bail them out, well before the financial crisis struck in December. If so, we would expect to see them taking large risks, gambling on resurrection. That is exactly what they did in the derivatives market.[35]

Under Mexican law and regulation of the early 1990s, it was illegal for Mexican banks to take foreign exchange exposure higher than 15 percent of capital. In his remarkable study of the Mexican crisis, Peter Garber showed that banks easily circumvented these rules by the use of derivatives such as those shown in the box on page 313. Garber estimated that the volume of *tesobono* swaps totaled $16 billion, which is about equal to the total amount of *tesobonos* registered with foreign

---

[33]Dresser (1997).

[34]Rojas-Suárez and Weisbrod (1995), p. 38.

[35]Material on Mexican derivatives is based on Garber (1998).

investors in December 1994. In other words, virtually *none* of the apparent *tesobono* sales to foreign investors represented true financing of the Mexican government by such investors; substantially *all* were swapped and represented the taking of *tesobono*/dollar risk by Mexican banks, financed by dollar lending from New York banks to Mexican banks. This insight is confirmed by the observation that after the devaluation there were huge new losses in Mexican banks but very few in New York banks.

The three derivatives transactions described in the box all took place in large quantity during 1994. They did represent different levels of exposure to a devaluation, however. The structured notes, equivalent to borrowing dollars and holding pesos on a leveraged basis, were the purest example of a foreign exchange risk. With the rates of *cetes* at 16 to 18 percent and dollar LIBOR at 4 to 6 percent during the April–December period, the apparent profit of this position was huge, say 12 percent less whatever spread above LIBOR the Mexican banks had to pay. Assuming a 1 percent spread, the net profit of 11 percent times about $2 billion exposure of Mexican banks under structured notes represents a possible profit of $220 million a year, assuming no devaluation. Of course, the existence of the large interest rate differential implies that the fixed exchange rate lacks credibility.[36]

The *tesobono* swaps had a somewhat lower risk/return profile. *Tesobonos* yielded 8–10 percent during this period, so the comparable net profit would have been 4 percent less a 1-percent spread, or 3 percent. However, the volume outstanding was about $16 billion, so the potential profit was $480 million a year, assuming Mexico did not default on its *tesobono* payments. Since *tesobono* payments were linked to dollars, the *tesobono* swap was essentially a speculation on whether Mexico would be able to service its *tesobono* obligations during a currency crisis. In the event, Mexico did have difficulty making such payments, and one of the main purposes of the U.S. bailout was to enable Mexico not to default on its *tesobonos*. This appeared to be a benefit to the U.S. banks that were the registered holders of the *tesobonos*. In reality, it was primarily a benefit to the Mexican banks, ultimately paid for by the Mexican taxpayers.

Garber also traced the consequences of the derivative holdings on the capital flow reversals. For example, *tesobono* yields rose from 18 percent to 24 percent during the late autumn of 1994, causing their market value to fall. Under the *tesobono* swap arrangements, the New York banks could then call for additional margin, which would force the Mexican banks to sell pesos for dollars. The same would be true of equity swaps in the face of a falling Mexican stock market. Both types of margin calls would create pressure in the foreign exchange market.

The Mexican authorities discovered the banks' uses of structured notes in September 1994. When they realized that these notes represented packets of illegal foreign exchange risk, they required the banks to cover their risks by buying dollars. Since about $2 billion of such notes were outstanding, this required the sale of pesos worth about $2 billion, adding to foreign exchange pressure.

Numerous observers have commented that the selling of pesos in the autumn of 1994, which appeared to be speculative attack, originated in Mexico rather than outside. The derivatives analysis clarifies who these speculators were: They were

---

[36]McKinnon and Pill (1999).

How Mexican Derivatives Worked

The creativity of capital markets led to an explosion of derivative products in the 1980s. In the 1990s this creativity was applied to EFMs in general and Mexico in particular. In Mexico, their net effect was (1) to increase greatly the risk of Mexican banks, (2) to give Mexican banks the possibility of large profits if Mexico did not suffer a financial crisis, and (3) to circumvent prudential regulations that were supposed to prevent Mexican banks from taking such risks. Following is a sample of the derivatives in question.

Tesobono Swap

A New York bank buys $1 billion of *tesobonos,* notes payable in pesos but indexed to the peso–dollar exchange rate. It enters into a swap agreement under which it remits payments on the *tesobonos* to a Mexican bank and receives payments (i.e., LIBOR plus a spread) on a notional loan of $1 billion in return. The Mexican bank puts up $200 million of collateral to secure its obligation under the swap.

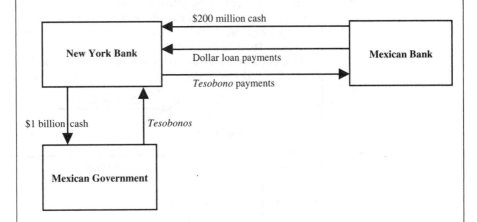

This appears to be a case of a New York bank agreeing to finance the Mexican government by buying *tesobonos,* earning the high *tesobono* return, and taking the related risk. In reality, the New York bank's risk is reduced by the $200 million of collateral and its return is reduced to a normal dollar loan yield. It is the Mexican bank that takes a risk equivalent to borrowing dollars to buy *tesobonos.*

Equity Swap

An equity swap does substantially the same thing, using a Mexican stock instead of *tesobonos.* Here the New York bank appears to be making a stock market investment in Mexico. But in reality it is flowing the total return on the stock (dividends and any appreciation or depreciation) to a Mexican bank in return for a loan of $1 billion secured by the stock plus $200 million collateral. The Mexican bank is investing $200 million and taking $1 billion of equity risk:

continued

concluded

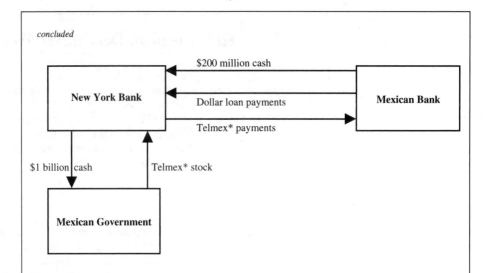

Structured Notes

Structured notes take many forms, but the basic idea of a "bullish obligation on the peso" is that a New York bank sells to the Mexican bank a note payable in dollars whose interest and principal are heavily indexed to the peso/dollar exchange rate under a complex formula. The note pays full principal and a large amount of interest if the peso does not devalue, but very little interest or principal is returned if the peso devalues substantially. The New York bank hedges its risk by buying peso securities such as *cetes*.

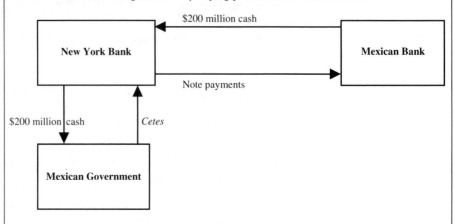

It appears as if the New York bank is financing the Mexican government by buying *cetes*, taking the foreign exchange risk and earning the high return on *cetes*. In reality, the New York bank flows most of the positive and negative consequences of owning *cetes* through to the Mexican bank, whose risk and reward are similar to those of borrowing dollars and buying *cetes* itself.

———

*The Mexican telephone company.

Source: Garber (1998).

primarily Mexican banks scrambling to come up with increased dollar collateral for their collapsing *tesobono* and equity swaps and cover for their structured notes.

This analysis lends considerable credence to the notion that excessive risk taking by troubled Mexican banks was a central ingredient in the Mexican financial crisis, whose ultimate cost to the Mexican government has been estimated at about 15 to 20 percent of Mexican GDP. Of course, this analysis does not imply that derivatives transactions in EFMs are a destabilizing factor in general. When domestic banks face proper incentives to use derivatives to hedge or diversify their risks, such contracts can be a stabilizing influence on EFM banking systems.

The Asian Crisis of 1997–1998

Facts of the Crisis

The financial crisis of East Asia was even more surprising than the one in Mexico because East Asia appeared to contain some of the most successful emerging markets. Real GDP growth for 1992–1995 had averaged more than 9 percent for the region as a whole, biased upward by exceptional growth rates in China. Indonesia, Malaysia, and Thailand all grew at more than 7 percent, and even the Philippines was rising toward 6 percent. Inflation was moderate throughout the region. Only the Philippines had fiscal deficits and inflation that reached double digits; Thailand had a fiscal surplus in every year from 1988 to 1996.

Japan had created a role model for East Asia in the 1960s and 1970s that included a highly competitive private economy, an intense focus on exports, restrictions on imports, bank-centered corporate governance and significant government direction of the economy through the banks. The model seemed extraordinarily effective throughout the 1980s, even as Latin America was grappling with its debt crisis and Central and Eastern Europe were struggling to rid themselves of communism. Japan was even outcompeting the United States in several key industries.

East Asian industrialization moved through a progression of increasingly sophisticated industries. It began with the most labor-intensive industries such as apparel, shoes, and toys where low local wages gave a large competitive advantage. As this succeeded and wages rose, production moved to more complex products such as consumer electronics. After that, the focus shifted to heavier industries such as chemicals and steel, and then to quite sophisticated processes such as automobile assembly where management skills and technology become increasingly important. Finally, production would be extended to include pharmaceuticals, computer chips, robotics, and aircraft, the most technically demanding industries of all.

By the 1980s, Korea and Taiwan had successfully followed this model and moved most of the way up the industrial ladder, so that they were increasingly referred to not as "developing" but as "newly industrialized." Singapore and Hong Kong were more prosperous and modern than many Western cities. Thailand, Malaysia, Indonesia, and the Philippines had moved through the lowest economic niche and were pressing upward. China, with wage rates one-tenth those of Korea and Taiwan, had awakened to its opportunities and dominated the labor-intensive bottom of the ladder through export-oriented joint ventures along its coast.

Countries further up the industrial pecking order invested in those further down. Thus, Japanese companies, freeing themselves from their national boundaries, invested heavily in Southeast Asia. In turn, the very prosperous Chinese business class of Southeast Asia was investing heavily in China. The entire region appeared to be an integrated economic machine of impressive strength. As late as December 1996, the IMF published a highly laudatory booklet titled *Thailand: The Road to Sustained Growth.* Net private capital flows into East Asia had increased steadily throughout the 1990s, reaching a peak of $110 billion in 1996.

Yet some signs of slowdown were in the air. Asian stocks on average had not risen above the levels reached at the end of 1993. Paul Krugman and Alwyn Young had published apparently heretical articles in 1994 and 1995 that questioned the sustainability of the "Asian miracle."[37] Japan, the locomotive economy of the region, had entered a major recession in the 1990s that it seemed unable to bring to an end. Foreign trade had slowed throughout the region. Serious levels of nonperforming loans were reported in banks throughout East Asia, including particularly those of Japan, China, Korea, and Thailand. Yet almost no one anticipated the size of the economic collapse that came.

Table 8.3 shows macroeconomic indicators in 1996 for the primary crisis countries. The slowing of both exports and imports from 1995 to 1996 is clear. But real growth in all five economies was continuing at an impressive pace and inflation was moderate. The current account deficit in Thailand had become quite large, but its debt was moderate compared to GDP, so it appeared the deficit could readily be financed. Government budgets (as measured through traditional fiscal accounts) were approximately balanced throughout the region.

The East Asian currencies were all pegged in one degree or another to the U.S. dollar. Hong Kong had a currency board and most of the other countries had some version of a crawling peg with trading bands. Before the second half of 1997 only two currencies seemed under pressure: The Korean won and the Thai baht had both appreciated through late 1995 and then depreciated substantially within their trading bands through 1996 and into 1997.

The Bank of Thailand intervened heavily to support the baht in May 1997, began to introduce capital controls, and allowed interest rates to rise. But these measures did not stem the tide, and heavy selling resumed in late May and June. On July 2, Thailand

TABLE 8.3   Macroeconomic Indicators in Selected East Asian Countries
(percentages)

	Thailand	*Malaysia*	*Indonesia*	*Philippines*	*Korea*
1995					
Growth of exports	25.1	26.0	13.4	31.6	30.3
Growth of imports	30.0	30.5	27.9	25.7	32.0
1996					
Growth of exports	−1.3	6.7	10.4	17.5	5.3
Growth of imports	11.6	1.3	11.1	20.9	12.2
Inflation	5.8	3.5	6.5	8.4	4.5
Current account / GDP	−7.9	−4.9	−3.4	−4.7	−4.8
External debt / GDP	19.8	28.8	38.9	N/A	11.2
Real growth of GDP	5.5	8.6	8.0	5.5	7.1

Source: Garnaut (1998).

---

[37]Krugman (1994) and Young (1995).

abandoned its exchange rate peg and allowed the baht to float, whereupon it fell by about 10 percent. The selling continued and quickly spread to the Philippines, which floated its peso on July 11; Malaysia, which floated the ringgit on July 14; and Indonesia, which floated the rupiah on August 14.

These actions did not lead to a new equilibrium, however. Instead, the selling continued heavily in all affected countries and spread to most other currencies in the region. All stock markets in the region also came under heavy selling pressure as capital flows went into reverse. Taiwan abandoned its peg of the Taiwan dollar on October 17, and the Hong Kong currency board was put to a severe test, much like Argentina's in 1995. Downward pressure on the Korean currency and stock market accelerated at the end of October. The Korean authorities widened the won's trading band from 4½ percent to 20 percent on November 20 and requested assistance from the IMF. Thailand, the Philippines, and Indonesia made similar requests.

Some currencies in the region, such as those of Taiwan and Singapore, recovered their equilibrium, and Hong Kong's currency board held fast. But the other currencies were in free fall from which no relief was in sight. From June 1997 to September 1998, currency declines against the dollar were 34 percent for Korea, 37 percent for Thailand, 38 percent for Philippines, 40 percent for Malaysia, and an astonishing 78 percent for Indonesia.[38] All countries in the region went into a major recession of the real economy, and bank failures were widespread.

How could this have happened? Certainly each of the countries was different and had its own mix of problems and opportunities, but there were also some common threads. Let us turn to our three generic explanations to see how well they fit.

Currency Overvaluation

The problem of overvaluation in East Asia was by no means as evident as it was in Mexico. The Asian currencies were generally pegged to the dollar, but the peg floated and inflation was moderate, so there was little opportunity for real exchange rates (nominal exchange rates relative to the ratio of domestic-to-foreign price levels) to rise.

Table 8.4 shows the evolution of bilateral real exchange rates against the U.S. dollar from 1987 through 1997. The year-end 1996 rates were slightly above their previous

TABLE 8.4   **Year-End Real Effective Exchange Rates versus the Dollar**
(Average 1990 = 100)

	Thailand	Malaysia	Indonesia	Philippines	Korea
1987	95.2	111.1	101.1	99.0	87.0
1988	97.3	100.5	98.8	101.7	101.9
1989	99.3	102.9	101.9	108.2	106.2
1990	102.2	97.1	97.4	92.4	96.1
1991	99.0	96.9	99.6	103.1	91.5
1992	99.7	109.7	100.8	107.1	87.7
1993	101.9	111.0	103.8	97.4	85.2
1994	98.3	107.1	101.0	111.7	84.7
1995	101.7	106.9	100.5	109.5	87.7
1996	107.6	112.1	105.4	116.3	87.1
1997	72.3	84.8	62.3	90.8	59.2

Source: J.P. Morgan, as elaborated by Chang and Velasco (1998).

---

[38]International Monetary Fund (1998).

highs in four of the five currencies, but there is no evidence of serious real exchange rate appreciation. Indeed, the dramatic collapse by the end of 1997 is the anomalous number, and suggests serious disequilibrium on the low side in 1997. Bilateral rates against the Japanese yen would show a somewhat different story, since the yen depreciated materially against the dollar in the two years prior to the crisis, from mid-1995 to mid-1997, and Japan was an important trading partner for all Asian economies. Indeed, a slowing of trade with Japan was the main reason for the decline in foreign trade noted in Table 8.3.

When real exchange rates are calculated against a trade-weighted blend of currencies (1988–1990 trade weights), the following picture emerges. Thailand, Indonesia, Malaysia, Korea, and Taiwan stay almost perfectly steady from 1988 through 1996. The Singapore dollar appreciates by about a third, the Philippine peso appreciates by nearly half, and the Hong Kong dollar appreciates by about two-thirds.[39] But Hong Kong and Singapore escaped serious damage and the Philippines was the least affected of the five crisis countries. Perversely for the overvaluation view, the four seriously affected economies were precisely those with no real appreciation on a trade-weighted basis.

It is tempting to conclude from the stability of real exchange rates that overvaluation was not a problem for East Asia, but such a conclusion neglects two important considerations. First, a constant real exchange rate may not be sustainable if a country is experiencing lower long-run productivity growth than the country to which its currency is pegged. Young (1995) and Krugman (1994) argued that Asian productivity growth was not sustainable, which implied a long-run need for the real exchange rates in Asian countries to depreciate. From that perspective, a constant real exchange rate against the dollar from 1995 to 1997 implied an overvaluation problem.

Second, a country's equilibrium real exchange rate can also be influenced by the real exchange rates of export-competing countries. When Thailand's currency depreciated in real terms, Indonesia, the Philippines, and Malaysia faced new competitive pressures in export markets, which forced them to depreciate their real exchange rates.

These considerations suggest that Asian currencies may have been overvalued prior to the Thai crisis and that the similarities in their export markets, combined with the Thai crisis, deepened the overvaluation problems in the region. Still, most observers argue that overvaluation cannot fully explain the depth of the crisis that gripped Asia in 1997.

Illiquidity

Liquidity risk certainly was high in the East Asian countries faced with financial crisis. First of all, the capital flows into the crisis countries during the mid-1990s were large, particularly in the form of bank lending, as shown in Table 8.5. By way of contrast, Taiwan was a net exporter of capital throughout the 1990s while China and Singapore relied almost exclusively on direct investment—and all three escaped serious damage.

Table 8.6 shows various measures of international liquidity. The first entry, foreign debt/exports, suggests that none of the crisis countries had exceptional amounts of foreign debt compared to their capacity to earn the foreign exchange to service it. From the perspective of these figures, sovereign insolvency does not appear to be a

---

[39]International Monetary Fund (1997), p. 8.

TABLE 8.5   **Net Private Capital Flows**
(percentages of GDP)

	1993	1994	1995	1996
Direct Investment				
Thailand	1.1	0.7	0.7	0.9
Malaysia	7.8	5.7	4.8	5.1
Indonesia	1.2	1.4	2.3	2.8
Philippines	1.6	2.0	1.8	1.6
Korea	−0.2	−0.3	−0.4	−0.4
Portfolio Investment				
Thailand	3.2	0.9	1.9	0.6
Malaysia	0	0	0	0
Indonesia	1.1	0.6	0.7	0.8
Philippines	−0.1	0.4	0.3	−0.2
Korea	3.2	1.8	1.9	2.3
Bank Lending				
Thailand	4.1	7.0	10.0	7.7
Malaysia	9.7	−4.2	4.1	4.5
Indonesia	0.7	1.9	3.1	2.7
Philippines	1.1	2.5	2.4	8.5
Korea	−1.5	1.7	2.5	3.0

Source: International Monetary Fund (1997).

problem. The structure of debt, however, does lean heavily toward short-term and foreign currency: About two-thirds to three-quarters of the debt is short term, and very little of it is denominated in local currency. Although short-term debt as a percentage of total debt remained approximately constant, reserves as a percentage of short-term debt declined materially in most countries between 1994 and 1997.

An important part of the liquidity theory of financial crises is the concept of self-fulfilling panic. The sudden quality of the Asian crisis is consistent with the view that illiquidity contributed to the collapse. Yet not all countries in the region suffered financial and economic collapse during the crisis. Taiwan was attacked and floated its currency, but soon restored equilibrium. Hong Kong resisted the attack and maintained its currency value. For the most part, Singapore seems to have been left out of the fray.

In other words, illiquidity probably played an important part in the Asian crises. But when the dust settled and the investors had a chance to look carefully at the facts, some countries (e.g., Taiwan) came out more or less unscathed while others (e.g., Indonesia) were damaged to a degree that will take years to repair.

Troubled Banks

To what extent were Asia's banks in trouble? The best broad measure of bank asset weakness is the fraction of loans that are nonperforming but, as we saw in Mexico, official figures often understate these. Table 8.7 shows some estimates of this measure in five countries, first as supplied by the governments in question to the Bank for International Settlements and then as estimated by two Hong Kong securities companies.

While there is clearly disagreement about the numbers between the private analysts and the public sector analysts, the overall pattern seems to suggest serious banking

TABLE 8.6   Measures of International Liquidity
(percentages)

	Thailand	Malaysia	Indonesia	Philippines	Korea
Foreign debt / exports (1996)	121.0	42.0	221.0	98.0	N/A
Short-term debt / reserves (June 1994)	99.2	25.2	173.0	40.5	161.0
Short-term debt / reserves (June 1997)	145.3	61.2	170.4	84.8	206.0
Short-term debt / total debt (June 1994)	74.3	59.1	61.1	44.2	72.5
Short-term debt / total debt (June 1997)	65.7	56.4	59.0	58.7	67.8
Percent of debt in local currency (June 1994)	5.87	10.91	2.73	5.39	6.61
Percent of debt in local currency (June 1997)	5.63	10.33	2.15	15.86	5.95

Source: Chang and Velasco (1998).

problems. The causes doubtless varied among the countries. In Korea, for example, a significant part of the blame can be laid on failing *chaebols* and continuing government interference in private credit decisions. In Thailand and Malaysia, 30 to 40 percent of bank loans were made to the real estate sector, primarily real estate developers,[40] a lending sector that has proven to be particularly vulnerable to bad loans in the United States and elsewhere. In Indonesia, a rapid financial liberalization led to more than 200 new banks and very high loan growth, from which substantial loan losses could be expected.

Table 8.8 displays information on nonperforming loans estimated one year later. Two patterns seem to emerge. First, there is much closer agreement among the sources on the size of the problem and, second, the greatest part of the nonperforming loans appears to have existed before the crisis broke. In other words, it seems from these limited data that the troubled condition of the banks substantially preceded the crisis. Of course, the crisis had not yet run its course, and ultimate levels of nonperforming loans became much worse as the crisis wore on. For example, the ratio of nonperforming loans to total loans in Thai banks was later estimated to have crested at 47.5 percent in 1999.[41] Estimates for Indonesia eventually reached 75 percent.

The high levels of nonperforming loans represent defaulting obligations of firms; that is, just behind the troubled banks there were troubled, overleveraged firms. The weakness of firms has been documented in some cases. In Korea, for example, 25 of the 30 largest *chaebols* had profit margins of less than 1 percent in 1996, half of which were running losses.[42]

Were Asian firms value destroyers? Table 8.9 shows some results of a World Bank survey of Asian public companies reporting financial results, averaged by country over 1992–1996.[43] Despite the inadequacies of accounting and disclosure in some of the countries, this provides at least a crude indicator of value creation or destruction by comparing return on invested capital (operating income over "balance sheet assets . . . minus financial items and fiscal items which are not considered as necessary operating capital") with interest rates. Wherever this measure is negative, we may infer that firms are not earning enough to pay their interest costs; that is, they are very likely to be destroying value. Note that a positive measure does not necessarily indicate value creation since cost of equity should also be taken into account.

[40]Goldstein (1998), pp. 7–8.
[41]*The Economist*, September 4, 1999.
[42]Corsetti, Pesenti, and Roubini (1998b), Table 8.8.
[43]Pomerleano (1998).

TABLE 8.7 **Precrisis Estimates of Nonperforming Loans / Total Loans, 1997**
(percentage estimates)

	Thailand	Malaysia	Indonesia	Philippines	Korea
Bank for International Settlements (official estimate)	7.7	3.9	8.8	N/A	0.8
Peregrine Investments	36.0	15.0	15.0	7.0	30.0
Jardine Fleming	19.3	15.6	16.8	13.4	N/A

Source: Goldstein (1998).

The important observation is that the *ROCEs* of firms were less than bank interest rates throughout 1992–1996 in Thailand, Indonesia, the Philippines, and Korea, and were substantially above the lending rate in Hong Kong and marginally above in Singapore and Malaysia. This reinforces the view that the Asian crisis was rooted in value-destroying growth, which is highly likely to lead to bank failures, which in turn can produce of financial crises.

Combining the Views

As noted above, the liquidity and banking stories are compatible. There was clearly a liquidity crisis in the autumn of 1997. But when the crisis passed, some countries had escaped serious damage and some had been flattened. The latter were generally those whose banks and firms had been in weak condition before the crisis struck. In the end, weak fundamentals determined who was significantly hurt by the crisis.

There is also a deeper connection between the liquidity and banking stories. As was the case in Mexico, some of the Asian countries made themselves vulnerable to liquidity risk by relying excessively on short-term, dollar-based bank loans, but others made different debt-management choices. Thailand, Malaysia, Indonesia, the Philippines, and Korea accelerated their use of short-term, dollar-based bank loans in the 1994–1996 period. They were also the countries with high levels of nonperforming loans and a set of public companies that did not appear to earn enough to pay for capital.

Who made the decisions? The capital inflows were not decided upon by governments as a matter of public policy, but rather by the private banks and firms themselves. This seems paradoxical. If firms are not earning enough to pay for capital, why would they seek more capital, particularly at short term and with foreign exchange risk? Similarly, one would expect responsible domestic banks faced with excessive nonperforming loans to restrain further lending, particularly if the borrowers as a whole look weak. Why would they expand risky funding to make more loans to risky borrowers?

Researchers have offered various explanations why the banks borrowed most of their funding in dollars. One is that the Asian tax and regulatory environment contained incentives biased toward foreign borrowing.[44] Another is that Asians fully believed that currency pegs would never break and were lulled into false security by previous successes. But a third explanation is simpler: There was no alternative available in sufficient quantity. Foreign banks fund themselves in dollars or other strong currencies, and they are typically unwilling to take the devaluation risk of lending in local currency.

---

[44]Chang and Velasco (1998), pp. 33–34.

TABLE 8.8   **Immediate Postcrisis Estimates of Nonperforming Loans / Total Loans, 1998**
(percentage estimates)

	Thailand	*Malaysia*	*Indonesia*	*Philippines*	*Korea*
Eschweiler, J. P. Morgan	17.5	7.5	11.0	5.5	17.5
Jen, Morgan Stanley	18.0	6.0	12.5	N/A	14.0
Ramos, Goldman Sachs	18.0	6.0	9.0	3.0	14.0

Source: Goldstein (1998).

Furthermore, dollar interest rates were substantially below local currency interest rates in most countries. A comparison of monthly deposit rates (local minus dollar) during 1994–1995 shows a negative spread in Malaysia but an average positive spread of 3.3 percent in Korea, 4.2 percent in the Philippines, 4.6 percent in Thailand, and 9.1 percent in Indonesia.[45] A firm that borrowed dollars instead of local currency would save these amounts; a bank that borrowed dollars and lent in local currency would earn these amounts. Of course, borrowing in dollars is only cheaper because the borrower is bearing the risk of a capital loss if the domestic currency depreciates. Why weren't domestic firms and banks more worried about that prospective loss (which turned out to be enormous)?

Another factor that begs explanation is why the borrowing was at short term, since foreign banks are normally willing to make term loans of five-to-eight-year maturities. The most likely explanation is that the lower spreads on short-term debt appeared to make that debt more desirable. But that explanation abstracts from the liquidity risk that short-term borrowing entails. Why were borrowers willing to undertake that risk?

The foreign exchange risk taking and liquidity risk taking by Asian banks is reminiscent of the activities of Mexican banks. One difference between the Asian crisis and the Mexican crisis is that Asian banks were overt about taking foreign exchange risk, since it was not prohibited. Explosive packets of foreign exchange risk that lay hidden in Mexican derivatives were more openly sought and accepted on balance sheet in Asia. But the motives were very likely similar.

As in the case of Mexico, Asian banks and industrial borrowers were willing to bear foreign exchange risk and liquidity risk because they believed their governments would absorb the costs of doing so. Banks with 15 percent nonperforming loans are likely to be insolvent or nearly so because losses on nonperforming loans are likely to exceed half the principal amount of the loans. If losses are 60 percent, then the bank is facing charge-offs of about 0.60×15 percent $= 9$ percent of total loans, a figure comparable in magnitude to total bank capital. It was very profitable to borrow in dollars and lend in local currencies, provided only that the local currency did not devalue. This gamble was the banks' best hope for restoring their balance sheets. Thus, moral hazard offers a plausible explanation of why weak banks, short-term borrowing, and currency risk join together to produce modern financial crises.

Governments, Safety Nets, and Bailouts

Up to now, our accounts of the Mexican and Asian crises have provided little detail about the actions of governments during the crises, as if their only role were to clean

---

[45]International Financial Statistics for local rates, Citibase for dollar rates.

TABLE 8.9   **Return on Capital Employed minus Interest Rate**
(percentages)

	1992	*1993*	*1994*	*1995*	*1996*
Hong Kong	15	14	12	10	7
Indonesia	−12	−10	−7	−8	−9
Korea	−3	−3	−1	0	N/A
Malaysia	3	3	3	3	1
Philippines	−13	−8	−8	−7	−10
Singapore	3	3	2	1	1
Thailand	−9	−9	−7	N/A	N/A

Source: Pomerleano (1998).

up the mess after it occurred. But government is typically a significant player from the very beginning in such crises, for two reasons. First, the government's willingness to monitor and discipline the banking system when it is weakening but has not yet collapsed goes a long way toward determining whether a financial collapse will occur. Second, government actions following a crisis will often be anticipated by players before the crisis and may well affect the behavior of the players.

Shocks do not always cause financial systems to fall apart; meltdowns require some preexisting fragility that magnifies the effect of shocks. In Figure 8.1 the "overextension of banks and firms" represents such a fragility, which reflects the absence of market and regulatory discipline in the banking system. Another element of fragility is a weak commitment to fiscal discipline (including growing bailout costs), which undermines the commitment to maintain the value of the currency. Together, these structural weaknesses create channels through which shocks are transmitted throughout the economy, growing in strength like a hurricane. The challenge in designing stable EFM financial systems, then, is to find ways to strengthen the commitments to market discipline and fiscal discipline.

In a world with no government-financed deposit insurance, the scenario described above for Asia would not be possible. Insolvent banks would not be able to attract deposits; they would soon experience a run and fail. Thus, the continuing existence and functioning of banks in which large loan losses are widely believed to be present implies that depositors feel quite safe, regardless of whether a formal system of deposit insurance is in place. In other words, government was an implicit player in the Asia story from the beginning.

If government does guarantee deposits, so that depositors do not need to monitor the health of their bank, then the task of monitoring the health of banks falls to the government. When the government finds that a bank is weakening, it must take action to close the bank or merge it. If it does not, insolvent banks will very likely expand rapidly through massive risk taking, a phenomenon that occurred in the U.S. savings and loan debacle of the 1980s and was evident in Mexico and Asia.

Furthermore, when the government intervenes with an insolvent bank, bank equity holders should lose everything and bank management should be dismissed with no exceptions. If this rule is not adopted, then the government is protecting not only depositors but also bank owners and managers. Knowing they have little to lose if the bets go wrong, bank owners and managers will take risks more freely and moral hazard will become far worse.

Many observers believe that Asian governments, though often acting with implicit rather than explicit agreements, did give protection against losses not only to depositors but also to bank owners and managers and indeed to industrial firms as well.

> Political pressures to maintain high rates of economic growth had led to a long tradition of public guarantees to private projects . . . With financial and industrial policy enmeshed within a widespread business sector network of personal and political favoritism, and with governments that appeared willing to intervene in favor of troubled firms, markets operated under the impression that the return on investment was somewhat "insured" against adverse shocks.[46]

This implicit protection explains why Asian countries have been so slow to adopt effective bankruptcy procedures and have allowed banks with large loan losses to go on operating. In Japan, for example, the government found it almost impossible until 1998 to grapple with massive and growing bank loan losses except by handing out money more or less to all banks, a program that seemed absurd in Western eyes but that made sense in terms of the implicit promises of the Japanese government. The connection between such promises and financial crises has now been formally modeled.[47]

As the 20th century ended, both Mexico and East Asia seemed to have regained economic stability: The financial crises had passed and economic growth had resumed in most cases. Indeed, the speed of economic recovery surprised many observers. Unfortunately, the speed of economic recovery also lessened the pressure for institutional reform. In particular, none of the crisis countries had dealt sufficiently with their troubled banks, and high levels of nonperforming loans seemed to continue in all of them. If the deepest connection between overvalued currencies, illiquidity, and troubled banks is moral hazard, then it would seem premature to declare that the period of financial crises is over.

References

Bernanke, Ben S., and Harold James. 1991. The gold standard, deflation, and financial crisis in the Great Depression: An international comparison. In *Financial Markets and Financial Crises*. Ed. by R. G. Hubbard. Chicago: University of Chicago Press: 33–68.

Brown, Stephen J., William N. Goetzmann, and James Park. 1998. Hedge funds and the Asian currency crisis of 1997. Working Paper no. 6427, National Bureau of Economic Research.

Burnside, Craig, Martin Eichenbaum, and Sergio Rebelo. 1999. Prospective deficits and the Asian currency crisis. Working Paper no. 6758, National Bureau of Economic Research.

Calomiris, Charles W. 1993. Financial factors in the Great Depression. *Journal of Economic Perspectives* 7: 61–85.

———. 1997. *The Postmodern Bank Safety Net*. Washington, DC: American Enterprise Institute.

———. 1998. Blueprint for a new global financial architecture. Working paper, Columbia University.

Calomiris, Charles W., and Allan H. Meltzer. 1999. Fixing the IMF. *The National Interest* 56, Summer: 88–96.

Caprio, Gerard, and Patrick Honohan. 1999. Restoring banking stability: Beyond supervised capital requirements. *Journal of Economic Perspectives* 13: 43–64.

Chang, Roberto, and Andrés Velasco. 1998. The Asian liquidity crisis. Working Paper no. 6796, National Bureau of Economic Research.

---

[46]Corsetti, Pesenti, and Roubini (1998b), pp. 2–3.
[47]Corsetti, Pesenti, and Roubini (1998a).

Choe, Hyuk, Bong-Chan Kho, and Rene M. Stulz. 1998. Do foreign investors destabilize stock markets? The Korean experience in 1997. Working Paper no. 6661, National Bureau of Economic Research.

Corsetti, Giancarlo, Paolo Pesenti, and Nouriel Roubini. 1998a. Paper tigers? A model of the Asian crisis. Working Paper no. 6783, National Bureau of Economic Research.

———. 1998b. What caused the Asian currency and financial crisis? Part 1: A macroeconomic overview. Working Paper no. 6833, National Bureau of Economic Research.

Daniel, Kent, David Hirschleifer, and Avanidhar Subramanyam. 1998. Investor psychology and security market under- and over-reaction. *Journal of Finance* 53: 1839–86.

DeLong, Bradford, Andrei Shleifer, Lawrence H. Summers, and Robert J. Waldmann. 1991. The survival of noise traders in financial markets. *Journal of Business* 64: 1–19.

Dornbusch, Rudiger. 1993. Mexico: How to recover stability and growth. In *Stabilization Debt and Reform.* Ed. by Rudiger Dornbusch. Englewood Cliffs, NJ: Prentice Hall.

Dornbusch, Rudiger, Ilan Goldfajn, and Rodrigo O. Valdés. 1995. Currency crises and collapses. *Brookings Papers on Economic Activity* 2: 219–93.

Dornbusch, Rudiger, and Alejandro Werner. 1994. Mexico: Stabilization, reform and no growth. *Brookings Papers on Economic Activity* 1: 253–97.

Dresser, Denise. 1997. Falling from the tightrope: The political economy of the Mexican crisis. In *Mexico 1994: Anatomy of an Emerging-Market Crash 1997.* Ed. by Sebastian Edwards and Moisés Naím. Washington, DC: Carnegie Endowment for International Peace.

The Economist. 1997. Banking in emerging markets, survey. April 12.

Edwards, Sebastian. 1994. Trade liberalization reforms in Latin America. In *Latin America's Economic Future.* Ed. by Graham Bird and Ann Helwege. London: Academic Press.

———. 1999. How effective are capital controls? *Journal of Economic Perspectives* 13: 65–84.

Eichengreen, Barry. 1992. *Golden Fetters: The Gold Standard and the Great Depression 1919–1939.* New York: Oxford University Press.

Eichengreen, Barry, and Jeffrey Sachs. 1985. Exchange rates and economic recovery in the 1930s. *Journal of Economic History* 45: 925–46.

Feldstein, Martin. 1999. Self-protection for emerging market economies. Working Paper no. 6907, National Bureau of Economic Research.

Fischer, Stanley. 1999. On the need for an international lender of last resort. *Journal of Economic Perspectives* 13: 85–104.

Garber, Peter. 1998. Derivatives in international capital flows. Working Paper no. 6623, National Bureau of Economic Research.

Garnaut, Ross. 1998. The East Asia crisis. In *East Asia in Crisis.* Ed. by Ross E. McLeod and Ross Garnaut. New York: Routledge.

Gil-Díaz, Francisco, and Agustín Carstens. 1997. Pride and prejudice: The economics profession and Mexico's financial crisis. In *Mexico 1994: Anatomy of an Emerging-Market Crash 1997.* Ed. by Sebastian Edwards and Moisés Naím. Washington, DC: Carnegie Endowment for International Peace.

Goldstein, Morris. 1998. *The Asian Financial Crisis: Causes, Cures, and Systemic Implications.* Washington, DC: Institute for International Economics.

International Monetary Fund. 1995. *Background Papers: Turbulence in Emerging Markets.* Washington. DC: IMF.

———. 1997. *World Economic Outlook, Interim Assessment, December 1997.* Washington. DC: IMF.

———. 1998. *World Economic Outlook.* Washington, DC: IMF.

Kaminsky, Graciela L., and Carmen M. Reinhart. 1999. The twin crises: The causes of banking and balance of payments problems. *American Economic Review* 89: 473–500.

Kindleberger, Charles P. 1978. *Manias, Panics and Crashes: A History of Financial Crises.* New York: Basic Books.

Krugman, Paul. 1979. A model of balance of payments crises. *Journal of Money, Credit and Banking* 11: 311–25.

———. 1994. The myth of Asia's miracle. *Foreign Affairs* 73, no. 6: 62–78.

————. 1998. What happened to Asia? Conference paper, author's website, Massachusetts Institute of Technology, **http://web.mit.edu/krugman/www.**

McKinnon, Ronald I., and Huw Pill. 1996. Credible liberalizations and international capital flows: The "overborrowing syndrome," In *Financial Deregulation and Integration in East Asia.* Ed. by Takatoshi Ito and Anne O. Krueger. Chicago: University of Chicago Press.

————. 1998. International overborrowing: A decomposition of credit and currency risks. Working paper, Stanford University.

————. 1999. Exchange-rate regimes for emerging markets: Moral hazard and international overborrowing. *Oxford Review of Economic Policy* 15: 19–38.

Obstfeld, Maurice. 1986. Rational and self-fulfilling balance-of-payments crises. *American Economic Review* 76: 72–81.

————. 1996. Models of currency crises with self-fulfilling features. *European Economic Review* 40: 1037–48.

Pomerleano, Michael. 1998. The East Asia crisis and corporate finances: The untold micro story. Policy Research Working Paper no. 1990, World Bank.

Radelet, Steven, and Jeffrey D. Sachs. 1998. The East Asian financial crisis: Diagnosis, remedies, prospects. *Brookings Papers on Economic Activity*: 1.

Rojas-Suárez, Liliana, and Steven R. Weisbrod. 1995. *Financial Fragilities in Latin America.* Washington, DC: International Monetary Fund.

Sachs, Jeffrey, Aaron Tornell, and Andrés Velasco. 1995. The collapse of the Mexican peso: What have we learned? Working Paper no. 5142, National Bureau of Economic Research.

————. 1996. Financial crises in emerging markets; The lessons from 1995. Working Paper no. 5576, National Bureau of Economic Research.

Soros, George. 1998. *The Crisis of Global Capitalism.* New York: Public Affairs.

Temin, Peter. 1989. *Lessons from the Great Depression.* Cambridge: MIT Press.

Thaler, Richard H. 1991. *Quasi-Rational Economics.* New York: Russell Sage Foundation.

Young, Alwyn. 1995. The tyranny of numbers: Confronting the statistical realities of the East Asian growth experience. *Quarterly Journal of Economics* 110: 641–80.

Building Financial Institutions

Introduction

The previous two chapters have been about problems and crises, of which there is an ample supply in the world of emerging financial markets. We end the book in this last chapter on a constructive note: There are many successes as well that can serve as models for the future. This book has emphasized fundamentals and the importance of institutions; armed with insights from previous chapters, we should be able to spot winning formulas. In doing so, we recapitulate the lessons for successful government policy from previous chapters and add new material focusing on the micro (firm-level) perspective on building financial institutions in EFMs.

We begin by summarizing the two fundamental messages of this book:

1. Finance creates value, in part by forcing firms to create value.
2. Successful finance requires strong institutions.

Let us examine each of these statements in turn.

Finance Creates Value

Economists have often undervalued the role of money and finance in economic development. We noted in Chapter 2 that classical economists viewed money as a thin overlay or "veil." Keynesian economics put more weight on the role of money, but treated it as an inert, profitless asset, which agents ought not to hold in excessive quantities. Increasingly, however, economists are recognizing the profound role of the laws, institutions, and policies that govern money, banks, and corporate finance for channeling capital to high-return projects and cutting it off from low-return projects. When the financial function is performed well, a great deal of value is created compared to systems in which it is performed badly. Firms, which are pressured to invest only in the highest-return projects, become more valuable. Investors, who obtain higher returns, capture this value.

Financial intermediation can be performed through two kinds of channels. One is the mechanism of securities markets, in which dealings between firms and investors are mediated by brokers, dealers, and underwriters. The other channel is banks, which stand between investors (who place their money on deposit with the banks) and firms (to which the bank makes loans or in which the bank owns an equity stake). Each form of intermediation has advantages and disadvantages.

The great advantage of securities market intermediation is lower overhead cost. Banks are an expensive form of financial intermediation because they require compensation for their ongoing services of screening and monitoring. When banks perform their function badly, allocating capital to low-return projects, they are subject to expensive collapse. We have seen that connected lending, moral hazard, and the long-run decay of franchise value greatly magnify the cost of such collapses.

On the other hand, securities markets are also subject to fraud and manipulation, and are highly dependent on legal and informational underpinnings. Countries that try to launch securities markets without proper legal and informational foundations often end up with public outrage over the exploitation of investors. Banks are better able to cope with legal and informational deficiencies, which is why banks tend to dominate finance in EFMs. Countries that try to build securities markets without first ensuring a sound banking system typically regret the choice.

Whether through banks or securities markets, financial intermediaries play the role of middlemen, mediating flows between savers and users of capital. One might have expected that this role would diminish as communications technology improves and users of finance grow in sophistication. After all, middlemen profit from inefficiency; the more easily buyers and sellers can find each other, the less important and lucrative is the role of a middleman.

But technological progress has not slowed down the financial services industry. In countries such as the United States, financial institutions are very strong and well supported by law, information, and a stable currency. They pay exceptionally high salaries, far higher than in most other industries. In doing so, they are able to bid aggressively for some of the most talented and motivated students in the universities. This is particularly true of securities firms and fund managers, though it is also increasingly true of banks as they become more sophisticated in the range and quality of services they offer.

Improvements in communications technology certainly lead countries to rely less on traditional bank lending and more on securities markets. This trend is unmistakable throughout the world. While banks provide the great bulk of finance in EFMs, securities markets are more important in the industrial countries and are centrally important in the United States. Securities services may seem to be less substantial than bank lending. They are of shorter term and primarily involve underwriting and distributing financial paper. Yet reputation and relationships also matter greatly to securities firms, and asset managers wield significant power in corporate governance. Increasing reliance on securities markets seems to be a sign of a stronger financial system, not a less substantial one.

Financial firms must be adding ever-more value to the U.S. economy, or they would never be able to grow and to bid so aggressively for talent. Indeed, one of the secrets of America's astonishing growth at the turn of the century seems to be its vigorous financial system. The financial function must indeed be adding important value to the American economy.

The source of that value is not hard to find. Successful banks and securities markets select and shower capital on successful, value-creating enterprises but deny it to failing, value-destroying enterprises. This presses firms to select projects that will attract the attention of capital providers, and gives investors the highest returns available. The process is imperfect, so investors can certainly lose in selected cases, but the overall effect is to direct capital to its highest and best uses. It is hard to exaggerate the importance to the economy of getting this process right.

No doubt financial markets sometimes overshoot, particularly in periods of rapid change. They are sometimes excessively optimistic, so that too much capital is showered on apparent value creators, and sometimes excessively pessimistic, so that too much punishment is exacted on apparent value destroyers. But these periods of exaggeration are unlikely to last for long. After all, any significant mispricing of financial assets creates opportunities for abnormal returns over the longer run, and such opportunities usually do not last for long. Modern financial markets are filled with well-paid, well-trained analysts looking for just such opportunities. Simply because financial markets may temporarily overshoot is no reason to reject their critical overall role or contribution.

The value-creating role of finance helps to put the emerging markets phenomenon into perspective. In the early 1990s, when countries throughout the developing world altered their previous policies and opened up their economies, privatizing state-owned enterprises and liberalizing their financial systems, global financial markets reacted with enthusiasm and showered capital on EFMs, driving up the values of their securities. When EFM crises began to happen in the second half of the 1990s, the markets reacted with equal and opposite force: EFM stock, bond, and currency prices fell, portfolio flows into EFMs slowed dramatically, and banks demanded their money back. No doubt there was some element of overshooting in both directions.

What conclusions can we draw from that experience? Some international economists have advocated capital controls to shelter EFMs from the effects of capital markets.[1] No doubt the short-term effects of capital mobility can be and have been destabilizing. Yet developing countries need capital for growth and want inflows to continue at a brisk pace; few have actually instituted capital controls. The great majority seem to accept that if they are able to put their fundamentals in reasonable order (e.g., by reforming their bankruptcy and governance systems and cleaning up their banks), then desirable capital inflows will follow.

As we move away from the bunker mentality of 1997–1998, we can observe a larger process at work. Financial markets are exerting a certain discipline on EFMs, forcing them to enhance the value-creating qualities of their domestic financial systems. On this broader view, finance is creating value, in part by forcing governments to create legal and regulatory environments that permit finance to operate effectively.

Successful Finance Requires Strong Institutions

The financial system is much more than a passive marketplace where investors and firms somehow match up their needs. The process needs to be intermediated by institutions: banks, securities firms, insurance companies, mutual funds, pension funds, and so forth. Intermediation is needed because of information problems; investors simply cannot gain enough information about their potential investments without the help

---

[1]For example, see Krugman (1999), Stiglitz (1999), or Eichengreen (1999).

of specialists. Financial intermediaries screen investments and monitor firms, both of which are difficult and time-consuming.

A central problem in emerging financial markets is the scarcity of information. Investors are given very little public information and need intermediaries, most often banks, to pry out private information. In industrial countries, the problem is often quite different: A flood of public information is available, but specialists are needed to organize it, interpret it, and turn it into insight and advice. In either case, both in EFMs and in industrial countries, investors and firms generally prefer to deal with strong institutions.

Size. To say that an institution is strong means several things. First, and most obviously, it may mean that the institution is of significant size. While there will always be a role for specialized boutiques, most financial systems are dominated by a few very large firms. Size is no guarantee of quality, but it does imply broad reach and a diversity of services. Success causes institutions to grow, so larger size is often the result of previous success. As the 21st century begins, financial institutions around the globe are merging into ever-larger enterprises. No doubt there are diminishing economies of scale in financial institutions, and some of the recently created giants may already have discovered this. But in a globally competitive marketplace, strength and capacity must be correlated to some degree with size.

Capital. Second, a strong institution has sufficient capital relative to its assets. Governments almost universally regulate banks, securities firms, and insurance companies, and the centerpiece of prudential regulation is capital requirements. Financial institutions necessarily take risks, and sufficient capital means that the shareholders, not the customers or the government, absorb losses resulting from those risks. When this is true, owners will behave more conservatively. We have seen how dramatically the risk of financial institutions can expand when capital is exhausted or nearly so, and the owners have everything to gain and nothing to lose from increased risk taking. Sufficient capital helps to ensure that risks are not extreme and that losses are absorbed by those responsible for them.

Reputation. But there is more. When asked during congressional testimony whether the foundation of credit is not capital, J. P. Morgan replied, "Sir, the foundation of credit is character." In our era we might use slightly different words, but the idea would be the same: A well-run financial institution is credible and trustworthy, deals with reliable customers, and inspires the trust and loyalty of those customers. Because customers cannot easily monitor the risks currently being run by a financial institution, they rely on the institution's reputation. Economists frequently study the benefits of reputation building by financial institutions. Loss of reputation, as happened in the United States to firms such as Drexel Burnham Lambert (1987), Salomon Brothers (1991), and Bankers Trust Company (1995), typically leads to major institutional change: replacement of the CEO, sale of the firm, or liquidation.

Certification. Reputation matters to the customers of financial institutions. Those entrusting capital to a firm need to feel confidence that their money will be carefully handled. Those needing funds typically want the strongest financial firms to supply them with it. Thus, the strongest financial firms are selective. Any first-class firm turns down more business than it accepts. To be among those chosen by such a financial firm has an important certification effect. In the early days of capital markets in the United

States, J. P. Morgan & Company was trusted to certify the prime firms in many industries.[2] A comparable certification function is needed in most modern EFMs. When it appears, it will be a sign that the market in question is maturing. Financial institutions with a concern for their reputation are those most likely to add value to the economy.

Skill and Knowledge.   Finally, strength in a financial institution implies that the staff has skill and knowledge. Finance is a service business, whose "product" results from the expenditure of time and imagination by its people. It is a technical domain that requires special training and experience, and about which many people are easily confused. Under financial repression, bankers do not require a high level of skill—they need only to follow orders and rules. But when financial systems are liberalized, banks need people far more skillful than before. Financial liberalization without sufficient skill preparation can lead quickly to massive losses, whether in the U.S. thrift industry (1982–1988) or the Mexican banks (1991–1994).

There is a subtle connection between strong financial institutions and financial liberalization. First, a repressed financial system will not have strong financial institutions, though they may be large. In a repressed system, securities markets scarcely exist except for government bonds, and banks do little more than follow government orders. Just as domineering parents usually produce weak and incapable children, so a repressive government usually produces weak and incapable banks.

However, a sudden, total, and uncontrolled liberalization will not lead to strength either, but more likely to a financial collapse within a few years. This is the pattern we saw in Chile (1976–1982) and in Russia (1993–1998). Unless legal foundations have been carefully laid and a sensible pattern of regulation established, financial institutions will likely indulge in massive connected lending or outright theft of assets. The subsequent collapse sets back the program of liberalization for many years to come.

Appropriate financial liberalization needs to do more than release banks from control: It needs to release them in a setting where pressures exist to perform well. The best form of such pressure is competition. By opening up local financial markets to international banks, a government raises the probability that sound managerial practices will enter the market and challenge local banks to improve. By encouraging the growth of securities markets, a government puts further pressure on banks to be efficient in order to compete.

Another form of pressure on banks to perform well is regulatory pressure. Activist regulators who examine banks and criticize poor practices where they see them increase the chances that banks will adopt the best practices. Regulatory rules on capital, provided they are well drawn and well enforced, will lower moral hazard.

But all of these market and regulatory pressures make it far more difficult for banks to earn a satisfactory return on capital. The easy rents available when governments coddle banks tend to melt away in the heat of competition. Banks need to define their strategies and hone their skills in order to make money. Life becomes harder but the best banks become stronger.

Inevitably, though, not all banks make a successful transition from sheltered life to aggressive competition. In Darwinian fashion, some banks will tend to fail along the way. This process needs to be monitored closely by the government because leaving failing banks in control of risk-taking decisions can undermine the entire economy.

Thus, the process of financial liberalization requires a well-conceived transition by both government and banks away from previous collusive patterns and toward a

---

[2]DeLong (1991).

new, responsible relationship, more arm's-length and more demanding than before. This transition is difficult and not all banks will make it successfully. No wonder there have been many crises and failures along the way. Yet there is no alternative if the outcome is to be strong institutions.

The remainder of this chapter discusses in more detail what can be done to build strong financial institutions. First, we address what governments can do to lay appropriate foundations. The answers given below in many ways summarize and restate the lessons of Chapters 3 through 6. Second, we consider what managements of financial institutions can do to become strong and effective in the challenging environment of emerging financial markets. The job of managing a financial institution has never been more difficult than in the present era. We propose four factors that good managements must always keep in focus.

What Good Governments Do

Separation of Business and Government

The first and most important principle of good government in a modern economy is that business and government have separate roles. The government should not try to own, operate, or interfere in the day-to-day running of any business, including financial institutions, and people with ongoing business and financial interests should not hold positions in government.

This principle is central because business and government have different jobs with different goals. The goal of business is, or should be, to create wealth and thereby create sustainable jobs and sustainable economic growth. The goals of government are many. Some are admirable (e.g., caring for those who are somehow damaged or disadvantaged, and preventing excessive concentrations of economic power) and some are not (e.g., self-preservation in power and often extraction of personal wealth). But all of these goals are distinct from and often in conflict with the business goal of creating wealth.

In a healthy economy, business and government each pursues its goals and negotiates the points of conflict. But if the upper levels of business and government are interwoven, distortions appear. The government can be found subsidizing firms, either directly or through cheap loans or bailouts, so that the hard budget constraint of financial markets is softened. Protectionism emerges, which benefits certain businesses but at a high cost to consumers. Business is deflected from its goal of value creation when government has too strong a say in how capital is allocated or how businesses are managed. It may feel obligated to make corrupt payments, make poor investments, hire excessive numbers of people, locate plants in remote regions, or make any number of other uneconomic decisions in support of government goals.

The result is a confusion of goals that makes both business and government less effective. The well-documented inefficiency of SOEs is, we believe, primarily a consequence of this goal confusion. Most economic models begin with firms that try to maximize profit, but with SOEs this cannot be assumed. Managers of state enterprises are trying to support all kinds of public and private agendas, but feel little pressure to create value. Since value creation is hard to achieve, a lack of pressure in this direction, and indeed pressure in other directions, nearly guarantees value destruction.

Business–government overlap can be crude (direct government ownership of banks and firms) or subtle. In Japan, for example, the Ministry of Finance successfully "guided" the private banks for decades with few formal command powers. In contrast,

Korea owned its banks outright in order to accomplish the same degree of guidance. Mexico privatized its banks in the early 1990s. However, the banks were sold at high prices to friends of the ruling party who continued to have a strong influence over government policy and managed to suppress effective regulation; this had a good deal to do with Mexico's financial collapse in 1994–1995. Even more paradoxically, Russia appeared to privatize rapidly in the early 1990s, but the business elites who got control were typically part of the previous state control group, or members of criminal groups with links to the government, or both, so that actual separation of business from government was far less than first appeared.

The overlap of business and government tends to enhance the power of government officials and the wealth of the private elite, so it is broadly popular with both. Furthermore, opportunities for corruption abound when such overlaps exist. These facts make "crony capitalism" extremely hard to break up. It requires strong political pressure from outsiders to effect real change, and that requires a measure of democracy that until recently has been rare in developing countries.

Even when government officials are not corrupt and are genuinely trying to further the public interest, their efforts may be counterproductive. For example, European governments, under the influence of a persisting socialist tradition, long ago enacted rigid labor laws designed to protect workers from dismissal and thereby to keep employment high. Industrial policies aimed at supporting dying industries such as shipyards and coal mines often have the same motivation. Yet such policies have led Europe to very high unemployment while the United States, with far less protection against employee dismissal and few cases of protecting dying industries, has very low unemployment—that is, government engagement in the economy produced the opposite of the result intended.

Similarly, government policies to foster maximum growth in a number of Asian countries led to many investments with inadequate returns, which produced banking losses and finally resulted in a financial crisis that brought growth to a standstill. Again, government engagement had an outcome opposite to the one intended. In the wake of the Asian crisis, many governments have resisted serious bankruptcy reform because they wish to revive economic growth and fear closing plants and liquidating companies. This effort to save jobs turns out to delay resolution of the financial crisis and so compromises future growth.

Many of these counterproductive government policies stem from a very human desire to avoid the harsh disciplines of financial markets. Governments most often intervene in the economy and the financial system because they fear that markets, in their heartless way, will lead to liquidation of firms and destruction of jobs. It takes considerable trial and error to establish that separation is a surer recipe for long-run success and that economic growth and job creation are better advanced by not intervening in pursuit of them.

Thus, good governments tend to separate themselves from business. They privatize SOEs and liberalize financial systems, but they do not vanish or play a minimal role; instead governments focus their energy on building strong foundations so that markets will work well. In particular, successful financial institutions can arise only when governments deliberately construct strong legal and regulatory foundations.

Law and Regulation

Those who live in industrial countries often take the rule of law for granted. They presume that commercial laws are well constructed and that courts will act promptly and impartially to enforce such laws and private contracts under them. But this cannot be presumed in EFMs, where rule of law itself is often in question and where adequate commercial laws and court processes are still being developed. Furthermore, the problem of adequate law is more severe in the case of financial markets. Financial contracts require more protection than normal commercial contracts because financial investors are uniquely vulnerable once they have parted with their funds. Governments are not always eager to afford them such protection.

Lenders need to have enforceable rights. As noted in Chapter 4, the government can do a great deal to stimulate lending by establishing a uniform commercial code with simple rules for registration of collateral interests in land, equipment, and inventories that give lenders strong rights to seize and sell collateral, and by establishing a public registry of collateral. A related need is for a strong bankruptcy law. When borrowers do not pay their loans, there must be consequences; creditors must have the right to enforce their claims without long delays. Otherwise lenders will be reluctant to lend in the first place. A well-written bankruptcy law gives confidence to lenders that they have remedies available if they do not get repaid. (See the box on the following page for Mexico's progress in debt and credit reform.)

Many EFM governments worry, however, that seizure of collateral and efficient bankruptcy procedures will result in excessive disruption and loss of jobs, particularly since collateral seizure and bankruptcies happen precisely during economic downturns. The close involvement of government with private firms adds further to government reluctance to move against firms that default on their loans. This often prevents appropriate laws from being written or adequately enforced. The result is frequently an impasse in which the government pays lip service to legal reforms but does not pursue them with any real enthusiasm.

Such governments need to understand that when a company is liquidated or when lenders take at least some of its assets, the assets do not vanish from the economy; they are simply sold to another management that can make more efficient use of them. Only if the assets in question are totally useless would they not find another buyer, and this is rarely the case—nor would lenders want to seize them in such a case. In other words, debt enforcement does not *destroy* assets or jobs but does *change control* over them. When governments fail to put strong creditor protection into place, they are really protecting those who currently control such assets and jobs.

In most countries, and almost always in developing countries, corporate management is concentrated in a small circle of individuals with the characteristics of a club. Such circles do not easily welcome outsiders into their midst, even when the outsiders are capital suppliers. Most often, the club of owners has significant influence over government policy and uses that influence to keep creditors and public shareholders at bay. That is why "crony capitalism," the excessive overlap between government and large private firms, is the enemy of legal reform.

This is particularly true in equity markets. One of the most difficult problems in corporate governance in all countries is how to protect outside shareholders. Such shareholders are even more vulnerable than lenders because their claims are more general and diffuse than those of lenders. So shareholders also need to have enforceable rights such as the "antidirector rights" enumerated in Chapter 4. Until these are provided, stock markets in emerging financial market countries are likely to be small and unstable.

Many economists undervalue the importance of well-functioning stock markets. John Maynard Keynes, for example, despite his success as a stock speculator, wrote that a typical stock exchange behaved so capriciously that its role in resource allocation was either insignificant or harmful. Certainly most capital flows within and into

Debt Resolution and Credit Market Reform in Mexico

Mexico has enacted a set of new policies to speed resolution of the overhang of bad debt from its financial crisis of 1994–1995 and to place new lending on a sounder footing. In April 2000, two landmark laws were passed, one establishing a new bankruptcy code, the other a new means for protecting the rights of creditors to collateral interests. The new laws are revolutionary for Mexico and they strengthen a financial reform program combining other complementary changes that were put into place earlier: the recapitalization of Mexico's banks, transfers of insolvent banks to competitors (notably, efficient foreign entrants like Banco Santander Centro Hispano, Banco Bilbao Vizcaya Argentaria, and Citibank), and the resolution of much of the uncertainty about debt repayment that has plagued the economy for years.

Following the peso devaluation and economic crisis of 1994, many debtors remained in limbo, refusing to repay or renegotiate loans. Creditors had little recourse owing to weak creditor rights and an inefficient and politicized judiciary that favored debtors. The failure to resolve payment uncertainty had costs beyond those suffered by creditors. It is hard to evaluate the creditworthiness of firms or individuals when it is unclear how much preexisting debt they will have to repay. Thus, debt overhang and repayment uncertainty discouraged bank lending, which was also hampered by the scarcity of bank capital and the lack of legal protections for new lenders. Bank credit growth was so slow that from 1995 to 2000 businesses relied mainly on alternative sources of finance (i.e., foreign direct investment, bond markets, and domestic nonbank lenders) to finance the robust growth enjoyed by Mexico over that period. But it was widely recognized that a continuing high rate of economic growth, particularly of firms that lack access to international capital, would depend on establishing an effective bank credit market.

The way forward required measures to resolve problems from the past and to avoid problems in the future. The *punto final* [final point] program—the last in a series of loan loss sharing arrangements between banks and the government passed in 1998—offered new incentives for debtors and creditors to resolve existing claims, providing that participants committed to the program by a certain date. The program gave debtors a last chance to receive government support, with the government paying creditors up to two-thirds of the unpaid portion of debt. While the program is generous (mortgage write-offs were as high as 50 percent), any bank expecting to recover more than what the government offered would not have sought to include that debt in the program. Thus, the incentives were designed so that the banks' own interests limited the extent of government-subsidized assistance in debt forgiveness. Furthermore, less generous half measures would have invited further stalling by debtors hoping to receive a better future deal. *Punto final* has succeeded in resolving over a million debt conflicts, mostly the eligible debts of individuals and small firms. Larger debts were not covered to the same extent by the plan and remain largely unresolved. Because of their size and the identities of the largest debtors, debt resolution of these claims is more politically difficult. After the election of 2000, it is believed that the pace of debt resolution will pick up for these debts.

Bank capital rose from 1997 to 2000, owing not only to government aid, but also to the post-crisis relaxation of barriers to entry and acquisition by foreign banks, and to positive bank earnings that have boosted capital. As of 2000, some domestic Mexican banks were still not adequately capitalized, but regulators seemed to be forcing insolvent or undercapitalized banks to increase capital, find suitors, or face government takeover and auction.

continued

Along with bank recapitalization and debt repayment, Mexico's new creditor protection laws should pave the way to restoring the proper function of bank credit in the economy. The new legislation not only promulgates good rules, but also ensures effective enforcement by overcoming constraints posed by Mexican courts. In Mexico as in other developing countries, bankruptcy and creditor rights reforms have sometimes failed because the courts refuse to administer them properly. The new laws are designed to prevent courts from undermining their intent. Among the provisions in the "guarantee" law is the creation of a new kind of collateral trust, which provides a means of liquidating collateral when debtors default, with minimal involvement by the courts.

The new bankruptcy law is even more promising as a means of protecting creditors. It permits distressed debtors to restructure (as in the Chapter 11 procedure in the United States), but it places limits on the length of time that a conciliator is allowed to arrange a restructuring plan approved by the firm and its creditors. If a firm's creditors do not agree to the terms of restructuring within six months, the firm will automatically move into liquidation, and liquidation (carried out by auction, to prevent corrupt sales procedures) cannot be blocked by the courts. This law places substantial power in the hands of creditors and makes it virtually impossible for firms to use the courts to help them avoid liquidation. Firms that are viable will face strong incentives to reach agreement quickly with their creditors, who also gain by avoiding the costs of unnecessarily liquidating a viable business. Mexico's banking and credit market reforms could usher in an unprecedented era of stable bank credit growth in Mexico.

developing countries are in the form of debt, which would seem to support the claim of irrelevance.

However, stock markets can have an importance disproportionate to the amount of new capital they provide to business because of their connection with corporate governance. When stock markets are well supported by law and institutions of information, observable declines in stock prices exert pressure on managers to disclose and defend their activities. It is not pleasant to explain failures to angry outside shareholders, particularly when they have credible power over management.

By supporting the rights of public shareholders, governments can diminish the clublike nature of corporate management and make it far more likely that management will focus on value creation as opposed to personal perquisites. As the 21st century begins, Western Europe is beginning to experience significant numbers of hostile takeovers, including cross-border takeovers, which disrupt the relationships within the European club. This is most uncomfortable for and aggressively resisted by many of the entrenched corporate managers. But it will no doubt accelerate the performance of Europe's corporations.

It does not greatly matter whether shares are traded in local stock exchanges, regional stock exchanges, or global stock exchanges. What matters is that they trade actively somewhere. In much of Latin America, local exchanges seem to be losing ground to regional exchanges and U.S. ADR listings. Conversely in Israel, the ratio of local stock trading to GDP (27 percent in 1998) is very high despite the fact that half the market capitalization of Israeli companies is listed in the United States.

A related issue is the availability of venture capital. Many governments have learned that their economies benefit greatly from a strong and innovative small business sector. Innovation, whether in use of the Internet or in better ways to produce more traditional goods and services, is a powerful engine of value creation and economic growth. Indeed, East Asia as a region may try to evolve a "new Asian model" in which technology-driven small businesses provide the job creation that used to be provided by industrial giants. Such thinking is becoming commonplace in Singapore, Malaysia, Hong Kong, and Korea.

But this requires financing, and in particular, equity financing. In some cases, governments are setting up funds to provide venture capital, but the record of governments making wise choices in this area is extremely poor. What is needed is a true venture capital industry. Venture capital funds, many of them international, have appeared in the stronger EFMs, but can hardly be sustained without the prospect of an initial public offering (IPO) of stock to provide the venture capitalist an exit. Thus, the success of venture capital is intimately connected to a strong local stock market.[3] Good governments will provide the disclosure laws and shareholder protections necessary to build such stock markets.

Banking Policy

Because banks remain the central financial institutions of EFMs, however, the greatest legal need is for strong banking laws and appropriate regulation. In September 1997 the Basel Committee on Banking Supervision published a document entitled "Core Principles for Effective Banking Supervision." While its recommendations are too lengthy to quote, its main ideas include the following:

1. Bank regulators should be independent and adequately funded.
2. Banks should meet minimum capital requirements.
3. Banks should have appropriate lending guidelines and procedures.
4. Banks should have defined procedures for credit audit and loss provisioning.
5. Banks should avoid excessive concentrations of risk with single borrowers or groups.
6. Regulators should monitor all connected lending.
7. Banks should have procedures for assessing and managing risk.
8. Regulators need to monitor senior management to ensure compliance with minimal standards of conduct.

In general, the greatest need is for intelligent, independent bank regulators who are provided with sufficient authority and resources to act decisively. In an ideal world, government regulation of banking might not be necessary, but so long as governments insure the liabilities of banks, governments also need to assume primary responsibility for monitoring their behavior. Even in those few countries that seem to have moved away from bailing out failed banks (as in Argentina, see box), the need for a strong central monitor of bank behavior seems in no way diminished. The commitment of such governments to the principle of market discipline could be undermined if the inspection and governance systems that guide appropriate market discipline do not develop quickly.

Accounting for nonperforming loans is a subject of particular concern. Governments need to press banks in this area because of a serious incentive problem: If bank managements candidly disclose all their nonperforming loans, they may be declaring themselves insolvent. Bank regulators need to ensure that the bank's credit audit function is strong and independent of loan officers, and support it with their own periodic inspections.

---

[3]Black and Gilson (1998).

Getting It Right: Argentina's Banking Reforms

Argentina is the largest country to have adopted a currency board. Its system came under severe stress in 1995, when the Mexican crisis caused a significant movement out of Argentine pesos into dollars. Peso interest rates rose with increased anxiety that the currency peg would break. The high rates and subsequent economic contraction led to many defaults and resulted in a banking crisis. For several months, Argentina suffered large contractions of deposits as money fled the country.

The currency board system made it difficult to provide a safety net to banks. Such a safety net is expensive, and can result in government obligations equal to a substantial percentage of GDP. The government had no obvious source of funds to implement a safety net unless it could borrow the needed capital abroad, which is unlikely at the crest of a crisis. At the time of its crisis Argentina had no deposit insurance and mustered little in the way of lender of last resort assistance. "Market discipline" prevailed as deposits flowed out of weak banks and into strong ones.

Many weak banks failed during the crisis. Nevertheless, the government's hard line appears to have paid off. In the aftermath of the crisis, the system strengthened, as foreign banks entered in force (in an apparent vote of confidence for the government), and many provincial government banks were either closed or privatized. The Central Bank continued the process of reform, including the following items:

- To provide liquidity in future crises, bank reserve requirements were raised to 20 percent of deposits, an unusually high level. However, this was not a tax since the reserves pay interest, which is also unusual.

- A "contingent repo facility" through which international banks provided potential liquidity protection lending to the government to cover another 10 percent of deposits.

- Capital requirements for banks start at 11.5 percent, to which are added requirements that link capital to loan risk (measured by loan interest rates) and market risk. Also, banks were obliged to issue subordinated debt equal to at least 2 percent of their deposits, to provide additional capital market risk assessment and monitoring.

- The bankruptcy laws were reformed.

- The banking supervisory process was strengthened to conform with the Core Principles for Effective Supervision issued by the Basel Committee.

- The *Central de Deudores* was expanded under Central Bank sponsorship to collect and disseminate the name of every corporate and individual borrower in the country together with its aggregate debt and credit rating on a scale of 1–6, and some information about the financial condition of borrowing firms. A monthly CD-ROM is sold that gives data on all persons and firms that have defaulted on debt.

- A modest private deposit insurance fund (SEDESA) was instituted to cover up to $10,000 per person, supported by each bank paying in 0.03–0.06 percent of deposits.

Argentina now has one of the highest rankings of all EFMs in most assessments of banking system quality. An index combining ratings for capital, loan classifications, management, liquidity, legal environment, and transparency rated Singapore, Argentina, and Hong Kong the strongest systems. Thailand and Indonesia scored the lowest of the countries reviewed.

Sources: World Bank (1998) and Calomiris and Powell (2000).

After nonperforming loans have been fully accounted for, the banks must maintain an amount of capital commensurate with their risk, since capital is the main defense against moral hazard and the main buffer between bank losses and claims on taxpayers. There should be prompt corrective action for undercapitalized banks and severe penalties for misstating capital, whether by underreporting nonperforming loans or otherwise. As noted in Chapter 7, it is not easy to define exactly what capital is or how much should be held against various types and levels of risk. But all forms of capital that credibly act as a buffer against depositor loss should be permissible, particularly subordinated debt held by knowledgeable investors who can be expected to assist in monitoring the bank.[4]

Governments must move promptly and decisively to close insolvent banks (i.e., those whose capital is probably exhausted by nonperforming loans). When a bank has failed, the equity investors must lose all their investment and the management must be dismissed. If that is not done and done promptly, the government is inviting banks to take excessive risk at the public's expense by protecting them against the downside consequences of their behavior. We have seen that moral hazard is a powerful engine of risk expansion. Nothing could be better calculated to create an even larger crisis in the future.

Given the awesome magnitude of bank losses in recent years, why do developing country governments not move decisively to close failed banks, replace failed bank owners and managers, and clean up these problem loans before moral hazard leads to another explosion of risk taking? If we imagine that government always acts in the public interest, this becomes a profound mystery. If we asked the governments in question, they would probably say that it would be too disruptive to close and restructure so many banks, and that their economies need the continuity of functioning banks for continued recovery.

Too often, however, the true reason is very similar to the reason why creditor and shareholder rights are not created and enforced: because governments do not always act in the public interest, but frequently act to protect a club of corporate owners and managers, in this case bank owners and managers. This is a direct consequence of inadequate separation of the financial sector from government. In the extreme case of state-owned banks and failed loans to state-owned enterprises, the government is engaged in connected lending on a grand scale, in which likelihood of repayment takes a back seat to continued functioning of the failed enterprises. In China, for example, the massive nonperforming loans in banks are largely loans to money-losing SOEs, and the government cannot prevent those losses from continuing since it benefits from their continuation. As governments around the world (including that of the United States) have learned, delay in enforcing prudential standards tends to make a banking crisis far more expensive than it needs to be.

Enforcing capital requirements and promptly closing insolvent banks are difficult and politically unpopular almost everywhere. Yet this is what good governments do.

Other Government Issues

Further actions of good governments to build their financial systems include supporting institutions of information. This begins with insistence upon accounting standards that are not only well written but, more importantly, well enforced. Unless banks can

---

[4]For a discussion of what should count toward satisfying the bank capital requirement, see Shadow Financial Regulatory Committee (2000).

see accurate numbers for their borrowers and investors, and governments can see accurate numbers for the banks, everyone is operating in the dark. Market-friendly governments such as those of Chile and Argentina also insist on banks obtaining a private credit rating, although ensuring that such ratings are of sufficient quality has proved a difficult problem.[5] A free financial press is also very important in disseminating information and ferreting out problems.

Much learning is taking place. Some countries such as Argentina have installed state-of-the-art law, regulation, and information standards for securities markets and banks, together with stabilizing their currencies, and may thereby have greatly reduced the chances of another financial crisis. The story of their success needs to be understood in detail.

A number of EFM governments are pursuing another type of reform with far-reaching consequences: privatization of social security systems (see the box on Chile, p. 342). Here is a reform that the United States and Western Europe are far too timid to initiate, yet it has had a huge and beneficial effect in Chile and has recently been introduced in Argentina, Mexico, Poland, and elsewhere. This transformation not only lowers inflation risk by relieving a major pressure on government spending, but also builds a class of local institutional investors that buttress local securities markets.

What Good Financial Institution Managers Do

Managers of financial institutions have many tasks to perform. A few, however, stand out as particularly worthy of focus by senior management: strategy, risk management, growth, and compensation. When financial institutions fail, it is usually because one of the four areas has been significantly mishandled. Getting these four elements right sets the foundations for success.

Strategy

The most important task in managing any enterprise is to have a viable strategy. Unless the strategy is good, all efforts to manage the institution will be wasted. People can work very hard with high loyalty and enthusiasm, but their efforts must be coordinated in a direction that promises the creation of value. Without this, they are like a crew on a ship that runs well day to day, but ends up near the South Pole.

Strategy is particularly important in the current era when technology and globalization have made the pace of change more rapid than ever before. Perhaps in a simpler time it was less necessary to devote resources to developing a strategy. Perhaps if one had a banking license and a banking franchise, one would need only to follow the formula that all good bankers followed in order to prosper. But such easy work seems to have vanished from the modern scene. Staid old businesses such as banking and electric power have become hugely risky. Indeed, one piece of evidence that strategy is more necessary now than ever is the high compensation paid to strategic consultants and the proliferation of such consultants. This is one of the few professions that rivals financial services in compensation.

Strategy is necessary because the creation of value is a difficult task, particularly in a changing and competitive world. In an efficient financial market, random actions will not lead to profitability. "Day traders," for example, who try to find and profit

---

[5]Calomiris and Powell (2000).

Chile: Pension Reform and Capital Market Deepening

In 1980 the total volume of fixed interest securities traded on the Santiago Stock Exchange during the entire year amounted to $614 million. In 1995 this amount was exceeded in two days of average trading. Chile now enjoys one of the most sophisticated capital markets in Latin America. Among several important reforms that laid the foundation for this success was the privatization of Chile's pension funds.

By the late 1970s it was clear that Chile's state-run pension system was nearly bankrupt. In 1980 the government established a privately administered program of mandatory retirement savings. Special corporations called *Administradores de Fondos de Pensiones* (*AFPs*) collected the contributions and administered their investment under tight government rules. Initially, they could invest only in bank deposits and fixed income securities. A special regulatory agency was created to ensure that AFPs were sufficiently capitalized and complied with the rules. At the end of 1981, total assets under AFP management of $264 million were invested 62 percent in term deposits, 28 percent in public sector bonds, and 10 percent in mortgage and corporate bonds.

In 1985, when the first wave of privatizations began, a ceiling of 50 percent was placed on the pension funds' public sector investments, a clear signal to the AFPs to support the newly privatized companies. The Risk Classification Commission (RCC) was instituted, which obliged all firms with public securities to obtain a risk rating from a private agency; the RCC had to accept the rating before the securities were eligible for AFP investment. An initial ceiling for equity investment of 5 percent was set.

By the end of 1986, total pension fund assets of $3 billion were invested 4 percent in equities, 26 percent in mortgage and corporate bonds, 23 percent in term deposits, and 47 percent in the public sector. In 1989 the ceiling on equity investment was raised to 10 percent, and in March 1990 the range of eligible securities was broadened to include equity in quoted real estate corporations, units of registered investment funds, commercial bills of exchange, and foreign bonds. In May 1990 the ceiling on equity investment was further raised to 30 percent of fund assets.

The rises in the stock exchange index during 1990–1991 were the highest ever on record. The real returns of pension funds in 1990 and 1991 were 15.6 percent and 29.7 percent, respectively. Between July 1981 and July 1996, the AFPs achieved for their account holders an average annual real return of 12.6 percent. By 1996 account holders who had reached pensionable age were on average able to retire with pension income equal to 78 percent of their last wages.

Chile's privatized plan has been compared with Brazil's traditional pay-as-you-go plan and Argentina's mixed plan, in which workers can choose between a traditional government program and a private alternative. By 1996 pension assets under management were 2 percent of GDP in Argentina, 12 percent in Brazil, and 40 percent in Chile. By the year 2011 these percentages are projected to be 20 percent in Argentina, 21 percent in Brazil, and 67 percent in Chile.[6]

---

[6]Heidelberg (1998), p. 37.

from patterns in short-term movements of volatile stocks, are unlikely to make sustainable profits unless they have access to information and insights denied to others.

Developing countries, of course, generally do not penalize inefficiency to the same degree as developed economies. Indeed, a few individuals have grown very rich in some EFMs by profiting from the "old" world of protectionism, subsidies, and local monopolies. But most of these games are coming to an end. In the dawning world of market efficiency and global competition, there will be few easy gains.

A recent book examined the strategies of a number of businesses in five Andean countries.[7] It noted that the businesses often could not sustain initial successes and that they relied excessively on "basic" or static sources of competitive advantage such as climate and geography, with insufficient attention to understanding customers and competitors. The winners in most businesses show intense focus on both customers and competitors, and have a "mental model" focused on flexibility and adaptation. Throughout the world, financial institutions need the same attributes. Few industries are consolidating as rapidly as finance, so few are as much in need of flexibility. Consolidation can create economies of scale and scope on both the revenue and cost side, but it can also reduce organizational adapatability. Adapting to a changing world is the essence of strategy.

Management also needs to be careful about strategic drift; that is, agreeing to one strategy but implementing another. This frequently happens in situations of rapid change as new people arrive in the firm and new events seem suddenly to offer new opportunities. It is a common phenomenon in developing countries, all the more so when the CEO is a strong figure with possibly excessive confidence in his or her powers. That a firm has succeeded *so far* does not mean it will succeed *at everything*. Occasionally strategy needs to be reassessed and revised, but opportunism is no substitute for anchoring the firm to a well thought-out, long-term goal.

Any viable strategy must be adapted to the particular strengths and weaknesses of the firm. If the firm has an expertise in trading, for example, one would look for trading-related strategies. If it has a wide network of branches, one must think out how a branch system can best be used; that is, all the ways in which branch-based services can be deepened or broadened. These might include insurance products, travel services, and asset management services as well as traditional deposits and loans.

Strategy comes from combining a careful appraisal of one's environment with an honest assessment of one's strengths and weaknesses. The idea is to grasp where the world is going and position oneself to benefit from it. In almost all countries today, banks have strategic opportunities. In developed countries, the change is in the direction of market-related services. A smart strategy for modern banks in these markets is to build the skills necessary to combine the bank's existing relationships with an increasing array of insurance, asset management, securities, and derivative products. Of course, this requires additional effort to understand and manage the risk characteristics of the new products, and the ability to tailor products to the environment of each EFM.

For example, life insurance is often the first financial product that new members of the middle class pursue. So a financial provider should track indicators of the growth of this segment of the population (e.g., monitor appliance purchases in the

---

[7]Fairbanks and Lindsay (1997).

country, as insurers do) to gauge the profitability of establishing or expanding this product line. Strategy must also take into account institutional constraints of the local legal system. For example, life insurance is a long-term liability of the insurer, which is typically backed by long-term investments as assets. In some EFMs, those long-term investment opportunities are lacking (e.g., consider the problem of property rights to real estate in China), which pose new challenges to entrants in the insurance industry.

A further test of strategy is whether it results in the creation of value. A basic problem with the inflation-related strategy of Brazilian banks before hyperinflation was tamed is that it did not create real economic value for customers. It simply capitalized on the private opportunities created by the high inflation tax that the government was imposing on the economy. A more viable long-term strategy for a less inflationary era would be one that creates real value for customers.

Similarly, too many banks in the late 1990s made a strategic decision to borrow low-interest-rate dollars and lend higher-interest-rate local currency. As we saw in Chapter 8, this had a great deal to do with the subsequent financial collapses in Mexico, Korea, Thailand, and elsewhere. Although such lending appeared to be profitable so long as foreign exchange rates remained fixed, it was not a value-creating strategy so much as the reward for assuming a massive devaluation risk. If you take such a large risk over a long period of time, sooner or later it is likely to create losses severe enough to destroy the institution. This is not a sound strategy.

Risk Management

Financial institutions cannot avoid risk; rather, they must take on the risks that they have a comparative advantage in managing, and be sure that those risks are well priced and well managed. This is a simple truism in any modern economy. The primary risk assumed by banks is default risk—the possibility that a borrower will not repay—but banks also thrive on managing interest rate risk and foreign exchange risk. Banks and securities firms alike trade a wide variety of instruments, so that they are exposed to changes in the instruments' value. But there are intelligent and unintelligent ways to take on these risks.

The first step is to ensure that management understands the risks being run. Too often, an institution-destroying risk lies hidden below the view of management. For example, Nick Leeson's trading activities (see box, Chapter 7) bankrupted Barings Bank before Barings' management could fully understand what had happened. Indeed, the maverick trader is a recurring figure in financial institutions. How can this problem be dealt with?

All well-run institutions impose limits on traders' activity. No matter how attractive some trade seems to be, traders are not entitled to take risks with unlimited amounts of capital. The practical problem is to have a record-keeping function that quickly detects and reports on limit violations. An elementary rule is that the record keeping must be independent of the trader and even of the trader's boss and colleagues—management needs a completely independent audit by people who have no vested interest in the trading profits. Barings violated this simple rule: Leeson was in charge of reporting on his own activities. It was an expensive mistake.

A related issue is that management must fully *understand* the risks to which the institution is exposed. Even if the risks are disclosed in general, the complexity of modern finance makes it all too easy to mislead senior management about the nature and extent of the risks. For example, many banks deal in derivatives, but the number of senior managers who clearly understand derivatives often is few. Or they may understand "plain vanilla" swaps but not leveraged swaps, equity swaps, or swaptions. The risks of derivatives are too serious to leave entirely to the traders, and appropriate trading limits cannot even be defined unless the underlying risk is clear.

Well-understood risks need to be *diversified.* A basic teaching of modern finance theory is that diversification can enhance the relationship between return and risk, in general lowering the overall risk for any given expected return. Banks that are concentrated in one region or one industry are needlessly risky compared to their more diversified competitors. Any financial institution that takes one large bet, which if wrong could destroy the institution, is guilty of very poor management. Indeed, one of the main tasks of a central risk management function in a financial institution is to add up all the risks and ensure that they are sufficiently diversified. Derivatives have also become a large element in diversification. They allow banks to lay off risks for which they lack competitive advantage, and reserve their capital to be budgeted for the bank's core competencies.

The analysis and management of credit risk is an art in itself. The breathtaking default losses in EFM banks during the 1980s and 1990s suggest that much remains to be learned about how to perform credit analysis carefully. As we have seen, financial repression reduces the need for any credit analysis skills, and sudden liberalization can sometimes leave banks unprepared for the depth of analysis required by private markets.

Furthermore, in many EFMs, private owners of firms are reluctant to share information and simply offer collateral instead. Some bankers see collateral and a high interest rate as substitutes for real credit analysis. Problems arise when the economy collapses and the collateral loses much of its value. Furthermore, collateral-based claims often turn out to be difficult to enforce in EFMs because of inadequate bankruptcy laws and collateral registries.

Real credit analysis is based on using detailed financial information to truly understand the business to which one is lending. It involves not only the standard financial ratios but also projections of cash flow with sensitivity analysis under various scenarios. A number of firms now offer credit-scoring models that attempt to automate this task. They use the firm's financial information as an input and give a default probability as an output.

Some of these models use the ratio of stock market value (when available) to outstanding debt as one of the key variables. This has proven to be highly effective in developed markets because, while standard accounting ratios look backward at the accounting record, the stock,price looks forward and estimates the present worth of future cash flows. Thus, a sudden change in a firm's prospects will show up instantly in the stock price while it will not affect the accounting ratios until some time has passed. To put it another way, the risks borne at any moment by lenders and equity investors are highly correlated. If the stock is strong, the debt is unlikely to be weak. Of course, this requires accurate stock prices.

In numerous other ways, banks are beginning to be more quantitative and scientific in measuring risk and estimating capital needs. The box on VAR and RAROC summarizes the most promising of these new directions for risk management.

Growth

How much growth is desirable? To many, the obvious answer is "as much as possible"! But we have seen in Chapter 3 that from a financial perspective not all growth is

VAR and RAROC

Financial institutions need capital because they take risks. They should maintain an amount of capital sufficient to absorb almost all losses. If capital were truly related to risk in this way, banks would hardly ever fail and losses to depositors would scarcely happen. But how do you decide what that amount of capital is?

Beginning in the 1980s, major banks have begun trying to measure *Value-at-Risk (VAR)*. This is the largest loss that each activity, asset, or off-balance-sheet commitment might incur during the next year, with a high degree of confidence such as 99 percent. VAR is a unifying concept of risk, directly related to the amount of capital needed. If VAR could be estimated for a whole bank, the bank could appropriately hold this amount of capital.

Progress has been made toward estimating VAR for market-related activities such as trading. Since securities and foreign exchange are traded daily, the record of their price movements over a long period of time can be analyzed statistically. There are competing ideas about how to make the calculations, but in principle such estimation is feasible.

Estimating VAR for credit risk is much harder. It requires some model that could plausibly show the distribution of possible credit outcomes. Numerous models have been proposed, very different from each other in concept and approach.[8] The securitization of bank loans (in which debt and equity securities are sold against a pool of loans) has given further impetus to careful default risk measurement.

Even if all of a bank's activities, assets, and off-balance-sheet commitments could have their separate VARs estimated, the problem of how to aggregate them still remains. One cannot simply add them up since correlations exist among losses in one area and losses in another. Even working out the correlations in a single pool of bank loans is a formidable technical problem. Nevertheless, the need for reliable answers is so great that progress is being made on this front as well.

Related to the VAR concept is *Risk-Adjusted Return on Capital (RAROC)*. The idea here is to create a ratio whose numerator is the expected return and whose denominator is the capital at risk. For example, if the transaction to be studied is a proposed loan, the numerator could be the lending spread less the expected loss (loss provision), and the denominator could be the worst-case unexpected loss that might reasonably occur (VAR). Most banks now compute RAROC for at least major transactions, and some refuse to enter into any transaction whose RAROC is less than some target number, such as 20 percent. If this concept can be perfected, banks will be able to select and price their risks much more accurately.

The statistical problem becomes much harder in EFMs, for reasons given in Chapter 1: EFMs are subject to jumps, collapses, and other discontinuities whose underlying cause is most often the weakness and instability of their financial institutions. The more sophisticated and forward-looking financial institutions in EFMs are beginning to embrace these concepts. Before much longer, all banks will need to understand and utilize tools of this sort.

good. A firm should only grow to the extent that it has positive-NPV projects. The related principle with financial institutions is similar. A financial institution only wants loans, underwritings, trading positions, or projects that promise a return sufficient to compensate for the risks involved; that is, that pass the RAROC test.

---

[8]See Saunders (1999) and the entire issue of the *Journal of Banking and Finance* 24, no. 1–2 (January 2000).

Bankers Trust Company and J. P. Morgan & Co. pioneered new risk-management concepts during the 1980s. The analysis led both banks to slow down the growth of their lending business and accelerate the growth of their securities business, where the returns appeared to be substantially higher relative to the risks. This required a massive change of culture in both banks. The idea that more lending was somehow not wanted did not sit well with the large staffs of trained loan officers. Institutional momentum tends to keep organizations doing the same things they have always done in the past; yet the analysis showed that future growth should be in a different business line.

In contrast, the Japanese banks greatly expanded their lending in the 1980s, both at home and around the world. As major Japanese corporations discovered the global capital markets, Japanese banks moved into real estate lending, project finance, and low-spread lending to U.S. and European corporations. Their balance sheets grew so quickly that by 1990 six of the ten largest banks in the world were Japanese.

But not all growth is good. It soon turned out that the Japanese banks had nonperforming loans estimated at more than $500 billion, even though neither the government nor the banks acknowledged any such figure for nearly a decade. But because the banks and their regulators knew the depth of their problems, bank growth eventually slowed. And because the problems were concealed rather than resolved, Japanese banks sank deeper into trouble during the 1990s. The highly bank-dependent Japanese economy stalled with them.

Similarly, excessive growth characterized the recently privatized banks in Mexico from 1991 to 1994, where domestic credit exploded and nonperforming loans quickly grew to unmanageable size. The same happened in Thailand, Korea, and Indonesia, and to a lesser degree in Malaysia and the Philippines. All of East Asia, it seemed, was addicted to rapid growth—a growth that was driven by banks. As East Asia's banks developed losses and as those losses became known, the related countries fell into financial crisis. As we saw in Chapter 8, all of the crisis countries had serious levels of nonperforming loans before the crisis struck, a hangover from their period of rapid growth.

One very good reason not to expand loans too quickly is that rapid loan growth virtually precludes sufficiently careful analysis of risk. Lending money is extremely easy; getting it repaid is the hard part. Lending organizations have a certain tone or culture, set at the top. If the prevailing tone is to "lend a lot," the quality of credit analysis will inevitably suffer and a later collapse may well occur. If, instead, the prevailing tone emphasizes a strong credit culture, no one will be permitted to lend until the loan passes a series of careful reviews. Banks in the latter category are much less likely to crash, and they grow at a more measured pace.

The pattern of lending boom followed by bank collapse has become all too familiar. It characterizes European banks such as Crédit Lyonnais (1988–1995) and Banco Español de Crédito (1987–1994). It characterizes the United States agricultural lending boom and bust of the 1970s and 1980s. It also describes the boom character of lending to developing countries in the 1970s followed by the bust of the 1980s.

Indeed, academics often use a lending boom as a predictor of later banking crises.[9] Research has also suggested that lending booms are a risk factor that is priced into the syndicated loan market.[10] The pattern is so clear that the rapid growth of lending is almost always a reliable warning signal of trouble ahead. In newly liberalized EFMs—where the end of financial repression offers many opportunities for profitable

---

[9]See, for example, Kaminsky, Lizondo, and Reinhart (1998) or Tornell (1999).
[10]Eichengreen and Moody (1999).

long-term growth—it is important to bear in mind the need for careful credit analysis, even if doing so means slowing the rate of loan expansion.

Compensation

Few subjects cause so much conflict in a firm as compensation. The amount and method by which firms pay their professional staff varies enormously from country to country, from firm to firm, and from function to function. Perceived injustice in compensation can destroy morale in a firm, and yet inappropriate generosity can create highly perverse incentives that all by themselves increase the risk that the institution will someday fail.

Traders, for example, are often given large cash bonuses based on their trading results. This practice is often justified by noting that traders make a clear, easily measured contribution to profits or losses, and are most motivated if they have some direct stake in their results. But there are problems with this practice. First, as in the case of Leeson at Barings Bank, a trader can easily make increased income by selling options or similar transactions that greatly increase risk; if the firm is not careful, the bonus will serve as an incentive to increased, and possibly inappropriate, risk taking. Second, a single-minded focus on one's personal bottom line can make people highly uncooperative with others in the firm, including their managers. Compensation schemes heavily oriented to personal results can fragment a firm and lead to destructive internal competition.

Incentives work; this is a fundamental truism. Management's problem is to be sure that incentives are focused on the right behavior. Incentives often focus on a single, measurable number that may not in reality capture the complexity of job performance. Salespeople, for example, are often compensated on commissions that are a mechanical fraction of their sales. The message of this system is that volume matters; sales volume is what the managers want above all other things. But is that the correct message? Do the managers want sales at all costs? Serious dysfunctions at financial institutions, such as the legal violations of Michael Milken in selling high-yield bonds at Drexel Burnham Lambert, often can be traced to compensation schemes that reward volume and implicitly don't care how the volume is achieved.

Compensating lenders is a subtler art, because lenders engage the institution in a long-term risk. It would be highly inappropriate to give cash bonuses to lenders based on the volume of their loans. This would encourage them to book the largest possible number of loans, whether the loans were good or bad. It would be a certain recipe for large loan losses. Instead, lenders should be given some bonus based on the overall performance of the institution and a broadly based assessment of their contribution to that performance.

A case can be made that all officers ought to be compensated in substantial measure through stock or stock options rather than cash because this ties them to the long-term performance of the firm and should make them less willing to put undesirable risks onto the books. Some banks have tried to connect cash bonuses to the VAR or RAROC measures of particular groups. But many of Wall Street's most successful financial institutions have long emphasized equity rather than cash as the appropriate form of payment, and overall firm performance rather than personal bottom lines as the determinant of amount. This tends to make officers think long term rather then short term, and to cooperate rather than to compete internally.

The Future of Emerging Financial Markets

Many people imagine that the story of emerging financial markets is a simple one: Investors became overly excited about the prospects of developing countries in the first half of the 1990s and showered unprecedented amounts of capital on such countries, setting the stage for massive losses and capital outflows in the second half of the 1990s. Having learned their lesson, this view says, investors appropriately packed up and went back home.

This view of the 1990s is far from the truth. The financial crises were undoubtedly a massive setback. Yet as noted in Table 1.1 of Chapter 1, net private investment continued to flow into the EFMs each year of the 1990s. This flow was driven by strong and growing direct investment by corporations, but portfolio investors also increased their net commitments to the developing world in each year of the 1990s. Only the banks showed a pattern of net outflows at times of crisis, reflecting the short-term nature of their commitments and the availability of money from the IMF and elsewhere that enabled short-term debts to be paid.

We have learned a great deal from the crises of the late 1990s. Most fundamentally, we have learned that a house built on a weak foundation is vulnerable. Storms come and go in financial markets as they do in nature, but storms usually knock down only those houses that are built on weak foundations. Following the recent storms, we can see more clearly what builds strong foundations. This book has been about those foundations.

The lessons of the financial crises must be learned because it has become too expensive to ignore them. Those who do not reform their financial systems are likely to have more losses and bank crises in the future. A great deal already has been learned and we think that the world of emerging financial markets will be stronger in the future than it has been in the past.

We have seen a number of countries climb from "developing" to "newly industrialized" status. We think that more countries will cross this threshold in the century now beginning, helped by effective capital allocations from modern financial markets. One benefit of our information-based age is that we can study and learn from successes and failures throughout the world, comparing different experiences and drawing up lists of best practices. Over the long term we expect actual practices to converge toward best practices in our ever-evolving, interdependent world.

References

Black, Bernard S., and Ronald J. Gilson. 1998. Venture capital and the structure of capital markets: Banks vs. stock markets. *Journal of Financial Economics* 47: 243–77.

Calomiris, Charles W., and Andrew Powell. 2000. Can emerging market bank regulators establish credible discipline? The case of Argentina, 1992–1999. Working Paper no. 7715, National Bureau of Economic Research.

Claessens, Stijn, Simeon Djankov, and Daniela Klingebiel. 1999. Financial restructuring in East Asia: Halfway there? Financial Sector Discussion Paper no. 3, World Bank.

DeLong, J. Bradford. 1991. Did J. P. Morgan's men add value? An economist's perspective on financial capitalism. In *Inside the Business Enterprise: Historical Perspectives on the Use of Information.* Ed. by Peter Temin. Chicago: University of Chicago Press: 205–36.

Eichengreen, Barry. 1999. *Toward a New Financial Architecture.* Washington, DC: Institute for International Economics.

Eichengreen, Barry, and Ashoka Moody. 1999. Lending booms, reserves and the sustainability of short-term debt. Working Paper no. 7113, National Bureau of Economic Research.

Fairbanks, Michael, and Stace Lindsay. 1997. *Ploughing the Sea: Nurturing the Hidden Sources of Growth in the Developing World.* Boston: Harvard Business School Press.

Heidelberg, Denise I. 1998. A comparative study of pension plans in Latin America: The case of Argentina, Brazil, and Chile. Working Paper no. 98–03, Center for International Business Education and Research, University of Connecticut, Storrs.

Kaminsky, Graciela, Saul Lizondo, and Carmen M. Reinhart. 1998. Leading indicators of currency crises. *IMF Staff Papers* 45: 1–48.

Krueger, Anne, and Aaron Tornell. 1999. The role of bank restructuring in recovering from crises: Mexico 1995–98. Working Paper no. 7042, National Bureau of Economic Research.

Krugman, Paul. 1999. Depression economics returns. *Foreign Affairs* 78:1.

Saunders, Anthony. 1999. *Credit Risk Measurement: New Approaches to Value at Risk and Other Paradigms.* New York: John Wiley.

Shadow Financial Regulatory Committee. 2000. *Reforming Bank Capital Regulation.* American Enterprise Institute.

Stiglitz, Joseph. 1999. Bleak growth prospects for the developing world. *International Herald Tribune,* April 10–11.

Tornell, Aaron. 1999. Common fundamentals in the tequila and Asian crises. Working Paper no. 7139, National Bureau of Economic Research.

World Bank. 1998. *Argentina Financial Sector Review.* Washington, DC: World Bank, Report no. 17864-AR.

Glossary

Following is a list of technical terms used in the course of this book. References to other glossary terms are italicized.

Adverse selection   A distortion to markets that occurs because the seller and buyer differ in the extent of their knowledge about the quality of what is being sold. Adverse selection refers to the way the market can attract participants in a distorted manner ("selecting adversely"), for example, by encouraging the excessive participation of unobservably higher-risk issuers of debt. Adverse selection affects prices and can close markets altogether. Applied to debt markets, adverse selection means that lenders charge higher interest rates and sometimes ration credit.

American (global) depository receipt (ADR or GDR)   A security that represents shares of a stock held by a trustee. ADRs and GDRs "translate" stock ownership in foreign countries to a standard form that meets a number of legal and tax problems, and are often tailored to meet the listing requirements of a stock exchange.

Antidirector rights   Powers given to stockholders over the directors and managers of the firms in which they hold stock. These include requirements that all shares have the same voting power, rights to vote in corporate elections by mail (proxy rights), cumulative voting rights that allow stockholders to concentrate their votes on a few directors, and the right to call extraordinary stockholder meetings.

Arbitrage   The simultaneous riskless purchase and sale of the same good or perfectly equivalent goods in two different markets. When markets are efficient, goods should have the same price in all markets, so arbitrage should not be profitable. The principle of arbitrage enables us to write down a number of important pricing formulas such as the *interest parity* relationship.

Asset substitution problem   The problem faced by a creditor who makes a loan and then finds that the borrower takes increased risk. This problem becomes severe when the borrower has little of its own money at risk, possibly because of previous losses, and hence has incentives to gamble heavily. The asset substitution problem is an instance of *moral hazard*.

Asymmetric information   A condition in which parties to economic transactions or relationships do not have the same information. *Adverse selection* is one of the major problems of asymmetric information. Another is the difficulty experienced by poorly informed outside shareholders trying to control well-informed inside shareholders and managers.

Bailout   The practice of using taxpayer funds to rescue insolvent private firms, typically insolvent banks. Government insurance of bank deposits leads directly to bailouts of bank depositors. Since the assets of an insolvent bank are worth less than its liabilities, including deposits, bailouts enable the deposits to be paid. Too often, bailouts rescue the bank's shareholders as well.

Bank for International Settlements (BIS)   An institution designed primarily to serve the needs of the world's central banks, the BIS is located in Basel, Switzerland. It serves as a forum for governmental negotiations on a number of financial subjects, including uniform bank capital requirements. For more information see the BIS website at **www.bis.org**.

Bank run   An effort by bank depositors to withdraw their deposits at one time, because of fear that the bank may not be able to repay. Bank runs have occurred throughout history whenever depositors have become worried about the safety and soundness of their bank, and they sometimes lead to the closing of banks.

Bankruptcy   A legal process that can resolve claims on a firm unable to service its debts. Ideally, a bankruptcy court determines whether the firm has a viable ongoing business or not. If so, bankruptcy may lead to *rescheduling* of debt or conversion of some debt to equity. If the firm does not have a viable ongoing business, bankruptcy should lead to liquidation of the firm.

Basel Agreement   An agreement among bank regulators of major industrial countries. It was reached in 1988 under the auspices of the *Bank for International Settlements* in Basel, Switzerland, and put into place a set of uniform capital requirements for international banks. These capital requirements attempt to take into account varying degrees of bank risk that different loans and derivatives imply, but the agreement is at best a first, somewhat crude step in that important direction.

Beta   A measure of a security's risk, specifically the part of its risk that should be reflected in its market price. Beta comes from the *Capital Asset Pricing Model*. The underlying framework assumes that investors hold widely diversified portfolios, in which the idiosyncratic risks of each security have little impact on the overall portfolio's returns. Beta measures what should then matter: the risk that when the market as a whole moves up or down, the particular stock moves up or down with it.

Bimodal   A characteristic of certain random variables. When a variable's distribution is bimodal, there is substantial probability of extreme outcomes, so that the probability density function has two humps, one at each extreme, instead of the normal bell shape.

351

Bond Rating   A letter grade assigned to the credit quality of a bond, such as AAA, AA, A, BBB, BB, B, CCC, and so on. Ratings are assigned by bond rating agencies such as Moody's or Standard and Poor's after studying the soundness of the issuer and the terms of the bond. "Junk bonds" are those with ratings of BB or below.

Brady bond   A bond issued by one of several governments in settlement of their defaulted bank loans in the period 1989–1992. Named for then U.S. Treasury Secretary Nicholas Brady, these bonds will pay all principal at the end of a long term, usually 30 years. The principal, but not the interest, of this obligation is fully secured by U.S. government *zero-coupon bonds* held in trust.

Capital Asset Pricing Model (CAPM)   A theory, dating from the 1960s, about how financial assets are priced. According to CAPM, the expected return on any stock equals the risk-free rate plus *beta* times the overall equity market risk premium. The equity premium, which is difficult to estimate accurately, is the excess return above the risk-free rate that investors expect or demand for bearing the risk of holding a broadly diversified portfolio of stocks.

Capital controls   Rules that restrict capital from flowing freely into or out of a country. They can take many forms, including taxes, *reserve requirements*, or outright prohibition. Capital controls may make capital more expensive or less available. They are sometimes instituted in an attempt to control the instability that occurs when capital suddenly flees during a crisis.

Capital flight   The sudden conversion of large quantities of local currency assets into a stronger foreign currency. Capital flight is not clandestine because the currency conversion typically goes through the local central bank. Capital flight often results from government policies that maintain an unsustainable currency peg (see *overvaluation*).

Collateral   Assets pledged as security for a loan. Collateral can be real estate, equipment, inventories, receivables, or securities. Governments encourage the use of collateral by establishing public registries where such liens can be recorded and by providing a legal framework that enables lenders to seize collateral when debts are not paid.

Commercial paper   A short-term promissory note (I.O.U.), this money market instrument is a class of substitutes for bank certificates of deposit in the portfolios of investors, as both are negotiable debts (transactable claims promising to pay a certain sum at a fixed point in time). Only companies with very high credit ratings are able to sell commercial paper, and they do so as an alternative to borrowing from a bank or from other debt markets. Since this avoids the high fixed costs of a bank, commercial paper borrowing is almost always cheaper than bank borrowing.

Contagion   The spreading of financial crisis from one country to another. At the peak of the Asian crisis, the "Asian flu" seemed to leap from country to country like a disease. Contagion may result both from rational concerns and from investor panic, but the effects of the former tend to endure and the effects of panic are usually transitory.

Corruption   The act of a public official who takes or demands private payments. Corruption is a conflict of interest between the official's role (serving the public interest) and his or her personal pocketbook. It has existed at all times and in all societies, but is far more tolerated in some societies and times than in others.

Crawling peg   A rule by which some governments attempt to manage the value of their currencies. The word "peg" implies that the currency is fixed against the dollar or other hard currency, but the word "crawling" means that the point at which it is fixed is subject to gradual adjustment, usually in frequent small steps, and usually because of inflation of the local currency relative to the hard currency to which it is fixed.

Credit rationing   Reduction in the quantity of loans available to a weak borrower, sometimes to zero. In a perfectly efficient market, it is assumed that weak firms could always borrow at some rate of interest. Credit rationing is a departure from that principle, as some credits are avoided rather than priced. *Asymmetric information* can explain credit rationing.

Creditor rights   Legal arrangements that enable lenders to collect some value on bad loans. These include the right to seize and sell collateral and the right to force defaulting borrowers into bankruptcy, as well as remedies available to lenders during bankruptcy proceedings. Such rights are needed to give creditors confidence to lend in the first place (unless government has implicitly agreed to keep them whole).

Cumulative voting   The right of shareholders to concentrate all their votes on one or a few candidates for a board of directors. Cumulative voting enables minority shareholders to elect at least one or a few representatives onto the board. Cumulative voting is often opposed by controlling shareholders and managements, who would prefer to control the entire election to the board.

Currency board   A very strong legal framework to fix the value of one currency relative to the value of another currency. In this arrangement, local currency typically can only be issued if an equivalent amount of dollars or other hard currency is held to support it and into which the local currency is convertible. Under a currency board, the government can no longer *monetize* budget deficits and indeed has no independent monetary policy.

Default   Violation by a borrower of a loan agreement, usually by failure to pay the interest or principal due in a timely manner. In some jurisdictions, violation of *loan covenants* is also an act of default. Borrowers typically have several months to cure defaults, but if they do not do so then typically the entire principal of the loan becomes due and payable.

Deposit insurance   The guarantee (typically by a government agency) that some or all deposits in private banks will be repaid. Federal deposit insurance originated in the United States in the Banking Act of 1933. Since that time, implicit or explicit government protection of some or all bank deposits has become nearly universal.

Devaluation   The reduction, by government action, of a currency's official value. A devaluation (as opposed to a depreciation in value) implies that the currency previously had been fixed in value to some degree against the dollar or another hard currency. Devaluation often follows a period of domestic price inflation that makes the currency peg unsustainable. The immediate precipitating influence is often a speculative attack.

Disintermediation   Avoidance of a financial intermediary. The rise of *commercial paper*, for example, disintermediates by enabling investors to save and firms to borrow by dealing directly with each other, saving the costs of using a bank. Disintermediation often lowers the *franchise value* of banks.

Economic and Monetary Union (EMU)   The unification of money and economic policy in the European Community (EC). Commitment to EMU was made by means of the Maastricht Treaty, which was negotiated in 1990–1991 and ratified by some but not all EC members during 1992–1993. EMU committed signatories to a single currency (the euro), which was launched in 1999.

Emerging financial market (EFM)   The financial market of a developing country, both for internal and external investors. EFMs "emerge" when they separate from domination by their governments; this requires the government's active support, based upon a commitment to capital allocation by private sector companies.

Exchange rate mechanism (ERM)   A system of semifixed exchange rates among European currencies. ERM was a subset of the European Monerary System, which in turn was a predecessor to *European Economic and Monetary Union (EMU)*. ERM involved fixed parities with broad and often-adjusted trading bands. Great Britain and Italy dropped out of the ERM in 1992, but by this time *EMU* was the new and far more ambitious goal.

Financial intermediation   The process of allocating capital from savers to users through financial institutions. The two primary forms are bank intermediation and securities market intermediation. Securities markets are more cost-efficient but require strong foundations in law, information, and currency. Bank intermediation dominates in EFMs.

Financial liberalization   The reduction of *financial repression* through *privatization* of financial intermediaries and deregulation of financial markets and intermediaries. Freeing financial institutions is akin to privatization of industry, but typically proceeds more slowly since poorly prepared financial liberalization has often led to crises and collapses. Financial liberalization is necessary if government wants a strong system of private financial institutions.

Financial repression   The domination of the financial system by government. This takes a number of forms, including interest rate controls, high bank reserve requirements, government ownership or domination of banks, and restrictions on capital flows into and out of the country. Financial repression tends to slow economic growth.

Floating rates   Interest rates or foreign exchange rates that vary from period to period. Floating interest rates, on a loan or derivative contract, are linked to some index, most often the *London Interbank Offered Rate*, or *LIBOR*. Floating foreign exchange rates occur when the government does not attempt to peg the level of its currency's value relative to other currencies.

Foreign direct investment (FDI)   A form of capital flow into a country resulting from foreign firms buying local firms, buying local assets, or building new plants, typically with the foreign firms playing a management role. FDI cannot easily be reversed, and so represents a more permanent commitment than bank lending or portfolio investment, the other two kinds of capital flow.

Franchise value   Applied to banks, the value of a bank charter. When banks have special skills or privileges, such as technical expertise, valuable customer relationships, government protection from foreign competition, or low government-mandated deposit interest rates, banks are more profitable, and those higher profits are reflected in a high ratio of market-to-book value for bank equity (which is the market's indicator of a high franchise value). Franchise value can be eroded when markets are opened to competition from securities markets and foreign institutions. But if competition produces entry by better-skilled banks and investments by banks in profitable customer relationships, bank franchise values may rise with increased competition.

Free riding   Making gains based on the efforts or sacrifices of others, which can discourage those sacrifices or efforts. Free riding can plague all schemes for wide cooperation among creditors as, for example, during the attempts to resolve the great debt crisis of the 1980s. It can be suppressed only if creditors can coordinate their actions effectively to prevent free riding, which sometimes occurs when an international authority or set of governments enforces cooperation.

Inflation indexing   Contract provisions that change the amount payable based on the level of inflation. In some countries where inflation is endemic, most wages, interest rates, and many other prices may be indexed to inflation. Inflation indexing attempts to protect people and firms from the uncertainties of inflation, but it also tends to perpetuate and institutionalize inflation.

Inflation risk premium   Extra interest to compensate lenders for the risk of creditor loss due to inflation. Lenders tend to incorporate expected inflation into their interest rates, but in many countries lenders require further compensation for the risk of unexpected inflation. Since lenders are usually risk averse, they must be compensated for inflation uncertainty wherever this is significant.

Insolvency   A condition in which one's outstanding debts exceed the value of one's assets. Insolvency is different from illiquidity (see *liquidity*), and implies a more permanent incapacity to pay one's debts. Insolvency should lead either to liquidation of a firm or to a reduction or *restructuring* of debt either voluntarily or through *bankruptcy*.

Interest parity   A relationship connecting foreign exchange rates and interest rates between two countries that do not restrict foreign exchange and borrowing transactions. It implies that hedged interest rates are always equal. For example, one cannot go into a foreign currency and earn a higher interest rate without taking a risk that exchange rates will change; if that risk is avoided (hedged), then the interest rate earned equals the interest rate of one's home country.

International bonds   Bonds that are sold outside the internal bond markets of any country. Such bonds are subject to no regulation or disclosure requirements. Once called Eurobonds, they represent a large and important form of international lending. They may have fixed or floating interest rates, and compete with international *syndicated loans*.

International Finance Corporation (IFC)   One of the five organizations in the *World Bank Group*. Based in Washington, D.C., the IFC invests debt and equity capital in private sector projects in developing countries. It also advises governments on private sector development and capital markets. It publishes the annual *Emerging Stock Markets Factbook*. For more information see its website at **www.ifc.org.**

International Monetary Fund (IMF)   The IMF was founded in 1946 to facilitate the establishment of a fixed exchange rate system (the so-called Bretton Woods system), and to encourage countries to maintain convertibility of their currencies for the purposes of international trade. With the collapse of the Bretton Woods system in the early 1970s, the IMF took on new roles, including involvement in the 1980s debt crisis, the transition problems of socialist economies in the early 1990s, and the management of financial crises in the mid- and late 1990s. For more information see its website at **www.imf.org.**

Liquidation   The termination of a firm's life, wherein the assets are sold and the proceeds used to pay off the debts in whole or in part. Liquidation terminates the equity and debt claims, but does not destroy the assets; that is, the plants may well continue to operate under new ownership, so that liquidation does not necessarily imply loss of jobs.

Liquidity   Having access to enough cash to pay all one's obligations in a timely fashion. One can be wealthy and yet illiquid if one's assets cannot easily be sold (e.g., because of *asymmetric information*) and do not pay out much current cash. Liquidity is enhanced by having short-dated assets and long-dated liabilities. Banks provide liquidity to the business system by financing relatively long-term loans with short-term debts. Poor management of liquidity by banks can risk a bank illiquidity problem, and possibly trigger a *bank run* in response (although bank *insolvency* generally is at the root of bank runs). Sovereign illiquidity can also lead bankers to demand repayment of short-term sovereign debt.

Loan covenants   Agreements by borrowers written into loan contracts. These include standard provisions such as an agreement not to pay out excesive dividends or a *negative pledge clause*, but may also include special lender protections such as an agreement to maintain a minimum amount of working capital or an agreement not to let total debt exceed some fraction of assets.

London Interbank Offered Rate (LIBOR)   The average rate paid by international banks on large deposits. Most loan contracts and many derivatives are indexed to LIBOR. Dollar LIBOR is announced daily by the British Bankers Association. It is actually a set of rates, one for each term of one month, three months, six months, nine months, and one year.

Loss allowance   A balance sheet entry designed to estimate future loan losses. Most bank balance sheets show gross loans and loss allowance, and then subtract allowance from gross loans to get net loans. Loss allowance is subjectively determined by bank managers, sometimes under pressure from government regulators to be more forthcoming about problem loans. In the absence of such pressure, loss allowance is often understated.

Loss provision   An income statement entry designed to show this period's increase in *loss allowance*. When a bank admits serious loan problems by taking a large loss provision, its net income is reduced, often to a significant loss, and this in turn reduces equity capital. Like the loss allowance, the periodic loan loss provision is subjectively determined within guidelines set by regulators.

Market discipline   The pressure exerted by markets on banks or other firms to control their risk. The strongest form of market discipline on banks occurs when the government credibly refuses to provide *deposit insurance*. In such cases, fear of a *bank run* tends to keep bankers conservative. An alternative form of market discipline is a requirement that banks have a certain quantity of *subordinated debt* outstanding.

Monetizing deficits   The practice of covering government budget deficits by, in effect, printing money. Monetizing deficits often seems more attractive to governments than raising taxes or cutting spending, but increasing the money supply leads to higher inflation. This is why controlling inflation in *emerging financial markets* requires credible limits on fiscal deficits.

Monitoring   Keeping track of loans or other investments after they have been made. Monitoring of firms by banks and large investors plays a significant role in ensuring appropriate behavior by the firm's majority owners and managers. Through monitoring of existing loans, banks and investors gain information that allows them to enforce contracts and to determine whether they will supply more capital in the future.

Moral hazard   A condition of skewed incentives. In debt contracting, it occurs when a decision maker who is also a debtor can score significant upside gains but suffer little downside loss from deciding to increase risk ("Heads I win, tails someone else loses"). Moral hazard results most often from government guarantees against failure, and is particularly severe when a firm's equity capital is exhausted so that it has little or nothing left to lose. Moral hazard predictably leads to greatly expanded risk taking and is an important cause of banking collapses and financial crises.

Negative pledge clause   A promise made to one creditor not to mortgage one's assets to another creditor. In the early stages of the evolution of a financial system, most loans are secured. As legal foundations and financial disclosure improve, lenders become willing to lend without security. But unsecured loans could easily be abused if borrowers could freely pledge assets, creating a layer of debt senior to the unsecured loans. The negative pledge is a standard *loan covenant* designed to prevent such abuse. It is a common feature of both private and sovereign debt contracts.

Net present value (NPV)   A measure of the *value creation* or destruction of a proposed project. According to the net present value rule, firms should project all expected cash flows into and out of the proposed project, and discount them to present worth (NPV) at a discount rate equal to the cost of capital appropriate to the risk of the project. If the NPV is positive, then implementing the project should increase the value of the firm by that amount.

Nominal rate   The actual interest rate or foreign exchange rate specified in a financial contract. Nominal rates need to be adjusted for inflation to determine the *real rate of interest* or *real exchange rate*. For example, a high nominal interest rate will create a purchasing power loss for lenders if the inflation rate turns out to be higher than the nominal interest rate.

Nonperforming loan   A loan that is not current in payment of principal and interest. Bankers can and often do avoid or cover up nonperforming loans simply by making new loans to weak borrowers so that they may stay current in their payments. Therefore regulators often need to audit banks to ensure that a sound set of credit audit policies is in place to uncover nonperforming loans and take *loss provisions* for them.

Organization for Economic Cooperation and Development (OECD)   A Paris-based organization of 29 member countries, primarily industrial countries. It collects and maintains substantial amounts of data, holds conferences, and publishes documents. See its website at **www.oecd.org** for more details.

Overvaluation   A condition in which a currency is priced above its long-term equilibrium level. Overvaluation can result from pegging (fixing the price of) a currency to the dollar or other hard currency in an effort to control inflation.

Portfolio investors   Those who purchase securities at arm's length. In contrast to banks making loans and *foreign direct investment*, portfolio investors have no direct relationship with the firms in which they invest. Governments often mistrust portfolio investors, fearing that they will cut and run in any time of trouble, but in the 1990s portfolio investors demonstrated more staying power than international banks.

Principal–agent problem   The problem encountered by a principal in getting an agent to act in the principal's interest rather than his or her own interest. Applied to corporate governance, shareholders (as principals) sometimes have great difficulty getting corporate managers (as agents) to act in the shareholders' interest.

Private equity   Equity investment arising from direct relationships rather than open market purchases. The main sources of private equity investment are banks and private equity funds. Private equity investments include venture capital (i.e., in young, high-risk companies) and leveraged buyouts (i.e., purchases of established companies using substantial debt).

Private placement   A sale of securities directly to private buyers, outside the public markets. Companies may choose to sell securities by private placement when the securities are complex and the buyers are sophisticated institutions. Private placements of equity are made to *private equity* investors. Private placements of corporate debt typically are sold to life insurance companies, pension funds, or investment funds. Private placements are less liquid than publicly held securities and usually require the promise of higher returns than similar public offerings.

Privatization   The sale by government of a *state-owned enterprise*. Such enterprises may be sold for cash to firms inside or outside the country involved, or to *private equity* investors. Alternatively, the government may sell shares in a public offering. The countries in transition from communism often distributed vouchers to their people for the purpose of buying enterprises being privatized.

Protectionism   The use of tariffs, quotas, or other devices of government to restrict imports. Protectionism shields domestic firms from external competition, which may bring short-term benefits to such firms but which in the longer term inhibits efficiency and economic growth. Free trade involves the dismantling of protectionism in the pursuit of efficiency and growth.

Proxy   Someone appointed to vote as directed on a shareholder's behalf. The use of proxies enables shareholders to vote at shareholder meetings without having to appear physically at the meeting, and so is an important *shareholder right*. Shareholder rights are further enhanced by rules that require management to distribute and take proxy votes on dissident shareholder proposals.

Purchasing power parity (PPP)   The idea that currency prices (exchange rates) should reflect the ratio of average goods prices across countries. PPP assumes that the *real exchange rate* between countries is constant; that is, exchange rates move in lockstep with the ratio of consumer price indexes.

Pyramid (or Ponzi) scheme   A classic investor fraud. The promoter of a pyramid scheme collects "investments" from gullible individuals, promising very high returns, sometimes without any underlying business. Initially, the promoter pays the high promised returns to early investors out of the proceeds from the investments of later investors. These payments appear to validate the scheme, thus attracting more victims until the scheme collapses, usually after the perpetrator has fled the country and the reach of the law.

Real exchange rate   The price of one currency expressed in units of another, adjusted by the ratio of price indexes in the two countries. Since the level of price indexes has no absolute meaning, the same is true of real exchange rates. What matters is change over time. Change in the real exchange rate implies that one country has gained competitive price advantage relative to the other, and this should affect real trade.

Real growth   Apparent or nominal growth adjusted for inflation. For example, if nominal GDP rises by 10 percent but inflation is 8 percent, the increase in real goods and services produced is only about 2 percent. Real growth of GDP per capita is the most widely used measure of whether people are better off economically than before.

Real rate of interest   The apparent or nominal rates of interest adjusted for expected inflation. For example, a nominal interest rate of 14 percent may be composed of an expectation of 8 percent inflation and an underlying real rate of interest of 6 percent. The real interest rate reflects the sum of the underlying riskless real rate and the *inflation risk premium*. However, none of these three components (expected inflation, the riskless real rate, and the inflation risk pre-

mium) can be directly observed, so identifying these components is a difficult exercise.

Regulatory discipline   The effort of government to prevent banks from taking excessive risk. Regulatory discipline is needed when governments reduce or eliminate *market discipline* by insuring bank deposits and other bank liabilities. Methods of regulatory discipline include required reporting and periodic on-site examination of banks.

Rents   Profits in excess of those that would prevail in open, competitive markets. Rents occur when markets are not open and competitive. For example, a firm with a local monopoly can extract rents because it has no competition.

Rescheduling   Changing the terms of loans by extending the repayment and/or lowering the interest rate. Lenders agree to rescheduling when they are convinced that the borrower cannot pay the full interest and principal, and are unwilling or unable to put the borrower into *bankruptcy*.

Reserve requirement   A rule that banks must redeposit a fixed percentage of their deposits at the central bank. In almost all cases the central bank does not pay the market rate of interest on such reserves. The original purpose of reserve requirements was to provide emergency funds for solvent banks facing a *bank run* or crisis of *liquidity*. In modern times, reserve requirements often are better understood as part of tax policy rather than prudential bank regulatory policy.

Restructuring (or reorganization)   Altering a firm's basic mix of assets and liabilities. Restructuring often implies selling underperforming assets or businesses, while reorganization often implies changing the claims of creditors and stockholders. A common pattern of restructuring in many countries is the scaling back or breakup of large conglomerates into more easily managed separate units.

Risk-adjusted return on capital (RAROC)   A measure to help bank management select appropriate opportunities. RAROC is a fraction whose numerator is the expected return on some transaction or activity and whose denominator is the notional capital required or *Value-at-Risk*. If RAROC exceeds some target return, such as 20 percent, management should accept the opportunity; otherwise it should reject it.

Safety net   Governmental protection against certain financial losses. *Deposit insurance* and central bank lending are nearly universal forms of the financial safety net, but some governments go much further and protect the shareholders and managers of banks or sometimes those of large industrial enterprises as well. Safety nets are supposed to make panics and crises less frequent, but because of *moral hazard* they often make such crises far more severe and expensive.

Shareholder rights   Legal devices to protect the interests of shareholders. Without adequate shareholder protection, management and inside shareholders can easily deceive or defraud outside shareholders. Shareholder rights include *antidirector rights* and also the right to receive full and fair disclosure of information and to sue to restrain fraud and abuse.

Soft (hard) budget constraint   The availability (unavailability) of outside cash to cover losses. Most firms and individuals are constrained to live within their means or face *bankruptcy*. When the budget constraint is soft, government offers easy money to cover up problems when earnings are low or negative. This almost always lowers the efficiency of capital allocation, enabling losses to continue and value to be destroyed.

Spontaneous privatization   Seizure of some or all assets by managers of *state-owned enterprises*. In the vacuum between the collapse of communism and the rise of appropriate corporate governance in transition countries, spontaneous privatization became a major social issue. In some countries (e.g., Hungary) it was deliberately arrested, while in others (e.g., Russia) it became institutionalized.

Spread   The interest rate margin on a bank loan or bond. To be profitable, banks must mark up the interest rate paid on their deposits to a higher interest rate charged on their loans. Deposit rates are usually close to *London Interbank Offered Rate (LIBOR)*, so banks usually price loans at a *floating rate* equal to LIBOR plus a spread. Bank spreads generally range from 0.25 percent to 3.00 percent.

State-owned enterprise (SOE)   A business enterprise owned by government. Such ownership is usually justified by the claim that it will reduce inequalities of wealth (socialism) or by the claim that free markets often fail to function properly (market failures). However, SOEs usually suffer from inefficiency, rigidity, and poor service. In some cases they are also vehicles for *corruption*.

Sterilization   Expansionary (contractionary) monetary policy by the government that offsets the domestic monetary effects of international outflows (inflows) of hard currency reserves from (into) the central bank. When a government supports the value of its currency, it must be willing to buy its local currency with hard currency reserves. When holders of domestic currency convert into hard currency, that shrinks the domestic money supply, which will tend to contract the economy. Sterilization means counteracting that contractionary influence of reserve outflows by expanding the money supply through purchases of domestic government bonds by the central bank.

Subordinated debt   Debt that is paid only after claims of senior and secured debt have been satisfied. Subordinated debt, like equity, provides protection for senior creditors, which is why some subordinated debt is counted as capital under the *Basel Agreement*. To increase *market discipline*, some economists advocate a requirement that all banks have some subordinated debt outstanding.

Survival bias   A distortion arising from the current observation of only the survivors from the past. Survival bias can make mutual funds or entire stock markets appear to be more profitable on average than they would appear if one also took into account all the failed and vanished funds and markets.

Swap   A contract under which two streams of financial payments are exchanged. For example, a firm can issue a yen-denominated bond and swap the yen payment obligation for one in euros, creating a synthetic euro-denominated bond. Alternatively, a firm can issue debt with a *floating rate* of interest and swap the payment obligation for a fixed interest rate, creating a synthetic fixed rate bond. Swaps enable firms to borrow where they can most efficiently borrow, but end with some different form of debt that they prefer.

Syndicated loan   A loan made by a syndicate of banks, some of which may have no relationship to the borrower. Syndicated loans are somewhat dangerous because many of the lenders may lack the information needed to make a sound credit and pricing decision. Instead, they rely on the credit and pricing judgment of the banks leading the syndicate.

Terms of trade   The ratio of a country's average export prices to its average import prices. If a country's terms of trade improve, it can obtain more imports for the same level of exports. Countries that produce commodities with volatile prices, such as petroleum, often experience wide fluctuations in their terms of trade.

Trading band   A price zone for some currency that its government commits to maintain. For example, a government may commit to keep its currency within ± 5 percent of a stated parity value. That means the government promises to buy the currency whenever it falls 5 percent below its parity and to sell it whenever it rises 5 percent above its parity. A narrow trading band approximates a fixed currency value and a wide band approximates a *floating rate* of exchange.

Tunneling   Theft of corporate assets by managers. The metaphor visualizes managers carrying out assets in secret. The reality usually involves selling or leasing assets at bargain prices to other firms controlled by the managers. Astonishingly, tunneling is legal in many jurisdictions, notably those of French origin, that lack a concept of fiduciary duty on the part of managers to shareholders.

Value creation (destruction)   Investment in projects whose rate of return is above (below) the cost of capital. The willingness of banks to lend to low-return projects accelerates short-term growth but creates long-term financial weakness and ultimately costly failure. Only growth that pays for its cost of capital can be sustained.

Value-at-Risk (VAR)   The largest loss that some activity might produce, with a predetermined probability (usually 95 percent or 99 percent). The idea is to create a "reasonable worst case," a quantification of the downside. VAR is a plausible basis for determining how much capital a bank ought to allocate to its risks, since capital provides protection against bad outcomes. Estimation of VAR, however, is fraught with practical problems.

World Bank Group   A set of five related international financial institutions, the first of which was established in 1944. The flagship is the World Bank (International Bank for Reconstruction and Development), which makes long-term loans to developing country governments. See its website at **www.worldbank.org** for more information.

Zero-coupon bonds   Bonds that do not pay periodic interest, but make one large payment only at some fixed future date. The U.S. Treasury has a program of "stripping" its own coupon bonds; that is, selling each coupon and principal payment as a separate zero-coupon bond or "Treasury strip." The availability of U.S. Treasury zero-coupon bonds made possible the *Brady bonds*.

Name Index

Subject Index